BRYAN EDWARD STONE AND JONATHAN L. FRIEDMANN, SERIES EDITORS

Also in the series:

Commodore Levy: A Novel of Early America in the Age of Sail, by Irving Litvag

Contesting Histories: German and Jewish Americans and the Legacy of the Holocaust, by Michael Schuldiner

Jewish Historical Societies: Navigating the Professional-Amateur Divide, edited by Joel Gereboff and Jonathan L. Friedmann

The Jewish Women Prisoners of Ravensbrück: Who Were They?, by Judith Buber Agassi

Karski: How One Man Tried to Stop the Holocaust, by E. Thomas Wood and Stanisław M. Jankowski

Love, Norm: Inspiration of a Jewish American Fighter Pilot, by Norman M. Shulman

"Non-Germans" under the Third Reich: The Nazi Judicial and Administrative System in Germany and Occupied Eastern Europe, with Special Regard to Occupied Poland, 1939–1945, by Diemut Majer

Pillar of Fire: A Biography of Stephen S. Wise, by A. James Rudin

Songs of Sonderling: Commissioning Jewish Émigré Composers in Los Angeles, 1938–1945, by Jonathan L. Friedmann and John F. Guest

The Tailors of Tomaszow: A Memoir of Polish Jews, by Rena Margulies Chernoff and Allan Chernoff

Transcending Darkness: A Girl's Journey out of the Holocaust, by Estelle Glaser Laughlin

Unwanted Legacies: Sharing the Burden of Post-Genocide Generations, by Gottfried Wagner and Abraham J. Peck

NEITHER FISH NOR FOWL

A MERCANTILE JEWISH FAMILY ON THE RIO GRANDE

MORRIS S. RISKIND

EDITED BY BRYAN EDWARD STONE

FOREWORD BY DR. PETER RISKIND

TEXAS TECH UNIVERSITY PRESS

Copyright © 2024 by Texas Tech University Press

All rights reserved. No portion of this book may be reproduced in any form or by any means, including electronic storage and retrieval systems, except by explicit prior written permission of the publisher. Brief passages excerpted for review and critical purposes are excepted.

This book is typeset in EB Garamond. The paper used in this book meets the minimum requirements of ANSI/NISO Z39.48-1992 (R1997). ∞

Designed by Hannah Gaskamp
Cover design by Hannah Gaskamp

Library of Congress Cataloging-in-Publication Data

Names: Riskind, Morris S. (Morris Samuel), 1911–1996, author. | Riskind, Peter Nathaniel, 1950– author of foreword. Title: Neither Fish nor Fowl: A Jewish family on the Rio Grande / Morris S. Riskind; foreword by Dr. Peter Riskind. Other titles: Jewish family on the Rio Grande Description: Lubbock, Texas: Texas Tech University Press, [2024] | Series: Modern Jewish history | Includes bibliographical references and index. |
Summary: "Autobiography of Morris Riskind, Jewish store owner in Eagle Pass, Texas"— Provided by publisher.
Identifiers: LCCN 2024018687 (print) | LCCN 2024018688 (ebook) |
ISBN 978-1-68283-230-1 (paperback) | ISBN 978-1-68283-231-8 (ebook)
Subjects: LCSH: Riskind, Morris S. (Morris Samuel), 1911–1996. | Riskind, Morris S. (Morris Samuel), 1911–1996—Family. | Riskind family. | M. Riskind, Inc. (Department store) | Jewish families—Texas—Eagle Pass. | Jews—Texas—Eagle Pass—Biography. | Family-owned business enterprises—Texas—Eagle Pass. | Eagle Pass (Tex.)—Race relations—History. | Eagle Pass (Tex.)—History. | Eagle Pass (Tex.)—Biography.
Classification: LCC F394.E13 R57 2024 (print) | LCC F394.E13 (ebook) |
DDC 976.4/435004924092 [B]—dc23/eng/20240802
LC record available at https://lccn.loc.gov/2024018687
LC ebook record available at https://lccn.loc.gov/2024018688

Texas Tech University Press
Box 41037
Lubbock, Texas 79409-1037 USA
800.832.4042
ttup@ttu.edu
www.ttupress.org

Morris S. Riskind
This book is dedicated to the memory of Miss Ida Bel Eby,
an extraordinary teacher and friend

Bryan Edward Stone
For my parents, Barbara Green Stone and Edward A. Stone

CONTENTS

ILLUSTRATIONS	ix
FOREWORD	xi
ACKNOWLEDGMENTS	xxi
EDITOR'S INTRODUCTION	xxiii
AUTHOR'S INTRODUCTION	xlv

CHAPTER 1:	FROM THE RUSSIAN EMPIRE TO EAGLE PASS	3
CHAPTER 2:	TEXAS BEFORE AND AFTER WE GOT THERE	21
CHAPTER 3:	A BORDER COMMUNITY	39
CHAPTER 4:	MY CHILDHOOD IN EAGLE PASS	51
CHAPTER 5:	WASHED AWAY	71
CHAPTER 6:	LOS ANGELES	83
CHAPTER 7:	THE HOME FRONT	103
CHAPTER 8:	BECOMING A FARMER	117
CHAPTER 9:	THE CATTLEMAN	131
CHAPTER 10:	FAMILY AND COMMUNITY	145
CHAPTER 11:	BRIEF CAREER AS A CRIMINAL LAWYER	163
CHAPTER 12:	MY YEARS AT THE STORE	173
CHAPTER 13:	THE TRAVELING MERCHANT	193
CHAPTER 14:	PUBLIC SERVICE AND POLITICS	203
CHAPTER 15:	SEÑOR RÍSQUIN RUNS FOR SCHOOL BOARD	217

CHAPTER 16:	AN ELEGY FOR MY PARENTS	229
EPILOGUE:	THOUGHTS ON THE FUTURE OF AMERICAN JUDAISM	243
	NOTES	249
	BIBLIOGRAPHY	329
	INDEX	343

ILLUSTRATIONS

xv	Riskind's storefront, prior to renovation, 2023
xv	Riskind's storefront exterior, prior to renovation, 2023
xvii	Riskind headstone, 2023
xviii	Morris Riskind, 1974
xxvii	Bird's-eye view of Eagle Pass, 1887
xxviii	Hand-drawn map of Jewish stores, ca. 1990
xxix	Hand-drawn map of Jewish stores, ca. 1990
xl	Riskind Building planned renovation, front, 2023
xl	Riskind Building planned renovation, rear, 2023
xli	Riskind Building planned renovation, reception, 2023
xlv	Downtown Eagle Pass, 1910
4	Nahum (Nathan) and Judith Riskind, wedding picture, 1867
7	Kalvaria, Lithuania, ca. 1870
8	Chatzkel Edelstein, ca. 1900
9	Miriam Fried Edelstein, ca. 1900
17	Michael and Rachel Riskind, wedding picture, 1907
26	Morris Riskind as a baby, 1911
29	Riskind's storefront, ca. 1915
31	Parade on Main Street in front of Riskind's, ca. 1917
32	Riskind's cash register, 1918
32	Riskind advertisement at entry point in Piedras Negras
36	Mike Riskind with employees, early 1930s
37	Riskind's advertisement, January 1922
53	Sam Schwartz with MGM Lion, 1927
57	Morris as World War I soldier, ca. 1920
61	Stephen F. Austin School, Eagle Pass, 1917
64	Michael Riskind, ca. 1920
78	Morris with his oldest son, John, and uncles Eli and David Edelstein, 1949
85	Riskind family portrait, Los Angeles, ca. 1924
99	Morris Riskind, 1932
100	Ruth Sholtz, 1936
113	Morris and Sam Meyer, Alaska, 1978
133	Morris looking rugged, ca. 1945
146	Morris and Ruth Riskind, wedding picture, 1944
150	Bimah at Eagle Pass Jewish Community Center, 1965
157	Michael Riskind, in costume for the Eagle Pass Centennial, 1949
160	Kickapoo settlement under International Bridge, ca. 1970

174	Main Street, Eagle Pass, ca. 1940
174	Riskind's storefront, ca. 1940
176	Mike Riskind with Ernesto Garza, ca. 1940
183	Riskind's flooded, 1954
184	Eagle Pass flood, downtown, 1954
190	Mural behind the store, 1960
190	Riskind's storefront, ca. 1960
195	Morris and Ruth in Oaxaca, Mexico, 1965
208	Roberto and Edna Bibb, 1950
238	Michael and Rachel Riskind with their grandchildren, Eagle Pass, 1966
240	Rachel Riskind, 1975

FOREWORD

This is the memoir of a most unusual man, my father Morris Riskind, who grew up in Eagle Pass, Texas, a small town on the Rio Grande on the US side of the Mexican border. Born soon after the turn of the twentieth century, he witnessed the arrival of automobiles and the first paved roads in the region, the tumultuous effects of the Mexican Revolution of 1910 to 1920, and the beginnings of the modern era. He details the remarkable story of his parents, who were Jewish immigrants from Eastern Europe, and their extraordinary transition to a vastly different and unique hybrid culture on the border. The Texas–Mexico border region is neither fully American nor fully Mexican. It is a society and economy foreign to the inhabitants of either country's interior. In Eagle Pass, Jews occupied an unusual social position, neither fully Anglo nor fully Mexican but partly belonging to both groups—neither fish nor fowl. This is the story of how my family learned to make Lithuanian pirogen with Bisquick and jalapeños and managed to remain Jews and become Americans in this tiny Jewish community on the edge of the United States.

Dad's father, my grandfather Michael, began peddling clothing in Eagle Pass in 1910. He and my grandmother Rachel tailored garments from wholesalers' samples, walking miles in extreme heat to sell directly to customers. He ultimately founded a very successful department store, which remained a leading regional business for almost a century. Trained as a teenager in Belarus, then part of czarist Russia, he was an expert tailor, but he probably had only the equivalent of a third-grade education. He learned to speak Spanish, the key language of commerce in Eagle Pass. A garrulous person, he developed lifelong friendships with Hispanic men, often drinking with them in the local saloon.

In contrast, my father Morris was a deeply introverted, profoundly scholarly man with a truly amazing grasp of the history and great literature of classical Greece and Rome, the Middle East, England, Europe, and the United States. He could recall the detailed plots of great English and French novels sixty years or more after reading them. He read the Torah in Hebrew, the *Aeneid* in Latin, Homer in Greek, Molière in French, and Cervantes in Spanish. He was especially interested in the history of the ancient Near East, subscribing to three professional archaeology journals on that topic. In the absence of an ordained religious leader, he was the lay rabbi of Eagle Pass.

M. RISKIND ("THE STORE") AND THE FAMILY THAT RAN IT

Dad originally wanted to become a classics professor, but his father insisted he go to law school. He dutifully became a lawyer. But after working unhappily for several years in Los Angeles during the Great Depression, he quit the practice of law. In his late twenties, in the 1930s, he returned to Eagle Pass, where he became a farmer-rancher for some years before entering the family retail business, M. Riskind Inc., named after his father Michael. After a few years of apprenticeship under his father, he became the store president. His younger brother, Reuben, became the vice president.

The store was divided into equal portions for men's and women's clothing. Dad ran the men's half of the store and Reuben the women's half, which at times also included a children's section as well as luggage, linens, gifts, tennis equipment, and vinyl records. Dad sold the Border Patrol their uniforms (at cost) as well as Boy Scout uniforms and equipment.

Riskind's sold very high-quality, relatively expensive clothing. We sold Stetson hats, men's and women's shoes, Western boots, ladies informal and formal dresses, handbags, men's formal and informal shirts and slacks, Levi's jeans, suits and sport coats. Hickey Freeman was a very expensive line we featured; most of the lines we carried were our exclusive lines in Eagle Pass.

Many of the salespeople lived in Piedras Negras, Eagle Pass's sister city on the Mexican side of the Rio Grande, and crossed the International Bridge to come to work every morning. We had both Hispanic and Anglo customers, but many of our customers spoke only Spanish. Our most important customers were from Mexico—politicians, generals, and wealthy ranchers and their wives who came to the store periodically to purchase their clothing for the season or even for the year. Riskind's advertised on large billboards as far as three hundred kilometers south into the interior of Mexico.

Hector Ruiz, a 1964 graduate of Eagle Pass High School and later CEO of Advanced Micro Devices, told a story about my father I have always remembered. After graduating from high school and before matriculating at the University of Texas at Austin, Hector worked at Riskind's department store.[1] He noted that Morris Riskind was a very strict boss but emphasized the importance of working hard to become successful. Dad once intervened when a customer who said "I don't want no Mexican" refused to be served by Ruiz. Dad promptly escorted the customer out of the store. Dad's standing up for his employee and refusing to cater to bigotry made a pronounced impression on Mr. Ruiz. Dad's actions were typical of his character.

M. Riskind Inc. had a prominent central location on Main Street. The store had bright fluorescent lighting and was extremely well air-conditioned, so that when you entered during the summer, when the outside temperature could range up to 114 degrees Fahrenheit, the cool air was pleasantly shocking. The upper floor, which had balconies that overlooked the street, was initially where my grandparents lived and later housed the store's administrative offices. It had several rooms and a kitchen that were used as a "Jewish Community Center," where we had all our community holiday and religious services. A billboard on the outskirts of Eagle Pass advertised, "The Jewish Community of Eagle Pass welcomes you!"

My grandmother Rachel's signature dish, served for all family occasions, was her Lithuanian pirogen. These were small, baked meat dumplings the size of potstickers, comprising finely chopped beef tongue, tomatoes, bell peppers, and onions. The wrapping was a flaky pastry dough, which turned reddish-brown from the meat filling. Served piping hot as an appetizer, they were genuinely delicious. They were clearly the tastiest part of any meals served in her home.

As Grandma Rachel aged and needed constant at-home care, the family recruited Licha Torres, a young woman who spoke only Spanish. The two women got along very well, and Grandma thrived. However, we began to notice a gradual change in the pirogen recipe as Licha took more and more responsibility for cooking. Some changes had already begun several years ago, such as the occasional use of ground beef when tongue was unavailable and the substitution of Bisquick or even refrigerated canned dinner rolls for the pastry dough. In a vain attempt to learn the recipe, one day I watched Licha making the pirogen. To my surprise she added a substantial amount of jalapeño to the mix. "How long has this been part of the recipe?" I asked. "A long time," she responded. The pirogen were still delicious but could no longer be deemed "Lithuanian"!

In later life my grandfather Michael did little exercise, loved salty food and sour cream, smoked cigars, and had at least one *schnaps* (a shot of straight Scotch) daily, probably in addition to a few beers. As a premed student, I was astonished by his incredible health and vigor in spite of so many bad habits. I never saw him visibly inebriated or ill. He always seemed physically indestructible. In his mid-eighties he snapped a solid oak walking cane in two when he became angry over a selection of men's ties my father had purchased for the store. Thus, it came as a surprise when we learned that he had stomach cancer and only a short time to live. He went to the hospital for routine blood transfusions during his illness but still went to the store for a few hours most days. His cognitive abilities seemed entirely normal. When he finally reached the end of his illness, he was hospitalized at our local hospital. I rushed home from college to see him. At first, he was able to respond to us in short English phrases. He had never been very talkative around his grandchildren, perhaps because he was not fully comfortable with English. It's also possible that he just had difficulty relating to young people from a background so different from his own. Strikingly, as he became even weaker, he lost the ability to speak and seemingly to understand English at all. We communicated with him exclusively in Spanish, the language he had learned for business and for most of his social outlets. This experience contributed to my interest in the human brain and resulted in my becoming a neurologist.

MORRIS AND RUTH RISKIND, MY PARENTS

Dad made up for his lack of an academic teaching career by providing highly intellectual lectures on ancient history to his children at every mealtime. It was common for us to hear a college-level discourse on the Hittites, Sumerians, Elamites, ancient Hebrews, or Romans. Invariably his lectures were much more interesting than what we were learning at school. Needless to say, my mother did not appreciate Dad's incessant monopolizing of mealtime conversation. After a few minutes of lecture, she would invariably interrupt with a comment like "Morrie, you are eating too fast!" or "Morrie, sit up straight!" in a vain attempt to derail his train of thought.

My father was always reading. In the evening, he sat in a recliner and browsed our twenty-four-volume set of the *Encyclopaedia Britannica* for entertainment. He was also an excellent tennis player from his California days and a lifelong enthusiast of the outdoors. Even in his last years, he walked so quickly that I had difficulty keeping up with him.

Mom had a strong, gregarious, warm, and friendly personality. She was famous for befriending everyone within earshot on plane trips, often gleaning their family histories and best recipes by the end of the flight. As a young woman she was a rebel, quite independent and "liberated" for her time. During World War II, she volunteered to work as an art teacher in a Japanese relocation camp in Arizona because she had friends from UCLA who had been interned. Later she worked for a movie producer in New York. One of her conditions for marrying Dad was that he agree to her previously planned six-week trip with another single woman into the interior of Mexico. This was remarkably brazen, independent behavior at that time, the early 1940s.

Mom had lifelong Mexican friends with whom she exclusively spoke Spanish—but only in the present tense, as that was all the Spanish grammar she had ever learned. She grew up in Los Angeles in a highly intellectual, artistic family. Famous musicians were family friends, and her father frequently had intellectual gatherings in their home. She demonstrated notable artistic talent at an early age. She was mentored by Peter Krasnow (for whom I was named), a well-known modern artist. She painted and sculpted, and her work was positively reviewed by art critics. However, when she realized that she was not going to be a great artist, she switched to studying art history. She was in graduate school at UCLA when our father finally persuaded her to marry him and go to Eagle Pass. After her children entered grade school, she had a long career as an art teacher at Eagle Pass High School.

My mother was extremely disdainful of clerics, whom she assumed to be hypocrites, of any and all persuasions. This disdain, of course, is ironic: her father was a highly regarded Jewish educator and scholar, and Dad was also a Jewish scholar and the lay rabbi of our town.

On several occasions Mom and Dad took us on long family drives down the Pan American Highway into the interior of Mexico. We drove through Saltillo and San Luis Potosí, visited San Miguel de Allende, Pátzcuaro, Taxco, Guanajuato, and Mexico City. I was fascinated and overwhelmed by our visit to the pyramids in Teotihuacán.

My parents' facility and ease in speaking Spanish and their deep knowledge of Mexican history and culture impressed me immensely. Mom taught us how to properly bargain in the Mexican markets, always making her offers and counteroffers with a smile. Both of my parents clearly had a profound fondness (*cariño*) for Mexico. When I was sixteen, our family rented an apartment in Mexico City for six weeks during the summer. This was an amazing time. We went to the National Museum of Anthropology, one of the world's best museums, numerous times. We joined the Centro Deportivo Israelita, the city's Jewish sports center, and we ate in many lovely Mexican restaurants. We had such a wonderful time that both my older brother, John, and I said we wanted to live there after we finished school. In fact, I once asked my father, "Where would you want to live, if it was not in Eagle Pass?" I thought he might answer somewhere in California or even New York City. Instead, he promptly replied, "Mexico City."

THE SAD FATE OF RISKIND'S DEPARTMENT STORE

Morris Riskind was typically modest and self-deprecating about his successes; nowhere in his memoir does he describe his substantial success as a businessman. Under his leadership, together with his brother, Reuben, M. Riskind, Inc., grew and prospered. At its peak there were two stores in Eagle Pass and another in McAllen, Texas, downriver from Eagle Pass. Additional stores were planned.

As best as I can determine, Dad and Uncle Reuben had a very good relationship when they were young men. Dad was eight years older and had been a virtual surrogate parent when he and Reuben were growing up in Los Angeles, as my grandfather Michael was absent much of the year, back in Texas running the business. Dad took Reuben with him to the tennis courts when he was a child, and Reuben later became a star tennis player. Dad also writes positively about Reuben in this memoir. However, over time their relationship, and that of our two families, became one of enmity and resentment. Eventually the tense relationship erupted into outright arguments between Dad and Reuben, causing my father tremendous stress. My father tried to patch things up with Reuben but ultimately gave up. He exercised an option in their legal documents that would force a buyout of one brother by the other. He finally sold his part of the business to Reuben in 1980.

Riskind's storefront prior to renovation, 2023. (Photograph by Bryan Edward Stone.)

Riskind's storefront prior to renovation, 2023. (Photograph by Bryan Edward Stone.)

My younger brother, Lorin, had been working with my father in the business since August 1978. After the split from Reuben, they took over the second, smaller store in Eagle Pass, the 21 Shop, and the Coed Shop in McAllen. Both stores were renamed Lorin's. At first, business was excellent in both stores. Dad and Lorin opened a third store, also named Lorin's, in the new mall on the outskirts of Eagle Pass in 1982. Unfortunately, the opening coincided with a disastrous unraveling of the Mexican economy. The peso had been a stable currency for decades, pegged at an exchange rate of 12.5 pesos per dollar. It was devalued in 1976 to 27 to 1, with significant negative repercussions on the border economy. Higher inflation rates in Mexico as compared to the United States helped the border economy to recover and prosper again for a time, but the situation worsened in February 1982 when the Mexican government instituted multiple more-dramatic peso devaluations. The peso fell to fifty pesos to the dollar; by January 1984 it had collapsed to 1,500 to 1. As a result, there was a catastrophic loss of Mexican purchasing power along the border, especially for retail clothing. These devaluations caused economic ruin throughout the border region. They had a devastating effect on hundreds of businesses along the border, including ours.[2]

Dad and Lorin closed the McAllen store in early 1982 and the remaining downtown Eagle Pass store later that year. With no foreseeable prospect for recovery of the border economy, Lorin was forced to leave Eagle Pass and moved to Dallas. My father closed the mall store, our last remaining business, in 1984. Riskind's department store struggled on under the leadership of my cousin Dan until finally closing in 2009, a year short of its one-hundredth anniversary.

DAD'S ILLNESS

During the last decade of his life, Dad went on several trips with his male friends, as my mother was not interested in some travel destinations. His last trip, in 1995, was to Alaska with his lifelong friend Sam Meyer. During the trip he began experiencing hip pain, which he initially dismissed as arthritis. However, the pain worsened. Medical investigation revealed metastatic cancer. As there was no possible treatment, he decided to have palliative care, mostly pain control, in order to have a good quality of life as long as possible.

His last years were productive and enjoyable. He was an active and enthusiastic member of the Texas Fine Arts Commission. One of his last civic endeavors was the organization of an Independence Day celebration in Eagle Pass. Though quite weak at that point, he was able to attend the celebration and was recognized by the speakers for his contributions.

For the last nine months of his life Dad remained in Eagle Pass. He continued to read avidly, never lost his intellectual curiosity, and was as physically active as possible. My siblings and I visited him in rotation so one of us was almost always present; each of us made frequent visits to help our mother and to see him. He met with my older daughter Rachel to discuss her Torah portion for her upcoming bat mitzvah, which he predeceased, and played chess with my children. With the help of videotape, we recorded blessings for each of his grandchildren and completed a series of interviews about his life and our family history. Our mother took wonderful care of him.

On one visit I went with my wife to the Walmart to get cleaning supplies. As we finished our purchases, I asked the young Hispanic woman at the register, "Is there somewhere nearby where we can we get some good *pan dulce* [Mexican pastry]?"

She gave me a hard stare and replied: "How do you know about *pan dulce*?"

Taken aback, I responded, "I am from here and grew up eating it my whole life. Why are you asking that?"

Burial place of Morris and Ruth Sholtz Riskind, Maverick County Cemetery, Eagle Pass. (Photograph by Bryan Edward Stone.)

In response, she said, "No, you are not from here. You can't be."

"Well, I am from here. I am from an old Eagle Pass family. My name is Riskind, from Riskind's department store. You must know it."

"No, I have never heard of it. I don't believe you are from here."

"You've never heard of my father, Morris Riskind?"

"No, I've never heard of him."

I persisted. "Morris Riskind? He has a mustache. He is about eighty-five years old now."

"Oh, that must be the old man who comes to the library every day. I used to work there and saw him coming in to read lots of different newspapers."

I recently learned that there is a Riskind Circle in Eagle Pass and a Mikulinski Road, named after one of our family's closest Jewish friends. This incident, however, brought home the fact that the Riskinds, formerly a prominent local family, had completely faded from popular memory among the younger inhabitants of Eagle Pass. In addition, as an "Anglo," I was now clearly perceived as an alien in Eagle Pass.

True to his own father's example, Dad never bemoaned his illness. Despite his increasing fragility and loss of independence, he somehow maintained dignity. He never expressed any self-pity and, remarkably, was able to tell jokes and funny stories to the end. When he last saw his oncologist, he thanked the team for all their help. They had tears in their eyes as he left. At my last visit with Dad, shortly before he died, I asked him, "Are you ready to go?" He quickly and unemotionally replied, "Yes." Dad died on July 24, 1996, at the age of eighty-five.

Morris Riskind in 1974. (Courtesy of Dr. Peter Riskind.)

Dad was widely admired and beloved by the Eagle Pass community. Remarkably, in a town still split by class and ethnic lines, our parents attended many social activities of the Hispanic community but also had friends in the Anglo community. Dad was very friendly with the Episcopalian minister, who gave him an annotated copy of the Old Testament. We were touched and immensely grateful in the days after his death when members of the Hispanic community, Anglos, Episcopalians, and others mobilized to bring food to our home.

Thankfully, Dad did not lose his mental faculties during his illness. During the weeks before his death, Dad helped to write his own funeral service and discussed with us various means to find a rabbi to lead the service. Dad had been the town's only "rabbi," performing funeral services, bar and bat mitzvahs, and officiating at all other Jewish functions. Who would officiate at his funeral? We were thankful that Rabbi Peter Tarlow, the rabbi of the Texas A&M University Hillel, volunteered. Rabbi Tarlow had met Dad through his friendship with my older brother, John. The funeral was held in a local funeral home—after the crucifixes were covered with drapes. Rabbi Tarlow drove seven hours to Eagle Pass from Texas A&M in College Station. He then conducted a moving ceremony in English, Spanish, and Hebrew.

My mother continued to live in Eagle Pass until October 1998, when she moved to Dallas to be near my brother Lorin and his family. She died on March 9, 2007, after a long illness. The rest of the family will be eternally grateful for the loving, supportive, and attentive care provided mainly by my sister-in-law Sherri Riskind and my brother Lorin. Our parents are buried side by side in the Jewish section of the Maverick County Cemetery.

THE MEMOIR

Dad had great respect for artistic and intellectual creativity and constantly lamented his own lack of achievement in that regard. He loved music but could not sing or play an instrument. He yearned to be a successful writer, and even wrote a short detective story, but he concluded that he could not write fiction. However, he was an outstanding storyteller. He decided that it would be an invaluable service to his descendants and to others interested in history to preserve our very unusual family story.

Perhaps as early as the mid-1970s, he began writing his memoir. At first, he wrote in longhand, as he was not a skilled typist. Later, he dictated to his secretary and edited the typed copy. Still later he had this document scanned and worked on an early Apple computer with three-and-a-half-inch diskettes. He had largely completed the memoir by 1993. At that time, he sent the manuscript to publishing firms that might have a special interest in Jewish history. Unfortunately, it was met with uniform rejection. To be fair, the document was not well organized and did not include sufficient explanatory material.

Dad remained deeply saddened by his inability to publish his memoir; it was clearly of great importance to him. As I was saying goodbye to him for the last time in 1996, shortly before he died, he asked me to do him a major favor. "Please see to it that my memoir is published." I assured him that I would.

After his death, I shipped several boxes of different typed and printed versions of the text, together with a floppy disk containing the latest version, to my home in Massachusetts. Over the years I had read various parts of the book, but I had not read it in its entirety. It was clear to me that it needed editing and reorganization. I performed some initial editing and sent samples to several publishing houses. One academic publisher in Texas expressed some interest but criticized aspects of the writing. At their suggestion I hired Victoria Woodruff, a professional freelance editor, to work with me and edit the memoir. We worked together during much of 1998 and 1999 and finally completed an edited version of the memoir. I added some wonderful photographs to the manuscript and then sent copies to my family and to some family friends who had known my father.

To my dismay, their reaction to the edited text was extremely negative. In an attempt to make my father's text clearer and easier to understand, we had completely washed out his "voice." I was devastated. I had spent many hours working on this project despite my busy medical career and family obligations, but I had actually destroyed what made it interesting and unique. I was so unhappy with this outcome that I stopped work on the memoir and did not take it up again for twenty years.

In December 2019, I retired from my job as professor of neurology at the University of Massachusetts (UMass) Medical School and director of the Multiple Sclerosis Center at UMass Memorial Health Care. I resolved to reedit and ultimately publish *Neither Fish nor Fowl*. To do this I wanted to use most of the document's structure from my work with Victoria Woodruff but replace much of the text with my father's original words. I also found new material as I worked with the various versions of original typewritten text. The Covid-19 pandemic gave me lots of time at home for this important project.

After six months of work, I assembled a restored text with much better organization than the original. I added many footnotes about events and persons mentioned in the text. I contacted a number of academic publishers and submitted samples. Texas Tech University Press (TTUP) expressed interest, but ultimately decided that the text needed extensive input from a historian to make it appropriate for an academic press. My family is extremely grateful to Travis Snyder, editor in chief at TTUP, who was invaluable in recruiting Bryan Edward Stone, an eminent Texas Jewish historian, to be the editor. We are truly appreciative that Dr. Stone has taken on this project.

The descendants of Morris and Ruth Riskind are widely dispersed. We live in California, Illinois, Massachusetts, North Carolina, Texas, Virginia, and Sweden. Our professions have been strongly influenced by our parents and grandparents; teaching has been a frequent career choice. We include two college psychology professors, a music professor, a neurology professor, a lawyer, a federal government official, and multiple business persons. All of us are Jewish and teach Spanish to our children. We continue to feel partly Mexican with much *cariño* for Mexico. I grow tomatillos and cilantro in my New England vegetable garden and make frijoles, *salsa verde*, guacamole, enchiladas, and tacos on a regular basis.

PETER RISKIND, MD, PHD
SON OF MORRIS RISKIND
NEEDHAM, MASSACHUSETTS
JUNE 15, 2024

ACKNOWLEDGMENTS

FROM PETER RISKIND

Many people have made invaluable contributions to the preparation of this manuscript. Most of all, I thank my wife, Dr. Carolyn Gayle. She has spent many hours proofreading and making key editorial comments and suggestions. This effort could not have gone forward without her. I also thank my brother, Dr. John Riskind, for his very helpful editorial suggestions, and my siblings Susan Riskind and Lorin Riskind for essential fact-checking. Together with my daughters, Dr. Rachel Riskind and Dr. Sarah Riskind, they have made many helpful comments and editorial suggestions. I must also acknowledge Victoria Woodruff, who worked with me over a two-year span to organize my father's original manuscript. Her contributions have been invaluable.

I also thank my cousin Miriam Riskind for her help identifying individuals in several old photographs. Special thanks go to Bryan Edward Stone, whose participation in this effort has been a godsend. *Neither Fish nor Fowl* could not have been published without his scholarly contributions.

FROM BRYAN EDWARD STONE

This book exists only because of Dr. Peter Riskind's indefatigable effort over many years to bring his father's work to publication, and I have had the distinct pleasure of taking these final steps with him. Peter has been constantly encouraging; generous with information, photographs, video interviews, and other materials; and patient through inevitable delays. My job was made much easier by the skilled work he had already done on the manuscript and the moral support he and his family gave me, and I couldn't be prouder to work with him in completing such an important task.

My thanks to Travis Snyder at Texas Tech University Press for inviting me to this project and guiding it with great appreciation of its importance. Christie Perlmutter, Hannah Gaskamp, John Brock, and Ryan Schumacher have also been invaluable in the preparation and promotion of the book. Mark Goldberg of the University of Houston wrote a marvelous review of the original manuscript, which has been a touchstone for me as I've sought to highlight the book's themes. As a newcomer to all things Eagle Pass, I could not have been more fortunate than to make the acquaintance of Jeff Taylor Sr., who runs the Facebook page "Eagle Pass, Texas ~ 'Back in the Day.'" Jeff not only shared his detailed knowledge of people and places Riskind wrote about, but he provided numerous photographs from his collection and gave me a personal tour of the Fort Duncan Museum, the contents of which he is largely responsible for preserving and curating. Jeff is the epitome of the dedicated local historian, without whom any small community would risk forgetting where it came from.

For specific contributions I thank Robb Packer and the members of the Synagogues of Chicago Facebook group, who helped me identify the shul Rachel Edelstein visited there. David Riskind, the son of Morris's brother, Reuben, provided invaluable photographs and detailed information on his father's role in the family business. David's daughter Rachel sent me a video link of an Eagle Pass press conference that was so compelling it now begins my introduction. Fort Duncan Museum coordinator Jerry Quiroz helped show me around the museum and provided ideas and insights. Jerry Suarez has been an important and knowledgeable contact in Eagle Pass. Barbara Green Stone, the best amateur photographer I've ever known, provided invaluable help with several historic photographs.

Many historians read portions of the manuscript and offered crucial insights and suggestions. I'm deeply grateful especially to Harriet Denise Joseph for her careful and encouraging peer review of the entire book. My thanks also to Derek Oden, Jonathan Friedmann, and my colleagues in the Community College Writing Group for their insights on specific chapters. Andrew Hernández went even further, correcting some of my misunderstandings about border history and recommending reading on regional topics where I badly needed direction. Finally, I could never adequately thank the librarians at Del Mar College—especially Vivian Brown, Mona Palmer, and Lisa Muilenburg—who helped me obtain countless necessary materials.

My wife, Shannon Dougherty, is my most constant source of support, encouragement, and common sense; she is a sounding board, an eagle-eyed reader, a friend. I'm immensely grateful for all she is and all she helps me to be.

In many ways this is a book about how much we learn from our parents, and I'm grateful for this opportunity to thank mine and to dedicate my share of this book to them.

EDITOR'S INTRODUCTION

In March 2021, a group of city leaders held a press conference on Main Street in Eagle Pass, Texas, in front of the empty storefront that had once housed the M. Riskind department store. Speaking through face coverings, the mayor of the Rio Grande border town, along with its city manager, congressman, and other dignitaries, celebrated the award of a $3.5 million grant under the CARES Act, which provided federal funds to help communities recover from Covid-19. The city had purchased the historic 1914 building, and the grant provided for its renovation into a 15,000-square-foot "small business incubator" that would hold office space, conference rooms, a restaurant, retail sites, an economic development office, and an expansion of the art and culture center next door.[1] It would be a place, Mayor Luis Sifuentes said, "that would provide jobs, create opportunities [for] entrepreneurs that wanted to open up their own business," and "bring people into the downtown area again."[2]

Mayor Sifuentes emphasized the appropriateness of placing such a facility in this particular building, where the M. Riskind store and the Riskind family had long been anchors of the city's commercial downtown. He recounted highlights in the life of the store's founder, Michael Riskind, "born in Orsha, Russia, son of Nathan and Judith Riskind, a Jewish-Russian couple." He told of how Michael Riskind moved from Chicago to Texas on the advice of his brother-in-law, "a street vendor near the border crossing between Eagle Pass and Piedras Negras." Michael began as a peddler, opened a small store on Commercial Street, and ran it successfully until 1914, when he bought a Main Street lot and built the storefront that still stands. As the city and downtown commercial district thrived, so did Riskind's. "By 1954," Sifuentes continued, during its peak period of growth, "the number of employees at Riskind's store grew from about ten to seventy-four—including my own mother, who used to work here at Riskind's building. So, this store, this front, has a lot of memories for me."[3]

After decades of success, lean years came in the 1970s and '80s with the advent of suburbanization, shopping malls, and catastrophic devaluations of the peso, which drove away most of the store's Mexican customers, a key share of its clientele. After a long decline and ninety-nine years in business, M. Riskind closed its doors in 2009. In a testament to the store's economic impact, Mayor Sifuentes noted that "its closure had a ripple effect on Main Street as other businesses closed as well."[4] It was fitting, therefore, that the historic building would now catalyze the recovery of downtown investment and development.

That storefront is imposing, even in inactivity a prominent feature of an active commercial block. Two stories high, its long, unadorned first floor is lined with large display windows facing the sidewalk and topped with an extended balcony overlooking the street. Set back on

XXIII

the balcony, six brick archways open to a covered porch and a large second-floor apartment, which was for many years the Riskind family home. It was also the site of Jewish worship services and holiday observances, which the Riskinds hosted and led, social gatherings of the city's small Jewish community, and an informal welcoming center for Jewish personnel stationed at nearby military bases during a revolution in Mexico and two world wars. For Mayor Sifuentes and thousands of other non-Jewish Eagle Pass residents, the Riskind building holds memories of family members who worked and shopped there, but the site holds an important place in Jewish memory. It is a remnant—perhaps the only remnant outside the county cemetery—of a small but constant Jewish presence in the border city.

As the themes of Jewish identity, family business, and the borderland intersect in the Riskind building, they also provide the foundation of this memoir by Morris Riskind, Michael and Rachel's oldest son and his father's successor in the management of the store, along with his brother, Reuben. Morris was born in Eagle Pass in 1911, just a year after his parents settled there, grew up in the apartment above the store, and lived his entire life in the town, with the exception of sixteen years in Los Angeles—a sojourn his mother demanded so he and his siblings could obtain a proper Jewish education. Riskind wrote his memoir in Eagle Pass, working intermittently from the 1970s until finishing in 1992, four years before his death at the age of eighty-five.[5]

Neither Fish nor Fowl is mostly set in one small Texas city, but Riskind chronicles a vast life experience, providing a wealth of detail about his parents and family history, his upbringing in Eagle Pass, his friends and schoolmates, the town's Jewish community, the growth and activities of the Riskind family business, his education and abortive law career in Los Angeles, his effort to succeed as a farmer and rancher during the war years, his own career managing the family store with his brother, his activism and civic leadership in Eagle Pass, and his world travels with his wife, Ruth. It is also a comprehensive family history—he begins and ends the book, in fact, with his parents, not with himself—and like all good memoirs, is not only a personal narrative but a reflection on the larger world the narrator inhabited. Riskind effectively places a particular family in a particular place where they were both deeply rooted and somewhat set apart.

MORRIS RISKIND AS NARRATOR

Neither Fish nor Fowl contains the recollections of a man with an unusual life trajectory—small-town Jewish boy, Los Angeles lawyer, West Texas farmer and rancher, borderland merchant, and world traveler—but also an uncommon sensibility and ability to observe. The book's uniqueness and importance derive from the distinctive point of view of Morris Riskind himself, the many ways in which his life diverged from the expected norms of both American Jewish history and borderland society. Riskind was extraordinarily well-informed, well-read in classical and modern literature, Jewish scripture and texts, and in local and general history; he was fluent in English and Spanish but also functional in Hebrew and Yiddish and literate in Latin, Greek, and French. He had a law degree from the University of Southern California; business associates in Dallas, Chicago, and New York; and traveled extensively in Mexico, Europe, and Israel. His point of view, then, was localized but hardly provincial.[6]

Until Morris's parents took a hard left turn toward Texas, their lives followed closely the well-worn path of most Eastern European Jewish immigrants of their generation. Born and raised in the Pale of Settlement, the expansive region of tsarist Russia where Jews were required to live, they came from communities steeped in religious and social tradition, albeit from different branches of Judaism. "My father's family were pious Orthodox, either Hasidim or close to the Hasidim in many of their beliefs," Morris writes. "My mother's family were Talmudic rationalists . . . who interpreted the scriptures through reason and laughed at folk tales of miracles." Both were large families—Michael Riskind was one of seven children, Rachel Edelstein one of ten—which would provide them an extensive family network in the United States once most of them had immigrated. Both families offer classic examples of chain migration, which directed the lives of most American immigrants, Jewish and otherwise.

As Morris relates, his parents followed different paths to America but ended up in the same place, the Jewish neighborhood on Chicago's West Side. Michael's father, Nahum (later Nathan), was his family's pioneer, arriving in New York in 1888, then finding his way to Chicago, and barely holding himself together until his more sensible wife, Judith, and most of their children could join him there. Twelve-year-old Michael remained behind in Russia to study for his bar mitzvah and apprentice as a tailor, reuniting with his parents in Chicago four years later. Far more astute and energetic than his father (at least according to Morris), Michael parlayed his tailoring skills into a successful career in the garment trade, the most common occupation for Jewish immigrants.[7] He experienced every side of the business, first as a worker in a suit factory, then in management, then caught up in a futile strike of Chicago garment workers that persuaded him to light out on his own. "The moral of the story, according to Pa," Morris recounts, "was never to go to work for anyone else again and to be his own boss." Here too, Michael Riskind hewed closely to a common immigrant pattern.

Meanwhile, worried about rising antagonism toward Russian Jews and her own declining marriage prospects, twenty-three-year-old Rachel Rose Edelstein, whose family were well-to-do landowners in Lithuania, moved to Chicago in 1903, where her brother Abe had established himself in the same neighborhood in which the Riskinds lived. Through contacts made at a nearby synagogue, she met Michael, who had set himself up in a small tailoring business, and they married in 1907.[8] Morris makes much of the differences in his parents' backgrounds, but the immediate connection between Michael and Rachel shows how quickly America had worked its magic on them: after only a few years in Chicago they were assimilated enough not to care about such differences.

What took Morris Riskind's parents to America were the same migration patterns that guided most Jewish immigrants; what took them to Texas was tuberculosis. Abe Edelstein, the brother Rachel had followed to Chicago, contracted the disease, which eventually killed him, and a Chicago doctor prescribed a common treatment: relocation to South Texas, where the drier climate was more conducive to recovery. Abe moved to San Antonio and began peddling a wide route that took him as far as Eagle Pass, on the Mexican border, where he opened a downtown furniture store in 1908. Back in Chicago, Michael Riskind lost his tailoring business in the Panic of 1907, fell ill, and received the same diagnosis and medical advice as his brother-in-law.[9] He followed Edelstein to Eagle Pass, lived for a while in the back of the furniture store, began peddling, and saved enough to buy a modest home. He then brought his wife and infant daughter from Chicago and opened his first small shop, filling the shelves with empty boxes and the family's own clothing "to give the illusion of a well-stocked business." Morris was born in their house the next year.

The Riskinds had much in common with the rest of the Eagle Pass population. Michael and Rachel, like many residents, were immigrants who became property owners, businesspeople, and investors in the town's growth and success. Morris Riskind was born and spent most of his life there, and as an adult, he was at the forefront of the town's commercial and cultural activities, a faithful civic booster. He was also a proud Texan, displaying in his memoir a lifelong passion for the state's history, especially of the borderland subregion where he lived. When his wife, Ruth, moved to Eagle Pass from Los Angeles and was hired to teach Texas history, she relied on Morris for help preparing her lessons. He tells us that he once offered to move back to California with her, but "she replied that I was happier in Texas, and she desired above all for me to be happy."

Yet there is much that sets Morris and his family apart from mainstream Eagle Pass, which gives his memoir its unique vantage point. Michael Riskind returned regularly to Chicago on buying trips, where his parents still lived, maintaining contact with a large and more traditional Jewish community; later he and Rachel made annual visits to Israel. Their son Morris lived for sixteen years in Los Angeles, in the Boyle Heights neighborhood that was then home to more than thirty thousand Jews.[10] He earned a bachelor's and a law degree and traveled widely. Though he always returned to Eagle Pass, these experiences affected his view of his small and remote hometown and gave him the objectivity to perceive flaws that might have been neglected by others among the town's biggest boosters. He is, for instance, troubled by the hardship his cultured and educated wife experiences in a place he describes as "a cultural backwater" and observes dryly that "if a tourist did find his way to Eagle Pass, it was because he was lost."

Morris's wish to promote his town motivates one of the book's longest and most revealing episodes, where he describes his effort to arrange the involvement of the Indigenous Kickapoo people in the town's 1949 centennial parade. He advocates their equal participation as members of the community but also sees them as resources to be exploited for tourism, potentially "a gold mine" for the town, a "bonanza" that could be "worth a fortune." He is brought up short when the planning committee doesn't agree. "To my astonishment," he writes, "neither the Anglo nor Mexican old families, nor the ranchers, showed any interest in what they termed 'a bunch of dirty Indians.'" When, after strenuous effort on Morris's part, the Kickapoo appeared in the parade anyway, they were greeted, to his great shame, with racist jeers from the audience. Riskind doesn't mention his own Jewishness in this account, but it is undoubtedly relevant. Being Jewish could explain why Riskind is more attuned than most to the value of ethnic difference, how the town's diversity gives it social and economic advantage. But his Jewishness also makes him unwilling to acknowledge consciously the town's embedded bigotry, potentially a threat to every member of any ethnic or religious minority.

THE SETTLEMENT OF THE JEWS IN EAGLE PASS

When historian Lee Shai Weissbach argued that "the full story of the American Jewish experience [cannot] be told without considering the history of small-town Jewish life," he was properly attempting to shift scholarly attention away from New York and other large and midsized communities. "Small communities," Weissbach says, "have always been fundamental features in the American Jewish landscape." In his study of small-town Jewish America, Weissbach placed his own focus on "triple-digit communities," those with between one hundred and one thousand Jewish residents, based on the presumption "that at least 100 Jews were needed for the maintenance of an active communal life."[11] Eagle Pass, however, never had more than sixty Jewish inhabitants; it was double-digit, not triple-digit. By Weissbach's standard Eagle Pass was too small a Jewish community to qualify as a small Jewish community.[12]

But Morris Riskind gives us tools to understand Eagle Pass as a real if indeed very small and highly mobile Jewish population, a group of dedicated families, some in place for generations,

Augustus Koch, "Bird's Eye View of Eagle Pass, Maverick Co., Texas," 1887. (Amon Carter Museum of American Art, Fort Worth, Texas. Gift of Charles Downing.)

others passing through briefly, who tried to maintain whatever degree of tradition and distinct identity was possible. Eagle Pass never had a Jewish congregation: the nearest synagogue when Morris was born was in San Antonio, 140 miles away, although one was established slightly closer in Laredo during World War I. There were no Jewish social, benevolent, or advocacy organizations, no regular prayer group, no rabbi for more than an occasional social visit. There *was*, however, a Hebrew school, a *sefer Torah* (the sacred scroll containing the first five books of the Hebrew scripture), several bar and bat mitzvahs, and regular observances of Jewish holidays and sacred events. It was a community limited by circumstances but not by ambivalence.

There has been a continuous Jewish presence in Eagle Pass since the town's founding, longer than even Morris Riskind was aware. After the Treaty of Guadalupe Hidalgo confirmed the Rio Grande as the international border in 1848, the US Army established a series of garrisons along the river, including Fort Duncan, at a long-used river crossing called Paso del Águila, or Eagle Pass. The town, which took its name from the crossing, began as a trading post in 1849, received a stage line from San Antonio in 1851, and grew rapidly with migration from both Texas and Mexico. The Mexican town of Piedras Negras ("black stones," named for the area's surface deposits of black coal) was established in 1850 directly across from Eagle Pass as a counter to the growing presence on the American side. Despite constant pressure from Comanche, Lipan Apache, and Kickapoo raiders, the town continued to grow, and during the Civil War it was an important export location for Confederate cotton smugglers

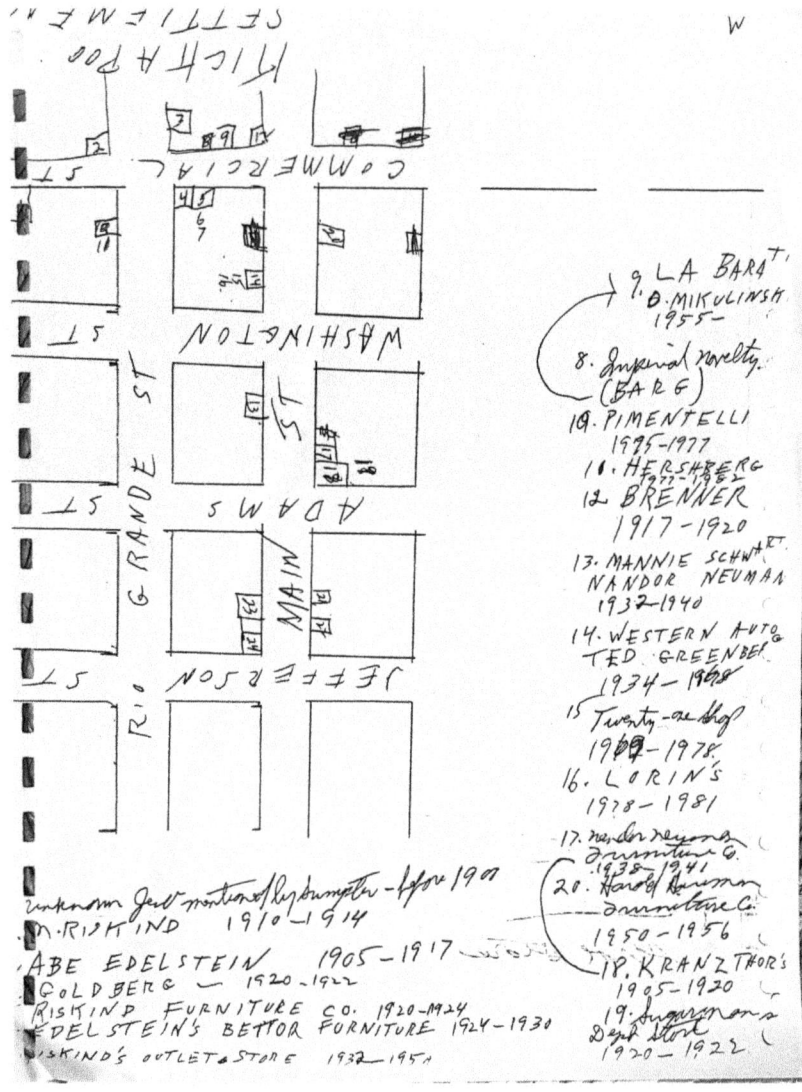

Drawn by Morris Riskind in the late 1980s or early 1990s, this map shows a fifteen-square-block section of downtown Eagle Pass. Morris indicated the locations of twenty-six Jewish-owned businesses in the area over an eighty-two-year period. (Courtesy of Dr. Peter Riskind.)

looking to evade the Union blockade. It became the seat of Maverick County in 1871, the railroad reached it in 1882, and by 1910 when the Riskinds arrived, it had a population of about 3,500, most of whom were of Mexican descent.[13]

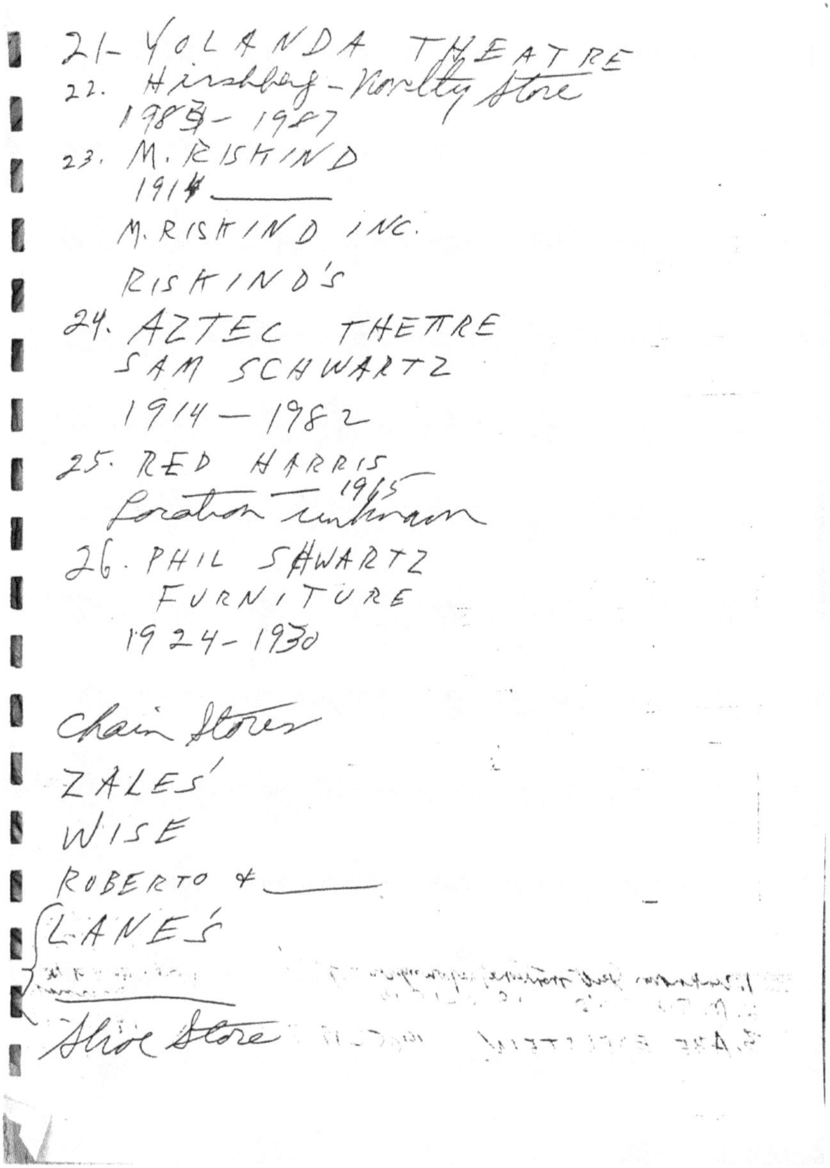

[Handwritten list:]

21. YOLANDA THEATRE
22. Hirshberg–Novelty Store
    1983–1987
23. M. RISKIND
    1914–_____
    M. RISKIND INC.
    RISKIND'S
24. AZTEC THEATRE
    SAM SCHWARTZ
    1914–1982
25. RED HARRIS
    1965
    location unknown
26. PHIL SCHWARTZ
    FURNITURE
    1924–1930

Chain Stores
ZALES'
WISE
ROBERTO & _____
LANE'S
_____
Shoe Store

The first Jewish resident arrived about 1850, just one year after the town's founding. In December of that year, E. Wolff wrote a letter from Eagle Pass to Isaac Leeser of Philadelphia, one of the nation's most prominent rabbis. "Revd Sir," Wolff began. He described himself as a longtime reader of Leeser's newspaper, the *Occident*, who now found himself "living in this Wild Indian region at a loss without it." Working through an officer friend at Fort Duncan, Wolff arranged to have ten dollars forwarded to Leeser to pay for whatever back issues were available, and "if there is any balance to imploy it in any Jewish tracts that may have appeared."

Signing himself "Your Brother in Faith," Wolff closed his letter and disappeared from the historical record.[14] Wolff's self-consciousness about his isolation from Jewish life, his hunger for community, and the brevity of his stay in Eagle Pass would become paradigmatic through the whole history of Jewish settlement there.

Subsequent accounts of Jews in nineteenth-century Eagle Pass are few. According to early resident Jesse Sumpter, there were two Jewish merchants, Behr Steinbock and a man named Cain, in town by the 1860s, both of whom met untimely and violent ends.[15] In 1881, a traveler through the region reported to a national Jewish newspaper that "there are but few Israelites in this section, and most of them are indifferent to religious matters." He found no Jews in Piedras Negras and in Eagle Pass met just one, Samuel White, "the only Israelite in the town, two-thirds of whose inhabitants are Mexicans."[16] White, born in Bavaria in 1837, was apparently unmarried, had been in the city for at least eleven years operating a dry goods store, and owned land in the surrounding country. In his pioneering history of Texas Jews, Rabbi Henry Cohen was compelled to repeat monotonously that nearly every Jewish settler was "engaged in mercantile pursuits," and Cain, Steinbock, and White established that pattern early in Eagle Pass.[17]

In the decades prior to the Riskinds' arrival, the Jewish community of Eagle Pass consisted of a small number of mercantile pursuers—all male, all single, none of whom remained in town more than a few years. These early cases also suggest the degree to which Eagle Pass Jewry was an offshoot of San Antonio, linked through family, commercial, and institutional connections. Nathan Sulzbacher, for example, was born in New York, moved with his brother to San Antonio in about 1879, and worked for the Jewish-owned Frank Brothers department store. He was briefly resident in Eagle Pass when, in 1887, he married a woman from San Antonio and returned to live there with her permanently.[18] Max Oppenheimer, born in Bavaria and related to a prominent San Antonio banking family, joined them in Texas in the early 1880s, then relocated on his own to Eagle Pass. In 1883, he married Texas native Rachel Ganz in a San Antonio wedding officiated by the city's rabbi and announced nationally in the *American Israelite*.[19] Rachel moved with him to Eagle Pass, where he ran a bank and they raised four children: Rachel Oppenheimer was probably the first Jewish woman, and theirs the first Jewish children, in Eagle Pass. The family returned to San Antonio, however, in about 1900.

In fact, all these early Jewish residents had left, most for San Antonio, and been replaced with others by 1901, when a correspondent to the *American Israelite* reported "only three Jewish families in the place," named Toziewitz, Baum, and Phillips. Two of these, the writer said, had recently traveled to San Francisco and New Orleans, where they had enjoyed what Eagle Pass could not offer, "the advantages of worshiping with those of their common faith."[20] The Baums have proven impossible for me to identify, but the Toziewitz and Phillips families were both engaged in mercantile pursuits and apparently related by marriage. Adolph Toziewitz and Yetta Phillips, born in Germany, married in 1891 in Eagle Pass, where they ran a dry goods store and had two sons; theirs was undoubtedly the first of a small number of Jewish weddings in the town. Prussian-born Jacob and Ada Phillips (their relationship to Yetta is unclear) arrived shortly later and lived on Washington Street, a block away from the Toziewitzes on Adams. Yetta Phillips Toziewitz may have died around 1909, when her husband Adolph adopted her maiden surname as his own, moved to Portland, Oregon, and remarried. Jacob and Ada Phillips relocated with their children to San Antonio, where Jacob died in 1909. None of these families remained long in Eagle Pass; all had left by the time the Riskinds arrived, and Morris makes no mention of having known or even heard of any of them.

The Jewish families Morris knew and wrote about began to arrive in the first years of the twentieth century and became critical to downtown retail. These include Jacob and Mary Kranzthor, immigrants from Hungary who ran a store called the Fair beginning in 1905 and later operated businesses in San Antonio and El Paso. Their daughter Ellen married Sam Schwartz, one of the city's most important business leaders, a longtime friend to Morris's parents, and the town's mayor in the 1920s. Schwartz, who figures as prominently in Morris's memoir as he did in the town, ran the Aztec Theater next door to the Riskind store on Main Street. The Kranzthors, Schwartzes, Riskinds, and Edelsteins formed the nucleus of a Jewish community on the verge of rapid growth. Riskind documents many of his personal recollections of its members, families named Mikulinsky and Spiegal, Lapin and Libson, Neuman, Levine, Hausman, Grossman, and Greenberg. The community remained highly mobile: "Even after the first group had moved on to other towns," Riskind writes, "new families came to establish prosperous businesses and contribute to the community." They were often joined at services in the 1920s and 1930s by members of the Stool family of Del Rio, augmenting their numbers to about ten Jewish families with twenty or so adults.[21] Many Jewish residents stayed only briefly; others lasted decades before eventually moving on. Few, such as the Riskinds, Schwartzes, and Mikulinskys, were multigenerational long-haulers.

One of the memoir's most important features is Morris's detailed description of this group's all-hands-on-deck approach to maintaining Jewish life in Eagle Pass. Services were held in the Riskinds' apartment above the store; on the rare occasions, as during wartime, when a larger space was needed, it was leased elsewhere in town. Services were led by lay leaders who had the necessary skills—Michael Riskind at first, Morris later—with cantorial support from whomever in the group could sing. Rachel Riskind, Morris's mother, "organized all the religious services in Eagle Pass on all the Jewish holidays" and, "with Falla Lapin as her lieutenant," arranged regular social activities for the group, including monthly dinners and a recurring weekly poker game.[22] Later, when the group had enough children to warrant a Hebrew school, Morris and his brother Reuben formed one and, because they could read Hebrew, became its teachers. Morris supervised the children's training for bar and bat mitzvahs and led the ceremonies. Notably, he says nothing about what happened at these religious observances or about their Passover seders, Hanukkah celebrations, or Yom Kippur services. And he observes, apparently without noting the irony, that the store was always open and "business was brisk" on Saturdays, supposed to be the Jewish Sabbath.

Of course, Jewish identity is expressed in many ways other than religious observance, and Riskind offers numerous examples of how the shared identity of Eagle Pass Jews created a strong connection not only among themselves but to a national and global Jewish community. Other Jews were the Riskinds' first points of contact in any venture. Michael traveled regularly back to Chicago to buy merchandise directly from Jewish manufacturers he knew—incidentally giving his store an early advantage in price and style over competitors who bought from Texas-based middlemen. When service personnel from elsewhere in the United States were stationed nearby, the Riskinds reached out to welcome and host those who were Jewish, and Morris formed lifelong relationships through these connections. Jewish friends in Eagle Pass became partners and investors in Morris's various land and agricultural activities; Jewish produce and cattle buyers were his main contacts in those industries; and Jewish apparel salesmen cut him deals on buying trips to Dallas or on their visits to the store.

Thus, Eagle Pass, as Morris writes, may have been "an isolated settlement" and "the end of the road," but its Jewish residents were embedded in an expansive network that connected them to Jewish society throughout Texas and the United States.

On the question of how their Jewishness may have isolated them from non-Jews in Eagle Pass, whether there was prejudice in the town against them, Riskind has little to say. By and large, it seems the small Jewish community of Eagle Pass was accepted without notice and always had been. "The few Jews here are not much subjected to . . . social ostracism or prejudice," a resident wrote to the *American Israelite* in 1901. "Indeed, the Gentiles realize the worth of the Jew in their midst."[23] Riskind might have seconded that sentiment, or even gone further. "The border has long had an easygoing, live-and-let-live atmosphere," he writes in his epilogue. "Such prejudice as existed was Anglo versus Mexican, Protestant versus Catholic, and so on. Jews figured very little in the picture—there just weren't enough of us to count."

When he does note encounters with anti-Jewish prejudice, Morris tends to focus on incidents that happened elsewhere, not in Eagle Pass. He tells, for example, of an acquaintance living in Mexico whose neighbors, upon discovering he was Jewish, forced him out of town, but "that," Morris emphasizes, "did not occur on the border and was certainly not typical of this region." He mentions only one case of "out-and-out antisemitism" in Eagle Pass, when an agricultural newspaper blamed "Jewish speculators" for farmers' hardships—but the editor, he stresses, "came from out of town" and "was a drunk with no credibility." In a 1995 interview, Peter Riskind asked his father directly if he had experienced antisemitism personally, and Morris spoke at length about something that had happened to him once in California.[24] Whatever antisemitism may have existed in Eagle Pass, Morris was committed to downplaying it.

Nonetheless, several antisemitic incidents sneak into Morris's narrative, things that happened to his parents and affected them deeply enough that they told him about them years later. In his early days peddling in the vicinity of Eagle Pass, his father was "ordered off the premises" of the Seco Mines, an industrial operation outside town. "We want no Jew peddlers here," they told him.[25] His mother told him how a woman came up behind her once and touched her head. "The padre had said in a sermon that Jews had horns and a tail," she explained, "and she was only trying to verify if this were true." And one case in Morris's own experience stood out in his memory. When he was running for school board, "a friend reported to me that an Anglo acquaintance had said he would vote for me even though I was a Jew. This remark made me furiously angry." These are, to be sure, microaggressions that seem to have done little lasting harm, and Morris holds fast to his view that "our relations with the Christian community were always excellent." Nevertheless, his own recollections imply a latent antisemitism in Eagle Pass, experienced personally by himself and both of his parents, that must have conditioned Jewish residents' experience there.

The Eagle Pass Jewish community Riskind describes was nearly gone by the time he wrote the memoir. "The older members of our community have all died or moved away," he says, "and virtually all of the children have moved to the big city. Now we would be unable to get together a minyan even if we included women and non-Jewish spouses." He accurately acknowledges in his epilogue that the disappearance of Eagle Pass Jewry was part of a national trend affecting small towns throughout the country. In Texas, for example, about 54 percent of Jews in 1900 lived in small towns outside the state's major urban areas; by 2000 that figure had fallen to just 3 percent.[26] Nationally, Lee Shai Weissbach estimated that one in ten of the triple-digit places he studied continued to flourish, but 90 percent diminished, merged into larger urban conglomerations, or disappeared entirely.[27] No doubt the loss was even more dramatic in communities as small and isolated as Eagle Pass. A great part of the appeal of *Neither Fish nor Fowl*, therefore, is the view it offers of a small, resilient, and self-sufficient rural Jewish community, something that barely exists today, at its peak.

A SORT OF INSTITUTION

Few features of Jewish history in nineteenth- and twentieth-century America were more ubiquitous than Jewish-run downtown stores, and another virtue of *Neither Fish nor Fowl* is the insight it provides into the inner workings of such a business.[28] "Beginning in the middle of the nineteenth century, across the United States and throughout much of the new world," writes Hasia Diner, "Jews played a conspicuous role in retail business in communities of all sizes.... In one town after another Jews owned all or most of the jewelry stores, optical shops, and dry goods stores, some of which transformed over time into department stores."[29] In Texas alone, the largest retail establishments in Dallas, Houston, San Antonio, El Paso, Austin, Corpus Christi, Brownsville, and countless smaller towns were Jewish-run; Zales Jewelry and Neiman Marcus, founded respectively in Wichita Falls and Dallas, became national institutions.[30] In this trend, Eagle Pass was no exception; in fact the path Michael Riskind traveled from peddling to store ownership was entirely typical.

The importance of Jewish shopkeepers to downtown activity in Eagle Pass was not lost on Morris Riskind, who describes many of the town's leading mercantile families. "Jewish merchants played an important role in the economic history of early Eagle Pass," he writes, establishing "shoe stores, furniture stores, fabric stores, clothing stores, and a host of other businesses that had a significant commercial impact all along the border." At some point (the item is undated), he drew a handwritten map of downtown Eagle Pass that marks the locations and proprietors of twenty-six Jewish-owned establishments in a fifteen-square-block area over about an eighty-year period.[31] Of these, Riskind's was the largest and the longest-lasting. He also describes how his mother's family, the Edelsteins, expanded their own Eagle Pass business into a successful chain of furniture stores throughout the Rio Grande Valley.[32] In detailing his family's businesses, Morris focuses on practices that might have seemed mundane at the time but fascinate in hindsight: how the Riskinds selected, acquired, and displayed their merchandise; how they built relationships with traveling salesmen and wholesalers; whom they employed and how they trained and promoted employees; how they arranged customer credit; and how they related and catered to a binational and bilingual clientele.

Much of the success and durability of the Riskind store should be attributed to Michael Riskind's energetic and innovative leadership. "All I know about business I learned from Mike," a former employee tells Morris, who undoubtedly could have made the same statement himself. The chapters in his memoir Morris devotes to his own years working at M. Riskind are replete with his father's efforts at "learning" his son the business. Michael's skill in tailoring gave him a deep appreciation for quality workmanship ("buttonholes in particular were a fixation," his son tells us), a selectivity that ultimately benefited his customers and allowed him to transform cheap remainders and samples cast off by salesmen into custom items he could profitably sell. He also strategically stocked goods with limited appeal in the hot, dry border town—rain gear, winter gloves, luxury furs—because, as Morris notes, "no other store bothered to have them," which would guarantee sales on those occasions when they were in demand. Riskind's carried prom dresses and bridal gowns and became the local source for uniforms for the Boy Scouts and the Border

Patrol. For such smart and effective practices, according to Morris, "Pa was referred to as 'M. Riskind,' a sort of institution."

However, throughout its history, the M. Riskind store was in every way a family operation. Mike was joined by his sister Rose in 1911 and brother Albert in 1917, each of whom brought essential skills. Albert became the business manager, credit supervisor, and, one gleans from the memoir, a kind of practical-minded antagonist to Mike's occasionally idiosyncratic and impractical leadership. Rose Riskind, Morris's Aunt Rose, was the store's "absolute arbiter of style, fashion, and manners." She "had a shrewd business sense and was most competent in getting along with the general public," and she "became the personal shopper for a doting following," no doubt influencing style and fashion sense on both sides of the border. Morris's account of Aunt Rose recalls Carrie Marcus Neiman, cofounder of a somewhat larger Jewish-owned store, and a woman of famously refined taste. Many of the latter's customers were the wives of suddenly wealthy ranchers and oilmen and, like Rose, Neiman not only sold high-quality apparel but taught her clients how to choose and wear it.[33]

Morris's descriptions of the different social positions he and his father held in the town further reveal the impact of Jewish-owned businesses on the local economy, as the owners became key figures in the town's civic life and leadership. Mike Riskind, as his son tells us, generally avoided politics, which he saw primarily as a way to make enemies, preferring an approach that was more convivial. He sustained friendships over drinks, socialized with customers, employees, and colleagues, and developed close personal relationships with the town's other business owners, Mexican officials, and local political leaders. "If he went into the saloon," Morris remembered in a 1995 interview, "first thing he'd do was to set them up for everybody in the saloon. He'd buy drinks for everybody. He said that was good for business."[34] One of his regular drinking companions was Roberto Bibb, the powerful county judge, through whom he maintained an avenue of influence without offering himself as a candidate or committing himself to any party. As a result, Mike enjoyed a wide popularity that sustained the store's name and reputation. Morris describes a memorable scene at the Moderno Café in Piedras Negras, where the Riskinds were such regular customers that the house band launched into a theme song for Mike whenever he entered the dining room. After a long visit to the bar to buy drinks for any store customers who happened to be there, Morris remembered that "Pa returned [and] would invariably get a lecture from Auntie. His reply would be that he was drumming up business."

In his own career managing the store, Morris's approach to "drumming up business" was less sociable but perhaps more professional than his father's, more on the model of their neighbor, Sam Schwartz. Schwartz operated movie theaters, including the Aztec (next door to M. Riskind), a hotel, and several other businesses, and in a long public career in Eagle Pass served on a bank board, headed the irrigation district, and was elected to the school board, the city council, and three terms as mayor between 1918 and 1924.[35] Morris followed Schwartz's example of wide-ranging civic engagement, as did his brother and business partner, Reuben, serving on a constellation of boards and commissions—the chamber of commerce, Red Cross, the public housing board, a music society, the library commission—and making forays into electoral politics. In a richly detailed chapter on the pitfalls of his tenure on the school board, it becomes clear that another generational change occurred: for Mike, social interaction with the public was a way to help the business, but for Morris the business gave him status he could leverage to help the public.[36]

After opting out of the law and washing out as a farmer-rancher, running the store was for Morris a third career—if not a fourth given his secret desire to be a writer—but once co-ownership of M. Riskind, Inc., fell to him, he committed himself fully to it. Many episodes in the book indicate how completely his working life absorbed his mind. In his travelogue of his various trips throughout the world, he comments frequently on the mercantile practices of the places he visits. In Taxco, Mexico, for instance, while Ruth bargains expertly over some handcrafted cloth, Morris occupies himself leaning against a tent pole and appraising the "cheap, gaudy blankets" for sale in the stall next door—"brightly colored, shoddy items [that] had long been sold in the U.S. in stores such as Kress for $3.99 or $4.99." Wherever he was in the world, the traveling merchant's thoughts were never far from Main Street, Eagle Pass.

Morris was also attentive to how, over a long career, his profession was changing. *Neither Fish nor Fowl* chronicles transformative generational change not only in the Riskinds' own business but also in the world of small-town commerce. He writes nostalgically, for example, of the traveling salesmen of his youth who visited the store personally, unloaded their trunks and sample cases for display, and went upstairs with the family for dinner, drinks, and a round of poker. Morris remembers their stories and jokes and the familiarity of the relationship between sellers and clients. World War II, however, "brought an end to the old days," he says. Rising gasoline prices and other travel expenses deterred personal visits, and wartime shortages and government-mandated allotments made it harder for Michael Riskind to purchase the goods his customers wanted. Relationships frayed as manufacturers were unable to fill every order for every customer and the quality of goods deteriorated as the best materials were harder to obtain.

By the time Morris took over the store after the war, visits from salesmen were a rarity. The relationship had reversed, in fact, so that buyers had to travel to the sellers, not the other way around. Morris regularly attended buying expositions in Dallas, where manufacturers displayed their lines to hundreds of large and small retailers at once. There was still a personal element—Morris describes cutting back-room deals with preferred sales reps (typically Jewish) in hotel suites—but soon enough even this degree of personal connection disappeared when the Dallas Apparel Mart opened in 1964 and introduced a degree of scale and standardization entirely unlike the practices Morris had learned from his father.

Writing in the 1980s and 1990s, when Riskind's, like local retailers everywhere, was suffering severe setbacks and nearing closure, Morris observes wistfully how much had changed from his youth through "the age of Walmart." Stores were once owned locally by residents who took personal pride in their businesses and their place in the community, contributing to the town with their time and energy as well as financially. Customers knew them and were loyal, and few would imagine buying anywhere else. "If an Eagle Pass citizen were asked fifty years ago to name a large business," Morris says, "they probably would have named the M. Riskind store." It succeeded, he says, "because it was made in the image of Michael Riskind," whereas shopping malls, chain stores, and amalgamated department stores "have a drab sameness." Riskind doesn't tell us anything here we don't already know, but his detailed recollection of the business he knew reminds us how much we've lost.

MEANS OF EXCHANGE

As merchants, borderland Jews like the Riskinds embodied the most characteristic quality of their region—exchange. Scholars have long distinguished "borderlands" from "borders" by noting that cultural impact does not stop where nations draw political boundaries. "A border is a line that separates one nation from another," writes Oscar J. Martínez. "A borderland is a region that lies adjacent to a border." Like the related term "frontier," a borderland is "a zone of transition," and residents occupy a place where cultural adaptation rather than essentialism is the rule. "In contrast to populations in national heartlands, where cultural homogeneity is the norm," Martínez writes, "people of border regions are more likely to live in heterogeneous environments because of greater ethnic mixing and more extensive migration between contiguous countries."[37] Borders are fixed and regulated; borderlands are fluid and transactional.

Alicia Dewey, who has written in depth about "the rise of a new class of diverse businesspeople" in the South Texas border region, describes a business climate in which the Riskinds were perfectly situated. In fact, she describes Riskind's uncle, Morris Edelstein, as "typical of the migrant entrepreneurs who moved into South Texas in the late nineteenth and early twentieth centuries." Dewey argues that conditions unique to the region, including the "porous nature of the US/Mexico border," created an environment conducive to "the emergence of a diverse, modern 'business class' along the South Texas border." Jewish peddlers-turned-merchants like the Edelsteins (and the Riskinds) were an essential component of that development, along with Italian, Syrian, Chinese, and of course Mexican and Anglo-American businesspeople. Together, Dewey writes, these entrepreneurs "remade the relatively isolated ranching society of the borderlands into one that was thoroughly commercialized, urbanized, and integrated into global markets."[38] By linking Chicago and New York manufacturers to Mexican consumers, the Riskind store certainly fit this description.

In many other ways, Jewish merchants were particularly well-suited for an environment marked by cultural and commercial transaction. Occupying a middle position between ethnic, religious, and national groups, neither entirely one thing nor entirely the other, their social identities were in a constant state of negotiation. Writing, for example, of the leading Jewish resident of Brownsville, Texas, Allison Schottenstein notes that Sam Perl "did not adopt a quintessential American white identity, but remained visibly Jewish. [Neither did he] adopt a Mexican identity in a border town in which the population was predominately Mexican." Like the Riskinds, Perl was a successful clothing merchant and a pillar of his town's business community. He was "the definitively 'in-between' Jew," writes Schottenstein, a position that enabled him "to bridge the gap between these two communities, ultimately causing cultural boundaries to blur."[39] The same was true in Eagle Pass, where, as Peter Riskind writes in his foreword, "Jews occupied an unusual social position, neither fully Anglo nor Mexican, but partly belonging to both groups."

With the exception of Dewey's study, Jews have been largely left out of border histories, as the border has been largely left out of histories of Jewish Texans. Scholarly examination of borderland Jewish communities is limited mostly to chapters in books on broader topics, unpublished manuscripts, and master's theses.[40] *Neither Fish nor Fowl* thus fills a number of conspicuous gaps in the historical record. It is the first published work about the Eagle Pass Jewish community, the most comprehensive about any Jewish community in the Texas border region, and a source of insight into how this unique environment shaped Jewish life and commercial activity.

Riskind observes that the store his father founded "was possible because of the peculiar conditions of the time and place," and he provides numerous examples of how the business benefited from its borderland setting. The Mexican Revolution, for instance, began in 1910 just as his family arrived at the border. Although the ten-year cataclysm was chaotic and violent, Morris acknowledges that it "brought an economic boom to Eagle Pass," turning the small border village into an unlikely commercial center. The local population grew rapidly due to the arrival of American military personnel deployed to guard the border and of wartime refugees from Mexico—the first sustained immigration from Mexico to the United States. These newcomers turned to Riskind's and other Eagle Pass businesses to supply their needs, giving the store a strong boost in its earliest years.

As a young boy Morris felt the effects of the revolution personally. Among his first memories was watching the passage of Mexican federal troops through Eagle Pass on their way to fight Pancho Villa's insurgent army, and he writes of the excitement stirred up in town by (incorrect) rumors of Villa's approach.[41] He was friendly with members of the prosperous Chuck family, Chinese immigrants who had fled the 1911 Torreón Massacre; Riskind remembers watching one of their sons play high school football. And when the Plan de San Diego—an attempt to incite Mexican and Indigenous populations in South Texas against Anglo rule—was exposed in 1915, the Texas Rangers began a campaign of violent suppression against Tejanos, and Riskind remembers his father securing guns in their home belonging to Mexican friends who feared their confiscation.

Eagle Pass may not have been cosmopolitan, but it was an international, multilingual, and ethnically diverse community, and the Riskinds were fully engaged with it. These close personal ties between the Riskind family and their non-Anglo, non-Jewish neighbors—as well as the bigotry Riskind frequently reports toward various minority communities—are a running theme in the memoir and one of its most important contributions to borderland literature and Jewish history. Morris claimed in an interview that his father "didn't particularly like the Anglo people," who mocked his flawed English, "and he got along much, much better with the Mexican people. His Spanish was much more fluent than his English."[42] To be sure, Mike's closest social and business contacts were Jewish, but most of those who were not were Mexican. Every member of the Riskind family was fluent in Spanish, became so early in their residence in Eagle Pass, and interacted freely with members of both major cultural groups. Relations with Latino communities is an aspect of the American Jewish experience that historians have neglected, and Morris provides here a wealth of anecdotes and recollections that reveal the friendships, working relationships, and mutual respect between a borderland Jewish family and their Mexican and Mexican American associates.[43]

The greatest avenue for interaction between the Riskinds and the Latino population of Eagle Pass was, of course, the store, most employees and customers of which were Hispanic. Eagle Pass's borderland location assured a binational and bicultural clientele that necessitated a multilingual sales staff. Riskind's owners, managers, and salespeople were all fluent in both English and Spanish—and often conversant also in the native Yiddish of the owners. Riskind's hired Latino and Latina employees in every position from delivery and carpentry to salesclerks, cashiers, bookkeepers, and department managers. Some of their employees lived in Piedras Negras and traveled daily across the border to work. Morris recalls by name many store employees who worked for Riskind's for decades, rising through the ranks to well-paid managerial positions. Most of these longtime workers came from working-class and immigrant backgrounds—as had the Riskinds—and the store offered them a path into the middle class. Thus, the store elevated not only the economic prospects of the Riskind family but also those of hundreds of employees and the community in which they lived.

How the Riskinds appealed to the unique tastes of Mexican customers in selecting stock and providing customer service is another significant theme in this story. "Our customers in Eagle

Pass had their own ideas of style," Morris writes. "Mexican women modeled their styles not on Hollywood but on Mexico City and Paris. Their standard was Parisian elegance."[44] They also tended to buy their shoes too small, he writes, an unhealthy preference perhaps, but M. Riskind went out of its way to provide what their customers wanted. In its effort to draw clientele from across the Rio Grande, Riskind's advertised heavily in Mexico, including signs posted on the Piedras Negras side of the border crossing and billboards as far away as Saltillo. In its early years, signs posted over the store's front entrance, and later even in the parking lot, were printed in both languages.[45] As a result Riskind's became a known brand not only in Maverick County but also throughout northern Mexico. Morris recalls sales to prominent Mexican generals and politicians including, in one especially memorable case, the president of Mexico, for whom he acquired a custom coat. At the same time, they devised individualized credit options that put their luxury goods within reach of poor and working-class Mexican and Indigenous buyers.

In such practices the Riskinds were part of a discernible trend among Jewish retailers in the Texas borderland, who all relied upon and catered to a Mexican clientele on both sides of a permeable border. Sam Schwartz expanded his theatrical business in Eagle Pass by opening a Spanish-language movie venue downtown. In Del Rio, the Stool family, who began their business in Mexico, operated clothing stores called El Remate and La Estrella, where they "did more business with Del Rio's Spanish-speakers" and with cross-border clientele than with local Anglos.[46] In Brownsville, Gabriel Pearl, whom locals referred to respectfully as "Don Gabriel," operated El Botega de Leon, and Sam Perl placed special emphasis on his store's open-door and one-price policies, adopting as a slogan, "We do love everybody!"[47] Adolph Schwartz, Sam's uncle, settled first in Juárez, where he ran a store known as Tres B, short for *Buena, Bonita, Barata*, giving him the wherewithal to cross the border into El Paso and open the Popular Store, which became one of the largest retail operations in the Southwest.[48] Many retailers, like Solomon Libson and Max Lapin of Eagle Pass, whose California Fruit Company Riskind mentions, ran businesses on both sides of the border simultaneously.

A theme Riskind returns to throughout the memoir, however, is how the border was changing, as it always does, and ease of movement was not available for long or for everyone. In an early example, he recalls his father's involvement in 1921 with a group of European Jewish refugees who were apprehended trying to cross the Rio Grande into Eagle Pass. The national quota law enacted that year severely curtailed immigration from Europe to the United States but left migration from Mexico relatively unrestricted. Many Jews seeking escape from dangerous conditions in Eastern Europe, or others simply wishing to reunite with relatives already in the United States, saw an opportunity in traveling to Mexico instead. Entry requirements there were comparatively lax, and it was often possible to find some way across the river into Texas. Hundreds were captured at border crossings, most commonly El Paso, and were deported—usually back to the maelstrom of Europe rather than to the relative safety of Mexico. Many others were stuck in Mexico without means or a community to support them, unable to find a way to cross without risking capture. El Paso rabbi Martin Zielonka was especially conspicuous in his efforts to help those trapped in Mexico build a sustainable Jewish life so they could remain there, giving root to permanent Ashkenazic communities in Mexico City and other parts of the country.[49] Michael Riskind seems to have followed Zielonka's lead, bailing these young men out of jail, employing them temporarily in his store, and helping them settle permanently in Monterrey. This little-known episode in Jewish immigration history demonstrates how increasingly rigid border enforcement affected Jews in a particular way.

The intensification of border enforcement over time is apparent in another aspect of Riskind's experience that resonates particularly strongly today. As a farmer during World War II, Morris often employed Mexican agricultural workers, who freely crossed the river under the noses of a mostly compliant Border Patrol. "The Border Patrol knew all of us were using illegal labor," Morris writes, "but they let us alone." When field workers were needed, Morris and other farmers would go to a spot on the river and wave toward a settlement on the other side. "All we had to do was raise an arm up and down to indicate the number of hands needed," he says. Beginning during World War II, the government formalized these processes, initiating the Bracero Program, in which Eagle Pass participated as a "reception center" for the distribution of migrant workers throughout the United States. Riskind notes the program's positive economic impact on the town but seems unaware of the harmful effect the program and its abrupt termination had on the workers themselves.[50] Riskind's outline of changes in border enforcement continues through the notorious Operation Intercept of the 1960s, a misguided Nixon administration effort to crack down on the importation of drugs by stopping and intensively inspecting virtually all traffic crossing the border.

Riskind's evocation of changing border conditions points toward recent developments more familiar to modern readers. In 2022, Texas governor Greg Abbott claimed that Eagle Pass had become "Ground Zero" for "illegal crossings" and visited the town to announce expansions to Operation Lone Star, the state's border enforcement initiative. The "strike teams," "miles of fencing and barriers," and "boat teams" Abbott bragged about would have seemed anathema and counterproductive to Riskind, who once advised a fellow passenger on a Mexican bus of the best places he knew of to sneak across the river.[51] "This country became great because people of so many diverse races and religions have learned to coexist," he writes at the end of his memoir. "This spirit of tolerance is perhaps our greatest accomplishment as a civilization." The militarized border of today's headlines seems miles away from Riskind's experience.

CONCLUSION

In his closing thoughts about the future of American Judaism, Morris Riskind writes of the need for change and adaptation, for modernizing Jewish practices not only to remain relevant in American society but meaningful for Jews themselves. "I am convinced that in the United States we are developing a distinct type of Judaism," he writes, and he pleads for "modernization of... the definition of who is a Jew" and for "tolerance" among Jewish movements, conditions he views as necessary for the survival of Judaism as a distinct faith. He adds that Jews in small towns like Eagle Pass (and by implication those in all borderland communities) are especially strong in these qualities. "American Jews raised in small towns and cities like Eagle Pass," he writes, are "more accustomed to living with non-Jews in everyday situations and do not think of themselves as apart from the majority population." Small-town Jews were forced to assimilate quickly, he says, to forge compromise with their neighbors, to find ways to remain separate without "remain[ing] in a world of their own." As a product of such a community, Riskind seems to view the style of Judaism practiced in Eagle Pass as a prescription for the larger population of American Jews.

And yet it is impossible not to notice, as Riskind does, that Judaism in Eagle Pass is no more. Indeed, in many ways *Neither Fish nor Fowl* is a chronicle not only of change but of loss. The Jewish community he documents is gone. The old-time cowboys, ranchers, and vaqueros he worked among and the mule-driven farming methods he employed—gone. The

Architect's plan for the renovation of the front of the Riskind Building, 2023. (Courtesy of Arturo Marquez, city of Eagle Pass.)

Architect's plan for the renovation of the rear of the Riskind Building, 2023. (Courtesy of Arturo Marquez, city of Eagle Pass.)

porous border binding Texas and Mexico into a single cultural and commercial unit—gone, or at least going. The downtown department store his family ran for nearly a century, the methods it employed, the durable personal relationships among owners, employees, and customers—all gone. Riskind's narrative captures a period of transition when entire ways of life were rapidly disappearing around him.

As of this writing, however, the renovation of the Riskind's storefront in Eagle Pass is underway. Behind the large display windows, now clouded with dust, there is a vast empty

Architect's plan for the renovation of the interior reception area of the Riskind Building, 2023. (Courtesy of Arturo Marquez, city of Eagle Pass.)

space that will be partitioned and subdivided for diverse new uses. Broken gaps in the deteriorating adobe covering the exterior walls show glimpses of the original brick below, soon to be revealed as the building's restored exterior surface. The decorative stamped-metal ceiling tiles Michael Riskind installed in 1914 are stacked neatly in front of the store, hopefully to be restored and reused. There is at the site a simultaneous age and newness, a sense of past and future occupying the same space. As Morris Riskind's memoir returns to life a vanished world, the store his father built will continue to sustain downtown commercial life long after the Riskinds and the rest of the city's Jews have gone.

A NOTE ON THE TEXT

This book represents the finalized version of a document that has gone through many iterations and many editors before finally reaching print. As Peter Riskind describes in his foreword, his father wrote the memoir over several decades and sought publication unsuccessfully in the last years of his life. Several versions of Morris Riskind's manuscript have survived in varying degrees of completeness, but there is a printed text dated June 27, 1992, that is typed, polished, formatted, margin-justified, and contains chapter and section titles. I consider this Morris's "final" version, and I assume it's the one he shopped to publishers.

After Morris's death, Peter took over the task of seeking publication of the memoir, and he describes in the foreword the extensive work he and a professional freelance editor completed, with input from other family members, in an attempt to make it publishable. Morris's original was episodic—almost a sequence of disconnected memories and events—but its editors shaped it into a more suitable chronological narrative and cut a good deal of extraneous material. These revisions vastly improved the quality and readability of the memoir. As Peter also explains, however, in the process Morris's colloquial and descriptive writing style was reduced to a succinct and bland academic prose. The substance was his, but the words and phrasing were substantially different. In this sense, the revised version was much worse than the original, and although Peter labored to return his father's voice to the text, this was only partially achieved in the version he submitted to Texas Tech University Press in 2021.

My role as editor was to begin with that submitted text, essentially an amalgam of the work of several editors over many years, and to try to shape it into a manuscript that is as true as possible to Morris's own words and intent while preserving the best of the improvements made by subsequent editors. I compared the submitted version line by line to the latest of Morris's originals and restored most of his words in place of the rewrites.[52] I believe it is crucial, both for the readability of the text and its credibility as a primary source, to let Morris speak for himself as much as possible without revision.[53] He was a good enough writer that there is no need to do otherwise.

The submitted version is much better organized than Morris's original, but I felt it still needed additional structural work, particularly in creating chapters that were more thematically coherent and more even in length. Therefore, I have moved many passages around, redesigned the chapter structure, integrated several appendixes into the main text, and added subheadings to strengthen transitions; where possible these subheadings are derived from Morris's original chapter titles. All the words are Morris's, but I have moved text around like jigsaw pieces in an attempt to reveal a clearer picture. I made a few cuts where I felt Morris was drifting onto unnecessary tangents (like spending too much time narrating historical events he knew only from books) and restored illuminating passages, such as his service as a delegate to the 1968 Texas Democratic Convention, that had previously been removed. I have also returned many proper names to the text that the previous editors, perhaps fearing offense to living people, replaced with initials: twenty-five years have passed since those elisions were made, few people included in the memoir are still living, and I see no reason not to identify Riskind's subjects by name.

Morris was an excellent writer but, unfortunately, not a great speller. He frequently misspelled the names even of people he knew well (including the high-school teacher to whom he dedicated the book). Furthermore, writing mostly from memory and basing much of his information on what others had told him, Riskind was naturally prone to error of fact. Part of my role has been to use the tools available to a modern researcher to discover and correct such errors. An irony of this task is that I have access to a great deal more documentary information about Morris's family and acquaintances than he had. He was mistaken, for example, about the year his parents married, but thanks to Ancestry.com I have a copy of their Cook County marriage license with the correct date. He relates confidently that his immigrant mother disembarked at Montreal, but according to a 1904 ship manifest he probably never knew about, it was definitely New York. Where possible, I've simply corrected the text; in many cases where the mistake itself is illustrative, I've left it intact and offered a (gentle) correction in the notes.

If Morris's English spelling is bad, his Yiddish is even worse, and I (not a Yiddish speaker) struggled to decipher his transliterations of his parents' Yiddish expressions. I have relied on *Harduf's Transliterated English-Yiddish Dictionary* as a standard reference, but most of the Yiddish represented here is my best guess of a proper spelling in English characters. With apologies to Yiddish experts, I hope they are adequate. Hebrew terms are spelled according to the *JPS Dictionary of Jewish Words* or the *Encyclopaedia Judaica*.

Neither Fish nor Fowl will appeal to readers with interest in the border region, Jewish history, and small-town business, but few will possess adequate knowledge of all three topics. I have tried, therefore, to supply detailed endnotes to help readers who may have previous understanding of one or two of these themes appreciate all three as fully as possible. The notes provide definitions of Jewish terms Riskind uses; capsule biographies of people he names; and explanations of his many historical, geographical, literary, and religious references. Finally, I have tried to show in the notes how this memoir fits into broader historical and historiographical contexts and to direct readers, especially those bent toward scholarship, to the most beneficial secondary works. The book concludes with a bibliography providing full citations to all of them.

BRYAN EDWARD STONE

AUTHOR'S INTRODUCTION

Eagle Pass, Texas, ca. 1910. (Courtesy of Jeff Taylor Sr.)

This is the story of my parents, Michael and Rachel Riskind, and how they happened to come to Eagle Pass, Texas, an isolated settlement on the Rio Grande, just as the bloody and violent Mexican Revolution of 1910 began. It is also an account of my experiences in the days when the Texas of the old-time cattlemen was giving way to modernity.

When my parents came to Eagle Pass, it was a quiet, sleepy village. It had a main street that had the appearance of a Western movie set, except that the buildings were constructed of native stone or Mexican brick instead of wood. Streets were, of course, unpaved and characterized by clouds of choking dust most of the year and adhesive caliche clay mud when it rained. There were few automobiles because there was nowhere to go in one. Travel was done by horseback, buggy, or wagon. The population consisted of a few thousand Mexicans, most of whom were very poor, and a small minority of Anglos, a large percentage of whom were Alsatians, Germans, or Scots. There was a smattering of Indians, Black Seminoles, and other Blacks who worked for the railroad.[1] I do not think there was running water yet. I can remember seeing people who went up and down the streets selling water from tanks drawn by mules. The town had electricity and a few telephones. A few of the original families from the founding of the town were still there in 1910, as they are today.[2]

MORRIS S. RISKIND

NEITHER FISH NOR FOWL

CHAPTER 1

FROM THE RUSSIAN EMPIRE TO EAGLE PASS

It is impossible, in my opinion, to understand my parents either alone or together unless one has some knowledge of their background in Europe before they came to the United States. They were born and raised before the automobile or airplane were known. In their time even the railroad was something new that terrified peasants when they first saw a train with its sparks spouting out of the chimney like some proverbial monster. They were raised before the old shtetl culture of Eastern Europe had been altered by modernity and were thoroughly immersed in ancient ideas and customs.[1]

My parents' backgrounds were very different. My father's family was pious Orthodox, either Hasidim or close to the Hasidim in many of their beliefs. My mother's family were Talmudic rationalists, Lithuanian Mitnagdim who interpreted the scriptures through reason and laughed at folk tales of miracles.[2] My father came to this country in a cattle boat, the cheapest possible fare. Mother came second class on a big luxury liner. Nevertheless, both were thoroughly steeped in a culture utterly different from that into which they were placed in the United States, particularly the unusual environment of Eagle Pass, which, when they arrived, was not yet culturally in the twentieth century. Certainly, their attitudes, their prejudices, their motives were determined by the culture and ideas of Eastern Europe in the nineteenth century rather than by those of America today.

How did my parents get to Eagle Pass, Texas, at that time an isolated village on the Mexican border, an American Timbuktu? It's a long story.

THE RISKINDS, MY FATHER'S FAMILY

My father, Michael Riskind, was born in 1877 in Orsha, a small town in tsarist Russia near Dubrovna, now in the Republic of Belarus.[3] He was born during Hanukkah, and we customarily celebrated his birthday on Christmas Day as a matter of convenience, since the store was closed and everyone was exhausted after the Christmas rush.[4] My father's parents were very pious Orthodox Jews, Hasidic in many of their beliefs. The origin of the name "Riskind" I can only surmise. Somewhere in our ancestry was an outstanding woman whose children were referred to as Risa or Raisa's *kind* or child, ergo Riskind. Remembering my

Morris's paternal grandparents Nahum (Nathan) and Judith (Ida) Sachs Riskind, wedding portrait. Orsha, Belarus, 1867. (Courtesy of Dr. Peter Riskind.)

Grandmother Judith, a true woman of valor, the existence of *beryes*, or exceptional women, taking charge of their families must not have been uncommon.[5]

Nahum (or Nochom) Riskind, my grandfather, spent his time at the synagogue or at home studying.[6] Grandmother Judith supported the family either with help from her wealthy brothers or by what she could earn. She worked as a cook catering weddings despite the fact that she had broken her hip in a fall and the break was never set properly. Even with this handicap, she was a dynamo of energy. She gave birth to twelve children, of whom seven (that I know of) lived to adulthood: Jacob, Aaron, my father Michael, Jennie, Albert, Rose, and Molly.[7] She saw to their welfare and directed their destinies with fortitude and resolution, despite the poverty and trials of the family.

To understand my grandfather Nahum, it is necessary to go back to earlier cultural traditions. Some two thousand years ago, the tractate *Pirkei Avot* or, as it is usually translated, *The Ethics of the Fathers*, set forth standards by which the rabbis who began compiling the Talmud thought that every Jew should be guided.[8] All males should be educated starting at age five, and this process should continue as long they lived. Work was important for all men, and many of the famous early rabbis were humble workmen, but no man should allow his work to interfere with daily prayer and study. When you consider that today the average college graduate may never look at a book of literature after graduation—or anything else for that matter other than a technical journal in his own field—you can appreciate the high ideal the early rabbis set. I am convinced that these norms had much to do with the character of the Jewish people wherever they were scattered and no matter the culture in which they were living at any time.

In large areas of Eastern Europe, the ancient norms became distorted because of economic factors caused by government restrictions. In the society in which my grandfather lived, men were supposed to devote their lives to prayer and study, probably because there were no jobs available anyway. An outstanding scholar would be married to the daughter of a wealthy family, and either her dowry would be sufficient or his father-in-law would continue to support the family. In the absence of a rich enough father-in-law, the family either starved or the wife had to support the family.[9] I know of no time when Nahum Riskind supported his family. That was left to my grandmother, Judith, a truly remarkable woman.

Whenever Grandfather Nahum would get into an argument with Grandmother Judith, which was often, he would draw himself up to his full height of five feet, seven inches and would declaim: "Woman, do you realize who you are talking to? Do you realize who I am? I am Nochom, Koppel, Abele Vielke," reciting his illustrious ancestors. In view of the fact that my grandparents were first cousins and were both descendants of the same illustrious ancestors, these words of Grandfather's always struck my grandmother as very funny, and when she recalled them, she was overcome with laughter.

Abele Vielke's son was a famous *magid* who must have lived sometime in the latter half of the eighteenth century. A *magid* was an itinerant preacher who spoke to the masses in Yiddish, something on the order of a modern revivalist. The usual theme of such a preacher would be hellfire. A true rabbi who gave scholarly dissertations was called a *darshan*. Unlike most *magidim*, Abele had a more cheerful theme. Providing they were good, faithful, and observant disciples of the rebbe, Abele guaranteed his listeners a place in the world to come, the *olam ha-ba*, seated near Moses and Father Abraham himself.[10]

According to Mother, quoting my grandparents, her in-laws, Abele was so eloquent that the flies on the wall stayed quiet to listen to him. As a reward for his efforts, whenever Abele was at the rebbe's court, he sat at the rebbe's right hand and had the privilege of eating food handed to him by the rebbe right off his own plate.[11] You can gather from this account that Mother was prejudiced against Hasidim and the ultra-pious.[12] I must confess that I was influenced by Mother also from an early age. Mother remarked to me once after hearing me give a dissertation to our assembled congregation in Eagle Pass on Yom Kippur, "Morris, what do you want to be, a *magid* or a businessman?"[13]

Whether because of hard times in Dubrovna or for some other cause, the family moved when Pa was a young boy. Grandmother Judith had a sister who was married to a man engaged in manufacturing and the wholesale trade. About this time gold was discovered in the Ural Mountains, and the sister's husband got permission to move his factory to Shadrinsk, on the Siberian side of the Urals. This was outside the Pale of Settlement, where Jews were permitted to live without special permission.[14] The wealthy brother-in-law secured permission for Nahum and his family to live there too, claiming that Grandfather was a skilled tailor needed in his manufacturing enterprise. Unfortunately, Grandfather knew nothing about tailoring, or any other skilled trade for that matter, nor did he learn enough about it to fake his work. It was a constant game of hide-and-seek with the authorities for the family to retain its resident status. If inspectors came, they were told he was out on a job; if they found him at home the excuse was that his machine was being repaired.

Finally, the not-too-friendly inspectors decided they had had enough of the runaround and summarily revoked the special permission for the family to live outside the Pale. Nahum and his family were ordered to leave forthwith and were hustled out of Shadrinsk with their few belongings. The family had to march on foot carrying their possessions, taking special care of their feather beds, their most precious property of all, until they reached the railroad depot, located out of town. They must have presented quite a sight going down the road: the two parents, children of varying ages from infant in arms to adult, and one daughter-in-law. The rail trip from Shadrinsk back to Dubrovna was some fifteen hundred miles, not made under the most luxurious conditions.

Back in Dubrovna they were faced with starvation, an embarrassment to their wealthy relatives, who solved the problem by giving Nahum and Judith three thousand rubles to emigrate to America—a case of out of sight, out of mind. It probably was a cheap way to get rid of a nuisance. My father always remembered this help. Years later, he heard from the children of his rich uncle. The Russian Revolution had stripped the family of their wealth. One of them wrote asking for money to buy a typewriter, with which he could get a government job and become a minor bureaucrat. Pa sent the money. Then he had a request from another cousin: if Pa would send money to buy a car, he could make a very nice living. Pa declined, offering instead to send money so the relatives could emigrate to America. After that, there were no more letters.

MY MOTHER'S FAMILY, THE EDELSTEINS AND THE FRIEDS

My mother, Rachel Edelstein, also came from an Orthodox Jewish family, but her background was entirely different from my father's.[15] By tradition the Edelsteins had come from Toledo in Spain—and therefore were Sephardic Jews—and had lived for some generations in Innsbruck, Austria. Mother recalled that her grandparents or great-grandparents had gone to Innsbruck to visit *kever avot*, the graves of their ancestors, before settling in Kalvaria, Lithuania, then on the east Prussian border.[16] According to Mother her family first arrived there toward the end of the eighteenth century. Mother's brother David recalled that a document was found in the Kalvaria synagogue archives recording that one Eben Yakar—Hebrew for "precious stone," or "Edelstein" in German or Yiddish—had performed a mitzvah, a good deed.[17] He had paid ransom for some Jewish captives, thereby earning the gratitude of the entire congregation.[18] As far back as anyone could remember the family had been in the wholesale grain business, not in the jewelry business as the name Edelstein would imply.

Kalvaria, Lithuania, ca. 1870, the home of the Edelsteins, Morris's mother's family. (Courtesy of Dr. Peter Riskind.)

During the Middle Ages, because of the feudal system and the Catholic Church, it had been impossible for Jews in Europe to own land. The occupation of this area by Napoleon, however, had brought the Napoleonic Code, under which Jews could own land.[19] The upheavals following the defeat of Napoleon and the revolt against the tsar by Polish nobles had resulted in Jewish ownership of considerable quantities of property. In this way, both sides of my mother's family were able to buy agricultural land.[20]

Mother's great-grandfather, Yossel, obtained the right from the local lord to build a flour mill. Sometime later, the lord had to sell his land and house in a hurry and offered it for sale: Yossel bought it. Yossel's grandson, my grandfather Chatzkel Edelstein, inherited the manor house with a garden of fifty acres. There he raised cucumbers, cabbage, and other produce. He also had a tract of one hundred acres on the other side of town near the Christian cemetery. On this land Chatzkel raised wheat and barley.

My mother's mother, Miriam Fried Edelstein, was the daughter of Reuben Fried, one of the great landowners in Lithuania. We don't know about the country of origin of the Fried family. Their name was variously spelled Fried, Freyd, Freed, Fred, and Freud, and some claimed Sigmund Freud as a relative. One of our Fried ancestors probably acquired the first of the family landholdings in the first half of the nineteenth century. According to Mother, a Fried was the steward for a Polish prince. The prince in question, for reasons, should we say, of his "health and safety," went to live in Monaco. There he spent his time gambling, with the result that he wrote constantly and hysterically to his steward demanding money. At his insistence, Fried sold all of the jewelry, then the silver and household effects, then all the livestock, so that it was no longer possible to work the land. When Fried advised that nothing was left, the prince ordered him to sell the land. There were no takers for such a large tract,

Chatzkel Edelstein, Morris's maternal grandfather. (Courtesy of Dr. Peter Riskind.)

and eventually the prince sold the manor house and land to Fried. Thus, my mother, Rachel Fried Edelstein, was part of a very prosperous, landowning family. This was not typical of most of the Jews in Eastern Europe at that time.

Another Fried descendant, possibly my mother's grandfather Reuben, added greatly to the family wealth by taking advantage of an opportunity later in the nineteenth century. The tsar had decided for military reasons to build a series of paved highways leading to the Prussian border for the purpose of speeding mobilization and troop movement in the event of war. On Reuben Fried's land were large areas of loose rock and boulders, making farming difficult. He made a low bid for the crushed rock needed in the construction of the highway and secured the contract. The rock was crushed by hand by a small army of peasants he hired. In this way he not only made a fortune selling the crushed rock, he also cleared his own land for farming.

With his new wealth Reuben bought the much larger estate and manor of Simna (now Simnas, Lithuania). This manor contained a private chapel, which Reuben turned into a synagogue. Many prominent scholars gathered in his synagogue for services followed by learned

Miriam Fried Edelstein, Morris's maternal grandmother. (Courtesy of Dr. Peter Riskind.)

discussions. Since Mother was a frequent visitor, she was able to listen to the discussions. Mother was a favorite of her grandfather Reuben. He praised her by saying that she had a *mansbil kop,* a male intelligence. Today, I do not think my wife, daughter, or daughters-in-law would be pleased by such a compliment.

The Edelsteins were Mitnagdim, Lithuanian rationalists in the tradition of the medieval scholar Maimonides.[21] Mother's father, Chatzkel, wore steel-rimmed glasses and had a Napoleon III beard, which was the current style. He was overly generous to friends and peasants, giving away or lending seed or money, to the detriment of his own wife and children. He was a well-educated man who spoke Russian, German, Polish, and Lithuanian, so that he was constantly in demand to read and write letters for illiterate peasants. My mother said he was asked to represent the town in the first Russian duma but declined, either for financial reasons or because he feared problems as a Jew.[22]

Although not an astute businessman, Chatzkel still retained some knowledge from his grain merchant ancestors. He subscribed to a Königsberg newspaper so that he was aware of the latest quotations on the wholesale grain market.[23] He had an arrangement with a Jewish grain merchant who arrived from Königsberg after his crop was harvested, and a deal would be made based on the dockside price less freight. In this way he received a much higher price than the peasants, who customarily sold their produce in the local market.

Chatzkel did not attend a yeshivah. Instead he studied Tanakh and Talmud under a private tutor.[24] A young Catholic priest, and perhaps others, also studied with him. The priest must have been an unusual man to have been interested in Hebrew studies. He secured permission from his superior and then persuaded Chatzkel's father, Hirsch, to allow him into the class. In any event, he and Chatzkel became good friends. In later years, the priest was ordained bishop of the diocese, and when he made his first official visit to Kalvaria, Chatzkel was standing on the steps of his house watching the procession. As he came by, the bishop left the procession, mounted the steps, and embraced Chatzkel, calling him "my dearly beloved son." This, of course, increased Chatzkel's reputation with the peasants.

There were ten children in my mother's family. Abe was the oldest, then Mother. Chatzkel couldn't keep track of his brood. One night he looked up from reading his newspaper and said very sternly, "Little boy, it is getting late. Shouldn't you be going home?" The little boy answered, "But Papa, I live here. I'm your Jake."[25]

Miriam (Mary) Fried Edelstein, my mother's mother, must have been a very unusual person before she was demoralized by a tragic accident that blinded her. Otherwise, the story of Michael Shalashudes would not have been possible. A non-Jewish peasant woman living in one of her grandfather's houses came to her with a most unusual proposition. "Mary," she said, "I have given birth to eighteen children, all of whom died in infancy. Obviously I am suffering from the evil eye. You, on the other hand, have ten children, all of whom are alive and healthy. Let me sell you my baby. If the baby is yours, it will share your good luck and will survive an otherwise evil fate."

When the baby was born, the mother sold him to Mary for a kopeck. The boy, Michael, or Micheleh in Yiddish, was raised in the house with the Edelstein children. Whenever he felt like doing so, he went to see his mother; otherwise, he played with the Edelstein children. He went to *heder* with them, the Jewish equivalent of elementary school, and he wore a tallis; in fact he became quite religious and wore a tallis all the time.[26] To all intents and purposes he was a member of the family. He survived alive and healthy until manhood.

Micheleh had one idiosyncrasy that drove his biological mother frantic: he was very fond of *shalashudes*, foods prepared for the traditional third Sabbath meal such as potato latkes, blintzes, and kugel.[27] He drove her crazy with demands that she cook *shalashudes* for him until she learned from Miriam how to cook the meal. By the time Mother left Lithuania Micheleh had grown and became a policeman, continuing to wear tallis underneath his uniform. I have often wondered what his fate was after the Nazis came.

The Edelstein home was one of the few buildings in town that did not have a thatched roof. In addition to many bedrooms, it had a large main hall with a huge fireplace and a large basement in which the cucumbers, cabbages, apples, and other foods were stored for the long winter. The big hall was the center of the family's social life. Mother's fondest memories went back to the days she sat near the fireplace listening to her grandmothers, Adela Fried and Deborah Edelstein, tell stories of bygone days. One favorite was the story of Napoleon's treasure. Mother heard the story from her grandmother, Adela Fried, who must have been eighty-five years of age, more or less, when she told Mother the story.[28] Adela lived to the advanced age of ninety-seven (a goal Mother set for herself), and when Mother told my son Lorin the tale years later, I asked him, "How many boys today have talked to a grandmother whose own grandmother saw Napoleon?"

The story goes as follows: When Adela was a little girl her parents operated an inn on the highway between Prussia and the Russian Empire at a point where the highway crossed the boundary at the Neman River. The tsar had dared to defy Napoleon's continental blockade against Great Britain, and Napoleon was determined to punish him. Crossing the boundary was an automatic declaration of war.[29] Napoleon and his staff spent the night at the inn before advancing into Russia. Soldiers in gorgeous uniforms paraded by on sleek, well-fed horses as bands played stirring music. It was an unforgettable sight. After a long interval the French returned, but they were a different army now, starving and dressed in rags. The weather was bitterly cold, and many were wearing women's coats to keep warm. The surviving horses, so beautiful before, were fewer in number and all skin and bones, barely able to keep their feet. Such was the disaster of the French retreat.

Life returned to normal, but a few years later came the story's second act. Adela's father was a close friend of the village priest; the two men played chess at the inn each night. One evening the priest asked to speak alone, at a place where they could not be overheard. It seems that a Frenchman had been arrested and thrown into jail. He fell ill and asked for the priest to make his confession. He told the priest that he had been in the paymaster department of Napoleon's army and that he and several others were in charge of a loaded wagon containing plundered gold and money to pay the troops. When they reached the border, the emaciated horses pulling the wagon died of exhaustion. There was no way to continue, so the officer in charge directed the men to bury the cargo. The soldier had returned, hoping to reclaim the treasure for himself, and before he died, he gave the priest a map indicating the burial place of the treasure. The priest showed the map to Adela's father and asked for his help to recover it. And so, by the light of the moon, the Catholic priest and the Jewish innkeeper hitched up a wagon, found the spot indicated on the map, and started to dig. After excavating for some feet, they hit an object. After more digging, they uncovered a large barrel. The barrel, alas, was empty. Someone else had beaten them to the loot!

Despite his broad education and modern ideas, Chatzkel refused to allow any of his children to attend a secular university on the grounds that such steps inevitably led to assimilation. This was in sharp contrast to his brother-in-law, my mother's uncle, Moshe Fried. Moshe sent his children to Swiss and French universities. Mother attended public school in the town, learning Russian, Polish, and some German. She read Russian and Polish literature and could recite poetry by Pushkin and Lermontov from memory. Her formal education was limited since she did not attend a gymnasium, a combination of senior high school and junior college. Higher education for Jews in the Russian Empire was restricted by a quota, and the Jewish community reserved the small quota for men.[30]

Mother learned all the customary accomplishments of a young lady of good family, and she was expert at sewing, crocheting, and embroidery. Her embroidery was exceptional. However, in one art she was totally lacking. She never learned to play the piano or any other musical instrument. This is unusual, but it could be that Jews of that area did not have this tradition, or perhaps her parents did not think music was important.

It was not customary in those days for a Jewish girl to get a Hebrew education. At most, a woman read a few Yiddish books containing a paraphrase of the Hebrew bible, or the *ma'asehbuch*, a collection of popular religious tales in Yiddish.[31] However, Mother was very much a Hebrew scholar with an excellent background in biblical Hebrew. She acquired this knowledge not by design but by chance. Her father, Chatzkel, had hired a teacher for his seven sons. They were supposed to learn Hebrew and Tanakh. The poor rebbe was terrified by his students, especially by her brothers Eli and Morris. To pacify the rebbe's fear of being injured by the boys, Rachel, as the oldest daughter, was placed in charge, with the unexpected result that she became the star pupil and acquired a remarkable knowledge, absorbing Hebrew and the Tanakh like a sponge. She had a prodigious memory for the Bible: even years later, if I asked the source of a quotation, she could turn to the correct text without hesitation. I don't know how much her brothers learned.

THE RISKINDS COME TO AMERICA

Wealthy relatives decided to rid themselves of a problem by shipping Nahum Riskind and his family to America. Accompanied by his eldest son, Jake, Nahum went first to find a location to settle. The advance party landed at New York in 1888, as best I can determine, during Benjamin Harrison's administration. At that time, immigrants entering the United States were processed at Castle Garden, later to be abandoned for a larger facility at Ellis Island.[32] Most of the immigration inspectors were either Anglo-Saxon or Irish, and they had great difficulty registering names that to them were exotic and unintelligible. Often a Polish or Russian immigrant would leave with a good Irish name completely alien to the new owner.[33] The Riskind family remained Riskind. Their cousins became Ryskind (such as the screenwriter Morrie Ryskind) or Riskin (such as the Israeli rabbi Shlomo Riskin).[34] However, Grandfather Nahum did not come out unscathed: he became Nathan, a perfectly good Jewish prophet but the wrong one.[35]

No sooner did Nathan step ashore in New York than his pockets were picked! Nathan and his son Jake were stranded in a strange country with no money. Fortunately, HIAS, the Hebrew Immigrant Aid Society, came to their rescue. Starting about 1880, there was a great mass migration of Jews from Eastern Europe that continued until after World War I. As a result of a deliberate tsarist policy of oppression to rid Russia of Jews, entire villages transported themselves to the United States with their rabbis to resume life in their new locations. In view of their poverty-stricken existence, the call of the *goldene medina*, the golden land, was irresistible. A horde of indigents, with their outlandish ways, descended on the shores of the United States, most of them at New York, to the extreme embarrassment of the old, established, mostly German Jewish community. They were anxious to avoid a large concentration of impecunious Jews in New York. Partly out of sincere charity, partly to avoid embarrassment, they created HIAS for the purpose of spreading the new immigrants throughout the United States. This proved to be a wise, beneficial policy. Although Nathan Riskind had no relatives or contacts in Chicago, HIAS sent him and Jake there.[36] When he arrived, he found that many from his area of Russia had preceded him, synagogues, rabbis, and all, and he was quite content. He immediately wrote to his wife, Judith, to come with their family.

Back in Dubrovna, however, a serious problem developed: it was found that the money Judith had been given was one fare short. Who was to be left behind? It could not be one of the daughters or one of the infants. There was a compelling reason to get the next oldest brother, Aaron, out of the country as soon as possible, otherwise he would be drafted into the tsar's army, a hideous fate, especially for a Jew. The term was seven years; drafted peasants were treated like animals, Jews even worse.[37] After much soul-searching, my grandmother decided to leave behind my father, Michael, age twelve, until money could be arranged for his passage. He was apprenticed to a tailor, a relative, who promised that Pa would be made bar mitzvah, taught his trade, and otherwise treated kindly.[38] This done, the rest of my father's family left for America to join Nathan in Chicago. According to my father's brother Albert, they went first to Königsberg in East Prussia where they took ship first to England then to America. They traveled, of course, in steerage.[39]

As a tailor's apprentice, Pa rose when it was still pitch dark and labored into the night, working under a lantern hanging from the ceiling. The tailor was himself existing in extreme poverty, he and his family barely above starvation level, so Pa had little to eat and was always hungry. The tailor's wife would mark their loaf of bread for fear that Pa would help himself to unauthorized food at night. The only decent meal he had in his years as an apprentice, he later told me, was when he was invited to a rich relative's wedding.

Pa spoke little about his youth. When I asked him once, he answered that life was *shver un biter*, hard and bitter. His only pleasure in life was some pigeons roosting nearby. Even in his old age, he spoke lovingly of *toibelach*, pigeons, and in Eagle Pass for a time he raised them. Once Mother served squab because the place was getting infested with them. Pa made a terrible scene when he discovered what was being served. As far as he was concerned, it was an act of cannibalism.

Pa told me once that he contemplated suicide during that period of his life, once even going down to the river for that purpose, but the water was freezing cold and he changed his mind. In all the years that I can recall, my father, no matter how difficult conditions were, never despaired, at least not on the surface. His experiences in Orsha molded his character and gave him fortitude as well as his feeling for those who were poor and humble.

The tailor had promised to teach Pa his trade, and this he did. Pa learned to sew with a close, fine stitch. He became an expert finisher, the elite of the trade. In his later business he used his knowledge of tailoring to train an excellent staff. He himself could take a suit apart and put it together again. When he bought lines of clothing, he would examine with great care their construction, paying particular attention to details of fine tailoring. Buttonholes in particular were a fixation, and he would hold forth on the merits of the handmade buttonhole, lamenting their sad state with the advent of machine-made clothing. He had profound distaste for shoddy fabrics or poor workmanship. These skills, I am sure, had much to do with his later success as a merchant.

Finally, when Pa was sixteen, his mother sent him the necessary money for his passage, which she had scraped together penny by penny. His journey to America was not exactly a pleasure trip. He came over on a returning cattle boat, the cheapest fare available because few people were willing to endure the stench. He landed in America in 1892 and joined his family in Chicago.[40]

CHICAGO

Meanwhile in Chicago, Nathan Riskind, my grandfather, with the help of HIAS or other aid organizations, opened a small neighborhood store selling candy and notions. He never learned to speak a word of English, and other than his family all his social contacts were with his synagogue. How he came to be a citizen is an interesting bit of Americana. An election in Chicago promised to be a particularly hot one. The ward alderman, whom Uncle Albert remembered was a political boss named "Hinky Dink," sent heavy freight wagons through the slum streets.[41] All the male immigrants twenty-one years of age or older were loaded and hauled before a cooperative federal judge and sworn in as US citizens. After the ceremony, they were taken to the polling place, handed an already marked ballot, and shown how to cast it. I am sure Nathan Riskind voted for the right candidate.

Both Albert and my mother concurred that my grandfather was a completely inept businessman, constantly losing money. The merchandise was not marked and he confused prices, selling the more expensive items too cheaply and asking too much for the cheap items so that they did not sell. The family hovered on the brink of poverty but endured because of income my Grandmother Judith made by catering food for weddings, banquets, and bar mitzvahs and serving meals to boarders. Her food was in demand as she had a reputation as a fabulous cook. In most cases when she catered food, she was allowed to take home the surplus, which helped feed the large family. When Albert was in the fifth grade, he quit school to get a job at two dollars per week, which he turned over to his mother. They all wore shoes donated by the aid society.

When my father, Michael Riskind, arrived in Chicago at the age of sixteen, he immediately went to work to support the family and became its mainstay. The average man's wage at that time was seven dollars a week. Pa found a job as a tailor with a suit manufacturer, and with his skill he soon became an assistant foreman at a higher wage. Then an event occurred that profoundly affected his life: a garment workers' strike of a very bitter nature. The strike was particularly uncomfortable since most of the tailors and most of the owners were Jews, often from the same villages and who attended the same synagogues.[42] These "owners" could hardly be classified as capitalists: most were just subcontractors who owned a few machines and were on the edge of starvation themselves. Pa was caught in the middle. He was accused by his boss of being uncooperative in disciplining the workers and was summarily fired.

A short time later his former boss sent word that all was forgiven. If Pa would return to work, he would be promoted to shift foreman at the wage of fifty dollars per week, a very large salary for those days. After much internal debate Pa turned down the offer—which was fortunate in the long run since only a few years later the manufacturer went out of business. The moral of the story, according to Pa, was never to go to work for anyone else again and to be his own boss.

Pa opened a small shop doing a combination of cleaning, pressing, and general tailoring. He made a bare living but soon realized there were much better opportunities. When not busy he stood outside the door and engaged the passersby in conversation. He had a pleasant personality and soon became friends with salesmen who came by with samples on the way to the manufacturers' offices or before embarking on the day's rounds with their customers. Pa asked them what was done with the samples when lines were changed at the end of each season, and he arranged to buy entire sample lines from the salesmen when they changed. These samples he put out for sale in the tailor shop at prices far lower than the stores were charging yet still permitting a very good markup. Gradually he increased his inventory until the shop became well stocked and the tailoring superfluous. He acquired a reputation for dealing honestly and fairly with his customers, and he had the advantage that he could alter clothing to make it fit.

Pa once described to me how some stores took advantage of their customers. If someone came in for a suit, the salesman would have him put on whatever he had, whether it fit or not, then hold the suit in back as the poor customer looked into the mirror so that he saw the suit only from the front, thereby selling him a complete misfit. Pa detested such tactics. If necessary, he would take a suit apart to make it fit. He took pride from the beginning in selling durable merchandise that was right for the customer.

Before long Pa was helping his mother substantially, and for the first time the family could live comfortably. He continued to build up his inventory, his business increased, and he was able to accumulate capital. I asked him once how much money he had when he met Mother. To quote Pa, he was "practically a milliner"—that is, a millionaire. Just how much did he really have? Well, said Pa, his assets totaled at least ten thousand dollars, a very respectable sum at the time.

MOTHER LEAVES FOR AMERICA

About 1903, my mother began to think seriously about migrating to America to join her brother Abe, then living in Chicago.[43] This was an emotional as well as a terrifying step to take. The idea of emigrating to America was not a new one. Between 1880 and World War I, many thousands of Jews left their homes in Eastern Europe. Most came to America; others scattered over the world. Mother had relatives in South Africa, Ireland, the Virgin Islands, and Canada. She related that there was an old man in her town everyone called *Yankel der Amerikaner*, Jake the American, because for a time he had lived in the United States before the Civil War. Unfortunately, he was peddling in the wrong area when the war broke out and managed to get tangled repeatedly between the opposing armies, finally deciding to go back home to a safer existence. He reported that Jews were treated well in America, that it was easy to make money in the United States without harassment or restriction by the government so long as you didn't mind the risk. And most interesting and astonishing was the fact that the Americans had a Jewish president named Avram Lincohlin.[44]

One important reason for emigrating is that Mother found herself in a most unfortunate situation as far as her matrimonial chances were concerned. Although not a great beauty, she was not bad looking and, very important for that time and place, her family had *yiches*, a Yiddish term that can be loosely translated as prestige or status.[45] In fact, under ordinary circumstances she would have been considered a most desirable catch. Twice she had been betrothed by family arrangement, as was the custom, to young men acceptable to her, but each time the young man had been seized and conscripted into the tsar's army for a term of seven years. Rachel Edelstein got the reputation of being an unlucky girl, a jinx to any potential husband, and her chances for marriage were nil. She was approaching her middle twenties and her only hope was to emigrate unless she would resign herself to be an old maid.

There was a second reason why Mother decided to leave her comfortable home to go to America. The tsarist government wished to rid the Russian Empire of Jews. To that end, it embarked on a deliberate policy of provoking pogroms, state-sponsored mob attacks against Jews joined in by the Russian Orthodox Church. Jews were not bothered in Lithuania, where she lived, but in Russia itself mobs ran amok in many areas, burning, raping, and killing as they went. It was not a happy atmosphere for Jews and certainly not a place for an intelligent

Jewish girl to contemplate spending her life. It was the reason, incidentally, why so many Jews joined the 1917 revolt against the tsar. They were branded communists in the United States when all they really wanted was to get rid of the tsar and his oppressive government. Mother mentioned once that although there were no pogroms in her area, the atmosphere following those in the Ukraine and other parts of the Russian Empire was such that she wanted to leave as soon as possible.[46] In addition to her passage money, her grandfather, Reuben Fried, gave her a gift of a thousand rubles, a considerable sum in those days.

Then there intervened a circumstance that caused bitterness for years. Mother never did get along with her younger sister Beilke, or Bertha as she was later called. Mother said that she was a spoiled brat. Beilke decided that she, too, was going to America and that her sister, Rachel, had to take her. Mother refused, but Beilke wept and carried on until Chatzkel ordered her to take Beilke with her. The result was a lifelong enmity on Mother's part.

Mother and Beilke departed for America from Lithuania in 1904, crossing the Atlantic in a second-class cabin on the German luxury liner *Kaiser Wilhelm der Grosse*. Her ship docked in Montreal, a route chosen as closer to Chicago, where she expected her brother Abe to meet her.[47] Furthermore, there were some Edelstein cousins in Montreal, and for some days the two girls stayed with these newly married cousins in their small apartment. Mother and her demanding, complaining sister were not a welcome addition. By the time the girls left, everyone was angry. After leaving, Mother never communicated with the Montreal cousins again, and as for Beilke, they parted in Chicago and Mother never spoke to her again either.[48]

Soon after Mother arrived in Chicago, she found a job in a blouse factory where the usual wage was three dollars a week. In a short time, she persuaded the owner to change her work to hand embroidery on the blouses on a piecework basis, and soon she was earning as much as fourteen dollars a week, a very big wage in those days. Looking for a better room to rent, she inquired at the Vilner Shul, the Lithuanian synagogue, and was directed to the home of Aaron Riskind, Pa's older brother.[49] Aaron was married to Sarah Block, and her father, Rabbi Block, also lived with them.[50] Aaron had no education and was making a bare living as a junk dealer, but both he and Sarah were pleasant, and Mother enjoyed living in their home with their children. There were five boys, the older ones going to school. By reading from the boys' schoolbooks and from newspapers, she soon acquired a good reading knowledge of English, although she never rid herself of a strong German-sounding accent. Mother also became very fond of Rabbi Block; he was a person she could talk to and they became good friends.

MY PARENTS

Sarah insisted my parents had to meet, and they were married in Chicago in 1907. Pa was twenty-eight or twenty-nine by then, Mother was twenty-five, both old to be unmarried by the standards of that time.[51] My daughter Susan once asked Mother if she had considered marrying anyone else before Grandpa. Ma said that she had been approached by a former resident of Kalvaria, who proposed she marry his son with the understanding that she would support the son while he attended medical school. After meeting the son Ma nixed the proposition: "He was the type who as soon as he graduated would run off with a pretty nurse." Susan then asked why she had married Grandpa. Mother answered that she was certain he would be a success, and besides, "He was so handsome." I asked my father once if he had ever taken Mother out to dinner when he was courting her. "No," he said. "We would go for a walk and I would buy her an ice cream corn." "How

Wedding portrait of Morris's parents, Michael and Rachel Riskind, Chicago, 1907. (Courtesy of Dr. Peter Riskind.)

much did that cost?" I asked. "A nickel." I would not be exaggerating if I were to say my parents were very frugal.

The food for the wedding was prepared by Grandma Riskind, who was in the business of catering food. After the wedding she announced she was exhausted and needed to go away for a few days' rest, so the newly married Rachel Riskind was asked to cook for the family. For the pièce de résistance, she made some gefilte fish.[52] In the process of seasoning the fish, the top fell off the pepper box and the entire box of pepper fell in. In a panic Ma took out all the pepper she could, but it remained so hot that she was afraid of the consequences. It was too late, however, to start all over. She served the fish with amazing results. "Rachel," said Grandfather, "for years I've been telling Yudke (his wife, Judith) she didn't use enough pepper. This is the first time anyone made fish the way it ought to be made."

For some time after my parents were married, Pa's business continued to prosper and expand. He was no longer just selling samples but going to various wholesalers and jobbers to buy regular merchandise. Then he embarked on a new project that was to prove catastrophic: he opened a second store, in Maroa, Illinois. Why Maroa I don't know. Pa's parents moved there with Albert, the youngest son, then about twenty years of age; Albert was one of the few of the children in the family who contributed to their support.[53] Out of respect for their father, the business was named "N. Riskind and Son." To the people of Maroa, that son was Albert, since he was the one they knew, but the money in the business was entirely Pa's, and he bought the merchandise, all on credit. Albert got along well with his customers and was well liked. As far as my grandparents were concerned, though, they were like fish out of water. Maroa was a small farming community. There were no other Jews with whom to associate and neither of my grandparents spoke English. They would only eat kosher food, which had to be sent from Chicago, often spoiling by the time it arrived. Grandfather missed his synagogue and his friends. Finally, they gave up and returned to Chicago, leaving Albert alone to run the business.[54]

Then came the depression of 1907. The entire country faced difficult times, and Pa's business became worse and worse.[55] He might have survived with only one store, but the combined debts of the two stores proved too great a burden and he was unable to meet his bills. His creditors put him into bankruptcy, and Pa lost everything. Making everything worse, my parents had a child, a son they named Herschel, probably after Ma's grandfather, who became sick and died. The death certificate showed that Herschel Riskind, an infant, died of a gastrointestinal disorder. The death of their son was a devastating blow to my parents.

Emotionally drained and destitute, they moved to Irondale, a steel mill district in South Chicago. They opened a small shop, with little merchandise, and lived in the back of the tiny store. The inhabitants of the area were steel mill workers, mostly Slavs of various kinds: Poles, Slovaks, Serbs, all from rural environments of a backward part of Europe. There was often violence, especially on Saturday nights or when there was a wedding. On one occasion a policeman burst into their place, ran into the bedroom, and hid under the bed. Of course, my parents were terrified.

To add further to their problems, Pa became ill. He had always had severe allergies, and with his emotional problems it developed into what Ma thought was tuberculosis, which at that time was common.[56] One night Mother wanted to get a doctor, but the only telephone was some distance away in a saloon. Through the years Ma told me the story how terrified she was to go in the dark to a saloon in a very rough neighborhood to make a phone call to the doctor. Either that doctor or a specialist recommended that Pa move to San Antonio, which was then being promoted for its hot, dry climate. Ma's brother Abe was already in Texas, and it was Abe who urged them to join him in Eagle Pass.

HOW WE ENDED UP IN EAGLE PASS

Abe had an interesting odyssey to Eagle Pass. While still in Lithuania, he had joined the Chovevei Zion, the Lovers of Zion, a group that believed that the way to redeem the Land of Israel was to go to Palestine, buy land, and farm as their ancestors had done.[57] Abe knew that his father would never agree to such a harebrained idea, so he deceived his father by telling him he wanted to go to Jerusalem to study. For this purpose, Chatzkel gave him money. Instead, Abe went to Palestine and joined his friends at the new colony of Hadera. In order for Jews to buy land, they first had to bribe Turkish officials for a permit then find an Arab effendi—a lord or noble—who would sell. While helping to drain swampy land they had bought, Abe became very ill with malaria. A doctor advised him to leave or die, and not wanting to return to Lithuania, Abe moved to the United States.

After leaving Palestine, Abe's boat docked in New York and he moved on to Chicago, where he worked in a cigar factory. According to Mother, Abe went to a lecture once, and when he was returning home it had turned cold and wet. He was in shirtsleeves, got thoroughly drenched, chilled, and became very ill. As a final blow, the doctor noted that he had contracted tuberculosis, probably from his employment in the cigar factory. The doctor urged that he move to a hot, dry climate—this must have been common medical advice—and, in the fashion of that time, he suggested San Antonio, Texas.[58]

In order to make a living in San Antonio, Abe started peddling, using the railroad as his means of transportation and stopping at all the small settlements along the route as far as Eagle Pass.[59] Among the items he carried were pictures of saints, of which the Mexican people were avid customers. Abe had an advantage over other vendors in that his pictures were tinted by a new process, better than the old black-and-white photographs—at least the customers preferred them. It happened that in Eagle Pass he sold a woman a picture of Saint Joseph, the patron saint of the town. She hung the picture above her bed. One night there was a violent electrical storm, and lightning struck the woman's house, moved down the chimney and the wall, and struck the picture of Saint Joseph over her bed. The lightning was deflected sideways by the picture wire, bypassed the woman in bed, and exited through the floor, leaving the terrified woman untouched. She reported the incident to the local padre, who pronounced that she had been saved through the saint's intercession. Word spread around the town, and when Abe made his next visit, he was swamped with requests for pictures of Saint Joseph.

Old Mr. Schmidt, the president of the First National Bank in Eagle Pass, told me that as teller of the bank he became friendly with Uncle Abe, who always made a deposit after completing his visit to Eagle Pass before returning to San Antonio.[60] Schmidt urged Abe to settle in Eagle Pass after Abe said that he was doing the major part of his business there. "Abe," said Schmidt, "there is an empty store on Commercial Street. Why don't you rent it, put a store in front, and live in the back?" Abe took Schmidt's advice and rented the building, which he bought a few years later. He called his business the New Furniture Company. This must have been in 1905 or early 1906, then Abe sent for his younger brother, Morris, paying his passage.[61] My parents joined them in Eagle Pass in 1910, when the Chicago doctor suggested that Pa should move to San Antonio for his health. It is on such chance events that a family's destiny is determined. How different it would have been had my parents located in San Antonio!

CHAPTER 2

TEXAS BEFORE AND AFTER WE GOT THERE

What sort of a place was Eagle Pass in 1910? I once saw an old magazine article written in the early 1880s in which an intrepid adventurer described the settlement as a collection of Indian jacales, straw-thatched huts. When the railroad was extended from points in Texas to Eagle Pass in 1882, where it connected with Mexican railroad lines to Saltillo and Torreón, the town began to change.[1] Importers and exporters began to build fine homes, and the number of Anglos increased. A few prosperous stores began to appear on Main Street and Commercial Street, closer to the Rio Grande. The most important of these was De Bona's. The original De Bona, Rocco, I think, had been an Italian immigrant. After running a candy stand in San Antonio, he moved to Eagle Pass and went into business. By around 1900, De Bona's occupied most of the northern part of the block, on Main Street from Commercial to Washington Streets. I remember it vaguely from my childhood. Most of the store was in ladies' and men's furnishings, but on one side was a meat market.[2]

By 1910, Eagle Pass was basically a trading post. The only importance it could claim came solely because it bordered Mexico and the much larger Mexican city of Ciudad Porfirio Díaz, now Piedras Negras.[3] Eagle Pass was an isolated settlement and continued to be so until recent years, which is one reason the people there were so unique. The town was the end of the road. Many of the people were outcasts, all gathered together with no place else to go. They either had to shoot each other, which some did, or get along. Whatever the reason, Eagle Pass had and continues to have an easygoing live-and-let-live attitude. It was some 160 miles to San Antonio via Uvalde on an unmarked trail, somewhat closer by the Laredo road, if you could find it. Chilo Rodríguez told me that his uncles, hauling freight in ox carts, took a week for the trip each way. The stagecoach from San Antonio made the trip in some three or four days of fatiguing travel. When the railroad was completed in the 1880s, the Pullman train to Torreón came through Eagle Pass until it was halted after the Mexican Revolution. When the automobile first came into limited use, a trip to San Antonio via unmarked wagon trail was a real adventure. Even if the brave traveler did not get lost, it was a journey of many hours, usually a day and a half or two days. When I was a boy, few in Eagle Pass had ever been to

San Antonio, let alone the world beyond. A boy in my second-grade class was much admired because he had actually been to Alpine and had seen "high" mountains.[4]

In my early childhood, there was only one feasible way to travel should one desire to go to San Antonio. Once a day, a freight train left Eagle Pass, which had one seating car attached at the end. This was a ramshackle affair straight out of a Western movie with antique lights and equally old seats, some with the springs popping out. The train creaked and jerked its way along at a speed of around twenty-five miles an hour until after some two hours of torture it reached Spofford Junction, about forty miles north of Eagle Pass. There you got off and waited for the passenger train to New Orleans coming from El Paso and California. In a Pullman car of that train, you could proceed in luxury to San Antonio or continue to Houston or New Orleans on your way north. In San Antonio you would get off at the bustling Southern Pacific depot, now deserted.[5]

PASO DEL ÁGUILA

The area between San Antonio and the Mexican border at Eagle Pass had always been isolated. Although the early Spanish explorer Cabeza de Vaca came through the area in the 1520s or 1530s, Spaniards did not fully explore the region for many more years.[6] A few expeditions passed through later in the seventeenth and early eighteenth centuries, usually friars seeking Indians to convert. One of the Texas historical journals carried excerpts from their diaries, which are rather humorous if one has lived here for any length of time. One Spaniard came by during a year of heavy rain and reported that the area was lush and verdant and could support a population of millions of Europeans. Thirty years later another padre who came through during a drought reported that the entire region of what is now northern Mexico and Texas was a worthless desert, not fit for a dog.

The first actual settlement in the area was made in 1699 with a military colony about thirty-five miles downriver from Eagle Pass at San Juan Bautista, also listed on old maps as Presidio del Rio Grande.[7] A few years later the French trader-smuggler-explorer St. Denis appeared and was arrested for trespassing. St. Denis saved his hide by marrying the comandante's granddaughter. The record does not mention if she was pretty.[8] The news about St. Denis so frightened the viceroy in Mexico of an imminent occupation of Texas by the French garrison in New Orleans that a number of settlements were founded on the south bank of the Rio Grande, and the colonization of Texas began. The most important settlement was San Antonio de Béxar, settled by Canary Islanders who rested for some time at San Juan Bautista before venturing into the wilds to establish San Antonio.[9]

After the Mexican War of Independence from Spain, which lasted from 1810 to 1821, the name of San Juan Bautista was changed to Guerrero, or "warrior," in honor of the heroes of the war. The village had a brief moment in history during the Mexican War against the United States when Captain Robert E. Lee oversaw the improvement of the old Camino Real from San Antonio to Guerrero, over which General Wool's army invaded Mexico and joined the army of Zachary Taylor at Saltillo.[10] Later, when the railroad bypassed Guerrero to enter Mexico at Piedras Negras, Guerrero faded from history. No one knew the location of San Juan Bautista until Mrs. Sarah McKellar, an Eagle Pass resident, suggested that Guerrero and its ruined mission was the site.[11]

The first settlement of civilians was called California Camp, located at what is now Commercial Street in the vicinity of the old ice plant. For a while, forty-niners tried reaching the California gold fields by cutting across Mexico to the Pacific and then continuing north by ship. I have followed this route a number of times back and forth, taking the road south to Monclova, then to Torreón and Durango, to Mazatlán, a distance of some eight hundred miles. By following this route, the gold seekers thought they could avoid high mountains and Apache Indians as well. What they did not know was that in following this route the trail would climb to over nine thousand feet, much higher than the road straight west from Eagle Pass.

Fort Duncan was founded in what is now Eagle Pass in 1849 to protect the region from the depredations of marauding Indians. The problem was that the soldiers stationed there were infantry and were useless against Comanches or Lipan Apaches riding horseback. Fort Duncan was not only the nucleus for the settlement of Eagle Pass, but it was indirectly the cause for the settlement of Piedras Negras directly across the Rio Grande. There had long been an Indian settlement at La Villita in Mexico because of the springs there. Many of the residents moved the three or four miles to the banks of the river directly across from Fort Duncan, hoping that the proximity of the American garrison would be a protection against Indian raids.[12] At first their hopes were unfounded. Jesse Sumpter, who came to Eagle Pass as a soldier in the original garrison in 1849 and was demobilized there, recalled in his memoir that soldiers standing on the American side could see mounted Comanche on the Mexican side spearing people and cattle. Sumpter's memoir pictures Eagle Pass as a violent, bloody settlement—it was no place for the timid.[13]

As a footnote to history, Robert E. Lee happened to be at Fort Duncan when he first received word of secession.[14] He had been engaged in trying to track down the elusive Juan Cortina, called by the Texans a bandit but regarded by the Mexicans as a patriot.[15] The building Lee used as a headquarters still stands in Fort Duncan Park. When the Civil War started, Eagle Pass acquired major importance. Money obtained from the sale of cotton became pivotal to the Confederacy to finance needed purchases. At first cotton was hauled to Brownsville, then crossed to Matamoros and shipped to England and France. Union forces briefly occupied Brownsville to stop this trade. Some cotton was then shipped through Laredo, but it was considered too close to the Union forays out of Brownsville, and the cotton export trade shifted to Eagle Pass. Cotton from East and Central Texas was arduously hauled via San Antonio to Eagle Pass, crossed to Piedras Negras, then hauled to the Gulf Coast at Matamoros for shipment to Europe. At one time Union supporters tried to capture Eagle Pass to halt the cotton trade, but they failed.

After Lee's surrender at Appomattox in 1865, the last Confederate force under arms and still flying the Stars and Bars was Shelby's Brigade. Shelby refused to surrender to the Union and hoped he could lead his forces to join Emperor Maximilian in Mexico, serving in the emperor's cause in exchange for grants of land to himself and his men.[16] Shelby led his troops across Texas and crossed the Rio Grande at Eagle Pass. In the middle of the river he buried his battle flags, weighted down with rocks, then entered into Mexico. But by that time, Maximilian's cause was lost, Shelby's force dispersed, and most returned to the United States. In this way, Eagle Pass earned the title of "Graveyard of the Confederacy." I suspect that some of Shelby's men remained in our area, since unlike other areas of northern Mexico, there are a number of Mexican families of importance with Anglo names, such as Boone (pronounced "Booneh"), Peary, Earnshaw, Ainslie, and Williamson. In any other town much would be made of being the Graveyard of the Confederacy; in Eagle Pass it is ignored.

Before the border quieted down, one of the last of the Indian wars took place in our area. The Kickapoo were a small tribe originally from the Great Lakes area. By the nineteenth century, the pressure of Anglo settlement forced them to move south and west. Some settled on a reservation in what is now Oklahoma, others migrated in about 1850 to the Mexican border near Eagle Pass, facing violent attacks from Anglo Texans as they went.[17] Proceeding under what they considered a flag of truce, they were attacked by frightened white civilians at a place called Dove Creek. The Kickapoo had a reputation as fierce warriors and easily drove off their attackers, at the same time vowing vengeance against white treachery.[18]

The Mexican government at that time was desperately trying to protect its citizens from Comanches and Lipan Apaches. It gave the Kickapoo a large tract of land some kilometers from the Seminoles at Nacimiento, in Coahuila 120 miles from Piedras Negras, in return for their promise to protect this area of northern Mexico.[19] The Kickapoo kept their word as far as the Mexicans were concerned and kept the peace within the boundaries of Mexico. On the Texas side, however, they sought vengeance, using their reservation as a springboard for attacks along the American border, murdering and robbing from Eagle Pass to San Antonio in revenge for the treatment they had received at the hands of the Texans. When I was a boy I saw numerous crosses that marked the graves of those killed by Indians.

The American authorities made repeated demands on the Mexican government through the State Department as well as the local Mexican authorities demanding that Mexico put a halt to the Kickapoo depredations, but to no avail.[20] So long as the Kickapoo protected Mexican citizens against the dreaded Comanche, Mexico turned a deaf ear. Since diplomacy proved fruitless, the military decided on drastic measures. General Philip Sheridan of the US Army sent Colonel Ranald Mackenzie to Fort Clark in Brackettville, Texas, in 1873 to put an end to the Kickapoo problem. Major Zenas Bliss was sent to the Seminole reservation at Nacimiento, where he persuaded a group of Black Seminoles to enlist as scouts for the US Cavalry. According to the Seminoles, he promised them land in Texas as a reward. The Seminoles were enrolled as scouts at Fort Duncan in Eagle Pass and put under the command of Lieutenant John Bullis, who later became chief of staff of the army.[21]

Traveling at night on a forced march, Mackenzie's cavalry crossed the Rio Grande, covered over seventy miles, and made a punishing attack on the Kickapoo village, which also sheltered a few Lipan Apaches. Mexico made an official protest, which the United States ignored.[22] In other fighting with the Kickapoo and other tribes, four of the Seminoles won the Medal of Honor for rescuing Lieutenant Bullis, whose horse had been shot from under him.[23] By 1880 the Indian wars were over, but the border remained no less violent.

Walter Prescott Webb's history of the Texas Rangers has much material about Eagle Pass and the surrounding area, including the bandit King Fisher, the terror of Eagle Pass.[24] I have been told that there used to be a scrawled sign on the wagon trail leading to Carrizo Springs, about forty-five miles from Eagle Pass, saying, "This is King Fisher's road. All others keep off." According to Webb, whenever the news came that King Fisher and his gang were approaching Eagle Pass, the county judge would dash home and hide under his bed so that he could not be called upon to act. It was King Fisher's boast that he had killed twenty-five men—not counting Mexicans, Indians, or Blacks. He once killed a man in an Eagle Pass saloon because he liked his fancy boots and the man would not sell them. As a result of our region's isolation, King Fisher is generally unknown. One history book gives Fisher a few lines as "a rancher and Sheriff of Uvalde." His ranching consisted mostly in cattle rustling. And so much of our local history is forgotten. Our outlaws are unwept, unhonored, and unsung. We have no O.K. Corral (reconstructed, of course) for tourists to gawk at.

Why was Eagle Pass such a haven for thugs and desperadoes? I learned the answer when the Mexican consul, Leopoldo de Samaniego, showed me a consular report dated around 1900 describing an extradition treaty between the United States and Mexico. Before then, the criminal elements of both countries gathered at the border. If the Mexican police, the rurales, came to Piedras Negras, the criminals had only to move temporarily to Eagle Pass; if the Texas Rangers came to Eagle Pass, the bad men were one step ahead of them and simply crossed to Piedras Negras. But when the treaty was signed, both border towns became quiet and peaceful.

The first Jewish merchant in Eagle Pass—it must have been around 1860—seems to have been a man who accidentally shot and killed himself while cleaning a gun mentioned by Jesse Sumpter in his story.[25] Sumpter says he had his business and lived upstairs in the red brick building that existed on the corner diagonally across from the present International Bridge. This old building was torn down about 1970 to make way for a new chain store. Sumpter tells another story about a Jew, apparently highly respected, who was courting a girl from Zaragoza, a Spanish settlement about forty miles from the border. One of the worst of the Anglo "bad men" was also courting the girl and challenged the Jew to a fistfight over her. When the Jew took off his pistol as agreed to and was ready to fight, his rival shot him dead. The Mexican townspeople were so enraged that they surrounded the offender and lynched him on the spot.[26] In 1887, Texas took an ethnic census that indicated that there were "one to nine" Jews inhabiting Maverick County.[27]

THE FAMILY GROWS IN EAGLE PASS

By the time my parents arrived, a complete transformation had occurred and Eagle Pass was a quiet, sleepy village where serious crime was unknown. The railroad arrived in the 1880s and brought more dramatic changes. Coal mining a few miles from town at Seco Mines became a major industry. In fact, the entire Southern Pacific system was fueled by the local mines. Railroad people, mining officials, merchants in the export and import trade, and wealthy ranchers all began to build imposing homes on Ceylon Street or its vicinity.

My father got to Eagle Pass some time in 1910 with twenty-seven dollars in cash, which he had borrowed from his mother, and a suitcase of odds-and-ends merchandise. Mother and my older sister Bess remained in Chicago. I never asked where he stayed; he must have slept in Abe's room, on the floor or on a cot, in the back of his furniture store. He started out peddling on foot, walking as far as the Seco Mines, which was then called the La Mar Mines, after the manager. This was a walk of over five miles from Abe's store, and coming from the climate of Chicago, the heat must have been an ordeal for a man in poor health. Our friend Chilo Rodríguez told me that his father recalled how Pa would sit exhausted in the shade of a mesquite tree in San Juan Plaza on his way back from the mines.[28] Rodríguez struck up a conversation and, as his house was across the street, offered Pa water. Our families have been friendly ever since. As soon as he could Pa bought a horse and buggy so that he could peddle the area quicker and in greater comfort. Even so, the heat in summer and the cold during northers caused much suffering.

Pa told me bitterly that the manager of the mines ordered him off the premises, saying, "We want no Jew peddlers here." The mining company maintained its own company store, which charged all that the traffic would bear, and they wanted no competition. Pa had been selling with a small down payment, the balance in weekly installments, and in the long run their treatment of Pa did them no good because their customers came to town to trade with Pa anyway. In a short time, he had accumulated enough money to rent a small wooden shack

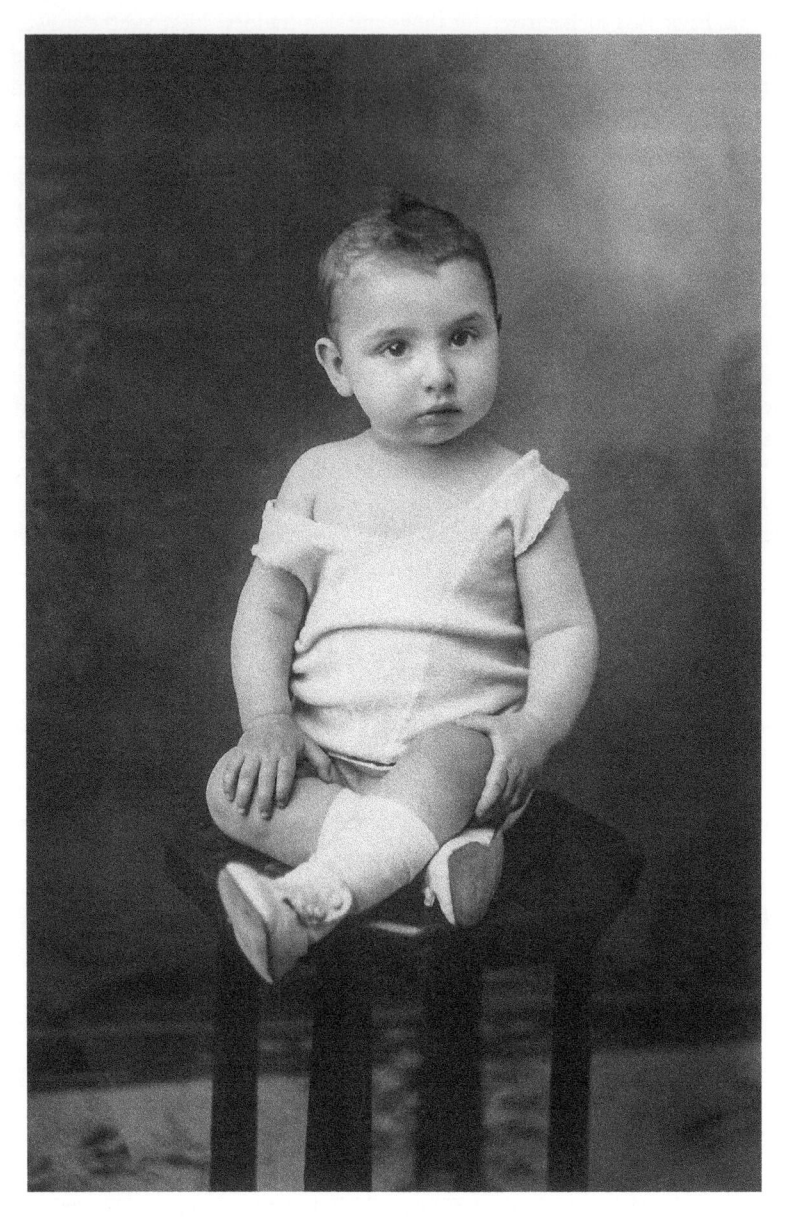

Morris Riskind, Eagle Pass, 1911. (Courtesy of Dr. Peter Riskind.)

of a store on the southwestern corner of Commercial and Rio Grande Streets, directly across from Abe Edelstein's furniture store. This edifice has since passed through the possession of many, and for years housed a small restaurant coincidentally called Mike's Cafe. In 1993, the old building was torn down to make way for a new Cerna's Money Exchange.

My mother and sister Bess arrived in Eagle Pass toward the latter part of 1910, and Pa was able to rent a house on the southwest corner of Rio Grande and Adams Streets. The house is still there, although it has since been remodeled several times.²⁹ I was born in this house February 8, 1911. The house was comfortable, although by no means luxurious. We had a covered cistern to hold drinking water, which was filled from a tin flume on the roof. The wooden house had its share of spiders, roaches, and scorpions. Mother was very nervous about the harmless garter snakes that were often living under the front steps.

The house is located at the edge of an arroyo, now called Eagle Pass Creek, which at that time marked the end of town. All sorts of small game were there, especially skunks, or polecats, as they were called. The skunks could make life miserable during the hot summer nights when the windows were open. Morris Fox, our neighbor's son, shot a bobcat in the arroyo behind their house and very proudly displayed the skin on the wall of his room. Our neighbors were very pleasant people, and we children often played in their yards. I remember the names of Fox, Gutiérrez, and Bonnet. They were Catholics, and my parents knew them only casually, but our relationship as neighbors was always on a very friendly basis.

Mother was sustained by the presence of her older brother, Abe, and her younger brother, Morris, who was known as a prankster. Abe had brought him over from Europe directly to Eagle Pass. Her brothers were regular guests for dinner, where Morris would delight in teasing my father. One night, Ma made potato latkes. Pa sat between Abe and Morris, and while Abe held Pa's attention in an animated discussion of business, Morris swiped the latkes off his plate as fast as Mother could replace them, until she finally intervened. Morris made the bill collections for Abe, making his rounds in a horse and buggy. At dinner, he would keep Mother in laughter with an account of his adventures, acting out a customer in the process of making tortillas, mimicking her patting the tortillas while spitting on her hands, alternating with scratching her head.

Morris himself told me the story of the cat. The mangy animal must have belonged to a previous occupant of the house and was there when they moved in. Ma couldn't chase it away, so she asked Morris to get rid of it as humanely as possible. The next day, when he went to make his collections at the mines, he grabbed the cat and left him there, five miles from town. When he came back for dinner the cat was waiting for him on the front porch. The next day he left it a few miles away on the other side of town; the cat was back by the time he arrived for dinner. Then he put the cat in a sack and took it with him to Mexico and released it there. When the cat again was waiting for him, Morris gave up.

There is another story about Morris Edelstein I learned from his son Ruben that bears on his character.³⁰ After moving to Brownsville, he was returning home from a visit to Galveston, where he had been courting his future wife, Yetta, when the train to Brownsville was stopped by bandits.³¹ Morris had been carrying on a conversation with a Mexican man and an American Anglo. When news spread through the train that the bandits had shot the engineer and fireman and were going through the train killing all Americans, Morris did some quick thinking. He told the Anglo to keep absolutely quiet, and when the bandits came he persuaded them that the man was a German, an *aleman*. This was confirmed by the Mexican sitting with them, and the man was unharmed.³²

M. RISKIND, INC.

Ma reminisced that during the first few years of the store, very little actual merchandise filled the shelves. To give the illusion of a well-stocked business, the family filled the displays with empty boxes and their own clothing. As soon as he was financially able, Pa made trips to

Chicago for merchandise rather than buying from jobbers in San Antonio, and he arranged for additional shipments as needed from Chicago. By buying directly, his prices were much better than those of his competitors.[33]

One of his biggest successes came from a shipment of black skirts he bought in Chicago at a very low price. Although of excellent quality, the skirts were all of one size—large in the waist and long. This would be an obstacle for anyone else, but not for him. He turned the detriment into a benefit. All the married Mexican women wore black skirts that were very much in demand. De Bona's sold skirts of similar quality for twenty dollars each. Pa turned his full skirts into garments made to measure, altering them for individual customers, and selling them for five dollars each in installments of one dollar down and one dollar a week. Pa soon became so busy selling that Ma had to help out, taking the skirts apart and resewing them in waist and length to fit each customer. With the proceeds, he ordered more and more merchandise from Chicago. Soon he had a large clientele among the laboring people.

About the year 1912, Morris and Abe ended their business partnership, probably because Abe was increasingly difficult to work with as his illness grew worse. Morris heard about the opportunities waiting in the lower Rio Grande Valley with the rapid increase of population, and he decided to strike out on his own. With the money Abe gave him for his share of the business, Morris opened a store in Brownsville, which he called Edelstein's Better Furniture. The business grew into a multistore chain in all the surrounding towns, and within a comparatively few years Morris Edelstein became one of the most important businessmen of South Texas.[34]

The Mexican Revolution, which began in 1910, brought an economic boom to Eagle Pass. All border points were critical to both sides as sources for the purchase of supplies, both for the military and the civilian populations. In addition, the hordes of refugees that poured into Eagle Pass at various times needed food, shelter, and clothing.[35] At first, the refugees were Porfirists, that is, those connected with the overthrown government directly or indirectly. Later there were those fleeing from Flores Magón, or the Huertistas, or Pancho Villa.[36] Pa began to get more business than he could handle in his tiny location. He no longer had to depend on house-to-house peddling, although for years later those in his employ continued to do it. The demand for blankets, pants, shirts, shoes, and other articles of clothing soared. Pa made an increasing number of trips east for goods. A larger store became a necessity.

In 1914, Pa took a decisive step in his business career. He bought a lot on Main Street from T. C. Wadsworth for five hundred dollars; the deed was recorded on March 23, 1914. On the same date Sam Schwartz, another Jewish businessman, recorded the deed to the adjoining corner property, later the site of the Aztec Theater.[37] The records also indicate that L. F. Sneed recorded a mechanic's lien on June 16, 1914, to construct a building on the newly acquired Riskind property. The original price of the building was seven thousand dollars; the lien was assigned to the Border National Bank and released on November 23, 1917. Sneed was an honest builder and constructed a very sound structure of hard red brick. The basement cross beams are solid twelve-by-twelve timbers, probably unobtainable today.

When the new store, named M. Riskind, Inc., and popularly called Riskind's, was completed in the fall of 1914, our family moved into the spacious apartment on the second floor. The front arches, still part of the store, were the original front of the building. In the kitchen was a huge wrought-iron wood stove in which mesquite logs were burned. In the winter on a cold day, this was the most comfortable part of the house; in the summer, it was a veritable inferno. Later, a second small kitchen was built in the back with a screened porch. By the time this was built, an electric stove was added and used in hot weather.

Original storefront of the Riskind store, ca. 1915. The showroom was on the ground floor, and the family's living space on the floor above. The one-story brick building on the right, added in 1915 or 1916, was originally used for furniture sales, and the store was also extended later into the empty lot adjacent to the left. (Courtesy of the Reuben S. Riskind Family.)

With the opening of the new store my father started a routine, which he continued for years. He opened the store early and closed late, coming upstairs only for meals. He worked long hours, and so did the help. By the time the farmers and ranchers came to town on Saturday, it was already late in the day. Business on a Saturday night was brisk. It was never before 10 p.m. that the last customer left and Pa finally came upstairs, exhausted. We children had little contact with our father except at mealtime. No one complained about the long hours. As far as my parents or the store personnel were concerned, it was the nature of things.

Riskind's was spacious enough to have a separate women's department, and this became the domain of my father's younger sister Rose, who came to stay with us in 1911.[38] Aunt Rose had a pretty face and was very intelligent, but she was unfortunate in that she had contracted some disease as a child, probably spinal tuberculosis, and remained a hunchback who was well under five feet tall. Her condition must have been extremely frustrating to one so mentally alert. As soon as she arrived, she became invaluable to my father in the business. My mother, meanwhile, whose health was not good, was banned from the business on the grounds that she should devote her time exclusively to the five children—Bess, Ruth, Sarah, Reuben, and myself.[39]

Aunt Rose increasingly became a thorn in Mother's side. Auntie, as we called her, took over more and more control, and with her domineering personality, she took on the proportions of a family tyrant. Pa had promised his mother he would take care of her, and to him Auntie could do no wrong. He shrugged off Mother's remonstrances that she was not the boss of her own household. Auntie was the cause of endless arguments that poisoned our family life.[40] The extent of Auntie's schooling was an elementary education, for which she earned a certificate from Hull-House in Chicago.[41] She was guilty of many malapropisms, such as calling cartons *cartoons*. Whenever possible in the evenings, she attended the Aztec Theater and would return home gushing over Clara Kimball Young or Theda Bara. In later years, her hero was Errol Flynn—"Flint, that handsome brute."[42] She had many pretensions and affectations of pseudo-gentility, one of which was to drink tea holding the cup with her little finger extended at an angle.

Auntie was the absolute arbiter of style, fashion, and manners in the family. We were all subject to her constant censorship on such matters as dress and conduct. In the business, if one were to think that Auntie was a comic figure or an object of contempt, it would be very much a mistake. She had a shrewd business sense and was most competent in getting along with the general public. She had a talent for making Anglo women feel that each customer was getting the best individual attention. Miss Rose became the personal shopper for a doting following, and those old-timers who remember her do not recall her as an object of ridicule. Far from it. Great as her authority was, however, she could not prevent Pa's frequenting of saloons, which was a horror to her. To be respectable with Anglos, she felt, this was just not done.

In 1917, Pa's younger brother Albert moved to Eagle Pass. Business had not been good in the small Illinois farming town of Maroa. Pa needed help in his rapidly expanding business, and he urged Albert to make the move. Albert proved to be an excellent asset in the business. He ran the office and was a first-rate credit manager. My father had little interest in the intricacies of bookkeeping or office management. To Pa, business was simple: You bought the right merchandise at the right price, you sold it at a profit, you collected the money. A difference in viewpoint on credit soon developed. Albert believed in large, thirty-day charge accounts. Pa wanted to continue small accounts, sold to the poorer part of the population, who paid only one dollar per week. In the end Albert prevailed. The jobs of the collectors were abolished, and the best of the small accounts were transformed into charge accounts.

As the store prospered, new additions were made. The building was extended to the east in 1917 by building on the lot between the store and the Aztec Theater, where we had a wooden four-seater swing and some trees Mother had planted. Mother continued to have her garden area in back of the store next to the Schwartz Building. Pa also bought the San Miguel Saloon building adjacent to the west side of the store from Sam Schwartz. The enlarged women's department was placed in the new east wing of the store. Pa also built a large screened porch with movable storm shutters on the second floor at the back, above the new women's building. This screened-in porch became a dormitory for all us children.

The most important store in Eagle Pass for decades had been De Bona's. The store had a reputation for fine quality. Sometime after my parents moved to Eagle Pass, De Bona's created a sensation by raffling off an automobile to the store customers. Since cars were practically unknown in Eagle Pass at the time, this was a big event. I recall my mother speaking of it years later. During the World War I years, old man De Bona died, and his two sons ran the business. They seem to have spent more attention lavishly entertaining the army officers stationed at Eagle Pass, vying to see which would be the town's social leader, rather than attending to their business.

Riskind's storefront displaying bilingual signs during a parade, ca. 1917. (Courtesy of Dr. Peter Riskind.)

In any event, De Bona's went bankrupt in the sharp postwar recession of 1920. In the liquidation of De Bona's, Pa bought a massive hand-cranked National Cash Register machine, the last word in technology at that time. This register served Riskind's for many years, until it was replaced by departmental electric registers in the enlargement and renovation of the store in 1957. Pa used to call the massive old machine "the organ," and he constantly wanted to know "how the organ was playing." The register, which played an important role in the commercial history of Eagle Pass, was finally given to the Fort Duncan Museum as a relic of the town's old trading days.[43]

With the closing of De Bona's store, M. Riskind quickly took its place as the quality leader of Eagle Pass and inherited much of the old De Bona clientele. It was after the De Bona closing that the store began to carry Hart Schaffner & Marx clothing, Florsheim shoes, and other high-quality items for both men and women.[44] Just about this time, the American Smelting and Refining mines in the Nueva Rosita area in northern Mexico began to operate at full capacity with a large American technical and administrative staff. Riskind's acquired these customers, along with the wealthy ranchers, politicians, and businessmen of northern Mexico. In subsequent years, northern Mexico continued to provide a substantial percentage of the store's customers. Billboards advertising Riskind's, in Spanish, of course, were placed as far south as Saltillo, 250 miles from the Mexican border.

At first we carried Packard shoes for men, a brand long since out of existence. We were also one of the original accounts for Friendly Five boots, which sold for five dollars a pair, and shoes from the same factory later called Jarman. When Packard shoes went out of business, we bought Florsheim. For women, what we carried in the early days, I don't know. At some point we started buying Red Cross, Carmo, Jacqueline, and Connie shoes. The store

The hand-operated, mechanical National cash register that Michael Riskind called "the organ," now on display in the Fort Duncan Museum in Eagle Pass. (Fort Duncan Museum. Courtesy of Jeff Taylor Sr.)

Advertisement for the M. Riskind store featuring their signature brand, Florsheim Shoes. The ad was posted in Piedras Negras on the Mexican side of the border crossing to Eagle Pass. (Collection of Bryan Edward Stone.)

also carried a large children's shoe stock. Pa originally bought either Buster Brown or Red Goose for children, but he changed to Poll Parrot when the greedy salesman opened another account in Eagle Pass.

Men's suits were hung in a recessed section against the wall, on racks that pulled out to better display the suits. Pa started buying Hart Schaffner & Marx probably in the early 1920s. He also carried cheaper suits such as Palm Beach. Silk and natural linen suits were important items. Once, I found an old advertisement dating from the early 1920s that advertised a sale on Hart Schaffner & Marx suits for $24.99 and silk suits for $19.99. On the women's side, there were a number of glassed-in areas against the walls where bridal gowns and better dresses were stored, as well as furs. There was a huge glass case facing the side entrance near the Aztec building. There were also numerous full-length mirrors for the customers' benefit.

The store as it appeared then would today be considered charmingly old-fashioned. The ceiling was quite high and was covered with painted tin squares stamped into a pattern. Every few feet there were large ceiling fans with dark brown wooden blades. There were no fluorescent lights at this time; instead, lights hung from the ceiling on long cords, giving a very dim, gloomy luminescence. The floor was wood, probably pine. Every morning before the store opened, red sweeping compound was thrown on the floor and it was swept, giving the floor a reddish cast. Merchandise was displayed on massive wooden counters, which my father hired local carpenters to build to his specifications, together with some smaller tables. In the center of the store was a long stationary display about five feet high and four-and-a-half feet wide. Merchandise was displayed on top of this apparatus. In the shelves, on the right-hand side, was the men's shoe stock. On the other side were the women's shoes. The customers' seats were on both sides, parallel to the display.

We had no air conditioning of any kind at the store other than the ceiling fans until late into the 1920s, when water-cooled blowers were introduced. Downtown Eagle Pass in midsummer, with all the heat absorbed by the brick buildings, was like the interior of a stove, and afternoon heat in the store had everyone suffering and gasping for air. Doors were kept closed as much as possible because of the pervasive dust.

In the center of the store area was a raised platform about two feet high with low railings. On one side was the huge hand-cranked register, "the organ," that Pa had bought from De Bona's. Usually, Albert sat there with his handwritten ledger containing the charge accounts. If he was out to lunch or otherwise engaged, Auntie sat there. From that spot one could survey the store, making sure all the customers were properly attended and keeping a sharp lookout for shoplifters. "*Mir muz ophiten*," my father would constantly admonish. "We have to watch out." In the back of the store was a narrow mezzanine measuring about thirty feet long, where Albert had his business office and his assistant worked. With Pa around, there was nothing very decorous or dignified about the store. He was always after the employees to keep working when not making sales. He admonished them to get to work in three or four languages, especially to clean stock. He would loudly denounce Albert or Auntie in Yiddish if anything in the store displeased him. Albert and Auntie would be embarrassed and try to calm him down. It's "*a shande far di goyim*," Albert would say, "a scandal in front of the gentiles."

It was Pa's theory that if an article did not sell in one place it would sell if moved to another location. I later found that even large department stores did the same. Sometimes just changing merchandise from one side of the aisle to another worked wonders. Once in New York I noticed that Macy's was selling a certain style handbag in quantity. At the same time a competing store across the street had the same bags in the window at a lower price but wasn't selling them because no one paid any attention to the location of the display.

In the fall, even before it turned cold, Pa always had a large display of mufflers and gloves, including fur-lined gloves. No other store bothered to have them. Pa's theory was that there was a need, even if it was only for the few days that it turned bitterly cold, and we had to provide them. This was especially true since we had a large trade area in the mountains of northern Mexico. If no other store had these cold-weather items, the customers had to come to him, and they would bring in new customers. Another item he carried was raincoats, even though in our frequent periods of drought rain might be a rare event. If it rained, Pa would hang a raincoat by the front door so that passersby could see it. When my brother Reuben came into the business, he objected to this practice as demeaning to a prestige store. As fast as Pa had a raincoat hung outside, Reuben would take it down until Pa gave up.

A sideline to the operation of the store was the sale of surplus wooden boxes. At that time merchandise was shipped in wooden boxes rather than in the thick paper cartons used today. The sturdy pine shipping boxes were of varying sizes, most of them about four or five feet square. The store received a constant stream of merchandise, and the disposal of so many large wooden boxes could have been a problem just as the disposal of waste is today. However, a solution immediately presented itself. The boxes were in great demand from the poor. Boxes sold for twenty-five cents and were used mostly for construction. Many houses in Eagle Pass were typical Indian jacales, but the better dwellings were constructed of native rock and adobe brick. The lumber from the packing boxes of the stores in town began to be used to build a different type of home for the poor, not very aesthetic in appearance, but nonetheless serviceable. Whenever I drive by the old neighborhoods, I wonder how many of the homes were built out of boxes sold by the Riskind store.

PA'S EMPLOYEES

In the store, Pa kept the clerks working continuously. If business was slow, he would put the men to work repainting the inside, outside, or upstairs. If nothing remained to be done and the stock was cleaned spotlessly, then he would put them to work rearranging the location of all the fixtures. A man might think he was hired as a salesman, but by the time he was with us long he became a jack-of-all-trades. Every night before closing, tarps were used to cover the exposed merchandise, otherwise a film of dust would cover the stock by morning. After badgering the men unmercifully, Pa would say, "Okay, boys, that's enough. Let's go have a beer." Then off they would go to the saloon where they would all end up plastered. It was more like a family than an employer-employee relationship.

Pa was never discreet in lecturing the clerks. He never seemed to care who might be listening. Sometimes he would lecture the men about getting rid of slow sellers and especially of odds and ends. He always maintained that the secret to making a profit was in selling off all the odd lots. It wasn't the original markup so much as getting rid of the odds and ends that counted. He called these items *chalerias* after the Yiddish cuss word for cholera.[45] Clerks would receive a bonus for selling them. Often a clerk would come up to Pa after waiting on a customer to report that he had sold a *chaleria*. Any of the clerks who were lax in obeying Pa's rapid-fire orders would get a merciless tongue-lashing in three or four languages. Sometimes when Pa was carrying on with the men, cussing them out loudly in Spanish, Yiddish, and Russian, Auntie or Uncle Albert would come to remonstrate with him, to no avail. *"A shande far di goyim."*

One would think the men would resent Pa or might even use violence after his abusive language, but they seemed to like him. Pa always paid his employees better than the other stores in town, usually giving a base pay and commission so that industrious workers were well rewarded. At a time when wages in Eagle Pass were miserably low, say seven to ten dollars per week, our salesmen were making at least double and sometimes triple the usual wage. The store was considered a most desirable place to work. In addition, Pa was far more understanding and considerate than the usual employer. If a man was caught stealing, and Albert demanded that he be fired out of hand, Pa instead would give the man a terrific tongue-lashing, then give him another chance. "He has a wife and children to support," Pa would say. "Besides, how do you know the next man is going to be any better?"

Anyone who ever worked for Pa would reminisce even years later about "the old man" and his eccentricities. Among Pa's various superstitions was the idea that if you didn't make the day's first sale in the morning, that day was doomed to be what in Texas vernacular would be called a "sorry" one. I heard this story from Ernesto Garza, a store clerk and later head of the shoe department, who was a participant in the events. One morning a Kickapoo came into the store just as it opened, and as luck would have it, he was the first customer of the day. This was in the 1930s, in the days when the Kickapoos came to town once a month to collect payments from the federal government. These payments were made in the bank at that time directly across the street from the Riskind store. The Kickapoo selected a pair of boots and a Stetson hat for a total of some $16.75. Then it developed that all the cash the Indian had amounted to $11.75. He was five dollars short. Since the Indian did not have the money, he turned around and walked out. Pa came up and asked Ernesto what had happened. Ernesto told him. "Run quick and get him back," Pa said.

Ernesto ran out and saw the Indian about half a block away. He chased him and returned with him a few minutes later, huffing and puffing. Pa asked the Indian his name and said, "Now, I am going to trust you. I'll give you the hat and boots if you give me your word you will pay the balance of five dollars next month when you get paid again." The Kickapoo promised. Pa made out a regular lease form, the Indian marked an X witnessed by Ernesto, and the Indian walked out, all dressed up in his new finery. Come the following month, all the Kickapoos were back in town to collect their government money, and Pa waited impatiently all day for the Indian. No Indian. Pa got very angry. "Ernesto," he asked, "where's the reservation?" Ernesto described how far away it was. "Tomorrow we're going," says Pa.

Despite Ernesto's remonstrances, off they went. First they took the train to Nueva Rosita, Mexico, about seventy-five miles. Then they took a ramshackle bus to Nacimiento, another thirty miles or so. In Nacimiento they hired a buggy to take them to the reservation, another three or four hours. Finally, they got there. The Indian was not hard to find. Pa started accusing him of not keeping his word. The debtor was very embarrassed. "I gave the money to my wife and she forgot to pay you. I apologize," he said, and he handed Pa the five dollars. Then they started the long trip back. By the time they returned to Nacimiento the last bus had already left. They had to continue on in the buggy to Nueva Rosita. Luckily they were able to catch a late train and were back in Piedras Negras by early morning.

"Well," said Pa, "we got the money."

"But Mr. Riskind," Ernesto said, "it cost you more than five dollars to get the money."

"It was the principle of the thing," replied Pa. "The man gave me his word."

One of our most valuable salespeople was Geraldine White, or Jerry. Jerry's husband, Alfred White, had been the most important sheep rancher in our part of the state.[46] One year, immediately after all the sheep and lambs had been sheared, there was a freak norther

Michael Riskind with staff at the M. Riskind department store, early 1930s. Pictured left to right: Dolores (Lola) Vela, Rose (Auntie) Riskind, Constancia Díaz, Federico Perez, unknown, Michael Riskind, Aurora Capitanachi, Valentín Daniel, and Albino Diaz. (Courtesy of Dr. Peter Riskind.)

late in the spring, something that happens once in a hundred years. All of his animals died from exposure. Overnight, Alfred White was transformed from a wealthy, respected rancher to a pauper. He got a job as district court clerk, and Jerry changed from one of Riskind's best customers to a sales clerk in the women's dress department. She was invaluable because she had the best contacts in the Episcopal Church and in Anglo society. She was a very pleasant person with one failing: there were days when she imbibed too freely of "cough medicine" during store hours. Jerry worked for us for many years until her death.

In addition to Jerry, some of the old-time clerks I can recall on the women's side of the store were Lola Vela, Cata Santos, and Constancia Díaz. Of the men, I can recall vaguely Grien Vann, Felipe Moncada, and Anacleto Torralba as well as Valentín Daniel, Federico Perez, and Ernesto Garza.[47] Our first display man was Abraham Seriff, then it was Mr. Karp, then Albino Diaz.[48] In our offices, I can recall the sister of Enriqueta Olivares, then Jesusita Cirilo, then René Barrientos. A complete list of those who at one time or another worked for M. Riskind would prove most interesting. Of our various collectors, I can remember by name only Charlie Johnson. Charlie would come in to announce an unsuccessful mission. After listening to Pa's dressing down and pep talk, Charlie would leave saying, "Mr. Riskind, I'll go out and read him the last chapter of the Bible." I also remember Demetrio Daniel, Valentin's father.[49] He worked for us sometime around 1918 to 1920, when we also carried some furniture in the store. There was a big shed on one side behind the store where some of the furniture was warehoused, and Maestro Daniel had a workshop where he repaired and touched up the furniture.

> **M. RISKIND**
>
> SALUDA A SUS FAVORECEDORES
> Y PUBLICO EN GENERAL
> DESEANDOLES
> PROSPERO Y FELIZ AÑO
>
> 1921   1922
>
> ERO 1º.
>
> S, TEXAS

New Year's advertisement for M. Riskind department store, January 1922, possibly the cover of a wall calendar. The message reads, "M. Riskind greets his preferred customers and the general public, wishing them a happy and prosperous New Year." (Courtesy of Dr. Peter Riskind.)

No description of the Riskind store would be complete without special mention of the role of Federico Perez.[50] Federico must have come to work for my father around the year 1915. He started out taking care of Pa's horse and worked as a yard man. By the time I remember him, he was already a clerk in the store. Federico was very Indian in appearance, and in later years he told me he came from Guerrero and must have been a descendant of the original mission Indians. According to Federico, any true native of Guerrero would drown in a bathtub, but come nightfall he could cross the Río Bravo (Rio Grande) with a bale of contraband under each arm.

Federico had a true gift as a salesman. I once saw him wait on a man who came in asking for a pair of shoelaces and walked out over an hour later loaded with all he could carry. Federico's customers varied from governors to workingmen (governors preferred), so long as he could sense the customer had money to spend. On only one occasion that I know of was he wrong. An Anglo came in attired in greasy overalls with several days' growth of beard. Federico, who was sitting near the door, let one of the junior clerks wait on him. The customer bought a huge stack of expensive clothing. He turned out to be an oilfield driller. Federico had to admit that one couldn't always judge a customer by their appearance.

One of Federico's best customers owned one of the biggest hotels in downtown Mexico City. Every few months he flew to Piedras Negras in his private plane and shopped. He would buy not only for himself but also for a regular harem of women. Whether it was suits, hotel linens, or lingerie, nothing was bought without Federico's opinion. Another of Federico's customers was a pleasant-enough Anglo rancher who owned over a million acres in Mexico near Del Rio. His interests, despite his age, seemed to be in girls. He was like a Turkish pasha buying for an army of wives. Federico was his consultant.

The fact that Federico was helping a number of elderly Casanovas in their purchasing once caused a scene out of a French farce in the store. One day, one of our best women customers marched in and demanded irately what was the meaning of certain charges, including dresses and lingerie, that had appeared on her monthly statement. It seems that through error, the items appeared on her account rather than being charged to her husband's personal account, which was not to be mailed. There was no way the errant husband's purchases could be hidden from the wife. She got even by buying and charging everything in sight.

My father, Aunt Rose (his sister), and Uncle Albert (his brother) always referred reverently to "the Store" as a living entity that had to be protected at all costs. Pa was referred to as "M. Riskind," a sort of institution. If Albert was at a chamber of commerce meeting, for example, and was asked for a commitment concerning the store, Albert would say, "I'll have to ask M. Riskind," as if my father was some sort of mythical personage. One of Pa's former employees often stopped me on the street to tell me, "All I know about business I learned from Mike."[51]

CHAPTER 3

A BORDER COMMUNITY

M. Riskind was located on Main Street in the heart of the commercial district of Eagle Pass, less than three blocks from the Rio Grande. The Aztec Theater, owned by the Schwartz family, was at the corner. Going east to west, next to the theater and incorporated into that edifice was the Schwartz Building, later bought by Pa. Downstairs was the Central Power and Light office, and upstairs were several apartments; later, when the Schwartz home burned, Mr. and Mrs. Schwartz lived in the front apartment. Then came the Riskind store, then Taylor's Saloon (later the San Miguel Saloon), which was also later bought by Pa and added to the store. Next was another business I can't recall, then Schuessler's Men's Store. Upstairs above Schuessler's was the telephone company. The building between was only one story, and from the store we had a clear view of the girls working the phone switchboards.

The International Grocery, operated by Mr. Gilliland, occupied the corner. This was one of the more popular stores of town, especially after the closing of De Bona's. I remember the soldiers from Fort Duncan coming there daily to buy fresh vegetables. They must have been his best customers. In front of the grocery, on the corner, an old Mexican man would come every morning to set up his portable glass case on a folding stand. There on the sidewalk, he sold a variety of homemade Mexican candies including several kinds of *leche quemada*.[1] Whenever I had a few pennies I would splurge on candied cactus and sweet potato, my favorites. Behind the International Grocery was a huge iron cauldron elevated a few feet above the ground. Every few days a fire was started using mesquite logs, and *chicharrones*, pork cracklings, were cooked in the cauldron. The smell was tremendous; when the wind blew toward you it could be overpowering.

Upstairs from the grocery was the Mesquite Club, to which all the high society of Eagle Pass belonged. There were all sorts of social affairs joined by army officers during the war years. I'm sure that in one of the side rooms the usual high stakes poker game was going on, played by the wealthy and those with pretensions who were always on the jagged brink of bankruptcy. My friend Dudie Bonnet remembered that his parents went to New Year's Eve parties at the club, his mother in a long evening gown with long white gloves, his father in top hat and tails. My parents did not belong. I'm sure that other local Jews, including Sam Schwartz and the Kranzthors, were members, but my parents took no part in Anglo society, even when Pa was one of the wealthiest men in town. In the 1930s, the Mesquite

Club was disbanded, and the Fort Duncan Club was organized using the old officers' mess for a building. By that time, the army was gone and Fort Duncan had been ceded to the city.

There was a sort of dirt alleyway behind the grocery so that vehicles could enter into the adjoining stores with frontage on Main Street. Later there was an alleyway from Jefferson Street directly into the store lot; on the side facing Schuessler's were the store's warehouses and our garage. Behind the store lot facing Jefferson Street was Murray Hardware, run by Murray and a man named Louden. What I remember about the hardware store, which I visited often, was the large display of pistols, rifles, and shotguns. Every now and then a customer would go to the back door to try out a gun, firing into a wooden target about six feet by six feet in the yard adjoining ours.

Next to Murray Hardware was Weyrich, the blacksmith, who worked in a galvanized sheet metal shed. I used to stand outside to watch him, in a leather apron, shoeing horses, an art one doesn't see anymore. The horse would stand there patiently while Weyrich heated the shoe in the hot forge, pounded it loudly on an anvil, then fit it to the horse's hoof, which he held in one hand. I don't know when Weyrich finally closed his smithy, but it must have been in the early 1920s when the use of the horse, except by a few vaqueros, declined and became obsolete.[2] On my return to Eagle Pass in 1939, the old shed was occupied by the Velásquez Body Shop. When Velásquez quit the location, the sagging shed was removed to make way for the Riskind customer parking lot, all of which represents the normal evolution of our culture.

Next door to the smithy shed was the Weyrich home. This was an old one-story house built of rough-cut native stone in the traditional Texas style and whitewashed. The high V-shaped roof was supported by massive mesquite beams almost a foot square. Mrs. Weyrich was a big, fat woman who was the town piano teacher; my sisters Bess and Ruthie were among her pupils. Many years later I asked Ward Wueste, our operations manager, to negotiate the purchase of the property for the store from Mrs. Schmerber, then the owner. We tore the structure down to make way for a parking lot we very much needed, although I was disturbed to destroy the old house since it went back to the original settlement of Eagle Pass or only a few years after.

THE REVOLUTION OF 1910

The Mexican Revolution beginning in 1910 was one of the great social cataclysms of the twentieth century, and it brought profound changes to Mexico. Our part of the border was in the middle of events that greatly influenced the fortunes of the Riskind family and the entire area. Unlike the separation from Spain a hundred years before, which placed power in the hands of wealthy Mexican landowners and the Catholic Church but did nothing for the great mass of the population, this revolution brought great social changes to Mexican life that continue to this day.[3]

During the revolutionary period, business was booming. There had been a time when Mexican merchants had imported clothing and other merchandise directly from Europe; in fact, there is evidence that in the nineteenth and early twentieth centuries, Eagle Pass residents did much of their shopping in Piedras Negras. With the revolution this came to an end, and the Mexican population started shopping on the American side. If I remember correctly, in the time of Mexican president Porfirio Díaz, the peso was worth a dollar.[4] There was no such currency as paper money: Mexicans paid in gold or silver, and Americans paid in silver dollars. Some of the revolutionary leaders, bereft of cash, did issue paper money, which was accepted only when they were present in the area; otherwise it had no value. I remember my parents laughing because Pancho Villa's currency was used to paper bathrooms.[5]

I can remember the excitement in the store when one of the great landowners came to shop with his family, with his *pistoleros* in attendance. There would be even more excitement when the governor and his staff or an important general came. I remember a visit by General Manuel Pérez Treviño and his staff. I recall the general wearing a gold-handled sword, and his aides also carried swords.[6] When a great man came, Pa and Albert would drop whatever they were doing and run to meet him. Then they and the senior clerk would follow the customer, taking care of his every whim. Such a customer might spend thousands of dollars on a visit, especially if his wife were along to be cared for by Aunt Rose.

When I was a boy, my father was offered an opportunity to profit substantially in the upheaval of the revolutionary years. I can remember a discussion between Pa and Uncle Albert over an offer made to Pa that would require him to put up twenty-five thousand dollars in cash to finance Osie Harper as purchasing agent for the Mexican government.[7] Pa would then receive half of the profits. It was a tempting offer, but Pa announced that he wanted nothing to do with this "*kunkel-munkel* business," or monkey business.

Those who survive from those chaotic days or recall what they heard from their parents have their own stories to tell. My friend Octavio Riddle told me that his father, Eduardo Riddle, a Mexican citizen, was imprisoned by revolutionaries and was told that he would be executed the next morning.[8] Riddle worked for the Mexican railroad as a stationmaster, and stationmasters were hated by the revolutionaries, perhaps because they were a symbol of the Mexican government. Some members of the family were able to talk to Riddle's guard and promised him a reward if he let his prisoner escape. The end of the matter was that both Riddle and his guard swam the Rio Grande to safety in Eagle Pass later that night.

Ben Chuck, from a Chinese immigrant family living in Piedras Negras, was a small child during the revolution.[9] Word got out that Chinese people were being massacred by mobs. His father assembled the family in their Piedras Negras home and sent word to his friend, Judge John Bonnet of Eagle Pass, that he needed help.[10] At this time it was illegal to bring Chinese people into the United States under the anti-Asian immigration laws. Judge Bonnet went to the Chuck home late at night with a big farm wagon. The entire family was hustled into the wagon and covered with a tarp. The terrified children were warned not to make the slightest sound.

In the darkness Judge Bonnet drove to the bridge, stopping only to carry on a friendly conversation at customs, then continued to his imposing home on Ceylon Street. At the back of the house, the passengers were unloaded and hurried to the third floor, where they were sheltered until the emergency was over. If I remember the words of Edith Bonnet, the judge's granddaughter, correctly, a total of thirty Chinese people were given asylum.[11] It later turned out that the rumors were true: Chinese people had been massacred but not in our immediate area.[12] Edith remembered that her father had to resort to all sorts of subterfuges when buying groceries because the grocer began to remark about the size of his purchases.

My personal recollections of that period go back to when I was nearly five years old, in 1915. The Mexican government secured permission to move troops through Eagle Pass in order to transport them on the Southern Pacific to Douglas, Arizona, to enter Mexico at Agua Prieta and thus to take Pancho Villa's forces from the rear.[13] I vividly recall going with my father in his buggy to the depot to see the trains go by loaded with Mexican soldiers. These soldiers were Yaqui Indians, part of General Álvaro Obregón's original army.[14] The cars went by loaded with men, women, and children, some on the roof. Many were in open flat cars where the women were cooking. They sang "La Adelita" as they went by, the most popular song of the revolution.¹⁵ My friend Ward Wueste, who lived in a house by the railroad tracks, recalled that the cars loaded with people went by all day and all night, and that the soldiers wore all sorts of clothing rather than a standard uniform.¹⁶

I have another memory of 1916 or early 1917, which relates to a closet I opened in one of the bedrooms above the new store where we then lived. On opening the closet, I found it packed with rifles, shotguns, and pistols of all descriptions. When Pa caught me playing with them, he was in a fury and threatened me with dire punishment if I ever opened the closet again. Since my father was afraid of guns of any sort, I could not understand what it was all about until years later when I read the history books of that period.

It seems that a group of Mexican ranchers in the lower Rio Grande Valley, provoked by their bad treatment at the hands of Anglos and the barbarity of the Texas Rangers toward Mexicans, were foolish enough to issue what they called the Plan de San Diego, from the town of San Diego, Texas, in the lower valley. This was a call to Mexican Americans and southern Blacks to rise in revolt and break away from the United States. The immediate result of this ill-advised action was the further suppression of the Mexican American population in the Rio Grande Valley. Among other punishments, the local authorities in the southern counties confiscated all arms from Mexican residents, even those who were citizens of good repute.¹⁷

When the news reached Eagle Pass, the Mexican residents feared that they, too, would be required to turn in all arms. Many of them came to my father and asked him to store their arms until the trouble blew over. Since Pa was terrified of guns, it must have taken some persuading. The result was that Pa had more assorted rifles, shotguns, and pistols than the hardware store, all kept in the closet I had opened.

The streets of Eagle Pass at that time were very colorful. American soldiers were everywhere, their uniforms quite unlike a soldier's today. Flared trousers narrowed below the knee and were wrapped in puttees, strips of cloth wrapped around the leg. Hats were peaked campaign hats that are no longer used by the army. Men were drilling not only in Fort Duncan but on the side streets. I used to go watch the sweating men drill in the extreme heat, the sergeant yelling commands, the men looking like they were undergoing an ordeal. Every so often, a man would keel over from heat prostration. The streets were crowded with all sorts of frontier types: Mexican refugees, vaqueros, American cowboys, Indians, and Mexican soldiers, mostly cavalrymen in gray uniforms wearing heavy leather leggings.

Sometimes cattle drives added to the excitement and the drama of life in Eagle Pass during the Mexican Revolution. Whenever word came of an approaching army, the larger ranchers in Mexico would round up as many of their cattle as possible and drive them to the safety of the border. They had learned early that cattle could be easy prey for both sides. One of the easily negotiable sources of cash needed to buy arms was cattle, which were confiscated with the slightest excuse. Usually, cattle brought to the border for safety were driven straight over the International Bridge, but sometimes if the owner was desperate enough, they were driven straight across the river. From the bridge cattle were usually driven down Garrison Street to the Southern Pacific corrals. I can recollect seeing them.

One of the side effects of the revolution was the appearance of many priests and nuns fleeing from the wrath of the revolutionaries. Since Spanish colonial days, the Catholic Church had had a dual character: the upper clergy had all been of the governing class, while parish priests were often on the side of the poor and oppressed. The church had been in effect an arm of the government and was bitterly hated by the leaders of the uprising. As a result of violence against clergy in Mexico, a sizable group of clerical refugees settled in Eagle Pass.¹⁸

I remember a convent on Hillcrest—it was on the left-hand side if you were coming from town—and a large wooden structure on Ceylon Street. After the revolution, when the refugees were permitted to return under restrictions, both of these edifices were abandoned and torn down. The Our Lady of Refuge church on Ceylon Street is now where a long, rambling convent once stood.[19]

This was also the time of the great influenza epidemic.[20] No one knew what to do about it. A great percentage of those who became ill almost invariably died. I used to go out on the store balcony to watch the military funerals. Every morning at about 10 a.m., there would be a procession of horse-drawn caissons loaded with coffins starting at the Fort Duncan hospital and proceeding to the cemetery. My recollection is hazy whether there was a band or a bugle corps preceding the caissons. I must have witnessed hundreds of coffins pass by.

PA AND PANCHO VILLA

The most excitement during those years was when we heard news of the approach of Pancho Villa sometime in late 1916 or 1917. His forces occupied Sabinas, in northern Mexico, about eighty miles from Eagle Pass. At first Villa had been very pro-American. When he captured Ciudad Juárez early in the fighting, he secured a base from which he could purchase supplies in unlimited quantities out of El Paso, just across the Rio Grande. Villa was also widely given favorable publicity in the United States. All he needed was diplomatic recognition by the United States, which he assumed he was soon getting. To his surprise in 1917, the Woodrow Wilson administration recognized his rival, Venustiano Carranza, as the legitimate president of Mexico, even though Carranza had been anti-American in his policies. The result for Villa was disastrous. After a number of military reverses, his army melted away, and he was reduced from a contender for the presidency to the status of a bandit. In his resentment against the United States, Villa was guilty of random murders of Americans who fell into his hands.[21]

My friend Arnold Schwartz told me the following story, which he heard from his uncle Adolph, who owned the Popular Dry Goods Store in El Paso.[22] Villa bought considerable quantities of clothing and other items from him. When Villa approached him with a request for ten thousand rifles and ammunition, Schwartz declined on the basis that selling him rifles and ammunition would be against American law. As a friendly gesture Schwartz suggested that Villa approach a certain merchant in Columbus, New Mexico. The merchant in Columbus accepted the order, receiving a substantial deposit against the future delivery of the rifles. When the agreed date for delivery arrived, not only were there no rifles, there was no refund of the considerable deposit made by Villa. In fury, Villa ordered a raid on Columbus.[23] There is a similar story that appeared a few years ago in a novel called *Tom Mix and Pancho Villa*, which accuses a Jewish merchant of Columbus of conning Villa out of money under circumstances similar to Arnold's story.[24]

Some years ago, I saw an old San Antonio newspaper account relating that the Torreón–San Antonio train had been stopped by Villa's advance cavalry at Allende, forty miles from the border. The terrified passengers were finally released and arrived in Eagle Pass to spread panic. Refugees began to arrive by the thousands, pouring over the International Bridge in an unending stream. Rumors flew through the town, increasing the panic. I remember my mother saying, according to the latest rumor, that the poor Mexicans in the big hats were really Villista spies and they were supposedly going around town marking houses to indicate those Americans who were wealthy so that Villa could hold them for ransom.

All the men of Eagle Pass, Mexican or Anglo, brought out their .30-30 hunting rifles and pistols. Hollis Fitch, a teenager whose grandfather owned the bridge, was collecting tolls and putting the money into a cigar box.²⁵ Hollis said that the entrance to the bridge was sandbagged with a few soldiers and a machine gun guarding it. Of course, anyone with knowledge of the situation would know that a cavalry force could cross the Rio Grande easily, either above or below the bridge. All they had to do was ford at a low point in the river.

In the midst of this hysteria, Uncle Phil Schwartz pulled the greatest coup of his career as a practical joker. Phil was married to my father's youngest sister, Molly. He was considered something of a black sheep because of his escapades and had been brought to Eagle Pass by Pa and given a job with the hope that in the new environment he would keep out of trouble.²⁶ Mother liked Phil; she detested Molly. Phil was a marvelous story teller, and Mother said he was like a Shakespearean actor. When Phil, Molly, and my cousin Joe moved away, Mother almost wept, saying that the only interesting man in town was leaving. Phil could fabricate the most outrageous stories with a straight face. The trouble was that we never knew when he was telling the truth.

The feared approach of Pancho Villa gave Uncle Phil the setting for his greatest triumph, the climax of his career. He filled an *olla*, a large clay stew pot, with gravel and had a confederate climb up and smash it on the tin roof of the building. The *olla* exploded with a bang; the gravel came rattling down the tin with a terrific clatter. Phil himself then came dashing into the apartment yelling, "Pancho Villa is bombarding the town!" It happened that Pa was hosting a poker game at the time with Sam Schwartz and other cronies. In an instant there was a terrific struggle for places under the dining room table. Pa never forgave Phil for this stunt.

Many years after the chaos of the revolution, I walked by Pa's favorite saloon, the Merchant's Cafe, and one of Pa's cronies came out. I slowed down to walk with the old man. Naturally the conversation turned to my father. "Your father is quite a man," he said, "*muy hombre*. He's got *cojones*! The way he handled Pancho Villa, now that was really something! It took nerve."

I couldn't wait until the store closed. As soon as I got home, I made my customary visit to my parents' home across the street from mine. "What's this story about you and Pancho Villa?" I asked. "He wasn't within miles of the border." After a pause, Pa said, "Let's have a *schnaps* and I'll tell you what really happened." Pa always had a drink before eating dinner, *tsu chapen der harts* ("to grab the heart"), and he would usually wait for me to return from the store to relate the day's events over a drink. He poured out a whiskey for each of us. He took a swallow. "*L'chaim*."²⁷

"It wasn't Pancho Villa," he began. "It was the general commanding the garrison in Piedras Negras. I sold him a lot of blankets. The total came to some thousands of dollars. I made him a good price, but I still came out okay—if he paid." He took another drink. "Trouble was, he never paid. I sent Charlie Johnson over to collect, and he came back shaking with fright and refused to go back. The general said he would kill him if Charlie bothered him again. It was a lot of money in those days. There was nothing else I could do. I had to go across and do the collecting myself."

Pa crossed the bridge and went straight to the general's home. After he knocked on the door persistently, a servant came out to say the general was not at home. Pa insisted that he had to see him. The servant went back into the house. Pa kept knocking on the door. The general's wife then came out. "The general isn't here."

"Where is he?" Pa insisted.

She named a saloon and sent the servant to lead the way there. The cantina was located next to the garrison. They entered, and the servant proceeded to relate Pa's insistence. This made the general very angry. "Miguel, you insulted my wife. I'm going to have to kill you," he said. With that he took out his .45 pistol. Pa was scared, as scared as one can be, but he managed to keep his cool. "*Mi generál*, don't do what you'll be sorry for later. Let's have a beer and talk it over." The general shrugged his shoulders and agreed. So, Pa and the general sat down and had a beer. Pa took his time to give the general a chance to cool down. When they finished, the general ordered a beer to reciprocate. Then Pa hastened to order another round. About ten beers later the general said, "You know, Miguelito, I really owe you the money. You're not a bad fellow and I'm going to pay you."

The general called over an officer and directed him to pay the money. The aide came back with a sack of gold coins and started counting them out. Pa calmly collected the payment, put it back into the sack, wrote out a receipt, then excused himself to make a run for the bridge as fast as the buggy could go. "And so," concluded Pa, "it wasn't Pancho Villa. But if they want to believe it was Pancho Villa, why not? It sounds better."

PIEDRAS NEGRAS POLITICS

Our neighboring city of Piedras Negras was fortunate in that there was no fighting in the city itself or the immediate area, although it was a time of anarchy and disorder. In 1911 some followers of Ricardo Flores Magón, an extreme leftist, occupied the mountains of northern Coahuila and for a time carried on guerrilla warfare, which caused some refugees to flee to the border. But it was not until the murder of deposed president Francisco Madero that large-scale violence became widespread.[28] On one day in 1913, more than eight thousand refugees crossed the International Bridge seeking safety in Eagle Pass, creating a problem for such a small town. Some of these refugees settled permanently in Eagle Pass, some with money continued on to San Antonio, while others settled in Piedras Negras as soon as they considered it safe to do so. Some families had members living on both sides of the river.[29]

Whenever refugees poured into Eagle Pass, most arrived destitute. Even the wealthy often arrived at the border with little money and tried to raise cash by selling jewelry. Pa refused to buy from these unfortunates, in part because he did not know how to value it, but he also had no stomach for taking advantage of these desperate people. Mother was never interested in jewelry, but the refugees brought with them all sorts of old coins, and these Mother was interested in collecting. At one time she had some old Spanish pesos in perfect condition, as well as Maximilian pesos.[30]

The 1810 Mexican revolt against Spain, led by Padre Hidalgo, was a political revolution primarily for the benefit of the *criollos*, the "pure," American-born descendants of Spanish colonists.[31] It had little economic or social effect as far as the general population was concerned. This was especially true in the time of Porfirio Díaz, who was president of Mexico intermittently from 1876 until he was deposed in 1911. Mining, industry, and business in general was in the hands of foreigners.[32] In many cases this still meant Spaniards. They used their monopolies to exploit the people, and as a result the *gachupines*, or uppity Spaniards, were hated.[33]

Piedras Negras was typical of the Mexican system. Different categories of businesses were controlled by monopolies owned locally, usually by Spaniards. Suppose someone decided to open a grocery. He would quickly discover that the wholesale grocery business was a monopoly in the hands of Spaniards, and if he wanted to open a grocery he had to deal with the Spanish middlemen. According to my friend Héctor Barrera, the Spaniards had a system all their own. As a man with a successful business grew older, he would send to Spain for a relative, or if he had none, for a young man of good family and reputation from his home town. The apprentice would sleep in the store premises, sometimes on a counter, and would receive a bare minimum wage. When the patron had made his pile and was ready to retire to Spain, he would turn over the business to the apprentice on a long-term purchase contract.

By the time the Revolution of 1910 was underway, the Spaniards in control of the various monopolies began to get nervous. To protect themselves, they associated with members of prominent Mexican families who were also of Spanish descent. In many cases, the next step was that the Mexican partners, once they learned the intricacies of the businesses, forced out the Spaniards. Then the revolution brought a new group into power and prominence: generals displaced the civil authorities. Not only did they possess the actual political power, they also became great landowners.

Of the various revolutionary generals, Manuel Pérez Treviño was the only one who was a man of education and culture. He was an engineer by training, and during the revolution was invaluable in organizing and mobilizing guns and munitions, thus enabling Obregón, the ultimate victor, to triumph. Pérez Treviño was the idol of Piedras Negras. His hacienda, La Calendár, was nearby, and he was considered a native son. However, the general had an Achilles heel. The other top generals (except Pancho Villa) all came from the south of Mexico and hated all *norteños*. Furthermore, these generals were rough, uncouth men who secretly resented the polished Pérez Treviño. Pérez Treviño had been minister of war under President Plutarco Calles. He was considered second only to Calles in importance and was expected to be his successor. Under the Mexican constitution the president served for a six-year term, during which he was a de facto dictator. However, one of the most important slogans of the revolution, incorporated into the constitution, was "No Reelection." The current president, Calles, was power hungry and had no desire to relinquish his office, so after his six-year term expired, he continued to rule through puppet presidents he chose himself.[34]

It was the custom in Mexico for the official candidate of the ruling party to be named about a year in advance of the election and then, even though his election was a foregone conclusion, the candidate would campaign vigorously throughout the country as though his success depended on it. Calles gave Pérez Treviño the nod, and the general set out to campaign on a special train. Before he left Piedras Negras, he invited Pa and Albert to dine with him on his train. Pa reported that the dining car was set in fine white linen, the service was all in silver, the glassware all the best crystal. The food was prepared by a French chef, the wines were the finest French wines.

At first, the general met with tremendous success. He was very popular and was everywhere received with true enthusiasm. Then disaster struck. Calles was probably disturbed by the candidate's popularity and feared that Pérez Treviño would not be an obedient puppet. In the midst of the campaign, Calles changed his mind and announced that the new president would be Lázaro Cárdenas instead, an obscure governor. Pérez Treviño withdrew in humiliation and died sometime later. Piedras Negras was greatly disappointed by the fiasco of its favorite son. Its politicians had already been savoring the spoils that would be theirs, and they were not sophisticated enough to disguise their anger and disappointment. This, of course, did them no good with the new administration. Piedras Negras always managed to be on the wrong side of national politics, with the result that it lost out more and more to Nuevo Laredo, another border town to the south.

The revolution, with its leftist and agrarian slogans, resulted in new social programs and a swarm of bureaucrats and politicians, some with high ideals but the majority poor men suddenly raised above their fellows. They proceeded to follow the old slogan: "Enrich yourselves." During my first year of college, I happened to read in the *Nation* a glowing account of a new irrigation project in the state of Coahuila near Piedras Negras. The head of the project was highly lauded for his great accomplishments in assisting the poor *ejidatarios*—communal landowners—to improve their lot. I wrote down his name and intended to ask Pa about him and the irrigation project. When I saw Pa a short time later, I inquired if he knew the man.

"Certainly," said Pa, "he's one of my best customers. He buys only my most expensive suits, the best of everything."

"What sort of a man is he?"

"A thief," Pa answered, "a gonif. He's the worst kind of gonif. If a poor farmer wants the water he is entitled to, this thief doesn't let him have any unless they pay him off first. That's how he gets all his money. The farmers starve and he's rich."

It was apparent that the reporter for the *Nation* had been duped, completely taken in and bamboozled. He had believed and reported not the truth but what he had wanted to believe. Thereafter, I began to be more skeptical regarding the truth of the printed word: It ain't necessarily so. That is especially true when Mexico or Latin America is the topic of the story. Be more than a little skeptical about revolutions or miraculous reforms.

THE JEWISH MERCHANTS OF EAGLE PASS

Jewish merchants played an important role in the economic history of early Eagle Pass. Even after the first group had moved on to other towns, new families came to establish prosperous businesses and contribute to the community. When my parents came in 1910, there were two Jewish merchants that I know of already there, one being Uncle Abe Edelstein. The others, the Kranzthors, had been in business first in Indian Territory, then in Shafter, Texas, in the Big Bend region, then they came to Eagle Pass around 1905.[35] Over the years, Eagle Pass Jews established shoe stores, furniture stores, fabric stores, clothing stores, and a host of other businesses that had a significant commercial impact all along the border.

I can recall only a few names from the early days. There were the Kranzthors, of course, but they held aloof from most activities since they came from Hungary and considered themselves "Deutsch," German Jews, a superior breed to the Eastern Europeans. I can remember the name "Red" Harris, another Jewish merchant who was in Eagle Pass around 1915 or a bit later. Other Jewish merchants were the Brenners, who were in business on the corner at Commercial and Main Streets in a space later occupied by Zales Jewelry; the Goldburgs, who had a store on the corner of Commercial and Rio Grande Streets they rented from my father; the Grossmans, who had a dry goods store on Main Street where Eagle Grocery is now; Sam Schwartz, who married Ellen Kranzthor; and the Hausman Brothers, Sam and Louis, and their families, who had a meat packing plant on Hillcrest.[36]

During the Mexican Revolution, the town's Jewish community got a temporary boost. There had previously been only a few companies of infantry at Fort Duncan, but after Pancho Villa's raid into New Mexico, Eagle Pass became a major garrison point. Not only was Fort Duncan filled to capacity, but there were tents all along the Del Rio highway from the present junior high and occupying what was later the Gates farm. According to Hollis Fitch, twenty-five thousand men were brought into Eagle Pass. Most of these were national guardsmen from the Northeast, including New York regiments.

Our home became a social center for Jewish boys, an unofficial USO for the Jewish servicemen. Some of them were given part-time employment in the store. There was one in particular I remember by the name of Epstein. Pa would give Epstein a series of staccato orders, some of these in opposite directions. I remember a sweating Epstein and another man carrying some heavy furniture up the steep stairs leading to the second floor while Pa was giving them instructions, and Epstein saying in Yiddish, "Mr. Riskind, *aher gai, ahin gai, in drerd gai* ("go here, go over there, go to hell")! Just what do you want us to do?"[37]

By the early 1920s many of the Jewish families who had been in Eagle Pass during the war left to go to bigger cities. The Brenners moved to San Antonio and founded the Solo Serve organization, a highly successful discount retail chain. The Goldburgs moved, I believe, to Corpus Christi. The Grossmans left after a 1920 hailstorm of terrifying proportions. Hail the size of tennis balls fell to a depth of around a foot on the ground with such violence that cattle were killed. Pa had people on the flat roof over the new part of the store shoveling off hail as fast as they could. The roof was new and it held, but the roof at Grossman's collapsed and Grossman closed the store and moved.

New Jewish families arrived in the early 1920s to take their place. There were the Lapins, Max and Falla, and Solomon Libson. Falla Lapin was the sister of Abraham Seriff, who had been my father's window trimmer until around 1925, when he was succeeded by Mr. Karp, who came with his family and stayed for a few years.[38] The Mikulinskys—Owsey (pronounced "Offsa") and Tanya and their son, Sam—at first lived in Piedras Negras until they were able to immigrate into the United States. In the late 1920s and 1930s, the Jewish community changed again: there were my Aunt Molly and Uncle Phil and my cousin Joe, the Morgensterns, and others whose names I can't recall.[39]

In speaking of border merchants, Solomon Libson and Max Lapin should be especially mentioned. Both came to the United States from Russia after the Revolution of 1905. Mr. Libson's family was murdered in one of the pogroms of that period. Libson and Lapin lived in Eagle Pass but went into the produce business in Piedras Negras importing fruits and vegetables under the name of the California Fruit Company.[40] Later, after World War II, they organized the gas company in Piedras Negras, obtaining the gas from the American side and distributing it to homes on the Mexican side. When the business was well established, a group of Mexican businessmen advised Libson and Lapin that Lapin, not being a Mexican citizen, could not own any part of the gas company under Mexican law. Libson was protected, as Eloisa Libson, his wife, was a Mexican citizen and title could be in her name. Max Lapin was forced out for what he considered a pittance. The embittered Lapin moved to Austin, which was a great blow to our community.[41]

Manny Schwartz, Sam Schwartz's younger brother, together with Sam's nephew Nandor Neuman, had a shoe store on Main Street next to Kress.[42] Later Nandor separated from Manny and opened a furniture store across the street, I think, in the corner building left vacant by Grossman or next to it. Ted and Gertrude Greenberg came to Eagle Pass in the early 1930s and established the Western Auto until around 1970 when he sold out.[43] After the war, around 1946, the Mikulinskys opened a fabric shop, La Barata, on Commercial Street. Tanya Mikulinsky ran the business while Owsey Mikulinsky was engaged in farming. Mr. Mikulinsky died around 1968, after which Tanya closed the store and moved to Pittsburgh to join her son, Sam Michaels.

Faye and Bennie Levine came to Eagle Pass after World War II. Bennie engaged in farming and cattle raising while Faye ran a fabric shop, first across from Riskind's, then at the present location of Pan American Fabric across from Kress. The Bargs came to Eagle Pass around 1970 and operated the Imperial Novelty Company on Commercial Street. Until he was too enfeebled by Parkinson's disease, Mr. Barg served as our cantor for High Holiday services. I believe he was in a concentration camp before coming to the United States. Bennie Spiegal, a bachelor, was also in business on Commercial Street for a number of years until his retirement about four years ago. David Pimentelli had a novelty store for a few years around 1975 on Rio Grande Street near Commercial. Finally, Mauricio Herzberg operated a novelty store on Main Street across from Riskind's. Herzberg, I believe, came from Argentina.[44] Despite their relatively small numbers, the impact of Jewish merchants along the border continues.

From the time they settled in Eagle Pass, my parents were the heart and soul of the Jewish community. There were few Jews in Eagle Pass, more than there are now, but still very few, constituting those hearty souls who found their way to the end of the world, which Eagle Pass was. Religious services were regularly held in our home above our store. The upstairs apartment had a combined living room–dining room, which served for many years as the semiofficial meeting place of the Jewish community. For High Holiday services during the Mexican Revolution, there were too many boys to hold services in my parents' apartment upstairs of the store, so the Jewish Welfare Board rented the Knights of Columbus Hall located upstairs of the old Marquez Wholesale Grocery on Adams Street across from the present Knights of Columbus Building. This old building still stands, the upstairs not in use for many years.[45]

My parents did not keep a kosher household, other than avoiding pork. There was a humorous incident once in which my mother, checking over the bills charged at the International Grocery, found a constant stream of charges for bacon. Upon inquiry the grocer showed tickets signed by one of the maids in our employ. Mother found the bacon neatly stacked under the girl's bed, waiting for her day off to take it home. The girl, of course, didn't know that Jews weren't supposed to eat bacon.

There was no Jewish school in Eagle Pass during that period. When my mother approached Solomon Libson about providing Jewish education for his children and the others, he told her that Jewish education in Eagle Pass was like the fifth wheel on a wagon. Sometime toward the end of World War I, when I was seven or eight years old, my father got a Jewish man—I can't remember his name—to be my teacher. All he did was teach me to read Hebrew haltingly, in what I later learned was a Galitzianer accent.[46] This lasted only a few months until the "teacher" left town.

Mother was undoubtedly the best-qualified person in town in her knowledge of the Jewish religion and certainly in her knowledge of the Hebrew Bible. Her command of the Tanakh was truly amazing. In the general field of Judaism, she had been raised by her father not only to know the practice but the "why" of the customs and rituals. Mother read Bible stories to us children. At an early age, we knew the stories of the Tower of Babel, Noah's Ark, Moses, David and Goliath, and many others. It was due to my mother's influence that I acquired a desire to learn Hebrew in order to read the Bible in the original. It never occurred to my mother, perhaps because she didn't have the time to teach me Hebrew herself.

A YOUNG SINNER

Until Prohibition closed the saloons, they were all very crowded and rowdy. Taylor's Saloon, later known as the San Miguel Saloon, was next to the Riskind store. I would stand outside and look into the bar. Often fights broke out inside. In a few minutes, a horse-drawn paddy wagon would arrive, a bell jangling on the roof, and military police dashed into the saloon and quelled the fight, usually by hitting the soldier in the head with a billy club. Then the soldier would be carried out, one MP holding him by the arms, the other by the legs. The unconscious soldier was tossed into the paddy wagon like a sack of potatoes, and the horse-drawn vehicle went on down the street, bell jangling.

I was also fascinated by the men drinking at the bar. The bartender poured out a shot glass of whiskey, which the customer gulped down in one swallow. Trying to emulate this process led to my downfall: I became a sinner at the age of six by succumbing to demon rum. My father's display man, called in those days a window trimmer, was a Jewish man named Abraham Seriff. Mr. Seriff never touched strong drink. He did, however, take a "tonic" for his health; I think the tonic was called Peruna.[47] Mr. Seriff kept his bottle of tonic and a shot glass in a cupboard of Mother's kitchen, and whenever he felt the need for a bracer he would go upstairs and take a shot. I had my eye on Mr. Seriff's tonic. One day when Mother was out and I was alone in the upstairs apartment, I decided to play saloon. I poured myself a shot and tried to drink it in one gulp as I had seen the men do in the San Miguel. This went on for some time until Mother came home and found me asleep on the floor in a sea of vomit. Alarmed by this spectacle, Mother immediately sent for Dr. Easton. After examining me, the good doctor turned to Mother and said, "Mrs. Riskind, I hate to tell you this, but your boy is dead drunk."

CHAPTER 4

MY CHILDHOOD IN EAGLE PASS

When I was a child, we lived in the upstairs apartment above the Riskind store. Behind our lot, on one side, was Ma's garden, where she worked herself. There was a small lawn, a peach tree, roses, and various plants in beds. That was her hobby and pleasure. There were some big hackberry trees, which I used to climb. In the yard we also had a large galvanized washtub where the maid boiled clothes using mesquite wood and a clothesline where the clothes were hung out to dry. Even after Pa had given up the use of his horse-drawn buggy for business, his old horse was kept there and cared for until it died. I also briefly owned a burro that the manager of the Indio Ranch gave me when I was six or seven years old. When I got into the saddle the burro wouldn't budge. Finally, I kicked him and was unceremoniously pitched off. The burro was returned.

I had a small menagerie in the yard. We kept chickens, among which I had some bantams, including a rooster. Other boys would bring over their roosters to match against mine, which proved to be the champion. In these rooster fights, the loser usually quit or we stopped the fight before either bird was seriously hurt. When I later saw a professional rooster fight in Mexico, in which the roosters had knives attached to their spurs, I found the spectacle disgusting. Someone gave me a tiny kitten—I believe it was a Maltese or maybe a Manx, which grew into a huge gray-blue tomcat with a very ferocious temperament. I called him Colonel Cootie. This cat never came into the house, preferring to live outside. He came only when I called him to feed him. Whenever another tomcat dared to come into the yard, the colonel sent him away all bloody and howling in terror. Once the Pilgrim boys came over with two fox terriers that belonged to a visiting uncle. The two dogs unsuspectingly chased Colonel Cootie into the furniture warehouse. Once inside, the cat jumped down on the two dogs and almost killed both of them.

My good friend Willie Chichester raised Belgian Hares in the back of his house, and I decided to get one too. The rabbit was kept in a cage in Mother's garden. Every day, I had to gather thistles to feed the rabbit. One day, I went to feed the rabbit and it was gone. I prefer to believe that he dug his way out. Another day, I brought a tortoise home and kept it in the garden. Although allowed to go freely, it did not stray away. I guess the living was easy and it preferred to remain there.

The Chichesters lived across the street from the Weyriches in a stone house that still stands. Willie had, unfortunately, lost the vision of one eye from a splinter he received while he was chopping mesquite kindling. Mr. Chichester, Willie's father, had participated in the Klondike gold rush and used some mementos to decorate the living room. I remember in particular some inlaid walrus tusks—scrimshaw, I believe it is called.[1]

Also living with the family was an aged relative, possibly Willie's grandfather. He had been a Confederate cavalry captain and had lost a leg.[2] Every now and then when I played with Willie in the house, the captain would hobble up on his crutches, put a finger to his lips, and motion us to follow. Once in his room, he would look into the hall to make sure the coast was clear, shut the door, put his finger to his lips again, take out a key he kept on a long chain, and open a big trunk he had in the room. This he would open only for an instant, so that we had only a peek, then he shut it tightly and relocked it. The chest was filled with Confederate paper money. I wonder what happened to it. Today I am sure Confederate money is worth much more to collectors than it was worth in the last days of the Confederacy.

ON THE *REJAS*

My father took me to the first movie I can recall. I must have been five or six years old. I can recall walking about a block from the store to an open-air theater located for a short time behind the present NBC Bank. We sat on ordinary benches. I must have accompanied Pa because Mother was not in the least interested in picture shows, preferring to stay home and read. The movie had to do with the nefarious activities of the devil, who was dressed in a skintight sort of leotard outfit, complete with horns and a tail. Only his mustached face was visible from out of the red outfit.

I saw many movies at the Aztec Theater, which was next to the Riskind store. The theater itself had a colorful history. When it was built in 1914 by our Jewish neighbor, Sam Schwartz, some bodies were exposed when digging space for the foundation. My mother told me that the bodies must have been Spaniards because they had swords. Years later, I found the true answer in Walter Prescott Webb's book *The Texas Rangers*. Some of the citizens of Eagle Pass decided that they had had enough of King Fisher, the notorious bandit.[3] The next time word came that Fisher and his gang were on the way, a large party hid in the mesquite brush in the general area of the present Riskind and Aztec buildings and ambushed their harassers. Members of Fisher's gang were shot out of the saddle and buried on the spot. Mother's Spanish swords were in fact Bowie knives.

Before the days of air conditioning, the Aztec Theater relied for cooling in the hot summer on large ceiling fans and on wooden door windows, which were opened to permit a flow of air to the gasping audience inside. These windows were on Jefferson Street, which at night was quite dark. I soon discovered that by peeking through the windows, the screen was visible at an angle. Every night, my sisters and cousin Joe Schwartz would gather with me to see the movie. This lasted until we were discovered by the janitor, Florencio Meza. Florencio would charge out menacing us with a broom and we would scurry away. It became a contest between us and Florencio until we became discouraged. Years later Florencio asked me for a job; by this time, he was a white-haired old man. He worked for us for several years, neither of us ever mentioning the theater.[4]

My favorite picture show was the Star Theatre across the street from the Riskind store. Every Saturday afternoon, I religiously attended, attracted by the serial shown along with the feature film, usually a Western. My favorite was Pearl White. I was thrilled by her narrow escapes from a horrible fate and awaited the next episode with ill-restrained impatience.[5]

Sam Schwartz, proprietor of Eagle Pass's Aztec Theater, posing in 1927 with Leo, the MGM lion, in front of the Aztec to mark the opening of *The Jazz Singer*, the first talking picture exhibited in Texas. Behind Schwartz is Dr. E. F. Gates. (Fort Duncan Museum. Courtesy of Jeff Taylor Sr.)

Then, for no reason, the Star embarked on a new policy. Instead of showing each installment in sequence on Saturday, they began showing entire programs consisting of three or four chapters in succession, starting on Monday and continuing all week. The new policy of the Star placed me in a desperate state. My Aunt Rose, the de facto boss of the family, refused to allow me more than five cents a week to go to the movies, ruling that one movie per week was enough. For years I carried a deep grudge against Sam Schwartz for this dastardly action until it dawned on me that Sam did not buy the Star until some years later, when the name was changed to the Yolanda and only presented films in Spanish.

What was I to do? I had left Pearl White tied to the railroad track with a fast train approaching and no money to learn what saved her in this desperate situation. But, as my mother said, quoting the Hasid, "God will provide."[6] The Star was located at a slight angle across from the San Miguel Saloon. The windows of the saloon were protected by wrought-iron *rejas*, or grills. I found that by climbing the *rejas* in front of the Star, I had a perfect view of the screen through a small air window. From this vantage point, I saw not only Pearl White but also Fu Manchu operating a machine that produced armed, pig-tailed Chinese by the thousands, ready to conquer the world until at the last moment the villain was foiled by the hero, Nayland Smith. I also saw a series in which the minions of a Turkish pasha were kidnapping beautiful

American girls for his harem. In one episode, a bride was seized in the midst of her wedding ceremony. With the hero and police pursuing their car, the villains drove right off the pier and were picked up by a waiting submarine. In the final installment, the wicked, lecherous pasha is bombarded in his palace and the girls rescued by the marines. It was unclear how the girls survived the bombardment and complete destruction of the palace.

Hanging on to the *rejas*, I also saw two of D. W. Griffith's memorable films, *Birth of a Nation* and *Intolerance*. This last film made a great impression, not for its message, but for the scenes involving Babylon. In the final scene Elmo Lincoln, as captain of Belshazzar's bodyguard, puts up a tremendous epic struggle against the entire Persian army. That is what impressed me about the movie.[7]

While hanging on to the *rejas*, I could also see into the saloon. I had a ringside seat into the activities of the drinking soldiers, vaqueros, and citizens. No matter how exciting the movie, I had to be especially attentive whenever a brawl started, since a thrown bottle or other object could splatter glass in my face from the shattered window. My theater-going activities ended with Prohibition. The San Miguel Saloon closed, and my father soon after purchased the building. It was added to the store and became the men's department.

THE PILGRIM BOYS

From 1920 until I left for California in 1923, my closest friends were the Pilgrim brothers, Charlie and Fred.[8] To get to their house, I climbed the back fence of the store, went through an empty lot behind Schuessler's store and the International Grocery, and crossed Adams Street to the Pilgrim house. A good part of the time either I was at their house or the Pilgrim boys were visiting me.

Pilgrim Jewelry was in a brick building on the corner facing Main Street. It was operated by Mrs. Pilgrim, a tall, thin, blonde lady, the daughter of Charles Hielscher, who had been superintendent of schools many years before. In the back of the jewelry store, Mr. Pilgrim had fitted out himself an office with an optometrist's chair and instruments. On the wall was a diploma proclaiming him to be a doctor of optometry. Mr. Pilgrim called himself "doctor," although I never saw a patient there.[9]

Mr. Pilgrim had come to Eagle Pass from Canada, ostensibly for his health, although he had a weird program of treatment that seems to have had a connection with the passage of Prohibition. He was supposed to be outdoors a lot, and the interesting thing is that he was always in the great outdoors in Mexico. On occasion, when school permitted, he would take Charlie and Fred along, and often I was invited. Pilgrim had a Model T Ford. Charlie, Fred, and I would occupy the back seat along with all sorts of fishing equipment and sometimes guns, which would be placed under the seat. We had some miscellaneous frying pans and cooking equipment but never any food except for a jar of pickled pigs' knuckles.

Our first stop after leaving the Pilgrim house was to pick up Rafael Bonnet at his home, which was later the Eidson house, on Del Rio Boulevard. Our second stop was at a liquor store in Piedras Negras, where they would buy all the firewater that could be crammed onto the floor in the back. We boys had to place our feet above this cargo. All necessities having been loaded, we set off, usually taking the dirt road south towards Guerrero. After some miles we turned off the road and drove through the brush, maneuvering in the high-clearance Ford until we reached a clear stream, probably the Escondido.

I remember the spot where we set up camp because it was marked by an outcrop of ammonite fossils in the stream bed and a dark area where there was a petroleum seepage.

The two men and the Pilgrim boys would set to work fishing. In no time, they caught a mess of fish consisting of perch and channel catfish. Mr. Pilgrim had a true gift as a fisherman. I don't know the technical name for that type of fishing. He had a small simulated fish with several triple hooks, which he would cast about fifty feet out and reel in. If there were any fish around, he had a magic touch for attracting them.

The boys sometimes loaned me a line, but try as I might I never succeeded in catching anything despite trying to imitate their example. I only caught one fish in my entire lifetime and that by proxy. I was at Padre Island with my children, who were fishing off the breakwater. I asked John to bait a line for Lorin, then only four or five years old. While John was busy I held his line, and while standing there watching him I caught a fish that was either very stupid or very unfortunate.

As soon as we had enough fish, they were quickly cleaned, and Mr. Pilgrim proceeded to fry them over the waiting fire. Mr. Pilgrim would eat his pickled pigs' knuckles along with the fish. The rest of us had fish only. I have never cared for catfish, but I remember the small catfish as delicious.

A good part of my time with the Pilgrim boys we spent just roaming around the countryside. Our group usually consisted of Charlie and Fred Pilgrim, Floyd Fitch, Junior Harper, and W. C. Gates. Some of our haunts were just outside of town; the town ended at the railroad tracks. In the arroyo behind the railroad station there were sometimes pools deep enough to go swimming, although the best swimming was a few miles upstream, where Elm Creek entered the Rio Grande. In order to get there, it was easier to walk on top of the cliffs that lined the river than to follow the bank. In passing Hopedale, I recall that the Mello family, which had come from Portugal, was growing onions. That was the first time I ever saw onions growing. We also entertained ourselves in the arroyo by catching a variety of crawfish. This was done by tying a piece of bacon to a string, which was then tossed into the water and jerked out. The unfortunate crawfish was then pulled out, hanging on to the bacon. I never heard of anyone eating the crawfish—we just threw them back into the water. The fun was in the catching. Unfortunately, our swimming hole in the arroyo was ruined when trains changed to diesel fuel. When the tanks were drained, oil covered the water, making swimming impossible.

Another place we played was the cliff side of Hillcrest Street. We clambered around and over the large chunks of sandstone broken off the cliff. I have the recollection that Hillcrest was a very high, steep hill. Years later, I brought my children there to climb the rocks and was shocked to discover how low the hill actually was. Steep it was, however, some fifty to seventy-five feet rising abruptly, and I found it to be excellent in training the children for ascending higher mountains. The only house in the Hillcrest subdivision at that time was Dr. McFarland's house, now the core of General Lewis's home on Olive Street.[10] Today the house is in the middle of town.

We spent time in Fort Duncan, which had been vacated after the Great War. For several years, the fort had been a bustling environment, teeming with thousands of men. During the day there were men drilling everywhere, even on Garrison Street outside the grounds. By night it was a lively place. A band would be playing and there would be boxing matches, heralded by posters hung at the entrance to the fort, as well as movies and other entertainment. The officers, of course, had their dances and other amusements. But with the war over, and as the threat from Mexico subsided, Fort Duncan became a ghost city. As I remember, there were only a sergeant and eight men stationed on the post.

There were many two-story wooden structures in the fort. Some had been hospitals, others probably barracks. We played in these abandoned buildings, climbing up and down the stairs, which were becoming daily ricketier and more dangerous. There was also a large swimming pool that the city obtained for its use and was a bonanza for us. According to my recollection, sometime before that the Weyriches operated a smaller pool in the direction of Hillcrest, but the former military pool was much better. In the 1930s, the army gave the old fort to the city as a park. All of the old wooden buildings were dismantled, leaving only the original stone buildings of the old fort.

GAMES WE PLAYED

As children we had no radio or TV. We were left to our own resources for entertainment. In my memory, we managed to enjoy ourselves. Perhaps the game we most frequently played, and played the year round, was marbles. We used cheap marbles made of glass, which we bought at Kress for a few cents. For shooters, however, we used more expensive marbles, the best being agates, which were pricey and highly desirable. Another popular game was tops. After buying a top, we would remove the point and replace it with the largest screw we could use without splitting the top. The screw was then sharpened to a wicked point over an inch long. The purpose of this was to use your top to destroy or damage your opponent's top. In the spring and fall when there were steady breezes we made kites. These were plain: I used wrapping paper from the store that was about a yard and a half long by a yard wide placed over two crossed sticks and tied together in the middle with string. The indispensable tail was made of scraps of cloth Mother gave me.

Pa owned a lot on Main Street where the Three Sisters store was later located. The lot was 150 feet wide, large enough for us to practice baseball. It was an excellent place to throw the ball high into the air to practice fielding. The eldest of our group was Charlie Pilgrim. Charlie later became a civil engineer and showed an early talent by putting us to work on Pa's empty lot. It must have been war movies that gave him the idea. First, we dug a trench about five feet deep, then against one side we excavated a regular dugout, large enough for all of us to gather for a few minutes at a time. This was our secret meeting place, our clubhouse. One time Ruby, the Pilgrim boys' younger sister, tried to enter and was rudely ejected. Years later, I read of some other boys doing this. The dugout collapsed, suffocating all of them.

Every Saturday and often other days when school was out, we boys explored the country within a radius of three to five miles from town in all directions. We paid no attention to posted signs. It simply never occurred to us that they applied to us. As for carrying and using guns where there were cattle, that never occurred to us either. I must have been eight years old when I bought my first gun, a BB gun that fired a round pellet. This had to be pumped manually before each shot. I soon graduated to a single-shot .22 rifle, a short Stevens for which I paid five dollars. Now I wonder how I managed to get permission and the money from Mother. A modern city-bred Jewish mother would be horrified at the very idea of a gun. But that time Mother, having been raised in a semirural environment herself, was persuaded.

There were certain procedures in using a gun correctly, which I soon learned from the more experienced boys, along with other lore of the woods. First, it was important for anyone venturing out into the brush to take their bearings against visible landmarks as they went along; otherwise, you could wander off in the wrong direction and get lost many miles from a human habitation. You had to learn how to carry a gun so as not to be a threat to your neighbor, and you had to learn how to get through a barbed-wire fence without impaling

Morris Riskind dressed as a World War I soldier, ca. 1920. (Courtesy of Dr. Peter Riskind.)

yourself on the barbs and tearing your clothes to shreds. By putting your shoe on the third strand of wire and pushing down, a sufficient space was opened for a person to slide through with care.

You had to learn how to cross a fence with a gun in such a way that you did not shoot yourself or your companions. This is done by placing the unloaded gun on the ground with the barrel pointing away from everyone before crossing the fence. We learned to unload our guns when not in use and never ever to leave a bullet or shell in the chamber. No matter how hot the weather, we learned discipline in rationing the water in the canteen each of us carried. To conserve water, you can place a small round pebble in your mouth to keep it moist. In case of another type of emergency, we learned to use a clean, round rock in place of toilet paper. Finally, and most important, we learned how to watch for rattlers and avoid locations where one could be lurking. Every little movement in the grass took on meaning. You never step into any spot deeper than the ground around it, and you never step into thick, knee-high grass without making certain first.

When I set out in the morning with my friends, I would take with me a small army canteen of water and a knapsack with my food for the day, usually a piece of longhorn cheese or a can of sardines and some crackers. I took my Stevens rifle, of course, and a supply of ammunition. Our favorite spot was a place called Thompson's Tank, some two or three miles out of town. The tank was a pond created for watering cattle. Cows tend to stay close to water, sometimes leaving thousands of acres of good grazing unused. For this reason, a well-organized ranch can greatly increase its production by spacing out tanks and windmills. There were always good shade trees around a tank where we could cool off and eat our lunches. On hot days, we went swimming. There were water moccasins in the tank, and their venom was deadly, but unlike the rattler, they kept out of the way if we left them alone. We never fished in the tank.

On one occasion, I recall we went out to Thompson's Tank on a cool February morning. As we approached, a flock of ducks came in and landed. We crept up as close to the water's edge as we could, staying in the brush. Some sound alerted the ducks, and most of them rose into the air. One of the laggards started to fly just as I approached the water's edge. It was about fifty feet in the air when I fired. Only an exceptional shot could possibly hit a flying duck with a single-shot .22, but I hit this unfortunate bird, and it fell dead in the middle of the pond. As punishment I had to strip and swim out about fifty yards in freezing water to retrieve the duck. I held the duck upside down by the legs as we started back to town. When we reached the dirt road, now Bibb Drive, a pickup truck passing by stopped and the driver admonished me: "Boy, don't you know this isn't duck hunting season?" I hid the duck under my jacket all the rest of the way home, scared that I might get caught by the game warden. When I got home and showed the duck to Mother, she cooked it and insisted that I had to eat all of it. To kill an animal and not eat it was a sin, she said. The duck proved to be very tough, all skin and bones, and it had a very strong, gamey taste. No more ducks for me.

At that time, we had a baker in town by the name of Luderus, a burly, big-bellied, red-faced man.[11] He lived on a chicken farm in the area where Jack Spence's house is now. One day, our group was wandering around near the Luderus place in the direction of a series of hills overlooking the Rio Grande flood plain. We had no particular destination in mind, just walking through the brush, when we came upon a covey of blue quail. These quail are larger than bobwhites and have different habits. Bobwhites tend to fly in a covey all at once, making a whirring sound, whereas blues run on the ground separately and regroup later.

We chased the quail right into Luderus's chickens. The ejector on my single-shot Stevens didn't work. Every time I fired, I had to use a ramrod to eject the spent cartridge then reload my gun. I was so intent on this operation and trying to follow the quail that I hadn't even noticed where I was. Next thing I knew Luderus came out of the house carrying a shotgun. He fired a shot into the air, which got our attention, hollering that if we didn't "git," the next shot would be in our pants. We got, running for our lives.

DOCTOR EASTON AND MRS. WILLIAMS

As a child, I caught every illness that plagued the town, starting with a simultaneous attack of pneumonia and diphtheria when I was six weeks old, followed by scarlet fever, mumps, measles, whooping cough, chicken pox, and other illnesses. There were few doctors for whom Mother had high regard; in fact, she had a grudge against doctors in general. In referring to a doctor she would say, "*Er farshteyt a krank*," which literally means he understands a disease, but in Yiddish slang it also means that he knows absolutely nothing. Her feeling about doctors was in large measure due to a doctor in San Antonio who told her in 1920 that unless she had major surgery immediately, she would only live a few months. Some years later that doctor died of a heart attack. Ma reminded herself of it when she was in her late eighties: "Ha ha! I have already outlived him by forty years."

She did respect Dr. E. S. Easton, however, who became our family doctor.[12] I was a frequent patient. The illness I remember with particular dread was an attack of shivering cold, even when covered with blankets, alternating with a high fever that consumed me with fire. Dr. Easton pronounced it to be dengue fever. The only hospital in town, the military hospital at Fort Duncan, was not available to civilians. When my sister Bess and I were operated on to remove our tonsils and adenoids, the surgeries were performed on our kitchen table.

About the year 1917, Uncle Abe Edelstein's tuberculosis became so advanced that he could no longer function in his business. At Dr. Easton's insistence, Abe no longer came to the house, and even though Mother and Abe had always been very close, she saw little of him. He sold out to Pablo Rodríguez and Arturo Flores and moved to a sanitarium in San Antonio. I recall going with Mother to visit him. We met out of doors. I sat on a bench apart from Mother and Abe, who engaged in a low-voiced conversation I could not hear. Mother was very sad and seemed on the verge of tears. I always thought that Abe died soon after, as I never heard Mother mention that she had heard from him again. Many years later, I was quite surprised to learn from Ruben Edelstein that Abe had died in 1933 in a Denver sanitarium.[13]

One of Dr. Easton's pronouncements, as understood by Mother, was that Uncle Abe's tuberculosis was highly contagious, so it was dangerous for us children to engage in such acts of affection as hugging and kissing. According to the good doctor, kissing was a bad habit anyway, causing the spread of much disease. Since Mother was not a demonstrative person to begin with, Dr. Easton's advice only served to reinforce the impression that she was very cold. One had to know her well to understand the depth of her feelings.

When my sister Ruthie was born in 1913, Dr. Easton recommended Mrs. Williams, a practical nurse, to help Mother around the house. Mrs. Williams was a Black woman whose husband was a Pullman porter on the Torreón railroad. The Williams family was one of the few Black families in town. Mrs. Williams and Mother become good friends. She told Mother a horrifying story about her family. Her grandmother had been a slave and had been forced to have six children fathered by her white owner. These children had been sold off by their white father, one by one. After emancipation her grandmother searched for her scattered children and managed to locate most, but not all of them.[14] The story made a deep impression on Mother.

Sadly, Dr. Easton had a tragic end. By mischance he slipped while boarding the San Antonio train and was caught in the wheels, losing a leg. Soon afterward he left Eagle Pass and was heard from no more.

SCHOOL

Public education in Eagle Pass was vastly different for most Mexican American children than for Anglos.[15] Those who could not speak enough English to qualify—which meant all who spoke Spanish at home—were enrolled in the annex, the adjoining building. In this building were only six grades. After that, a few continued by choice in the Anglo school, but most Mexican American children ceased their education at this point, since there was no state requirement for further schooling. The state at that time contributed little to local education. Since schools cost money, more schooling meant more taxes. The attitude of school boards was why waste money on those who didn't want to go to school in the first place? The truth was that few of the Mexican American parents saw any need for the further education of their children. Their horizons were very limited. Even years later when I was on the school board and argued with parents to keep their children in school, the answer would be, "What good does education do in harvesting onions?" Except for the few tuition students from Mexico and a scattering of students from the "better" Mexican American families, the students were all Anglos.[16]

The Spanish language was not permitted on the school grounds. A child caught using Spanish, even on the playground, was punished. This, plus the fact that the Anglo children treated the Mexicans with open contempt, did not serve to create a healthy atmosphere. Even today some of our elderly Mexican American friends bear a deep resentment against their childhood treatment. I certainly do not subscribe to the old program, but neither do I look with favor at present-day methods. Years ago, as president of the school board, I practically forced on a recalcitrant board the acceptance of an English as a second language program, but I do not subscribe to the program as it has been practiced throughout the nation. It seems to me that the program has served to create a bloated, overgrown bureaucracy rather than to teach English even as well as the old system, brutal and uncivilized though it was. The present system certainly does not produce results commensurate with its excessive cost. It is my considered opinion that TV has done more to teach English than the schools.

I started school at the age of seven and a half. In order to attend school, you had to have attained the age of seven before the start of school in the fall, and my birthday was in February. I was taken to school by my Aunt Rose and handed over to Mrs. Dena Graves, the first-grade teacher who was also the school superintendent's wife. She was a stern, gray-haired woman who ruled her class with an iron hand.[17]

Mrs. Graves held a daily singing session, which each of us had to lead in turn. When my turn came to stand in front of the class, my voice came out somewhere between a croak and a screech, perhaps because I was scared. The class roared with laughter, and I was deeply humiliated. Since that time, I have never been able to sing in public, even in the midst of a crowd. In later years, whenever I performed a Hebrew service or read from the Torah scroll, I was unable to chant or sing. I read the text, nothing more. Sometimes driving along in the car by myself I would chant long sections from the Shabbat service, doing a quite creditable job if I kept my voice in a low register.[18] There is something cruel in forcing a child to sing solo in public. There must be a better way to teach singing, sparing a child from such a psyche-scarring experience.

For a time, I was not doing too well in school. Then my second-grade teacher notified Mother that I was having trouble seeing the blackboard, even when I sat in the first row. A short time later, an itinerant optometrist came to town. His tests showed that I was not only nearsighted but was afflicted with astigmatism. With glasses my schoolwork immediately improved. I have worn them ever since.

The Stephen F. Austin School, built in 1917 on Madison Street in Eagle Pass, where Morris began elementary school in 1918.

I began to read with pleasure after I was fitted with glasses. I was encouraged by my mother, who bought me books whenever she went to San Antonio. By the time I was in the fourth grade, I was given a *Life of Alexander the Great*, which I still have, as well as English and American classics such as *Alice in Wonderland* and *Tom Sawyer*. I also was an avid reader of the *Wizard of Oz* series and borrowed from my friends such masterpieces as Horatio Alger, the Rover Boys, and Tom Swift. An encyclopedia set that greatly influenced me was *The Book of Knowledge*. It contained excellent, well-written articles on history, literature, art, and science. I dearly loved this set and read it from cover to cover.[19]

These books proved to be an excellent starting point for further reading. When I finished *The Book of Knowledge*, I started on the encyclopedia Mother had. I have always enjoyed reading encyclopedias, constantly looking for errors, which are not uncommon. There was no library in town, and books were scarce. In my opinion, reading is essential to the proper education of children. The schools, if they do their job, can do much to teach a child to read if they have the cooperation of the parents. The problem today is that in most cases neither condition prevails.

The school I attended was the old Stephen F. Austin School, which was torn down around 1975. It was then called "the new school," having been completed in 1917 or 1918.[20] It was during World War I, and the country was on a physical-fitness binge, being exercised (to use a pun) over the news that so many men were being rejected for the military service. We entered into one of our periodic frantic attempts to solve a problem overnight, as though a national condition developing over many years can be solved quickly with no true understanding of the problem or its cause. Every day, the entire school lined up in front of the school facing San Juan Plaza and went through a period of rigorous calisthenics. After a few months of this, the war ended and so did our physical-fitness program. It was forgotten and life went back to normal.

There were two adjoining buildings comprising the Austin School, both two stories and built of a hard, light tan brick. Between the two edifices, there was a gap filled in part by wide slides coming down from the second floor intended, I suppose, to serve as fire escapes. The regular school was on the corner of the Madison Street side of the grounds. The lower grades and the principal's office were on the ground floor. On the second floor the classrooms started with the sixth grade and continued through the eleventh and final grade, what was then the senior year. There was no twelfth grade at that time.

Classes were small, perhaps as many as twenty-five or thirty in the entire first grade to as few as seven or eight in the senior class. The curriculum was taught with no frills. Students were well-drilled, and most of the few who graduated went on to the University of Texas at Austin, although a few to Texas A&M. It was expected that a student who graduated from Eagle Pass High would be an honor student at the university.

In the fourth and fifth grades, we studied several courses no longer taught or since changed in substance. For one thing, we were taught geography as a subject. Even today I am fascinated by maps; judging from my own children, unless there have been recent changes, children today cannot read a map. I heard on TV that in a survey made last year, New York high-school seniors thought that the state south of Washington, DC, was Mexico. My own sons, until I took them in hand, could have ended up driving to Seattle on the way to New York.

We were taught Texas history, but not the same Texas history as is taught now. Then there were the good guys and bad guys. The Texans were all heroes of superhuman stature. The Mexicans were all villains, tyrants, and cold-blooded killers. No mention was made of the Mexican Texans who died fighting for the Texas cause in the Alamo or otherwise participated in the War of Independence. Incidentally, I have yet to find a Mexican history of the period that is any more truthful than the old Texas ones. Good histories of the period are few and far between.[21] We also studied a text called *King Cotton* and for a semester learned about the history and growing of cotton and its importance to the state of Texas. Sometime later the boll weevil began to take its toll, and because of other more profitable crops, cotton ceased to play such a paramount role in the economy of the state.

At no time during my schooling, either in Eagle Pass or later in Los Angeles, did we ever pray in school. I never heard of such a practice. It could be that school prayer took place in rural communities where everyone was of one denomination, but I had never heard of praying in public schools until after it was declared unconstitutional some years ago.[22] I thought that if parents desired their children to pray in school, they sent them to a parochial school. It is true that in a town such as Eagle Pass there are invocations and other public religious practices that can make a non-Christian child uncomfortable. In my opinion they are not important enough to cause public protest. At such a practice as a high-school baccalaureate service, a Jewish child can stay home. I see no point in stirring up a hornet's nest with neighbors with whom I have lived at peace. One has to bend a little. If I put up a fight, let it be for a truly important issue.

The size of the school made athletic teams a problem. Any boy who could walk was expected to be a football and baseball player so we could field a team. The football field was nothing but an empty dirt field, gravel and all, with goal posts at each end. By the end of a game all the participants would be bruised, bleeding, and well battered. Ward Wueste told me that in order to have a full team for the high school, Jimmy Chuck was drafted, even though he had never seen a football game or had any idea what it was about.[23] The Chuck family were

Chinese immigrants who lived in Piedras Negras, and the children were tuition students. In the big game with Del Rio, Jimmy turned out to be the star. He was exceptionally fast, and the Del Rio team chased him all over the field with little success. Ward recalled that the Del Rio stands started to yell, "Kill the Chinaman! Kill the Chinaman! Kill the Chinaman!"[24]

In Francis Aldridge's graduating class of seven seniors, he was delegated the job of hiring a band for the senior prom. At the dance the principal asked, "Francis, where did you get the band? It's the best I've ever heard." Francis innocently replied, "I got the band across the river in the Zona," the red-light district. Were it not for the fact that he had already graduated, Francis would have been in trouble.

ADVENTURES IN MOTORING

In 1918, Pa bought his first automobile, a Studebaker four-door sedan. By this time, Pa was a prosperous businessman, but when it came to buying what he considered a luxury, he was super cautious. The best policy, he believed, was to sell on credit but buy with cash. "Never buy what you can't pay for in cash," he said once. "When you have the money in the bank, then you buy a car."

For a few days we drove around town, but Eagle Pass was small, and when you drove down a street, the air filled with dust. In a few days the novelty wore off. Pa had hired a driver and was ready to venture farther afield. We made a trip to Allende, about forty miles into Mexico south of Piedras Negras. The road was fairly straight and level: it had been the old stagecoach road to Saltillo. We left a huge cloud of dust behind us as we drove for over an hour. After the barren countryside near Eagle Pass we were amazed at the vegetation closer to Allende. Watered by springs with an ample flow of water, there were tall cypress and pecan trees, and many homes had gardens where avocados and papaya grew. In Eagle Pass, only a few miles away, we couldn't grow either since they froze almost every winter.

Next, we embarked on a true adventure: we made a trip to San Antonio. There were five of us in the expedition: our driver, my parents, the store's window trimmer Mr. Seriff, and myself. Before the railroad came, it was a week's trip each way to San Antonio hauling freight by oxcart and probably a three- or four-day exhausting trip by stagecoach. The "road" was a mere wagon trail through the brush. There were no signs of any kind giving directions; you either knew the road or you didn't. If you got lost, it was no joking matter. You could go for hours without seeing human habitation or meeting a soul. There were no bridges, so when you came to an arroyo or creek you had to hope there was no water in it. After a rain, the traveler had to wait until the water went down to cross.

Between Eagle Pass and La Pryor, there wasn't a habitation to be seen for forty-seven miles. It was all one or two huge ranches. La Pryor got its name, I believe, because it had been the headquarters of the Ike Pryor ranch. There were few houses in La Pryor, and I remember a blacksmith shop that sold gasoline pumped by hand from a fifty-gallon drum. A milk cow tied to a tree was resting in the shade. After filling the car with gasoline, we continued on toward Uvalde, crossing the Nueces River on the way. Whenever I cross the Nueces, I think of its significance in Texas and American history. Before the Texas War of Independence, the Nueces had been the boundary dividing the northern Mexican states from the province of Texas. Had Mexico been willing to negotiate rather than fight, the boundary could very well have been fixed at the Nueces rather than the Rio Grande.[25]

There were three main hazards on the trip to San Antonio. The first was the danger of getting lost. The second was mechanical failure or running out of gas. The third was

Michael Riskind, Eagle Pass, ca. 1920. (Courtesy of Dr. Peter Riskind.)

the problem of flat tires. Cars were high off the ground and rode on thin, narrow tires. Mesquite thorns pierced the tires as though they were made of paper, and the driver had to take care not to drive over branches of mesquite and other chaparral. On the round trip to San Antonio, we had twelve flat tires. The process of removing a tire and repairing it would take an experienced man about a half an hour. Everyone got out of the car, it was jacked up, and the tire was removed, patched, replaced, and inflated with a hand pump. Any driver who embarked on a trip without checking his tire equipment could be stuck in a very sad predicament.

The road through Uvalde went past the cemetery, where it became confusing, and for a time we went around and around the cemetery. But other than flat tires, our progress after passing Uvalde was uneventful since the road followed the railroad track, and we arrived in San Antonio by the end of the day.

On the way home we decided on a different route, intending to take the Laredo road as far as Dilley or Devine, then to Carrizo Springs and home. As we left San Antonio there was a landmark I recall: a wooden shack on the right-hand side of the road with a sign reading "Last Chance Saloon." For a few hours after we left San Antonio, all seemed to go well. Then, as the day progressed, it became more and more evident that we were lost. It is possible that we had gotten onto the military road Robert E. Lee had cleared through the brush for General Wool's army on its march to Saltillo in 1846. Lee's road went to Guerrero on the Rio Grande about forty miles south of Eagle Pass. We traveled all day and into the night without reaching any settlement. I can remember the car moving slowly through the brush, Mr. Seriff walking in front carrying a flashlight or lantern. The scene gave an eerie feeling, especially since we didn't know where we were.

Some time about daybreak we came upon an old man collecting *leños*, mesquite logs, in an oxcart. We questioned him hysterically, and he advised that we were only a few leagues from the town of Águila, by which he meant Eagle Pass. We continued on for what seemed an age. When the sun was well above the horizon, we came to the edge of one of the seven hills overlooking Eagle Pass. This was our last trip to San Antonio for a long time.

Sometime later, Pa tried driving the car himself. He drove to Elm Creek, about five miles from town, where we stopped and the children played. When it was time to go home, Pa couldn't start the car. We sat there, Pa in a fury, until someone came along to crank the car for us. The next day Pa sold the car. Not until my father could get a car with a self-starter did he buy another one.

Around 1919, Pa bought an immense Hudson seven-passenger touring car. There were two folding seats in the back between the front and back seats. Two of us children sat on the folding seats when the entire family was aboard. In addition, Pa had a rack attached to the back to hold suitcases and sometimes a tent, cots, and cooking utensils. Pa bought the car from Dr. Hume, who not only practiced medicine but also was a Hudson-Essex dealer. He had a reputation as a speed maniac and could often be seen tearing down the streets at high speed followed by a cloud of dust. He drove an Essex Phaeton with the top down, which he turned over on several occasions without getting hurt. By reputation he imbibed liberally, and it may be that he escaped injury because he was well relaxed. In fact, Dr. Hume did end up getting himself killed, not by the Essex but by being thrown from a horse and landing on his head.[26]

By the time Pa bought the Hudson, there had been a pronounced improvement in travel to San Antonio. The main roads had been graded, although not yet graveled or paved, and there were some signs. Unless the roads were muddy from rain, a trip to San Antonio, about 150 miles, could be made in six hours or less. If it rained, however, that was another story, as streams and arroyos were dangerous. Gauges had been placed at every potential water crossing. These were poles driven into the ground indicating the potential depth of the water. A depth of more than a few feet presented the danger of getting stalled, and a fast current could sweep the car away and drown the passengers. Some intrepid souls would try to cross by hitting the water at a high speed, hoping their momentum would carry them across.

After he bought the new car, Pa hired a driver, a young man named Jesús. The trouble with Jesús's driving was that he knew only two speeds—slow and fast—and couldn't seem to get the hang of anything in between. One afternoon Ma and the children went for a drive on the Del Rio road. After Elm Creek, the road wound between a series of low, graveled hills covered by sage and thorn brush. Jesús was driving at his usual slow pace when Ma said, "Jesús, drive a little faster." Jesús slammed his foot down on the accelerator, lost control of the car around a curve, and slammed into the brush. We all yelled and screamed in terror and general pandemonium until the dinosaur of a car came to a stop. Jesús backed up and nonchalantly continued on our way.

Some weekends, we drove to the town of Del Rio, fifty-five miles away, and continued on to Devils River.[27] This was a beautiful spot with large, old pecan trees, many islands, and crystal-clear water. Sometimes we left after the store closed on Saturday night and camped out all day Sunday. Once we drove to Del Rio because a small vineyard was nearby. This was during Prohibition, and Pa tried to make some wine with no previous experience, which turned out badly.

The trip to Del Rio was a leisurely drive at around thirty miles an hour, and we always made several stops. Ten miles out of Eagle Pass was a wide swinging bumper gate that marked the Green Davidson Ranch, which we drove through for miles. Since there was little traffic and we drove slowly, we didn't scare the wildlife. One trip I counted around seventy jackrabbits near or crossing the road. There were many deer, especially in the late afternoon and evening, occasionally javelina and wild turkey. Coyotes were common. The cattle were all longhorns. When we got closer to Del Rio, sheep and angoras replaced the cattle.

Our camping trips to the Devils River ended after the flood of 1922, which washed away many of the pecan trees and obliterated the islands.[28] That location lost most of its charm, but there was probably another reason we changed the location of our camping. A customer of Pa's, Dr. Cantú, invited him to camp on his property on the banks of the Rio Escondido near La Villita in Mexico. It also had large pecan trees and clear running water, was close to our home in Eagle Pass—and Mexico had no Prohibition. Passing through Piedras Negras, Pa would stop to buy a keg of beer and plenty of ice to keep it cold. When we reached the chosen spot, Mother would spread a blanket in the shade of a pecan tree. The adults spent the day drinking beer and playing poker. Mother prepared food, strolled around, or read a book. We children swam in the clear, cool water of the Escondido.

On some of these trips we were joined by Mother's brother David, who was living in Piedras Negras waiting for a visa.[29] Mother had brought him from Europe, but he could not enter the United States because of the newly passed immigration act.[30] David did not care to play cards, so he spent his time either talking with Mother or swimming with us. I was impressed by David; he was strong and muscular, and swam using the breast stroke rather than the crawl. David waited over a year in Piedras Negras before he was able to get a visa, then after a short stay with us he moved to the lower Rio Grande Valley, where his brothers Jake and Morris Edelstein helped him open a small furniture store in the town of Mission.[31]

SAN ANTONIO

Around 1920, my father bought a house in San Antonio for his sister Jennie and his parents, who were still living in Chicago. Jennie had contracted tuberculosis and had been told by the doctor to move to a warmer and drier climate. Aunt Jennie's husband, Jack Schrager, was a shadowy figure who seldom made an appearance. He was supposed to be peddling between San Antonio and the lower Valley.[32]

My grandparents were unhappy about the move from Chicago, especially my grandfather, whose life was built around the Russian shul, or synagogue, where he was accustomed to spending the day with his cronies. He felt uprooted and had no interest in the small Orthodox synagogue in San Antonio.[33] We made frequent trips to San Antonio to see them. Usually, Grandmother Judith met us at the door. She would pursue me, hobbling on crutches and offering a variety of foods she always had ready for us. As she chased me about the room she would hold out one plate of food after another, saying, "*Es, zunnike, es,*" "Eat, little son, eat!"

Grandpa Nathan Riskind was oblivious to our presence. He had one constant routine. He would line up five, six, or seven cups of hot tea with a generous spoonful of Grandma's *malinkes*, raspberry preserves. Seated in his chair at the table, he drank cup after cup of tea while he read his book, sucking the tea through a lump of sugar held in his front teeth. This, I understand, is the Russian manner. I suppose if Grandfather had been raised under different circumstances, he would have been an efficiency expert.[34]

There were two Schrager children.[35] The doctor urged that they be moved out of the house to avoid contact with tuberculosis. We seldom saw Aunt Jennie, who was in a back bedroom. Occasionally, we had glimpses of a wan face peering out of covers. After a discussion, Mother offered to care for the Schrager children, and they came home with us.

San Antonio in 1920 was still very much a cow town. It was the center of Central and South Texas cattle ranching, and the cattlemen were much more important then than they are now. On weekends, especially, the stores were filled with country people. The Hispanic population, although much fewer than now, was very much in evidence. If we stayed at a hotel, it would be the Gunter, the Menger, or sometimes the Travelers.[36] My favorite was the Menger because it had a patio planted with tropical vegetation and a pond, in which for a time there was a small alligator. Unfortunately, the alligator grew up and disappeared from the pond.

The Alamo had recently been turned over to the Daughters of the Republic of Texas.[37] In the 1920s, the surrounding area had not yet been changed to the extent that it has today. Alamo Street was one of the city's most important business streets. The most important store was the Joske's department store, four stories high and a block square. At night, the block-long wall facing the Alamo was lit up by an electric sign, which consisted of a cowboy on horseback who threw a lariat of moving lights to rope a large steer.[38] I had not seen anything like it and was fascinated by the sign. Joske's itself was the gathering place for all the ranchers and farmers. I don't believe such an assemblage of types could be assembled anywhere in the world today. Another major attraction of San Antonio at the time was the Buckhorn Saloon located downtown on Houston Street. In addition to an old bar, they had a large collection of animal skins.[39]

During the summer when we visited San Antonio, we camped in Brackenridge Park.[40] At that time, there was a large campground along the San Antonio River. It was a very rustic setting with many trees giving the feeling of being far from any city. We had a large surplus army tent with a peaked roof and pole in the middle, which could comfortably hold six or seven cots. One night there was a severe storm with high winds, causing the tent to blow over on all of us with resulting pandemonium and drenching.

Other than that unhappy incident we had a great time. It was cool in the shade of the trees. We swam in the San Antonio River or played, and Ma cooked the meals as though we were home. At night the city provided entertainment: across the river was a screen, and at night they showed old two-reel comedies. There was also community singing with words on the screen. I particularly remember a song about "K-Katie Over the C-cow Shed."[41]

At night, when we were camping, we often sat around a campfire and Mother would tell us stories. We were fascinated by her descriptions of life in Kalvaria, and we listened entranced, over and over again, as we sat around the flickering campfire. The escapades of her brothers were also a topic very much in demand. On clear nights, she would point out the constellations. In later years, I would recall these evenings with nostalgia.

A TRIP TO REMEMBER

In the summer of 1920, Mother took our Schrager cousins to visit their sick mother in San Antonio. After staying for a day, we started back. Jesús was driving the seven-passenger Hudson, filled to the brim with Mother, my sisters Bess (about eleven years old), Ruthie (seven), and Sarah (five), me (nine), my brother Reuben (two or three), and the two Schrager children, the oldest of whom, Bessie, was around my age. There were nine of us in all, including Jesús. If all went well, we should be home before dark.

At first, we made excellent progress. The road had been recently graded and we were able to speed along at thirty or thirty-five miles an hour. We passed the town of Hondo and were approaching Sabinal when the sky clouded ominously and grew menacingly dark. Ma looked at the sky apprehensively. She was a good weather prophet and decided that it would be too risky to continue. In Sabinal, we finally located a house that had clean rooms for rent. The problem was Jesús. At that time in Texas, Mexicans and Mexican Americans were not admitted into restaurants or hotels. This was especially true in a German community such as Sabinal. Jesús assured Mother that he could take care of himself in the Mexican barrio, so we parted company until the following morning. We went to bed early after our meal.

No sooner had we fallen asleep than we were awakened by an extremely violent storm. At breakfast we heard that the cloudburst had covered a wide area, including the Hill Country in Central Texas. Rivers were rising and would soon be impassable. We were urged to be on our way as soon as possible. Jesús appeared early, and we started out. Travel conditions had greatly changed from the previous day. The road was not graveled and had become black, slippery mud. Jesús drove with increasing difficulty, the car sliding all over the road, and even in low gear he had difficulty making headway. Jesús advised returning to Sabinal and tried to turn around, but the car became stuck sideways across the road. He tried rocking the car back and forth. The car stalled and, to make matters worse, the starter had broken.

Nowadays when one sees a car stalled on the side of the road, the tendency is to step on the gas unless you recognize the unfortunate in need of help. In 1920, we were living in an unsophisticated society. If one saw his fellow man in distress (an Anglo, that is) the natural and expected course of action was to help without hesitation—and most certainly if it were a woman with small children. A short time after we stalled, a pickup truck came along driven by an Anglo rancher and accompanied by a ranch hand. With rope attached to our car they quickly pulled us out and got us on the road facing Sabinal. They gave us a push to get the engine started, and we were on our way.

In Sabinal, we left the car in a garage to be repaired. We had a wait of at least an hour and it was lunch time, so we were directed to the town's best restaurant, the Cow Bell. After lunch and a short walk, we were on our way. By this time the hot sun had dried the road sufficiently to provide adequate traction, and we reached Uvalde without incident. But at a gas station, we were advised that rainwater pouring down from the Hill Country had completely covered the Nueces River bridge and that it would probably be several days before the flood receded. The only way to reach Eagle Pass was by train. The problem again was Jesús. He would have to be left behind with the car to continue when possible.

To reach Eagle Pass, it was necessary to take the Sunset Limited coming from San Antonio on its way to El Paso and Los Angeles. At the Uvalde station we were advised that the Sunset wasn't due for four or five hours. Jesús was going to wait with us until we left, but Uvalde was a notoriously anti-Mexican town, and Jesús soon found the atmosphere at the station inhospitable. At that time there were segregated waiting rooms for White and Black people, and in Uvalde, Mexican people had to stay in the Black section. There were a number of tough characters in the waiting room who glared at Jesús and loudly made threatening remarks directed at him. It was apparent that there would soon be violence. Jesús had good reason to be frightened and wanted to leave at once. As soon as Mother gave him money for gasoline, food, and a room, he was on his way. For us it seemed an endless wait until the Sunset Limited arrived. Mother hustled seven tired, sleepy children on board. An hour or so later the train made a brief halt at Spofford Junction, just long enough for Mother to shepherd us off the train as quickly as she could. It must have been at least 11:00 at night, and the local to Eagle Pass wasn't due to leave until morning.

The few buildings in town were all dark. Only a few railroad men were on hand. One of them directed us to the hotel nearby, a two-story wooden edifice with a second-story porch that could have served as a Western movie set. At the desk there were several kerosene lamps, already lit, and a notice advising any late guests to register in the nearby book then help themselves to any vacant room. Mother registered for two rooms, took a lamp, and marched us up the stairs. We were divided up, put to bed, and were almost immediately sound asleep.

Before six in the morning, Mother woke us. We hurriedly dressed and were marched off to the station. We boarded the train for Eagle Pass, taking our seats in the antique car attached to the end of the long freight train. Some of the seats in the car had the springs popping through. Although it was only some thirty-five miles to Eagle Pass the slow, jolting ride took well over an hour. Finally we arrived and our ordeal was over.

To our surprise Jesús returned in the early afternoon, the unrecognizable Hudson completely splattered with mud. Jesús had shown initiative. Rather than wait in Uvalde for the water to recede, he had driven south on side roads as far as Devine, inquiring as he went along about how to cross all the streams, and arrived in Eagle Pass much earlier than expected.

CHAPTER 5

WASHED AWAY

My childhood in Eagle Pass was a time of remarkable physical independence and innocence. I was able to wander and explore the environs over substantial distances with my friends, without adult supervision. I felt accepted, and at home my family owned a respectable, prominent local business. I spoke fluent Spanish and was comfortable with the border culture and the unusual things that occasionally happened there. The 1920s, however, brought some upheavals.

REFUGEES

Sometime after the end of World War I, probably in 1919 or 1920, Pa received an urgent call from the head of immigration at the International Bridge asking him to translate for a troupe of Russians called the Russian Cossack Choir, who had appeared at the crossing and asked for entry into the United States. Pa returned after a long interval, very excited about his meeting. This had been his first opportunity to speak Russian since he left his native country at the age of sixteen. In later years, reminiscing about his youth, he said to me that he always liked the Russian common people and remembered them as friendly and kind.

Mother, on the other hand, was not enthused at the prospect of assisting Cossacks. Word was beginning to come out of Ukraine of terrible atrocities committed against the Jewish population, the worst since the seventeenth-century massacres. The rumors, later authenticated, were that a Cossack extremist, acting in the name of the tsar, had declared that all Jews were communists and were responsible for the revolution. He had murdered more than a hundred thousand innocent Jewish men, women, and children.[1] "How much Jewish blood do these Cossacks have on their hands?" Mother asked.

A different group of refugees came to Pa and Uncle Albert's attention sometime later. In late 1921 or early 1922, after the immigration laws had been changed to restrict Jews from coming into the United States, Albert learned that a group of Jewish boys from Eastern Europe had been caught attempting to swim the Rio Grande to enter the United States and had been jailed.[2]

Under the law there wasn't much Pa could do, but he secured the release on bail of the young men, all about twenty years of age, and gave them jobs in the store until the hearing. Their deportation to Mexico was inevitable: the question was how to give them long-term help. Pa recommended that the boys give up any expectation of entry into the United States, since a second capture could lead to severe punishment. Rather they should settle in Monterrey, Mexico, the largest city in the region, and he would assist them by lending them money and giving each of them a small stock of merchandise to start a business. To my knowledge, all of this money, as well as the cost of the merchandise, was repaid. Some of them later became very wealthy businesspeople.

About this time Mother's cousin, Isaac Ramberg, came to Monterrey with the help of Mother and her brothers. My parents and I made a trip to Monterrey to visit him. With the assistance of Uncle Morris, Isaac opened a furniture store he called El Fenix. He was immediately successful and stayed in Monterrey until he was able to enter the United States. In the 1930s, Isaac moved to Los Angeles, where he opened a furniture store on the Eastside, which was rapidly changing from a Jewish to a Mexican neighborhood. This store was also called El Fenix and was very successful. After I completed my legal education in California, I was Uncle Isaac's attorney.[3]

THE INTERNATIONAL BRIDGE

Almost every year, usually in June, the Rio Grande rose suddenly. Within a few hours the water would overflow the banks of the river to fill the valley. The Kickapoo Indians, camped near the International Bridge, would move to higher ground. In some years, the water came close to Commercial Street. People who lived on the block just to the south would be forced to abandon their homes until the water subsided.

In 1922, the water rose until it came within a foot or so of overflowing into Commercial Street. Once the water came over the crest of the river valley, it was downhill to the center of town. Luckily the rise halted. But before the floodwaters crested, people spread the word that all the debris carried by the torrent was damaging the bridge and that a collapse was imminent. About 9 p.m., when it was already dark, I accompanied my father in the car as far as he could drive up Rio Grande Street, near the river. He was able to approach Commercial Street, where he was stopped by the police and a dense crowd of people. Pa called out to Mr. Fitch, then the owner of the Eagle Pass side of the bridge, who said that the bridge could go down any minute.[4] Pa asked if it was insured and Fitch said that it was. Just then there was a tremendous cheer. Bystanders said that Mr. Pilgrim had just come over the bridge, nearly waist deep in water, by holding onto the guardrail. Even though the bridge had been closed to traffic, Pilgrim had managed to get across to Piedras Negras for one last drink, this being the days of Prohibition. A few minutes after Pilgrim staggered back across, there was a cracking, tearing sound from the bridge and a section was swept away by the torrent.

After cresting, the water briefly paused then rapidly subsided. A day later the water was back to normal, but it was not business as usual since the collapsed bridge isolated us from Piedras Negras. Until the bridge was repaired, it was a return to the old days before the bridge was built. Townspeople stretched a heavy rope across the Rio Grande, and large rowboats called *chalanes* were poled across and attached to the rope to keep them from being swept downstream. I used to walk over to the riverbank to watch them being poled across, but I never had the experience of crossing in a *chalán* myself. Pa would never permit such a foolhardy venture.

After the flood carried away the International Bridge, the franchise for the bridge was purchased from Fitch by Francisco Estrada, an Eagle Pass personality who had a significant economic impact on Maverick County life.[5] My good friend Héctor Barrera, who was for some years Estrada's private secretary, told me about him. He said that Estrada was of such a suspicious nature that from time to time he would go to the bridge and station himself where he could spy on the tollbooth without being seen. He would make a tally of every car and truck, and at the end of the day check against the receipts. If the toll taker was short on fees, he would be dismissed.

Estrada came from around San Luis Potosí. He never spoke about his past, but on his desk was a photograph of himself as a boy in an expensive charro costume astride an obviously good horse.⁶ He must have come from a well-to-do family. As a young man during the era of railroad expansion in Mexico, he learned that the railroad ties they used originated from mills in East Texas. He managed to get an exclusive contract for all railroad ties and with this monopoly opened a lumberyard in Eagle Pass. In a few years, Estrada was a multimillionaire.

When the Maverick Irrigation District was created, Estrada bought large acreage both above and below town.⁷ On Saturdays, Héctor Barrera had to deliver to the various foremen the payroll for hundreds of men employed on the farms at Rosita and at the Quemado Valley. Héctor described Estrada as a recluse with few friends. When not at work, Estrada occupied himself reading his extensive library on American history.

Then a strange thing happened. After many years as a solitary bachelor, the cloistered man went to Spain and returned with a much younger wife. Gossip was that she had been a cabaret singer or dancer. The Estradas continued to live in retirement until he died a few years later. After a period of mourning, Mrs. Estrada went on a trip to Mexico City, then, to the shock of the town, the widow returned with a new husband. To the scandal of the good Catholics on both sides of the river, the new husband was not only a younger man than the bride but also had been a priest who left the church to marry. After a period of quiet, the new husband began to pressure his wife to liquidate Estrada's property and move to Spain. A few years later the ex-priest notified Héctor that she had died and that he was now the sole owner of any Estrada property remaining.⁸

Coincidentally, a short time before, Francis Aldridge, as the Viguera insolvency trustee, had sold the Del Rio Bridge to that city.⁹ When Uncle Albert learned that the Eagle Pass–Piedras Negras International Bridge was being offered for sale by the former Mrs. Estrada, he arose at the next Rotary Club meeting and suggested that the city of Eagle Pass likewise should purchase the International Bridge at Eagle Pass. The matter was pushed, prominent citizens were enlisted, and the city made the purchase. However, better speakers than Albert were the frontmen; when all was over, Albert, the instigator of the deal, was not even appointed to the new bridge board. Perhaps it was because the board members were entitled to various forms of pecuniary compensation or perhaps others felt that he was not entitled to such a post. I always felt that Albert should have been given some recognition as the father of the purchase of the bridge by the city. Without the bridge income, the city could not have grown the way it did. Albert was another prophet without honor in his own country.¹⁰

DR. McFARLAND

During the war years and after, Dr. McFarland was an important figure in Eagle Pass.¹¹ I remember him vaguely as a tall, thin, dour Scotsman. He was probably the most successful doctor in town since he lived in one of the nicest homes. This he constructed on Hillcrest in what was then an isolated area. I was told by Thurman Roberts of Dripping Springs in the Hill Country that McFarland's parents had been cotton sharecroppers in East Texas. They were given an offer to sell them the land they farmed but refused since more acreage could be bought in the Hill Country for the same money. Several years later they heard that the Spindletop well had been found on the land they had declined to buy. That's what can be called bad luck.¹²

This was in the middle of the Texas oil boom. Spindletop and other big fields had recently been discovered, and it was a period of wild speculation: everyone expected to find a gusher in his backyard. It was similar to the fever of the California gold rush. Eagle Pass was not immune, and McFarland was badly bitten by the oil bug. He decided there was oil near Eagle Pass and resolved to find it. The good doctor spent his fortune in wildcat drilling. He organized a company using mostly his own money and sold stock to all interested parties in Eagle Pass. I don't know if Pa was involved in his projects, but I remember that the town was wild with rumors that McFarland's well was about to come in. Handfuls of mud were brought around for everyone to smell. I recall going with Pa in his buggy to see the well "spudded in," whatever that meant. The whole town was there waiting expectantly. I believe nitroglycerin was dropped down the well to break the last layer of rock, which was supposed to bring the oil in a gusher. The crowd waited breathlessly, but nothing happened, and people left. Dr. McFarland went broke and moved from town.

OUR TRIP TO CALIFORNIA

In 1922, Pa had severe allergic attacks, probably aggravated by business worries. His sister Jennie in San Antonio was dying of tuberculosis, and Pa constantly visited her. Ma feared for his health and insisted he see a specialist, who recommended that Pa take time out from his business and get out in the open, maybe a long automobile or camping trip. We embarked on a trip to Los Angeles.

Pa bought a four-cylinder Dodge touring car for the trip, a very sturdy vehicle that was practically mechanically foolproof. He added a wrought-iron rack in the back that was sturdy enough to hold considerable weight. A flexible, removable iron frame was added on the driver's side along the running board to hold luggage. The members of our expedition were Pa, Ma, Ma's brother Jake, my brother Reuben (then three or four years old), me (age eleven), and our driver Jesús—six of us in all. When fully loaded we had a large tent, folded in the back rack together with five folded army cots. In addition to our luggage in the side rack, we had all sorts of pots and pans, including a cast-iron dutch oven. In front, over the radiator, was a large water bag. With this grotesquely loaded vehicle we were ready to start.

At that time, there were no highways or even roads as we know them today, nor did road signs exist. As an aid for the trip, Jake had purchased a printed and bound guide giving detailed directions on how to find the road to California. It was something like the pilots' charts used by early navigators. It went something like this: "On leaving town X, going westward, you drive 3.2 miles until you reach a cattle gate. Pass through the cattle gate, not forgetting to lock it, then drive 1.6 miles until you reach a windmill. Circle the windmill to the right and drive 4.7 miles until you reach a crossroads, taking the road to the left," etc. Along with this description came a strip map indicating that information for the stretch of road. I was fascinated by Uncle Jake's maps and studied them carefully. I can still recall vividly a section in Arizona marked Dragoon Mountains. Even today I have only to study a map, and I get the itch to go to that area to see what's there.

Finally, when all our preparations were ready, we set forth on an afternoon in December 1922. Pa and Jesús sat in front. Jake, Ma and I sat in the back, with Reuben on Ma's lap. We stopped the first night at our usual camping spot where the road crossed the Devils River. Pa demanded a hot meal. My job was to find firewood and chop it into usable pieces so that Jake could start a fire. Ma was busy getting dinner ready, cooking it in the dutch oven, while Jesús was unloading the tent and cots. Jake and Jesús put up the tent, and I put up the cots as soon as I had the firewood ready. While all this activity was going on, Pa would be giving directions and making himself comfortable. This was the procedure the first night and every night for the duration of the trip.

After leaving Devils River, we drove up the river canyon for a while through wild country until we came to a tiny place called Juno, then we proceeded toward Ozona and Sheffield. We stopped at several stores trying to buy milk for my brother, only to be told disdainfully that milk was for calves, not human beings. In driving along, Jesús kept our speed at around twenty-five to thirty miles per hour, speeding up to thirty-five on some good stretches. There were so many twists and turns that I doubt if we averaged twenty-five miles an hour. That night we stopped at Sheffield, no great distance for the day. After we were through setting up camp, I went off with Uncle Jake to look over the town. The center of the town's activity was a combination one-room barber shop and pool hall. We were awakened early the next morning by the braying of mules. It turned out that in the dark we had pitched camp right by the town corrals.

After several days of more travel, we came to a crossroad. The turn to the right was a good graded road, to the left was unimproved. Pa wanted to go right, but Jake pointed out that we were going west, which was to the left. After an angry debate, we decided to stop for the night where we were. A norther had come up, and it had turned quite cold. We all went to sleep still dressed in our clothes to keep warm. When we got up, we discovered a large sign by the road with directions on the side facing away from us. We learned from it that the good road to our right led eastward to Fort Worth. We turned to the left and continued toward El Paso. One of the small towns we passed, I think it was Van Horn, had a sign as you entered that announced, "This town is so healthy we had to shoot a man to start a cemetery."

In no time we arrived in El Paso, which at that time was a town of around one hundred thousand people. El Paso had a large public campground with faucets for water and public restrooms; we marveled at this luxury. We spent a day visiting Mother's cousin Harry Uspitz, who had changed his name to Spitz because of constant ridicule in the army. He had opened a furniture store in El Paso called the Overland Furniture Company, and in a few years it was quite prosperous. Ma and his wife, Hannah, were good friends for years.[13]

As soon as you cross the Rio Grande in New Mexico, the road goes up a long hill to get out of the river valley, then as you proceed toward Deming, the soil becomes very sandy. Several times most of us had to get out of the car and push to keep it from getting stuck. Later, in Tucson, Jake decided to change our route. A caravan was forming to go to Yuma through the mining town of Ajo. This is a road seldom traveled even today. It goes for 180 miles through the Tohono O'odham Indian reservation, passing near the Organ Pipe Cactus National Monument, and crossing the road called El Camino de los Muertos that goes south to the Gulf of California. In summer, temperatures in this area are over 120 degrees, but fortunately it was winter and the weather was very pleasant.

Our caravan consisted of about ten automobiles and one motorcycle. One car had a small trailer hauling a wooden water barrel; one was an expensive Haynes sedan. The cars proceeded in a single file, spaced a short distance apart. The road was horrendous—up hill, down dale, and curvy and bumpy simultaneously. Every so often we passed an Indian hogan, the Indians coming out to watch us pass.

The trip from Yuma to San Diego was also an adventure. First, the unimproved road became increasingly sandy. Every little while, we had to get out and push. Then we came to the sand dunes, an area that looks more like the Sahara than the actual Sahara does. The landscape is fine, glistening sand in shifting wind-driven dunes, some of them fifty to one hundred feet high and lacking any vegetation whatsoever. A wooden road had been constructed through the dunes about ten feet wide. At distances about a block apart there were widened areas so that if another car approached on the one-lane road you could pull over to let it pass.

The Imperial Valley is bordered on the west by a peninsular range. The road rises sharply out of the desert until it enters an area of sparse pine trees in a pleasant valley. Before reaching the pine trees the road crosses a deep canyon littered with enormous chunks of rock, the largest I have ever seen. Someone preceding us had painted "Jesus Saves," "Repent," "Prepare to meet thy Maker," and other religious slogans on the rocks. For the weak-kneed already terrified by the passage of the canyon, it did not help to learn that "the end of the world is nigh."

Near San Diego we reached a paved road and were able to speed to Los Angeles, arriving after dark. The next day we set out to find Sonya Levitansky, Mother's cousin. Sonya had an administrative job at the Jewish Home for the Aged on Boyle Avenue. At that time, Boyle Heights was the Jewish neighborhood of Los Angeles.[14] There was also a small Jewish neighborhood around Temple Street downtown and a nicer Jewish residential area on West Adams on the west side of town. The affluent were already moving into the Wilshire area, and Fairfax Avenue did not even exist yet. We stayed about two weeks in Los Angeles before returning home. The trip back is a complete blank in my mind. It took us twelve days to reach Los Angeles, but much less time to return home.

I went back to school, Pa immersed himself in the business again, and Jake married Sophye Harris of San Antonio and went into business in McAllen, Texas, where he soon became a leading merchant.[15] Then in January 1923, soon after our return, Mother announced her intention to move to Los Angeles. She said that the constant alkali dust in Eagle Pass was bad for her health and that she had felt better in California. I was twelve years old, nearing bar mitzvah age at thirteen, and she insisted I be given a proper Jewish education. I also suspect, although she didn't say so, that she wanted to free herself from Auntie's domination and bullying. Pa remonstrated that he could not leave his business, on which the family depended for support.[16]

Pa offered to buy the De Bona house on Ceylon Street, the most pretentious residence in town. Then he suggested that the family move to San Antonio, to no avail. Constant arguing and bickering took place during meals, with such tension that I began to have severe indigestion every meal. Finally Pa capitulated, and it was agreed that as soon as school closed in late May, Mother and the children would leave for Los Angeles. Pa would follow in June or July, as soon as he had finished his fall buying in New York. He would return to Eagle Pass toward the end of September, remain until after Christmas, then rejoin us until early March. During Pa's absences in California, Uncle Albert would be in charge of the business.

When I look back on this arrangement years later, I begin to appreciate the sacrifice made by my father. Not many men would have done the same. To be separated from one's wife and children for months on end and to make the long train ride back and forth—this was certainly no easy life. At the time I did not begin to realize the extent of his sacrifice or feel proper gratitude for his love for us.

One humorous recollection of this period. I happened to be with my parents while a real estate agent was rhapsodizing over the benefits of the California climate. After listening to him go on and on for ten or fifteen minutes on the subject of the California sunshine, Ma interrupted him to say, "Mister, don't talk to us about sunshine. We have too much where we come from."

MY UNCLES

Other than Albert, I was never close to my father's brothers. Pa's older brother, Aaron, or Otto as he was sometimes called, I saw occasionally. In their old age Uncle Aaron and Aunt Sarah moved to Venice, California, near Los Angeles, and my parents saw them frequently. Once, Uncle Aaron visited Eagle Pass and complained that the scotch Pa served was too weak for his taste, "like water." As a joke, I bought Aaron a bottle of Waterfill & Frazier made in Mexico, a very raw whiskey, which, during the war, the army had warned enlisted men not to drink because it contained too much fusel oil (if I remember correctly).[17] Uncle Aaron tasted this fiery gut burner, smacked his lips, and pronounced, "Now *that's* whiskey!" Despite my protests, Uncle Aaron insisted I get more. He must have taken a full case back with him. Whether this hastened his demise at a ripe old age I don't know.

The oldest son in Pa's family was Jake, who lived in South Chicago. He had started out as a watchmaker, then had expanded into jewelry, and in the family's early days in America, Jake was by far the most prosperous. My father corresponded with him but seldom saw him. Ma did not care for Jake's wife, Aunt Ida. According to Ma, instead of sending her children to school, Ida put the family money on their back, with fancy clothes and jewelry.[18] Despite the fact that Jake was the only one in the family with an education, none of his children to my knowledge went past high school. On the other hand, Aaron, who had probably had the least education, managed to send his children to the university, with three prominent lawyers and a medical specialist among them. This was probably due to the fact, according to Mother, that Sarah's father was a highly learned man and Sarah had been raised to respect and value education.

In his old age, Jake was placed by his family in a nursing home. Pa used to send him money—twenty-five dollars a month if I remember correctly. From time to time, Jake wrote letters to Pa thanking him for his help. I saw a letter from Jake written, I believe, when he was 105 years old. His handwriting was beautiful—much better than mine ever was.

I was much closer to Mother's family. Although Ma refused to have anything to do with Beilke, or Bertha, who lived with her husband and children in Corpus Christi, she kept in close contact with her sister Malke (Mollie) Benkaim, who lived in Scranton, Pennsylvania.[19] I met Ma's brother Louie only once, when I was an adult, when he came to Eagle Pass to visit my parents about 1960. By this time, Mother had acquired a grudge against Uncle Louie because of the way he treated his older daughter, Adelle, whom he did not care for. For one thing Adelle had married an immigrant named Alexander who was a short man, shorter than Adelle, not well educated, and a tailor, to boot (no *yiches*, to use the Yiddish expression). Louie lavished money and affection on the younger daughter, spoiling her, according to my mother, but he refused to help Adelle.[20]

The Alexanders moved to Los Angeles during the time my parents lived in Santa Monica. Ma became a parent by proxy for Adelle, her niece. My father, for his part, did not mind that Alexander was a tailor, since Pa himself had been trained as a tailor. He and Alexander got along very well, in fact. Alexander was quite handy with tools, and if anything needed fixing Alexander would rush over and take care of it. In his tailoring business, Alexander was a hard worker who began to specialize in uniforms of all types and soon was doing very well.

Of my mother's brothers, Morris, Jake, Eli, and David all lived in the Rio Grande Valley and kept in close touch with us. I was friendly with all of them, especially Eli and David, but Uncle Eli, my mother's second youngest brother, was my favorite.[21] I regarded him with awe as a combination of Dumas's d'Artagnan and Stevenson's Alan Breck Stewart.[22] I don't

Morris holding his son John, with his uncles Eli (left) and David Edelstein (right), 1949. (Courtesy of Dr. Peter Riskind.)

know when Eli first joined us in Eagle Pass, but I presume Mother brought him over from the old country. It must have been by 1917, as there is a photograph of the store taken then with all the personnel standing in front, and Eli is in it. Uncle Eli was not a big man, standing about five feet, nine inches, and was not heavy but powerfully built, and he was red-headed with a light complexion.

Unless angry, Eli had a perpetual smile on his face, as though life were a huge joke, and as children we would all gather around him to watch intently while he performed the amazing feat of wiggling his ears. He was quite volatile, however, a hothead, Pa said. I remember once when Eli went across the river with Pa and persuaded him to try mescal. Eli had a saying, "Tequila is t'kill ya; mescal must kill ya." The next morning at around 2 a.m., Eli and Pa were sitting on the sidewalk in front of the store singing duets until Aunt Rose came down and gave them both hell. Ma didn't like it but said nothing. Eli, of course, thought the stunt uproariously funny.

Pa, in contrast, was very straight and not very humorous. Once Pa asked Eli to recommend a hotel in a certain town. Taking Eli's advice, Pa got off the train late and checked into the Hotel De Italia. When he went to bed he was bitten unmercifully. Later, when he complained to Eli, Eli laughed and said that the hotel was not the Hotel De Italia but the Hotel De Utilee, which means "Bedbug Hotel" in Lithuanian.

One time, before I was married, Eli and I walked across the bridge to Piedras Negras for dinner. On the way back, Eli walked with coat slung over his shoulder and wore a bright green tie worn loose with the knot about six inches down from his collar. He wore no hat so his red hair was quite conspicuous. When we got to the American customs, an immigration inspector asked him, "Are you an American citizen?"

"What the hell do you think I am?" demanded Eli.

"I don't know," answered the inspector, who fortunately had a sense of humor. "Maybe you're from Dublin."

I drove to San Antonio once with Eli. At the Nueces River crossing, where there were some people camped, Eli decided it was a place to wash the car, which was covered with dust from the dirt road. There was no bridge over the Nueces, just a narrow concrete road base over the stream. Eli pulled off the concrete and we proceeded to wash off the car until we noticed that one end had sunk about a foot. Eli ran to a trucker camping nearby who helped us pull the car out before it sank. Then we proceeded on to San Antonio, stopping for the night on the side of the road and eating some food Eli had prepared. All in all, I had a great time with Eli.

Eli, then about twenty-five, persuaded Mother that he could drive a group of us—consisting of Mother, the five Riskind children, and my cousin Ida Ramberg—to California without any trouble.[23] Ma had recently brought Ida over from Europe. She was around eighteen, and I remember her as having a fair complexion and rosy cheeks, not a raving beauty but quite pretty. We started off in June 1923, the four-cylinder Dodge touring car loaded with luggage and cooking and camping equipment. We immediately started fighting in the back seat over space.

Several days after we left Eagle Pass on our move to California, we detoured to see the Davis Mountains, which Mother had heard about and wanted to see.[24] It began to cloud up, so we returned to the El Paso road and camped by the roadside. Mother was in the midst of preparing dinner when it became obvious we were in for a violent storm. Eli put up the side curtains on the car and drove us to the highest point he could find on the highway, turning the car with its back end toward the wind. We were all huddled in the car as the rain came in torrents. Lightning came in terrifying flashes. When the storm abated, one of the most violent I ever experienced, we were all thoroughly terrified. Eli somehow drove the car to an empty section house by the railroad track. He had to carry the smaller children through high water to the platform. We spent the night on the floor of the section house, thankful to be alive.

The next day Eli drove us to a place between Balmorhea and Van Horn called Wild Horse Creek, normally a fairly wide dry gulch. I have passed the spot on numerous occasions but have never seen it since with a drop of water in it. But on this occasion, it was a raging torrent. Dozens of cars, all headed west, were waiting to cross.

We waited at this spot for three days until it was safe to pass. Fortunately, Ma had a supply of food and we were able to eat. Other people had to forage for food or hunt rabbits, birds, and other small game. On the second day of our wait, a large car tried to cross. The owner became impatient and hired three cowboys to help him cross. The cowboys tied their ropes to the car and with their horses pulling with all their strength, attempted to guide the car across. The driver got about halfway over before the force of the water swept his car over an edge. He barely got out alive. The yelling cowboys had to cut their ropes to save themselves and their straining horses as the car was swept away.

After three days the water receded rapidly and we were finally able to cross, a double stream of cars moving in two directions over the rock-littered creek bottom. Then we hurried toward El Paso. Once on the paved road near El Paso, we flew at maybe fifty miles an hour.

We spent a day in El Paso visiting with our cousin Harry Spitz and his wife, Hannah. I remember that Eli and I went to visit Harry at his new business, the Overland Furniture Company. When we came out with Harry, he discovered that his car, a Ford Model T roadster, had a flat tire. Harry had no jack and was going to get one, but Eli said that it wasn't necessary. He picked up that end of the car and held it up for Harry to change the tire.

Mother decided that she had had enough car travel for a while and bought tickets on the train to Los Angeles. She was one seat short, however, so Ida had to continue with Eli and me by car. After Mother and the children left on the train, Ida stayed with her cousin Harry while Eli and I were camped in a public campground. There were any number of people in the camp, most with rickety old cars and all their belongings, all headed west for California. This was before the days of the Dust Bowl but even then, in 1923, there were swarms of dispossessed and uprooted people moving west. Eli soon made friends with our neighbors in the campgrounds. One of them had taken the head off the engine of his battered car and was busy grinding the valves. Eli proceeded to take the head off the Dodge and cleaned out all the carbon.

From the general conversation among the people making the trek west, Eli decided to head north before going west, in order to avoid the heat of southern New Mexico and Arizona. We followed the Rio Grande north through small towns founded in the Spanish colonial times, turning off at Springerville, then we joined the main highway somewhere before the Grand Canyon after passing through the Petrified Forest.

As we drove, Eli and Ida argued incessantly and emotionally in Yiddish, which I understood imperfectly. Eli wanted Ida to marry him, but Ida vehemently insisted that she was already engaged to someone else. Eli's attitude and responses varied from impassioned pleas, all the while driving along on terrible dirt roads, to sullen silences. When we got near the Grand Canyon, Eli announced that he wanted to see it and turned off the road to drive an extra two hours or so to get to it. Ida had hoped to get to Los Angeles as soon as possible.

After the Grand Canyon we headed for Needles. As anyone who has been there knows, Needles in midsummer is hotter than Hades. After the coolness of the canyon area, the heat was cruel. Past Needles a few miles, we stopped at a small railroad section house set in a grove of big cottonwoods at a spot called Amboy. Eli joined other travelers waiting for dark in the shade. After resting among the trees for half a day, we started west in a long caravan of cars, stopping at Victorville before descending the mountains to San Bernardino. Eli drove the twisting switchback in daylight.

Once past the mountains, we sped toward Los Angeles on paved roads, where we found Mother waiting for us. Eli was despondent because Ida had rejected him. He announced there were too many people in Los Angeles and left for home the next day. Ida was also angry and announced she was leaving immediately to locate her fiancé and get married. Ma was very disturbed and perplexed, and she was irritated with Ida for leaving.

Once we moved to California, I saw very little of Eli until I returned to Texas in 1939. He would come through Eagle Pass, sometimes with Uncle David, sometimes with several of his friends. They would stop on their way to go camping in the Devils River Canyon near Del Rio. Then he announced that the Devils River country was becoming too crowded. According to Eli if you could see someone else's campfire at night, the place was too crowded and no longer desirable.

Eli came to see Mother frequently, and my parents' apartment was full of life whenever he visited. Sometimes Eli and Mother would laughingly converse in Lithuanian, a language no one else around understood. I'm sure that after all the years since they had left Lithuania, it was an exercise in memory for them. Eli's presence could be heard even in a quiet pursuit. His loud hee-haws reverberated through the house as he sat reading. Whenever Eli was asked to do anything he did not wish to do, he'd say, "It's against my religion." If he was asked to do something to which he was amenable, he would say that he would do it "*mit main tefillin handt,*" with the hand to which phylacteries were bound when an Orthodox Jew says his morning prayer.²⁵

When World War II started, Eli was past draft age, but his "official" age was younger because he had entered the United States illegally on his younger brother David's birth certificate to avoid the Russian army draft. He didn't say a word about it when he was drafted. Eli went to Fresno, California, and he immediately made waves. First, he tried to be assigned to combat duty and was turned down as too old; he was officially forty-five. To prove that he was able to qualify, Eli insisted on going on an overnight forced training march, with the result that he ruined his feet. For the rest of his life, he could walk only with pain and was always seeking shoes that would help, including handmade boots and shoes.

When his attempts to volunteer for active duty failed, Eli went to the captain and advised him that eight men were unnecessary in the mail room. Eli could do all the work himself, freeing the other seven for active duty. Of course, this hardly pleased the captain, whose chance for promotion was based on how many men he had under his command—nor did the prospect of combat thrill the seven enlisted men. Finally, Uncle Eli found something useful to do in the army. There were many Spanish-speaking boys in the camp at Fresno from Texas, New Mexico, Arizona, Colorado, and rural California. Most spoke very little English. There was an official interpreter, a *gachupin* professor who spoke only Castilian. The boys couldn't understand him, nor he the boys. When the boys complained to Eli, he resolved the problem with the wisdom of Solomon. The Spanish-speaking boy explained his problem to Eli in the professor's presence, Eli translated for the boy to the professor, the professor passed the message to the captain, the captain gave the professor his answer, the professor told Eli the response, and Eli gave the captain's decision to the boy. In this way everyone was happy, especially the professor, who was terrified of the alternative, namely combat duty.

Eli did not take part in Jewish community life in the Valley. Once he attended a function of the Jewish congregation in McAllen, where one of the dear ladies asked him why he wasn't wearing a tie. "Can't your rich brother-in-law in Eagle Pass give you a tie?" she asked. "Lady," answered Eli, "a tie is what a horse wears behind him." That settled his social career.

On another occasion, Eli somehow got the responsibility of showing some important visitors to the Valley areas where there was interesting wildlife, including getting permission to go into the King Ranch.²⁶ A short time later, by way of appreciation, Eli received a letter advising that he had been made an honorary member of the Audubon Society. He wrote back that he was sorry, but he was not a society man.

Eli never seemed interested in making a great deal of money or getting rich. Eli once described his furniture business in Weslaco, Texas, as "a dollar down and a dollar whenever I catch you." As soon as he made enough to support his random style of life, he turned his business over to the management of a few employees. He spent most of his time either moving around wherever he felt inclined or setting up on Padre Island in a shack made of driftwood, which met his needs. When the hotels began to build on South Padre Island, a delegation came to Eli and asked him to improve his dwelling place. Eli answered that he was there first and suggested the hotels move.

Eli was a great teller of stories, many of an anticlerical nature. I don't know where he heard them; he didn't drink beer or frequent cantinas. One story I remember concerns a poor Indian who comes to see the village padre.

"Padre, please lend me the image of Jesus," he requested. The padre, of course, was shocked and surprised. "I can't do that. It just isn't done."

"Padre," said the Indian, "it hasn't rained in weeks. My milpa, my field, is burning up from drought. If I don't get rain soon I'll lose my crop and my wife and ten children will starve to death. I have to take the image of Jesus out to the milpa so that we can all pray for rain."

Finally, the padre consented and loaned the Indian the image of Christ out of the church. The Indian went out to his cornfield and prayed for rain. That night there was a terrible storm. The rain poured down in sheets. When the Indian took a look at his field the next morning, he was shocked to learn that everything had been washed away. Nothing was left.

The Indian went back to the padre. "Padre, I want to borrow the image of the Virgin," he said.

"My son," replied the padre, "what's this? Yesterday you borrowed the image of Jesus. Today you want the Virgin. Why?"

"Padre," said the Indian, "I want to take the Virgin out to my milpa to show her what that son of hers did to me."

When Eli passed sixty, he became more and more eccentric. He would arrive unannounced, unload a crate of Rio Grande Valley citrus, and go to visit Mother. Sometimes, as soon as he told his latest stories, he would announce that he was ready to go home. It would take all of Mother's power of persuasion to get him to stay for the night. From his youth he suffered from high blood pressure. He had medication he was supposed to take, but most of the time he ignored it. He must have had a series of small strokes. Finally, he could no longer take care of himself and ended his days in a nursing home, a sad end for a most unusual man.

Eli's younger brother David was his exact opposite. Where Eli was rough and brash, David was shy and retiring. At the end of World War I, the German free companies, private military groups that had taken over after the retreat of the German regular army, adopted the practice of conscripting able-bodied civilians to dig trenches on the Russian and Polish fronts. David was a powerfully built blond, about five feet, nine inches in height, and spoke German. Not at all the stereotype of the European Jew, he looked more like a German than most Germans, which may have saved his life.

David had been very much in love with a cousin. She denied him, however, and refused to venture through war-torn Europe to the United States to be with him, preferring to make her way to Paris instead. Although a handsome man, David never considered marriage again. Interestingly, in the Edelstein-Fried family there were many marriages of first and second cousins; it seems to have been a family trait. I think this occurred in great measure because in the old country there was a lack of mobility. One knew people from at most fifty miles around, and these were usually relatives who saw each other on all sorts of family gatherings. A wedding or other simcha was a big family event, and families were very close-knit.[27] My paternal grandparents were first cousins. Eli and David both fell in love with first cousins, and when they were turned down neither ever looked at another girl. They both died bachelors.

CHAPTER 6

LOS ANGELES

In Eagle Pass, even boys in the higher grades were wearing knee britches buckled below the knee over long white socks. When we moved to Los Angeles and I entered school, I appeared wearing this attire. All the other boys in Los Angeles were wearing pants. Not only that, but over the summer I had undertaken a spurt of growth, and I wore knee britches several sizes too small, so I gave the impression of something between Ichabod Crane and a stork. Until I was sent some pants from the store in Eagle Pass, my days at school were not exactly pleasant.

An exception to such unpleasantness was Miss Ida Bel Eby, who turned out to be the finest teacher in my many years at school. In a way she ruined me for college, since I expected my college professors to be of equivalent quality.[1] When I first enrolled in Roosevelt High School on the Eastside of Los Angeles, I signed up for a world history class.[2] The next day I changed my mind, because the semester before, in junior high, I had gotten credit for a year of world history by exam. My friend Saul Rittenberg was signed up for a class in Latin at the same time, so I decided to change to Latin also.

I was assigned a seat in the very back, sat down, and waited. Miss Eby, our teacher, began to call the roll. As each name was called, the student answered something incomprehensible to me. I nudged the boy sitting in front of me and asked what the word was that I was supposed to answer. That devil replied with a word that didn't make sense, but when in Rome do as the crazy Romans do. At the very last my name was called, and I cried out "hot soup." A stern Miss Eby called me to her desk and demanded if I thought I was funny. It took a while for me to discover that the correct reply was *adsum*, meaning "present."

Under Miss Eby I took four years of Latin and studied Aurelius, Cicero, Ovid, Terence, Plautus, and Virgil. She also persuaded Miss Dozier, a teacher in another field, to teach me Greek after school, and I read Xenophon's *Anabasis*. In Miss Eby's classes we were taught much more than so many lines per day of some long-dead author. We were given insight into the society in which the writer lived. We were taught something about the structure of good style. Not only did we learn to scan poetry, but we had to write poetry ourselves. I remember how, starting with the description of Rumor in the *Iliad*, she read us the same lines in translation in Latin, Italian, and English as used by Virgil, Dante, and Tennyson.

Even the best teacher has no luck with some students. One day, one of the best students was reading a comic book in class. Miss Eby had him come forward and spend the remainder of the hour in a Socratic dialogue on the difference between good literature and comic books. Why is one book so enduring and another trash?

Miss Eby and I became very good friends. With Mother's permission, I invited her to our Friday-night dinner, and for years I visited her at her home. Once she gave me a tongue-lashing because I did so poorly in my first years in college. When I tried to explain my problem, her answer was that this was no good excuse to waste my life.

She traveled every summer throughout Europe. She described how she had gone to France with the high-school French teacher. That teacher had insisted that she alone should do the talking as she was better qualified. Upon their arrival at the rail station in Paris, the French teacher directed the taxi driver to take them to their hotel. The taxi driver couldn't understand a word and demanded to know if anyone spoke French. Finally, Miss Eby intervened, and in the French she had learned by experience in her travels she succeeded in getting them to their destination, to the humiliation of the French teacher. I might say that we had a similar experience in Oaxaca when my wife Ruth had to act as an interpreter for the head of the Spanish department of Tulsa High School. The ability to conjugate a verb does little good in an emergency.

One of Miss Eby's last trips took place when she was at least eighty. She sent me a postcard she wrote on a bus on the way to Kyiv. Finally, she retired to a nursing home in Cupertino, California, where I visited her for a short time before her death. To paraphrase the *Pirkei Avot*, or the *Ethics of the Fathers*, I honor her memory because of what she taught me.[3] Would that there were a multitude of teachers like her in America! She was not a beautiful woman, far from it, but she was beautiful when she taught.

MR. MIRKIN

Soon after we settled in Los Angeles, Mother secured a Hebrew teacher for me, Mr. Abraham Mirkin.[4] On his business cards he called himself "Reverend." I suppose Mr. Mirkin had attended a yeshivah in his youth, a Jewish academy, but he had never managed to obtain a certificate of ordination, called a *semikhah*, which would allow him to call himself a rabbi. As far as I was concerned, he had two duties: to teach me Hebrew and to prepare me for my bar mitzvah. I was twelve years old, which gave me about a year of preparation. At first, I was in an after-school class along with about ten other boys who were also in the elementary stage of learning Hebrew. Most of the boys were there at the insistence of their parents; as soon as they learned a smattering of the language and their bar mitzvah was over, their parents were satisfied and the boys quit. That, sadly, is what happens with most children today, and in my opinion is at the bottom of much that is wrong with the condition of Judaism in the United States today.

I was joined in my Hebrew class by my neighbor Saul Rittenberg. We were not only close friends, but were classmates in Miss Eby's Latin classes for three years. Saul was an outstanding student, and after a while we practically ran the class ourselves, Mr. Mirkin serving to guide us in our translations. Saul later became an outstanding member of the California bar, the dean of experts in entertainment law.[5]

As part of the class, we attended services on Friday nights and Saturday mornings. Most of the time we attended the Breed Street Shul, the largest Orthodox synagogue in Los Angeles.[6] Not a word of English was used, the service was in Hebrew, and if the rabbi gave a *droshe*, a sermon, it was in Yiddish. Coming from an environment with few Jews, I was struck by the seeming chaos of the service. Men would go right on talking or come in and go out while the cantor was chanting. Latecomers would start from page one, swaying back and forth and chanting loudly for their own benefit, all while the hazan was performing the service on page fifty.[7]

Riskind family portrait, Los Angeles, ca. 1924. Top row: Bess and Morris. Bottom row: Reuben, Rachel, Sarah, Michael, and Ruth. (Courtesy of the Reuben S. Riskind Family.)

We also attended various small congregations made up of Jews from diverse European backgrounds. All of these used various accents of Ashkenazi Hebrew.[8] The worst accent among these were the Galitzianer, the Jews from Galicia in Austrian Poland. On one occasion, for Simchat Torah, the celebration of the giving of the Law, we attended a service in a Hasidic synagogue. By the time the service was over, the entire congregation was dancing all around the synagogue, some of them in an ecstatic trance.[9]

The most famous hazan of the time was Yossele Rosenblatt. I had the good fortune to hear him perform a Saturday service at the Breed Street Shul. He had an exceptional, lyrical tenor voice and chanted with a sense of timing to emphasize the meaning of the words. My only criticism was that at times he employed a falsetto, which might have been typical of Eastern European cantors, but which I could have done without. Many lesser old-time cantors seem to have been spoiled by listening to Italian opera and tried to emulate the tenors.[10]

As I came to understand the words of the Hebrew services, I began to enjoy them. Most of the language is magnificent, furnishing a libretto of the first order, fitting for Bach. The trouble is that often it is simply butchered. Of all the services I attended with Mr. Mirkin, the ones that I enjoyed most were at the Talmud Torah, an elementary Hebrew school.[11] The principal, Mr. Moses Tolchinsky, had recently come from Poland, where his family had been killed in a pogrom.[12] He had an excellent voice and sang the words of the service with no frills, allowing the language of the psalms and prayers to speak for themselves. I do not ordinarily care for choirs used in the service. However, in this case, Tolchinsky had organized the boys into a choir, not to interfere with the service, but to sing the responses. In some cases, such as the medieval hymn *Adon Olam*, "Lord of the World," the chorus sang alone.[13]

I can recall only two instances of services I enjoyed as much. One was in Jerusalem at the Har El synagogue. It was considered radical because men and women sat together, women participated in the service, and the entire congregation sang the responses. The other was at the Harvard Hillel, which I attended with my son Peter one Rosh Hashanah.[14] At this service, the hazan was a young woman who had a beautiful contralto voice and enunciated the Hebrew perfectly. I would guess that her father had been a cantor and had trained her.

A major part of my first year with Mr. Mirkin was occupied with preparing for my bar mitzvah. I had to learn to chant the benedictions both before and after the Torah is read, and I learned the *trope*, the musical notations for chanting the section from the Prophets to be read on the date of my bar mitzvah. In my case, I was to chant the opening chapter of the Book of Isaiah. When I later studied Latin in high school and read Cicero, I could not help but compare his invective with that of Isaiah—and the result was very unfavorable to Cicero. His denunciation of Catiline cannot begin to compare with Isaiah.[15] I finally learned to read and chant the service without any mistakes. The trouble was that my voice could only be described as "sour," and my chanting came out as a variety of croak.

The final step was to prepare my speech. This was in Hebrew, written by the Reverend Mr. Mirkin himself. In later years, I prepared some twenty boys and a few girls from Eagle Pass for the ceremony. I always insisted that the boy or girl write the speech themselves. After all, it wasn't my bar mitzvah.

My bar mitzvah was held at the Jewish Home for the Aged, then on Boyle Avenue in Los Angeles, a few blocks from where I lived.[16] The synagogue had a raised platform in the middle of the room, fenced in by a low railing, very unlike most synagogues in the United States but similar to some of the old European buildings. I was called up, recited the first blessing, listened to the reader chant the section from the Torah, then proceeded with my part of the ceremony. I gave my speech to an audience of blank-faced old men and women, very few of whom, I am sure, understood enough Hebrew to follow Mr. Mirkin's speech.

To Mother's surprise and delight, I continued my Hebrew studies for three years after my bar mitzvah. I had read so much ancient history and heard so many Bible stories from Mother that I was anxious to learn. The experience of reading the Tanakh, the Hebrew Bible, was one of the great experiences of my life. Since the days of my initial Hebrew studies, I have had a keen interest in translations of the Old Testament.[17] None of them equal the King James translation, a great work of literature in its own right. It is writing of the greatest felicity and has an archaic quality matching that of the Hebrew. No translation, however, can equal the beauty of the Hebrew text.

Strangely, in some instances where the Hebrew is rather ponderous, the King James is beautiful; sometimes both original and translation are writings of the first order but are two quite different pieces of literature. Modern translations are more accurate and give the original meaning with more clarity, but as literature they are sadly lacking. The latest translation published by the Jewish Publication Society is an example. Perhaps it should be read along with King James. Because of its archaic English, the King James can have strange or humorous readings. My choice example is from the Book of Judges: "Speak, ye that ride on white asses, ye that sit in judgment, and walk by the way."[18]

Mr. Mirkin taught us only a minimum of Hebrew grammar. We began reading the Hebrew by plunging into the text. Since the narrative parts of the Tanakh have a limited vocabulary and, for the most part, a repetitive grammatical structure, it is possible to translate most of the narrative with minimal knowledge. It is a different story when reading the Prophets or the Book of Job. They are far more difficult to translate. We had been studying the Tanakh for several years before I ever saw a Hebrew grammar. It happened that Saul was taking a social sciences course from John Sholtz, a prominent Jewish educator in Los Angeles and later my father-in-law. Mr. Sholtz loaned him a Hebrew grammar, and in turn, Saul loaned it to me. I found the grammar most complex. Perhaps we were fortunate in not having studied grammar early in our studies. We could not conjugate a verb, but we had read most of the Tanakh.

When we read the Prophets, most of our time was spent in reading Isaiah, and this book made a profound impression on me. The part that critics call First Isaiah is the most powerful writing I have ever read.[19] When God speaks, there is no question it is God speaking. No one else in my experience has written so convincingly. Of Isaiah's prophecies, the one that influences us the most today is a brief prediction of a perfect world in which war would be no more. This vision, diluted in Christianity and still more in Marxism, has tantalized Western man to this day. I have often wondered how many devoted radical leftists know they are disciples of Isaiah at third hand.

I am reminded of the disputation forced on the Jewish scholar Nachmanides. The Dominicans challenged him to a debate before the king of Aragon, James I. The topic: Was Jesus not the messiah predicted by the prophet Isaiah? Nachmanides was in a precarious position. He said he did not doubt that Jesus was the true messiah of the Christians, but as far as Jews are concerned, he could not be the messiah promised by Isaiah since he did not answer the description. The Jewish messiah, according to Isaiah, would bring a perfect world and an end to war. It was evident to all that the world was far from perfect and war was raging in all parts of the world. Alfonso the Wise ruled that Nachmanides had won the debate—then he ordered Nachmanides to leave Spain immediately. I was once asked to speak to a church group on the subject of why Jews do not accept Jesus. I thought of Nachmanides and decided to beg off.[20]

As I see it, the Tanakh contains the evolution of religious thought since neolithic times. The Book of Genesis is a gold mine of information concerning the early days of civilization. There are those who point to ideas from the most primitive days of this evolution and can see only a God of cruelty and vengeance. Gandhi did this: to him the Jewish God was a monster. He said the Holocaust was the Jews' great opportunity to show the moral force of passive resistance.[21] I know what my mother would say by way of answer. There is a Yiddish expression she sometimes used to the effect that the Jewish people would readily relinquish this honor to Gandhi and his followers.

Some religions set forth the idea that the ultimate good is for the individual—by himself and only for himself—to attain enlightenment. The Bible offers a contrasting program. The message of the Tanakh is a simple one. There is one God, who insists and demands a world of social justice here and now, not in the next world; a world of kindness and consideration for our fellow men including the stranger in our midst; a world in which we are our brother's keeper. If the world is far from perfect, it is our fault, not God's. We are not born in sin. The world is good. If man makes a shambles of it, then he must cure himself. God operates in and through history. Man exists in society. As an individual concerned only with himself, he is worth nothing. Also, the Jews are a chosen people, a nation of priests given the task, whether they like it or not, to teach these ideas to the rest of mankind.

Many scholars have objected that these teachings have had unfortunate results for the Jewish people. The prophets constantly denounced the Jewish people for their deficiencies, insisting on a level of conduct superior to that of their neighbors. Certainly, the Jews were far from perfect; however, a double standard of conduct was created that exists today. "The Jews are a terrible people, doesn't the Good Book say so repeatedly?" And at the same time, they are expected to set an example today better than anyone else. The Germans and the Japanese are forgiven for their errors but not Israel.

The final period of our studies with Mr. Mirkin covered a number of tractates of the Mishnah.[22] We started with the readings of the *Pirkei Avot*, the *Ethics of the Fathers*. These pithy sayings of the early rabbis were a joy to read. The most famous of these are the words of the great Jewish sage, Rabbi Hillel: "If I am not for myself, who will be for me? If I am only for myself, what am I? And if not now, when?"[23] It was also apparent to me from reading the Mishnah that the early rabbis, or Pharisees if you wish to call them that, had much free discussion in their schools and arrived at majority and minority opinions that are remembered and recorded. They developed a system of logic of their own, an idea they must have gotten from the Greeks.[24] What I object to is their attitude toward educating women. I understand their reason, which arose from the ancient struggle to rid Judaism of the fertility cults; however, it is a tragedy that nothing was learned from the example of Rabbi Meir, who, having no sons, educated his daughters.[25]

In later years, it also occurred to me that the rabbis of the Talmud and their antecedents were quite revolutionary. Their egalitarian ideas led to universal education, at least for men. "An ignorant man cannot be truly religious." A father was enjoined to start the education of his male children at age five. No age limit was set for an end to education. A man should continue to study as long as he lives. This insistence on mass education has had a profound effect on the Jewish people and their influence on Western society and culture to this day. Education and learning are the right of everyone, not only of those who gain them by reason of wealth or birth into a priestly class. Even today in a secular society, the culture established by the ancient scholars influences young Jewish men and women to pursue higher education.

LOUIE RITTENBERG

I soon found another teacher, less traditional than Mr. Mirkin, but who would also influence my learning. My friend Saul Rittenberg lived in a house on Hollenbeck Street facing the park.[26] Their house was directly behind ours, and both families were constantly together. The family included Saul's mother, Mrs. Rittenberg, who was a widow, Saul, his brother Syd, his sister Bea, and his uncle Louie Rittenberg, a middle-aged bachelor. Whenever I came over in the evening, Louie would be reading in a comfortable chair.[27] He had little formal education but read widely, mostly in history and economics. I can recall seeing such books in his hands as Gibbon's *Decline and Fall of the Roman Empire* and Trotsky's *History of the Russian Revolution*. Louie would interrupt his reading from time to time to make observations on the contemporary scene. This was in the days of the Coolidge and Hoover administrations. He was laudatory in speaking of Russia and thought that a revolution here in the United States was inevitable, even not too far off.

Every weekday morning, Louie would take the Fourth Street car to downtown Los Angeles. He spent his mornings in the brokerage office of Hutton & Company, where he worked as a small-time trader. Then he would go to Pershing Square, at that time the local Hyde Park.[28] All sorts of radicals and political crackpots gathered there: communists, Trotskyites, socialists, single-taxers, plus members of splinter groups.[29] Some, like Louie, just met with cronies on a park bench and talked. Others, Hyde Park–style, harangued anyone who would listen. In the background lurked "Red" Hynes of the city Red Squad.[30] Hynes saw revolution brewing under every bed. Sometimes Hynes and his goons would raid the park, arresting everyone unfortunate enough to be there for any reason at all. On such occasions, Louie would phone to advise the Rittenbergs that he would be home late. On his release, like a returning hero, he would recount his experiences as a dangerous radical.

My parents were very friendly with the Rittenbergs. Mother decided that since there was a famous scholar in Kalvaria named Rittenberg and our neighbors came from a village nearby, they must be related. As for Louie's ideas, my parents did not take them seriously. For my part, I had never heard or read such ideas, and hearing Louie expound on them prepared me for later experiences at the university.

Louie unwittingly played an ignoble role in an important Riskind event. When my older sister Bess was married, she insisted on a big wedding at the Beverly Hills Hotel.[31] For the reception in the ballroom, Pa bought some cases of real Scotch from a "reputable" bootlegger at a fancy price. While the ceremony went on in one room, the cases of scotch were stacked up behind the bar in the ballroom, and Pa stationed Louie there with the admonition to guard this treasure with his life. After some delay, the ceremony went on without a hitch, "Oh, Promise Me" was sung, and the crowd stampeded to the ballroom and bar. But Pa received a crushing blow. Louie was sound asleep, all five feet six of him stretched out on the floor behind the bar, snoring, his face ruddy, his glasses still perched on his nose. As for the treasure, it had disappeared lock, stock, and bottles, except for one empty.

MY SOUR SIXTEEN

In the summer of 1927, at the age of sixteen, I enrolled at the University of California at Los Angeles, but my time there started inauspiciously. I had gone through junior high and high school in four years. I was president of the honor society and had been chosen by the faculty as an Ephebian, one of those expected to make a mark in the world and to be an outstanding citizen of the city. As I look back at my disastrous career at UCLA, it appears to me that the fault was mine. I was just too young and naive to enter a major university.

I advise my own children, please do not send your children to a large school before they are mentally and emotionally prepared for the transition. Either send them out to work for a year or to a small college where there are personal relationships and small classes. Even to an older and more mature student, the first years of a large, impersonal university can be devastating. At UCLA, I was ignored. I was a sort of zombie, an inconsequential sixteen-year-old kid to whom no one said as much as hello. All the girls were older, and to them I did not exist. I had thought of myself as homely—now I was convinced of it. No Jewish fraternity took notice of me.

Even my classes were no help. At this point in my life, I have no awe of professors, having learned better. Besides, two of my sons are professors, and I know their failings well. But I arrived at UCLA with the misconception that my professors would all be sages with long beards, uttering words of profound wisdom. I signed up for a Greek class on Homer's *Odyssey*. Based on my experience with Miss Eby, I expected this to be a most exciting class, but no such luck. Every day, we were given so many lines to translate, and each line was mechanically translated. Nothing was said regarding the historical background or literary criticism. If we came to any lines that might be classified as the least bit naughty, as the story of Vulcan trapping his wife Aphrodite in the act of having sex with Ares, they were omitted from the lesson.

One of the worst disappointments came from my class in beginning political science. The professor seemed to think it was his duty to utterly destroy any preconceived ideas or values the class held, and to replace these values he offered nothing. He scoffed at religion, political parties, and the existence of right or wrong or any morality whatsoever. He would pick out particularly naive students, submit them to Socratic questioning, and make them objects of ridicule. To make matters worse, there was a student of about twenty-five years of age in the class who was an official in the local communist party. The professor fawned over him, and his remarks were treated with profound respect. He was excused from the final exam and given an A. I later learned that this individual was caught red-handed (pun intended) dealing in stolen goods and sent to prison.

I also enrolled in a course in logic, thinking that this would be a good way to begin to study philosophy. This was a lecture class with some five hundred students, taught by the head of the philosophy department. I never found out what the purpose of logic was or the role it played in the development of Western thought. The big moment of the course was the dean's annual discourse on the True Meaning of Christmas. The class for which I had had such high expectations turned out to be somewhere between a joke and a waste of time.

From listening to Louie Rittenberg, I had acquired an interest in learning something about economics. This was another lecture class of five hundred students, held in a small auditorium and taught by the head of the department. The professor stood on a dais and, in a monotone so dry it raised dust, would lecture like this: "Today we take up the Industrial Revolution: 1, 2, 3, 4, 5. We have now covered the Industrial Revolution. And so we shall move on to 1, 2, 3. Incidentally, there was a man named Karl Marx who wrote a book called *Das Kapital*. He was of no real importance. Pay no attention to him."

There was one course I did truly enjoy, taught by the provost of UCLA. Ernest Carroll Moore was a rather big man with a large head, on top of which perched a black Homburg hat.[32] He wore horn-rimmed glasses that made him look like an owl. He would walk around the campus in a seemingly aimless fashion and was ridiculed by the students behind his back as he passed by. He gave a series of orientation lectures to entering freshmen on the purpose of a college education. He read excerpts from Plato's *Apology* and from Crito dealing with the trial and death of Socrates. I had read references to these philosophers but had never been exposed to their ideas. Socrates, as a person, impressed me as being in the same category as the Hebrew Prophets. A new world opened to me.

Nevertheless, by the end of my first year at UCLA I was approaching a state of depression. My grades were mostly C's. I just couldn't study and had no interest in my schoolwork. Two things saved me: I spent the summer reading, and I took up tennis.

I began by reading every work by Plato in the library. I read *Republic*, especially his discussion of justice, with pleasure. I was bewildered by his description of the ideal society, which I found too regimented; years later I sympathized with Bertrand Russell's analysis of the *Republic* as a form of fascism, although that view may be perhaps too strong.[33] I contrasted Plato with Isaiah's vision of a perfect future society in which war would be no more.[34] The ancient rabbis amplified that idea by placing the scholars at the top of society, with no mention of the military caste. In Plato, first come the philosophers, then the warriors: the philosophers are assumed to be part of the military, and war is taken for granted since the ideal society is the Greek polis, the city-state, constantly at war with its neighbors.

After Plato's *Republic*, I began reading a list of utopian works. I think the most interesting of all, although naive, was Bellamy's *Looking Backward*.[35] The example of Soviet Russia has cured me of utopian fantasies or any belief in a quick fix to the ills of our society. Miss Eby once showed me a copy of George Bernard Shaw's *An Intelligent Woman's Guide to Socialism*, indicating that she thought it an insult to talk down to women as though they were inferior beings.[36] Shaw himself didn't prove very intelligent when he made his trip to Soviet Russia and was duped by Stalin. He returned to Britain to announce that Russia was well on the way to becoming the utopia of the future—at a time when Stalin was killing millions of innocent people.

I read much else that summer vacation, and for years to follow, in the field of economics. Louie Rittenberg had mentioned Henry George's *Progress and Poverty*, which I found to be a lucid exposition of classical capitalism except that his proposal for a single tax on the value of rent as a panacea seemed to be dated.[37] I read some of Adam Smith and John Stuart Mill, and I jumped to Karl Marx's *Das Capital*. I frankly had difficulty in following and wondered if Marx himself understood it. Later I read the writings of the Fabian socialists such as Cole and Laski. When I became a farmer and rancher and then a businessman, the glaring errors of Marx and the Fabians became apparent.[38]

I have a habit of reading two or three books at once. At the same time I was reading Plato or economics, I was reading Gibbon's *Decline and Fall of the Roman Empire*, Herodotus, and Thucydides's *History of the Peloponnesian War*, followed by Livy and Polybius. I particularly enjoyed Thucydides, whom I regard as the historian par excellence.[39] I read all of Darwin I could find in the library, and I have been fascinated by the study of primitive man and early civilizations ever since.

After Plato I tried Aristotle, whom I found dull. Then I read Spinoza and Maimonides, the twelfth-century Jewish sage.[40] I was most impressed by Maimonides as a man. I still wonder, how in the world did he find time to accomplish so much in one lifetime? He was a leading physician of his time, with a busy medical practice; codified Jewish law, which would be a full-time career for any scholar; acted as the spiritual leader for the Jews of a large part of the world; wrote a volume of responsa, scholarly Jewish commentaries, profoundly and beautifully addressed to Jewish communities in widely scattered areas giving sensible, practical advice; and yet he wrote *The Guide for the Perplexed*—this is what I find difficult to understand. The man must have worked day and night. What is astounding to me is the completely modern approach he took to analyze the origin of ancient Jewish religious practices. He was truly a remarkable man.[41]

As I think back to my reading, the thinker who made the most sense to me was a writer forgotten in our time by the name of Vilfredo Pareto. He was an Italian sociologist who proposed that society is influenced not by rational ideas but by what he called "residues."[42] A certain course of action that has its origin long before, under completely different conditions and ideas, continues to motivate people even though the original events have long since been forgotten. We are motivated by these residues, which may have no logical relation to the present situation. This is true of Christians versus Jews, French versus English, Mexicans versus Americans, and so on. There are cultural differences and animosities resulting from a long history, and these residues explain events better than Marxist economics or Freudian analysis.

Besides books, I proceeded to cure myself of depression through tennis. It happened that the varsity tennis courts on the old UCLA campus were located near the classroom buildings. Every day I would watch the team practice, sometimes standing there for hours at a time. I had played tennis of a piddly variety in high school and at the nearby public courts. After watching the college team, I decided to learn the game properly. I approached Bill Ackerman, the coach and the tennis pro at one of the smaller country clubs, for private lessons, and I embarked on a series of lessons for something like four or five dollars a week, a laughable sum based on the present-day prices. I soon learned the fundamentals of the forehand, backhand, serve, and volley. I could tell that Bill had no hopes that I would ever make much of a player. At the end of my series, he left me with the advice to go out and keep practicing.

The interesting and strange thing about any sport is that one can play for years and never improve beyond a certain point. On the other hand, some people seem to have a natural aptitude. My brother Reuben would follow me out to the tennis court, and at the age of eight, by holding the racket halfway up the handle, he picked up the game without any effort. Soon he was beating most of the older boys and then many of the men.

I entered Reuben in a major under-thirteen juniors' tournament in Santa Monica. He easily won every match until the finals, when he met a boy named Bobby Riggs.[43] Reuben was tall and thin; Riggs was smaller and wiry. Reuben took the offensive, expecting to win easily. Riggs was like a jackrabbit, running all over the court and sending the ball back. I became so excited that I began yelling instruction and encouragement. The tournament director came out, gave me a dressing down, and warned that if I opened my mouth again, I would be ushered off the grounds. I kept quiet. Reuben lost in three long, hard-fought sets. This was the beginning of a rivalry that was joined by another boy by the name of Joe Hunt. For the next five or six years, the three were rivals in every Southern California tournament. In the semifinals, Reuben would meet either Hunt or Riggs and would be beaten in three hard-fought sets. Then, in the finals, Riggs would beat Hunt. The loss was no disgrace to Reuben, though. As soon as they were out of juniors, first Riggs then Hunt became men's national champions, and Riggs also won at Wimbledon.

I became hooked on tennis to the extent that I neglected my schoolwork. I happened to make friends who were exceptional tennis players. At first, they played tennis with me as a favor, but I improved rapidly against such competition, and soon enough I became a good practice partner, and they did not object to playing with me frequently. I could have become a good player except that I lacked stamina. I was slightly under six feet tall but weighed 135 pounds. Against an equal opponent with superior stamina, I could not make the effort required in the third set. In a close match, I would be exhausted. Today, one would jog to improve stamina, lift weights to strengthen muscles, and stuff oneself to gain weight. I would play all day with nothing to eat but an Eskimo pie.

One of my friends was Frank Westsmith, a UCLA star. Frank and I looked remarkably alike, except that he was three inches taller. He had a vicious serve, a good volley, and beautiful ground strokes. Frank and another friend, Orv Shotz, with whom I played frequently, had won many doubles titles. One day when I had acquired considerable skill as a player I was playing at some event and noticed that a small crowd of spectators had gathered. I was very flattered, thinking that they had come over to watch me play. My ego was deflated when I heard one of the bystanders say, "I don't know what's the matter with Frank. He's not playing as well as usual today."

MY BRIEF, INGLORIOUS MILITARY CAREER

When I enrolled at UCLA in 1927, two years of training in the Reserve Officers' Training Corps (ROTC) was mandatory.[44] This was during the days of the Oxford peace movement, and morale in ROTC was not good.[45] There was so much protest that compulsory ROTC was finally abolished—after I left and just in time for World War II. In addition to drill, we were taught how to clean and assemble our weapon, an old Springfield rifle. We were given a short period of target shooting, we had classes in map reading using ordinary and topographical maps, and we learned the use of the compass, either by itself or in coordination with maps. I did quite well at this phase of the work. I was already accustomed to caring for a rifle, and I was a fairly good shot, although we were required to shoot while tangled up in the rifle sling, which was supposed to give added support and to steady one's aim. I can't imagine anyone in the heat of combat using a gun sling as we were taught. As far as maps were concerned, I had always been interested in reading maps from hiking in the mountains, and I found that information practical as well as useful.

It was the drill that was not my strong point. I felt a resentment against the regimentation involved. It was as though we were being forced to participate in a structured, unthinking mass. Three days a week we were required to appear in uniform for an hour's drill. I believe that in World War II the type of drill was changed, but in my time, we learned the old, more involved system from the days of the Civil War, marching in columns or forming a line of skirmishers. Among other things, we were trained to form into phalanxes and fire in volleys, as though this antique system of making war was still practical. For my part, I was in the second line of the squad. All I did was follow the man in front of me without bothering to learn correctly.

At the end of each school year, we had a grand review of the corps. Our battalion was made up of two regiments. For weeks we practiced. The band played Sousa marches, student officers pranced in their shiny boots and swords, and we were polished to perfection. It was an exhilarating time as we went swinging along like West Point cadets. Then came the day of the review. The stand of the football field was filled. In front were members of the university brass, together with military uniforms of all sorts, even a French officer with a chest full of decorations. The band struck up a march, and the parade was due to begin.

In front were the color guards. Immediately behind was my squad. As second-year men, we had the honor of leading the parade. At this exciting moment, a catastrophe occurred. The squad corporal, who was supposed to step out on command and then pivot in a left turn to march around the athletic field, had a nosebleed. He poured blood all over his uniform in an uncontrolled stream. Everything was halted, the corporal was rushed off the field, and the next man behind him—me—moved up. The further catastrophe was that I hadn't any idea what to do. As soon as order was restored, the band struck up "Semper Fidelis," the commander barked out an order, and I was supposed to start, then make my pivot. Unfortunately, my manner of pivoting was not according to the book, and in an instant my squad was in a state of confusion. An officer dashed up, I was yanked out, order was restored again, and the cadets marched off. The remainder of the parade was very hazy to me.

I TRANSFER TO USC

In my junior year I transferred to the University of Southern California. USC was a small school, financed in large measure by football money. Although USC's School of Liberal Arts had no reputation and was scorned by students at UCLA, the law school was considered the best in the area, and I was planning on going to law school. This was not my choice, but my father's decision. When I told him that my interest was in ancient languages, he vetoed my wish, saying that this was no business for a Jewish boy. Later, when I was already enrolled in law school, he announced that I should transfer to medical school. The Depression was well under way, and he had been told that lawyers were starving but doctors were still doing well. I refused to change since I would have had to take chemistry and biology first as prerequisites. I learned later that I should have taken his advice. I was young, and another few years would have mattered little.

My classes at USC were small and the instruction surprisingly good. I began to enjoy my classes, and my grades improved to all A's. Every Friday, after my last class, I spent at least an hour in the library reading newspapers from all over the United States and some from England and France. What was apparent was a wide difference in the facts reported in the various papers. In the *Daily Worker*, the police and hired thugs of the Ford Company were beating up striking workers, none of whom had lifted a finger in violence.[46] In the *Chicago Tribune*, hordes of violent strikers were beating up the police trying to maintain order. In the *New York Times*, the strikers were being led foolishly by union bosses, but it was true that Ford "security" was behaving with excessive brutality. In the *London Times* the French Foreign Office was up to no good. In *Le Temps* of Paris everything wrong in the world was the fault of the British, who among other misdeeds, in all parts of the world, were conniving with the Germans against France.

I began to be highly skeptical of the veracity of the press. Then, when I began to do the same with political magazines, I found them no better. When it came to something truly controversial, such as the Spanish Civil War, it was exceedingly difficult to learn the facts. My conclusion from all this reading was that it is probably impossible to arrive at the absolute truth, but with diligence one can reach a fairly accurate picture.

Across from USC is Exposition Park. Whenever I had a few hours to spare I walked to the Los Angeles County Museum, which at that time housed an art collection in addition to its exhibit of paleontology from the La Brea Tar Pits. The art collection was small but did contain some fine works, including Monet's famous water lilies. By studying the exhibit brochures and publications, I managed to learn a considerable amount about art and after a time began to go to private exhibits. Since that time, I have gone to museums all over the world, and they are still the greatest attraction when I visit a city. While I attended law school, I also discovered the philosophy library across the street, which held a philosophy forum every Tuesday afternoon at which members of the faculty or visiting speakers gave dissertations on various subjects.[47]

I have always been amused by people who join Mensa or some such organization and spend the rest of their lives in narcissistic self-admiration and little else.[48] To me, the creative person is to be admired above all else. All my life I have wanted to create, without success. An original idea, a work of art, a great musical composition, a literary work, a scientific discovery—such were what I admired and hoped to emulate. In my education, I tried to emulate the Renaissance man: to know something about the world around me rather than concentrate in one narrow field. My only accomplishment in my youth was to become a walking encyclopedia, like a human version of the *Jeopardy* program. Of originality I showed little, to my frustration and bitter disappointment.

At the University of Southern California, I took a graduate test in two parts. The first session was the general information test. Early the next morning, I was to continue with an intelligence test. The night before the second test I took part in a bridge game and at midnight, when I wanted to quit, there was a howl of protest. I had to continue, and unfortunately, I continued to win, and the game lasted until the early hours. When I arrived at the university for the test at 8 a.m., I kept awake with difficulty. The test was a blur. I finished as best I could and returned home to sleep.

About six months later, I was called into the psychology department. I was ushered to a seat in the designated office and sat there for some minutes under the stare of a man seated behind the desk. "Mr. Riskind," said the man. "I wanted to meet you. I can't understand your tests. You made the highest score on the general information test anyone has ever made since we started giving them. In almost every field, your score was as good as majors in that field. But," he said, stopping and looking at me again, "in the intelligence test you were barely average. I wanted to meet you." Sometimes when I think over my life and some of the stupid things that I have done, perhaps the test was right. I did not play bridge again for many years.

LAW SCHOOL AND AFTER

You may well ask, if I were playing tennis, reading so much outside material, going to art exhibits, playing bridge, and so on, when did I study? How did I manage to get through law school? My freshman law class was quite large, with more than three hundred students. By the time the second year started, the class had shrunk by half. I did fairly well, actually, after a fashion. In my freshman year I got a C in what was supposed to be a cinch course, Legal Ethics, taught by an old judge. This, and some other stupidity, kept me off the law review, which might have been my salvation.

Teaching Contracts was a gray-haired man, Professor Orville P. Cockerill.[49] "Cocky," as the class called him, would rock back and forth on his heels with his fingertips pressed together at the level of his waist while he mumbled his lecture. The class would soon be lulled into a somnambulant state. "The test under the law," Cocky would say, "is what would a reasonable man do?" Then he would let out a roar, causing the drowsy class to jump a foot out of their seats. "A reasonable man? Have any of you ever met a reasonable man? Is there such a thing as a reasonable man?"

Another teacher I remember with much respect is Professor William Burby, who taught Property Law, reputed to be the most difficult course taught in law school.[50] I made an A, perhaps because I enjoyed the instructor, perhaps because of my knowledge of medieval history and feudalism. Burby terrorized the class. When he walked into the room, the class shivered so badly that the floor shook. Burby had a long, thin face. When he grinned, he could have passed for the wolf when he met Little Red Riding Hood. Woe betide the poor devil who was called on to recite. More than any other professor, Burby taught us how to analyze in legal terms.

In most of my courses, I was able to judge when I would be called on to recite, in which case I was well prepared. Otherwise, I took notes in class, both on the recitation of the student called on, and on the professor's comments and heckling. I made A's in some of the most difficult classes because I was interested in the subject matter or enjoyed the professor. All in all, I wasn't too far down the grade list. To say that I had a burning desire to become a lawyer was not the case. Considering the conditions by the time I graduated, during the Depression, I would have been better off if I had taken my father's advice and switched to medicine. Doctors at least were still getting paid.[51]

In 1933, I graduated from law school and passed the bar exam without difficulty. The exam, in my view, was more a test of physical stamina than of knowledge. A question would give a statement of facts that included completely extraneous material. Unless relevant to the legal question involved, it made no difference what a man ate for dinner or what color tie he wore. Anyone who could recognize the material facts had only to apply the law, and for me that was easy. The exam lasted three long days, and many could not endure the strain. The top student in my class did not last the three days.

I was very young and naive, just twenty-two by the time I was sworn in and received my license. Other members of the class were mature men. I had never held a job and knew nothing about the world around me. The Great Depression was in full swing. People were starving, and there was a general air of hopelessness in the country. Some members of my law class had been smart enough to prepare for graduation. One, for example, had gone to the public defender's office as a freshman and volunteered his services, so by the time he graduated he had been promised a job. Another had been in contact with the US Attorney's Office in Hawaii for several years and had a job waiting. They may have known much less of the law than I did, but they knew what was going on in the world.

Soon after graduating, I was notified by the law school that I had been recommended to a Hollywood law firm. I went for an interview. It was a small firm of men in their thirties who were just beginning to make it in Hollywood. They offered a salary of fifty dollars per month. I showed no enthusiasm and someone else took the job, so I went out on my own looking for a position. There was no use going to most of the large offices—they did not hire Jews—so I went to small firms. They hired no one or offered an office and use of a secretary in return for work. I took an exam for a civil-service job advertised by the newly created State Inheritance Tax Department. I was at the top of the list and went for an oral interview, but I was told by my friends that I was wasting my time. The interviewers could select for the job anyone from the top five candidates. The man selected was already working in the department under a temporary appointment. I took no more exams.

During the next seven years, I fluctuated between three jobs in addition to working for myself or with a partner. In my employment, I had the misfortune to work for men who were eccentric or worse. I know there are attorneys who are fine, cultured people of ability and character, but each of my employers was in a class by himself. The most competent was Abe Gold. He was a short, pugnacious, and uncouth man with a strong New York accent. He had a broken nose, which he had earned either as a pugilist or by his conduct. He was an excellent lawyer but could get along with no one. After handling the bankruptcy of the largest drugstore chain in California, which earned him a huge fee, his partners had all left him and he was practicing alone.[52] I grabbed a job for twenty-five dollars per week and the right to have my own practice. I didn't know what I was in for. Work was heaped on my desk, to which I did not object; but if I did manage to get a paying client Abe complained loudly that I was taking too much time away from his work.

There were facets of Abe's personality that were hard to take. In the midst of a conference, he would let off a stream of exhaust and continue nonchalantly with his instructions. He had a mania for rearranging the furniture in the reception room. Every so often I would get a peremptory order to move the sofas and chairs. Once he nearly lost his best client, who was waiting to see him, by ordering him to help me move a desk and sofa. I angered him by showing no enthusiasm in a labor case he was handling. I prepared a law brief as requested but did not volunteer to sit in and assist in the trial. I had volunteered to give talks at various organizations in favor of the new National Labor Relations Act, and I had no heart for the task of asking for an injunction against a union.[53]

The final blow-up came when he handed me a file and told me to appear in divorce court in half an hour for an uncontested divorce hearing. I knew nothing about the case and had not even as much as seen the clients. They turned out to be a wealthy, elderly couple who after a few weeks of marriage had decided they were incompatible and mutually agreed to divorce. There was no property settlement involved. Unknown to me, the judge was an old, gray-haired man well known to be a leading Catholic layman and a vocal enemy of easy divorce. Had I known this, I could have asked for a continuance well before the hearing, even if I had to get sick myself. Instead, I presented my case, not suspecting what would follow.

First of all, the judge gave my witness on the stand, the wife, a tongue-lashing. "Who do you think you are?" he asked. "A Hollywood actress, that you can change husbands every few weeks?" Then he turned to me and said I was a disgrace to the bar for bringing such a case before him. I returned to the office in a daze and reported what had happened. Abe gave me more hell, saying that I had to be utterly incompetent to lose an uncontested case. I quit. Sometime later I heard that Abe had been shot and killed by a mentally unbalanced man he was sitting next to on a plane to New York.

The years I enjoyed in the practice of law were spent in partnership with Dave Mohr.[54] Dave was a few years behind me in law school. Our families had been friendly, and after I left my employment with Gold, Dave proposed we form a partnership. He had been on the debating team at Los Angeles High School; yet, from some psychological quirk, he was terrified by the idea of trying a case in court. Dave got most of our cases and we worked on them together, but I made the court appearances. We had a good winning score without making much money. These days plaintiffs in California seem to earn huge judgments in the flimsiest cases, but during the Depression neither judge nor jury were very generous.

Unlike today, it was illegal for lawyers to advertise in any way. I had a strong suspicion that some attorneys paid press agents to get their names into the press as society news, never failing to mention that so-and-so was a prominent attorney. For the run-of-the-mill lawyer willing to take chances rather than starve, there were ways to evade the code of ethics. One firm I knew of had "detectives" on their payroll who were quick to arrive on the scene of an accident, make friends with the injured parties, and then steer clients to the office. They were then paid to investigate the accident.

Dave and I strictly adhered to the code of ethics. As a result, we were always just one step ahead of the bill collector. I managed to get a few business clients and probated a few estates, but we never did much more than pay our expenses. The strange thing is that after I quit the practice and decided to return to Texas, Dave became a success. Since I wasn't there, he had to try cases himself and became an excellent trial lawyer, winning some large verdicts in insurance cases. Some years after World War II, Dave's reputation was such that he was appointed to the superior court bench. Unfortunately, when his career seemed assured, poor Dave died of a heart attack.

HOW I MET RUTH
Throughout the thirties, I was dissatisfied with myself. My ambition was not to have an outstanding career in the law, but I burned with the desire to be a creative person, a writer—by my standards the ultimate in creativity. Try as I might, I produced nothing. I thought I had a brilliant new insight in the interpretation of economic history only to discover in my research that a German economist had published the same idea fifty years before—and more humiliating still, it had had no effect on economic thought. Then I considered a new approach to Jewish history. I wrote a summary and showed it to one of the leaders of the Los Angeles Zionist organization. He glanced at it and snorted something about precocious young men with newfangled ideas. Convinced I lacked the mental capacity to write on serious topics, I turned my hand to detective fiction, then very much in demand. Several times I worked up excellent plots without any success. After writing a few chapters I would have mental block and couldn't continue.

To add to my anxiety, I was hoping to get married and settle down to a blissful matrimonial state. The trouble was I just couldn't support a wife on my income, so my prospects were dim. Some of my friends recommended marrying a girl who had a good job. My two cousins, both doctors, with whom I shared an apartment after my parents returned to Eagle Pass, argued that the only solution for me was to marry a rich wife. They introduced me to the daughter of a prominent movie producer, expecting me to do the rest. I took her on a date, but all I could think of was Gilbert and Sullivan's song about the rich attorney's older, ugly daughter who wasn't so bad in the dusk with the light behind her.[55] They gave up on me and left me to my fate.

A few years after I graduated from law school, my friend Saul Rittenberg invited me to a lecture on Jewish mythology. The lecture was given by the noted Jewish philosopher S. M. Melamed in the home of a Jewish educator and former teacher at Roosevelt High School, John Sholtz.[56] Mr. Sholtz was a colleague of Melamed's who sometimes wrote articles for Melamed's philosophical journal.[57] Surprisingly, Melamed delivered the lecture in a very formal manner, despite the audience of only two persons, Saul and myself. In the middle of the lecture, Mr. Sholtz's daughter Ruth, aged seventeen, came into the room. She was clearly angry about something, but Melamed unwisely tried to tease her into a better mood. She stalked out of the room in a fury. I thought she was extremely attractive.

Sometime later, I was president of a Zionist youth group and asked Mr. Sholtz to be our speaker. For some mysterious reason, Mr. Sholtz brought Ruth to the meeting. Although she was not yet allowed to date, her father gave her permission to attend Zionist youth group meetings with me. Eventually she was allowed to date, and we spent many wonderful evenings dancing to big band music. We dated intermittently over several years, but the relationship did not seem to be extremely serious. Our relationship almost came to a complete end after one extremely embarrassing evening.

One year, in an affluent moment, I had splurged by purchasing season tickets, two mezzanine box seats, to the Los Angeles Philharmonic orchestra series. I invited my sister Ruthie to many of the programs. However, for the performance by the famed Monte Carlo Ballet Russe on its first American tour, I invited the young woman I was dating, my future wife Ruth. Tickets for this event were at a premium. I had choice seats, or so I thought. At the Philharmonic, I led Ruth straight to my accustomed seats, not bothering with the usher.

Morris Riskind, 1932. (Courtesy of Dr. Peter Riskind.)

When I got there my seats were occupied. I showed the people sitting there my tickets; they showed me their tickets; both sets were for the same seats. In the midst of our hot discussion, the usher came up. After looking at the tickets, he explained that for this special event (as I supposedly had been advised), I was required to exchange my season tickets for tickets specific to this particular event. I had no seats. There I was with a special date and no seats. The usher advised that we search for two empty seats, if we could find any. We stumbled and floundered in the dark all over the auditorium, finally locating two seats in the top balcony in

Ruth Sholtz, 1936. (Courtesy of Dr. Peter Riskind.)

a corner near the roof. It was my most humiliating moment. Of the Ballet Russe I remember nothing. I was so embarrassed that my relationship with Ruth almost ended forever.

Then, in early 1939, I had an experience that was too much to handle in my already unhappy frame of mind. One evening I received a call from a girl I knew from one of the Zionist youth groups. She asked for my help, telling me that her father had not come home and could not be located anywhere. He had last been seen going to the bank in the morning for the weekly payroll of his manufacturing business, a substantial sum of money. I rushed to their house to obtain more information and found the girl's mother wildly hysterical. The hours went on, but the man had still not been heard from.

After consulting with Dave Mohr I went to the police, who believed the man had been kidnapped for his payroll and issued an all-points bulletin. The next day the man was found in his car, dead from carbon monoxide poisoning. The day he disappeared, he had driven off the highway into an orange grove between Los Angeles and San Diego and had run a hose from the exhaust into the closed car. The money was found with him. He had been spending liberally and had bankrupted his business to finance his standard of living. To postpone the inevitable day of reckoning, he had borrowed money on the security of the same accounts at two different banks. Finally, his financial juggling caught up with him. His first thought must have been to take all the cash available and run for Mexico. Then, on the way, the enormity of his conduct dawned on him and he decided to take the easy way out.

As soon as his wife recuperated from her first shock, she began to proclaim that I had killed her husband. If I had not notified the police and made them put out an all-points bulletin, she claimed, her husband would have gone to Mexico and safety. It was all my fault. Had I been toughened to reality, I would have shrugged off the whole affair. No experienced lawyer should or would take the accusations of such an obviously disturbed woman seriously. As it was, I was deeply troubled by the incident and decided that the practice of law was not for me. I decided to return to Texas to go into farming and ranching on a tract of land my father owned. Around the same time, by late 1938 or early 1939, I had become convinced we would inevitably be involved in the war in Europe.

CHAPTER 7

THE HOME FRONT

I was concerned about European hostilities from what I read in the American press, but when my mother started to receive letters from relatives telling her about the savagery in Europe, I was appalled. Except for a period during World War I, Mother was in regular communication with her family in Lithuania. She received some news at first hand when her brother David made his way from Lithuania to Mexico in the early 1920s. Around 1930, her El Paso cousin Harry Spitz made a trip back there and reported that Lithuanian officers were strutting around dressed in fancy uniforms and carrying swords like comic opera extras. Jews were restricted economically and politically, and their treatment was as bad as it had been under Russian rule. Many of the large estates had been expropriated from Jewish ownership, theoretically to give land to the peasants, but in some mysterious way, they had ended up in the ownership of generals and politicians. Harry pressed Chatzkel, my mother's father, to emigrate as soon as possible, but he refused to go to America. Mother wrote letter after letter urging him to go to Palestine instead and take her brother Isaac, who had been denied permission to enter the United States, with him.[1] Chatzkel again refused, saying that he wanted to be buried with his ancestors.

For years Mother had been sending money to her relatives, as had other members of her family. After her death, I found a bundle of bank draft receipts. All during the Depression, even when we were faced with financial difficulties, she was regularly sending fifty dollars each month. During this period, I never heard mention that her mother had passed away. It was too difficult a subject for her to discuss. Years later I learned about it from Aunt Yetta, the wife of my uncle Morris Edelstein, who showed me a letter saying that Miriam Edelstein had died.[2]

After Russia occupied eastern Poland and the Baltic countries in 1939, Mother received a letter from her father. The Russians had confiscated his land, leaving him only the house and a garden plot, which Chatzkel and Isaac worked for food.[3] Mother's checks became more important than ever. Sometime after World War II, Jack Benkaim, Aunt Mollie's son from Scranton, met a man from Kalvaria who had made his escape only a short time before the Nazis came.[4] By coincidence he was Uncle Isaac's best friend. He said that Isaac had more pocket money than anyone else and was always dressed like a dandy. He also had the reputation of being the best card player in town. When news of the Nazi atrocities in Poland reached them, he urged Isaac to join him in trying to reach a safe haven from which they could get to America or some other country. Isaac refused, saying that he could not desert his aged father.

VOICES OF THE DEAD

Mother received a wealth of letters from family members—carefully saved and now still in our family's possession—that chronicled family squabbles, made pleas for charitable help for various neighbors or acquaintances, told about weather and crop conditions, and, above all, offered words of encouragement and support for a family separated from each other by years and miles. Especially in the context of such mundane news, the firsthand accounts of the evil befalling my mother's homeland were harrowing. We especially treasured their letters after their deaths at the hands of the Nazis. These are the "voices of the dead," translated from the Yiddish.[5]

November 15, 1939

Dear Rochel [my mother, Rachel]:

Today I received a letter from our cousin Dvora, of Los Angeles. She told me that you had written to her that you were very much worried about us because we did not answer your two letters. I want to let you know that Father and I got the fifty dollars you sent us and wrote twice to Los Angeles, telling you that we had received the money you sent. We are sure you will get both letters. It took us from October 4th to November 11th to receive the package from Dvora. Anyway, I am sending by registered mail.

We thought having lived through the bad time during the war between Poland and Germany we would now be able to live peacefully. But now an even greater calamity has come upon us Jewish refugees. The Germans are evidently chasing the Jews out of the Suwalki area, which they took from Poland. They are taking from the Jews whatever they possess. They remove all their clothes and chase them out. Most Jews have left the area. They are naked, without any clothing. The evil ones spare neither women, nor children, nor old people. We don't know what to do for these unfortunate people. The savagery of the Germans is indescribable. Kalvaria is filled with refugees. Every house is packed. We have put up over twenty families, mostly women and children. The Germans have so far managed to chase Jews from Senno, Pinsk, and Suvalki.[6] Their awful plight is indescribable. Even before they came here, they had suffered so much, sleeping in the mud of no-man's land. We hope that we will somehow manage to help them establish themselves here in Lithuania. We also hope that their relatives would help them go to America, to Africa, to Palestine, or to other countries.

Let us hope that you will get this letter. I am also writing to Dvora. Do answer me soon. Regards to all of you. Papa also greets you. He is working in the fields.

Itsik [my mother's brother Isaac]

March 13, 1940

Dear Sister,

We got your letter a few days ago and are very happy to hear you are all well. Yesterday was Yom Kippur.[7] Let us hope that this year their prayers will bring a better year to the Jewish people than they had last year. It is about time God gave them something better.

Do not send us any more money for the time being. We can manage without it. I didn't get the fifty dollars you sent me. The letter was probably lost, as has happened so often in the past year. Please do not worry about us. Be well. Regards from all of us. So, *g'mar chatima tovah*, May you be inscribed for a good year![8]

Itsik.

June 3, 1940

Dear sister, may you live long!

I received the last two letters you sent me. Many important events have happened in the world recently, though not here. We did, however, have one scare, but luckily it was only a scare. At present our thoughts are pointed toward the Western Front. These are fateful days for France, for us Jews, and for the whole world. If the evil foe should win, we Jews will go under. His hand will reach us Jews everywhere.

Father and I are feeling fine. He had been sick earlier, so it is hard for him to write. But he sends his regards and will add a few words in his own writing. We haven't heard from the children in a long time. Malke had stopped writing to us a few years ago. Despite these difficult times, she doesn't even call us up. We did get a letter from Benkaim's daughter.[9] They haven't heard from Scranton in a long time. I haven't as yet received your fifty dollars. As soon as I receive the money I will let you know by airmail.

My best regards to you and your family. I hope to get a letter from you soon.

Itsik.

Dearest Rochel

Heartiest regards to you and the family.

Your father, Chaim Chatzkel Edelstein.

July 1, 1940

Dearest Daughter Rochel,

We got your letter and are happy to hear that all of you are well. We are anxious to hear how you get along, especially in these troubled times. We don't get any letters at all from the children in America. Moyshe does write often.

I should describe to you the horror of what our foe has done to the Jews of Poland, but I simply cannot get myself to put it down on paper. Unless one sees with one's own eyes, one cannot conceive of what it is like. The Germans took these people and murdered them and crippled them and didn't let them take anything with them when they chased them out. Those Jews who didn't manage to escape were caught and either murdered or else sent away to Lublin and interned in its concentration camp, where they are dying of hunger and cold. In Lithuania, and especially in Kalvaria, we got only that part of them who had managed to run away. We house them and are giving them whatever we have. They lack nothing here. America and England are helping them by sending money.

We only hope that the Germans do leave Lithuania alone so that all will be well with us.

Our winter has been extremely cold. The mercury dropped to below thirty degrees on some days.

My warmest regards to your husband and to the children.

Your well-wishing father,
Chaim Chatzkel Edelstein

August 22, 1940

Dear Sister Rochel,

We wonder why we do not hear from you. I had sent you an airmail letter on the fifth. During this period much has changed here. We now have a new government. At present we are going through a transitional stage, but with time, we hope things will straighten themselves out.

Only thirty hectares of land [about seventy-five acres] were allowed to us. We do hope that this will be enough for us to make a living.

We have no other news to tell you. We are all well and wish the same to you. Answer us by airmail.

Regards,
Itsik.

March 12, 1941[10]

Dear Sister,

I can't understand why you didn't answer our last letter. Father and I are feeling very well. We hope that all of you are well likewise, and that you will write soon.

We had a very cold winter as well as a cold, late spring. Today Father went to work in the fields for the first time. We have seven hectares of land, a couple of horses, and two cows, and we hope to have an income from these.

Write news about yourselves and how you are feeling. That is the most important thing. We expect your answer soon.

Heartiest regards to all of you,
Itsik.

Dearest Rochel

I am sending my heartfelt greetings to your family.

Your loving father,
Chaim Chatzkel Edelstein

Some time ago I got your fifty dollars, which was paid to me in rubles. You don't have to worry about it any more.

Itsik.

Dear Niece Rochel,

I received your letter five days ago and was happy to hear that all of you are well, thank God. Why are you so upset because the tombstone has not yet been put up? I got a letter from Itsik just before Pesach [Passover]. He writes that he had ordered a monument in Kalvaria. Beautiful stones are made there. It's funny to hear you say that the graves of Grandfather, Grandmother, Moyshe and others have very beautiful stones. Twelve years ago while you were there I found the stones all smeared over. Don't you know your brother Itsik yet? Don't you know that he is honest and wouldn't touch the money for himself if it was earmarked for a stone?

I can write to you that I saw Aunt Blume in Kovno when she was sick. Because her son Mayer is a doctor in Vilkovishk, they took her there to stay with her daughter Mary.[11] After her daughter Chaya had visited her she called me up to come there too. And so, Itsik and I went to pay a sick call on her. They were all very happy that we came. Her daughter Chaya has had a very harsh life. She is married to David Mirkes. Had Moyshe been alive, he would not have let him become his son-in-law. The husband is living with a *goyische* [non-Jewish] woman and demands a divorce from Chaya. Chaya is a very fine woman and I resent what he is doing to her. Blue told us that she herself is a very good age and her husband says she is a fine woman and treats her well. Everyone in that family is devoted to each other. Mary also leads a very good life. She has a beautiful daughter and a very good husband.

I'd like to write you a long letter in answer to your letter of the past winter. Please forgive me for not answering sooner. Because you have been sending money to Itsik quite often, I waited, thinking that it will surely come. You haven't sent any money for some time, and so, naturally I had no money to send on to Itsik. He wrote to me that he expected to come to Kovno and I invited him to come to see me as he hasn't been here for a long time.

Do you expect to go to Los Angeles soon? If you do go there, please try to get together some of your children's worn clothes and send them to Moyshe's Khaye. You can't imagine what a mitzvah you would earn by doing this. Their distress is great. I try to help her by giving her anything I can. Occasionally I give her money, for what else can one do? She confides in me, telling me everything to ease her ache. She has gallstones and has no money to pay for a doctor. How can one describe her suffering? She has a son in America. I forgot the name of the city where he is. He hasn't written to her in years. Her letters to him are returned undelivered. He could have supported her, but evidently he does not want to. If he would send just five dollars a month, he would make her happy, for that would be enough for her to live on. Forgive me for telling you this.

Now I want to know how you are and what you are doing. What do you hear from your brothers and sisters? The situation with Dvora is still one and the same. It hasn't improved. Can one help it if one has no luck?

All the children are well, thank God. I feel so old and weak with my [word cut off].

Give my regards to your husband and to your children.

Your Aunt,
Yehudith

June 14, 1941
Dear Niece Rochel, may you live long.
I got your letter last week. The next day I sent a check to Itsik. I made sure I sent the check at once, in case he needed the money. Forgive me for not answering your letter before Pesach. This is the first time that I did not answer at once. I was sick. One grows older, not younger, and my illness grew worse. One doesn't live forever. Your brother Itsik came to see us before Shavuos, and stayed a few days.[12] We spoke to him, saying it was time he got married again. He said he couldn't afford it, as he needed the money to repair his home. We also spoke to him about your father. My son offered to go to Kalvaria to speak with the father about leaving Itsik half his estate. Itsik had agreed to this at first, but before my son started his trip, Itsik told him not to go because he was going to speak with his father himself. Who knows what he had in mind? As for myself, as long as I am alive, I would like to see him married and leading a happy life. I can't wait too long, but he refuses to listen to me.

I just got a letter from Dvora. She writes to me that they have sold their business and are going to settle in California. They had suffered enough trying to make a living. All her life she has worked hard. I am looking forward to a letter from them saying that their luck has changed for the better. They never had a good day. But if one is not fated by God to have luck, one can't do anything about it. Hershl could have helped her out a bit, but it seems he is not interested. In past years he sent them money twice, ten dollars each time. They have lived through a lot. My Itsik has helped them with more money than Hershl did. I am impatient for a letter from Dvora, telling me where they have settled and whether her husband got a good job. I have never waited for a letter more eagerly than now.

Now about Baila Chaye. They bought a big house in Palestine. You surely know from newspapers that there is a great unrest in Palestine. Today's papers report that Arabs threw a box of dynamite into a train, wounding fourteen Jews. Who knows when the trouble will be over? Shloyme is doing well and so is my Golde. Hanna is not well and she left for a cure at the baths. Itsik and his family are all well. I feel weak. The doctor found sugar in my blood, and I have to go for injections every other day. Thus we spend our lives suffering. Best regards from all of us and to all of you. Be well.

Your well-wishing Aunt,
Yehudit

Best regards to your husband, children and your grandchild.

After the war, news finally came regarding the fate of Chatzkel, Isaac, and the other Jews of Kalvaria. It was one of the first Lithuanian towns occupied by the Nazis, who with their Lithuanian nationalist helpers rounded up the entire Jewish community—men, women, and children. They were marched out of town, and the men were forced to dig a long trench. Then they were ordered to remove their clothes and made to line up at the edge of the trench, where they were all shot. Their bodies either fell or were thrown into the trench, and they were covered over with dirt. Such was the horrible fate of the Jews of Kalvaria.[13]

A PASSOVER STORY

Many families have similar stories. Some years ago, while visiting my son Lorin in Dallas for Passover, we were invited to a seder at the home of a friend. At the table were our hosts and the wife's father, an older man of uncertain age. He was either a young-looking old man or an old-appearing middle-aged one. All through the service he sat at the table, saying little. My wife Ruth attempted to engage him in conversation, only to be answered in monosyllables. When the meal and the service were over and we were about to rise, he began to speak in a low voice and told us this story.

His father had been a wealthy merchant in Warsaw. When the Nazis entered the city, at first all was quiet. Then one day the entire family—his father, mother, younger brother, and him—was moved to the ghetto. Then they were ordered to appear at the railroad station and were transported to a concentration camp. After some time in the camp, he began to notice that people his family knew were disappearing day by day. It became clear that they were being killed. He was a teenager and his brother a few years younger. There was no way to save his parents, but he was determined to save himself and his brother. He embarked on a tour of the camp to find a way of escape.

At one spot, he discovered that there was a house against the concentration camp wall; the house had a porch, on which there was a table and chairs. He estimated that by putting the table against the wall, then placing the chair on the table, he could pull himself over the wall. He waited until there was a dark night, and then about 2 a.m., he and his brother quietly left the barracks and made their way to the house and the wall. Careful to make no sound, they placed the table next to the wall and the chair on the table. The house kept the spot in the shadows, protecting it from the searchlights. As he had planned, by getting on the chair first, he and then his brother were able to climb over the wall.

All night long they kept moving to get as far away as they could. By the time it was light, they came to a town that was entirely deserted. They selected a large mansion and moved in. First they helped themselves to food, which was abundant. Then, by going through the closets, they were able to find new clothing and changed from their camp uniforms. In the house they stayed for some days, eating on fine china and using the best silver. If the food was not to their liking, they had merely to go to an adjoining house to help themselves. Then, one day, they heard the muffled sound of artillery fire in the distance. At first, they thought this was the sound of distant thunder, but it became clear that the front was moving closer. There had been rumors in the concentration camp that the Germans were not doing well at the Russian front. Much as they did not want to leave their pleasant surroundings, they decided to leave and head west. At first, they were tempted to take some valuable property with them, but this would impede their travel and the idea was abandoned.

Taking only some canned food, they headed west, and as they came to settled areas they continued only at night. They had traveled for some time and had eaten all their food by the time they reached the Sudeten area of Czechoslovakia or some other German-speaking region. By this time, they were desperate from hunger. They knocked on the door of a house. The woman who came to the door spoke to them in German. Fortunately for them, they spoke the language well. He told the woman they were running from the advancing Russians, were tired and hungry and asked for food. She invited them in, fed them, and gave them a place to sleep. She acted suspiciously, as though she did not entirely believe their story. He was a little leery of her, but thought that even if she suspected they were Jews, she might consider them insurance against the approaching Russians.

After they had been there for a day or so, there was a loud knocking at the door. When their host answered, there were several German soldiers demanding to know whether there were any old men or teenaged boys in the house. When the boys presented themselves, speaking in German, the soldiers announced that they were being drafted into the home guard, the Volkssturm. They were taken to a barracks, and after being sworn in were showered and dressed in uniforms. Then they were told that the Russians were approaching and they were expected to fight to the death to protect the Fatherland.

For some days, they adhered to a routine of military drilling. He and his brother were terrified lest it be noticed in the shower that they were circumcised and had tattooed numbers on their forearms. This routine continued until the sound of artillery fire could be heard. As the sound got closer, most of the unit, the two boys included, decamped, heading west toward the American lines as fast as they could. When they reached the Americans, they all surrendered en masse. Each man or boy was interrogated, and when it was the turn of the two brothers, they tried to explain they were Jewish refugees. This claim was not believed, and they were ordered to join the other prisoners behind barbed wire. Protesting loudly as they went, they were heard by a Jewish officer. He spoke to them in Yiddish and heard their story. They were released as refugees and finally were able to get to the United States. He concluded ironically that he was not only eligible for reparations as a concentration camp victim, but was also eligible for a pension as a German war veteran.

TRYING TO ENLIST

Since I felt strongly about the situation, I tried to enlist in early 1939. As a practicing lawyer, I might have succeeded had I tried through the Judge Advocate General's office, but I was thinking in other terms.[14] I went to the office of the California National Guard, expecting that I could enlist with my ROTC certificate. An elderly sergeant was sitting behind the desk in an otherwise empty office. When I was able to attract his attention from the sports page of the daily paper, I stated that in view of the war in Europe I was certain that we would also be involved. I handed him my ROTC certificate and said that I was ready to enlist. The sergeant handed me back the certificate, saying that no one had told him of a war anywhere. In any case, he was interested in signing up husky eighteen-year-olds, and I did not qualify. He then went back to reading his newspaper.

Following this episode I tried the various branches of the armed services but to no avail. In desperation I tried the FBI, not because I was an admirer of Mr. Hoover, but I thought I could hunt Nazi spies.[15] The FBI advised me that with my poor eyesight there was no use filing an application. The other services did not bother to answer.

Sometime later, the selective service law was passed and in due course I received a notice to report for a physical.[16] The examining doctor turned out to be a bald-headed old man who, from his talk, must have been a retired army doctor. He checked my heart and lungs, pronounced me sound, and gave me a lecture to the effect that the army would make a man out of me. Then he said, "Take your glasses off and read the chart on the wall." I dutifully removed my glasses and looked around. "What chart? What wall?" The doctor flew into an absolute rage. "Don't pull that stuff on me or I'll see you go to the pen." I assured him that without my glasses I simply could not see well enough to do what he asked. He controlled his tantrum long enough to write a note to another doctor. I kept protesting my inability to read the chart.

"We'll soon find out," he said, handing me the note with an address written on it. The second doctor turned out to be an ophthalmologist. He read the note and then gave me a searching look. "Let me see your glasses." He used a gauge on the lenses, then flashed a light into my eyes. "That doddering old fool. Calls himself a doctor. That idiot should have been able to tell you were telling the truth." "What chance do I have of being drafted?" I asked. "Practically none. If you broke your glasses, you could shoot the wrong side. Of course," he continued, "if we get into a long war, you might be drafted, but it would turn out to be a desk job." I thanked the doctor and left. By late summer 1939, I was back in Eagle Pass.

We entered the war in December 1941, and six months later the young men of Eagle Pass were all gone. People began to look at me as a "slacker," a draft evader, whenever I came to town. Once again, I attempted to enter some branch of the service in a useful form. I wrote to my congressman but again to no avail.[17] I heard of an army language school in Colorado and wrote there, but all my efforts were fruitless.

Finally, late in 1943, I was ordered to report for a medical exam by our local selective service board. I asked Dr. Montemayor what the situation was like.[18] He replied that he had been instructed to pass anyone who could walk through the door. The next day I drove to Fort Sam Houston in San Antonio.[19] I was directed to a room where a sergeant was interviewing a number of teenage boys, all waiting their turn. When it was my turn, he took me to the side and made a face. "I don't want you, mister. I want eighteen-year-old kids."

"If you don't want me, why should I be drafted?"

"Hell if I know," he said.

"What would I do if I were drafted?"

He scratched his head. "Can you type?"

"No," I answered.

He held up two fingers. "You'll type."

"Isn't there any place I can volunteer?" He sent me to another office. I knocked on the door. An officer was seated at the desk. I explained my problem. I said I was a lawyer and wanted to volunteer. Wasn't there anything I could do? "We're full up on lawyers," he said.

He took my name and address and told me with no enthusiasm that he would let me know if anything opened up.

I drove back to Eagle Pass and claimed my exemption as a farmer and rancher. At least I was doing something useful in that capacity. The townspeople continued to regard me as a draft-dodger, and I suffered from their opprobrium for at least ten years after the war, when they finally accepted me.

SERVICEMEN AND THEIR FAMILIES

About six months after the war started, construction began on an airfield to be used as a single engine training school ten miles north of town, off the Del Rio highway.[20] About five thousand personnel, including staff and trainees, were stationed there. A larger field for bomber training was built near Del Rio.[21] During construction there was a flurry of excitement when Charlie Lindenborn, a local man, and another security guard got into a heated argument and a regular old-time shoot-out. Charlie was badly wounded. The other man was shot dead.[22]

The town soon became crowded, and when the Eagle Pass Army Air Field opened, military personnel came pouring in, adding to the housing shortage. Every available space was sought. My parents rented their back apartment to a Jewish lieutenant, Wally Mendelson, and his young wife, Marge. This apartment was a self-contained unit with its own bathroom and kitchen. Marge Mendelson proved to be a friendly person. She had a degree in journalism from a major university and soon got herself a job as editor of the *Eagle Pass News Guide*, which she handled very capably until she had a baby and quit. Lieutenant Mendelson, on the other hand, was very aloof and made no friends in town that I knew of, nor did they participate in the Jewish community. After the war, he became a professor of political science at the University of Texas at Austin.[23]

The shell of the old Yolanda Hotel, which had been destroyed by fire in the early 1930s, was rented to the USO by Sam Schwartz.[24] The building was reroofed and the inside rebuilt. Most of the building was one huge room, like a big dance hall. Sometimes there were dances. On most days there were small tables and chairs.

For some reason, the Jewish Welfare Board was placed in charge of the USO. The first director was Ozzie Baum of San Antonio.[25] Ozzie was a quiet man who did his job efficiently and soon had the USO well organized and running smoothly. In no time it was crowded with boys from the airfield. Eddie Klein of Seguin, Texas, followed Ozzie as director. Eddie was married to a sister of Max Mandel, later the president of the Laredo National Bank.[26]

In decorating the inside of the building, one wall had been turned over to Sue Jaffe, wife of a lieutenant on the airfield staff. Sue was a talented artist already of some reputation in New York. She painted a mural on one entire wall depicting local scenes relating to the military. It was a very competent piece of work, and it would have been preserved anywhere else. Not in Eagle Pass. As soon as the USO vacated the building it was painted over.[27]

Sue Jaffe herself seemed to delight in shocking the townspeople. At that time, women wearing shorts was unknown and most shocking. Sue not only wore shorts both in Eagle Pass and in Piedras Negras, but she squeezed herself into rather short shorts. She caused a sensation whenever she pranced down the street. You could sense the men's eyes popping out and hear the women's tongues clacking.

As soon as Ozzie Baum had the preliminary organization of the USO in hand and soldiers began to participate in numbers, he appealed to the townspeople to help entertain them. I'm sure the military men were more interested in girls, but since I had nothing much to do in the evenings, I made a practice of dropping in to play checkers or chess with those interested. One boy went around asking if anyone could play pinochle, a game commonly played by Jews, and I volunteered. I took it for granted that the boy was Jewish and invited him to come to services at my parents' home. The soldier was completely mystified by my invitation. It turned out he was a Catholic boy of Slavic descent, which made me reappraise my judgment of individuals based on ethnic stereotypes.

It dawned on me that much of what small-town people consider to be "Jewish" characteristics are actually manners of speech, dress, and conduct associated with big northern cities. The most "southern" man I ever met, with the thickest accent, was a Jew from Natchez, Mississippi. In my own case, I have not been taken for Jewish in other parts of the country, even by my fellow Jews. When I was in high school in Los Angeles, I came across two boys having a heated argument over whether I was Jewish, one insisting that with my accent, I could not be Jewish.

At the USO, I soon learned that there was much dissatisfaction in the ranks. Job placement was the principal cause of discontent. At first the services had attempted to place men based on ability and previous training, but soon the vast scope of the task was too much and placement had gotten completely out of hand. If a unit needed a cook, for example, but one was not available from the personnel at hand, a man would be picked at random. Then, if subsequently a qualified chef arrived, the file would indicate that no such position was open and the trained cook, even an expert chef, would be placed elsewhere rather than be substituted for the unqualified man. In no time, jobs were filled by unhappy misfits. Men were performing tasks for which they had no skill or inclination. One man told me he had been an assembly line foreman at General Motors. He enlisted to serve his country and was placed sorting mail. This man was bitter and resentful because he felt that his sacrifice had been in vain.

Two Jewish men I met solved their problems in a sensible way and made arrangements on their own without going through channels. One was a master butcher who had been designated an electrician. His friend was a professional electrician placed as a butcher. Every day after hours the men swapped jobs. Each checked the other's work and corrected any errors. This they did while waiting to rectify the situation through channels.

Another matter that caused much discontent was the barracks construction. Apparently, the barracks must have been designed for some post in Greenland or Iceland. The buildings were covered with black tar paper to retain heat, and there were few windows. By midsummer the barracks were like stoves, hot enough to cook on the floor. Only by taking their cots outside were the men able to survive. This was against regulations, but the officers looked the other way.

When the first cadet class arrived at the field, the commander, Colonel Bundy, came to Riskind's department store and told Albert that he wanted to put the entire cadet class into cowboy boots with the words "Eagle Pass, Texas" stamped on them, each man paying for his own.[28] This wasn't exactly according to regulations, but Bundy was the boss. Boots were rationed by the factory, and ordinarily the store could not get the 250 pairs that the colonel asked for. Albert got on the phone with the Justin Boot Company, and after a lot of talk was able to get the boots. Of course, Albert was very proud of his coup and told me that Colonel Bundy would naturally be given his boots free, with his name and "Eagle Pass, Texas" stitched on them.

When the day came to deliver the boots, Albert, unfortunately, was out and Pa took care of the matter. When it was Colonel Bundy's turn to get his boots, he expressed great

Morris (right) with his lifelong friend Sam Meyer during a visit to Alaska, 1978. (Courtesy of Dr. Peter Riskind.)

pleasure and prepared to leave, whereupon Pa announced the price for the specially made fancy boots. Colonel Bundy got a funny look on his face, paid up, and stalked out. When Albert returned, he tried to argue with Pa. Pa answered that he did not like *kunkel-munkel* business and wasn't going to *shmeer* (bribe) Colonel Bundy or anyone else.

Back during World War I, the Jewish Welfare Board had sent a rabbi to Eagle Pass for the High Holidays. He held services in the Knights of Columbus Hall, which they rented. But during World War II, services were held as usual at my parents' home upstairs from the store, and any officers and enlisted men who wished to come were welcome. It was at such a service that I met Sam Meyer, from Laredo, who became my lifelong friend. Sam had gone into the store and introduced himself to my father. After hearing that he was a Jewish boy from Laredo, Pa merely said: "Go upstairs and tell Ma to give you something to eat."[29]

Sam came originally from Rochester, New York, but his mother's family, the Alexanders, had come to Texas from Alsace, landing at Indianola around 1870, before it was destroyed by a hurricane, then settling first in Victoria and by about 1880 in Laredo. When his mother died, his father sent Sam to Laredo to live with his aunt, Frances Alexander. Sam studied Spanish and Spanish civilization at the University of Rochester and later in Austin, and his education and life on the border, plus extensive travel experience in Mexico, Central America, and South America gave him an unusual knowledge of Spanish at every level, from border *pocho* to elegant Castilian. Sam said that the rule was that the further from the border, even as much as crossing the bridge, the worse the Spanish became. The further west, also, the poorer the Spanish until by the time you got to Los Angeles the *pocho* bore little relation to Castilian.[30]

Sam came to Eagle Pass as a seaman placed in naval censorship. His job, along with various civilian workers, was to listen in on all phone conversations between Eagle Pass and points in Mexico. In the course of his duties, he had occasion to overhear such momentous matters as the intimate conversations between some of our prominent local citizens and their Mexican girlfriends.

There are few people I have ever met with Sam's ability to make friends. He traveled more than anyone I ever met, to the most diverse cultures and environments. His knowledge of geography was remarkable, as was his interest in botany. This background served him well during the war. After being transferred from Eagle Pass, he ended up in Hawaii via San Diego. Unfortunately, he suffered all sorts of indignities from noncommissioned officers who seemed to delight in torturing an educated man who was also a Jew. Then, one day, as he was working in an office in Hawaii, an admiral happened to ask where a certain island was located. No one on his staff seemed to know. Sam, however, recited from memory the approximate longitude and latitude of the island. He then added that he thought he was qualified to be an officer. The astonished admiral asked Sam about his background. Several weeks later, Sam received a notice to report to Officers' Training School.

Another Jewish boy I got to know well was named Goldberg, a New Yorker.[31] Goldberg took my parents literally about making himself at home. He slept on the back screened porch of the upstairs apartment, saying he couldn't stand the heat of the barracks, and he helped himself at all hours to the contents of Mother's refrigerator. Goldberg announced at an early point in our acquaintance that once the war was over, he was moving to a kibbutz in Israel. When the war ended, he wrote to me that he had married and moved to Israel. Then we lost touch.

One of the boys Goldberg brought around was Ladislas Ruza, a non-Jewish Hungarian.[32] Ladislas had an interesting story to tell. He had gone to the recruiting station to enlist and had asked the sergeant in charge, "In what branch of the service do I have the best chance of seeing action?" The recruiting sergeant, a relic of the old cavalry, signed him up for the horse cavalry. Next thing he knew, Ladislas found himself at Fort Ringgold in extreme South Texas.[33] As part of their training, the men had to take off on a charge; if they fell off the horse, they had to walk back carrying their saddle. Since Ladislas had little previous experience with horses, he spent a good part of his time hiking with a saddle on his shoulders.

One day, the fort commander, old General Augur, a true relic dating back to the Indian wars, decided that he was going to prove that a cavalry division could move faster than motorized troops.[34] He tried to move his entire division on a forced march from Fort Ringgold to Fort Clark at Brackettville, a distance of over 350 miles. The division got to somewhere around Carrizo Springs, then collapsed from fatigue. The horses and men had to be trucked into Fort Clark. Then the cavalry division was disbanded and sent off to other pursuits.

Ladislas got a lucky break. He was transferred to Eagle Pass in military intelligence. As such, he was provided with a jeep, and every day he drove over to Piedras Negras, where he collected the *Diario* and other Mexican publications.[35] Then he drove back to Eagle Pass, placed all these publications in a folder, and mailed them to headquarters, after which his work was through for the day.

We were all very proud of Ladislas over his feud with Colonel Bundy. The colonel had issued an ukase that no enlisted man could wear any uniform or part thereof other than regulation attire for such enlisted personnel.[36] This was because cadets had complained that the enlisted men were wearing uniform trousers and caps as good as or better than theirs. The MPs were very zealous in enforcing this order. When Ladislas was nabbed for flagrantly disobeying the dress code, he insisted that he was not under Colonel Bundy's command and was not bound by any of his orders. The matter finally went by direct communication to

Ladislas's superior who, it turned out, was an old army cavalryman with a positive hatred for the Air Force. He directed Bundy to leave his "cotton-picking hands" off his men. And so, to Bundy's fury, Ladislas wore boots and an officer's cap set at a jaunty angle that would have made MacArthur envious, and he even carried an English officer's whip in his hand.

On a few occasions, I took Jewish servicemen out to the ranch. Once, I brought some boy out and left him to his own devices while I sat inside the house to read some reports. The next thing I knew there was a terrific blast a few feet away. The idiot had picked up my vaquero Agapito's shotgun, which had been left propped up inside the door, and without checking to see if it was loaded, he pulled the trigger. The blast missed me by inches. I could feel the buckshot go by, and it literally blew a hole a foot in diameter through the door. I don't know who was more frightened, me or the boy. It seemed strange to me that one could be in the service without any knowledge of guns or how they worked.

On another occasion, I brought two of the soldiers to the ranch on a day we were moving some cattle. After watching the slow proceedings for a while, the men asked me if they could borrow some horses to go riding. I warned them that the horses were rather wild. They assured me that they knew how to ride well. They took off and were gone for quite a while. I began to worry about them. Finally, they returned on foot, leading the horses. "The horses in Central Park weren't at all like this," they confessed.

CHAPTER 8

BECOMING A FARMER

In September 1939, I entered upon my new career as a farmer and rancher. My father owned a tract of land eighteen miles from Eagle Pass. About 1920, he bought it from some Spaniards, who had acquired the land some years before with the idea of going into cotton farming, still a lucrative crop at that time. The Spaniards cleared several hundred acres near the Rio Grande and put in what they thought was a proper irrigation system. They installed a centrifugal pump connected to an ordinary clay pipeline, which they extended to the top of the line, about seventy-five feet above the level of the river. When the pump started up, the clay pipeline exploded like a giant torpedo mine. Even many years later, chunks of clay pipe covered the ground along the path of the pipeline. One can only wonder how many were killed in the horrendous explosion. The Spaniards were ruined. They owed Pa several thousand dollars for credit extended at the store, so Pa had the land appraised, made a deal, and bought the land, deducting the debt. The place was called El Retiro ("the Retreat") and still remained isolated and quiet. During good cattle years Pa leased it out for cattle grazing; otherwise it was completely idle.[1]

EL RETIRO

El Retiro bordered the Indio Ranch to the south and the Loma Linda ("Beautiful Hill"), farmed by our friend Owsey Mikulinsky, to the north.[2] The Indio Ranch in the old days was a wild and isolated area. Other than a few vaqueros, it was known only to cattle rustlers and smugglers. There were constant raids across the river in both directions—those from Mexico who felt they were only taking back their own, and bandits such as King Fisher who made a living out of cattle rustling. In the days of Prohibition, smuggling liquor was profitable business for those on the Mexican side. Once during the Depression, a woman applied for a job as a government trapper and got the job. She caused a sensation when she managed to trap a mountain lion in the Indio area near the river that measured well over six feet in length from the nose to tail, the largest animal of its kind on record in the area.[3] Later the name "El Indio" was applied to the whole area, which is now a suburb of Eagle Pass.

I knew absolutely nothing about farming or ranching, so I consulted the county agent, Walter Sellers.[4] He was an elderly mild-mannered man, always dressed in a business suit. If I had to guess, I would have said he was a schoolteacher. He had a map of the county, indicating the types of land in each area. He discussed the soil at El Retiro and gave me government pamphlets. First of all, he said, I had to get water. El Retiro was not on the irrigation canal, and without irrigation, farming in our area is not feasible. He said I would need to contact a concrete pipe manufacturer. At his suggestion, I made a trip to San Antonio to the Mission Concrete Pipe Company. There I explained the problem to a graduate engineer from Texas A&M University. We made an appointment to meet in Eagle Pass so that he could make an on-the-spot survey.

Meanwhile, my brother Reuben and I went out to the ranch. To get there, we took the road south toward El Indio for about fourteen miles along an unpaved road full of rocks, bumps, and caliche. Whenever it rained, the clay became a slippery, sticky mess, causing the car to slip and slide. After passing the old Evans Ranch, we came to a fork in the road and took a dirt trail that turned to the right toward the Rio Grande. The path went up hill and down dale, through wild-looking brush country that gave one the feeling that bandits or Comanches could be hiding in ambush. The road followed the barbed-wire fence line of the Evans Ranch and the Loma Linda, until it finally came to the El Retiro fence line and a rickety gate.

The first task facing us was to cut a passageway through the brush into the El Retiro. Taking turns with an axe, we cut a path about ten feet wide through the brush, so that it was easier to drive toward the river. A few hundred yards from the gate was an an arroyo, which was no problem in dry weather, and the brush was not too dense as we reached the area the Spaniards had cleared years before.

It is difficult for a city dweller to grasp the size of tracts of land in this area. In California, anyone who had an acre of land with a few chickens called it a ranch. In this part of the country, or in Mexico, one could drive for miles and still be on the same property. El Retiro had some 1,050 acres, a very small ranch for Maverick County. Still, it constituted an oblong tract about a mile wide and a mile and a half long, with more than a mile of river frontage. On the south side near the Indio Ranch fence, there was a sharp fault scarp, from the top of which one could get a magnificent view of the surrounding country.

It was apparent that my first task was to get a proper road inside the ranch. In wet weather, the arroyo would be impassable. I solved the road problem by having a plot of the ranch prepared indicating a road, then filing a dedication of the road to the county. Once this was done, I could request that a road grader be sent to cut a straight passage through. I made an appointment to visit Judge Bibb, the county's political boss and my father's friend, and got very quick results.[5] Not only was a grader sent, but a drain was installed in the arroyo to make it passable in all weather. And so I had a road—not graveled, but it was adequate.

Before I could start actual farming operations, I had a number of priorities to accomplish. First, I had to get a foreman and some workers. Land had to be cleared and farm machinery purchased. But neither of these steps would mean anything unless I could get water for irrigation. A concrete pipeline would have to be built and a pumping system installed. That phase of my task would prove a monumental project. Only in my ignorance could I undertake such a major public works program and, also amazingly, I succeeded.

After making inquiries, I went to see a local tractor driver by the name of Atanacio García.[6] He proved to be a heavyset man of about fifty with a solemn countenance. He always wore the same outfit: a pair of old-fashioned denim overalls with straps crossed over the shoulders. I agreed to pay him fifty dollars per week as foreman and promised him a bonus if we had a successful season. Atanacio secured a crew of about ten men, many of them relatives, to be paid the going rate of three dollars per day.

In the winter, there was no shortage of labor, but starting in March each year a major part of the work force went north as migratory labor. Around the end of September or early October, the families of migrants returned. If they had a good year up north in Michigan, Idaho, Montana, California, Oregon, or Washington, some did not work again until their money gave out. Most migrants, however, worked in the local winter harvest on a contract basis. Entire families from grandparents to small children would work cutting spinach on a piecework basis at so much per basket. A good worker could make much more than three dollars per day. A large family with an army of children and grandparents did very well by local standards. After spinach came onions and then cotton. Those who had not left earlier worked in the onions and cotton, then followed the cotton harvesting north toward the Texas Panhandle. Those who left earlier went to work in the sugar beets or to pick fruit in California and Oregon. Many of the better workers had jobs waiting for them. Often the boss would advance them money for the trip.

I traded in my Pontiac two-door sedan for a heavy-duty Dodge pickup truck. Every morning at 6 a.m., Atanacio would collect all the men, who sat on removable benches on the bed of the truck. Then he would come for me, waiting in front of the store, where I was living with my parents. Sometime later, I bought an old Ford sedan from Martin Kelso to give us more freedom and mobility. At first, I had difficulty communicating with the foreman and men, since I had forgotten my childhood Spanish. Furthermore, the sort of Spanish the men used wasn't exactly the same found in a Castilian grammar or dictionary. After a while, I learned the necessary farm and ranch terminology.

The engineer at the Mission Concrete Pipe Company worked out a blueprint of the proposed pipeline and detailed instructions controlling construction. He explained the mandatory requirement that we keep an even grade along the entire length of the line. From the pump to the top of the rise was about two hundred yards in length. Starting from the top we worked downhill, the men digging between two lines of cord. As they excavated, Atanacio and I had to keep them to a perfect grade by using marked poles as the engineer had trained us to do. The men dug until the bottom of the ditch reached the mark on the pole representing the surface. The bottom of the ditch had to be even, ready for the pipe to be laid.

Simultaneously with the building of the long pipeline, I had to install a pump and build a pressure tower. The best pump man in the area was in Asherton, fifty-two miles from Eagle Pass. He recommended a well pump rather than the centrifugal pump generally used by the local farmers. After a few years, I discovered why centrifugal pumps were generally used in the area. While the well pump was more efficient, the heavy Rio Grande salt wore down the impellers every few years so that they had to be replaced.

The most difficult part of building the pipeline was the construction of a pressure tower. This was necessary as a pressure escape in case of a sudden change in the pressure in the line, which is called water hammer. It had to be taller than the top of the pipeline, ending about two hundred yards uphill, a vertical height of over seventy feet above the river. The bottom concrete joints were about five or six feet in diameter, weighing at least half a ton, and tapering toward the top until the tower ended in pipe of about two feet in diameter. As the tower rose higher, we built a scaffolding around it so the men could mortar the joints of pipe in place. When we got above fifty feet the job became scary. Fortunately, the crew finished without an accident.

Once the tower was completed, we dug and installed a windmill at the top of the ridge near the irrigation discharge, where we were going to establish our headquarters. The water turned out to be brackish—drinkable but not palatable. With the tower completed, we had to run a twelve-inch steel pipe from the pump into the river, about fifteen to twenty feet away. Finally, a massive steel gate valve had to be bolted to the steel line underwater. It took three men working together to do this. We decided to pump the river water into a small brick-and-concrete storage tank about ten feet square, out of which the water could be distributed using steel gate valves.

As we constructed the tower, another crew was at work to clear the land. The area the Spaniards had cleared had grown back in scrub mesquite brush. This the men cleared using axes and grubbing hoes to dig up the deep roots, all the time keeping a sharp eye out for *viboras* (rattlesnakes) and *alicantres* (coral snakes).[7] The coral snakes were rare but deadlier than rattlers, and the men were terrified of them. The cut brush was collected in mounds every fifty or hundred feet or so and burned. Think of all the mesquite charcoal-broiled steaks this could have made! As soon as the land was cleared, it was plowed and leveled. I had learned from government pamphlets that the planted area should also be contoured to avoid excessive soil erosion. I bought a surveyor's instrument and learned to use it. After contouring the land, making ten-foot beds, digging ditches, and fertilizing heavily, we were finally ready to plant onions.

I bought my farm equipment from Eagle Hardware in Eagle Pass. Hite and Larry Harper ran the company.[8] Sales were handled by Hite. He was a tall, thin middle-aged man, very genial and friendly in manner. During the Mexican Revolution he had been living in Mexico City as the resident purchasing agent with the Mexican government for all sorts of supplies, while his older brother Osie Harper did the purchasing in the United States. Whether because of his Mexican stay, or because he already had it, Hite spoke English with a slight Mexican accent.

Hite sold many thousands of dollars of farm machinery on credit to customers located in a wide area of northern Mexico. I could never understand how he could afford to do this, but years later I learned the secret. If a customer reneged on his debt, a squad of soldiers would appear a few days later at his hacienda and remove all the equipment—probably with a few pieces extra. From the days of the revolution, Hite was on a first-name basis with all the generals, and it took only a phone call. Payment of debts to Eagle Hardware was promptly made.

At Hite's suggestion I bought an International diesel tractor, which had huge rear rubber tires rather than tractor treads and could pull a large plow. I also bought a tiller, a tooth harrow, a border maker for irrigation, a ditch digger, a broadcast seeder, and a raw crop seeder.

HOW I MADE A BIG STINK IN EAGLE PASS

Around December 1, we started planting a huge load of Bermuda onion sets that Atanacio had secured from a source near La Pryor. Atanacio was able to get a contractor with a trained crew of planters. The onion plants were set out in rows twelve feet long and three feet apart— an old-fashioned way to plant, since the narrow rows do not permit cultivation by even a light tractor. Atanacio said we would get a better yield if we planted in narrow rows. We bought two mules and found some old-fashioned mule cultivators. We planted about thirty-five acres of onions.

Three things happened that I had not counted on. First, we ran out of onion sets with about six or seven acres still unplanted. Second, after I had taken care of this problem and the land was fully planted, the seed company salesman persuaded me to plant an additional five acres with a new type of onion called Barbosas. He offered me the plants for free if I would plant them. Unfortunately for me, I agreed. There was a patch of land about five or six acres near the pump outlet. We hastily prepared this area and planted the Barbosas.

The third issue is that I ran out of money, so I looked around for a partner. In 1939, the Western Auto Parts Store in Eagle Pass was operated by Ted Greenberg, and after some discussion, Ted and I arrived at a deal. He agreed to purchase the necessary onion plants and to pay the costs of growing and harvesting the crop. At the harvest, he would get back his investment, then we would split the profit fifty-fifty. Ted had come from a small town in upstate New York. During the Depression he came to Texas, first to San Antonio, then to Eagle Pass. He opened the Western Auto in an empty building next to the old First National Bank. Ted was an immediate success. He had a very genial personality—a schmoozer, to use my father's terminology. The Western Auto became a meeting place for his customers, presided over by Ted, the local cracker-barrel philosopher. He kept up a constant chatter with the small farmers, and Mexican customers did not slow him down. He could jabber away in the most barbarous Spanish.

By the time the irrigation system was ready, we had planted all the onions. We started up the pump engine on Christmas Day. The Buick engine engaged with a roar.[9] It did not have a muffler, and the noise was amplified by the sound echoing from the cliffs on the Mexican side. In an instant the solitude changed to a cacophony of exploding sounds. As the pump took hold there was a brief air lock, which the line withstood with no problem. After the pressure adjusted, water poured out the other end to a flow of around two thousand gallons a minute. The men commenced irrigating and worked day and night. Watering onions was a slow job, and we wanted to be finished before the end of the month. I had been told that January 1 was a deadline for adequate time to grow a crop of onions.

From the first, the crop did beautifully. There was a set procedure to follow. In the absence of rain, the crop had to be irrigated; if the crop dried, growing would stop. The onions had to be cultivated using the two teams of mules. If all went well, the onions put on good healthy tops. Then, when the weather turned hot around mid-April, the onions were given a dose of nitrate fertilizer, and water was poured to them. Harvest date ideally came around May 5.

At that time only Bermuda onions were widely grown in South Texas. The Bermuda is a flat onion, and our area produced from 200 to 350 bushels per acre. The benefit of the Bermuda is that it matures early, which can be all-important. In contrast, the Grano onion produces double or triple the yield, but it comes in later. Before the Grano onion appeared on the scene, all the farmer had to worry about was a shortage of water, hail, and thrip. Thrip, an onion grower's nightmare, is a tiny insect that sucks out chlorophyll and turns onions yellow. Hail can get a farmer worried every time he sees a cloud in the sky, especially from March 1 on. Sometime after I quit growing onions, a spray was developed to control thrip, and the new Grano onions increased crop yields so much that prices dropped and onion growing practically ceased. Less can be better, or at least more profitable.

My particular project was the five-acre field of Barbosa onions. The patch was near the pump outlet, and I went there constantly. When first irrigated, some onion plants had washed out of the bed, as always happens. I was so disturbed by the sight of loose plants that I got down on my knees to replant them myself. By the time I was through, I had just about a perfect stand of onions, a model field. One day when I was on my knees planting onions, a local farmer, Ed Ritchie, and his foreman came by looking for me.[10] I could tell he was a little surprised to find me at such a task. The usual Anglo farmer did no labor himself. He was a "planter" in the old southern sense. We talked a bit about tractors, and I went back to work on my onions.

Onion harvesting began in South Texas around the first week of March and moved north from the Coastal Bend to Zavala, Laredo, Crystal City, and then to Eagle Pass. The harvest always opened with high prices; if the crop was poor, prices remained high, but if tonnage was heavy the price soon dropped, often breaking by the time the Laredo harvest got underway. By the time it was our turn we were often lucky to make back our costs.

I started harvesting onions on May 5. It had been my understanding with Ted Greenberg that my crop would have priority over his. My foreman recommended an old man, Manuel Moncada, as the best onion harvesting contractor in the area.[11] Moncada was now in the grocery business on Commercial Street and had retired from contracting. I went to the Moncada home and argued with Manuel until he agreed to supervise the harvesting of my crop.

I had ordered fifty-pound onion sacks with my own label, El Retiro; they cost fifteen cents each. The field hands had to be paid on a per-sack basis for pulling, clipping, and sacking the onions. Workers plowed between the rows with mules to loosen the soil, then a crew of some fifty men, women, and older children pulled the onions out of the ground by the tops. The pulled onions were then stacked in windrows on top of the irrigation borders and left overnight to dry. Next day, they were clipped—the tops and the roots were cut using garden shears. When this was done, the onions were sacked and checked off by the contractor. They were then carried to a hand-cranked grader placed in the field, and they were poured out onto the moving grading table where any damaged, seed-stem, or off-colored onions would be removed. The remaining onions were then sacked, tied, and loaded onto a truck for hauling to the railroad in Eagle Pass. At the railroad station a US government inspector opened the sacks at random and graded them. My crop was almost perfect—95 percent US no. 1. The trouble was that by this time the price had taken a disastrous tumble. There were too many onions.

Each railroad car of onions consisted of around five hundred fifty-pound sacks. The onions had to be loaded into the car in a certain pattern so as not to be thrown around and damaged as well as to provide adequate air circulation so that they would not rot. Usually, it took two men to unload the truck and stock the freight car. In my case, the job was handled by a man named Robles, who loaded five cars a day all by himself, a prodigious feat.

The resident onion broker in Eagle Pass was Joe Alvarez, who represented a South Texas broker named Tebbe.[12] Joe was quick to tell me he was not Mexican. He was from Asturias in Spain and was rather contemptuous of Mexicans. They in turn called him El Gachupin, the uppity Spaniard. Alvarez had a dour look on his face and pontificated, gesturing with a cigar in his right hand as he walked back and forth. As soon as Joe heard I had an onion crop, he started reporting daily on the latest quotations. By mid-April, he began to give pessimistic reports: "The price is $2.75 now and Laredo is still harvesting heavy. It looks bad for Eagle Pass."

I had made an estimate that my growing costs, not including depreciation, were about fifty cents per sack, plus harvesting costs of another fifty cents, which included the sack, the labor, the contractor's commission, the trucking, and the loading. At one dollar a sack, I would just about get my money back, not counting the depreciation of equipment.

By May 5, Joe reported that the price for onions was $1.25 and dropping at least five cents per day. By the time I loaded the first car, I sold for $1.15 per sack. Joe would call me at night and say, "Hurry, hurry." The last part of my crop was sold for $1.00. I explained the dire situation to Ted. "Don't worry about me," he said. "Sell and get your money out."

By the time we loaded Ted's onions in the first car, the price was down to ninety-five cents—but he refused to sell for that low price. He wanted his money in full. The next day the price was ninety cents. We continued harvesting until we had three cars loaded with Ted's onions, but he still obstinately refused to sell. Joe Alvarez came to see me. "Tebbe has instructed me to stop buying. The price is eighty-five cents. I'll still buy yours and tell him that I had already made a deal." I argued with Ted, whose loss had increased considerably. Finally, he agreed to sell.

And so I was out of the onion business, but only temporarily. There yet remained the crop of Barbosas. These onions had not matured yet, growing larger and larger every day and yielding a very heavy tonnage per acre, much more than the Bermudas. I had a regular onion monster on my hands. When I asked Joe Alvarez what to do with the Barbosas, he shook his head with a grimace. "Arizona is coming in, and then California. Plow 'em under and you'll save money."

I wouldn't dream of plowing under my special project, my beautiful crop I had personally replanted on my knees to maintain a perfect stand. To plow it under would be abhorrent. Out of just a small patch we harvested a bumper crop. The problem was, what to do with it? When I asked Joe Alvarez, he shrugged his shoulders. The last price quoted for Texas onions had been sixty-five cents. "You could try rolling a car," he said, "but I advise against it." I loaded a car and sent it on its way to New York. When it reached St. Louis, I wired a produce firm and received an offer of fifty cents. This just about covered the freight. I sold the car.

But what could I do with the rest of the onions? I had a bear by the tail. My father owned a large building on Commercial Street, which he had built in 1920 for the Riskind Furniture Company. About 1925, Pa sold the business to his brother-in-law, Morris Edelstein. A branch of Edelstein's Better Furniture was operated in the building until around 1930, when Uncle Morris was in financial difficulty and closed the store. After keeping the building empty for a while, Pa had a partition built across the rear two-thirds of the store. In the front he opened El Palacio de Hierro (the Iron Palace), a dry goods store selling mostly odds and ends from Riskind's. The manager was Anacleto Torralba. In mid-June, we hauled the unsold onions to town and stacked them in the back of El Palacio de Hierro, turning it into a regular onion warehouse. Then I waited for the price of onions to change. It didn't.

About July 1, I received an urgent phone call from Torralba. He sounded hysterical. I made an immediate trip to see him. As I walked through the front door of El Palacio de Hierro there was a powerful, pungent smell of onions. "Mr. Riskind," he said, "the merchants of Commercial Street say they will kill me unless I get rid of these onions. They can't stand it anymore." In desperation I called up Mr. Libson of the California Fruit Company in Piedras Negras. "What will you give me for the onions?" I finally made a deal for thirty-five cents a sack, with the understanding that they would be regraded. We sifted through the onions in the back of the store and found that perhaps half of them were spoiled and couldn't be sold. I had to get rid of the ruined onions, too, so we hauled them back to El Retiro and spread them over the newly plowed fields. It was the most expensive fertilizer I had ever heard of.

CHANCAQUILLAS

The next year, from 1940 to 1941, I planted onions again, but with very different results. In growing onions, there are many variables. A slow steady rain in March could increase yield by 25 percent, but a torrential rain could wash out the crop. A hailstorm could wipe out the crop in five minutes. One of the worst enemies was the thrip. A failure in the pumping system at the wrong time could bring ruin. And finally, even if you raised and harvested a crop, there was the ultimate question of price at the moment of harvest. After hearing all my problems, Pa remarked that he would rather be in business under a roof.

That year the crop in South Texas had been a failure. Onions were in short supply, but for me everything went right. It rained at the right moment. There was no hail or thrip. I produced a beautiful crop even though I had cut back on the acreage. Even Joe Alvarez smiled. Every day he gave higher quotations. I sold the crop at a good price and went on to other problems.

About a week later I received a call from Tebbe, Joe Alvarez's boss. Did I have any onions, any onions at all, even a partial carload? I thought a bit and answered that we still had onions out in the field we had graded out. A good part of these were *morados*, that is, purple onions that were graded out of yellow onions.[13] "Right now," said Tebbe, "any onion that's sound, whatever the color, will bring $3.75 a sack." I went out to the field to check. There was a mound of onions that had been graded out. Some had been damaged. The majority were off-color or seed-stem onions. Some were boilers, too small to pass grade.

I put a crew to work regrading and sacking anything that was sound. Then I thought of other possible sources to tap. During the harvest a patch of about a quarter of an acre had been abandoned. The strip was infested with *chancaquillas*, a type of grass burr you have to experience to appreciate, if that's the proper term. When dry, the burr clings to your clothes, gets in your shoes, penetrates anything but tough leather, and is excruciatingly painful to the hands.[14] O. Henry must have been thinking of *chancaquillas* in his short story "Shoes," about a man who opens a shoe store in South America only to discover that everyone went barefoot. He solves his problem by importing a shipload of Texas grass burrs and spreading them at night. The next day everyone rushes to his store to purchase shoes.[15]

The harvesting crews refused to work in the infested patch. I offered a bonus to no avail. Then I bought some heavy gauntlet-type gloves and told my foreman to put some men of our crew to work pulling onions. He came back to say that the men said they would quit first. My mother was with me the day we were packing the culled onions and wanted to know why the unharvested patch had been left there. When I explained the problem, she replied, "Nonsense. We'll harvest those onions ourselves." And so Ma and I put on our gloves and went to work pulling onions in the burr patch. Once we had them out, the men clipped them and sacked them. In this way we were able to salvage three hundred sacks of onions and sold them for over a thousand dollars. A crazy business, the onion business.

Some months later we had a cotton crop of fifty acres. We had the same problem with some areas: they were infested with *chancaquillas*. Ma and I put on huge cotton-picker sacks, which have a strap that loops over one shoulder and you drag the sack after you. We picked cotton that no one else would pick. Ma must have been over sixty at the time. I can just imagine what the society ladies of Eagle Pass would have said if they could see her.

THE MIKULINSKYS

Adjoining El Retiro on the north was Owsey Mikulinsky's farm, the Loma Linda. Owsey had a most interesting story to tell. His family had been prominent in the lumber industry of western Russia around Gomel, the same area where Ruth's grandfather had been in the same industry. After the Russian Revolution, Mikulinsky's older brother was appointed commissar of the lumber industry, a job he couldn't refuse without dire consequences. Owsey worked under his brother in the field.

One day when Owsey was coming home from work, he was met by a frightened member of the family with the news that his brother had been arrested as a traitor for "not meeting his norms"; that is, he was not producing enough lumber to meet the communists' demands.

Owsey was given as much money as was available and advised to run for his life, leaving behind his wife, Tanya, who was expecting their first child. Mikulinsky ran for the border, slipping under the wire at the frontier, and made his way to Czechoslovakia, then to Germany, and finally to Mexico. He was initially unable to enter the United States, as the new immigration law had severely limited immigration into the country.

In Mexico, he started peddling to make a living, ending up in the Rosita area of northern Mexico, about seventy miles southwest of Piedras Negras. About a year after he left Russia, Tanya joined him in Mexico with their infant son, Sam. They moved to Piedras Negras, and when Sam reached school age, he went to school in Eagle Pass. The Mikulinskys became members of our Jewish community and were very good friends of my parents.

Mikulinsky often told me about his experience in Mexico. In partnership with several other Jews, also from Russia or from Poland, he built up a considerable business selling radios. Owsey went directly to one of the biggest radio manufacturers in Chicago—Majestic, I believe—and contracted for a variety of models, including a large console unit. He gave the radio consoles the name Ultramar. These radios turned out to be of excellent quality. They were so well promoted by Mikulinsky and his partners that for years afterwards, as he told me with a chuckle, his former customers drove merchants on both sides of the river crazy by insisting on the Ultramar brand as the very best.

When the Mikulinskys were finally able to emigrate to the United States, it was their intention to move to a large city. However, by this time their son, Sammy, had become the close friend of Richmond Harper, whose father, Osie, went to see Owsey to convince him to stay in the border area. "Why, the idea," said Osie, "to go live among all them damned Yankees! The horror of it!"[16]

GROWING SPINACH

Somehow Owsey was persuaded to stay in Eagle Pass, going into the business of planting and selling spinach, of which he knew absolutely nothing. By the time I knew him and became his next-door neighbor in the fall of 1939, he was already doing well as a spinach planter. The Loma Linda consisted of about 1,100 acres, about 150 of which was in river *vega*, meadow, too rough for farming. Above this was five hundred acres of farmland on two levels: on top was the arroyo and below a tract of brush land. By double-cropping some of the land, Mikulinsky raised around seven hundred acres of spinach a season. When I later started running cattle, I made a swap by which I used the *vega* and the upper land for cattle, and in return Mikulinsky farmed about 150 acres of El Retiro, which he could irrigate from his second lift pump and upper storage tank.

The farming on the Loma Linda was under the supervision of Tony Mello, who had gone to grammar school with me years before.[17] Tony was an excellent farmer and did his end of the operation very well except for his one failing: he drank too much. Once he bent double the steel pole carrying the telephone to Indio Ranch headquarters by ramming it with his car, which was demolished. Tony told me, very dramatically acting out all the parts, about how once in the brush he had come across a whole family of javelina, which charged him on sight. According to Tony, he saved himself by using his .22 rifle as a club and fighting his way through the pack.[18]

The theory of large-scale spinach farming was that by planting in successive plots starting in late August, the planter would have a continuous flow of spinach for the market, allowing him, theoretically, to take advantage of prices over a long period and average out better than in a one-shot crop. The trouble with this system of growing spinach is that it depleted the soil, not rich in humus to begin with, ultimately causing falling yields and increasing crop diseases over time.

Mikulinsky planted successive spinach crops in fifty-acre plots, providing a steady supply from November until late spring. At peak production, and using my unused upper land in exchange for his range land, he planted more than nine hundred acres. Mikulinsky loved the spinach business. The part he cared for most was the *handlen*, in the Yiddish expression. That is, he loved the wheeling and dealing. He sold his crop himself, unlike most of the other planters of his size, who sold through brokers like Ritchie or Tebbe. During World War II, when spinach was in great demand, Mikulinsky was in his glory, dealing with the various brokers' agents who flocked to Eagle Pass, the Spinach Capital of the World, according to our Chamber of Commerce. The Anglos all called him Mr. Micky or plain Micky. The Mexicans called him *Miskulín*.

Especially after the war started, farm labor became increasingly scarce.[19] We, along with Mikulinsky, solved the problem by getting our labor from the pool on the Mexican side. At the point where the common boundary of the Loma Linda and El Retiro reached the Rio Grande, the river narrowed. Its course followed an ancient fault scarp as it wound between cliffs on both sides, a little higher on the Mexican side. There were a number of slate-like layers of rock at an angle in the river, making it easy to cross, especially in periods of low water. Directly across from us on top the cliff there was a Mexican settlement. It wasn't difficult to attract someone's attention there. Whenever we needed help, all we had to do was raise an arm up and down to indicate the number of hands needed. The Border Patrol knew all of us were using illegal labor, but they let us alone with the tacit understanding that none of the workers left the area.

Mikulinsky had a crew of about fifty men, women, and children who came over every morning and after cutting spinach would go home at night. One day, we got a new crew of Border Patrol men in the area. One of them happened to drive up in the evening just as the harvesting crew was taking off their shoes to cross back over the river. Why he did what he did I don't know. Perhaps it was some superior's orders or maybe the man was just malicious. Anyway, he made the entire crew march over a mile and a half all the way to the Loma Linda gate. He had radioed for some vans, and the entire crew of some fifty people were then hauled eighteen miles back to Eagle Pass, driven to the International Bridge, and told to go back to Mexico. Next day, they were back again at work, cutting spinach at the Loma Linda. I don't know how they got back, whether they walked or hired someone to take them home. In any event, they were back at work, perhaps a little later than usual.

The harvesting of spinach was an interesting operation. A harvesting crew was usually around fifty people, including children who learned to help their parents. If the crew was from town, they were hired through a contractor who furnished trucks and brought the labor. Each spinach cutter had a special sharp knife, which severed the plant at the top of the root. The cutters were paid by the basket, which had to be tightly filled before the basket tops were forced down and closed. If the *espinaca*, or *acelga*, or *yerba*, as the crop was variously called, was thick and of good quality, an expert could cut and fill baskets with amazing rapidity. If the crops were poor, or if this was the second cutting, the cutter would have to be paid a higher rate per basket.

The baskets were then loaded onto trucks that had specially constructed wooden railings about eight feet high on the truck bed, permitting about two hundred baskets at a time to be hauled to town. The trucks would stop at the refrigerator railcar, and each basket was opened and given to the icer, a worker who tossed a shovelful of chopped ice into the basket, which was closed and loaded into the car. It took trained men to load each car with about eight hundred baskets, placed in such a manner that they would not fall all over in transit.

Mikulinsky was having much more success by raising spinach than I was in farming, so I decided to try growing spinach also. I planted a fifty-acre field on my best land. The stand was perfect; I was going to have an excellent crop, estimated at fifteen cars. Prices were excellent. Two competing Jewish wholesale produce firms from New York had sent their buyers to Eagle Pass. For lack of younger men, they had brought out of retirement two older men in their seventies. They were fiercely competitive and watched each other like hawks. Every move of the other, however innocent, was regarded with suspicion. One would think that the two of them were the only buyers in Eagle Pass by the way they disregarded the activities of the many other buyers. As soon as the markets closed in New York in the late afternoon, the two rivals declared a truce and had T-bone steaks and french fries together night after night in the Eagle Coffee Shop.

First one buyer got word of my field of spinach, and then came his rival. Each insisted I had to take them for an inspection and drove me half out of my mind by insisting that I had to promise an exclusive on the crop. Since I had expected to sell through Joe Alvarez, this presented a triple problem. Then a bombshell fell and my golden prospects collapsed. Mikulinsky reminded me that I had better go to the stationmaster, J. C. Carraway, and arrange for refrigerator cars, as they were in short supply.[20] Mr. Carraway was my neighbor, and I anticipated no trouble. When I went to the station to see him and explained the purpose of my visit, his smiling face fell as he explained that since the start of the war, there had been a shortage of refrigerator cars. Locally, because of the great number of cars required for vegetable crops, a quota system had been set up. Growers such as Ritchie Brothers, who were the big shippers before the war began, had the largest share of the quota. Small growers, such as Mikulinsky, were given a proportionate number of cars based on prewar shipments. Upstarts like me had to wait for a car not in use. My fifteen cars of spinach vanished like smoke.

The produce buyers kept hounding me to sell them my crop. Mikulinsky regretted that he had his own crop to ship. My foreman informed me there was evidence of disease in the field and I had to act quickly. I went to Carraway and pleaded. Finally, I was given two cars. In the end, I got back my costs and a small profit.

TOMATOES, CASTOR BEANS, AND PEANUTS

In addition to spinach and onions, one of the big crops of the area at that time was fall tomatoes. I had previously grown tomatoes with some success and sold them to Joe Alvarez at his packing shed. The tomatoes had to be picked at the right moment. If picked green, they would not mature properly. If picked too late, they would ripen too soon to be shipped east and could only be sold to canneries as "ripes" at a low price. Tomatoes generally started to mature between October 20 and 25, changing on the bottom from green to a shade of white. After that the tomato starts to turn pink. We had to pick the fruit as the green tomatoes started to whiten, not before, not later. At that time, we were planting a variety of tomato called Rutgers, a medium-sized tomato with good carrying qualities.

The first pick of tomatoes was called "cleaning the field." A large proportion from this pick would be misshapen, damaged, or worm-eaten tomatoes, which would be graded out as culls. After this first pick, most tomatoes picked by an experienced crew would be of good quality. The tomatoes would be placed in large lugs, loaded on a truck, and hauled to the packing shed. At the packing shed, each farmer's crop in turn was dumped, lug by lug, onto the grading table and run through. Meanwhile, Joe Alvarez usually was in his office calling New York or other markets. His crew chief supervised girls wearing gloves who graded out the culls. The good tomatoes were passed on, to be wrapped individually and packed in boxes of forty to fifty pounds. The price of graded tomatoes varied from around five cents to eight or nine cents per pound, depending on market conditions.

I remember one occasion when Sam Schwartz was there with a load of his tomatoes. Sam was president of the local irrigation district and also had a farm where he grew tomatoes. Every time the graders threw out a tomato, Sam picked it up, held it forth for all to see, and demanded to know what was wrong with it. Then he threw it back on the grading table. The graders gave a howl and threw it out again, but Sam put it back. The graders yelled for Alvarez, who, in accented English, demanded that Sam leave the girls alone. Sam yelled in Yiddish that Joe was a gonif, a thief. I don't know the final result of that comedy act. I left.

Sometime around 1942, Mikulinsky proposed to me a joint deal. I would grow fifty acres of tomatoes on my land. The cost of the crop would be evenly divided between us, with an allowance for the rent of the land. I had the responsibility for growing the crop; Mikulinsky would handle the money and pay all bills. Mikulinsky would sell the crop, endeavoring to make some direct deals, thereby eliminating Alvarez, the middleman. From the beginning all went well. It rained just after we planted, and we had a perfect stand. It was cool and the plants began to bloom early. We started to harvest around October 20 with heavy yields. Mikulinsky made a deal with a Dallas produce man to sell the tomatoes loaded on the farm for five dollars a lug, field run, that is, ungraded.[21]

On the night of November 1, I had dinner with the Mikulinskys. After hearing Owsey's latest joke, we got down to business. It seems that we were breaking even, almost to the penny. From then on it would be all profit. The usual season started November 1, and with luck, we would have a month before frost. The next morning three trucks were arriving to pick up an estimated fifteen thousand dollars in tomatoes. That night it froze and all the tomatoes were lost. A sad ending after a very promising beginning.

During the war my mother showed me an article in the San Antonio paper that reported that castor beans were badly needed for the manufacture of oil for military aviation. It just happened that Ma had for years grown castor beans as a purely decorative plant in her garden behind the store. The castor bean might grow into a regular tree in the tropics, but in Eagle Pass it grew into a shrub about six or seven feet tall with flat leaves about a foot wide, growing like parasols. The plant has a red bloom and produces a round pod with about four large seeds from which the oil is derived.

Taking seeds from her garden, Ma personally seeded castor beans all along the main irrigation canals until she had a long line of plants. In a few months the seeds began to mature. Without bothering the farmhands, Ma and I picked beans until we had sacks and sacks full stacked in the barn. When my brother Reuben came home on leave, he too was taken out to pick beans. By the time the first frost came we had a small truckload.

I went to see Mr. Sellers, the county agricultural agent, and asked where I was supposed to ship the load of castor beans. He was taken aback. "What are castor beans?" he asked. I explained about the article Ma had seen. He expressed ignorance of the entire project but said he would look into it. He reported back a few days later that none of his agricultural contacts knew anything about a castor bean program. The castor beans were emptied into one of the fields and as they sprouted were plowed under. They were cheap fertilizer, having cost us nothing.

Despite this setback, I still wanted to help the war effort, so I asked Mr. Sellers to give me a list of crops considered necessary by the government. One such crop was peanuts. I suppose peanuts and peanut candy were valuable foods for the military. Also, peanut oil was in demand. The soil at El Retiro was sandy and suitable for peanuts, which are easy enough to grow. I planted some fifty acres of the crop. They are planted in rows wide enough apart to cultivate mechanically. The peanut itself grows underground. The plant grows about a foot and a half tall and has the general appearance of clover or alfalfa.

At harvest time I had a new headache. The closest area where peanuts were extensively grown was the Pearsall region, about a hundred miles east of Eagle Pass. No one from Pearsall wanted to bring his thresher to Eagle Pass. Unless I could buy a thresher there was no way I could harvest my crop. I threw my problem back in the lap of the county agent, who had gotten me into this in the first place. After a few days, Mr. Sellers reported that he had secured a permit for me to purchase a stationary thresher. The catch was that I had to sign a statement that I agreed to harvest any crop in Maverick County where the owner did not have his own thresher. The thresher was delivered at a cost of around twelve hundred dollars, and I was ready to go. Nowadays no one would dream of using a stationary thresher: in order to harvest the crop, the peanuts had to be brought to the thresher. It would simply be too costly. However, at that time it was the latest stage of farm technology.

First the rows of mature plants were plowed with a row cultivator, then the plants were manually pulled, shaken to loosen dirt, and windrowed to dry. When the plants were well dried and brittle after about a week in the hot sun, they were ready for threshing. The peanut plants were lifted with pitchforks onto the flat-bottomed wagon we had made for carrying bundles of hegari and hauled to the thresher, which had been set up in an open field. One man had to be on top of the thresher to attend to the proper feeding, another man had to be at the discharge to sack peanuts, and a third man had to sew the sacks up and stack them. The thresher was run from a pulley belt attached to one of our tractors. The load of peanut plants would be hauled up to the thresher and peanut plants would be forked up to the top, where the man above fed them into the machine. The thresher, activated by the tractor and pulley, quivered and shook. Inside the thresher a series of revolving steel rods tore the peanut plants apart. The peanuts fell downward to come out the discharge. Peanut hay blew out one end of the thresher to stack up there, accompanied by a horrendous cloud of sandy, white dust. Everyone had to wear a bandanna over his face, and in a few minutes all of us looked like white-faced clowns. By the time I came home I was covered in about ten pounds of dirt.

It took us a week to harvest the crop, then the sacks were loaded onto a huge trailer truck to be hauled to Pearsall, where the nearest warehouse was located. Except for the peanut hay, which we stacked into a huge rick to better protect it against the elements, we were finished with peanuts, or so we thought. Then Mr. Sellers dropped the bombshell that a man in Quemado, about twenty miles from Eagle Pass, had four acres of peanuts, and I was obligated to harvest them.

It took us all day to haul our equipment to Quemado to the farm at the far side of the valley. In a few hours we had threshed his crop, barely earning enough to cover my costs. The farmer was an old white-haired Anglo with a long walrus mustache. He was very happy about the entire proceeding, since he planted, irrigated, cultivated, and pulled his crop entirely by himself and the result was all profit. Before we left, he said to me, "Mr. Morris, next week there's going to be an auction of some Quemado land. I sure wish y'all would bid on it. I don't want to see any of them damned Yankees from North Texas coming down here and taking over our land."

CHAPTER 9

THE CATTLEMAN

The end of World War II marked a sharp transitional period in the culture of Eagle Pass. It coincided with the disappearance of the old-time cattlemen who had previously dominated the life of the area. They were a rough, tough bunch, something like the characters depicted in Larry McMurtry's novel *Lonesome Dove*. Their sons and successors were a different breed. I was fortunate to meet a few of the old-timers before they all died off. These were men born in the old days of Indian wars and cattle drives, and a wide gulf exists between them and the businessmen who operate the ranches today. The same ranches still exist, with their thousands of acres, but the old glamour is gone.

The old-timers were a self-reliant breed who in their time had been working cowboys. Most of them were unpretentious, plain-speaking men who had survived good times and bad. When adversity brought drought, natural disaster, or financial crisis, they simply picked themselves up and started over again. Such men had very little contact with the government in their youth. They were suspicious of government, asking for no help and bearing any governmental restraint with fury. Since World War II, the ranches have mainly been owned by men with a few cattle for show, who couldn't ride a horse, and knew little of the practical side of raising cattle in the old manner; they were mainly interested in hunting leases so they could put on shiny new boots and hunt deer from a blind.

When I was a boy, there were thousands of longhorn cattle on the ranches in this area. They were all horns and a tail on long legs. They were tough like jackrabbits and their owners. They were wild and difficult to handle. Only a skilled cowboy or vaquero could round them up in the brush country. Many of the old-time vaqueros used dogs to get them out of the thickets. The longhorns began to disappear when English breeds were brought in. After the longhorn came the shorthorn, which gave way to mixed breeds such as the Santa Gertrudis, Angus, and the Charolais. The domesticated breeds are docile and even when allowed to roam are much easier to control than the old wild cattle.

One of the unfortunate consequences of the windmill and other improvements is overgrazing. Cattle will eat what tastes best, much as a child will go for candy. The result is that many of the best native grasses have disappeared. In this area, between fifteen and twenty acres of range land are needed to raise a cow and a calf on an annual basis. The trouble is that greedy men in a strong market will overstock following a good rain. For a while all goes well, but then a dry period comes and the land is seriously overgrazed.

For many years, the customary meeting place for cattlemen from both sides of the border was the Eagle Hotel in Eagle Pass. Over coffee, deals were made, and cattle were bought and sold. It was an informal market. There was a definite caste system among these men based on the amount of land they owned and the number of cattle. First of all were the cowmen. Some of them had ranches larger than some of our smaller American states. The largest were in northern Mexico. Hal Mangum had over a million acres. Old Man Meir had as much. At one time, the Sánchez Navarro family held 16,500,000 acres, and the Terrazas family had five million.[1] On the American side, none of the ranches in our area were over a hundred thousand acres, but there were some from twenty to fifty thousand acres. When I was a boy, the land between the outskirts of Eagle Pass to the intersection of Highway 57 and Interstate 35, nearly to San Antonio, was uninhabited except for a few isolated ranch houses. Even today this expanse of a hundred miles has only a sprinkling of inhabitants. Cattle ranches do not support many people.

Next in line in the caste system were the ranchers who bought stocker calves at around 250 pounds and let them run in fenced-in range country. This annually required about ten to twelve acres per animal. If there was enough rain to provide good pasture, these calves would get fat rapidly, reaching 750 to 800 pounds in less than a year. From local ranches stocker cattle were sold to slaughter or shipped to Kansas to be put on grass or, if good quality, to go to feedlots. Lowest on the totem pole were farmers, who planted winter oats and grazed cattle. In our part of the country this could only be done on irrigated land. The great ranchers spoke with a certain arrogance and a condescending attitude to anyone who was not a cowman.

The old-time cattlemen and cowboys dressed in simple fashion. The only man in Eagle Pass who clothed himself in anything resembling a dude-ranch outfit was known as Cowboy Fitzpatrick. He bred horses near town. The old-timers wore olive drab pants in various fabrics. These were stuck into their boots, which came to their knees. Shirts were usually white, with long sleeves in winter or summer. If they wore a tie, it would be a string tie. Hats were huge, with brims sometimes three and a half to four inches. I have seen old-time vaqueros and cowboys with antique, old-style high-peaked hats of the sort now only seen in photographs. I don't know where they bought them. No one that I recall wore either a black hat or a white one.

Since the Spanish days, the great landowners lived like lords of creation. In Texas, they dominated politics for generations. But by the end of World War II, it was clear that power was no longer in their hands. It was not the ranchers who gave the orders. New economic forces had more money. So far as I know, there are no more Anglo cowboys in this area. Pay is too low, life too lonely. Vaqueros must be brought in from Mexico, where they are still plentiful. Whether special permission must be secured to hire them, I don't know. The old Eagle Hotel was torn down, like other historic buildings in town. One no longer sees the cattlemen making deals for herds about to cross from Mexico or coming in at night to eat huge T-bone steaks. Perhaps it is just as well. In the period after the war, oil money and hunting leases seemed to be more important than cattle.

There is a story that is appropriate at this point. Three men were having drinks in the first-class lounge of a 747. The first one was a tall rancher in a big hat and boots. "I have a hundred thousand acres in West Texas," he boasted.

The second man, also a rancher wearing a Stetson and boots, said, "I have a fifty-thousand-acre spread in South Texas."

"And how about you?" the ranchers asked a little Jewish fellow, also in big hat and boots.

"I have four acres," he said.

"Only four acres!" they exclaimed. "Where?"

"Downtown Dallas," he replied.

Morris in about 1945. (Courtesy of Dr. Peter Riskind.)

THE AZULEJO

When I went into the ranching business my first task was to repair the barbed-wire fences and to have a windmill installed to provide water. I found the fences at the boundary with the Indio Ranch next door were in bad condition, and the Indio was not using the adjoining pastures. I repaired the fence at my expense. My next task was to stock El Retiro with cattle. For this purpose, I enlisted the help of Osie Harper, a neighbor and friend of my Uncle Albert.

Osie was a most unique person. He was six feet four and thin, with a long, gaunt face. He always wore an enormous wide-brimmed Stetson, which I never saw him remove. I wondered if he took his hat off when he went to sleep. His boots reached his knees. With his tall hat, cadaverous face, and high boots, Osie was a truly impressive sight. His voice was rasping, and when he spoke, there was no nonsense about his pronouncements. As long as he was alive, he ruled his three sons, Junior, Richmond, and Tito, with an iron hand.[2]

During the Mexican Revolution, around 1915, Osie had been a purchasing agent for the Carranza government. I vaguely recall discussions in the family regarding a proposal from Osie to make Pa a partner in his business. Pa was afraid that Osie might do something illegal, there being restrictions at that time on exports to Mexico, and he declined.[3] In any event, Osie and his brother Hite made a great deal of money. Osie used his share to buy the Azulejo ("bluebird"), a ranch of about a hundred thousand acres, from the Madero family.[4]

I went with Osie into Mexico to look for cattle. We drove to the edge of the mountains on the other side of Múzquiz to a ranch called Las Rusias—meaning either "the Russians" or a breed of silver-gray horses—but found nothing satisfactory and returned.[5] After our unsuccessful trip, Osie announced that he had seen no satisfactory cattle for my purposes and would have to sell me some of his own. He left me saying he would let me know when he had the calves rounded up. Sometime later I received a message to meet him at the Azulejo the afternoon of the following day to inspect the cattle that had been rounded up. Osie didn't ask if this was convenient. He said: "Be there."

It happened that my brother Reuben, on leave from the US Army Air Force, was coming to Eagle Pass the day following my appointment with Osie. He had only a few days' leave, and I was most anxious to see him. There was another problem: I had not yet bought a second vehicle, and my pickup truck was needed to carry hands back and forth to El Retiro. I asked Hite to loan me a truck or car for the trip and was given an aged, dilapidated International pickup that seemed to be held together with baling wire.

From El Retiro, the road to Azulejo heads south some forty miles, more or less paralleling the Rio Grande; there is now a paved road from Piedras Negras all the way to Laredo. At that time, the road was a dirt wagon trail. In wet weather, cars driving to Guerrero had cut a number of side trails, like the fingers of a hand, looking for higher, passable ground. Since there were no signs, it was most confusing. The road was deserted, weaving in and out of the mesquite brush.

After some thirty miles the trail passed the turnoff for Guerrero, visible on the left, and it continued on toward the Azulejo. About twelve miles from the ranch house, the road was blocked by the Azulejo gate. It was the old-fashioned variety that one had to get out to open. Unfortunately, by the time I had opened the gate the old pickup had stalled, its battery dead. There was nothing to do but walk. I covered the twelve miles to the ranch house on foot in three hours, walking at a fast pace. I was walking in boots that originally had tall heels, but I had the heels lowered as much as possible and they were not too uncomfortable. The walk was quiet and uneventful. There were no cars and no visible signs of life other than occasional quail, a few rabbits, and hawks flying overhead.

When I arrived at the ranch, Osie was waiting for me. After my explanation, he led me to the bedroom to wash up. There was a washbowl and a pitcher of water on a small table. Other than the bed and dresser, the room was bare; the walls were whitewashed, and there were no pictures or decoration. The Azulejo was not an impressive place. I have seen old-time Mexican haciendas that were quite imposing, consisting of a pretentious house, a church, a school, storehouses for food, and satellite homes for the vaqueros and field hands, the peones. The Azulejo had nothing of such splendor. It consisted of an unpretentious house and a number of adobe houses for vaqueros.

Osie led me into a large room that served as the dining room. By this time, I was ravenously hungry and had been looking forward to the prospect of eating a juicy steak at the famous Azulejo. To my shock the cook served me a plate containing two boiled doves and some grits. It happens that I dislike dove, especially boiled, and grits are not one of my favorite foods. But there was no choice—it was eat the dove and grits or go hungry, so I ate. While I was eating an old man came in and introduced himself as Osie's father. This was a surprise because he was not too tall and very cheerful, unlike Osie, and he did not seem old enough to be Osie's father.[6] Then he left the room and I did not see him again. In the corner of the room I noticed an old double-barreled shotgun, the largest I had ever seen, probably an eight-gauge. Sometime later I saw Osie's son, Richmond Harper, and asked him about it. He called it Old Betsy and proceeded to tell me the following story, acting out all the parts himself:

An American general in San Antonio got an invitation to visit the Azulejo from Osie's brother Larry. The general arrived with his staff, expecting to be royally entertained, only to find that Osie couldn't care less. A general meant nothing to him. The bored general decided to go hunting at night using flashlights, something strictly illegal in Texas. Carrying Old Betsy as his weapon, the general went off with his staff through the brush in search of deer. In order for them not to get lost in the dark, Osie sent a Mexican vaquero with them. Unfortunately, he could not speak English, and the general did not speak Spanish. After they tramped around in the dark for at least an hour, the vaquero led them back toward the ranch without the general knowing. All at once he saw two huge eyes shining at him. Despite the protestations of the vaquero (which no one understood), the general raised the old shotgun to his shoulders and fired both barrels. The gun went off with a terrific clang, followed by the sound of breaking glass. The general had shot out the headlights of his own Cadillac.

As soon as I had eaten, Osie rushed me to the corrals, which were quite large. To my surprise the calves he had collected were of excellent quality, much better than I expected, as I had been warned that Osie was a tough man to make a deal with, and I had no experience buying cattle. These calves weighed on average three hundred pounds, were of mixed Hereford breed, and would grade from good to choice, excellent for my purpose. It was my option to reject any calves I did not want. As a matter of form, I declined a few, accepting around 275 of them.

This done, I was ready to go home, as it had already turned dark, but Osie had more to show me. He handed me a flashlight—because I had arrived late, they had to do this job in the dark—and ordered me to stand astride the top of a chute, shining the light on cattle running through the chute in the dark. The cows in question were not calves but huge, full-grown Mexican longhorns. As each steer ran through the chute, I had to practically jump in the air to avoid the long, sharp horns. In the middle of this, a norther had come up. It was October, usually quite warm in that area. I had not expected such weather and was wearing only a short-sleeved shirt. I was freezing. The vaqueros temporarily stopped work, and one of them made some coffee. Along with the others I took mine out of a discarded Campbell's soup can I found on the ground nearby. Under the circumstances, sanitation was unimportant. The coffee was delicious.

By the time we were through with the longhorns, it was about midnight. I requested a lift to the stalled truck and a push to get it started. The drive back was uneventful until I got near to the lights of Guerrero, where I came to a fork in the road. I turned left, only to realize that the road I had chosen was going inland rather than north toward Piedras Negras. I started to turn around, got the truck across the road, and again it stalled. I had no success trying to restart it so I just dozed in my seat. About an hour later, I saw the lights of an approaching car. I got out and stood in front of the truck. The approaching vehicle turned out to be a pickup with two men inside. I walked over to the driver, who stuck a pistol the size of a cannon in my face and asked what I wanted. After I explained my predicament, they helped me turn around and gave me a push to get started. This time, when I came close to the lights of Guerrero, I made the correct turn and continued my odyssey.

All went well, and after a while I could see to my right the bright glare of the furnace of La Consolidada, a steel mill in Piedras Negras about five miles away.[7] Then my troubles began anew. The trail to the highway divided into a series of tracks, and I could not tell which was correct and kept going toward the glare of the furnace. The trail I took went through thick mesquite brush, then went down into a creek bottom. I tried desperately to extricate myself, but the truck stalled, completely dead. I opened the hood and discovered that a battery cable was on fire. I tried throwing dirt to no avail; then I grabbed the cable as high up as I could and yanked it loose. There was nothing to do but abandon the truck.

I climbed the other wall of the arroyo and looked around. The wind was blowing and it was freezing cold. I headed off through the brush toward La Consolidada as fast as I could. As I approached Piedras Negras after about an hour's walk, my way was obstructed by barbed-wire fences. These were easy enough, but I began to pass jacales, all of them guarded by mean-looking dogs. With dogs yapping at my heels, I finally reached paved streets. At around 6 a.m. I arrived at the International Bridge looking dirty, bedraggled, and tired. The immigration inspector at the bridge took one look at me and said admiringly, "Boy, oh, boy! You must have had one hell of a night in Boy's Town!"[8]

TRAVELS WITH TIPPIE

Perhaps because I had repaired the boundary fence at my expense, Scales, the manager of the Indio, allowed my vaqueros to graze the cattle on the Indio's *vega* adjoining El Retiro. This was a strip of some one hundred acres of Bermuda grass along the river outside the Indio fence. Most of the year the grass on the *vega* was green and lush; even in dry weather it was excellent pasture. Together with the Loma Linda acreage I leased, I had a substantial tract of land, between eight hundred and a thousand acres, on which to graze cattle.

Occasionally, I explored the area on horseback, but I much preferred to go about on foot. It was an exhilarating experience to walk through the country with my dog Tippie at my heels. I soon learned that not only were there wet and dry cycles, but the normal year had its progressions of development. Especially if there were rains, the land came to life toward the end of February. Grass turned green and trees and brush started to put on leaves, the mesquite last of all. If there was rain, wildflowers appeared overnight. By the middle of March, there would be a profusion of birds and other wildlife. Raccoons, armadillos, turtles, opossum, red fox, coyote, cottontails, and jackrabbits were in abundance. There were also traces of more exotic animals, such as the Rio Grande beaver, now a protected animal. Once, at a distance, I saw a large gray animal, much too large for the average coyote. I took it to be a wolf, but my encyclopedia said the gray wolf is not found east of New Mexico; I wondered if it could have come out of the high mountains of Mexico. By midsummer all this beauty had gone. If the rains came around September 1, it cooled down and everything again came to life once more.

I am no botanist, but soon I was able to recognize the common vegetation: the sage, the guajilla, the white brush, the black brush, the lantana, the cat's claw, and all sorts of wildflowers. All along the river, the trees put out leaves: the willows, the elm, the hackberry, and the mesquite, which grew to a respectable size where there was water. I became observant of the various kinds of grasses and learned from our vaquero, Agapito, the difference between the edible grasses and needlegrasses, which cattle could not eat.[9] A good rancher soon learns that if he overgrazes his pasture, the cattle quickly eliminate the grass that has value as food, leaving only trash vegetation. Soil erosion becomes a fact rather than some theoretical threat once one truly inspects the terrain at hand. In my opinion, soil erosion and soil depletion are the greatest threats facing the human race.

One day Tippie and I were at the southwest corner of the ranch in the Indio area, a very isolated spot. Coming through the arroyo we came upon some large fresh paw prints about the size of a man's hand in the sandy area near the river. We tracked the animal until Tippie got very excited. I looked ahead to see a large shape about a hundred yards away. The beast—perhaps a mountain lion—stood there looking at us. Then we took off in the direction we came from as fast as we could run.

Although there was much game of all kinds in the area, I did little hunting. I have no use for those who kill beautiful animals for no reason at all. I include the so-called hunting safari in this category. Shooting at game to eat I can understand; I didn't hunt deer or dove because I didn't enjoy eating the meat. But I did like quail, and El Retiro was covered with many dense thickets, thick with quail. I attempted to train Tippie, a beagle, which are usually used as rabbit dogs, to be a pointer, but I had little success. Carrying a double-barreled .410 shotgun Uncle Eli had given me, I would approach a thicket slowly, hoping Tippie would stand and point to the quail. Instead, Tippie would dash in, the quail would fly in a sudden whirl of sound, and, if I fired at all, I would be so afraid of hitting Tippie I'd be way off target. Finally, I gave up trying to make a pointer out of a beagle.

One of my favorite areas to visit was El Retiro's southern boundary with El Indio. From the top of the fault scarp hill there was a magnificent view of the Rio Grande channel and of the farmland below. I would stand there and dream of building a house to take advantage of the view. My special pride and joy was a flock of wild turkeys that had flown over from Mexico and had made a home in one of the isolated thickets. The birds were elusive and it was a game of hide-and-seek to get a glimpse of them. Then, when I returned from a vacation, I learned that Billy Ritchie, without asking permission, had appeared with a pack of dogs and chased the turkeys back to Mexico. They never returned. I could have killed Billy then and there.

RAISING CATTLE

After studying Morrison's *Feeds and Feeding* and discussing my problems with Mr. Sellers, the county agent, I decided to divide my cattle into two groups.[10] I put about eighty calves in a feedlot I constructed, and I let the rest, about two hundred calves, roam free under the watchful eye of Agapito, the vaquero. At Agapito's insistence, we went to the ranch of one of his former employers, situated some miles from Eagle Pass, to try to find him a horse for herding cattle. We found John Mason, the foreman, and a group of vaqueros gathered around a fire trying to keep warm on the cold day.[11] After much palaver between Agapito and Mason, we bought a beautiful-looking horse and a Heiser saddle for some nominal amount, I think about seventy-five dollars.[12] At the same time, I couldn't understand why the horse was sold for so little, but I soon found out. This horse, which Agapito called Johnnie, was as close to a schizophrenic as a horse can be. Most of the time Johnnie was a superb cow horse, strong, fast, and well-trained. But now and then, for no apparent reason, Johnnie would go berserk. He even managed to throw Agapito, a superb rider, and broke his leg, although Agapito insisted it was not the horse's fault since he had tripped in a gopher hole.

I went riding on Johnnie once, which was enough for me. All of a sudden, Johnnie took flight and tried to knock me off by going under low mesquite limbs. Frank Dobie describes in one of his books about how experienced vaqueros in the South Texas brush country were sometimes killed by their horses pulling this stunt.[13] I managed to flatten myself along the side of the horse, getting badly scraped and bruised in the process, but hung on. When this didn't shake me off, Johnnie tried hurling himself against the side of the corrals, trying to mash me against the heavy corral boards. I finally was able to dismount, and I decided I'd had enough of Johnnie. After that I rode an old mare with no vicious tendencies.[14]

I must confess that I was a complete failure as a cowboy. Whenever I tried to help move cattle I always zigged while the calf zagged and never managed to be where the action was. On one occasion we were working inside a corral and I had the bright idea that I could help out on foot. I was promptly knocked down by a five-hundred-pound calf, coming at me at full speed. My ribs hurt and my teeth rattled. I never tried anything so stupid again.

One day the men were working on the corrals and I came over to check on their progress. I heard someone speak in a perfect old-time Texas accent and turned around, expecting to find some paunchy middle-aged Anglo rancher. Instead, it was one of the men digging a post hole. His name was Salvador Dovalina, and he said that he had been educated in the Uvalde elementary school. His brother Natividad, who also worked for me, couldn't speak a word of English.[15]

I decided to try to put my farming experience to use, growing my own fodder for the cattle and to experiment with feed. After the onions had been harvested, I planted a crop called hegari. This is a member of the sorghum family, similar to milo. Milo is all seed head with very little plant, and today it is about the only sorghum grown because the grain is a perfect height to be mechanically harvested with a combine. Hegari had more leaf and stalk, and I planted it as a source of bulk ensilage. The hegari was planted in rows in the same fields where we had harvested onions. There was so much fertilizer remaining in the soil that the hegari crop turned out to be a fantastic one, the sorghum growing to a height of around six feet with large heads of grain.

The next step, according to Morrison's *Feeds and Feeding*, was to build a silo to house the ensilage. I decided to build a trench silo. Using the diesel tractor and a drag, we dug a silo measuring about a hundred feet long from entrance to exit. It started at ground level, reached a maximum depth of from twelve to fifteen feet, and exited at a gradual rise to the ground level. When the hegari crop was mature, the next step was to harvest and fill the silo, which was a little more difficult than I had anticipated. For one thing, a black cloud of starlings, which was joined by more compatriots daily, settled on the hegari and proceeded to eat the maturing grain. I got out the double-barreled shotgun Uncle Eli had given me, but after a few days the birds learned the range of the gun; as I banged away at one end, the damned birds flew over to the other end of the field, well out of range. I kept chasing them around until I finally gave up, deciding it best to put all efforts into harvesting as quickly as possible.

I managed to buy a used row binder and hammermill. Such equipment is no longer used simply because it requires too much labor. We also made two flatbed wagons, which were pulled by tractor and our two mules. One tractor pulled the row binder, which cut the hegari row by row and tied it in bundles. The bundles were loaded on the wagons and pulled to the hammermill. There the hegari was chopped into one-inch pieces, leaf, stalk, and grain, and automatically dropped into the trench silo.

Morrison stressed that the ensilage had to be packed very tightly or it would spoil and suggested running a tractor over it, back and forth, to pack it down. We had no available tractor so I tried another idea. We attached a heavy weight to a pole, and the idea was that a man would spread and vigorously pound the ensilage as it was cut by the hammermill. It was a very hot day, about 110 degrees in the shade, and the men taking turns pounding the ensilage showed no enthusiasm. I decided to get down into the pit myself to show them how it should be done. I worked away very vigorously until I quit with heat prostration and was able to get home only with difficulty. Atanacio, the foreman, continued to fill the trench silo then covered it with dirt. The remaining bundled hegari was staked in large ricks about fifteen feet high and left to dry. Some of this we later used ourselves, but most of it we sold to ranchers who needed feed in dry years.

About eighty calves were brought into the feeding pen we had built and fed a daily ration of ensilage dropped into a trough for the cattle to eat at the rate of so many pounds per animal per day. This was supplemented with cottonseed cake, very rich in protein. After we harvested peanuts, we had self-feeders with dry peanut hay, which was also very rich in protein. The eighty calves in the feedlot grew rapidly and soon were fat and sleek. I followed the instructions in *Morrison's* with care, increasing the quantity of feed constantly as the cattle grew. The self-feeders were kept filled with peanut hay, and the combination worked wonders.

Some months after the calves were placed in the feedlot, two Jewish men, cattle buyers from Denver, showed up. They offered a firm contract to purchase my stock at fourteen cents per pound, to be delivered in six months at the railroad in Eagle Pass. They offered a deposit of two thousand dollars cash. I had read in *Morrison's*, my bible, that there had to be a price spread of some cents between the price paid for the calves and the fatted cattle. Since I had bought the calves for ten cents a pound, I thought I was doing well selling at fourteen cents a pound. I didn't take into account the war that was going on, and that there would be an inevitable inflation of prices.

I happened to see the younger of two cattle buyers from Denver sometime after I delivered the cattle. He told me that they had sold the cattle in San Antonio for twenty cents a pound; and he also confessed, shamefacedly, that I should have received a large government bonus intended for the producer of cattle fattened to choice grade. His partner, he said, had collected the bonus, falsely signing a statement that he was the producer. I knew nothing about such a bonus and was furious, but it was too late.

A QUARTER HORSE NOT WORTH A NICKEL

I used to buy gasoline and get my car serviced at Ward Wueste's service station at Main and Monroe. Across the street, where the American Legion is located now, there was a large lot, empty except for a grove of very old, twisted, and gnarled mesquite trees. One day when I stopped at the gas station I noticed a crowd gathered on the empty lot. Out of curiosity I crossed the street to discover what was going on. A horse was tied to one of the trees—or it might be more correct to say the horse was leaning against the tree, which seemed to hold the creature up. The horse was what in the local expression we would call a "sorry animal": sway-backed, shaggy-haired, and skinny, its bones visible, and very sad looking.

Standing by the horse were two tick inspectors who periodically came by El Retiro, "Pockets" Mason, who was about five feet, six inches tall, and Kraft, his associate, who was about six feet five. They both wore white shirts stuck into their Levi's, which in turn were tucked into their boots, but the effect each gave was very different. Together they were like the comic strip "Mutt and Jeff."[16] They were very pleasant in doing their job, neither officious nor nasty, as some were, and I always enjoyed chatting with them. As river riders, it was their duty to impound all horses found on the riverbank and, if not claimed, sell them at auction.

A customs man in uniform was trying to hold the auction of the horse leaning against the tree. Every time he called out "What am I bid?", the crowd of loafers broke into jeers. One of them yelled, "Who will bid a nickel for a quarter horse?" The auctioneer was getting more and more exasperated. Despite his efforts, no one bid.

"Morris, why don't you make a bid to start it off?" Pockets suggested to me.

Without thinking I said, "Five dollars" and went on into the post office across the street.

When I came back a few minutes later, Pockets and Kraft had wide grins on their faces. "The horse is yours," Pockets said, congratulating me.

"Wait a minute, wait a minute," I protested. "What do you mean the horse is mine? I don't want it."

"Too bad," said the auctioneer. "You got the horse," and he gave me a slip with the instructions to go upstairs to the federal building, show it to the customs cashier, and pay five dollars.

Grumbling loudly, I went across the street. I found the customs office on the second floor, showed my paper to the cashier, and paid the cash. "You sure bought a horse cheap," the cashier said, to which I replied, "You haven't seen the horse."

I went downstairs worrying about the damn horse. What was I going to do with it? I doubted it could be ridden eighteen miles to El Retiro. To truck it in alone would cost money, ten dollars at least. And what would I do with the animal once it got there, just let it die a natural death?

As I reached the front of the federal building, a man was waiting for me. He wore a black hat, like a villain in a Western movie. He had a thin Leo Carrillo mustache, and his eyes were shifty and nervously looking from here to there as though expecting something dramatic to happen.[17]

"Señor," he said, "will you sell the horse? I want a gentle horse for my little girl." (The horse was gentle enough—it could barely move.)

"Why didn't you buy the horse at the auction?" I asked.

"I am afraid of *el ley*, Señor. I don't want nothing to do with the law."

"What will you give me for the horse?"

"Eight dollars," he said. I might have gotten a little more, but why tempt fate? I took the eight dollars, endorsed my title, and ran.

A FEUD AMONG MY CREW

In addition to Atanacio, the foreman, and Agapito, the vaquero, I hired Demetrio Daniel, a carpenter.[18] When I was a small boy of six or seven, Demetrio had worked for my father assembling and repairing furniture in a large galvanized-iron warehouse behind the store. While he worked, he would sing songs from the Mexican Revolution or tell old stories about *el gato y el ratón*, the cat and the rat. As a boy, I was fascinated by him. I needed a carpenter at El Retiro, and when I heard that Demetrio was unemployed, I gave him the job. By this time his hair had turned gray, but he still had his fierce-looking mustache. He was a short man, still thin and spry as ever. Demetrio built not only the irrigation discharge but a small house and outhouse, a barn, and the cattle corrals and chutes.

A serious feud soon developed between Atanacio, Agapito, and Demetrio. Atanacio regarded Agapito as a loafer. According to Atanacio, Agapito did nothing all day long but sit on his horse while others were doing physical labor. Agapito, for his part, had a vaquero's traditional contempt for the farm laborer. He was a horseman, a caballero, and he considered himself superior to the others, including the foreman. As for Demetrio, he was in a rage because Atanacio did not require the men to refer to him as "maestro." Atanacio was also angry at Demetrio because on Monday mornings Demetrio was never ready to work, having celebrated on Sunday like a good old-time revolutionary.

At some point, ducks became part of the controversy. Someone had given my mother a pair of Muscovy ducks—large, white ducks known for being quackless. The ducks did very well in the yard behind the store and soon had multiplied to eight, too many. There were many complaints about the ducks, which had acquired an aggressive and possessive attitude regarding the backyard, which they considered their territory. The ducks were gathered up by Atanacio, who took them out to the ranch and turned them loose by the house and barn. All went well for a while. The ducks prospered and became regular denizens of the area. The big white birds waddled around as if they owned the place and liked to congregate around the house where Agapito lived, where water was always available. I paid no particular attention to them.

One day Atanacio stopped me and, in a conspiratorial voice, accused Agapito of eating the ducks. "Count them, Señor Morris. Count them and you'll see for yourself." Sure enough, the ducks had been reduced to seven. Sometime later I saw Agapito. He also took me aside as if someone were listening. "Listen, Señor Morris, I have to tell you this. That man is stealing your ducks. Just count them and you'll see for yourself."

The next day there were only six ducks, and it was clear that something was making the big white birds nervous. Demetrio was working on the corrals. He beckoned for me to draw near, and even though no one else was around he whispered, "Señor Morris, you know I am a friend of yours and can be trusted. Those two men are bad. They are stealing your ducks." The next day there were only five ducks. The men glared at each other and gave me knowing glances, mentioning ducks at every opportunity. In a few days, the obviously excited ducks had all disappeared. What happened to them? It was a mystery.

Very often in the early morning on the way to the ranch I used to give a ride to one of our local characters, Bill Bond.[19] He would squat on the ground on the arroyo bridge near the old Estrada warehouse and wait for a lift. Bill was thin and wiry, with a seamed face cooked by the sun. He always wore the same outfit, a matched pair of khaki pants and shirt that looked as though he never changed them. Every Christmas, Bill was given a new shirt and pants by Travis Ferguson, a local planter. By the end of the year his clothes were again in tatters. Bill always carried a beat-up old shotgun. His hat looked like he had found it somewhere. All in all, he was a wild-looking individual. I used to refer to him as Daniel Boone when speaking of him to my boys.

The first few times Bill was my passenger, he rode without saying a word except when he wanted to get out. After a while he became more loquacious. It seems that during World War I, Bill was the driver for a general. Bill indicated that being the chauffeur for an important personage was the only job he could hold. No other employment would be fitting and proper for him. Once, said Bill, he had broken his rule and at the instigation of a local benefactor—either Hite Harper or Travis Ferguson—he had accepted a job as a hunting guide for a Houston oilman. The oilman promised Bill a large reward if he would help him kill a deer. According to Bill, this man had noisily clomped through the brush in his new boots and squeaky whipcord britches, scaring every animal within a mile. Bill placed him up in a tree downwind from where Bill knew the deer was and instructed him to sit tight until Bill could circle around and drive the deer by. After a while, a deer appeared and the oilman fired, but he had gotten so excited that he fell out of the tree and broke his leg. That was it, said Bill. No more such jobs for him.

One night, my Aunt Rose went to answer a knock at the door. She returned a few moments later in a state of shock holding a wild duck by the legs. A wild man had handed her the duck, she said, claiming it was for me, and had immediately left. It was Bill, showing his appreciation to me the only way he knew how.

So, I mentioned the case of the vanishing ducks to Bill one day while giving him a lift. Bill suggested I take him out to the scene of the crime. He briefly examined the area around the house, studied the ground, and then took off toward the arroyo. In a while he returned, then gave me a demonstration of all sorts of animal tracks, pointing out the differences between dog, coyote, fox, rabbit, raccoon, and opossum marks. "Come with me," he said. He led me to an area of heavy brush near the arroyo. The ground was littered with duck feathers and bones. "You got a fox and her pups in that burrow over there. Them's the ones who ate up your ducks," he said. "What did you expect, leaving them unprotected like that? Some varmint had to get them sooner or later." And so Bill Bond solved the mystery of the disappearing ducks.

I always considered Bill to be the last true Texan, proud to the end, resistant to government interference or anything that smacked of charity. In his later years. when he was a sick man, I tried to help him, a war veteran, move into a nursing home for old soldiers. He refused proudly, and I left him in despair. A few weeks later we had a strong norther, and Bill died huddled near the door of one of the downtown stores.

THE COWS FROM PHARAOH'S DREAM

In the fall of 1944, I struck a deal with Osie Harper to fatten about 150 calves on oats. The procedure was to broadcast oats in early September when rain was expected and nights began to turn cool. Around December 1, the field should be ready for grazing, and by dividing the field, one part would be grazed while another area would be irrigated. In this way, the cattle would always have ample feed. I also added clover to the oats. As long as there were oats the cattle would prefer them to clover, but when the oats finally failed because of heat in the spring, then they would be forced to eat the clover, which was very fattening. Later the uneaten clover would be plowed under as a green manure.

Harper agreed to send me calves of the same quality as the ones he previously sold me. The deal was the customary one at the time: I had all the expense of growing the crop of oats, Harper furnished the cattle, and we split the increase of weight. Calves were worth fifteen cents a pound, while fat cattle were worth twenty cents. The calves Harper provided entered weighing about five hundred pounds each, and after the feeding period, they weighed eight hundred pounds. After some cost calculations, I figured that Harper might make about fifty-five dollars per head, while I might make about thirty dollars per head, or about 4,500 dollars total—not much, even if all went well. I couldn't help myself because I was out of money and didn't want to ask my father for a loan.

Almost immediately, things went wrong. I discovered why no one had used deep well pumps on the river. There was so much silt that the pump impellers soon got chewed up and had to be replaced at heavy cost. The crop itself, on the other hand, went well. By November the oats were green, high, and beautiful. All we needed were the cattle, which were due to arrive soon. Then calamity fell. Hoof-and-mouth disease was discovered in Mexico, and an embargo was placed on importation of all Mexican cattle. Harper's cattle had been rounded up and were ready to ship only a few miles away. but they were on the wrong side of the Rio Grande. Osie told me that the only cattle he had on the American side were some wild Mexican cattle he had grazing in Oklahoma. He would bring these to graze if I wished, but he had to point out that they were not the type specified in our contract. I was desperate and consented. A few weeks later the cattle arrived.

Harper's cattle were huge beasts—all horns, bones, and tail. Even if fat they weren't worth very much. Not only that, they descended on my oat field parched and famished from a long rail trip. Had I been more sophisticated about these things, I would have insisted they be weighed before they were given water. They must have added a tremendous weight in water by drinking at my expense. And that wasn't all. Like Pharaoh's cows, they ate everything in sight.[20] Nevertheless, the more they ate the skinnier they looked. My men were busy irrigating; the Mexican steers ate and ate. By April, when it started turning warm, they had eaten everything down to the ground.

Harper sold his cattle and we sat down to divide the proceeds according to the contract. My share was less than growing costs by a considerable amount. Osie added a few dollars more as conscience money, I suppose, and I was left to try and pay my accumulated bills. This was the coup de grâce to my farming and ranching career. I decided to accept my father's offer to work in the store. "At least," said Pa, "everything here is under a roof."

CHAPTER 10

FAMILY AND COMMUNITY

Several years after I returned to live in Eagle Pass, while I was working at El Retiro as a farmer-rancher, I revealed to my friend Sam Meyer that my only meaningful romantic relationship had been with the young woman I had dated in Los Angeles, Ruth Sholtz. Sam urged me to contact her and rekindle the relationship. I visited Ruth in Los Angeles and begged her to come to Eagle Pass for a visit. She agreed to see me on the condition that her visit would not interfere with an extensive trip she had planned to Mexico.

At that time it was highly unusual for single American women to travel in Mexico, and Ruth did not speak a word of Spanish. Nonetheless, her trip was consistent with her rebellious, independent nature. On one occasion during their trip, she and her friend Maria Riddle flew into Oaxaca in a converted World War II bomber and landed in a corn field.[1] Oaxaca is in the central highlands of southern Mexico and was definitely off the beaten path for American tourists at that time.

After returning from Mexico, Ruth came to Eagle Pass, and throughout her visit I waged an intensive romantic campaign, fearing that she would return to California without committing herself.[2] Thankfully, at the end of the visit, Ruth agreed to marry me, and we were married by a justice of the peace in San Antonio on March 30, 1944. We were later married again by a rabbi in Los Angeles so that our families could attend.

In the first years of our marriage, I asked Ruth if she would be happier if we returned to Los Angeles to live. Her reply was that I was happier in Texas, and she desired above all for me to be happy. Ruth was not a girl one would expect to find living in Eagle Pass, a cultural backwater. Her home had a highly intellectual atmosphere. Her sister, Jeannie, was an accomplished musician who had recently won a statewide piano contest and had been a soloist at the Hollywood Bowl. Ruth herself was a talented artist. When still in high school in Los Angeles, she was part of a group of gifted young artists who were selected for special training by famous European artists and architects in exile. She earned a bachelor of arts degree from UCLA in fine arts and then a master's degree in art history. She was the student assistant to Dr. Isabel Creed Hungerland, then the president of the American Society for Aesthetics.[3] She was a close friend of Lotte Klemperer, the daughter of Otto Klemperer, the famous conductor.[4] She had met world famous composers and musicians such as Arnold Schoenberg and Ernst Toch.

At the time Ruth received her degree from UCLA, Japanese people in California were being sent to "relocation centers," a euphemism for concentration camps. Included were

Morris and Ruth Sholtz Riskind, wedding picture, 1944. (Courtesy of Dr. Peter Riskind.)

UCLA students, some of whom were Ruth's friends. She was deeply troubled, since this was so similar to the actions of the Nazis with regard to Jews in Europe.[5] Ruth applied to serve as a teacher in an internment camp. In addition to a teaching credential, she also had a supervisor's credential in art, and she was hired as art director at the Gila River Relocation Center in Arizona, where she organized and taught classes.[6] Ruth later insisted that the staff did not treat the inmates brutally; on the contrary, the staff showed much kindness in their relation to the prisoners.[7] Nonetheless, the Japanese were prisoners denied their freedom and certainly were not there as a matter of choice.

After being at the camp for some time, she struck up a conversation on a flight to Los Angeles with the man seated next to her. He introduced himself as Frederick Ullman, the RKO Pictures producer of the *This Is America* movie series, and he offered her an executive job in New York.[8] Because of the war, he said, qualified men were scarce, and he believed the time had come to give women a chance. In Los Angeles, Ruth thought it over. The offer sounded most attractive, but she worried that the man was an impostor. She called New York, the offer was verified, so Ruth left for New York and entered upon a new career that promised so much.[9]

She soon learned the reality. At that time, women had no jobs in business or industry other than as secretaries. The result was that the men with whom she worked made life miserable, implying that she must be Ullman's mistress.[10] In addition, life in New York was lonely. After a few months she could endure no more and returned to Los Angeles and the life of a schoolteacher. It was at this point that she received a letter from me.

RUTH ADJUSTS TO LIFE IN TEXAS

At first Ruth found life in Eagle Pass to be difficult. My parents showed resentment since they held her responsible for our elopement. A Jewish girl should have a proper wedding with both families present, they thought. People in town laughed openly at any examples of her work. To them, "art" meant a photorealistic style, i.e., representational drawings of familiar subjects such as bluebonnets or horses. Modern art was unknown.

Most Anglo women in Eagle Pass knew very little Spanish, but I wanted Ruth to learn it as quickly as possible. I bought her a book, but this did not work for Ruth. She learned orally. As soon as I was able to rent a house on Nueces Street, which I later bought, I asked Atanacio, my ranch foreman, to help us find a maid to help with the housework. He found one from a ranch in Mexico. The girl had never seen running water and thought the commode was a place to wash dishes. Since the girl spoke no English, Ruth was forced to learn Spanish, and the kitchen Spanish she picked up was augmented by visits to Piedras Negras. Because she had a good ear, she acquired a perfect accent and intonation. As time went on and Ruth made friends with upper-class Mexican women, her conversation became fluent. One thing Ruth never learned, however, was grammar. She had close friends with whom she conversed only in Spanish, but almost exclusively in the present tense.

At first, while I was at the ranch, Ruth spent her time walking around the Piedras Negras business district. Soon she knew every little shop and was on friendly terms with the owners. Her favorites were an old couple named Ávalos who had a tiny jewelry store on the main street near the plaza. Mr. Ávalos was a gray-haired old man who wore steel-rimmed glasses and always beamed a bright smile like an aged cherub. His wife was younger, also always smiling. How Ruth managed to communicate with them I don't know.[11]

Ruth had the features and skin tone of a Mediterranean woman. In Greece people thought she was Greek, French in France, and Spanish in Spain. Some people undoubtedly thought she looked Mexican. In Eagle Pass, few Anglo women spoke Spanish beyond a few words, nor did they make the slightest effort to learn. The upper-class Mexican women refused, as an act of patriotism, to learn a word of English. In contrast, in the interior of Mexico many were anxious to show that they spoke English, however brokenly. Ruth was easily accepted by her Mexican peers since she was friendly and spoke to them in Spanish.

Ruth also soon became a friend and protégée (perhaps more like a daughter) to Cora "Coco" Ostrom, an older, well-established woman in the Anglo community.[12] Mrs. Ostrom dabbled in art, painting on china, but she had true artistic talent. She painted a large panorama of historic Fort Duncan, which hung in the old Fort Duncan Club before it was destroyed by fire. This painting by Mrs. Ostrom was superior to the usual daub of an amateur artist and showed fine potential.

It was through Mrs. Ostrom that Ruth gained acceptance into the town's Anglo society, and soon she was in the middle of activities. She was secretary of the newly organized hospital board. She became a charter member of the Pan American Round Table, which included both Anglo and Mexican women, later serving for a few years as director.[13] She and Carolina Cerna organized a chapter in Del Rio at Ruth's suggestion.

Sometime after her arrival, Ruth started a free art class on Saturday mornings for high school students. About fifteen students enrolled, some Anglo, some Mexican. Ruth used her own ideas in teaching, stressing design and creativity. After some months, she heard of a national interscholastic art contest; the regional contest was held in San Antonio. Ruth secured permission to enter her students in several categories. They won a number of first-place prizes against students from San Antonio, Austin, and Corpus Christi high schools. One of the entries won an honorable mention in the final competition in New York. Unfortunately, none of this particularly impressed the people of Eagle Pass.

Ruth was also able to return to teaching school for a time before our kids were born. It happened that occasionally I played tennis with Jimmy Garland, then the Eagle Pass school superintendent.[14] I mentioned one day that Ruth had a teaching credential and had taught in Los Angeles. Garland called Ruth and offered her a job teaching history in the junior high school. Ruth wanted to teach art, but art was not offered in the curriculum. Ruth agreed to teach a half day, one class in world history and another in Texas history.

Ruth had attended school in California and had never studied Texas history. The textbook she was supposed to use turned out to be utter garbage, still teaching the old hero-villain version of the Texas War of Independence. I advised her to junk it and replace it with materials I gave her, from which she could lecture to the class.[15] Frankly, neither the Mexicans nor the Texans told the truth about the facts and events leading up to the conflict.[16] All went well in Ruth's class, until it was time to study Reconstruction. When Ruth said that the Ku Klux Klan was an evil organization, there was a howl of protest from several of the Anglos. They had been taught by their parents that the Ku Klux Klan was a most noble organization, only seeking to redress grievous wrongs.

When our son John was born, Ruth stopped teaching until all four of our children had entered school, then Louis Bernal, the school superintendent, offered her a job teaching art in the high school.[17] She could not resist. She was given a free hand. Her classes were small and select, a pleasure to teach. She stressed individual creativity, which had gratifying results. Ruth would repeat over and over to me her belief that Mexican children showed amazing artistic ability. It was her belief that if their talent could somehow be channeled into an industrial vocational field, unemployment along the border could be solved. Her curriculum included discussion of how art fits into daily life, in the decoration of a home, no matter how poor, or in choosing clothes or makeup to wear.

Ruth had a wonderful rapport with her students. For years afterward, former students would come to visit her at our house; sometimes one would say they had gone on to art school or had developed a business in the art field. Ruth laughed and said that if she were stopped by a policeman, the odds were he would be a former student. After a discussion about his family, he would wave her on.

But, as the Book of Exodus says, "A pharaoh came who knew not Joseph."[18] A new high-school principal came, a former football coach, who thought art was a waste of time. From a small class of select students, she was given jammed classes composed of all the school's problem cases. Also, whereas before she was allowed free rein in teaching, she was placed under the new bureaucracy devised by the state, whereby a teacher spends more time filling out forms no one reads than teaching anything of substance. Ruth retired.

THE JEWISH COMMUNITY AT ITS PEAK

Before we left for California, my mother had organized all the religious services in Eagle Pass on all the Jewish holidays, and with Falla Lapin as her lieutenant, she also arranged for the entire Jewish community to meet once a month at members' homes in rotation. It was the duty of the host to provide dinner, either at their home or at a restaurant, usually the Moderno Café in Piedras Negras. Following the dinner, the company would divide, most of the women in one room and the men in the other. When my parents moved to California, the practice of holding Jewish community dinners ceased and never resumed.

When they moved back to Eagle Pass in 1936, however, a new ritual started—a rotating poker game every Sunday night.[19] Neither the Lapins nor the Greenbergs played poker, so they were left out unless they cared to come merely for a social hour. At the poker game, Pa was the tsar. The other participants were Uncle Albert, Aunt Rose, Sam Schwartz, Solomon and Eloisa Libson, Tanya and Owsey Mikulinsky, sometimes Nandor Neuman, and Louie Hausman.[20] Pa did not like more than seven or eight in the game, so this made the playing fate of some uncertain. On some occasions during the war, one or the other of the two Jewish spinach buyers, Spector and his colleague, also played. The only non-Jew ever allowed to play was Joe Alvarez, the produce buyer. My father called him "the Spain."

The game itself was a very noisy, wild affair, usually seven-card stud with deuces wild. They played for pesos, and since there was a limit, no one could lose very much. At first, Sam Schwartz tried to pay off in theater tickets, but he was sternly admonished by Pa and resorted to the currency of the realm. There were two in the game who seldom lost. Mrs. Mikulinsky sat very quietly, but if she ever bet you could be sure she had at least four aces. Eloisa Libson also played very carefully. She was a bridge player of tournament caliber and usually won back what Solomon Libson lost.

Soon after we were married, Ruth joined the game, although I did not. The rest of us, including Ma and Ellen Schwartz, sometimes joined by the Greenbergs and a few others, sat around talking until about 10 p.m., at which point the game was suspended for refreshments for about half an hour. Then the game resumed until midnight. After the refreshments the nonplayers left.

There was always one other interruption. At some point after 9 p.m. the phone would ring and Sam Schwartz would get a report of the theater attendance. On rarer occasions, there might be a long-distance call from a spinach broker for Alvarez. And on one Sunday night, a short time after I was married, my mother-in-law called Ruth from Los Angeles. At that time, there was no automatic dialing, and my mother-in-law was astonished to have the Eagle Pass telephone operator tell her about Ruth's whereabouts. "She's not home," the operator advised her. "You can reach her at Mikulinsky's. They're holding a Jewish prayer meeting."

The bimah at the Eagle Pass Jewish Community Center, a large room connected to the living space above the Riskind store, 1965. The cabinet behind the altar holds a *sefer Torah* (Torah scroll) acquired from San Antonio. Left to right: Lloyd Munter, Morris Riskind, Owsey Mikulinsky, Tanya Mikulinsky, and Ruth Riskind. (Courtesy of Dr. Peter Riskind.)

By the time of World War II our Jewish community had dwindled considerably from its peak. Many left during the Depression, moving in some cases to a large city; my brother, Reuben, the youngest in the family, left for college. But there was still a core of old families. High Holiday services resumed in 1936 in our home upstairs of the store. We were joined sometimes by the Freed family, who operated a cannery in Crystal City, and a considerable number of air base personnel, both officers and men and women, so we had no trouble finding a minyan.[21] Mr. Libson was the chief cantor, assisted by my father. I gave a talk at one service on the significance of the occasion, and before long I began to serve as lay rabbi of the community. At about this time I became acquainted with Rabbi David Jacobson of Temple Beth-El in San Antonio.[22] He was able to get us a gift of a Torah scroll. At High Holiday services, and later at bar mitzvahs, I read from the scroll, calling up various members of our congregation for the *aliyahs*, their turns at reading from the Torah. Since the old-timers always deemed it an honor to be called up for Torah reading, I always had to be a diplomat in deciding whom to call on and in which order.[23]

After the war, the nature of our Jewish community changed again. My brother Reuben and his wife, Esther, returned to Eagle Pass, and other younger members married and stayed in town.[24] Lloyd Munter married Yolanda Schwartz, Bennie Levine and his wife, Faye, arrived, and Dr. Harry Kaback, his wife, Edna, and their family joined us. Arnold Schwartz married Edythe, a girl from El Paso. Rosalie and Bennie Spiegel were already in Eagle Pass and also joined us, as did Max and Libbie Stool from Del Rio and Michael and Ann Stool.[25] Relatives came and went, marriages took place, and children were born.

As soon as my children were old enough, I organized a Hebrew school meeting every Sunday morning. At first, there were only my children and Reuben's. Gradually we were joined by others until we had about twenty children in attendance. Reuben taught the elementary class in Hebrew while I took the more advanced students. A few who were not as interested were taught some elementary Judaism in English. By the time my older boys and Reuben's children were in high school, most were fairly well advanced, and I commenced teaching them Tanakh. We were able to read Joshua, Judges, and Samuel before the older children graduated. My son Pete went on to study Hebrew at university and won a prize as top student.

In teaching the children I used my knowledge of archaeology and anthropology to explain the Hebrew text, giving them a twentieth-century view rather than medieval pietism. In doing so I have been accused of not teaching true Judaism. I feel, on the contrary, that this is the only correct way for modern people to understand the Bible, and Judaism as well. Such teaching may not please some Hasidic rebbe with his mind bonded to the Middle Ages, but frankly, I don't give a damn.

The first boy to be bar mitzvah in my class was Reuben's older son, David, followed by my sons, John and Pete, then Reuben's younger son, Dan, and my son Lorin. They all performed the bar mitzvah ceremony in the traditional Hebrew form except for chanting the haftarah itself in the traditional way.[26] I have a terrible voice and was afraid I could not teach them properly. My own boys had additional help on visits of my father-in-law, John Sholtz, who was not only a Hebrew scholar but an excellent musician as well. We participated in the bar mitzvahs of at least eighteen Eagle Pass boys, and later, with the help of my daughter-in-law Sherri, the bat mitzvahs of several girls.[27] I remember the bar mitzvahs of David Kaback, the two Greenberg boys, Arnold Schwartz's two sons, the three Levine boys, Ben Spiegel's boys, Max Stool's boys, and Jerry Abram's two boys. Neither my niece Miriam nor my daughter Susan had a bat mitzvah, but Sherri trained Alexia Bres and supervised her bat mitzvah, and I prepared Stephanie Bres. The last bar mitzvah held in Eagle Pass was that of Carlos Bres.

In the 1960s, we had as many as sixty men, women, and children in attendance at High Holiday services and our community Passover seder, including Jews from Del Rio, like the Stool family, and Jewish servicemen from the air base. However, at the time I write, the older members of our community have all died or moved away, and virtually all the children have moved to the big city. Now we would be unable to get together a minyan even if we included women and non-Jewish spouses. At one of the services recently held, my wife observed that of those present, two were official converts to Judaism, and half of the others were wives of non-Jewish origin who were now part of our congregation. What has happened here is, I believe, typical of what has happened elsewhere.

PAPPY O'DANIEL

Perhaps because of its nature as the end of the known world, Eagle Pass had more than its share of colorful, even eccentric, characters, and because of the prominence of the store in the town's social and economic life, we had an opportunity to observe a great cross section of people during the high and low tides of Eagle Pass life. It is a footnote to Texas history, for example, that Lee "Pappy" O'Daniel and his family were tenants of my father before O'Daniel became governor. The family lived in a large upstairs apartment adjoining ours.[28]

In the 1930s the federal government made it difficult to advertise quack medicines over American radio stations. Mexican stations were quick to take advantage of the situation.

They were cheap and cared little about the content of the advertising. Powerful stations were erected all along the border from Brownsville to Tijuana.[29] The program that achieved the most notoriety was that of Dr. Brinkley from Villa Acuña, across the river from Del Rio. The "doctor" promised renewed youth and sexual vigor through the use of goat glands.[30] In Piedras Negras, a powerful fifty-thousand-watt station was built by Claudio Bres, one of Pa's best customers. Through Bres, Pa rented the large apartment upstairs to one Lee O'Daniel.

O'Daniel advertised his own brand of flour over the station in Piedras Negras. A hillbilly band composed of O'Daniel, his wife, and four or five children entertained, and at every intermission, the band called out, "Pass the biscuits, Pappy!" He came to be known as Pappy O'Daniel. After this slogan, Pappy would launch into a rhapsodic description of the merits of his flour and tell listeners how it could be bought. Since his program was a long one, O'Daniel began to pad his time with his homespun comments on religion and politics. On his program, at least, he was the champion of good old-time religion and moral rectitude in politics. He had hit upon just the right note to reach the lonesome country people. Texas at that time was still basically a rural society. He received a flood of mail urging that he run for governor and throw the rascals out.

In 1938, O'Daniel formally announced he was running for governor, using his popular program to promote his candidacy. The station reached all over the state, and Pappy also toured the state with his family band, campaigning with little expense. To the frustration of the professional politicians, he was elected. The radio program ended and the family packed up to move to the governor's mansion.

My parents, living in the small adjoining apartment, could hear everything that occurred in the O'Daniel household. Mother came to loathe Pappy. She said he was loud, vulgar, and abusive to his wife and children. "A terrible man," she said, although she liked Molly, O'Daniel's daughter. Mother was happy to get rid of the O'Daniel family.

SHOWCASING THE KICKAPOO

Such brushes with celebrity were rare enough in Eagle Pass, and we should have taken better advantage, but even our extra-bad men were unpublicized. We were what an old-timer would call a "snake-bit" community, completely unknown in the world at large. Once, as an experiment, I asked people in San Antonio for the road to Eagle Pass: no one seemed to know. On the highway from San Antonio, there were no signs telling how to get here. The Texas Highway Department had evidently forgotten us, along with everyone else. If a tourist did find his way to Eagle Pass, it was because he was lost.

No tourists came to Piedras Negras either, our adjoining Mexican city, despite the fact that it was much more typically Mexican than other border cities. Tourists seemed to only be interested in "red-light" districts. Having lived in Los Angeles, where a supermarket opening or similar momentous event was greeted with klieg lights and hoopla, I decided that something had to be done to advertise my hometown. In a surge of patriotism, I resolved to cure the situation single-handed.

At the annual dinner of the chamber of commerce, I rose during a lull in the program and suggested that we should hold a centennial celebration in 1949.[31] As a reward for my suggestion, I was appointed chairman of the Eagle Pass Centennial Celebration. I suppose no one else wanted the job. My fellow chamber members may have expected that the whole project would quietly be forgotten as usual, but I was stubborn, and I went to work with enthusiasm. First, I selected a committee representing the old families, both Mexican and

Anglo. Then I asked Harold White, the head of the local Texas Employment Office, to be the parade chairman. Harold was a ham actor at heart, and putting on a parade was the next best thing to acting. I prepared a tentative program for the celebration, starting with such events as a beard-growing contest.

We had one significant asset, in my judgment, that should have been a gold mine. We had the Kickapoo Indians in our midst—the real ones. What couldn't a Hollywood press agent do with such a bonanza? It made my head swim. Every child knew about the Kickapoo, who were featured in Al Capp's cartoon "Li'l Abner." The concession for "Kickapoo Joy Juice" should be worth a fortune![32]

Sometime after the turn of the century, under an act of Congress settling Indian claims, the Kickapoo at Nacimiento, Mexico, about 120 miles from Eagle Pass, were given restitution for their rights to their American lands.[33] Payments were either monthly or quarterly to all registered tribal members. Toward the end of World War I, and for some time thereafter, one of the most colorful sights in Eagle Pass was the periodic visits of the Kickapoo to collect their payments from the US government. They received their checks at the bank across the street from the Riskind store.

For a few days, whenever the Indians came for their payments, they were very much in evidence all over town. The women would sit on the sidewalks near the National Grocery offering beaded moccasins and baskets for sale. Hollis Fitch, who was old enough to remember them well, recalls that the men wore buckskin britches with fringes, while the boys went around dressed only in buckskin aprons. All the Kickapoos wore buckskin moccasins, some elaborately beaded.[34] The boys would set up shop in the empty lot where the First National Bank now is, and with bows and arrows tipped with .30-30 cartridges they shot at coins put up by bystanders. Hollis said the boys scorned to shoot at pennies. The target had to be a nickel or more.

While this was going on, the men would be out shopping. In the store a brisk business was done in two items in particular: cheap, gaudy blankets and assorted beads sold in narrow glass vials. I used to tag along behind Federico Perez, at that time a young clerk, while he waited on a solemn-faced Indian. Federico would turn to me, make a face, and whisper something like *hekervenee hemenee*, mimicking the sound of the Kickapoo language. Once a Kickapoo family marched into the backyard of the store and, without a by-your-leave, used the water hose to wash themselves off, the children all stripped nude.

The Kickapoo were always very distinct from the Mexican population in appearance and habits. On the street, they always walked in single file, the husband first, then the wife, then the male children, then the girls. Over the years, changes in costume began to appear. The men, the older ones at least, continued to have their hair cut in a distinctive way, with a pigtail in back, but their clothes changed to Levi's and work shoes. The older women wore Mother Hubbard dresses in a flowered gingham pattern, and many still wore moccasins. Increasingly, the girls began to change their dress. For a while, they seemed to prefer saddle oxfords.[35]

Then the payments terminated and the visits stopped: there was no longer a reason for the tribe to come out of Mexico. Nonetheless, a few Indians continued to come, camping on the river bottom near the International Bridge. Gradually more and more came to work as seasonal farm laborers in the United States.[36]

The highlights of the Eagle Pass Centennial Celebration, as I saw it, would be a parade, an Army Day program, and a Kickapoo village. The Kickapoo already had a traditional camping ground by the International Bridge. This could be cleaned up a bit, and perhaps a ramada (an open shelter) could be built out of river cane, under which the Indian women could sell their handicrafts. The boys could set up a bow-and-arrow shooting range like they used to have in town when I was a boy. Finally, we would have a day of Indian dances, which would bring more tourists than we had ever seen before. Stands could be put up selling "Kickapoo Joy Juice" (spiked with tequila, of course) for the thirsty tourists. It was a natural.

When I presented my tentative program to the committee, there was no argument over the parade: everyone loves a parade. As for Army Day, our town had originated as an appendage to Fort Duncan, an army post where Robert E. Lee had been stationed when he got the news of secession; later many famous generals, including Philip Sheridan, had been stationed in Eagle Pass. We hoped that an Army Day would bring the return of many who had been stationed in Eagle Pass during World War II.

To my astonishment, however, my committee showed absolutely no interest in the Kickapoo portion of my proposal. Neither the Anglo nor Mexican old families, nor the ranchers, showed any interest in what they termed "a bunch of dirty Indians." Even Chris Benavides, who as notary made copies for them of their tattered passes—issued over a century before by the commandant of Fort Dearborn stating that "the bearer, a Kickapoo Indian, is friendly and entitled to free passage throughout the United States"—warned against it, arguing that it would be impossible to get their cooperation.[37] He had once arranged for them to perform some Kickapoo dances at the opening of the irrigation canal, but they had failed to appear. "Better not get involved," he said. "All you'll get out of it is aggravation." When it came time to work up a budget, the committee was adamant. Not a cent for Kickapoos. It was a crushing blow, but I could not give up on my dream. I would proceed on my own. At least I could organize a Kickapoo representation in the parade.

I tried desperately to contact someone in authority. Under the bridge, I found that everyone seemed to be gone harvesting. I heard that one of the minor chiefs was with a group harvesting at Monty Montgomery's farm. I found a sickly old man under a ramada, watching a number of women, boys, and girls working in the adjacent field. Addressing him as "jefe," I launched forth in my best Spanish explaining my plan for Kickapoo participation in our centennial. I got no reply and finally gave up.

I decided the only thing left to do would be to make the expedition to the Kickapoo reservation some 130 miles into Mexico, and for this project I enlisted the help of my close friend Sam Meyer of Laredo. Sam had traveled all over the world and was intrigued by the idea of going into the wilds of Mexico to visit the reservation. He even volunteered his car, a Buick coupe. My wife Ruth, Sam, and I set forth and headed south. We turned off the main highway at Rosita and drove to Nacimiento, a town originally settled by Black Seminoles from Florida.[38] The village was a direct transplant from the old Deep South of the United States. The houses were copies of log cabins one saw in old photographs. In front of the cabins Black women sat smoking corn cob pipes, their hair in red bandannas.

From Nacimiento, we traveled on a poor dirt road, muddy from a recent rain. As we continued the road became worse, the runoff from the nearby Sierra Madre turning low areas into a slough. I found a long pole or tree branch and proceeded on foot in front of the car, poking the road to see if it was passable. All went well for some distance, then I made a serious mistake of judgment and we were mired over the hubcaps of the car. As we sat there, stuck fast, a Black man appeared with a team of mules as if by magic and introduced himself as "John Payne, Juan Valdez." All the English he knew was "OK." For a consideration of five dollars, he set his team of mules to work and we were soon on dry land. After a brief conference we decided to return home. On the return to Laredo, Sam found it advisable to trade in his car.

Back in Eagle Pass, I heard that the Kickapoo chief, the real one, was at Mike's Cafe near the bridge, where the Indians congregated. Dropping everything, I hastened to the cafe hoping to confer with the chief. He was pointed out to me, a dour-looking old man in a fringed buckskin jacket. I introduced myself and went into my spiel. The chief finished his coffee, got up, paid the cashier, and walked out. I followed along. He walked to the bridge and headed for Mexico. I continued to talk but was ignored. Halfway across, I gave up in despair.

A few days later I received a call in my office from the floor of the store. A Kickapoo man wanted to see me. I hastened in anticipation. Perhaps this was the break I had been hoping for. The Indian was holding a pair of *teguas*, deerskin moccasins. "Here are the moccasins you ordered," he said. I examined the *teguas*. Unlike the ones I had seen years before, these were not beaded, and they were much too small for me; they might have fit a child. I didn't want to argue. "How much?" I asked. "Five dollars," he replied. I paid the money, then launched into a rhapsodical account of how many moccasins, beaded shirts, and other goods could be sold if the Indians would only join in our centennial celebration. He listened impassively and then walked off.

Some days later, I received a call from the chamber of commerce. Some Indians wanted to see me. I hurried over. A Cadillac sedan was parked in front of the chamber of commerce. In the back was seated an elderly Indian, his hair in two long braids hanging down from a high-crowned black hat. A young man was in the driver's seat. Inside, an Indian in a fancy get-up was impatiently waiting for me. He also wore his hair in two long, heavy braids hanging down in front and had massive silver and turquoise ornaments, including bracelets, belts, and a bolo tie. It was a case of overkill.

"I understand that you want an Indian program," he said without preliminaries. "What are you running, a fair or a rodeo?"

"Where are you from?" I asked.

"Oklahoma. We put on a good show. The best trick riding. Big attack by the war party. The crowds love it," he said proudly.

"I'm sorry," I replied. "I want to put on a program with our local Kickapoo."

He looked at me with amazement. "The Kickapoo can't do nothing. They can't put on a good show."

I shook my head. "I am not interested in outsiders."

He stalked off in disgust, got into the front seat of the Cadillac, slammed the door with fury, and drove off.

By this time, I had given up on any Kickapoo program. Then, unexpectedly, someone introduced me to a Kickapoo I had seen around town with his wife and two children. They always walked, according to tradition, in single file with the man at the front, but there was something a little different about this family. The man wore conventional work clothes, although his hair was still in the traditional pageboy haircut, and his children wore ordinary shoes. Only the woman wore traditional clothing. I guess they were what you would call a progressive family.

I can't remember the man's name exactly, but I'll call him Minnehoa, which sounds something like I remember. Minnehoa was a man of around forty years of age, I couldn't really tell, and he listened very solemnly. It was too late for any organized program, as the parade was only a few days off, but I pleaded with him to help get some Kickapoo representation for the parade. Minnehoa said he thought he could persuade twenty or thirty men, women, and children for the parade; they would be in our town for the parade in any event. I was overjoyed. We agreed to meet in front of Kress at 10 a.m. on Saturday, the day of the parade.

I hastened to check with Harold, the parade chairman. He told me that every phase of the parade had already been worked out in detail. The parade had been divided into divisions, with marshals in charge of each. Every float, every band, every marching unit had its place. The Kickapoos were to march in a division that was to assemble in San Juan Plaza. I had to have them there not later than one o'clock in the afternoon.

Harold then reminded me that, as centennial chairman, I was to ride in a car behind the color bearers and the military band leading off the parade. The car would drive me to the reviewing stand, where I was to sit between Congressman Lloyd Bentsen and former Representative Maury Maverick, the two guests of honor, to review the parade.[39] "Remember," Harold warned. "You have to be in your tour car no later than 1:15."

Early Saturday morning, the chamber of commerce called me. Two truckloads of Kickapoos on their way north for the harvest wanted to know what I was paying per head if they marched in the parade. When I told them there was no budget for that purpose, they announced they were leaving town. At eleven o'clock, punctually, I was at the rendezvous in front of Kress. Minnehoa assured me that he had invited twenty men, women, and children for the parade. However, they demanded that they be fed at Mike's Cafe before they assembled. I took out my wallet and emptied it in front of Minnehoa. A total of only twenty-five dollars. Minnehoa eyed this amount dubiously, then decided that it would have to do. We agreed to meet at 12:30 on the dot in front of Kress.

After a hurried lunch and a phone conference with Harold, I was back at the rendezvous by 12:25. There was no sign of Minnehoa or the others. The seconds and minutes went by as I stood there looking at my watch. At ten minutes past one, Minnehoa appeared. In addition to his wife and two children, he was accompanied by an old man and another woman. "Where are the others?" I asked. Minnehoa had a sheepish look on his face. "The men took the money and got drunk," he said.

By this time, there was no use arguing. The assembly point was over two blocks away and we had only seconds to get there. I marched my crew at half-trot to San Juan Plaza. Then I had to find the divisional marshal. I shepherded them to the right spot with stern warnings to the marshal not to let the Indians out of his sight. This done, I was off at a run for the head of the parade. By this time, they had given up on me, and the lead band and the color bearers had started to march. I jumped into my slow-moving car, sweaty and breathless.

When we reached the reviewing stand and I took my place between the guests of honor, all I could think of was the Kickapoos. Were they going to appear? Division after division of the parade passed us by. Finally, I could hear what sounded like "ki-yi-yi" with miscellaneous other hoots and yells. Then the Kickapoo passed by—to the sound of "ki-yi-yi, I'm an Indian!" coming from the schoolchildren in the crowd. First came Minnehoa striding jauntily along in fringed buckskin britches, a feather in his hat and carrying a new bow and arrow. Behind him came the old man with a surly, unhappy look on his face, followed by the two women and the children. I breathed a sigh of relief when they passed. The Kickapoo affair was over, or so I thought.

The parade over, with no further strain or worry, I relaxed. The concluding event was the Army Day banquet. All arrangements were in competent hands, and all I had to do was attend. The next few days were uneventful. The celebration had not been what I had

Michael Riskind in cowboy costume for the 1949 Eagle Pass Centennial celebration. (Courtesy of Dr. Peter Riskind.)

hoped for, but it was over, and I was overjoyed to be released from an oppressive burden. Then the final blow fell. I answered a long-distance call from San Antonio. It was one of the newspapers. "Was the Kickapoo program to be held on Wednesday and at what time?" I was dumbfounded and sputtered, "What Kickapoo program?" "The Kickapoo program announced on the centennial program," the reporter replied. I had completely forgotten the draft program I had worked out for the committee nearly a year before. I don't know what impelled me to answer the way I did—some evil demon, perhaps. "Oh, the Kickapoo program. That will be at the San Juan Plaza tomorrow at eight o'clock."

Sometime later the phone rang again. It was an elementary school teacher. "Should classes be dismissed for the Kickapoo program? What time will it start?" And once again I told the same fabrication. Having stuck my neck in the noose I had to extricate myself. Dropping my work, I went searching for Minnehoa. After an hour or so, I found him and explained my predicament. Could he get together some of his people to put on some typical Kickapoo dance? Minnehoa shook his head. All the men had left for the harvest up north. I pleaded with him in my desperation. Couldn't he get anyone at all, even a small group? I was persistent despite his refusal. Finally, he agreed to meet me the next morning early in front of Kress to discuss the matter further, after he canvassed the available Indian population. I spent a sleepless night.

At ten the next morning we met. Minnehoa showed no great enthusiasm for my project. There were only a few people available. Besides, he added, there was no drum. A drum was essential, and all the drums were back at the reservation. I knew very little about drums. "I'll borrow a drum from the high school band," I suggested hopefully.

"Wrong kind of drum," he said, shaking his head.

"Can't you adjust it?"

He shrugged his shoulders. "Maybe."

So I set forth to the high school to borrow a drum. The band director refused. He could not loan a drum for such a purpose. I threatened to go over his head to the principal or even the superintendent of schools. He reluctantly agreed and handed over a drum. "Remember, you are personally responsible for the return of the drum like you got it." I promised, took the drum, and left.

That night, at 7:30, I was at San Juan Plaza with the drum, my wife, and Dorothy Worrell, a member of the centennial committee and a feature writer for our local weekly newspaper.[40] I had told Ruth very little about my problems with the program. When we got to San Juan Plaza, the Indians were already there. It was the same group that had participated in the parade, Minnehoa, the glum old man, the two women, and the two teenage children. I gave Minnehoa the drum. He passed it over to the old man. The old man grunted something, then he began to loosen the drum. He practically dismantled it trying to get the right sound, as I stood by having a heart attack thinking about what the band director was going to say. Finally, the old man got the drum to give a dull thumping sound and looked up with approval. Next, the old man engaged in what sounded like a violent argument with Minnehoa. "He says you have to pay the Kickapoo money."

"How much?" I asked.

"Thirty-five dollars." Why this sum, they did not say.

I counted out money and handed it to Minnehoa. Now, I thought, we were ready to start. A large, impatient crowd had gathered in front of the kiosk that served as a bandstand. It was already eight o'clock. The old man and Minnehoa held another conference. "Not enough women. Need more women for dance," he argued.

"How many women do you need?"

"Two more," he said.

I held a quick conference with Ruth and Dorothy Worrell. They were intrigued with the idea of being Kickapoo dancers. They came up on the band stand and joined the two Kickapoo women.

"What now?" I asked. Minnehoa indicated all was ready. I turned on the bandstand lights. The two men sat on the floor, the old man with the drum. In front of them, the four women lined up across the bandstand: first Minnehoa's wife, then Ruth, then the older Indian woman, then Dorothy. The old man started thumping on the drum with a low boom, boom, boom. Minnehoa emitted a high, wailing chant. The four women started shuffling across the floor in a particular swiveling movement, putting their heels on the floor together, then swinging their toes back and forth while pointing them outward. They moved slowly from one side of the bandstand to the other, perhaps twenty feet, then they swiveled back to the starting point, where the Indian women broke ranks and walked off, leaving Dorothy and Ruth by themselves. The two men also got up and started to leave.

"But the dancing." I protested. "How about the dancing?"

"That's all," said Minnehoa, and they left. By this time the crowd in front was turning into an angry mob. Beer and soda bottles were coming through the air. I pushed the two women to the back, turned out the bandstand lights, and we ran for our car.

About a week or so later, on Main Street, I saw Minnehoa walking along the sidewalk followed by his family. He stopped directly in front of me. He had a sheepish look on his face. "Someday maybe we have a real Kickapoo program," he said. Then he and his family walked on.

THE SEMINOLES

One day, during the early 1950s, I got a call from Dorothy Worrell asking me to accompany her to Brackettville to meet with the Seminoles there. The Seminoles had first come to the Eagle Pass area in 1850. Cora Montgomery wrote about the Seminole arrival in Eagle Pass, led by their chief Wild Cat, in her 1852 book, *Eagle Pass; or Life on the Border*. At the end of the Seminole War in Florida, Wild Cat had refused to be moved to a reservation in Indian Territory. With his followers, he journeyed all the way to Eagle Pass and crossed into Mexico.[41]

Accompanying the Seminoles was a band of Black families who had escaped slavery. They called themselves "Allies of the Seminoles" and were led by a man they called Gopher John, whom Mexican people later called Juan Caballo, or John Horse. In Mexico the Seminoles were given land in return for a promise to protect the border from the attacks of the Comanche and Lipan Apache. A few years later the Seminoles decided to return to the United States, leaving behind the Black families, who were afraid to return because of the Fugitive Slave Act.[42]

In 1870, the raids of the Kickapoo Indians were making the area from the Rio Grande to San Antonio unlivable. Major Zenas Bliss was sent to Nacimiento, some 120 miles south of Eagle Pass, and he enlisted a group of scouts with the promise that they would be given land. As a guarantee, the Seminoles were given a written document, which according to one account was filed with the legal records of the town hall, the *municipio*, at Nacimiento, but unfortunately these records burned during the Mexican Revolution of 1910. The scouts were sworn in at Fort Duncan, transferred to Fort Clark, and they and their families were given plots of land. The Seminole scouts performed prodigious acts of valor in the fighting to subdue the Kickapoo and participated in Mackenzie's Raid against the Kickapoo and were largely responsible for its success.[43]

In 1910, the commandant at Fort Clark decided that he no longer needed Indian scouts and ordered all the Seminoles off the military reservation. The unfortunate Seminole families

Kickapoo residences, or wikiups, in the Rio Grande floodplain beneath the International Bridge, ca. 1970. (Courtesy of Dr. Peter Riskind.)

were left to their own resources. Some were employed as cowboys on the surrounding ranches, but, by and large, they led a difficult existence. Their justified feeling that they had been cheated and deceived rankled them. Many felt that if they could only locate the document Bliss left them, all their problems would be solved. In their suspicions they fell into cliques, each claiming that the other was holding out "the papers."

Dorothy Worrell had become interested in the Seminoles and thought that I might help them determine whether they had a legal case. Before going to the meeting I did some quick research using the few resources available. An important question was first: Were the Seminoles in fact Indians or were they African Americans? This was in the early 1950s, before the civil rights movement, and it would be difficult to enlist aid for the Seminoles if they were perceived as Black. If they were Indians, the courts in the old days had held that all agreements with Indians were treaties and as such had no value unless approved by the United States Senate. Furthermore, in 1910, Congress had put an end to all legal claims by Indians.[44]

The meeting was held at Brackettville in an old wooden church. It was crowded, every seat taken by a sea of expectant Black people. What I had to say was not what they expected to hear. I had no words of encouragement. They could either go the legal route, which I did not recommend, or they could go to their congressman and ask him to introduce legislation on their behalf. Dorothy and I drove back to Eagle Pass in a subdued mood, leaving behind a vociferous crowd arguing about "the papers."

Sometime later, a federal judge finally ignored the 1910 act of Congress and granted relief to an Indian tribe. By the 1970s, Indians had become popular. A Hollywood group looking for a cause fastened onto the Kickapoo, resulting in a reservation being bought for them some miles downriver from Eagle Pass. Many of them objected, saying they did not want to be removed from the spirits of their ancestors, but the Kickapoo were moved there from their camping ground of generations, which had been located on the flood plain near the International Bridge.⁴⁵

As for the descendants of the Seminole scouts who saved the border from Kickapoo raids, they received nothing. Such are the jokes of life.

CHAPTER 11

BRIEF CAREER AS A CRIMINAL LAWYER

During all my years of legal practice in California, I had never tried any criminal cases, not even one. The closest I ever came was when I accompanied a colleague whose client had been accused of indecent exposure and was being tried in a night court. The defendant was an elderly man who had stopped his car to relieve himself behind a billboard. A patrol car happened to come along at just the wrong moment. Fortunately, the judge was an older man himself, and after admonishing the defendant to pick a less conspicuous spot in the future, released him.

Around 1950, before the days of the *Gideon* and *Miranda* cases, there were few lawyers in Eagle Pass.[1] Soon after I became a member of the Texas bar, Judge Roger Thurmond started appointing me to defend various indigents, mostly illegal immigrants.[2] At the first appointment, I thought I should try to get out of the responsibility on the basis that I was not trained to handle criminal cases. Then I decided that the experience would prove interesting, even though I was never appointed to defend a murderer. The court clerk would phone and tell me to get to the courthouse pronto because the judge was waiting to start the trial. In most cases, the appointed attorney conferred with his client for ten minutes then proceeded to plead him guilty, feeling that he had done his duty by talking Judge Thurmond into a lenient sentence. I was so intrigued with the novel experience that I always pled not guilty and insisted on fighting the case to the bitter end. In retrospect, this may have resulted in the defendant receiving a more severe punishment.

There are three cases in particular that stay in my memory. The first involved a burglary at the turkey farm of a man with the unlikely name of Tom Sawyer. Sawyer and his wife had gone to town to see a movie. When they returned, they found the farmhouse ransacked and a rifle, pistol, radio, and similar small items missing. Sawyer reported the crime to the sheriff, who notified the authorities in Piedras Negras. A short time later a former employee of Sawyer, an illegal immigrant, was arrested in Piedras Negras trying to sell Sawyer's stolen rifle and pistol. He was tried in a Mexican court for a *crimen en extranjero*, a foreign crime, and found guilty. After serving some time in a Mexican jail, he was released. A few months later, he got a job painting the Mexican side of the International Bridge. As he was diligently painting away, the sheriff waited for him on the bridge. As soon as he stepped past the boundary marker into the United States, he was nabbed.

I was given about half an hour to confer with my client before the trial was scheduled to begin. I pleaded not guilty, to Judge Thurmond's annoyance, and asked for a jury trial. A panel was duly waiting for such eventualities. Instead of spending a great deal of time selecting a jury, I thought I would try the English practice. After a few basic questions I told the first twelve men that I relied on their fairness and proceeded with the trial.

At first, I was completely at sea regarding what to do, then on an extemporaneous basis I arrived on a plan. In presenting my case, I first called the Mexican consul as a witness. He read the Mexican statute specifying that a Mexican citizen who commits a crime in a foreign country can be tried in Mexico, following the laws of the country in which the crime was committed. Judge Thurmond, however, ruled that the defendant had not been in jeopardy when tried and punished in Mexico, since by American law, the Mexican court would not be a court of "competent jurisdiction." Thurmond was right, but I had made my point. I had conveyed to the jury that the man had already been punished.

Then I had an inspiration. I remembered the Abraham Lincoln story about his use of an almanac to disprove a witness's story in a murder trial.[3] I called Sawyer to the stand and asked him if it had been light or dark when he left for town. Sawyer said that before he got to town, he had to turn on his car lights. I produced a statute that read that night time starts a half hour after sundown. The sun, by Sawyer's testimony, had not yet set when he left his farmhouse. That being the case, and with no evidence to show when the crime had happened, we had to presume that the burglary took place in the daytime. Judge Thurmond overruled my motion to dismiss, but the jury listened to my argument and found the defendant guilty of "burglary in the daytime," which has a different, lesser legal status than a theft at night. He was sentenced to several years in the penitentiary and shipped off to Huntsville.[4]

I appealed the case on the record, and after six or seven months, the court of appeals reversed the case on the grounds that the indictment was drawn so that if the defendant was not found guilty of burglary in the nighttime, he was not guilty of any crime. It was a personal triumph. The defendant, however, not being able to raise bail, had spent the intervening time in Huntsville and probably did not appreciate the fine point of law involved. He was released and booted over the border, probably a few months sooner than if he had been released in due course for good behavior.

The second case that stays in my memory occurred after *Gideon v. Wainwright*, which found that defendants have a constitutional right to counsel, and courts were taking more care to ensure that indigent defendants were provided with proper legal representation. An eighty-year-old man had been arrested for embezzlement. It seems that a friend of his had died, leaving the widow a modest estate. My client, acting as a *notario*, a Mexican judicial officer, assumed control of the estate, not going through probate, and paid himself some generous fees while doling out money to the widow in small sums. Finally, the children started to investigate and complained to the district attorney.

His family secured his release on bail but claimed they could not afford an attorney. I was appointed to defend him. The defendant proved to be an obstinate, opinionated old man, probably in the first stages of senility. He insisted that he had authority to act as he did because he was a *notario*, and he showed me his notary seal to prove it. He could not get it into his head that a *notario* under Mexican law and a notary public in Texas were not the same thing. I tried to explain to the old man the procedures involved in defending him, to no avail. He insisted that under the law he had full authority to act as he had; further, he claimed that I was not advising him properly.

On the day set for his arraignment I appeared in court early. My client was waiting for me holding a sheaf of papers. He handed me one. It was a typed declaration stating in Spanish his name, residence, and so on and declaring that as a *notario* he had full legal authority to assume control of the estate in question. By the time I had read my copy, the defendant was busy handing out copies to the clerk, the judge, the district attorney, the sheriff, and a few bystanders. I ran around grabbing the sheets as fast as the defendant handed them out, over his protests. Around this time, the case was called. I pulled my man forward, listened to the reading of the indictment, pleaded him not guilty, and pulled him back as soon as the judge pronounced him to be held for trial.

My client continued to make howls of protest to the annoyance of the judge and his clerk, claiming I was preventing him from making a "declaration," as required in a Mexican legal proceeding, and denouncing me as incompetent. At the first lull in the day's calendar, I approached the bench and asked Judge Thurmond for a conference in chambers with him and the old man. I explained to the judge the difficulty I was having with my client. Judge Thurmond assumed a most stern, foreboding appearance and proceeded to lecture the old man on the general subject of obeying my advice. This was all very fine, except that the judge spoke only English, of which the old man understood nary a word. This burlesque over, the judge resumed his place on the bench and I was left with my stubborn client.

The problem was ultimately solved in the most satisfactory manner. Either by design on the part of Judge Thurmond or by chance, the case was postponed repeatedly and never went to trial. After a lapse of time the widow died, and the district attorney dismissed the case for lack of a prosecuting witness. I called the old man's daughter and drew a grim picture of life in Huntsville. She promised to throw away the old man's notary seal and keep him out of trouble. As far as I was concerned, that was the end of the matter. I am sure that Judge Thurmond was satisfied also.[5]

The third case I remember involved an interesting legal matter. There were several cases of men, sometimes Anglos, sometimes Mexicans, having wives on both sides of the river. It was more common for them to have girlfriends, but sometimes the girlfriends insisted on marriage. If the Anglo was Protestant, there was an easy solution: the Catholic Church in Mexico simply ignored the American Protestant wedding and a second, Catholic wedding could take place.

A Mexican traveling man had a wife in Eagle Pass. When she heard that he also had a wife in Guadalajara, she went to the district attorney and filed bigamy charges. I was appointed to defend him. My client couldn't see anything wrong with this arrangement. After all, one wife lived in the United States and one wife in Mexico. What was wrong with that? After some discussion, he agreed to plead guilty subject to immediate deportation to Mexico. I guess he preferred the wife in Guadalajara. She was younger.

THE HUMES

No legal history of Eagle Pass from the 1920s to the 1970s would be complete without a mention of the Humes—David Hume, Junior and Senior. David Hume Sr. dominated the legal scene for many years.[6] He was over medium height, heavyset, and had a stern, dour expression. On cross-examination, he asked questions with sardonic, biting humor that stripped the witness bare, all delivered with a stern and forbidding appearance. The entire town was terrified of lawyer Hume. The Southern Pacific Railroad and Eagle Pass Lumber Company kept him on generous retainers to neutralize him.

When I returned to Eagle Pass in 1939, I visited the local district court out of curiosity. I was shocked by the informality of the proceedings. Only Judge Montague and Hume wore a coat and tie.[7] During an intermission, one of the lawyers had his feet on the table while he studied papers. Worst of all, Hume was acting not just as an attorney but also as the judge. If an opposing attorney made an objection, Hume would overrule the objection and proceed, while Judge Montague just sat there smoking a cigarette.

When I decided to take the Texas bar exam, I asked Mr. Hume if I could use his library in the evenings to study. He said I was welcome, and the key would be above the door. Then he proceeded to tell me about a trial he had conducted in San Diego, California, a few years before. One of his clients, Señor Alfonso Bres, owned a radio station in Tijuana.[8] Most of the advertising was beamed to the United States. Congress passed a law prohibiting the use of mailboxes in the United States by Mexican radio stations. Mr. Hume filed suit in federal court in San Diego, testing the constitutionality of the law. During the trial he behaved in a very loose manner. He must have ignored the necessary proprieties, and as a result he ended up in jail for contempt. The federal court, where the rules are strictly enforced, is no place to take liberties. Hume was very bitter when he recounted this experience.

His son, David Hume Jr., had had an interesting career before returning to Eagle Pass.[9] After graduating from the University of Texas Law School, he went to Washington, DC, where he became a trial lawyer for the Department of Justice. Then he became attorney general of Maryland, where he compiled an outstanding record for honesty in a corruption-riddled state. He married the daughter of Cyrus Eaton, the wealthy industrialist, and seemed to be on top of the world.[10] Then he chose to run for governor against Spiro Agnew, later Nixon's vice president. He lost, his wife divorced him, he got lung cancer, and he had one lung removed. He drank excessively and smoked constantly. He was a broken man. He returned to Eagle Pass and went into practice. No one knew of his past or cared.

I first got to know David when I became a member of the Eagle Pass school board. He was board attorney; as such, he came to meetings. Every so often he would interpose in some discussion to say that such an action could not be legally taken. I remember an occasion when an irate parent accused a teacher of child molestation. There were board members who were ready to fire the man summarily. Hume intervened to say that the accused was entitled to a hearing or his rights would be violated and the school district would be subject to a suit. At the hearing, it turned out that the teacher had done no more than hold a crying child in his lap to soothe him. That was all. I wonder how many teachers are unjustly accused. How many high-school girls, wanting attention or excitement, make false accusations? Of course there are legitimate cases of molestation. How to tell the real from the false, that is the question.[11]

Hume was an unusually capable trial lawyer, probably the best I have ever seen in action, including lawyers with great reputations I saw in Los Angeles. In my opinion, it is necessary to be a ham actor to be a first-rate trial lawyer, especially when before a jury. I have seen defense lawyers who created such a turmoil that they had the jury ready to convict the arresting officer. The criminal himself was by this time completely forgotten. He could have sneaked out and gone home. No one would have noticed. Hume had one fault, to my taste: he retained something of the old-time southern orator and at times was too flowery in his language.

David and I became close friends and saw much of each other. In one respect, we did not agree. He believed in an interpretation of civil liberty that I considered close to anarchy.

Liberty within the meaning of the Bill of Rights is based on the ideas of Locke and Jefferson, and it does not concern itself with local mores of a nonpolitical nature. It seems to me that such matters as pornography should be left for various localities to regulate for themselves. I do not believe that Berkeley, California, and Fredericksburg, Texas, would handle pornography in the same way. As far as I'm concerned, if a young, good-looking girl wants to run around in the nude, that's her business, so long as she realizes what she faces. I am more offended by a 180-pound, five-foot-tall, middle-aged woman appearing in a bikini; to me that is very bad taste. But I do believe that a community or a state has the absolute right to regulate what the community considers pornography, violence, or violent movies and television as a proper function of police power.

In the field of law, David was much better versed than I. When it came to history or general information, however, I had the better of the discussion. One summer David and his second wife, Margaret, went to Scotland. After their visit I asked if he had visited the home of David Hume, the philosopher. He said that he had been to the site of the Battle of Flodden, and went on to say that this was a great victory for the Scots against the English. I interrupted to remonstrate that Flodden was not a Scottish victory; on the contrary, it was the worst defeat in Scottish history. The Scottish king and many of the nobility were killed by English archers in the first battle in which archery was used. David said that this was impossible. "If the English had won the battle, they would have bragged about it on the monument and there wasn't a word." When I offered to read the *Encyclopaedia Britannica* section to him, David insisted on going home to get his own copy. As soon as he was home, he called back. As he read the article his voice began to fail, since it agreed with what I had said. The last sentence of the article read: "After the battle the Humes were accused of plundering both sides."[12] After a pause he said, "Damn you, Morris, you think you know everything!" Then he slammed down the phone.

One of Hume's most successful cases was also his last. A woman had come into town who said she was a refugee from Chile. She opened a fabric store on Main Street called Los Chilenos (the Chileans) next door to a small restaurant run by a man named Parra. About a year or so later, the woman was arrested under federal warrant and accused of international transportation of illegal drugs. David Hume Jr. was retained to defend her. The fee he charged was based on the supposition that she would be tried in the Del Rio federal court, about fifty-five miles from Eagle Pass. To his shock, the attorney general's office claimed that her trial was involved in a larger conspiracy involving the Mafia of New York. The case was transferred to the Brooklyn federal district. In a quixotic moment, David said that since he had accepted a fee to defend her, he was obligated to go to New York. He should, at least, have insisted on his expenses in advance: he stayed in New York for weeks.

At the trial, the evidence was that cases containing furniture shipped to the woman from Chile also contained large amounts of heroin hidden in the furniture. The government had the shipment under surveillance because of a tip from an informer. To further implicate the Chilean woman, there was much testimony that she had repeatedly called Santos Parra, the Colombian drug lord, on numerous occasions. Evidence was also given by an expert that the furniture shipped from Chile was old junk and had no intrinsic value, being only a subterfuge and a container for the drugs.

On cross-examination, the "expert" admitted that he was only a junk dealer and had no knowledge of antiques. Hume's client then took the stand to testify that she had left behind her handmade antique furniture in Chile and had written her brother asking him to ship the furniture to her. More than that, she knew nothing. If her brother took advantage of the situation to smuggle drugs, she had no part in it. Furthermore, the Santos Parra she had called on the phone was her landlord next door, whom she called frequently to complain about the plumbing or the leaking roof. David then called a licensed New York antique dealer, who testified that the furniture was not only antique, but the fabric on the sofas was handwoven. In sum, the furniture was valuable. In his argument, David practically laughed the district attorney out of court.

The end of the story was not so funny. The Chilean woman never paid his expenses, and David was heavily in debt. He became despondent, drank heavily, and smoked without a letup. Finally he caught pneumonia and died.

LEOPOLDO DE SAMANIEGO

Of all the eccentric characters inhabiting Eagle Pass in bygone years, the most interesting as far as I am concerned was Leopoldo de Samaniego, the Mexican consul.[13] He was distinguished in appearance, reasonably tall, thin, very Spanish. In addition to his handsome, imposing appearance, he was a man of intelligence, charm, and culture and was considered an expert on Cervantes. He had a beautiful and mellow speaking voice, which had earned him a position as a commentator on a leading Mexico City radio station.[14] By touting one of the successful candidates for president of Mexico early in the game, he had been rewarded by being given the post of consul in Eagle Pass, a spot chosen probably because his wife came from nearby Múzquiz. Señora Samaniego was a very quiet, very proper lady who kept very much in the background. In contrast, Samaniego was a complete rogue, a character right out of a sixteenth- or seventeenth-century picaresque novel.[15]

Samaniego and I hit it off very well from the first. We discussed Spanish literature and early border history. Once, in his office, he showed me the official consular reports from around 1895, which contained much information about Eagle Pass and Piedras Negras at that time. To use the words of Bernard Shaw, Samaniego oozed charm from every pore except when he was drunk, which unfortunately occurred whenever he had access to free booze. When drunk, he became a slobbering Mr. Hyde.

My father and Uncle Albert had been good friends of General Pérez Treviño, and after the general's untimely death, Señora Pérez Treviño and her sons continued to be good customers of the store. She had been quite a beauty, and even in her older age was a very handsome woman of presence. Ruth and I were invited to the wedding of her oldest son, held at their hacienda. It had rained heavily the day before, and the dirt road to the Pérez Treviño ranch was in terrible shape. Tractors and trucks were used to pull out the stalled cars. We came with Bill Kane, the American consul, and were able to get through without getting mired in the mud.[16] At the hacienda, there were already hundreds of guests milling about. The wedding presents were all on display in one room facing the courtyard, with soldiers on guard both inside and outside.

Unfortunately, because of the rain, the barbecue had been delayed, and there was no food—plenty of drinks, but no food. One o'clock went by, then two o'clock and three o'clock—still no food, and the large crowd began to get restless. Finally, some food was brought out, but the crowd lost all sense of discipline, and the mob almost went to blows over the plates of meat.

Meanwhile, Samaniego had proceeded to get drunk as a hoot owl in broad daylight. He followed Ruth around, speaking to her in a very suggestive and insulting manner. We had been married only a few years; Ruth was young, and quite a beauty. At first, we tried to get rid of Samaniego by merely going elsewhere, but he persistently followed, and Ruth began to anger perceptibly. I was in a dilemma. If I did nothing, I would be in trouble with Ruth for not protecting her. If I gave the drunken Samaniego a beating, there could be an international scandal. I was saved by Bill Kane, who grabbed Samaniego by the collar and hustled him out of the area.

Some days later Samaniego came into the store as though nothing had happened and hailed me as his buddy. He was carrying a new Nikon camera in a leather case with an assortment of lenses. He bragged that he bought the items on credit in Laredo, merely on the basis that he was the Mexican consul. Of course, he never intended to pay the bill. He offered to sell me the entire outfit for two hundred dollars. The value of the gear was at least a thousand dollars. I declined but thanked him, not saying that I did not buy stolen property.

One day Samaniego was walking by the Eagle Hotel. Dick Lane, himself an eccentric, called out, "Hello, you son of a bitch." An enraged Samaniego immediately went to the district attorney, claiming that Mexico, in his person as consul, had been grievously insulted. He demanded a criminal slander suit be brought against Dick Lane.[17] It came to a trial, at which Lane was represented by David Hume Sr., also quite an eccentric. At the trial, Samaniego testified that as he passed the veranda of the Hotel Eagle where Dick Lane was seated, Lane had called out in a loud voice: "Hello, you son of a bitch." When it was Hume's turn to cross-examine, Hume had him repeat his testimony, then he asked if there were other persons present at the time of the incident. "Oh, yes, there were others present. That is what made the insult especially serious to the person of the Mexican consul." Whereupon Hume asked, "Mr. Samaniego, if there were other persons present, what makes you think that you are the only son of a bitch in Eagle Pass?" The jury went into convulsions of laughter and proceeded to declare Dick Lane not guilty.

THE GREAT JAIL BREAK

When Richard Nixon campaigned for president in 1968, he made much of the drug problem and promised to clean it up. As soon as he took office, he announced that drugs were pouring into the country from Mexico, which Mexico was doing little to stop. The Mexican attitude was that the problem belonged to the United States. If North Americans did not buy the drugs, there would be no drug problem. No Mexicans had forced them to use drugs.[18]

Nixon then ordered that every car coming from Mexico, without exception, had to be searched at the border. At the border crossing stations, from Brownsville to Tijuana, there were long lines of cars waiting to be searched. Previously, courtesy had been extended on a reciprocal basis to Mexican officials; now, even the Mexican governor had to get out of his car and wait while it was searched. There was a cry of outrage from Mexico. The Mexican president denounced this flagrant insult, and publicly announced that if the president of the United States wanted strict enforcement of drug laws, then that is what he would have. He then instructed Mexican officials to search every American car crossing into Mexico. The police and judiciary were told that any North American caught for even the slightest infraction of the drug laws would be jailed and punished. What this meant, in effect, was that instead of the old practice of ignoring minor violations, now even an American boy caught smoking a marijuana cigarette would be thrown into jail.

Mexico followed a legal system based on Roman law, which meant that if one were arrested and the *procurador* (prosecutor) believed there was sufficient evidence, a person could be jailed indefinitely without trial. The Mexican jails were not the Plaza Hotel. Food was a plate of beans. If the prisoner wanted more, he had to buy it himself. For a rich man a Mexican jail wasn't too bad, but for a poor man it was hell.

This was the situation when, one day, Father Shulhafer, the Episcopal priest in Eagle Pass and a good friend of mine, came to talk to me as the leader of the Jewish community.[19] Two American boys were in jail in Piedras Negras, accused of drug possession. One of the boys was Episcopalian, which was how he became involved, and the other one was Jewish. Did I wish to join him in seeing what we could do for the boys? Both boys were from the Midwest. They had driven to Acapulco and then, with several pounds of marijuana, they had started back to the border. Driving between Monclova and Piedras Negras they were stopped by the police, who found the marijuana. In previous times this would have required only a *mordida*—a "bite," or bribe—and not too large an amount. Now they were thrown into the local jail and transferred to Piedras Negras, despite their loud protests that they were Americans and entitled to their constitutional rights. After discussing the possibilities with Father Shulhafer, we decided that he would look after the needs of the boys in jail while I investigated steps to obtain their freedom.

Father Shulhafer agreed to call the parents belonging to his church, while I called the Jewish parents, introduced myself, and explained what Father Shulhafer and I had undertaken. I said that attorney's fees and probably a bribe would cost in the neighborhood of five thousand dollars. They replied that they were people of modest means but would raise the money.

After due consideration, I decided to try political means first. One of the customers in the store with whom I was on friendly terms was a high official in Mexico City. It just happened that in a short time I would be taking the family to Mexico City for a vacation.[20] In Mexico City I called my friend, an assistant cabinet minister, and invited him to lunch. I explained the situation and asked for his help. After listening to my story, he said that in a few days he had to talk to the chief justice of the Supreme Court about another matter and would sound him out as a special favor to me. A few days later, I got my reply. The chief justice had been told by the president of Mexico himself that nothing was to be done for Americans who violated the drug laws. If Nixon wanted strict enforcement of the law, he was going to get it.

Back in Eagle Pass, I decided to see what I could do locally. Another of the store's customers was a prominent criminal lawyer in Piedras Negras. He came to the store frequently, when he would discuss local news and other subjects. He came into the store a few days later, which gave me the opportunity to explain the situation. After listening to me he said that he would talk to the judge in charge of the case so that he could intelligently discuss the situation. He returned several days later. The judge had agreed that the boys would be released on bail pending their trial. What they did while on bail was up to them. Technically they were supposed to remain within the boundaries of Mexico. My friend, the *licenciado* (lawyer), told me the amount of bail fees for each boy and the additional amount of "expenses." I hastened to call Father Shulhafer, and after reporting this news, I urged him to call the parents of "his" boy to get a check from them as soon as possible. I then called the Jewish parents. In a few days we had cashier's checks for the required amounts. I called the *licenciado* and on his arrival handed him the checks.

The *licenciado* told me later that when he went to the jail with an order for the boys' release, he had a taxi waiting outside with instructions to take the boys and run straight to the International Bridge without delay. The boys were told to keep moving until they were safely back in the United States. The Mexican jail must have made quite an impression on them: they seem to have run right through Eagle Pass without stopping. Neither Father Shulhafer nor I ever heard from either of them or their parents again.

One more incident reflects the sort of event that can only take place on the border. It did not happen in Eagle Pass but in another border city. A woman bought a new Chrysler Voyager van and drove it across the border into Mexico to visit a relative. When she returned to where she had parked the van, it was gone. She reported it to her insurance company, received a check, and bought a replacement van. Some days later, she drove across the river again and parked the van. Once again, when she returned the van had been stolen. She reported the theft. Sometime later, she was visiting Mexico in someone else's car, and she saw a van parked in the street that looked just like hers. She tried her keys, they worked, and she drove home. That night she received a phone call from the chief of police of that Mexican border city. "I do not hold it against you that you took back your car," he said. "After all, you paid for it. However, I would appreciate it if you would give to my deputy the *pistola* I left under the front seat."

CHAPTER 12

MY YEARS AT THE STORE

Quitting the farm and ranching business in 1946 was a bitter pill to swallow. I loved the outdoor life. However, it was obvious that with the end of the war and the resulting drop in agricultural prices, a marginal area such as this could not survive. I was only one of the first of many to quit because of financial difficulties. Accepting a job in the store was humiliating, but I now had a wife and future family to support. I knew that Ruth would have preferred to move back to California or to a big city. Ruth knew that I was not happy about returning to California, and she insisted that I accept the job in the family business.

At first my tasks were minor. I became an assistant to Albert in the office. The bookkeeper's office was located at the back of the store in a mezzanine, which was about ten feet wide, where there were several Burroughs business machines, a large safe, filing cabinets, typewriters, adding machines, and work tables. The mezzanine was open above the height of the tables, so one could see the entire floor of the store. All invoices were entered by hand into a ledger with pertinent notes: amount due, applicable discounts, and due dates. In a second ledger all charge accounts were entered by hand, indicating the customer's name (listed alphabetically), the total amount, and the amounts delinquent, if any. Albert kept this ledger in the cashier's area on the main floor—a raised platform on which there was the huge hand-cranked cash register Pa had bought in the De Bona liquidation around 1920. Here on this platform, Albert reigned. If a customer paid on an account, Albert would make an entry indicating the amount paid. If a clerk made a charge, Albert either approved and entered the amount in the ledger or, if there was a credit problem, the customer would be brought over to discuss the matter with Albert. In Albert's absence, Aunt Rose would take over. At the end of the day, all cash and charge tickets would be taken to the mezzanine to be tallied or entered on Burroughs ledgers by trusted employees.

FRANCIS ALDRIDGE

Our bookkeeper was Francis Aldridge. For many years, he was the de facto manager of the Eagle Pass Lumber Company at a salary not at all commensurate with his duties or worth.[1] After hours and on Saturday afternoons, Francis kept the books for Riskind's and a few other businesses, and when I returned to Eagle Pass, he also kept the books of the El Retiro ranch and farm. Francis told me that when he prepared the store tax return, he always left a

Main Street business district, Eagle Pass, ca. 1940. (Collection of Bryan Edward Stone.)

Riskind storefront, ca. 1940. (Courtesy of Dr. Peter Riskind.)

small but glaring error where it could be easily found in case of an IRS audit. According to Francis, by the time an IRS man came to Eagle Pass he would be anxious to get home. All the auditor wanted was to report some correction in our books that called for a small penalty. This would indicate to his superior that he was doing his job. Otherwise, Francis said, the auditor would become suspicious of books that appeared to be too perfect and would keep searching until he found something.

If there ever was anyone who was the "reasonable man" of the legal fiction, it was Francis Aldridge. He was the epitome of common sense and honesty; as such, he was universally respected. He was a big man, about six feet tall and around 250 pounds. He never owned a car, and it was a common sight to see Francis shuffling slowly down the street in a pair of baggy shorts, holding an antique tennis racket. The trouble with Francis was that he did not understand his own worth. As a bachelor with very limited financial requirements, he needed little and did not ask for much.

My contact with Francis continued when I entered the store and we became good friends. When World War II got underway, Francis was mayor of Eagle Pass. When he was drafted, he was in his forties and a big, heavy man, completely out of shape. Fortunately, he was placed exactly where he was most suited—as an accountant. Francis thoroughly enjoyed his years in the service; to him it was the big moment of his life. After the war, his one indulgence other than beer was to attend the annual reunion of his army group, after which he would go to see a big-league baseball game. Although most of the men in the local American Legion post were Mexican Americans, Francis was always elected commander.

Some years after his return from the army and to work at the lumber company, Francis asked his employer, Mr. Meyer, about a pension upon his retirement. In the ensuing argument, which was quite heated, Francis either quit or was fired—this after many years of service. He continued to keep the books at Riskind's for some time after, then one day he told me that corporate tax returns were becoming so complicated that he could not do our tax return any longer. Francis gave notice that he was retiring. His social security was too little to live on, he said, and he asked for a small pension from Riskind's, fifty dollars per month, which we voted to give him. A few years later, he hesitatingly asked me for ten dollars more per month as a cost-of-living increase, and we gave it to him.

At one point, Francis was offered his brother's International Harvester agency. Although the deal would have made him a rich man, Francis declined, saying he was too old and didn't need it. Instead he suggested Fred Pilgrim, my boyhood friend. And so overnight Fred was on his way to becoming a millionaire, while Francis remained as poor as ever. Later, when Francis was ill and needed help, I don't know if he even asked Fred for anything.

Francis had a notebook, which he used to methodically prepare a monthly budget. Every expenditure was entered and checked against his budget. He included one bottle of beer per day. He discovered that rooms were cheaper in Piedras Negras than in Eagle Pass. He rented a room in the San Carlos Hotel a few blocks from the bridge. Every morning, Francis could be seen shuffling ponderously along from the San Carlos across the bridge to the legion hall. Every evening, he reversed his trek. Francis also figured out that in the winter he could take the bus to Veracruz and live cheaply in a hotel room. Once, Ruth and I happened to be in Veracruz sitting at an outdoor restaurant near La Parroquia. I remarked that Francis was in Veracruz, and just then I saw him standing some distance away. I walked over and invited him to a beer, for which he thanked me profusely but declined, saying that on that day a beer was not in his budget.

Michael Riskind in the store with Ernesto Garza, ca. 1940. (Courtesy of Dr. Peter Riskind.)

BUYING IN DALLAS

I continued helping Albert at the store for some months until I was heartily tired of it. Then I noticed that one department, the women's shoe department, did not receive the attention it merited. Ernesto Garza was the head salesman in charge, and he felt dissatisfied because the potential of the area was not being realized.[2] It was a neglected department; Pa gave his own attention to the men's department, which was excellent, while Auntie and then Reuben devoted their full attention to the women's and children's departments. We also had excellent household and luggage departments. On the other hand, shoes and handbags were neglected; we did not carry the best lines for a quality store, with the result that sales volume was far from its full potential. I approached Pa with the proposition that I be allowed to manage this department. Pa hesitated at first, but after some discussion, he agreed and I took on the job. I guess he felt that with Ernesto there I could do no harm. Ernesto and I developed a close relationship, more than business associates. We became good friends.

First, I asked Ernesto to instruct me in the proper way to fit shoes. He was very meticulous about fitting, more so than anyone I have ever seen. Even in stores that sell expensive shoes, I have not seen any clerk take the care that Ernesto used in properly fitting a customer. The usual clerk merely asks the customer her size or takes a look at the size of shoe already worn and brings the same. Ernesto always measured a customer's foot with great care. Once his customer, few women went to another store.

One of the problems we had to face was that as late as the 1940s, women, especially Mexican women, insisted on wearing shoes too small for their feet. Some persisted in squeezing into shoes several sizes too small, as small as three-and-a-half. Most of the older women had horribly mutilated feet, on which they tottered around with difficulty, reminding one of the Chinese practice of foot-binding. It was too late for Ernesto to convince many of them to change. For the younger women Ernesto would slip on the correct size, no matter what size they requested, and then get the customer to walk around for a few minutes. In this way he made many converts.

After a course of instruction, I embarked on a brief career as a shoe clerk. I learned by doing. It was hard work. Pitching hay was in many respects easier. After this apprenticeship, I was ready to become a shoe buyer. At first, I merely accompanied Ernesto as an observer. After a day's work buying at the Dallas Shoe Show, we would walk from one downtown store to the next, studying the display windows, both for the shoe styles and their display. I would also watch to see what mature women, as well as teenagers and children, were wearing.

What struck me, both from Dallas window displays and by observing the styles women wore there, was that our customers in Eagle Pass had their own ideas of style. They were not wearing what was in style in Dallas. There were two factors I had to consider. First of all, Mexican women modeled their styles not on Hollywood but on Mexico City and Paris. Their standard was Parisian elegance. We sold few closed casual shoes; local women wanted high heels to make them taller, and they wanted styles they considered elegant.[3] Second, we had to search the shoe lines for very small sizes (which were actually common in our customers), as small as a three-and-a-half, with a heavy emphasis on sizes four-and-a-half and five. Very few manufacturers offered these, and as time went on, they became more and more difficult to obtain. Most young women no longer crammed their feet into tiny shoes.

We finally were forced to the expedient of getting smaller sizes by buying salesmen's samples, which for convenience in packing came in small sizes. We also arranged a swap system with salesmen with East Texas accounts. Increasingly, shoes were being sold in prepacks that included sizes up to ten or ten-and-a-half. We arranged to trade all sizes above eight-and-a-half or nine in exchange for five, five-and-a-half, and six.

My other main accomplishment was to abandon some cheaper lines and replace them with better, moderate-price or medium-expensive ones. By simple mathematics, I would work out a break-even point for expensive lines of shoes. Then I would discuss with Ernesto the shoes he could sell at regular and sale prices. If he thought that he could sell a sufficient number at regular price, then we bought the line.

In two years, we had an excellent shoe department offering prestigious lines, and our volume had greatly increased. In addition, we upgraded our handbag assortment. Before, under Auntie, with the exception of a few expensive items, we had bought handbags to match shoes, as that was the way Mexican women bought their bags. After discussing handbags with Ruth, we began to buy a more extensive assortment. In a few years' time, I had also succeeded in transforming the handbag department into a contemporary one, with a significant increase in volume.

Ernesto and I went to Dallas for every shoe market. At first, we would take the bus to San Antonio, leaving Eagle Pass on Saturday at around 5 p.m. and arriving at about 9 p.m. Then we would walk a few blocks to the Manhattan Cafe on Houston Street near the Majestic Theater. We would both order the special, a filet mignon and baked potato, for $1.65. I would ask for medium rare, Ernesto for well done, and invariably mine was well done, his medium rare. We would solve the problem by swapping. After a leisurely meal, we would take a taxi to the MKT Depot to take the night Pullman train to Dallas, which left at midnight and arrived at 6 a.m.[4]

Our first trip by Pullman did not go well. Ernesto had never been in a Pullman before. I took the lower berth, telling Ernesto to take the upper. Next morning, I discovered that he had spent the entire night sitting in the restroom because he could not figure out how to get into the upper berth. Eventually, I must say, Ernesto became a sophisticated traveler. Our last trip to market via railroad was a memorable occasion. We had boarded the train in Dallas at around 11 p.m. and gone to sleep. The next morning when I awakened and dressed, I carried my bag to the front of the car as usual. The train was moving slowly through the outskirts of the city, as it always did on arrival into San Antonio, and I presumed we were about to enter the station. Just then the conductor arrived to announce that due to a severe storm in the Waco area we were still in Dallas! We did not arrive in San Antonio until that afternoon. Such was our last trip by rail. We either drove or flew to Dallas on subsequent trips.

In Dallas, we would check into our hotel, usually the Adolphus or the Baker, then we would go to work at a frenetic pace. The women's exhibits were in the Adolphus, the men's at the Baker.[5] Most of our work was in the Adolphus. Before buying, we would make a quick survey of the market by starting on the fourteenth floor of the Adolphus and going from room to room to get an overall idea of what was being shown. Some of the most expensive lines were always closed, open only to their own accounts. We were sometimes granted admission to other closed lines by explaining that we might be interested in them at a future time. We would always make appointments to see our most important accounts. After our survey we set to work.

After working for so many years with my father, Ernesto had developed some unusual habits. Whenever we saw something he thought was particularly good or bad at the market, he would give me a confidential appraisal in Yiddish, which he had learned from Pa. Clearly this was a very functional approach in Eagle Pass, but not in Dallas! I would answer in Spanish, telling him that the salesman was Jewish!

Ernesto had but one failing: he had no tolerance for liquor. When he had more than one drink, he lost control of his faculties. It happened that on Tuesday night of each market, the Salesman's Association gave a banquet, usually at the Adolphus Hotel ballroom. At first, I would excuse myself early to attend an attraction such as a performance by the Dallas Opera, leaving Ernesto with one or more of the salesmen.[6] On this occasion, I returned to the hotel after midnight to find no Ernesto. About 1 a.m. the phone rang. It was the police station calling for me to come and get him. They had found him sitting on the curb in front of the Adolphus Hotel. After that experience, I never left Ernesto by himself. When the day's work was over, we would have dinner, look at store windows, and go to a show or some event I wanted to see. I remember *The Caine Mutiny* in particular. After watching the captain manipulating the steel balls, Ernesto nudged me and asked, "What's the matter with him? Is he crazy or something?"

On only one other occasion did Ernesto go astray. It happened that the men's market that season came before the shoe market. Ernesto was supposed to go to San Antonio on the bus and take the plane from there for Dallas. At the appointed time he did not arrive, showing up finally on the next plane. It seems that at the airport he had met a customer; deep in conversation, he had followed the customer onto his plane, which was departing for Chicago. Fortunately, the error was discovered before the plane took off, but in the confusion he missed his own plane and had to wait for the next flight.

Ernesto developed a wonderful rapport with many of the older salesmen, especially the Jewish ones. There was one in particular by the name of Jack Altman, who had a line called Deb. It was a youthful, moderately priced, all–calf leather line of excellent quality, and it was quite unique in that Jack would allow the customer to have shoes made to the customer's specifications. We could order a sample made in any heel style, color, or combination of colors and trim that we wished. We sold his closed flats at $9.95; today they would retail for at least $100. After we became established customers, and after we had completed our selection for that market, Jack would motion us to follow him into the bathroom of the suite. This was the hush-hush procedure if other buyers were in the showroom. The bathroom would be filled with boxes of samples, each box printed with size and quantity information. Jack said that these were orders on which his credit department had stopped shipment. He offered to let us have whatever we wanted at very low prices. On the first occasion, there happened to be a big delegation outside in the showroom from one of the major department store chains. "What about them?" I asked. "The hell with those bastards," answered Jack. "They can pay regular price."

We continued to buy from Jack as long as he was in business. Once when he was in San Antonio, he made a special trip to Eagle Pass just to see the store and take us to lunch at the Moderno, the finest restaurant in Piedras Negras. One of the major shoe manufacturers finally eliminated Jack as a competitor by buying out his business and giving him the title of "style coordinator." By then Jack was getting old and was in poor health. He was one of the last of a vanishing breed.

Another salesman with whom I became friends was Ken Diamond, a Princeton graduate. Ken had an expression: "He eats like a buyer." To understand this remark, you have to understand that in most cases, department store buyers, or buying office representatives, were not paid that well. Consequently, any free meals were a benefit. In fact, companies often bribed buyers by entertaining them lavishly at expensive restaurants, where they ate and drank the best.

Meanwhile, I had also been going to the men's market with my father. At first we went to the market by bus out of Eagle Pass. For some time after the war, cars were unobtainable unless bought used. Less than a year after the end of the war, Ralph Jones, the Eagle Pass Buick dealer, told Pa that he had a car for him. It turned out to be a huge sedan, the largest car Buick made. It had a new feature, a Hydramatic transmission, which was the first automatic transmission on the market. Pa kept the car a few days but then decided it was too big. Instead of taking the car back to Jones, Pa sold it to Eugenio González, who worked with Jones as a salesman and as an independent agent in selling Buicks to Mexican customers. Pa sold the car to González innocently, not realizing how difficult it was to get cars. Jones was furious; he had given what was considered a choice car to Pa at list price as an old customer, and Pa had sold it to Eugenio thinking that was the same as returning the car to Jones. Jones refused to get Pa another car.

Finally, I was able to get a car. Kenneth Thompson, a local rancher, had secured the Kaiser-Frazer dealership. The Kaiser went out of existence in a few years, but not because it was a bad car. It was just ahead of the time in that it was lighter and had a low center of gravity and better suspension. The car I bought had a six-cylinder engine with adequate power based on standards of that time. It was much closer to a present-day BMW than to the clumsy cars of the day.

Going to the men's market with Pa was a harrowing experience. We would leave on a Saturday night after the store closed, usually at 10 p.m. This was before the time of freeways.

The road was narrow and traffic heavy at times. Pa would sleep and I would drive, arriving at the hotel in Dallas around 7 a.m., dead tired. At 8 a.m., Pa would wake me up to say we had to go to work. "Time is money," he would call out in Yiddish. Sunday and Monday, we worked at a furious pace. We always ate at a nearby Jewish delicatessen. Tuesday morning, we would check out, leave our luggage in the car, and continue working. As soon as we completed our buying, it was back to Eagle Pass. Once again Pa would sleep while I drove. Sometimes we stopped in Austin at an all-night restaurant. I remember one occasion when Pa ordered a two-minute soft-boiled egg to exacting specifications. When Pa refused two successive eggs, the exasperated waiter returned from the kitchen to advise that we had better leave at once.

On a few occasions after we bought the car, Pa also went to the men's shoe market, which immediately followed the men's clothing market. Before I could fully recuperate from the first trip, the whole scenario would repeat. If I complained of being fatigued, Pa would mutter some remark about young people having no stamina.

THE OLD-TIME SALESMAN

Nowadays, when a merchant goes to the Dallas Apparel Mart, it is a time of rush and stress.[7] Expenses are high, both to the seller and the buyer; time is limited, and pressures are great. Not so in the old days. When I was a boy, it was a major event when an important salesman came to town. The great man would walk into the store to be greeted by Pa, Uncle Albert, Aunt Rose, and the clerks. Pa would take the visitor upstairs for a *schnaps*. A wagon, or later a truck, would go to the depot for the traveling man's trunk or sample cases. These were brought to the store and unpacked by the clerks.

Meanwhile, the visitor would be upstairs having his leisurely drink, while he gave Pa the news about business conditions in his territory and around the country. The salesman would then proceed to tell his repertoire of jokes, most of which were very good. If it was early enough, Pa would go down and take a look at the man's line, then Ma would serve dinner, followed by the inevitable poker game. The visit was an event for both the salesman and the merchant.

I recall a couple of stories I heard from salesmen. Soon after the war, there was a brief craze for pink pants and pink shirts. Then, as suddenly as it came, the craze was gone. No one wanted pink pants, and this manufacturer was left with thousands of pairs. Ruin stared him in the face.

He called in his sales manager: "Mose," he said, "We have a critical situation. We have five thousand pairs of pink pants in the warehouse and they don't move. You have to do something."

"I know, boss," said Mose. "I've talked to all the men on the road and threatened to fire them unless they sell pink pants. They can't sell a pair."

Just then a secretary came in. "Mr. Cohen, there's a man from the Smith Company who wants to see you."

"Show him in."

The visitor came in and introduced himself. "I'm the head buyer for the Smith Company, and I need some pink pants. Do you have any available?"

Mr. Cohen kept his cool. "It so happens that I have some in production," he says. "They're sold, but I can steal a few for you."

"The Smith Company doesn't buy just a few pairs. We have over a hundred stores. When we buy something, we buy. I need seven thousand pairs."

Mr. Cohen gulped. "Well," he said, "I'd like to have you on our books. I'll do whatever I can and can guarantee you at least five thousand pair."

Whereupon they made a deal and filled out an order. When this was done the customer started for the door.

"There's one little hitch," he said. "I haven't talked with my controller yet. I'm pretty sure that everything's OK, but in case I can't get my money I'll let you know. If you don't hear from me by five o'clock today, you can start shipping tomorrow." And with that he walked out the door.

Mr. Cohen and Mose sat there looking at each other. "What time is it?" asked Cohen.

"Four o'clock," said Mose.

Cohen took out a decanter of whiskey and they took a drink. "What time is it now?"

"A quarter to five."

"Send everyone home and close up."

At five o'clock the two of them were sitting there sweating. There was a knock on the door.

"Who is it?"

"Western Union."

"Go away, we're closed."

"Better let me see what it is, boss," said Mose. "You can never tell what it's about."

The messenger boy slipped the telegram under the door. Mose opened it, read it, broke into a smile, and threw the telegram into the wastebasket.

"What is it?"

"It's nothing, boss. Your mother died."

Another joke I remember is more of a Texas story. In the old days a group of itinerant actors came to a small town in Texas to put on a play. On the day of their performance, the stage manager came to the director with bad news. The girl who filled in for miscellaneous parts was sick.

"Go out and find a girl," said the director.

The stage manager came back a short time later with a gorgeous girl. The substitute was bubbling with enthusiasm at the prospect of a part in the play. The director said to her, "It's a very small part. All we can pay is five dollars."

"It doesn't make any difference," said the girl. "I've always wanted to be an actress."

The director explained, "Now, when the curtain comes up, you're all alone on the stage. A minute later a man comes in, points a gun at you, and fires. Don't worry, it's only a blank. You can't get hurt. Just fall over and lie still. That's all you have to do."

When the girl was ready to go on, the audience was seated, the curtain went up. The new girl was up on the stage all by herself. She made all sorts of dramatic poses. Then the villain came out to the center of the stage, pointed his pistol at her, and fired with a loud bang. She fell, went into contortions for five minutes, and finally lay still. The villain stood there, distraught, holding his pistol. "My God, what have I done? What have I done?"

A drunk got up from the audience and yelled: "What have you done, you SOB? You killed the best-looking whore in Waxahachie!"

World War II brought an end to the old days. Salesmen had little gasoline and could not see their accounts in the old manner. In addition, merchandise, especially good, desirable merchandise, was in short supply and quickly placed on allotment. Not only that, prices were frozen, and if a manufacturer could not make a profit, he either ceased making the item or resorted to subterfuge, such as altering a design to create a new lot of goods (change a stripe, for example, and you have a new item) or reducing the quality of goods under old lot numbers.

Markets were centralized. Pa had to go to Dallas and New York. At first, the older salesmen tried to maintain the existing relationships—the drinks, the stories, the jokes—but then the pressure became too great. Pa had heated arguments with old friends over allotments. He might get twelve pairs of wool gabardine pants or flannels when he needed many times more. He would insist on a larger order, calling on years of friendship and customer relationships. The salesman would protest, swearing on his mother's grave that the matter was out of his hands. Pa would then insist that the salesman steal the merchandise from some big department store order. "They won't know the difference," Pa would say.

Sometimes a salesman did have plenty of some item, usually because there was no demand for it. In that case he would resort to camouflage. He would place the item under his bed with just a little sticking out. The other subterfuge with, say, men's socks would be to put the socks in his pants pocket with just a little showing. Upon inquiry, the salesman would say that the item had been withdrawn as sold out. In that case, after an argument, he would agree to sell the customers some of the merchandise, "dating back" the order. Pa was too sophisticated for such stunts.

THE FLOOD OF 1954

In late June 1954, a severe hurricane formed in the Gulf of Mexico.[8] The normal course for hurricanes is to devastate the coasts of Texas and Louisiana. This aberrant storm turned inland and was heading straight for Eagle Pass and the Big Bend. We did not pay much attention, thinking it only meant rain, which we always needed, and winds of fifty or sixty miles an hour. So what? In 1932, a storm had come our way and dumped thirty inches of rain, washing out the newly completed irrigation canal in Maverick County. Surely such events occurred once every thousand years. We certainly expected nothing catastrophic.[9]

A day or so later, we had a hard rain accompanied by winds that lasted for a few hours. Then all was over—or so we thought. That night we heard news that around Sanderson in the Big Bend, there had been sixty inches of rain. This strained credulity. Next came word that the Southern Pacific had suspended train service from the west because water had gone over the top of the Pecos River canyon, closing the bridge. How was this possible? The canyon was ninety feet deep!

The next morning, as I was walking down Main Street, I noticed two men with surveying instruments marking the walls of buildings. Upon inquiry I learned that they were from the International Boundary Commission and were marking where the water was expected to reach at the crest of the coming flood.[10] "That's not possible. Water in all of recorded history has never reached higher than the western edge of Main Street," I protested. They assured me that the Río Bravo, or the Wild River, was already rising and would flood the downtown by the next afternoon. I rushed back to the store with the news. My father scoffed. Federico Perez, one of our oldest employees, said that such a thing had never happened. It was impossible.[11]

Reuben and I talked it over. The basement was crammed with merchandise, mostly Reuben's reserve household department stock and my reserve stock of white Arrow shirts for the men's department. These were in high demand by Mexican customers, who would buy as many as a dozen at a time.

First, we began to move our valuable household department merchandise. This consisted mostly of blankets and sheets, all very heavy. The women clerks worked on the main

Riskind's during the 1954 Eagle Pass flood. (Courtesy of Dr. Peter Riskind.)

floor trying to protect merchandise there. The able-bodied men were put to work handling merchandise in a chain from the basement up the steep stairs to the main floor, where the women worked at finding a place for it. The older men worked stacking shoe boxes on top of counters in the hope they would be protected. For that day and part of the next, we worked in a frenzy until we all were exhausted.

The river was getting ominously high, and it was said that the International Bridge would soon be closed. We told our employees who lived in Piedras Negras, a significant percentage of our staff, to go home, as well as those who were worried about their families. The business district was a ghost town.

While all this was going on, I had troubles of my own. First, we were expecting our fourth child, Lorin, any day. Judge Bibb, the Maverick County political boss, had offered to take Ruth to San Antonio by helicopter if necessary. In addition, I was worried about my home. At that time, we were living on Nueces Street, which was near Eagle Pass Creek. If the creek went over its banks, my house could be flooded. We settled this danger by moving the family to my brother Reuben's house on Hillcrest.

One afternoon. as the flood reached its crest, we sent all the rest of the employees home. The only ones left in the store were my brother Reuben, Federico Perez, and myself. Federico was an old man, at least in his late seventies; nevertheless, he refused to go home and stayed with us. Reuben had ordered a load of sacks filled with sand. We placed these behind the front and back doors of the store. They did such a good job that no water entered. As we worked inside, the street began to fill with water. Soon the water was deep enough so that rowboats began to go up and down the street.

Downtown Eagle Pass during the flood of 1954. The Yolanda Theater was owned by Sam Schwartz. (Courtesy of Jeff Taylor Sr.)

While this was going on, Federico kept talking to himself. "This is impossible. It just can't be," he kept repeating. He had lived in Eagle Pass all his life, and no flood like this had ever happened. Every so often I would interrupt his monologue. "It may not be possible, but it's happening," I told him.

At this point we heard water pouring into the cellar. How it got in, I still do not know. Reuben and I decided we had better get out while the getting was good. Who knew how deep the water could get? We had to move all the heavy sacks of sand we had so carefully stacked behind the door. Then we had to force open the front door. It took all three of us to get it open against the force of the water. Outside, we had to wade through waist-deep water to get to the Eagle Hotel, about a block away. We arrived thoroughly wet but safe. There were six or seven steps up to the veranda at the front door, well above the water. We stayed in the hotel for a while, then Reuben and I went to his home, where our wives had been apprehensively waiting. How we were able to get across town to Hillcrest I can't remember, except I do recall that in back of the hotel and going north the town was higher. We probably had to go on a wide circuit to stay on dry land.

The next morning, Ruth said we had better go to San Antonio. Even if we had wanted to go to our local hospital for the birth, it was under water. Besides, her doctor was in San Antonio. We left our children in Eagle Pass with our maid, then I took Ruth to the Nix Hospital in San Antonio, driving as fast as it was safe to go. Lorin was born some hours later, on the Fourth of July.

Over the radio, there was constant news about the Rio Grande flood. No deaths were reported in Eagle Pass, but Piedras Negras was reported to have been devastated, with many fatalities. San Antonians were shipping truckloads of food and blankets, as well as medicines. I decided I had better get back to the store. I left Ruth and the baby in San Antonio and returned to find Eagle Pass in chaos. The high water had gone down as quickly as it came. It had taken the bridge with it. Eagle Pass was cut off from Piedras Negras except by boat. For a few days, the old-time *chalanes* (barges) operated across the Rio Grande. A rope had been stretched across the river and rowboats were poled across and attached to the rope to prevent the current from carrying the boat downriver. Some people desperate to reach their families were venturesome enough to make the crossing.

I spoke to a man who had made it across. He had a horror story to tell. There were dead horses and other animals everywhere. In wading through the water, he had stepped on numerous human bodies. The older parts of Piedras Negras are in a bowl-shaped depression. Once the river went over its bank, the water flowed downhill to reach a depth of over ten feet in the downtown. To complicate matters, there was a creek going around the back of the town, and water had poured in from two directions. People had been warned to vacate the area, but many had refused to leave either because, like Federico Perez, they refused to believe such high water was possible, or they were afraid their homes would be ransacked if they left. Those who lived in stone or brick homes were saved by getting on the roof or second story. Those unfortunates, the poor, who lived in jacales or in adobe huts had their houses swept away, the adobe disintegrating. Some saved themselves by climbing into trees. I heard that as many as five hundred people drowned. I had no way to verify this number, but it was certainly possible.[12]

Reuben had been able to determine that Lola Vela, one of our longtime employees, and other employees were safe.[13] There were thousands of people on the hills outside of Piedras Negras, some in tents, some in makeshift shelters, and the majority just out in the open. Sanitation and water were a problem. Relief supplies from San Antonio and other points were being brought in by helicopter. Stories began to circulate that politicians and the Mexican army were taking away the relief supplies, selling them, and pocketing the money. Mexicans have a mean sense of humor about their politicians, with reason. A story was going around that the general of the garrison asked an army patrol if they had seen any thieves. "Only your sons, *mi general*," was the reply.

In a few days, the Army Corps of Engineers appeared in Eagle Pass loaded with truckloads of equipment. I guess that Judge Bibb had used his influence to have them rushed to town. They had never helped in previous floods. First, they quickly constructed a pontoon bridge over the Rio Grande, as well as a road from Commercial Street to the International Bridge. Then they went to work to patch the span of the regular bridge, which had been swept away. Soon traffic returned to normal. A new bridge was finally constructed by the city, wider, stronger, and with no superstructure.

In Eagle Pass, the Red Cross and the Salvation Army quickly sent representatives to help those unfortunates left destitute. The Salvation Army did much good work on a person-to-person basis. The Red Cross had good intentions; however, there was an element of unintentional humor in their efforts. Under their program, any poor family was entitled to have its losses in clothing and household effects replaced at no cost. The Red Cross representative did not know that many of the poor had very few possessions. I spoke to a friend who helped move families threatened by the flood. He said that it was not uncommon to find in their shack a big refrigerator with very little in it. This seemed to be a status symbol. Everyone in the family had his or her personal radio and a small television. There was no other furniture in the house. All slept on the floor. The Red Cross "replaced" the lost furniture by giving each family a complete house full of furniture. The furniture contract had been given to Harold Hausman as the low bidder. With this bonanza, Harold, after filling his contract, closed his furniture store and built a motel, the Holly Inn.[14]

My home on Nueces Street came through the flood unscathed, the water reaching a few inches below the entrance level. The only damage was to those objects stored in a chest in the garage which, unfortunately, was lower than the house and ruined by the water. I brought the children home. Ruth and the baby came home to Eagle Pass a few days later but had to stay in a rented room in the Eagle Hotel because one of our older children had developed chicken pox. Finally, when it was safe, they came home.

At first the store was in utter chaos. The floors were covered with a stinking layer of mud and filth, the floor covering was ruined. The high water in the store had made all the wooden counters float, overturning all the merchandise so carefully stacked on them. Water had reached suits and jackets we had thought were sufficiently raised, covering them with mud, reaching above the level of the pockets. Sheets, blankets, pants, work clothes, and expensive shoes in wet boxes—all were in the mud on the floor. When Pa saw the mess the shock put him into a frenzy. He gave me a verbal lashing which went on for hours. When I tried to reason with him that I had not personally caused the flood, his answer was that if we had not had so much merchandise we wouldn't have had so much damage. Why did we have to have the basement so full?

When I explained that Reuben had bought most of the merchandise in the basement, which was household merchandise that had to be purchased in quantity to get a low price, he replied that he had never bought in such quantities and did not approve of the practice. I asked why he did not speak to Reuben directly. Why give me hell for it? "Who can talk to Reuben?" he replied. As his older brother, it was my responsibility to control him. The ancient Canaanites and related Semitic peoples had a practice to which the Prophets objected vehemently. Whenever a situation became desperate, such as in a famine or the siege of the city, the oldest son was sacrificed to Moloch or another deity to appease his wrath. In a Jewish family, the eldest son was loaded with all sorts of responsibilities and was not especially appreciated by his siblings. I was foolish enough, or stupid enough, to be my parents' lieutenant in all sorts of thankless situations. Pa blamed me for the 1954 flood. If it were only true that I could start floods—think how much money I could make with all the droughts in progress!

We had thousands of damaged items, from suits and expensive jackets to slacks and work clothes. What to do with them? It was my father who had the bright idea to rent an empty store a block away, further east on Main Street. We left the more expensive items, still in fairly good condition, in Riskind's. The balance of the merchandise was moved to the rented store. We had a heavily advertised sale on all damaged merchandise. The discount depended on the condition of the item and usually ranged from 40 percent down to a dollar for a pair of water-damaged shoes.

Since work clothes were washable, they were grabbed by a mob of customers at bargain prices. At Riskind's, people came in a swarm to buy expensive merchandise at 40 or 50 percent off. In a few days most of the damaged merchandise had been sold. When we made an estimate, it appeared that we had substantially recovered the cost of the damaged merchandise.

RUNNING THE STORE

After the flood, life finally got back to normal. Ruth and Lorin were home and the store was back to the customary routine. After Uncle Albert and then Pa fully retired, I became president of the company in the late 1950s and continued to manage the men's and shoe departments. As vice president, Reuben continued to manage the women's, household, luggage, and gifts departments. Ward Wueste, Albert's son-in-law, became my assistant, supervising store operations as well as serving as credit manager. Ward had no experience in merchandising retail lines, but soon he was handling his duties expertly. Ward not only spoke Spanish fluently, he also was related to many of the ranching families and was invaluable in greeting customers. What Ward did not learn to my father's satisfaction was a knowledge of merchandise. If Ward did not seem to have learned a lesson after my father had lectured him, Pa would yell: "*Der Daitsh mit der aizeneh kop*!" (The German with the iron head!)

Pa used to take a break from the store by going to the Sabinas Inn or to the Merchant's Cafe across the street. Both Mr. Vann of the Sabinas Inn and Mike Chorgas of the Merchant's were old friends and customers of the store.[15] One day Pa came back very disturbed. "What's the matter," he asked me, "why don't you mangle with the people?" "Pa," I said, "I mix with people." And I gave a list of organizations I belonged to. "Not the high-polluted people," he said, "the common people. You got to know the common people. I was in the saloon and not a soul there knew you."

Over the years, we had many prominent Mexican politicians as customers. They ranged from men with elegant manners, such as members of the Madero family, to some rather uncouth individuals, who were fortunately only a small minority. My worst experience was with a governor who had started in politics as head of the teachers *sindicato*, or union.[16] This man ordered a Hickey Freeman suit, our most expensive brand, made to his measurements. He was fat as a hog, and the suit was as big as a tent. After he was notified that the suit was ready, he came into the store with his entourage. Without even trying on the suit, he announced that it did not fit and he would not take it. He then made a series of insults, which his courtiers laughed at uproariously and he left.

Sometime later this boor got his comeuppance. Maybe his position had given him delusions of grandeur, or maybe he was just stupid, but he went to Mexico City uninvited to see the president. When told that the president was in conference, he brushed the attendants aside and entered the president's office. During his term of office, a president of Mexico is next to God; the offender could have been shot on the spot. He was forcibly removed and on his return to Saltillo was arrested for embezzlement. A search revealed misappropriation on a fantastic scale; such conduct by a governor is relatively normal in Mexico but not to such excess. With a little urging from the president, he had the book thrown at him. As far as I was concerned, it couldn't have happened to a more deserving man.

The Riskind store had always done a certain amount of special-order business. I developed this aspect of business considerably. We spread the word that there were many items we did not carry in stock but could custom order and charge only an in-stock price. In some cases, if I considered it good public relations, we charged much less. For example, I outfitted the Piedras Negras *aduana*, the customs office, as well as supplying new uniforms for the Mexican national police responsible for Highway 57 from Piedras Negras to Mexico City. I gathered many swatches of fabric for their approval, then charged them only cost and freight, plus 10 percent. The profit was hardly worth the bother. Of value to us was the possibility that on seeing a Riskind bag filled with merchandise, the customs inspector would look in the other direction. In the case of the highway police, one day the *jefe* of the patrol came into the store and gave me a gift of museum quality on behalf of his department.

One day I received a phone call from a customer, a prominent politician in Mexico City. The Mexican president had expressed a desire for a pearl-gray cashmere topcoat made by Hart Schaffner & Marx.[17] My customer wanted to give the Mexican president a gift of such a coat. Could I get one? I promised to get the coat within four days. This was a rash promise, since it was around the first of March and the winter season was over. Besides, light gray, or pearl gray, was not a stock color. I had a plan. All I needed was luck.

First, I called the Riskind stock department and, as expected, learned that no such coat was available. Then I called Hart Schaffner & Marx and asked to speak to the president of the company, at that time a member of the Hart family. I offered many explanations and was transferred many times before I reached Mr. Hart. I explained that I needed a pearl-gray cashmere topcoat for the president of Mexico and gave him the size. I went on to say that if the president wore a cashmere coat made by his company, it would soon be imperative for every Mexico City politician to own one. Far better that the label in demand be Hart Schaffner & Marx than some competitor's brand. (I did not mention, of course, that the label would also list Riskind's.) Then I suggested that he might have the coat in one of Hart's retail stores. Mr. Hart answered that I could expect the coat within the next few days. The coat arrived by air express the following day. The pleased customer sent a car from Saltillo to pick up the coat and gave it to the president the next day.

Despite such successes, we always had problems with complaints, especially after Ward Wueste, who had managed them, retired. My new assistant came to me after a week on the job threatening to resign if he had to handle complaints, saying it was "just too hard on the nerves." There was no way out. I had to take over myself. Now, there is a general mythology that all merchants are crooks taking advantage of the poor, innocent consumer. I soon discovered that a surprising number of the innocent consumers have a strain of larceny in their hearts too. My father had established a policy of guaranteeing the quality of all merchandise. This was the best form of advertising, he believed. The question always was, however, was the claim a legitimate one? Was the merchandise truly defective?

One woman indignantly claimed that a suit her husband had bought was defective because it had developed moth holes within a few weeks. "Only a few weeks," she said indignantly. I answered that we could not guarantee against moths. The suit was all wool. It was up to her to protect the suit. Finally, since she had been a good customer, I settled the dispute by giving her husband a half credit on any new suit he bought.

The biggest outright crook I ran across was an elderly man from Piedras Negras who insisted on being called by the title of *licenciado*, a title given to lawyers. I discovered later that he was only a *notario*, much lower in the hierarchy.[18] He was also a man with a reputation as a crook. This man would come in periodically, display a sales slip for a certain style of Florsheim kangaroo shoes, then bring out a used pair that he claimed had given insufficient wear. The first time the matter came to my attention I told the clerk to give him a replacement pair. Sometime later he was in again, only this time I remembered his name. Wueste had instituted a system whereby every complaint was recorded, so I checked the record and it became apparent that this rascal followed a pattern: he would buy a pair, then ninety days later would bring in an old pair and use the new sales slip as the basis for a claim. Anyone who knew about shoes could tell the used pair had some three years of use. I not only refused the claim, but I invited the customer to do all his shopping elsewhere in the future.

Another colorful character was a Riskind's business rival in town. During the period from around 1925 to his death, A. D. Eidson was a considerable force in Eagle Pass.[19] He was a big man, Scandinavian in appearance, showing little emotion but a cold, blue-eyed stare if he didn't like you. His store was perhaps the largest store in town until it burned down around 1960. It was a single-story brick building at the northeast corner of Main and Commercial Streets. Eidson was in competition with the Riskind store in only one field: he was the largest dealer in Stetson hats in town, one reason being that he did not sell at the advertised price. My father finally complained about this practice to the Stetson salesman, a man named Stewart. Stewart had no desire to quarrel with Eidson and put Pa off with all sorts of delays. When Pa pressed the issue, Stewart demanded proof. When Pa showed him a ticket from Eidson's, Stewart returned with word that Eidson said it was an error on the part of a clerk. At that time, Pa had to swallow the obvious lie.

We had another source of friction with Eidson. On several occasions, Pa had rented El Retiro to Eidson for cattle grazing. Every time, Eidson had promised to keep the fences in good repair. He never did, with the result that Pa received complaints from neighbors about Eidson's straying cattle. When I was farming, I had a large field of hegari, a tall sorghum used as cattle feed. The county agent advised me that the hegari should be cut with a row binder for better storage and handling. I was told that Eidson had a row binder. When I asked him to rent the machine, he readily agreed and told me where to get it. But my foreman told me that the row binder didn't work and needed extensive repairs, so I bought a used machine in nearly new condition from a local farmer. I sent Atanacio, my foreman, to return Eidson's, explaining that it was out of order and that I had bought a new one. Some days after we had completed the job, Eidson's foreman asked to borrow our machine, which we lent. A day later the machine was returned in terrible condition, reportedly no longer working.

On the other hand, if Mr. Eidson liked you, he could be very generous. He loaned many small farmers or businessmen money (at interest, of course), which they could never have gotten from Mr. Schmidt at the bank. Such beneficiaries swore by Eidson as by a saint, but woe betide anyone who crossed him! So popular was Mr. Eidson with part of the population that he was elected mayor and served very credibly for a term.

I used to frequent the lunch counter in Eidson's store every day to have coffee with Mikulinsky since La Barata, a fabric shop operated by Mrs. Mikulinsky, was located across the street. Next to the lunch counter were a few pinball machines, the first, I believe, in Eagle Pass. Every afternoon Padre Jáuregui, later Monsignor Jáuregui, was there playing the pinball machines with his coat and clerical collar removed. He would play very intently, as though it were a life-and-death matter, his face and silver-rimmed glasses giving him a cherubic appearance despite the sweat from his efforts in the heat.[20]

Late in 1952, the Eidson store caught fire at night, either because of a short in the wiring or spontaneous combustion: Eidson carried a huge stock of piece goods, fabrics woven in fixed lengths for sale, stored in the basement. By about nine or ten o'clock at night, if one stood on Hillcrest, it seemed that the entire downtown area was on fire. Flames reached a hundred feet in the air. It was a terrifying spectacle—not, perhaps, of the magnitude of the burning of Atlanta, but a show nonetheless. In a relatively short time, Eidson was in business again, on a more modest scale, at the southwest corner of Main and Washington Streets where years before Sugarman's had been located.

Mrs. Eidson was an eccentric in her own right.[21] During the war, my mother helped roll bandages at the Red Cross and was shocked that Mrs. Eidson presented a bill for materials she used. Dottie, as her friends called her, was a heavyset woman, usually with a smile on her ruddy face. She loved music, especially opera, and for years attended the opera in San

Mural on the back exterior wall of the Riskind building, visible to the parking lot, painted about 1960 by Eagle Pass High School art teacher E. O. Mackey. The mural is still intact and was included in the renovation of the building that began in 2023. (Courtesy of Jeff Taylor Sr.)

Riskind storefront, ca. 1960. (Courtesy of Dr. Peter Riskind.)

Antonio, Dallas, and Houston. On all these excursions, she was accompanied at her own expense by Carolina Cerna, then the Eidson office manager; in later years, Louis Bernal would sometimes drive her car in return for a free trip to the opera.[22] When Ruth and I organized a civic-music program in Eagle Pass, Mrs. Eidson would give a post-concert party at her home, with refreshments that were not lavish but more than ample, all prepared by Carolina. Where music was concerned, Dottie was more than generous.

When Ward Wueste retired at age sixty-five, my life increased in difficulty. Bertha Riojas, our senior clerk in the office, was made credit manager.[23] Since she had been in charge of the records, Bertha was thoroughly conversant with the job, and everything went smoothly. A short time later a problem arose when there was a sharp devaluation of the Mexican peso, and customers often insisted on discussing the amount due on their charge accounts. We established the rule that the accounts were due in dollars; in cases of hardship, we extended time for payment, and in a few cases, such as that of a recent widow with small children, we forgave the debt entirely.[24]

The headaches arose when the debtor, a man, refused to talk to Bertha, a woman, and insisted on a meeting with me. One man I remember in particular came into my office very belligerently and insisted that he owed his bill based on the peso rate at the time of purchase. When I pointed out as politely as I could that we were situated in the United States and sold in dollars, his answer was that I was *maleducado*, badly reared or impolite, that is, with no manners. These are fighting words. If used in Mexico, the parties draw their *pistolas* and start shooting. I agreed with him that I was *maleducado*, but this had nothing to do with his problem. He had two choices: he could pay his account in full, in which case he still had an account at Riskind's; or he could pay what he thought he owed only or pay nothing, in which case he no longer had a charge account and the balance would be a bad debt reported to the credit bureau. He stalked out in a fury.

The period from around 1900 to the 1970s was the golden age of small business, especially in rural communities. According to modern government statistics, a small business is any business under two hundred million dollars in capitalization. But in a rural community like Eagle Pass, a small business is a mom-and-pop store. If an Eagle Pass citizen was asked fifty years ago to name a large business, they probably would have named the M. Riskind store. Most of the successful businesses were locally owned. A chain store manager, with few exceptions, stayed for years and was part of the community. Civic offices such as president of the chamber of commerce were rotated. It was taken for granted that in any community endeavor, such businesses as the bank, the lumber company, Eagle Drug, Eagle Hardware—and M. Riskind—would not only take part but would contribute liberally.

Today social and economic conditions have changed. A new order exists. Wherever one travels in the United States the same chain stores and fast-food franchises meet the eye. One town looks like the next. Chain-store managers have no roots. In most cases they are biding their time, hoping to be transferred to a larger and more lucrative post. Stores today, except for a few specialty shops, lack character. Chain stores and big department stores have a drab sameness. In the old days, there were more stores with character, each stamped with the individuality of the owner. The Riskind store was a success because it was made in the image of Michael Riskind. The store that he founded and developed was possible because of the peculiar conditions of the time and place. Now we live in the age of Walmart.

CHAPTER 13

THE TRAVELING MERCHANT

One day not long after the 1954 flood, Captain Juan Salinas was in the store on a scheduled trip from Mexico City. During World War II, Salinas had been the ace of the small Mexican air force, sent by Mexico to join MacArthur's army in the Philippines. Salinas shot down a large number of Japanese planes and became "Mexico's Lindbergh."[1]

At the time, Captain Salinas was working for La Consolidada, the steel mill in Piedras Negras, flying the company plane. He was in the store often with a list of purchases for people in Mexico City, and I got to know him fairly well. When he saw me in the store, he asked me what was wrong, as I looked completely exhausted. When I explained about the flood and its aftermath, he suggested that I get away for a while. He said that he was due to fly to Mexico City in an hour and offered me a ride. I drove to my house and asked Ruth if she objected to my going. She thought it was a good idea, so I quickly packed a case with clothes for a few days and rushed back to the store to await Salinas. We took off about an hour later.

The plane Salinas flew was a small two-engine aircraft, unpressurized. I sat next to him. After flying for a few hours, we were close to Mexico City and entered a dense fog with no visibility. The plane started to climb. Salinas kept looking at the altimeter. We soon reached an altitude of over fourteen thousand feet. Since some of the peaks in the proximity were well over that height, I began to get nervous. For a while the plane strained, then the fog began to lift and we could see the city below. A few minutes later, we landed at the airport. I gave Salinas my thanks and went on my way. At first, I could only walk staggering like a drunk and I had a severe headache caused by the thin air in an unpressurized plane.

The owner of the Hotel Regis in Mexico City was a store customer. The Regis was an old hotel, but well situated directly across from the new art museum.[2] Although I said I was a friend of the owner, the desk clerk said the hotel was completely filled, this being the height of the tourist season. The only available space was the janitor's room in the basement. I could have it for the next few days, but he warned me the room was spartan. I didn't care. All I needed was a place to sleep and a bath. The room proved to be next to the boiler room. It had a comfortable bed, a bureau, a small bathroom, and a bare concrete floor. The bed was comfortable, which was all that mattered.

Every morning, I got up early and, after a light breakfast, started walking. First, I visited every museum. Then I walked for miles at random over the old area surrounding the cathedral. I ate in Prendes and other good restaurants.³ One night I went to see a comedy starring Cantinflas, the famous Mexican film comedian, and had a good laugh even though I could not understand most of his double talk.⁴ Other nights, I just walked along the Paseo de la Reforma, stopping only for an occasional beer.⁵ In three days, I had lost my haggard look and considered the best way to return to my wife and children. I decided to return by train. The Pullman to Laredo was sold out, so I decided to go chair to Saltillo, then by bus to Piedras Negras.

The train was supposed to arrive in Saltillo around 11 p.m. I sat next to a shoe salesman from one of the León factories. We had a long discussion on the shoe industry of Mexico. My Spanish is quite adequate for such a conversation and fairly grammatical as well. Where I am sadly deficient is in expressing myself in the more ornate language used by educated Mexicans. It is more like eighteenth-century English in its nature, and I can't seem to get beyond a stilted matter-of-fact use of the language.

The train arrived in Saltillo almost three hours late. Tired and yawning, I fortunately got not only a taxi but also a room. I fell asleep exhausted and slept late, had breakfast, and strolled to the bus station, only to find that the air-conditioned express bus had already left. There was a four-hour wait for the next express. However, there was a third-class local leaving in a few minutes. On impulse I bought a ticket.

The bus was jam-packed with people, luggage, packages, and animals of various descriptions. The man sharing my seat was a field hand. Books dealing with the Middle Ages speak of the "odor of sanctity," referring to holy men who never bathed. My companion definitely had a powerful odor, whether from holiness, sweat, garlic, or all of the above. To make matters worse, as we descended the high plateau, the weather warmed rapidly until it became like a stove in the bus. We proceeded in a pandemonium of sound from people talking, children crying, and animals protesting. Every time we came to a hamlet, the bus stopped for ten or fifteen minutes. No one that I saw got on or off. The bus driver would lean against a wall and talk to a pretty young girl who always seemed to be waiting. Then we would proceed to the next stop.

My seat companion was on his way to the border to smuggle himself over to look for a job. I discussed with him the best places to cross the Bravo.⁶ The statute of limitations having long run out, I freely confess my crime. My companion took out a *lonche* (lunch) and offered me some, which I declined with thanks. He also had a bottle of hard liquor, *aguardiente*, from which he took a frequent swig, always offering me the bottle, which I also declined.

We arrived at the Piedras Negras bus station about 6 p.m. The temperature was over one hundred degrees, but after getting out of the bus, it seemed cool. I boarded a taxi and soon was home to be met by Ruth and the children. I was overjoyed to be home. The world was wonderful.

WORLD TRAVELERS

Ruth and I have also had some interesting experiences in various parts of the world. Many years ago, she and I were in Taxco, Mexico. While wandering around town, we discovered a path that led down a steep hillside near the Santa Prisca church to an Indian market with a variety of shops clustered along the hillside. Ruth soon located a stall containing handwoven and hand-embroidered fabrics of various types. In a short time, she became engaged in bargaining over a large bedspread made of handwoven cloth and decorated with a variety of local Indian motifs in bright colors. It was truly a choice piece. After much bargaining back

Morris and Ruth Riskind in Oaxaca, Mexico, 1965. (Courtesy of Dr. Peter Riskind.)

and forth, Ruth made a deal. Then she asked the seller if she had another or similar piece. The proprietor explained that the Indian women came down from the mountains only once a month, and it took a woman a month's labor to make such an item.

While this transaction was in progress, I was leaning indolently against the pole separating the stall from the adjoining shop. The stall contained a stock of the cheap, gaudy blankets that were then just beginning to be manufactured in Mexico. These brightly colored, shoddy items had long been sold in the United States in stores such as Kress for $3.99 or $4.99. As I stood there gazing at the scenery, an Indian woman came up and began to examine the merchandise. After being told the price she complained loudly about the high cost. I was close so I could easily hear the conversation. "*Muy caro!*" she protested. "This is very expensive!" The stall proprietor answered her vehemently: "*Señora,*" he declared, "this is not some of that handmade junk. This blanket is guaranteed machine-made!" I was only able to contain my laughter with difficulty.

We went to Athens in 1960, soon after the Greek film *Never on Sunday* came out. Ruth loved the film's bouzouki music and was excited at the prospect of hearing more in Athens itself.[7] Where else? As soon as we got settled in the ancient city, Ruth was impatient to go to a nightclub where she could hear bouzouki being played. She organized a group from the tour to go with us. They wanted to go to the Plaka, in the old city near the Acropolis, where they had been told all the nightclubs were located. Ruth persuaded them otherwise.[8]

Our group crowded into three taxis. Ruth and I were in the lead. "Take us to where you Greek people go," she instructed our driver, "not just a tourist spot. We want to go to a true Greek nightclub." Our taxi started off, the two others following in a row. We drove for miles at a fast pace all the way to Piraeus, turned right, and drove a distance along the beach until we came to an outdoor bandstand.[9] In front of the bandstand were tables and a dance floor. The band was blaring forth rock and roll in a deafening outpour. Ruth stood by the taxi, stunned for a moment, then demanded indignantly: "What is this? We asked you to take us where they play real Greek music." He replied, "Lady, you asked me to take you to where we Greek people go when we go out. We don't want to listen to the old Greek music. That's for tourists. If you want to hear the old-fashioned stuff, go back to the Plaka."

Furiously angry at Ruth, the group of tourists reentered the taxis, turned around, and went at a fast clip back to Athens. After another long ride we arrived at the Plaka, not too far from the hotel where we had started. We had a painful taxi bill, and we left no tip. At the nightclub we were ushered onto the flat roof, where the tables and bandstand were in the open air. Facing us, and not too distant, was the Parthenon, all alight and truly magnificent as it looked over the city. An orchestra was playing bouzouki music. The food was good. We calmed down and enjoyed ourselves.

On a trip to Morocco, Ruth decided to purchase some of the local handmade rugs. On a free afternoon in Meknes, we sallied forth from the hotel, enlisted the aid of a small boy who spoke a few words of English, and went in search of a rug merchant.[10] We ended up in what seemed to be one of the larger establishments in the souk. In addition to an enormous stock, it had a posted credential advising that the shop was recommended by the country's ministry of tourism. The proprietor ushered us inside with effusive gestures of welcome. We were seated in a domed room where there were stacks of rugs over ten feet high. There was not a breath of circulating air. The temperature was oppressive, like the inside of an oven.

First, we were offered mint tea in tiny cups. This seemed to be an essential part of the ritual. The proprietor ordered an assistant to take rugs off the top of the stack. There was a wide variety of colors and patterns. When Ruth saw one of interest, it was laid aside in a separate stack for final determination. Time went by, and I sat there suffering from the heat. More tea was served. After what seemed like an hour but might have been less, and after examining countless rugs, Ruth made her selection. Then the real fun began, if you want to call it that.

We had to have more mint tea. By this time, I was beginning to hate mint tea. Finally, they got down to business. Ruth had experience with bargaining in Mexico, and she had been coached by others. Nevertheless, the actual experience proved harrowing. Ruth asked the price of the rug. The proprietor quoted a price of 1,000 dirhams. Ruth said that he must be joking. He asked for an offer. She said 150 dirhams. He practically cried and said that his wife and children would starve to death at that rate. Ruth then asked for his best price. He said 800 dirhams. Ruth countered with 200 dirhams. During this bargaining (or altercation) I was getting more and more impatient. Not only was the process wearing, but the heat was getting to me. Ruth was so involved that the heat seemed to have no effect on her at all.

After Ruth's offer of 200 dirhams, the merchant threw up his hands, imploring heaven, and cried that 700 dirhams was the very best he could do. Ruth by this time was getting exasperated, since the price he asked was higher than she had seen in New York. She rose and announced that we were leaving. I was overjoyed. I grabbed her by the arm and rushed for the door and fresh air. The proprietor followed us outside, imploring us to return and promising to give us the correct price. We reentered the domed oven, sat down, and had some more mint tea.

Ruth then asked what was his price. He said 500 dirhams. Ruth answered that this was still too high and said that she would pay 400. They finally settled on 450 dirhams. Then,

Ruth selected a stack of smaller rugs and asked for a price on the entire stack. This time the deal went through rapidly. I guess the profiteer knew that he had a tough customer, it was getting late, and procrastinating would only result in losing the sale. We paid the man and arranged for shipment to Texas.

The entire transaction took many hours—Ruth says at least four—but she was satisfied that the prices, including shipping, were better than what she could find in New York. As for the rug dealer, I am quite sure that he got the better end of the deal. The rugs arrived a month after we got home. In my opinion, every American diplomat should be required to buy a rug in Morocco or another Middle Eastern or North African country before being posted to that area.

ISRAEL

Following the independence of Israel in 1948, my parents made an annual trip there in the summer. They spent most of their stay in Jerusalem, where Pa enjoyed the climate and visiting relatives in other areas. Pa also especially enjoyed the sea voyage, but Ma, for her part, would describe on her return the prodigious amounts of food eaten by the ship's passengers—Jews, Italians, and Greeks. She herself ate little and thought the gorging aboard ship was disgusting. Pa's comment about the food was, "Not too bad, only they had no chile."

The usual procedure was that they first went to New York and stayed for a few days, where Pa bought such items for the store as novelty hats and caps, mufflers, and gloves. These items were left to him to buy. Pa considered them important, reasoning that if no one else in Eagle Pass had them in the winter, then the customer would have to come to us. Following the short stay in New York, they would board a ship and continue their journey. If my sister Sarah Robson and her family were in Europe, they would first stop there. Sarah's husband, Mark Robson, was a Hollywood movie director and had made a number of films in Europe.[11] Following their visit with Sarah, the folks continued by rail to Italy, and then traveled by air to Israel. If Sarah was not in Europe, then they went to Israel by ship from New York, either on an Italian, a Greek, or the ZIM line.[12] Usually they would stop at Gibraltar, Naples, and Piraeus, finally docking at Haifa.

In 1967, I agreed with my parents to meet them in Jerusalem on June 7 at the King David Hotel.[13] They left New York on the Greek ship *Olympia*, expecting to arrive some days before Ruth and I were due to arrive. When the ship reached Haifa, an American consular agent came aboard and advised the American passengers not to disembark since war appeared to be imminent.[14] He must not have expressed the urgency of remaining on board the ship forcefully enough, as Ma and Pa disembarked and caught a *sherut*, a sort of shared taxi or shuttle service running between cities, to Jerusalem. As my mother later explained, "Morris said that he would meet us in Jerusalem on June 7, and Morris is always on time."

Meanwhile, in Eagle Pass and Los Angeles, the family was frantic. We had been following the Israeli situation with apprehension. First, we thought that the *Olympia* would surely not proceed into a war zone, and if it did, they would not allow the passengers to disembark. To make sure, we tried to reach the *Olympia*, but all phone lines were jammed. We tried to reach the American embassy in Jerusalem, but no luck. We could only hope that Ma and Pa would not disembark in Haifa.

When they arrived in Jerusalem, Pa and Ma noted that the city was unnaturally quiet. That condition didn't last. Soon all hell broke loose. They were staying in the President Hotel in downtown Jerusalem, not too far from the Old City, which was then under Jordanian control.¹⁵ King Hussein of Jordan stupidly joined President Gamal Abdel Nasser of Egypt in attacking Israel after he should have realized that Egypt had already lost the war. Hussein attacked despite direct pleas from the Israeli government to stay neutral in the conflict. In a short, bloody fight, the Old City, including the historic Jewish area, was captured and Jordan was driven out of the West Bank, losing all the territory it had conquered in 1948.

During the fighting and bombardment of Jerusalem, my parents remained in the basement of the President Hotel along with the other residents. After a few days, when there was a lull in the bombardment, Pa went out to look around and see if he could find some food and cigars. He succeeded in both endeavors, returning home with two eggs and a pocket full of cigars. When a man in Arab dress burst into the basement, Ma thought the end had come, but the "Arab" yelled: "We won! We won!" And dashed out again. At this, everyone came out of the hotel basement into the street. Soon the city was bursting with life again.

A few days later, and after the worst was over, my parents decided to return home. They walked to the American consulate and joined a mob trying to get back to the United States. Most of these people were longtime residents of Jerusalem, mostly Hasidim, who had allowed their American passports to lapse. The consul himself was not in. Supposedly he was in the Old City getting information for our government. The staff of the consulate seems to have been utterly and completely confused. The person my parents spoke with never asked to see their passports but instead advised them to apply for visas. Perhaps in a year or so they would be granted.

My father had enough sense to go to the Jewish Agency, which was connected to the United Jewish Appeal (UJA).¹⁶ For many years, my parents made an annual visit to the agency office, at the invitation of the UJA, and each year they had been provided a car and driver for a day. Mr. Venitzky, in charge of the agency office, listened to their story and arranged for a flight the next day to Athens. There they rejoined the *Olympia* for its return voyage to New York. Unfortunately, on board the ship, Ma seriously hurt herself in a fall and never fully recovered. This was their last trip to Israel.

About a month after the Six-Day War, Ruth and I were able to make our trip to Israel. Theoretically, we went as delegates to the Zionist Organization of America (ZOA) in Jerusalem.¹⁷ The bus taking us from Lod to Jerusalem stopped near the airport to get fuel. Inside the complex was a Wimpy's restaurant. It was hot and we went in to get a cool drink. The counterman looked like a Mexican. Ruth spoke to him in Spanish, and to my surprise he answered in Spanish. It turned out that he was from Majorca, a chueta descended from Sephardic Jews.¹⁸ His ancestral community had been forcibly converted to Christianity in 1391. They continued to be mistreated and shunned by the rest of the population and consequently kept to themselves. In 1948, after they learned of the independence of Israel, a group moved there asking to be admitted under the Law of Return, which grants Israeli citizenship to any Jew. After pondering the question whether they were indeed Jews, the rabbis solved the problem to the satisfaction of all by passing them through a mikveh and then pronouncing them Jews. He was *bautizado*, the counterman said, "baptized."¹⁹

We registered for and attended all the cultural events of the ZOA convention; however, I confess that we never attended a single session of the convention itself, nor was anyone there seemingly interested in our doing so. I suppose the politicians were happy enough to be left undisturbed. Also of interest to me, Ruth and I were supposed to be delegates of the South Texas district of the ZOA, but no one ever asked for our report on the convention. I made a good slideshow record of what we saw, including photos of the debris of the Egyptian army, which I presented to the Eagle Pass Jewish community and a few church groups.

Along with several other delegates we got to see much of the newly occupied territories. In Nablus, in particular, the local people were very sullen. The Israeli forces had entered the city from the north, and the people had initially welcomed them, thinking they were Jordanians or Syrians. It was too late when they realized their error.[20] In Hebron we found the crowds also very sullen. We managed to visit the Cave of Machpelah, where the Jewish patriarchs Abraham, Isaac, and Jacob and the matriarchs Sarah, Rebecca, and Leah were reportedly buried. Under Muslim rule, this site was altered to become a mosque, and under the British mandate Jews were not allowed to enter.[21]

In Jerusalem, I debated paying a visit to the American consulate with a thought of telling them off for their treatment of my parents, but ultimately I decided not to go. The consular staff must have gone through enough already. I hope that American consulates are better prepared for emergencies in the future. I did go to see Mr. Venitzky at the Jewish Agency to thank him for his help to my parents and to deliver a gift from them. "Please," begged Mr. Venitzky, "don't let your parents come to Israel anymore. They are too old."

Jerusalem is a fascinating city at any time, but the amount of devastation done to the former Jewish parts of the city under Jordanian occupation was horrifying. All the ancient synagogues were destroyed. According to Jewish tradition, the resurrection of the dead will begin at the Mount of Olives. In 1948, when the Jordanians captured the Old City of Jerusalem, they tore up the ancient Jewish cemetery on the Mount of Olives and used the tombstones to build latrines for the Jordanian Army.[22]

The most shameful part of this is that during the years of Jordanian rule (1948–1967) not a single voice was raised in the United Nations in protest over this religious desecration or the Jordanian prohibition against any Jewish visitation to their most holy places. In contrast, Israel gave control of Muslim and Christian sites to those religious groups. Nonetheless, once Israel took over, the chorus of imaginary persecution of Muslims and Christians began. Later, I stopped at the Intercontinental Hotel for a cup of coffee. The Jordanians had built the hotel on the crest of the Mount of Olives, and as I sat drinking coffee and admiring the magnificent view, I wondered if I might be sitting on the graves of my ancestors.

In 1970, I was in Israel again, this time by myself. After a few days in Jerusalem, I rented a car and set off. First, I stopped in Jericho and walked around the town.[23] Then I sat down in a cafe and ordered coffee. The other customers in the place, all men, glowered at me. I was definitely not welcome. After my coffee, I drove north in the direction of the archaeological zone, stopping at a soda stand to ask directions. A good-looking boy of about twelve volunteered to show me the way. After viewing the ancient walls—no trace of any tumbled down—my guide asked if I wanted to see the ruins of Caliph Hisham's winter palace. I had never heard of it, but he said it was only a short distance away, so off we went. The palace must have been a spectacular complex in the days of its glory, but soon after it was built it was destroyed in an earthquake and abandoned.[24]

Following a short viewing of the ruins, which was very worthwhile, I returned the boy to the soda stand, paid him five dollars, for which he was overjoyed, and continued on to the ruins of Qumran, the site of discovery of the famed Dead Sea Scrolls.[25] I was tempted to climb up to one of the caves, but it was getting late and I had yet much to see in the few remaining hours of daylight. Then I drove along the Dead Sea to the Ein Gedi kibbutz for a walk up the canyon.[26] I was tempted to stay there for the night at the kibbutz, but decided to continue to Masada.[27] It is undoubtedly one of the most spectacular sights on earth. However, by the time I reached the top on the cable car, it was already dusk, so I decided to return the next morning. I must have been the last person to leave the top.

As I started to drive away, I noticed two women at the bus stop. It was getting dark, and the place seemed to be completely deserted. I stopped and offered them a ride. The women were German tourists staying at the nearby hotel. A few minutes later we arrived at the hotel. I left my suitcase in my room and went down to dinner. The maître d' ushered me to a table where three women were seated. They were obviously a grandmother, mother, and daughter, a girl of about eighteen. All three had Titian hair, medium-fair complexion, and could have stepped out of a Renaissance portrait of Tuscan women. They were speaking Italian. I asked one of them in Spanish to please pass the salt and pepper. They thought I was speaking Italian and answered in a flood of words. When I then spoke English, the young girl answered, also in English. I asked where they were from. They were from Lugano, in the Italian-speaking part of Switzerland. After a while, I asked if they were Jewish. They were surprised at my question. Of course they were Jewish. Then one of the older women, speaking through the girl, asked if I was Jewish. They were most surprised at my answer. It seems that they had decided that I was a German, which explained their initial reluctance to speak to me.

We embarked on a discussion regarding whether it was possible to tell a Jew from a gentile based on their appearance. I remarked that most Jews could be distinguished not merely by physical features but by mannerisms. I further asserted that the two men seated at a nearby table were definitely not Jews. They were conversing in an upper-class English accent and were very restrained in their mannerisms. They were classically British in appearance.

The next morning, as I prepared to leave the hotel for a return to Masada, I noticed one of the men who had been at the next table waiting at the bus stop. I offered him a ride to Masada and he joined me. It turned out that he was from San Diego, California, from a thoroughly assimilated Jewish family. His parents had owned the big department store in San Diego and had sent him to an English prep school. He had not been interested in retailing, but instead devoted himself to yachting and one-man sailboats. He was a bachelor and one day, for no particular reason, decided to move to Israel. His previous contacts with Jews had been slight. In Israel, he was engaged in the manufacture of star-class boats, most of which he sold to the Israeli navy. All naval cadets, both men and women, had to commence their training by learning to sail a boat. If I were to go to Eilat, he said, I could see the cadets returning to harbor in the evening.[28] Each had to land the boat alone and furl the sails. This I saw later in my trip.

I asked about the other man at the dinner table with him. He was a retired non-Jewish Englishman who occupied himself with visiting archaeological sites. He had come to Israel after visiting South America. From Masada, he was on his way to the newly excavated site at Arad.[29] Well, in the end I turned out to be 50 percent correct in guessing who was a Jew.

It is very sad to me what has happened in Israel since those days in 1967, when the future seemed to hold so much promise. For one thing, a short time after the Six-Day War, the Arab countries at the Khartoum Conference announced that there would be no peace and no cooperation of any kind with Israel.[30] This was followed by continuous acts of terrorism against civilians. The strange thing is that the Israelis, not the Arab governments, have been accused of intransigence. The political left all over the world, including many Jewish liberals, have engaged in a vicious anti-Israel and thinly disguised antisemitic campaign. Their program seems to be that the Israelis should simply capitulate on Arab terms. What is never taken into consideration by those who demand unilateral actions by Israel is this: How do you make peace with someone whose political terms are that he be permitted to kill you, your wife, and your children?

We Americans are accustomed to vast open spaces, and Americans cannot comprehend a situation where dangerous areas are only a few miles away. It is difficult to grasp a situation such as Jerusalem, where Israelis couldn't have open windows on the side of the house facing Arab territory because rifle shots into the house would be inevitable.

The Israeli government, for their part, missed a golden opportunity. They should have taken a gamble, a calculated risk, and given full equality to the Israeli Arabs. It is true that compared to the brutal way Jews have been and still are treated in Arab countries, Israeli Arabs are treated relatively well. But that is not enough. The Israelis missed the chance to offer the Arabs real de facto equality, including serving in the army and involvement in politics. The Israeli Arabs felt, and still feel, like second-class citizens, and with some justification. The situation facing Israel is not a happy one, but then the Jews have faced adversity for millennia. At least in Israel they are in their own country.

CHAPTER 14

PUBLIC SERVICE AND POLITICS

In my younger days, I was trained by my mother to believe that one did not compromise with right and wrong, especially if one were a public servant. From reading the historian Livy's account of the early Romans, I was filled with stories of rectitude in public life. Reading about Washington, Jefferson, and Lincoln further strengthened my ideas of political conduct. However, my father always warned me: "Morris, don't get mixed up in politics. It's bad for business." I should have followed his advice. Pa was probably motivated by other considerations than business. To a Jew of his generation, it was better not to be involved in politics. Politics created enemies. Jews should be as inconspicuous as possible. To get into politics was only to draw attention to oneself, which in Europe had bad results.

My own involvement in politics got off very innocently when Mrs. Russell persuaded me to become president of the local chapter of the American Red Cross.[1] No one else would take the job. Under normal conditions, and barring a disaster, the local Red Cross had few duties. If, for example, there was a death in the family of a local serviceman who was stationed in Germany, the Red Cross would locate him and arrange leave, transportation home, and eventually his return to duty. That was Mrs. Russell's job, and she was a pleasant woman and very efficient. The problem came from a new job that had been thrust on the Red Cross, which was not one of our former duties. In about 1950, before the organization of the United Fund, no public relief agency existed. When a charity case arose, Mrs. Russell handed me the problem. Charity cases involved relatively few people and fell into a pattern. Every year starting around the end of March, some thousands of migratory workers and their families went north. Most of them were hard-working and frugal people, such as our back-fence neighbors the Jiménez family. We had a very friendly relationship with them, and their children played in our yard and our children in theirs.

Most *migratorios* used their earnings to improve their homes or buy cars and trucks; some went into business. As Red Cross president, my concern was with a minority, the same people over and over again. When they came home from El Norte they usually came in a flashy new car or station wagon. Every member of the family bought a large new radio. The father lived it up in the saloon. By the middle of January, they came to me with a pitiful story: they had no money for food or to buy shoes so that the children could go to school. Their rent was in arrears and they were threatened with eviction. "Quick, give me money or my army of little children will starve."

I learned to handle the situation out of our limited Red Cross budget after consultation with the priest who knew them. We gave them just enough to survive until March, cooperating with the priest to make sure that the head of the family didn't spend the money in the saloon. By the middle of March, the migratory workers would be ready to go north again. By this time, of course, their car had been repossessed. If the family had a reputation as good workers, the expense of the trip would be taken care of by a local labor contractor. Usually, the entire family traveled in one of the contractor's trucks. There were a few families to whom I had to donate money to go north. I handled this job for two years before I resigned.

CIVIC MUSIC

In the late 1950s, at Ruth's prompting, we set about organizing what came to be called Civic Music of Eagle Pass. I can't sing a note and I can't play an instrument, but music has always been my opiate. I can listen to music day and night, reading a book or just stretched out, relaxing. Mozart is my particular weakness; however, I can enjoy composers as varied as Vivaldi to Bartók and orchestras as diverse as the New York Philharmonic to Duke Ellington. Gilbert and Sullivan is my delight, as is Cole Porter. I must admit that much of Wagner is hard for me to take. I once listened to four days of the Ring cycle and came to the conclusion that if a listener left in the middle of an aria and returned an hour later he wouldn't notice the difference. When I lived in Los Angeles, I had a season ticket to the Philharmonic series and had the good fortune to hear such concerts as Stravinsky conducting his own music.

Organizing a civic program was no easy task. Ruth and I got together a small nucleus that became the board of directors of the organization, and we managed to sell enough season tickets for a small series. I insisted that programs be of good musical quality, booked through a New York agency. In the course of several years we brought to Eagle Pass some excellent violinists, pianists, dancers, and groups, and even presented the full San Antonio Symphony. On one occasion we booked a small touring group of flamenco dancers, but for some reason they had to cancel their booking. We had a guaranteed program with the New York agency, which advised that no similar program was available, therefore they were sending us the José Greco Dance Group, which happened to be in Texas. This was quite a bonus, as their cost was far out of our reach.[2]

Ruth believed that for such an organization as Civic Music to be a success, it had to be socially prominent, so we held parties after the programs to which all season ticket holders were invited. We hosted the first of these parties, then they were taken over by Mrs. Eidson, who loved music and traveled all over the state of Texas to follow opera or symphony performances. Although the parties were given at the Eidson home, the actual organization was done by Carolina Cerna, then in the employ of Mr. Eidson as bookkeeper in his store at the corner of Main and Commercial Streets.

All went well in the Civic Music organization for several years until Ruth decided that we had done our share. It was time for someone else to lead the group. The organization struggled for a few years and then died. Without someone devoting much time and effort to it, it couldn't exist.

ON THE PUBLIC HOUSING BOARD

Around 1948, I was appointed to the public housing board. This was another case of no money and little glory. No one wanted the job. For most of the eighteen years I was on the board I declined to be the president; yet I played a leading role since I felt that in Eagle Pass, at least, public housing was a necessity. I worked very closely with Jake Mabe, the paid director, and was constantly consulted on day-to-day operations. The first board president was Rudy Marquez. The next two, Max Medley and Bruce Thomson, were Republicans at a time when the Republican Party loudly opposed public housing.[3] Fortunately, we had no discord, and for many years all decisions of the board were unanimous.

We had perhaps a unique situation in Eagle Pass. Rental housing was very scarce and the average Mexican home was horribly crowded with two or three families crammed into a small shack, but there was no way to finance new home building, even for a person with means. The First National Bank made neither home loans nor car loans. The bank president, Mr. Schmidt, told me once that the bank invested a major part of its money at 8 percent in large banks in Monterrey and Torreón, Mexico.[4] Since it paid 4 percent or less to savings depositors, the bank was able to net 4 percent with no expense. They made few business loans in Eagle Pass. My father, he told me, was one of the few businessmen who could borrow. Schmidt was very proud of his financial statement and the fact that he netted some thirty to forty thousand dollars a year profit, a pittance of the potential if he had operated as a modern bank.

When I built my own home, I had to trick Schmidt into giving me a ten-year home loan. I did this by telling his son Edward casually over coffee that my friend Sam Meyer, the largest stockholder in the Laredo National Bank, had helped me arrange a home loan there. Actually, I had not even discussed the matter with Sam. When I got back to the store, I received a call from Schmidt telling me that he wanted to talk as soon as possible. A half hour later, I went to the bank. He demanded to know why I had to go to Laredo. Why didn't I speak to him about the loan? The loan was arranged before I left the bank. Usually, if anyone sought a home loan, either the request was turned down summarily or one of the directors might make the loan personally.

In building our first housing-board project, the directives were that we were supposed to eliminate substandard existing homes. This was easy in Eagle Pass since a major part of the housing would be considered substandard. The problem was finding a place to start. We decided on one of the oldest areas, the Loma de la Cruz. No sooner did the word get out than the dilapidated shacks in the area suddenly became very desirable, expensive properties. We had to resort to a combination of diplomacy and trickery to buy a compact block of land. We could always tell the stubborn owner that we were leaving him out, since there was a plethora of shacks available. The last demanding owner of a shanty finally capitulated.

Our first project got underway and was completed around 1950. I was not the president but was asked to make the dedicatory speech. I recall that my remarks were short and to the point. I disliked flowery oratory. The units we built filled immediately, and there was a clamor for more. Perhaps half the population was eligible, incomes being among the lowest in the country, and available housing very limited.

Mr. Mabe mentioned that a very important housing conference was taking place in Washington and asked me to go.[5] It happened that the conference took place only a few days before I was scheduled to go to New York on my buying trip. I agreed to accept only enough expense money to compensate for my stopover in Washington—a room in the hotel where the conference was taking place, taxi from the airport, and meals, most of which were at the conference. The conference itself was very disturbing to proponents of public housing. The problems discussed bore little relation to ours. Complaints came from all sides that the program had resulted in the destruction of long-existing neighborhoods and their replacement by high-rise apartment buildings in which there was no sense of neighborhood or communal responsibility, and where violence from hoodlums became increasingly a problem. The program was clearly a failure. Serious reform was in order.[6]

One constructive thing I learned was that nothing in the law or regulations required that a project be built as a compact unit or as a tall building; in fact, one of the experts recommended that units be scattered so as not to destroy existing neighborhoods. I took this recommendation to the next meeting of our board and moved that our impending project be spread out over a wider area and that units be made to look like private homes or duplexes. The motion carried.

I also suggested that once a year the entire board divide into teams for the purpose of inspecting properties room by room and talking to the tenants to hear any complaints or suggestions. Such an inspection enabled us to ensure that maintenance was as it should be. It was our intention to ensure that tenants were financially qualified and that when the project eventually became the property of the city as provided by law, it would be in good condition so that the city would acquire a valuable property rather than a shambles. The board kept completely out of politics.

It was on either my first trip or a subsequent trip to Washington when an episode occurred that stays in my memory. I decided to pay a visit to our congressman. His office was packed, no sitting room, but when I told the receptionist I was there to pay my respects, she immediately called the congressman on the intercom. A moment later, the person who had been talking to the congressman was ushered out and I was ushered in. I still wonder why I received such VIP treatment. Perhaps he thought that because I was a prominent businessman, I also played an important political role. He must have thought I had my fingers on the local political pulse. In any event, I was welcomed royally.

Somehow, the conversation got around to the fact that the congressman was waiting for a House roll-call vote on the controversial Voting Rights Act, one of the most important pieces of legislation in recent years. The congressman confided that he believed passage of the bill was inevitable; it might be delayed, but opposition under the political climate that prevailed nationally was futile. Not only was it futile, he said, but action was long overdue.

Just then the buzzer sounded, and he had to hurry to take his seat. He instructed his secretary to give me a ticket for a choice seat in the very center of the House visitors' gallery so that I could watch the historic vote. A few moments later the voting commenced. One by one congressmen answered to their names, northern and western congressmen voting for the bill, and southerners as a bloc voting against. When it came my congressman's turn, he also voted against it. I was a little astounded, since he had just stated that the bill was long overdue. It was one more case of what counts being not what you say but what you do.[7]

It is now many years since I have been on the public housing board. Since that time local public housing has gone from bad to worse, from being completely out of politics to being a festering mess, as it has been nationally. The sad state of affairs does not mean, in my opinion, that public housing should be abolished. The problem and the need on a national scale is greater than ever. The lack of housing for the poor is approaching a crisis.

Sometime after I left the housing board, there were rumors of hanky-panky in public housing in Eagle Pass, and two well-dressed young men came through the door, introduced themselves as FBI agents, and began asking questions regarding one of our neighbors, who happened to be an officer of the housing board. Under a law passed during the Reagan administration, the housing board, instead of building new units, could rent existing apartments to qualified tenants, the rent being paid by the board, which, in turn, charged the tenant a subsidized rent based on income and family size. There were rumors that units had been double-rented, that is, rented to nonexistent tenants and then re-rented.

The FBI agents wanted to know if we knew the neighbors' maid. Had we seen her around the premises? Ruth answered that she had seen a person carrying out the trash, and when she taught school, she had given a pupil, who said he was the maid's son, a ride to and from school. Sometime later a young woman and one of the FBI men returned. She introduced herself as one of the trial attorneys in a coming criminal proceeding against our neighbor. The FBI agent read from a notebook Ruth's words from the previous meeting, and the attorney asked if they were correct. Ruth hemmed and hawed. The last thing she wanted was to testify against her neighbor. At this point the FBI agent noticed some Pre-Columbian art pieces we had on a shelf, and we launched into a discussion on archaeology, after which our visitors left.

A few days later, when I was out of the house, the FBI agent appeared with a subpoena for Ruth to appear in federal court in Del Rio the following Tuesday. Ruth told him that she could not go because she was hosting her club's poker game that day. The agent then said the odds were that she would not be called to the stand until Wednesday. Ruth answered that she could not go Wednesday because she was hosting her bridge group that day. The FBI agent must have been completely nonplussed. After some hesitation, he said that a plea bargain deal was under discussion. The case might not go to trial. He would phone her if she were going to be called to testify.

When I returned home and heard the story, I had visions of Ruth being arrested and jailed by a federal judge not known for his sense of humor. Fortunately, the next day Ruth had a call. The accused had plea-bargained. There would be no trial. Now when Ruth mentions the FBI she says, "They are such nice boys."

JUDGE BIBB

For over thirty years—from 1932 to 1963 and again from 1967 to 1969—Judge Roberto "Bob" Bibb dominated politics in Maverick County.[8] Judge Bibb was one of the most interesting men I ever met. During his heyday, he had many bitter enemies as well as devoted followers. Bibb was born in Mexico, the son of an American Southern Pacific Railroad conductor who married a very light-skinned Mexican woman of Spanish descent, a Riojas, from Monclova. He spoke Spanish like a native Mexican, but he could pass for an Anglo anywhere. He had only a fourth-grade education, which made his accomplishments all the more remarkable.

Before Bibb's time, Eagle Pass politics had always been the exclusive business of a small Anglo clique. Policy was determined by a tacit program of keeping taxes as low as possible and maintaining the status quo. They liked the town as it was and had no particular interest in seeing it grow for fear that a larger population would mean the Anglos would lose control. And they certainly had a point. Although poverty-ridden and dormant, Eagle Pass was still a quaint little town in the 1930s, very pleasant to live and do business in, provided you had money yourself. I must admit that since the town grew rapidly after World War II, it has lost much of its old charm.

Through the years, a small group of Anglo men rotated civic offices. Local government was small, efficient, and honest. The only paying jobs of a policy-making nature were the county judge and the commissioners court. The most powerful or prestigious citizen was the county judge himself, who would sometimes operate through an obedient deputy. In Texas's

Maverick County Judge Roberto Bibb with his wife, Edna, ca. 1950. (Fort Duncan Museum. Courtesy of Jeff Taylor Sr.)

unique system of government, carried over from its frontier days, the state constitution gave the county judge a dual function: he was not only the executive officer and chairman of the county commission but also had jurisdiction over both civil litigation and criminal cases, including misdemeanors and probate and juvenile matters. In addition, the county judge was automatically county superintendent of schools.[9]

When I was a child, the de facto political boss in Eagle Pass was William Hollis of the First National Bank. I remember hearing that Hollis once threw an FBI agent into jail for daring to come to town before his boss got permission from Hollis. This, of course, was before J. Edgar Hoover's days of glory. For a while, Hollis made his son-in-law county judge, but his efforts proved unsatisfactory.

During the early days of the Roosevelt administration, Bob Bibb was given the job of foreman for the Works Progress Administration (WPA).[10] He did such a good job that Hollis, who was looking for a good candidate for county judge, decided he would pick Bibb. Of course, Bibb was elected. For a while Bibb was subservient to his mentor, then it dawned on him that he did not need Hollis. In the first place, the Roosevelt welfare programs placed great sums under the control of the county judge. For the first time, there was big money available, not just the meager sums that the businessmen and ranchers had made available to pay low wages to a few. Not only that, but under Texas law, Bibb was like a dictator, with power to pass out patronage to his own people.

Bibb persuaded the Mexican population to register to vote, which was a scandal in itself. Even though they had the legal power to vote, few except the educated had ever exercised that right. Judge Bibb encouraged the mass of the population to vote, and he made sure that they got to the polls and voted as instructed. In short, the power of Mr. Hollis and the Anglo oligarchy was gone. The Anglos considered this an outrage. They dreamed of the day Judge Bibb would be overthrown, not realizing that the world was changing around them.[11]

The remarkable thing to me is not that Bibb got the power, but what he did with his newfound authority. He used every trick to get votes. Every Mexican American, including some who were not citizens, was registered, and on election day all the taxis in town were hired to take voters to the polls. In addition to those who held public offices or who worked for a government agency, paid workers, usually women, were enlisted to get every conceivable voter to the polls. Everyone had marked ballots to aid their voting, and if necessary, a voting official would go into the booth to vote for you. If the voter was aged or infirm and stayed in the taxi, the election official brought out the ballot and obligingly filled it out for them—properly, of course. And under the old system of voting, which was not changed until fairly recently, the voter had to sign his name, or his X, on the back of a numbered tab on the ballot, to be torn off and thrown into a box. Theoretically, this was to ensure in a contested election that the voter was properly registered. In practice, the voter feared that if he double-crossed Bibb and voted for someone else, he or his relative could lose a scarce political job.

The fact is that Bibb would have won even without the shenanigans. The Mexican voters and a good many of the Anglos would have voted for him in any event. Bibb was a master of buying off the opposition. By flattering their egos through honorary positions, throwing business their way, and finding jobs for them or their relatives unable to support themselves, Bibb bought their silence if not their enthusiastic support. In the commissioners court, Bibb very astutely divided representation. The Indio area was represented by an Anglo rancher, Quemado by an Anglo farmer, and Eagle Pass was divided into multiple areas represented by either Mexicans or Anglos. Bibb as chairman was the real power.

Judge Bibb used to spend much of his time, especially mornings, in the Sabinas Inn, then he would have lunch in the Fort Duncan Club restaurant and would receive anyone who wanted to talk to him there for part of the afternoon. Some mornings, Pa was one of Bibb's drinking buddies. He would come back from a session with Bibb and tell me, "Judge Bibb says you can have anything you want. Do you want to be mayor or county attorney?" "Pa," I would answer, "didn't you tell me to keep out of politics because it wasn't good for business?"

Was Judge Bibb corrupt? Did he steal? Let me put it this way: he was no saint. For many years, he did not overtly interfere in either city politics or the school board, where Anglos continued their dominance, but it was tacitly understood that there were limits to their independence. I never heard that Bibb embezzled money or took illegal funds; if he had done so, his enemies would have made much of it. He did, however, avail himself freely of the perks of his office. County judges all over Texas regarded it as a universal custom and matter of right that they would get 5 percent over the bid price from all bridge and road contracts. In addition, even though Maverick County had an independent school district, Judge Bibb voted himself five thousand dollars a year as superintendent of a nonexistent county school system.

Early in his career, Bibb became friendly with Lyndon B. Johnson. Johnson would come to Eagle Pass to confer with Bibb or just relax, and he would sit in the Moderno Restaurant in Piedras Negras with Bibb as a companion, eating and drinking for hours. If Bibb wanted favors for himself or for friends that involved a larger theater than the limits of Maverick County, he asked Lyndon for help and usually got it.[12]

When LBJ first ran for Senate in 1941 to fill an unexpectedly available term, he was expected to win but was defeated at the last minute by ballot boxes stuffed in favor of Pappy

O'Daniel. When he ran against Coke Stevenson a few years later, Johnson was more careful. He arranged with Boss Parr of Duval County (and Bibb in Maverick County) to wait until all of Stevenson's votes were in. Then a large enough vote was announced for Johnson to assure his victory. His enemies called him "Landslide Lyndon." Of course, Lyndon could have answered that he had done unto others as they had done to him, only better.[13]

After his election, Johnson was able to help Judge Bibb through the Bracero Program, which Congress passed after World War II when it became apparent that we were facing an acute shortage of farm labor. Temporary Mexican laborers (braceros) were brought into the country by contract with the Mexican government. With Mexican consular officials supervising, braceros were brought in, registered, processed, and sent to farm and ranch employers. At the end of their term of employment, they were sent back to be reprocessed, discharged, and returned to Mexico.[14]

Bibb was able to get Eagle Pass selected as one of the prime bracero processing centers. This brought employment to Eagle Pass in many forms: government personnel, both American and Mexican, doctors, food kitchens, camp personnel, insurance companies, and so on.[15] Bibb also managed to channel money into his own pockets. Using Fred Smith as his partner, he got the contract to feed thousands of braceros.[16] He had a hand in such concessions as photographing braceros and in selling insurance to farmers and ranchers as required by the regulations. In short, Bibb made money very quickly.

On one occasion, he got himself in trouble. At the same time that the bracero camps were operating, meat was being packed in Piedras Negras to be shipped to Europe under the Marshall Plan to alleviate the postwar food shortage. Bibb discovered that there was either no duty or very little duty on imported dog food, so he bought canned meat in Piedras Negras, labeled it "dog food," and brought it across to feed the braceros. Then someone noticed that the cans were marked "dog food." There was a tremendous outcry from the Mexican consul, then the press. Papers from New York to Mexico City reported the "atrocity." Bibb was in a jam. If he admitted that the meat was regular Marshall Plan meat, then he was in trouble with customs; but if he failed to admit it, then he was in trouble as a victimizer of unfortunate braceros. I remember we laughed at Bibb's dilemma, but finally it all quieted down. LBJ was able to quash the investigation.[17]

Sometime after that, the Bracero Program was canceled at the insistence of labor unions. According to them, the Mexican laborers were being exploited. As a matter of common sense, this was a little mystifying. The braceros were better paid than native Mexican American labor. They were insured against accidents or loss of life or limb. They worked under strict rules governing their employment. For example, if they were transported to work in a truck, it had to be supplied with seats. In view of the fact that native labor had no safeguards at all or medical insurance, it seemed to me that the unions and native labor should have begged to be exploited likewise.

The Bracero Program did much good for Mexico. In the course of our travels in Mexico, in the remotest villages, the man who had the best garden patch, the newest taxi, or the best boat had been a bracero. The returning braceros almost all carried back with them old-fashioned, foot-propelled Singer sewing machines, which then created new jobs in Mexico. So, we killed the Bracero Program, and in its place we have a horde of illegal immigrants, completely out of control and doing American labor far more damage than the organized program. The unions sowed the wind and have reaped the whirlwind.

My first run-in with Judge Bibb occurred in 1950 over the census. I argued that the city limits should be extended to Eagle Pass's true boundaries. By doing so, we would show a population of over ten thousand people. If we continued to total only 7,500 inhabitants, we would not be listed on most maps or in the atlases consulted by business for their local or regional offices.

"Morris," Judge Bibb answered, "don't worry. You're too nervous. I can tell by the way you drink your whiskey. Take it easy."

For some reason, Bibb did not want the city limits changed until after the next election. I think the reason was that if the census showed a small population we would be entitled to low-interest "rural" loans, greatly aiding those selling subdivisions of cheap lots to poor immigrants. These lots were sold out in the country with no water or sewerage. These *colonias* were to be the curse of the entire border and later cost the state and federal governments huge sums for water and sewerage provided free to their owners.

"I can fix it up," he assured me. "All I have to do is ask Lyndon." However, in the 1950 census we showed less than ten thousand.[18] In May, after the election took place, the city limits were extended, but Lyndon or no Lyndon, the census bureau refused to alter its earlier figures.

Periodically, I would have arguments with the judge over his failure to hold court. To my knowledge, in thirty years he held only one criminal trial. His reluctance was understandable. In holding a criminal trial in a small town, you are sure to antagonize someone: the best way out was not to hold court. One day he called me in. "Morris," he said, "I'm going to hold court just like you wanted. I've got a case that's just right. The man doesn't have one single voting relative. It's some fellow by the name of Spiller, the manager of Lane's."[19]

"My God," I said. "Spiller was a concentration camp victim. He's so nervous he shakes. What has he done?"

It seems that Spiller had suspected some girls of shoplifting. Instead of asking one of his women clerks to watch them, the fool had the idea of watching them himself from above the open-top dressing rooms. The girls saw him, made a commotion, and filed charges. Instead of the girls being arrested for shoplifting, Spiller, the peeping tom, was arrested and Judge Bibb rushed him to trial.

It just so happens that Spiller was my tenant in my old house on Nueces Street. The Spillers had only recently been married, and Mrs. Spiller had little experience in cooking. She cooked with an excess of grease and poured it down the sink. Every few days the sink clogged with thick grease, and she called for a plumber. If the plumber did not show up at once, I got calls every few minutes. The plumber reported back in exasperation that there was no remedy unless she ceased pouring grease. After a few months of this, I refused to send the plumber again, and Spiller said he wasn't going to pay rent. At this point, his arrest occurred.

I and other members of the Jewish community tried with no avail to reason with Judge Bibb. "No voting relatives," he said. "Besides, you were the one who wanted me to hold trials." The jury found Spiller guilty. This satisfied Judge Bibb. We arranged for Lane's to transfer him to a distant town, and he got a suspended sentence. Judge Bibb never took a criminal case to trial again.

Eventually, failing health and bad luck combined to cause Judge Bibb to lose control of his political fiefdom. For one thing, a new priest came to town. He was a Spaniard, very strict, dogmatic, and greatly disliked. He was unaccustomed to the mores of border society and was easily shocked by the open displays by Bibb's lieutenants of their young girlfriends. One lieutenant not only flaunted his girlfriends but mistreated his wife and children. The Spanish priest fulminated from the pulpit. No one liked the priest, but for Bibb it hit at the wrong moment. The truth of the matter was that Roberto Bibb was no longer the man he had been twenty or thirty years before. Too much beer and whiskey had eroded his brain and given him cirrhosis of the liver. His wife, Edna, a shrewd supporter, had also been affected by too much liquor. Everything began to go against him, and he did not run for reelection.

A good friend of mine, Dan McDuff, had sold his insurance business and was at loose ends. He decided to run for county judge. At that moment in time, he was the ideal candidate. He had a friendly, outgoing personality. He had no enemies. He spoke Spanish fluently and was well-liked by the Mexican population. He was the right candidate at the right time and won the election. Dan took his job seriously. He read manuals on how to hold court. He studied the problems of the county.[20]

Unfortunately, right at the start he made a terrible mistake. It happened that Jerry Rhodes, then president of the school board, was elected a county commissioner.[21] When someone objected that under state law, he could not hold both offices, he resigned as commissioner. It was up to Dan McDuff, as county judge, to appoint a replacement to complete the term. Dan asked the advice of a number of his friends on whom to appoint. I urged him to choose Raul "Peanuts" Rodríguez, the man Rhodes had defeated in a close election. I believed he deserved to be appointed and also that Dan would gain the loyal support of the important Rodríguez family. Without Mexican American support, Dan would have no power base.

Dan ignored my advice and appointed an Anglo, a good man but persona non grata to the mass of the population. It turned out to be a catastrophe. Dan presided over the commissioners but lost control. At the next election, Bibb was reelected. He was a shadow of his former self, and not too long afterward was hospitalized and died of cirrhosis of the liver. So ended the career at a comparatively young age of a remarkable man. With him ended a whole era in our local history.

I remember reading a book by the muckraker Lincoln Steffens. His observation was that there is nothing in the Constitution or in the American system of government to provide for coordination between the various elements of government. We talk of a separation of powers. Even in city government, there is no legal coordination between various agencies and bureaus. The political boss has arisen as an American institution to fill this void. Under someone like Boss Tweed, the boss can do great harm. Under the benevolent leadership of Judge Bibb, we had comparatively good government until "drink and the Devil," as the song goes, caused Bibb to lose his touch. With the fall of Judge Bibb, Eagle Pass and Maverick County have suffered a period of corruption and chaos with no end in sight. Nowadays, whenever I meet a fellow old-timer over a cup of coffee, my companion sooner or later brings up the state of present-day Eagle Pass politics, and he invariably says with a sigh, "If we only had Judge Bibb back again!"[22]

HOW I HELPED SHAPE STATE AND NATIONAL POLITICS

Sometime in the 1960s I was asked if I would be a delegate to the Texas Democratic Convention. As a college major in political science, I had read all about conventions. I was most anxious to participate in one. What actually happened in a convention? This was my opportunity to learn.[23]

First, there was a local meeting in Eagle Pass to determine who would be the delegates to the state convention. I don't recall whether this was by precinct or at one meeting. In previous years, few had attended except local office holders: delegates were all hand-picked by Judge Bibb. This year it was obvious that Bibb's rule had disintegrated and Art Flores, then the mayor, determined to take control. I came to the meeting to find a large crowd of Flores's followers there. The Bibb forces were overwhelmed, and Flores's slate was elected.[24]

Some weeks later, along with the rest of the Eagle Pass delegation, I was in Austin, where the convention was held in the ballroom of one of the Austin hotels. There was an open bar, and attendees stood around with glasses in their hands and talked while a meeting was in progress in one of the side rooms. I guess that would be the "smoke-filled room" of the old days—now, of course, it can be found without the tobacco smoke. Only Art Flores of our delegation attended in this sanctum.

It was an open secret that John Connally, the governor, controlled the convention. After what seemed an interminable length of time, the door of the inner sanctum opened, the participants filed out, and the general meeting was called to order. The proposed platform was read and a list of delegates to the National Democratic Convention named. Motions were made to approve them. Everyone dutifully voted "Yah," after which the meeting was soon adjourned. I then went back to my hotel room and next morning returned to Eagle Pass. Most of the delegates remained in the ballroom and continued drinking as long as the supply lasted.

This recollection is probably incorrect in detail, but it is how I remember the momentous event in which I participated in the affairs of the nation.

THE COMMUNITY ACTION PROGRAM

Among other legislation passed in Lyndon Johnson's first term was the community action program.[25] The mayor of Eagle Pass then, Art Flores, appointed my brother Reuben to head the program. Reuben then appointed me to the board of directors. The theory behind community action, the brainchild of a sociologist in Chicago, was that the best method to cure poverty was to involve the poor in local politics. The rationale of the program was that if the poor become involved in fighting for their political rights, they would inevitably consider their poverty and take steps to improve their economic situation.[26] Community action brought to the forefront a host of would-be orators, some of whom were talented rabble-rousers. Most of these were self-styled saviors of the poor. One of the most vocal of these was Queta Díaz, a real firebrand. Many years later, in an odd turn of events, Díaz was elected county judge, ostensibly as a Republican.[27]

How Lyndon Johnson, a most astute politician, was persuaded to adopt such a program I cannot understand unless it sneaked by him in a maze of other legislation. The life's blood of politics is money; it is the grease that oils the political machine. When a group of people are paid to engage in politics, it is like throwing meat to a tiger. In no time at all, there is a political machine competing for power with the existing one. Perhaps it was thought that in each locality the local political boss, through the power of appointment he was expected to wield, would control the political-action organizations.

It happened that the new mayor of Eagle Pass, Art Flores, was a bitter personal enemy of Judge Bibb. Flores was closely connected to John Connally's conservative faction of Democrats, who were doing everything they could to replace the liberals in power. The irony of the situation was that my brother Reuben was a devout Democrat of the liberal persuasion. All he took into consideration was that this was a program passed by a Democratic Congress, so he assumed it must be good, and he was going to carry it out honestly and efficiently. Almost immediately, Reuben was at loggerheads with Judge Bibb. Hitherto, Bibb had been the sole source of important patronage. Now there was a rival source of money in great quantities competing with him. Bibb came to one of the meetings of community action to ask that the program be conducted through consultation with him. Reuben refused, and I had to back up my brother although I was most unhappy over the situation.

Through the community action program, a considerable sum had been allocated to the city for the purpose of building a community center. The only auditorium in the city was at the old high school. It seated only some 450 people and was not air-conditioned. Unlike Laredo and other border cities, no convention of any size could be held in Eagle Pass, simply because there was no place available to hold one. To my exasperation, the saviors of the poor managed to waste the available money allocated. Instead of a true community center, the money was divided. Part was spent on a useless multipurpose center, which had a flat floor suitable for a basketball court. It was thought that the area could also be used as an auditorium, using folding chairs when needed, so at one end was a small stage. The trouble was that the stage was too small, and from the flat floor no one could see it.

The balance of the money was used to build small buildings scattered about town with the idea they would serve as neighborhood meeting centers. In a short time, it was apparent that the neighborhood centers were a disaster. Each one required a janitor and administrative staff, and the city had no money for staff, maintenance, or repairs. In no time, the centers were abandoned and finally used by the city for offices or rented or sold for such purposes as evangelical churches. The "multipurposeless center" has also been used for offices. After all these years, the poor have not been saved, nor do we have a civic center. As for the community action program, it was quietly dropped.

GEORGE DE MOHRENSCHILDT, THE SCOUNDREL

In addition to Judge Bibb, I have met all varieties of men in my lifetime, good ones, bad ones, wise men and fools, learned men and illiterates, but the status of the biggest scoundrel I have personally met I award to the late George de Mohrenschildt.[28] Ruth and I met George and (I believe) his fourth wife, Jeanne, through our good friend Tito Harper, a son of Osie Harper.[29] When Tito was a student at St. Edward's, in Austin, he shared an apartment with de Mohrenschildt, then studying petroleum engineering at the University of Texas. From what Ruth and I have gathered, it was he who first introduced Tito to drugs and other destructive habits.

George was born a Russian baron in one of the Baltic states. After the Russian Revolution, he was at the court of the king of Belgium, one of his relatives. The Second World War brought him to the United States, penniless but with the best of social connections. He soon managed to marry one of the DuPont heiresses. After a divorce, he married a lesser heiress. This union also did not last. Finally, no longer able to live off women, and a mature man, he returned to school to learn a profession.

By the time we met George, he had the unique distinction of having been personally friendly at one time or another with most of the principals in the Kennedy assassination. In his days of high social standing, he had been friendly with the family of Jacqueline Kennedy. Later, in Dallas, through contacts of his wife Jeanne among the Russian exiles, he became close friends with Lee Harvey Oswald and his wife, Marina. I am certain that he was also acquainted with Jack Ruby.

We met the de Mohrenschildts at Tito Harper's home in Piedras Negras. George was tall and handsome, with courtly manners when he chose to use them. He also proved to have a propensity for malice and making sneering and belittling remarks. Jeanne, on the other hand, proved to be a rather plain, good-hearted woman who was obviously disturbed by George's actions. She made her living designing tennis dresses for one of the Dallas manufacturers.

George, at the time, was teaching petroleum engineering at a Black college near Dallas.[30] I wondered what George and his wife had in common other than they were both Russian. She deserved better.

At first, we were much intrigued by the de Mohrenschildts and their contact with the Kennedy assassination. George remarked that if Oswald had only agreed to buy Marina a new refrigerator, the assassination would never have taken place. According to him, he witnessed a violent quarrel between them the day before. Oswald had refused to buy the refrigerator after constant nagging, saying that he did not have the money, and then stormed out of the house in a fury. If he had not been in a mental turmoil, said George, he would not have turned to assassination. That you can believe or not.

The de Mohrenschildts told us that a few years before they had made a trip through the length of Mexico on foot, accompanied by a small dog and a burro carrying all their equipment. Jeanne said that she had hoped to get a children's book published in which the journey was described from the standpoint of their little dog. Ruth was skeptical and insisted to me that a more sinister reason must have been involved in their trip.

On a number of occasions, I was obliged to play tennis with them. They were enthusiastic but terrible players. In Dallas, we were often invited to their home, where we were introduced to a combination of assorted radicals involved in various causes. One of George's friends was a conservative insurance executive, and I wondered how he fit in with the rest of George's motley collection of guests.

On their trips to the border to visit Tito, they would often leave some of their belongings with us before crossing into Mexico. I introduced Jeanne to my mother. Both were delighted, since it gave them an opportunity to speak Russian, a language Mother had not used since leaving Lithuania. Jeanne brought Mother a Russian book on a subsequent trip, but I doubt Mother could see the print well enough to read it.

One New Year's Eve we were invited by the Harpers to a party in Piedras Negras. The de Mohrenschildts were also invited. We had given our children, then of high-school age, permission to have a party. The de Mohrenschildts stopped at our home with a daughter from one of their previous marriages.[31] She was a teenager and quite pretty. George asked if she could join our children's party, and we readily consented. We then all left for the Harpers' party. A few hours later we received a hysterical and incoherent phone call from my son John, the oldest of our children. We gathered that the de Mohrenschildt girl was either on drugs or in a wild frenzy for some other reason. In any event, she was throwing things, screaming, and otherwise causing a commotion. We notified George, and the de Mohrenschildts left to get her and rescue our children. The girl's parents had unloaded her on George for a good reason.

We became increasingly uneasy about George as we saw more of him. The final break occurred at a dinner at the Harpers'. For no reason at all, George started to ridicule Concha Harper, Tito's wife and the hostess, on the Catholic religion, making one contemptuous remark after another. Concha took his taunts without a reply although it was apparent she was enraged. Tito said nothing. To Ruth and me it was unpardonable to be a guest in someone's home and then repay hospitality with gratuitous insults. George then proceeded to make a remark insulting to Jews. Ruth had been hiding her anger with difficulty over the gratuitous insults to Concha; she could no longer conceal her feelings and proceeded to vent her wrath. Jeanne had been trying unsuccessfully to restrain George, but she also lost restraint. The dinner was ruined. We never saw the de Mohrenschildts again.

In my view, George was an Iago. He liked to see people squirm, like a cruel boy who runs a pin into an insect. He thoroughly enjoyed provoking those who were susceptible, either to push them into a course of conduct through suggestion or merely to make them squirm. As far as Oswald was concerned, George might very well have influenced him in certain directions. In an unguarded moment, George said that he knew who had had unsuccessfully tried to assassinate General Edwin Walker prior to the Kennedy assassination and strongly implied that it was Oswald.[32] He never admitted he himself had any part in the Kennedy assassination. One thing is certain: George was not a nice person.

Sometime later, there was a revival of interest in the Kennedy assassination. In various books alleging sinister machinations, de Mohrenschildt is described as an FBI agent, a Cuban agent, and a Russian agent. Either because they had some evidence or merely were suspicious, the FBI seems to have hounded George until he became completely paranoid. He killed himself with a shotgun. I do not know what became of Jeanne.[33]

CHAPTER 15

SEÑOR RÍSQUIN RUNS FOR SCHOOL BOARD

My own first entry into elective politics as a candidate was relatively harmless. About the year 1960, a delegation of Main Street businessmen came to see me and asked if I would run for city council. They were unhappy about the caliber of men on the council, blaming Judge Bibb. Officially, Bibb did not involve himself in city elections, but all the winning candidates nevertheless were from his party.

The incumbent I was to oppose was Pete "The Greek" Mathiwos, who operated the Merchant's Cafe, Pa's favorite saloon and hangout.[1] As a councilman, Pete was neither good nor bad. Everyone knew that he slept through most of the meetings of the council. Pete seemed to be interested only in the patronage attached to his position. Although there was little by way of accomplishment in his record, neither could he be accused of responsibility for bad legislation. To those who believed in as little government as possible, Pete was an ideal councilman.

Despite my better judgment I agreed to run. It is very pleasing to the ego to be asked by your fellow citizens to represent them in public office, and in my weakness, I succumbed to the implied flattery. However, I did no campaigning whatsoever. In my vanity, I felt that if the citizens of Eagle Pass would not choose me over Pete, so much the worse for them. I was swamped in the election.

How I got subsequently involved in school politics is a long story. The nature of the schools in Maverick County had changed by 1960. Due to state laws that took part of the burden of financing schools from local school districts and made education compulsory to age sixteen, enrollment had ballooned. Under the new state law, the subsidy to the local districts was based on average daily attendance.[2] It became advantageous to school districts to corral as many students as possible and keep them in school. Since Maverick County has only one school district for the entire county, school enrollment exploded over the next ten years. The high-school graduating classes grew to over one hundred, then to over two hundred. Grammar schools were opened in every neighborhood. With increasing enrollment came more teachers, janitors, cafeteria personnel, and other staff members, until the Eagle Pass

Independent School District became the biggest employer in the county. Patronage became an important factor in school politics.

As enrollment increased, a new high school was built on Webster Street. This soon proved too small and yet another new high school was built on the Del Rio highway, the Webster school becoming a junior high.[3] Elementary schools were at opposite ends of the county, at Quemado in the north and at El Indio in the south. The Lee School and then the Graves School were built in Eagle Pass for additional elementary school classes. Population continued its rapid growth because of a high birth rate and the flood of new immigrants.

With the growth in enrollment came a gradual decline in aggregate test scores. This was only natural: a school merely reflects the general population, so the more students, the greater the scope of the results. An increasing number of students, made greater by an influx of immigrants from Mexico, couldn't speak English. In a substantial number of cases, the parents were not only illiterate, but they were completely uninterested in the schooling of their children and took them out of school at harvest time or left with them as migratory workers, since the children also worked in the harvests and earned money. To be fair, the quality of education was steadily declining throughout the United States; Eagle Pass was just part of the total picture, no better and no worse.

Until the early 1960s, the school board continued to be the exclusive preserve of the most prestigious male citizens, almost all Anglos, whose only true interest was to keep taxes as low as possible. Their idea of supporting the school was limited to attending football games and betting on the home team against their counterparts from rival towns. In most small Texas towns, the football team is all-important.[4] I used to laugh over the similar situation in Arkansas in the time of Governor Orval Faubus. When he closed Little Rock's Central High School after the Supreme Court ordered an end to segregation in the schools, Faubus allowed the football team to play out its season.[5] Just think how much money could be saved if Texas high schools were closed except for the football teams!

With the huge increase in enrollment, more teachers were needed. Good teachers who were willing to come to Eagle Pass, with its low salary scale, were increasingly hard to find. The level of teaching fell. Some of the faculty could only be classified as unsophisticated provincials. When my son Pete asked at the high school for information on Stanford University, the answer was, "Stanford? Never heard of it. A bright boy like you should go to a good school like Texas A&M."[6]

SCHOOL POLITICS

The superintendent of schools in the early 1960s was Jimmy Garland.[7] Jimmy and I played tennis and were on friendly terms. He was, as I later found out, a much better than average small-town superintendent. He had a pleasant personality, got along well with people, and ran an efficient school system. After leaving Eagle Pass, he became the head of a small college in South Texas. At this point in his career, however, Jimmy brought about his own downfall: he decided to zone the various elementary schools. Because of neighborhood location, most of the poorest Mexican children, a major part of whom were from migrant families, went to Lee. Most of the Anglo children, as well as the middle-class Mexican children, attended Graves, Webster, or Austin.

The Rhodes family lived on a farm immediately outside of town, zoned to attend the Lee School. Susie Rhodes, unlike the great majority of Anglo women, spoke fluent Spanish and raised her children to speak it correctly.[8] Her father, Dr. Gates, was practically sanctified by the poor Mexican population.[9] Jerry Rhodes, a Harvard Law School graduate, was also very popular with the Mexican population. Certainly, neither Susie nor her family could be considered anti-Mexican. Nevertheless, Susie asked Jimmy Garland for permission to send her children to the same school as their friends. Jimmy refused in order not to be accused of favoritism, and this led to a great controversy that convulsed the town for years and into which I was innocently drawn.

Susie pressured her husband into entering school board politics in order to gain revenge, and he and his slate won the next election, with the result that Jimmy Garland was summarily fired and replaced by a new superintendent, Curly James.[10] The Garland forces in turn plotted revenge, and at the next election they gained control of the board, and Curly James was fired. A new superintendent was brought in from the lower Rio Grande Valley, but at the next board election the Rhodes faction won by a landslide, the new superintendent was summarily fired, and Curly James reinstated.

I was on the sidelines during this burlesque. I had friends on both sides of the controversy. I was disturbed by the controversy in the school system, especially since I had three children going to school in Eagle Pass. One day in 1966, a delegation came to see me and asked me to be a candidate for the school board. They said that the town was split over the ongoing controversy and the downtown businessmen had decided to intervene. If I would run on a ticket with Jack Spence, the owner of the Style Shop, the committee pledged that they would finance the campaign.[11] I was genuinely surprised by the offer and answered that I would need time to think it over.

After discussing the issue with Ruth and my brother Reuben, I decided to enter the race. Maybe I could do something to improve the schools. I held a meeting with Jack Spence over coffee at the Eagle Drugstore. Jack was a graduate of Rice University and a fine choice for the school board. We had never been intimate friends, but he was a person I respected. From all I saw or heard, no one had a bad word to say about him. Unlike me, with my more aloof personality, Jack had a smile for everyone and would unquestionably be a great vote-getter. We agreed to run and, if elected, to serve as a team. We decided that neither one of us would take any action unless it was mutually acceptable. With this decision we formally announced our candidacy and embarked on the campaign.

In planning the race, this was my idea: I was going to carry the campaign to the common people. I was running against Jerry Rhodes, then president of the school board and very popular with the Mexican voters. Unlike Jack, I had no church behind me to provide a base. A woman working at the 21 Shop, which Riskind's then owned, mentioned to me that she had at one time worked for Judge Bibb in his campaigns and that she had a wide acquaintance in San Luisito, a part of town where most of the migratory workers lived. She agreed to introduce me to some of the key people in that neighborhood.

After the store closed, I went with her from house to house to meet people. All the conversation was in Spanish and with people who exhibited the expression of a blank wall, so I would come home in a state of absolute exhaustion. After a week or so, I could take no more and gave up. I doubted my message counted at all. What turned out to be of the utmost importance, however, was that word spread that the great "Señor Rísquin" actually came to see them.

One of the disappointments was the realization that in entering the race I had alienated some of my good friends and customers. The people I had allied myself with were neither good friends nor customers of any consequence. Most of them were Anglos who considered themselves too important to buy their clothes in Eagle Pass. From a business standpoint, Pa was right: politics wasn't good business. However, once I entered the race, Pa did everything he could to help. When we held public meetings, he would be in the crowd shaking hands with all the old-timers and telling them proudly that I was his son.

As a political campaigner, I would not give myself high marks. In an intimate group I was a better than average speaker if discussing a topic I believed in. Before an outdoor crowd, especially after a rabble-rouser of the old style, I sounded dull and flat. I just could not make myself mouth out-and-out baloney. One of my recollections of the election and the campaign: A friend reported to me that an Anglo acquaintance had said he would vote for me even though I was a Jew. This remark made me furiously angry.

It was the local custom on election day for each candidate to establish his base as close to the voting place as is legally permissible. We put up our signs and banners on the corner by the Eagle Hotel facing the Maverick County Courthouse. Our opponents stationed themselves on the opposite corner of Quarry Street. I stood out on our corner all that long day greeting those who came past. Usually, it was easy to tell who would be the winner by counting those voters who greeted one candidate or the other. In this election it was soon apparent that the outcome would be very close. Too close for comfort.

Some zealous person in our "reform" party had called the Texas Rangers, saying that not only violence but vote tampering was expected. As a result, a gruff Ranger appeared to keep an eye on the courthouse. It just happened that my wife Ruth kept walking across the street to look into the courthouse to see how many were voting. Finally, Ruth, of all people, was ushered off the courthouse grounds by a nasty Ranger as a suspicious character interfering with the election!

At 7 p.m. the polls closed. A short time later word came that Jack and I were leading by a narrow margin. Only Quemado and El Indio remained to be heard from. A short time later our victory was confirmed. I had won by some sixty votes, Jack by a larger margin. Our group was wild with enthusiasm. Jerry Rhodes, my opponent, came over to congratulate me, and as we shook hands one of Jerry's rivals came up, shook his fist in Jerry's face, and said, "I told you I would get even with you." I felt terrible. Here I thought I was running to improve the schools, and I found myself the tool of a vendetta. It was not an auspicious way to begin my term.

ON THE BOARD

When I became a member of the school board in 1966, the administrative staff of the school system was very small. The central office was staffed in an old wooden building that at one time had housed the entire school system. The Hielscher School was named after a nineteenth-century superintendent. It was no longer used as a school but served as a central office. The entire staff consisted of Curly James, superintendent of schools; Ofelia Sepulveda, his secretary; Cliff Butler, the business manager; Humberto Torralba, tax collector; Cecilio Rodríguez, tax appraiser; and four secretaries. There was also a coordinator of federal programs, a recently established position as federal assistance was just being offered.[12] As I write, there is now a building packed with administrators, and periodically there is an announcement of yet another new assistant superintendent or director of some new program. With all of this, test scores have become worse, and there are students who graduate and cannot read, write a simple sentence, or do the simplest math. If one wanted to be facetious, he could say that if this continues there will be more administrators administrating than teachers teaching.

At first, I was all in favor of the use of federal money for the schools, but used improperly, it has become a curse on the school system. We were not given money to hire more teachers or to raise teachers' salaries, which were pitifully low. Instead, positions were funded to implement programs that might have been needed in New York or Chicago but not in Eagle Pass. We were told that a secretary should be paid "not more than ten thousand dollars per annum," the prevailing wage in big cities, leading one of our board members to protest that his secretary, a very good one, was paid only five thousand dollars.

It was pointed out that these inflated salaries cost the town nothing; the funds were, so to speak, "dollars from heaven," and if we didn't use them some other town would. Job after job was filled, whether needed or not, and the bureaucracy grew. All sorts of reports for the classroom teacher were devised, with the net result that the teachers spent more time on useless reports than on teaching. The reports became part of a never-ending stream of reports or ended up in the trash. Federal programs did serve a purpose, albeit perhaps not the one that was originally intended. They served to raise wage scales in low-wage areas and created a new middle class made up of school personnel and other government-office holders. The town is certainly more prosperous as a result.

In fact, the problems of the schools have less to do with money than with the system of education based on warped ideas of "civil liberties," under which all discipline in the public schools has evaporated. If a student disrupts the class, or even threatens the teacher with a gun, it is the teacher's fault. Any attempt to discipline or to maintain order is followed by a lawsuit. It seems to me that a voucher system, as many people want, would result in a complete destruction of the public schools, which would be left with all the problem cases.[13] If I sound bitter, it's because I am.

I soon learned that even a well-intentioned school board member could have little influence on actual teaching methods. Our time was so filled with all sorts of business and related matters that a meeting would start early and adjourn at midnight with unfinished business. In checking the law, I found that my authority as a board member was limited to my voice and vote at a meeting or if I were officially empowered by the board or the president to perform some designated action. I had no authority to go out on my own and order school personnel to do anything the board had not officially required. On the humorous side, I soon learned from talking to school personnel that, although no one seemed to know who Plato was, everyone was a philosopher. The superintendent had his philosophy on how to handle the "kiddos," and the football coach had his philosophy on how to play football. Everyone had a philosophy.

Soon after I was elected, unexpected problems erupted. When the federal programs were first offered in the previous year, the board had appointed a local young man just out of college as federal coordinator at a fancy salary. The new coordinator had gone at his task with great enthusiasm before taking the trouble to read the fine print. He proceeded to order all sorts of "aids to education" without bothering to get prior approval from on high, so we had a warehouse full of overhead projectors and other devices for which we owed $250,000, with no means of payment. The young man resigned; nevertheless, we still owed the money. We secured a loan from the bank, and Mr. Schmidt, the bank president, warned me that we could expect no more money. We had to live within our means.

Next, we had a problem with our superintendent. Curly James was an excellent public relations man. He failed when it came to the details of administration. For years, he had been accustomed to leaving day-to-day business to his very competent secretary, Ofelia Sepulveda.[14]

Ofelia was the de facto superintendent. Then a catastrophe occurred: Ofelia married a sergeant in the army who was transferred to Turkey and took Ofelia with him. Without Ofelia everything fell apart. The board was made up of Curly's friends, but they had no recourse. Curly was asked to resign, and a new superintendent had to be selected.

It was the usual practice for small-town Texas school boards to select a coach, preferably a football coach, to be superintendent. The board reasoned that a coach would be able to maintain order and run a tight ship. I never at any time in my years on the board heard a word said about a candidate's cultural background. It was presumed that the candidate had taken the requisite education courses. No one cared whether he knew anything about literature or art or music, nor even the basic facts about what was going on in the world. A new superintendent would immediately be swamped by routine problems and have little time for anything other than to keep abreast of the flood of work. It would be an exceptional superintendent, even in a big city, who spent time thinking about the cultural content of school teaching.

The man selected as the new superintendent was the football coach, Kenneth Moore.[15] He proved to be a hard worker, and he soon met with the board to report on an urgent problem facing us, the rate of growth of the school population. He concluded that the existing schools were becoming excessively overcrowded and school construction was an urgent necessity. I had heard about the overcrowded conditions from Ruth, who was teaching in the high school, and the lower grades were mushrooming at an even faster rate.

Since we had been elected as an opposition party, Jack Spence and I were treated with open hostility and were consistently outvoted. Jack and I agreed that, at a minimum, a new high school was a necessity. The board voted unanimously to retain an architect to plan a new high school and to compute the cost, taking into consideration that ours was a poor community. Under Texas statute, we were required to advertise and to hold hearings before making a choice. Half a dozen architects applied, and we scheduled a time for each of them to give a presentation of their previous work. As conscientious board members, Jack and I spent many hours away from our businesses. Then we noticed that most of the time we were the only members of the board in attendance. Upon inquiry, we discovered that the architect had already been selected. Our board president had been asked by Democratic Party leaders in Austin to see that their nominee was selected. Needless to say, Jack and I were furious.

The actual plans submitted to us turned out to be quite good. Political hack or not, the man had done a competent job. One of the architect's suggestions was to build the gymnasium underneath an auditorium. I stressed to him that the entire town had no true auditorium. If the new high school had an auditorium to serve its needs, it could serve the schools and the town as well. The architect planned an auditorium to seat about fifteen hundred people, a feature very much needed by the town and within our budget.

Strangely enough, I became the leader of a fight for passage of the school bonds, even though I had started my term of office as an open enemy of the majority of board members.[16] The president of the board was Richmond Harper, then at the height of his prestige as one of the leading cattlemen of the area. His brother, Tito Harper, was one of my best friends, and I had done business with their father, Osie. However, as president of the board, Richmond did little more than preside at meetings, nor did anyone else of the old party show any leadership. Whenever I wished to talk to Richmond about school business, I had to go to his office in the basement of the Eagle Hotel and wait until the great man deigned to speak to me. The result was that I was the one who went to Quemado or to PTA meetings to present the urgent need of the bond issue.

The *Eagle Pass News Guide*, the town's only newspaper, attacked the proposed bonds in the most intemperate language, arguing that there was no need for more school building projects which would be a waste of the taxpayers' money. There was plenty of room in the schools we had, if only the school administration would make efficient use of the available space. The board, they said, was a bunch of evil men seeking to divert the taxpayers' hard-earned money for our own purposes. I was the worst traitor of all, since it was with their help that I had been elected. The bond issue was defeated. So ended my first year as a board member.

SCHOOL BOARD PRESIDENT

After the next school board election we were required to select new officers. I had told Jack that I would support him for president. Jack declined, saying that he would support me, working with me as before. To my surprise, the two carryover members from the old administration also voted for me, and I became school board president. I found myself in the unenviable situation of having to lead the fight for new school construction. This paramount problem was delayed, however, by a host of minor issues demanding our attention.

First of all, I was pestered by job seekers. The school district was the largest employer in town. In the past it had been a matter of "to the victors belong the spoils." Jobs were filled with the friends and relatives of the president and board members. I merely told job seekers to go to the proper personnel officer and apply. There was a scream of outrage from the applicants—hadn't they voted for me and so on. There were some who just asked for money or "loans."

Before I could get settled comfortably in my chair as president, a storm broke. A teacher got into a dispute with the principal of his school. The teacher happened to be related to Judge Bibb and appealed to him for help. When it came to my attention, I told the board that the whole matter was most unseemly. Teachers claimed to be professionals. They were educators. If so, then there should be a dignified procedure to settle disputes should a teacher feel that he or she had a grievance.

I knew from talking to Ruth, who was then teaching, that teachers were often badly treated by their superiors and were in constant fear of losing their employment. I asked the board to draw up a code of procedure under which a teacher could appeal directly to the board in case of a grievance. The more conservative members of the board objected, saying that this was socialism. After much discussion, a procedure was adopted. Even if the board supported a teacher with a grievance, it was pointed out, the teacher's position was untenable if they antagonized their principal or other superiors. Today, of course, the teacher would sue the school district and recover a juicy settlement.

After we set up the appeal process, I was stopped on the street by one of our leading citizens, an Anglo, who accused me of promoting socialism. When I mentioned how little teachers were paid after many years of school, he replied that a man who taught school did so because he was incompetent to do anything else. Besides, he commented, in most cases both husband and wife taught; between the two of them they earned a good salary. When I asked if his wife was forced to work in order to earn a decent standard of living, his reply was that he was in a different category, and furthermore, for me to suggest that his wife, a lady, should have to work was insulting. Sometime after I left the board the matter was settled to this man's satisfaction. He was able to get the grievance procedure canceled without the teachers realizing what was being done to them—all accomplished with a little hanky-panky, of course.

The next crisis came with the sudden resignation of our latest coordinator of federal programs, a man from out of town. In my mind, the best local candidate for the job was Louis Bernal, who was not only capable but deserved the job. He had been roughly handled by the previous administration in a most unjust manner. At a teachers' meeting, Louis had asked Curly James when teachers were to be given sick leave, since most school districts had long since given sick leave to teachers. James answered curtly that sick leave was not in the budget. At the next teachers' meeting, Louis again asked about sick leave. Curly ordered him to shut up and sit down. Shortly after that, Louis was transferred from the fourth grade to teach a first-grade class, with the expectation that he would resign.

When I asked Kenneth Moore, the current superintendent, if he would consider Bernal for the federal coordinator's job, his answer was that Bernal was a known troublemaker. When I asked that he place Bernal's name on the panel of nominees as a favor to me, he reluctantly agreed. Then I asked a carryover member from the previous board to vote for Bernal. He refused, also saying Louis was a troublemaker. Then I spoke to Marcos Fuentes, also a carryover member. Marcos worked for the irrigation district. I had noticed that whenever there was a vote, Fuentes always waited for his fellow board member, who was also on the water district board, to vote, then voted the same. First of all, I asked Marcos if he knew Louis Bernal. He nodded and added that Louis had taught his children, who all said that Louis was the best teacher they ever had. I then asked him to vote for Louis when the vote came for federal coordinator. Marcos pledged his vote. With this bit of Machiavellian politics out of the way, at the next board meeting I had Moore read off the panel of recommended names, and after saying that I personally favored Bernal, called for a secret ballot. Bernal won.

One of my first acts as board president was to visit every school to see its condition for myself. Most of the school visits were routine, but I was deeply disturbed by what was then called "special education." These were classes made up of all types of children with disabilities. What troubled me was the cause of these problems. Could they be prevented by proper medicine and proper diet? I was horrified by what I saw. In my view it would take nerves of steel to teach in these classes, as well as true compassion. At the next board meeting, I insisted that teachers in such classes be given an increase in salary. They deserved it.

The next controversy had to do with the new federal programs. Louis Bernal, the new coordinator, reported that money was available to provide preschool breakfasts for elementary school pupils.[17] A national study had shown that a large percentage of children were suffering from malnutrition. The proposed grant was based on the proposition that students could not learn on empty stomachs. Once again, there was an immediate charge of "socialism" from some on the board. I managed to get the board's approval to apply for the necessary federal money. We were one of the poorest areas in the country. If anyone needed such a program, we did.

Then Bernal recommended that we apply for federal money to implement an English-as-a-second-language program. I had always thought that the old system, under which students were actually punished for speaking Spanish on school grounds, was very wrong. Most of our teachers were bilingual, so I thought it would be simple for a teacher to use Spanish in order to make it easier for a student to learn English. Again, I used all my powers of persuasion to convince the board to adopt the program. What I did not yet know, and what I am now very much against, is that an elaborate bureaucracy has arisen in the program, stretching from Washington to the local level, involving an army of unnecessary personnel. The program has done more to create jobs than to teach bilingualism. In a border town such as Eagle Pass, I believe that every child, whether Anglo or Mexican, should be taught in the schools to speak and read both English and Spanish correctly. It is very sad that most of our children go through our school system without speaking either language properly. What is most shocking is that so many of the Mexican children speak an illiterate dialect of Spanish and cannot read or spell simple words in either language.

Toward the second year of my term, it seemed apparent to me that the school system was approaching an unmanageable state of affairs. I asked Superintendent Moore to prepare a full assessment of the condition of the school buildings and to make a proposal of what should be done considering the rate of growth of the school population. Moore presented a careful, analytic report that recommended that a new high school be built, in which case the existing high school could become a new junior high, and the existing junior high could become a much-needed elementary school.[18] By adding an additional elementary school in the rapidly expanding new neighborhood along El Indio Road, Moore concluded that there would be sufficient classroom space for the next ten years. At the next meeting, I stated that I thought the time had come to arrive at a definite decision; it seemed to me that we had talked endlessly. If the board decided not to build additional schools, then we had to decide how we could make do with what we had. After deliberations, the board voted to act according to Moore's recommendations.

The next step was to find a site for the new high school. A committee selected a tract in an unsettled area on the east side of town, but one of our board members urged a tract near El Indio Road instead. He gave an emotional description of poor, barefoot children trudging long distances to the committee's proposed site: in fairness to the poor, he said, the new school should be near their neighborhood. I said nothing but went out to the site he wanted, and with a scale map I measured distances. I privately asked him to use the scale of the map to compute distances from the two sites to various poor neighborhoods. After a few minutes he handed me back the map and left. At the next meeting, he said nothing as the board voted to accept the committee's recommendation. The purchase of the land was negotiated, after which I received an anonymous message informing me that the board member in question had a financial interest in the tract he had wanted.

If we were to propose a bond issue to build new schools, it was first necessary to determine the costs of such new construction. In order to do this, we had to hire an architect. But just as we were about to embark on this project, it was again time for a school board election. Every year, two new members were elected, the idea being that there would always be a core of experienced members on the board. The trouble was that the new members could hold up action for months on the basis that they were entitled to be informed fully before any action was taken. If this were kept up from year to year, a determined opposition could long delay action no matter how desperately needed. In order to avoid a long waste of time before acting on what I considered a critical situation, I invited all school board candidates to our final two meetings, which were spent in detailed reviews of problems we faced, the action we wanted taken, and what would face us in the next term.

The two new men were a slate that had been backed by the *Eagle Pass News Guide* and were dedicated to the proposition that new school construction was unnecessary. If new construction was approved nevertheless, they wanted as little spent on it as possible. One of these men was from out of town, the manager of a temporary enterprise in Eagle Pass, and he left some two years later. The other new member was Leon Miller, the owner of a large farming and cattle-feeding operation. At first both men were belligerent, insisting they were not satisfied with the lengthy presentation they had attended and wanted to go back to the beginning of the question whether new schools were needed. I was supported by the rest of the board, which voted to proceed. When a motion was made to hire an architect, they proposed an amendment that an architect was not required and would be a waste of taxpayers' money. They wanted the contractors to provide plans. Any good engineer, they said, could design the needed school buildings. This was voted down.

As time went on, Miller became less and less belligerent. Before many meetings, he dropped his role of opposition and soon was participating with the rest of us in trying to solve the problems we were facing. We set up a series of meetings with interested architects, and when each architect gave his presentation, I insisted that all board members attend. When it came time to vote on the choice of an architect, the board selected the man whom Jack and I had voted for some two years before.

This time around, there was a difference. Prices of materials, as well as costs of labor, had risen considerably. To make matters worse, interest rates had gone up. The net effect of the delay in building the necessary schools was that we were getting less for more money. Instead of an auditorium, the school would have bleachers on a basketball court. It's sad, but those were the conditions that prevailed.[19]

Another problem the board faced during my tenure was the tax assessment of ranch land, which was assessed at five dollars per acre, a rate grossly unfair to owners of city property, which was taxed at a higher rate. In making the assessment, Judge Bibb was only doing what other Texas county judges had done for over a century. Concessions were made to the big ranchers in exchange for their financial support. This was a statewide political accommodation going back to the old days when the ranchers controlled state politics. Judge Bibb kept their tax rate low, and in return the ranchers provided ample financing for his reelection campaigns—money he could either spend or pocket as he saw fit. The voters received a free barbecue, where beef was plentiful and beer flowed freely.

In addition, if the high-school football team wanted to go to the Cotton Bowl or the band needed new uniforms, Judge Bibb always managed to squeeze the necessary money from the reluctant ranchers. After all, if a man owned many thousands of acres, the difference in the taxes saved from even a few dollars an acre in appraisal added up to a juicy sum of money. It was certainly cheaper to donate to a worthy political cause—such as reelecting Judge Bibb. What the ranchers did not seem to realize was that times had changed: except in a few sparsely settled counties the balance of power was now in the hands of other interests with as much or more money as them, people such as the town merchants, oil investors, insurance companies, and manufacturers. The ranchers had their day. It is over now.

Having been in the ranching business myself, even though on a small scale, I had a certain sympathy for the ranchers' problems. It was becoming increasingly difficult for the large ranches to make a profit at cattle ranching. Vaqueros were hard to find; costs were escalating continuously with no corresponding increase in the price of cattle. Big corporations were buying up land purportedly for recreational use—as for places where big executives could hunt deer. The price of land was booming to the extent that it was too expensive for cattle ranching. Of course, the ranchers did not mention that those who wished to do so could lease their land for hunting, and many ranchers also received large sums from oil leases.

Hoping to reach a peaceable agreement, I contacted a rancher with among the largest acreage in the school district to try to meet with the ranchers' representatives to discuss setting a more realistic rate, since the present rate was totally unacceptable. I received an answer implying that I should travel to a region that was abnormally warm. I was put out by this reply considering I was skirting improper conduct to even suggest such a meeting, and I had done so to avoid the political conflict and costly litigation I knew would follow. Soon thereafter, when I was out of town, the board voted to place a value of twenty dollars an acre on all ranch land. This was followed some months later by a suit brought in district court against the school board.

The ranchers' suit, titled *Dolph Briscoe et al. v. Morris Riskind as President of the Eagle Pass Independent School District, et al.*, came to trial in the local district court. Briscoe, a banker from Uvalde, owned large acreage in Maverick County. He was a candidate for governor, and the lawsuit was embarrassing to him. He was angry that his name had been placed first in the alphabetical list of plaintiffs.[20] On our side, David Hume Jr., as school board attorney, defended. On the day of the trial, a battery of lawyers from Austin appeared, representing the ranchers. They strutted into the courtroom as though a bugle was blowing a fanfare to announce their arrival, and they condescendingly acknowledged Hume's presence. They had apparently not taken the trouble to learn his background as one of the chief trial lawyers for the Department of Justice and his tenure as attorney general of Maryland. By the time the trial was over, they had been thoroughly beaten and their attitude had changed.

As in the action that led to this lawsuit, it seemed that every time I left town, the board availed itself of my absence to take some drastic action that my moderating influence would otherwise have prevented. On one occasion, I returned to learn that Superintendent Moore had been fired. Moore had not been my choice for superintendent, but he had worked diligently, was doing a creditable job, and was at the least entitled to complete his term. To me, the continuous hiring and firing, with no regard for existing contracts, was not only financially unwise, but destructive. Now we had to hire a new superintendent. We advertised, held lengthy interviews, and hired a man from San Antonio who at the time was the principal of a large high school.[21]

During my last year on the school board, I managed to get myself into yet another hot controversy. I learned that as president of the board, I was supposed to be in charge of a federal vocational retraining program for veterans.[22] To my knowledge, no other board president had ever bothered himself with the details of the program. It had been left entirely to the program's administrator. Since I was theoretically responsible, I decided to investigate. In doing so I noticed that there were a few people listed on the rolls as attending one school after another. After attending the initial class of house painting, for example, that person would no longer attend. Every month, however, the enrollee would receive a check as though he had dutifully attended class. When that course was over, he would sign up for another class, never attend, and get paid for attending. I proceeded to instruct the administrator not to enroll these thieves in any further classes and not to pay any enrollee when absent without proper excuse. I was soon met with a storm of protest from the veterans' organizations, who complained that the men were veterans and entitled to participate. When I pointed out that the program was for retraining, not for welfare, my argument was ignored. I decided to let discretion be the better part of valor. A properly run job-training program could accomplish worthwhile results, but this was just another well-intentioned program that accomplished little and wasted vast sums of public money.

For weeks, the *News Guide* had carried feature articles on the front page about my alleged misdeeds as president of the school board. I could not be accused of either financial or sexual hanky-panky, so the *Guide* had to show great ingenuity. I was accused of wasting the taxpayers' money, and they vividly portrayed me as a veritable Roman tyrant, a Nero, a ruthless dictator who lashed the board until they bent to my will. The implication was that something horribly evil had occurred. Ruth was greatly disturbed each week as she read the *Guide*: one issue literally made her cry. She begged me not to run for reelection, and since I was sick and tired of the whole business, I readily agreed. My failure to run must have been a serious loss of material for the *News Guide*.

After I was off the school board, there were two other events of a political nature that followed from my school board career. At the next meeting of the public housing board, of which I was then president, I came to the meeting to find that the mayor had replaced me after nearly twenty years on the board. The two new members acted as though I wasn't there. As soon as I called the meeting to order and swore in the new members, I left. A few days later at a library board meeting, a similar procedure occurred. I had taken my duties as board vice president very seriously, and only a short time before I had gone to Austin to straighten out a problem with the city's application for funds to remodel the old federal building as a new library. At the library board meeting I again found myself replaced and the new members acting as if I wasn't there.

I resolved never to have anything further to do with politics. It seemed apparent to me that I was not cut out to be a politician. Whenever I read that a businessman has entered politics, I think to myself, "Is he in for a shock!" Politics and business are totally dissimilar skills. In business, costs and potential markets are all-important; business requires making decisions, implementing them promptly, and correcting errors in judgment quickly. Politics, on the other hand, is the art of convincing the voters or fellow legislators to adopt a course of action acceptable to conflicting interests. This necessarily involves compromise. Errors in judgment may require years to correct and may never be corrected. A foolish program goes on and on simply because conflicting interests cannot agree on a compromise. Politics is simply the art of arriving at the possible.

CHAPTER 16

AN ELEGY FOR MY PARENTS

When my father was about seventy, I suggested that he should take steps to reduce a possible heavy inheritance tax on his estate. Many people in his generation were superstitious about discussing such eventualities. To my surprise, he discussed the subject and ended up going beyond my expectations. Pa divided most of his property among his five children, keeping only enough to live on comfortably. Then he retired to California, leaving Reuben and me with the business.

At that time my sister Sarah was living with her husband, Mark Robson, in Brentwood near Wilshire Boulevard. Pa bought a home about ten blocks away in a very nice, but less affluent, neighborhood in Santa Monica. At first all went well. Pa and Ma saw Sarah and her children every day. They joined two different congregations, a more traditional one where Pa went on Saturday mornings and Ma to another that was either Reform or Conservative on Friday nights. They also made a few new friends. Mother's cousin, Isaac Ramberg, lived on the other side of Los Angeles, and they exchanged visits. Mother's niece, Adelle Alexander, Louis Edelstein's daughter, moved with her husband to Los Angeles and were frequent and welcome company. My sister Bess was living at that time in the San Fernando Valley, a long drive away, and my parents usually saw Bess and her family at Friday-night dinner, when the entire family gathered.

Then problems arose. Pa had an automobile accident in which he broke his leg. He decided to stop driving, which greatly restricted their activities. Pa became increasingly bored. In Eagle Pass, he was an important man to whom everyone deferred. In California, he was a nobody. When he walked down the street no one said hello. Around the house, he was no longer a man who commanded and made people jump. He was just someone underfoot, relegated to being somewhere in status between a yard man and third-class kitchen help. For lack of anything to do, he trimmed a bougainvillea that had almost covered the kitchen window until it was reduced to a stump. Finally, Pa decided against all protests to return to Eagle Pass.

In Eagle Pass, my parents bought a house across the street from mine. Every weekday, Pa kept to the same routine. After he recited the morning prayers and had breakfast, he was picked up at 10:30 a.m. and driven to the store. Most of the time he sat in a comfortable chair in the men's department, from where he took command. He harried the men unmercifully, especially Chema García, who was unfortunate enough to supervise the nearby department.

Poor Chema had a young man to help him and did most of the physical labor in arranging stock and lifting boxes of shirts in the adjoining stock room. Pa was constantly after Chema, demanding to know why he didn't do some of the work himself instead of just standing around. Chema, as well as the other senior clerks, was paid extra for sales beyond quota. With Pa harassing him, plus his rivalry with another senior salesman named Galindo, Chema could have had a nervous breakdown.

My assistant was Ward Wueste, Uncle Albert's son-in-law. Whenever Ward would tell Pa that something he demanded was contrary to my instructions, Pa would yell, "Morris's orders! What does Morris know?" Pa would pound his cane in his rage; once he did this with such force that the cane broke. He would launch into a stream of cussing in a variety of languages. He would yell at Ward—"Wueste! *Der Daitsh mit der aizeneh kop!*" (the German with the iron head)—then Ward would return as best he could some of Pa's imprecations. It was a kind of charade that all the participants enjoyed, except it had no place in the store.

In the first few years after his return, Pa would go to the Merchant's Cafe every day at around three o'clock. Then he began to go infrequently. "Most of my friends have died," he said very sadly. Instead, he would go home. Once I found my father reading one of Mother's books. It was the first time I had ever seen him read anything other than the daily paper.

When I described his activities to Mother, she would tell me the story of the South Sea islanders who took people too old to be of service to their society and left them outside to die. As a man approached the fateful day, his activities became more frenetic as he sought to prove he was still capable of activity. "Don't mind Pa," she would say. "He just wants to prove he's still able to work."

Once a Jewish woman from Mexico City happened to be in the store during such a performance. "Why don't you throw that old man out? Do you realize the terrible language he is using?" "We can't," replied the clerk. "That's the boss."

My brother Reuben was angry at Ward for showing disrespect to our father, but as far as Pa was concerned, he was having a good time and would be the first to object if Ward were punished. Ward was genuinely fond of the old man, and he was always the one Pa called on for help. Years later, after we had both retired, it was always reminiscences of Pa that Ward discussed when I saw him.

MY FATHER, THE ECCENTRIC

Anyone well acquainted with my father knew him to be a kind man, generous to a fault, especially to his family, and quick to forgive. He was also a most eccentric man with many foibles all his own. For one thing, he was superstitious in ways acquired from the family's time living among Russian peasants. If I whistled, especially in the house or the store, he went into a regular frenzy; according to folk belief, I was calling up demons. He also stopped us from playing leapfrog for the same reason. His most annoying folk belief to Mother, and later to Ruth, was his fear of bringing on the evil eye by praise. If Mother made an exceptional dinner and he remarked that it was good, he would hasten to add, "But not as good as last time." This never failed to infuriate Ma. If business was good and Uncle Albert or Auntie remarked on it, Pa would hasten to add, "But not as good as it used to be."

If any of us children did anything praiseworthy, we always received a left-handed compliment. When I entered the business, Pa would frequently call me and proceed to give me a lecture on merchandise quality, selection, or display, always concluding by saying, "Morris, I'm learning you, Morris." A short time before his death he said to me, "Morris, for years

I've been learning you this business. You're finally learning." Then he hastened to say, "A little, not too much." I believe this was the most praise I ever received. I was very flattered.

Pa had his own unique way of describing people. When he told me that my sister Sarah was getting serious about Mark Robson, whom she later married, I asked him for a characterization of the candidate. "He's a 40 short," answered Pa.

Pa was a most charitable man. He was by far the largest contributor to the United Jewish Appeal in the Eagle Pass area. A group of Lubavitcher Hasidim used to come every year to be well entertained and go away with a generous contribution.[1] As far as I know, there was no denomination on either side of the river that he failed to give to. Every Christmas he sent a check for ten dollars, a lot of money during the Depression, to every minister or priest. He gave a larger check to Lola Vela, who worked for us for over fifty years and was considered a part of the family, to deliver to Padre Jáuregui in Piedras Negras.[2] Padre Jáuregui, later Monsignor Jáuregui, once gave a sermon on charity to his congregation, naming don Miguel Riskind as an example.

In later years, when my parents were residing in Santa Monica, Pa learned that his son-in-law, Mark Robson, was routinely giving quantities of Rodeo Drive clothing to charity. In his business as a film director, Mark had to constantly change his clothing or be considered either penurious or eccentric. Pa could not bear to see such clothing go to waste. He would surreptitiously extricate sport coats out of the giveaway stack and wear the clothing himself. His combinations became quite outlandish. When he returned to Eagle Pass, he continued wearing his ill-fitting, mismatched clothes until, at the insistence of others in the family, we put a stop to it.

During our childhood, we saw little of Pa during the day except at mealtimes. Whenever Pa wanted to speak to any of us individually, he had difficulty in remembering our names, so he would have to call the roll until he came to the right name. Discipline was left to Mother or Auntie. Once I misbehaved and he threatened to spank me. He actually took off his belt and made dire threats, but he never gave me a blow. He just couldn't hit me.

Pa's use of the English language, inflected with an Eastern European Jewish accent, was something out of a Leo Rosten book.[3] He used words such as "school driver" for screwdriver and "ayen" for an iron. What was worse was that he knew that his English was poor, and was very self-conscious about his deficiency. Pa also used antique terms that had long gone out of daily use. Food was "grub." A delinquent was put in the "hoosegow," an old border word derived from the Spanish *juzgado* (convicted). Pa dearly loved the Yiddish theater. Whenever he was in a city where he could attend a performance, he was sure to go. Once he saw a Yiddish version of *King Lear* and came home convinced that his children, by that time adults, were out to get him. Fortunately, he changed his mind in a short time.

Pa had no sense of humor in the usual meaning of the word. I once took him to see a Marx Brothers movie. He sat through it impassively. Everyone else in the theater was roaring with laughter. When we came out, Pa asked, "Tell me, what was the moral of that picture?" At the same time, he had his own sense of humor. Once he was stopped on the street by a man notorious for being in and out of business every few months. This man told Pa that he was doing very well in his furniture business. In fact, it was expanding so rapidly that he lacked working capital. If Pa would only invest in the business, the man claimed, he would get a handsome return for his money. Pa answered that he had good advice to give: If he had such a profitable business, he would share it with no one. He would keep it all for himself. The next week the business was in bankruptcy.

One of Pa's private jokes concerned a fiesta he attended in the Mexican town of Guerrero. An auction was started for the benefit of the local church, and Pa donated the hat he was wearing. Everyone thought that surely the great M. Riskind would be wearing at least a hundred-dollar Stetson, and men were bidding for it accordingly. In fact, Pa was wearing a Stetson "second," sold in the store for five dollars.

I can remember only one actual joke I ever heard my father tell: a businessman calls up a banker at three o'clock in the morning. "Mr. Smith, remember my fifty-thousand-dollar loan that is due tomorrow morning? I just wanted to tell you that I haven't got the money and can't pay."

"My God!" exclaims the banker. "Why did you have to tell me at three o'clock in the morning? Now I won't be able to sleep a wink worrying about it."

"Good," says the businessman. "You stay awake and worry. Maybe I can sleep now." Then my father went on to say: "It is better to be in a position where you don't have to do the worrying. Let the other fellow worry."

Pa had a problem with drinking. From what I have seen, there seem to be two main types of those who drink to excess, social drinkers and solitary drinkers. He was strictly in the category of a social drinker. At home he had one scotch before lunch and another before dinner. On Friday night when the family gathered, we had wine with our dinner. Pa's problem arose once he entered a saloon, usually either the Merchant's Cafe, situated where the addition to the Walgreen's is now located, or the Sabinas Inn, which was later torn down to make way for the NBC Bank. If he met any of his cronies, such as Judge Bibb or Mike Chorgas, the men took turns buying each other drinks. Sometimes Pa would set up drinks for everyone in the place. This he considered good public relations.

Whenever Pa wasn't home by dinnertime, someone had to be sent to extricate him from the saloon. In the old days it would be a store employee, Albino Diaz.[4] In my time it was usually Ward Wueste. It took much persuasion to pry him away from the bar, and he would be completely plastered. Auntie would lecture him; Ma would only say *farshnoshket*—drunk—with contempt. To her generation, drinking to excess was gross and inexcusable. She would proceed to tell me the story from the midrash in which Satan teaches Noah how to make wine. Satan says, "One drink and you feel better. Two drinks and you feel like a lion. Three drinks and you behave like a monkey. Four drinks and you become a pig."[5]

Pa never ate at restaurants in Eagle Pass. He liked a Jewish-style delicatessen in Dallas or Jewish restaurants in New York. Unless there was no way out, he refused to eat *goyische essens*, gentile cooking. The only restaurant on the border Pa would patronize was the Moderno in Piedras Negras. The original Moderno was run by a Chinese man. About once a week Pa would say, "Let's go to the Chinaman's." His motive for wanting to eat there was the advent of Prohibition: Pa liked beer with his meal. Across the street from the Moderno a cousin of "the Chinaman" had a competing restaurant, but Pa preferred the Moderno, perhaps because the proprietor was a Riskind's customer. Pa bought only from customers. If anyone asked him for his patronage, he usually agreed—provided the man would reciprocate.

I have a vague recollection of the original Moderno. One memory is of a parrot on a perch inside. In the hot season, most of the year, we ate outside, usually at night. In the back of the restaurant there was a large open space, now used only as a parking lot, and there was a bandstand with its back to the street and tables in front. It was very pleasant in the cool of the evening with the band playing. Inside the Moderno were two sections, a large room with tables where the band played in the winter and a smaller room with a long, old-fashioned bar. The ceilings were very high, perhaps fifteen feet, and the walls were whitewashed adobe with a pastel tint. The leader of the band was old man Díaz, although he was not so old when he started. He played a small upright piano situated on the left side of the bandstand, and there were a drummer, a violinist, and a trumpet player. Díaz always played deadpan, without any show of emotion or movement other than his hands kept flat. The music was much better than it is today.

Pa had a regular ritual when entering the Moderno. First, the band let out a fanfare. In later years, my daughter Susan recalled that in her time the band launched into Agustín Lara's "Te Vendes" ("You Sell") whenever Pa made his entrance.[6] This wasn't exactly appropriate, since it referred to a woman accused of selling herself, but apparently it was the only song relating to merchandising they could think of. When Pa arrived, the Moderno, which might have been in the doldrums, immediately became a beehive of activity. The head waiter, Cruz, was Pa's favorite. He came running to set up a table at a spot Pa designated. As soon as we were seated the fun started. Men came running with beer and *bolillos*, small individual loaves of French bread. Usually the beer was cold enough, but invariably the *bolillos* failed to pass the test. They were either not hot enough or they were stale. Pa would let out a roar. Cruz and the waiter would apologize profusely and scurry to get proper bread. This ceremony performed, Pa would always order the same meal, broiled chicken and guacamole salad. The food was always excellent.

After ordering, Pa would often leave us to head for the bar. If there were men standing at the bar, especially if they were Riskind's customers, he would buy drinks for all. If the band was taking a break, he would often send them beer. Should the food come before Pa returned, the waiter would be sent for him. This never worked. After repeated trips the waiter might finally get him back by saying his food was getting cold. When Pa returned, he would invariably get a lecture from Auntie. His reply would be that he was drumming up business. Then the waiter would be called because his food was cold and had to be reheated. After dinner when we were ready to leave Pa would first check the bill carefully, then sign it to be collected in the store, adding a generous tip.

Once, in about 1960, I met my parents in New York on their return from Israel. I had driven to New York, showing Civil War sites along the way to my two older boys, John, who was twelve, and Pete, who was ten. The evening I was to meet my parents the great New York blackout occurred. We were all staying in the Manhattan Hotel. I secured a flashlight and made it to my parents' room. Pa insisted he wanted to go to a Jewish restaurant. The phone book listed one some three blocks away. Fortunately, the elevator was running. We descended to the street where all was in confusion. There was more light in the street from car lights than in the hotel, where we had only candlelight. After a struggle we fought our way through the crowds and reached Gluckstern's Restaurant. It was dimly lit by a few candles.[7]

The waiter attending us apologized that their menu would be limited due to a lack of electricity. I studied the menu. It was quite lengthy with fancy prices. There was little my sons would be accustomed to or enjoy. They wanted the $1.69 charbroiled steaks being prepared in the windows of some of the chain restaurants. I asked my mother what she wanted. She had been silent up to that point.

"Nothing," she said.

I turned to Pa. "What do you want?"

"*A teler zup*," a bowl of soup.

"Nothing else?"

"Just a *teler zup*."

I exploded. I was stuck with a substantial bill for the three dinners the boys and I had to order and that they did not eat.

MY MOTHER, THE STORYTELLER

My first recollection of my mother is of her singing. There were several songs she would sing around the house. One went like this: "Oh! Bedelia, Delia, Delia, I've made up my mind to steal ya."[8]

There was another song in Yiddish that was her favorite:

Oi! Chob ich a cousine!
Oi!, oi!, oi!, die grieneh!
Beckalach vie riete pomerantzen,
fieselach vas beiten sach tsu tanzen!
Oi!, oi!, oi!, die grieneh.

Oh! Do I have a cousin!
Oh! Oh! Oh! That greenhorn!
Cheeks she has like red pomegranates.
Feet that beg to dance.
Oh! Oh! Oh! That greenhorn![9]

After we had a car and a driver, Ma would take us on short outings or longer trips, and when we set out she would sing, "My wife has gone to the country. Hurray! She took the children with her! Hurray! Hurray!" In later years, I heard her sing no more.

Mother was also a marvelous storyteller. At night before we went to bed, she would tell us stories from the Bible or read us Mother Goose. When we were out camping, all of us sitting around the campfire, she would keep us enthralled with stories about the old country. Her family was very religious by today's standards, but rationalists rather than mystics. She had a large fund of stories ridiculing the superstitions of the Hasidim and the ignorant.

One of her stories had to do with the golem, which could have been the source for Mary Shelley's story about Frankenstein.[10] The legend is that at a critical moment Rabbi Loew of Prague saved the community by creating a golem, an artificial monster, that terrorized the king. According to this folktale, Rabbi Loew was a great kabbalist, an expert in Jewish mysticism.[11] He created a huge man out of clay and powered the figure with the secret name of God. According to Mother, when the rabbi of Vilna heard about the golem, he decided he was not to be outdone. He was going to make a golem also. The trouble was that he was not a mystic nor a student of kabbalah. He went about manufacturing the figure of a man, dressed it in proper clothes, performed the proper abracadabra (or so he thought), and was ready to put his golem to the test.

"Golem, go fetch water," he ordered. The golem didn't budge. "That's all right," he said. "You rest. I'll get it myself." Then he said, "Golem, go chop wood." The golem didn't budge. "That's all right," he said. "I'll go do it myself." In this way, he and the golem continued to get along amicably for years. After telling this story, Ma would say that getting any of us children to do any housework was like getting the Vilner Golem to help.

She had another story for when the question came up of whether a certain person was a Jew. "That is an interesting question," said Mother. "Just who is a Jew? What determines who and what is a Jew?" And she proceeded to tell me the following story. Yankel made a deal with a peasant to take him and one other Jew to the market in the next town in his wagon. A few blocks later, another man climbed aboard the wagon. A short distance more and still another man got on board. "Wait a minute," said the peasant. "You said you and one other Jew." "That's Moshe," Yankel replied. "He's no Jew. Ask anybody." A short distance further and still another man climbed aboard. "Hold it," yelled the peasant. "You said one other Jew and there are already four of you." "That's Shmerl. Whoever said he was a Jew? He never comes to synagogue. How could you call him a Jew?" And so, Ma said, "Look around you. How many are real Jews, especially these days?"

One of our favorite stories was one about talking too much. A prankster put up a sign in the town's public bath house: "All fools must leave the bath house." This stupid fellow took a look at the sign then angrily accosted the owner. "What's the matter? Isn't my money as good as anybody else's?" The moral of the story, Mother said, was that it's better to keep your mouth shut when you are not sure what's involved. "The odds are that you're going to make a fool of yourself." That was Mother's advice.

At night, out in the country, she would point out the various constellations and tell us stories about them. Mother loved nature and the outdoors. Even when we lived in California, we did not stay in the city. On weekends, holidays, and in the summer we would be out exploring the side roads. Her special favorite spot in California was Yosemite. In the 1920s, it was possible to camp in midsummer right on the banks of the Yosemite River. We hiked for miles and swam in the freezing water. I believe that I knew more about the backcountry in the park than most of the park rangers.

There used to be huge, open Pierce Arrow tour buses that drove tourists around Yosemite Valley showing them the sights. Mother would convulse with laughter every time a tour bus came by on the paved road outside the camping area and you could hear the driver on his megaphone calling out that to the right was one thing, to the left was another. "How can you possibly appreciate the beauty of Yosemite by looking for an instant to the right and then to the left as you drive by?" Mother asked.

In her arguments and discussions with my father she used some pithy Yiddish expressions I can recall. If she did not agree with Pa's solution to a problem she would say, "*Es vel hilfen vi a toiten bankes*" (it will help like a dead leech). Or she might say, "*Chochem fun der Hagode*" (wise one from the Haggadah), referring to the wise son in the Passover story. Her clever pun poked fun at my father: in Hebrew, a *chacham* is a wise man, while in Yiddish, a *chochem* is a "wise guy," a smart aleck or know-it-all. If Mother referred to someone who had disappeared, her remark was, "*Er hat antloifen vu der schwartze pfeffer vakst*" (he ran away to where the black pepper grows). If you say the rule or the law did not allow something to be done, her remark would be, "*Die Rebetzin meg*" (the rabbi's wife is permitted), meaning the rabbi's wife was the exception to the rule because the rabbi was afraid to tell her no.

She called a story that stretched the truth a *bubbe maise*, one of Grandma's stories. One of Mother's favorite stories in her later years was the story of the *bubbe*'s pretty penny. The old lady told her grandchildren that she had saved a "pretty penny" and hinted that her *yerushe*, her inheritance, would be divided depending on how her relatives cared for her in her last years. "Take care of me and you will get a pretty penny," she said. As a result, the grandchildren vied in taking good care of her. When she died, they all gathered to divide the pretty penny. After a search they found a handkerchief with a shiny new penny wrapped inside.

Mother never kissed us or gave any demonstration of affection. Thinking back, I cannot say whether she was just inhibited or whether it was because Dr. Easton had warned her not to allow anyone to kiss us children because of fears about tuberculosis. Mother was a very kind person, always helping relatives and friends and seldom getting any credit or appreciation. She did what she did with so little ostentation that the recipients paid no attention and probably gave someone else the credit. When the doctor caring for Aunt Jennie, who was in the last stages of tuberculosis, warned that the two Schrager children should be taken out of the house immediately, it was Mother who took them into her care and raised them. When the daughter of a relative by marriage had to move to a drier climate, it was Mother who cared for her.

As I think back, one of the lasting influences Mother had on my personal development was encouraging me to read at an early age. At first, it was simple Bible stories and fairy tales. I was in no more than the fourth grade when she gave me a biography of Alexander the Great that I still own. Although there was no library in Eagle Pass, she gave me a steady stream of books: *Tom Sawyer*, *Gulliver's Travels*, *The Arabian Nights*, and *Grimms' Fairy Tales*. There was a volume of French fairy tales, too, the name of which I cannot remember. One story had to do with "east of the sun and west of the moon."[12]

I dearly loved the Wizard of Oz series and read everything that L. Frank Baum wrote, passing them on to my siblings. When my children were old enough, I first read Baum's books to them and then bought them their own copies. Unintentionally, Baum made two prophecies concerning our present-day culture. Professor Woggle-Bug gives his students pills from bottles marked "History," "English," and "Mathematics" after which the students are free for the day. Also, the army of Oz, with one private and numerous superior officers, is a perfect description of a present-day federal program: by the time all the bureaucrats are well provided for, there is very little left for the program.

Mother bought me a set of books called *The Book of Knowledge*. It probably is long out of print. It was in ten or twenty volumes and contained well-written articles on a large variety of subjects covering history, English and American literature, and science. It included condensed versions of many of the classics. It featured excellent coverage of Western culture. By the time I was in the fifth grade, I had read it avidly from cover to cover and acquired a thirst for more.[13]

All her life Mother enjoyed reading Tanakh, the Hebrew Bible. She believed it was the foundation and basis of Judaism. The Talmud interested her little. Once, in Los Angeles, my parents went to visit some friends. The husband was learned in traditional Judaism and soon their discussion centered on the true meaning of Judaism. The man claimed that the most important aspect of Judaism was keeping kosher; in other words, if you follow the forms and ceremonies, everything else follows automatically. This is the point of view of perhaps most Orthodox Jews and, I might add, many Christians and Muslims. Very few stop to ask, as the Haggadah asks on Passover, "What is the meaning of all this?"[14]

Mother was horrified by this answer. According to this man, true Judaism was not the social legislation of Moses demanded by God, nor the demand of the Prophets for justice and kindness toward one's fellow men. All the martyrs through the centuries died over a bunch of kosher pots and pans. Perhaps in protest of this point of view, Mother soon afterward stopped keeping kosher.[15]

The next day my mother was still very disturbed by the direction the argument had taken. She admired the story in the Talmud concerning a prankster Greek who asked the great sage Hillel to tell him the essence of Judaism while standing on one foot. Hillel replied that the essence of Judaism is, "Do not do unto others what you would not want done to you." In other words, Hillel believed that it was too much to insist that we act perfectly; only a saint does that. But we can have a decent world if we do not mistreat others, a very practical outlook on humanity.[16]

It was Mother's opinion that what saved the Jewish people was their ability to laugh at the world and at themselves. If you can't laugh you lose your will to live. Mother dearly loved the Yiddish humorists and would often tell me some story from Mendele Mocher Sforim or Sholem Aleichem. *Tevye der Milchiker*, or Tevye the Milkman, from which *Fiddler on the Roof* derived, was her favorite.[17] She would laugh as she recalled Tevye's conversations with his horse and his constant misquotation of scripture. She preferred Mark Twain among the American authors, saying that he was the American Sholem Aleichem.

Her observations on American society could be quite caustic. "In the old country," she said, "the lowest kind of a thief was a *tsibele* gonif, an onion thief who came in the dark of the moon and stole onions from your garden." A *ferd* gonif, a horse thief, like in America, was of a much higher category. There was a story going around when I was a boy that Mother enjoyed. It seems that in Arkansas a man killed another in an argument, and in trying to escape, he stole a horse in Texarkana, Texas. Arkansas wanted to hang him for the homicide, but in Texas they wanted to hang him for stealing the horse.

According to Mother, criminals in the United States weren't punished for moral reasons but for getting caught. "Never be a *tsibele* gonif in the United States," she joked. "If you must steal, steal on a large scale. Should you embezzle a small sum, you will surely be severely punished, as was the hero in *Les Misérables*, who went to the gallows for stealing a loaf of bread. But steal a million at least, hire a good lawyer, and not only will you be acquitted, you will be highly respected and can be a pillar of your church."

As I look back at my mother, whom I adored, I must say, as Cromwell said to the portrait painter regarding his warts, that a true picture of her must include her cultural limitations. She was interested in a subject if it was between the covers of a book or could be viewed in nature, but she had a complete blind spot in her intellectual and cultural horizon for art and music. She could not grasp the world of fancy and make-believe; to my knowledge she never entered a museum or attended a concert. She just wasn't interested. When we children went as a group to the Hollywood Bowl, she did not accompany us, preferring to remain at home and read. Literary discussion or a disputation on politics or economics interested her, not the theater or the ballet. I suppose that the culture in which she was raised determined her interests. Once I took her to see a movie, *The Texas Rangers*, based on incidents recounted in Walter Prescott Webb's history. In one scene the Rangers ambush some smugglers crossing the Rio Grande in the Quemado Valley, which is about twenty-five miles north of Eagle Pass. The scene had been filmed somewhere in Utah. Mother became excited and protested loudly, "That's not the Quemado Valley!"

When I invited Mother to attend the theater with me, she answered by telling this story. A peasant took a trip to the city and, at the recommendation of a friend, went to the theater. When he returned to the country and was asked about the sights of the big city, he told them about his visit to the theater. "First of all," he recounted, "a big tablecloth was pulled up. A man and a woman were on the platform. First, he wanted her but she didn't want him.

Michael and Rachel Riskind with three of their grandchildren. Left to right: John, Rachel, Peter, Michael, and Lorin Riskind. Eagle Pass, 1966. (Courtesy of Dr. Peter Riskind.)

Then she wanted him but he didn't want her. Finally, after a lot of talk they both wanted each other. Just as I thought something interesting was about to happen, the tablecloth came down and you couldn't see a thing."

THEIR LATER YEARS

After my parents moved back to Eagle Pass and bought the house across the street from mine, I visited two or three times a day. In the evening, after the store was closed and before I had dinner, I was expected to give a full report on the day's business. Often Pa would interject with criticism. If Ma remarked that in similar circumstances Pa had done the same, Pa would say, "Never." Ma would come back with, "Never?" Finally, Pa would admit that "sometimes" such things were unavoidable. Ma would keep him in line with caustic remarks. It was like a scene from *Pinafore*.[18] As long as Pa was alive, my parents spent a good part of each day rehashing and arguing about events of many years before. There was no point in such recriminations, but they did serve a beneficial purpose in that they passed the time away.

Pa looked years younger than his actual age. In his eighties, he continued to have the appearance of a man at least ten years younger. He always delighted in comparing his age with that of strangers. Once in the store, a customer came hobbling in and soon was enticed into a conversation with Pa. "I'm old," the man said. "I'm seventy-five years old."

Pa said nothing. Finally, the customer asked, "And how old are you?"

"Oh, I'm eighty-eight," he replied. On hearing this, the customer almost collapsed. He tottered out of the store in a state of shock.

When Pa was ninety, he began to complain of pains and not feeling well. I drove him to San Antonio, accompanied by Mother and Ruth. After an examination and X-rays we were told by the specialist that he had advanced cancer and that it was inoperable. The prognosis was that he had a year to live and that all we could do was to make him as comfortable as possible. During the remainder of Pa's life, he was in complete command of his faculties. Whenever he was in pain the doctor would give him a sedative, which became more potent as time went on.

All this time, Pa maintained the same routine, refusing to be an invalid. Every day he continued to go to the store at 10:30 in the morning, returning home when he was tired. Although he was subdued in his conduct, he continued to sit in his chair, from which he could survey the men's department and issue a stream of directives like a commander on the field of battle. This went on for about a year. I do not recall one word of complaint about his condition or his fate.

This state of affairs became so much a matter of routine that we in the family ceased to worry about it. Then, in February 1969, after I had driven alone to a Dallas men's market, I received a call from my sister Sarah telling me that my father was in the hospital and that it was probably the end. I drove back to Eagle Pass at ninety-five miles an hour, stopping only for gasoline. The family gathered in the hospital. We all agreed to instruct the doctor that if there were no hope for Pa, he should not resort to any attempt to prolong his life through the use of inhalators, tubes, or other devices. We wanted our father to die in peace.

When we all went to pay our final respects to Father, he insisted that he wanted to say goodbye to the store personnel. We had the employees brought to the hospital, and one by one they filed in to see him. After speaking to the men, Pa demanded, "Where's Chema?" We explained that Chema was afraid to come because the day before Pa had given him a dressing down for being lazy. Pa insisted that Chema come. Chema arrived and walked in with downcast eyes. Pa took his hand and said, "Chema, if I hurt your feelings, I am sorry. Please forgive me." A short time later, Pa lost consciousness and died. It can be said that he left this world with dignity.[19]

When my father died, Mother showed no sign of grief or emotion. Whenever I came to see her, she would be sitting at the window of the breakfast room looking out at birds perched on the tree. This she would do for hours at a time. She showed a return to a normal existence by renewing her interest in flowers and gardening. She would garden in the mornings before it became too hot. One day when she was over ninety, she was out chopping weeds in the garden facing the street. The next day a neighbor stopped me. "Morris, can't you get your mother a gardener? It's a shame to make a woman her age work in the heat!" I had to explain that Mother enjoyed gardening. To stop her would take away one of her few remaining pleasures in life.

After Pa died Mother was so lonely and bored that she would invite in missionaries who came to her door. In most homes, when Jehovah's Witnesses or Latter-day Saints knock on the door, it is slammed in their faces. Not so in Mother's case. She would welcome in the delighted missionary, seat them at the table, and offer them tea and cookies. To convert a Jew is especially meritorious, a real mitzvah that would earn them points in heaven, but these good missionaries were in for a shock. When they started their pitch, Ma answered them with counterarguments. When they quoted texts, Ma replied with counter texts. As a final blow Mother would take out her Hebrew Bible, read them the text, and show them where the King James had made an error in translation. At this point, her adversaries usually fled. Mother enjoyed the visit and always followed them to the door urging them to return. Perhaps some did to rest their weary feet and drink a cup of tea.

One day Mother announced that she wanted a book to learn correct Spanish. Licha Torres, the Mexican woman taking care of her, spent her free time watching telenovelas

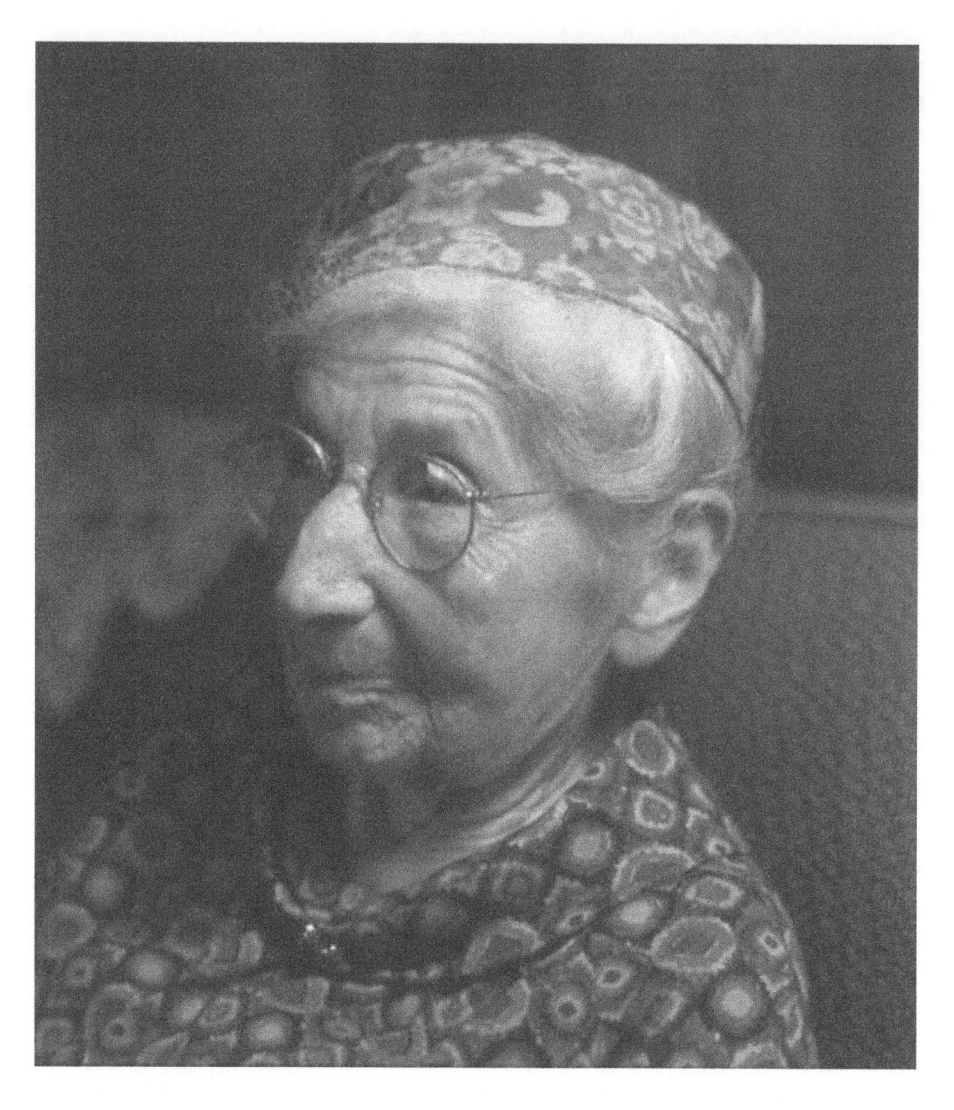

Rachel Edelstein Riskind, Morris's mother, in 1975. (Courtesy of Dr. Peter Riskind.)

on TV, and Mother in her boredom also watched them. The telenovelas were difficult for her to understand, especially since many had been filmed in Argentina, where the Spanish differed from that of Mexico. I spent some time searching for a grammar book adequate for her purposes, then Ruth hit on an idea to keep her occupied and happy. Ruth bought a set of *lotería* cards, a variety of bingo that instead of numbers had pictures with the Spanish word at the bottom of the card. The game was used in Mexico to teach little children spelling. Mother was delighted with the game and played it constantly.[20]

    Mother had never had cataract surgery, as her eyesight had always been adequate with glasses. By the time she was well into her nineties, her vision had deteriorated. We were told that nothing could be done to remedy her failing vision. I then secured for her books with large type from our library, but their list of such books was extremely limited, so I ordered more from Austin. When she increasingly resorted to the use of a handheld magnifying glass, I secured for her a new type of reading stand that contained a movable magnifier with a strong light. By using the reading lamp, she was able to read with considerably less effort.

When Mother was about ninety-five years old, she fell with a disintegrated hip. We rushed her to the hospital for emergency surgery. She was brought home some days later in a confused mental state and may have even suffered a stroke from the shock. For a number of days after her return, she hallucinated. For hours Mother would recite what must have been Russian poetry she had learned as a child in school, or she would recite from the prophet Isaiah. It was apparent that her mind was failing at an accelerating rate.

One day I went over to find the house in an uproar. Mother was demanding to know who had taken her large-print Tanakh. I showed her the one I had bought her some years before with the largest print I could find. Mother insisted this was not the correct large-print Bible. It took much persuasion to calm her down and to use the magnifying lamp. A few days later when I came to see her, she put down her Tanakh and remarked, "You know, our father Jacob wasn't really such a nice man."

In her youth Mother had done beautiful work in embroidery and crocheting. To occupy herself in her last years she would knit for a few hours each day. At first, her work was of excellent quality. Ruth would replenish her supply of wool yarn in a variety of colors, and Mother would crochet the yarn into squares of about eight inches. Licha combined these squares into afghans of various sizes, which were distributed to all the family. Then I discovered that Mother had stopped reading and was using the strong light of the reading lamp to provide light for crocheting. Her eyes were failing and she was deteriorating mentally as well.

One day, my son Pete came from medical school to introduce Carolyn, a fellow student and the woman he married. When he introduced her to Mother, Mother took one look at Carolyn and asked, "Where's your elephant?" Carolyn nonchalantly replied, "I parked it outside."

The gradual decline of her condition continued until I was one of the few she could recognize. When my sister Sarah visited her, she was deeply hurt because there was no sign of recognition. I saw her three times a day, and she continued to recognize me. Finally, Mother reached a stage of utter senility. This condition continued for over a year until she died in her sleep at the age of ninety-nine.[21]

One of the ancient Greek writers said that a man who died in battle in the flower of his youth was blessed by the gods because he would always be remembered as young, beautiful, and healthy. While I do not subscribe to such a standard, I have a horror for the fate suffered by so many of us in this enlightened age as a result of increased longevity. To me it seems cruel that a woman of such intelligence as Mother, who was able with fortitude and determination to survive such difficult trials in her lifetime, should have to suffer such degradation in her final years. I only hope and pray that like my father I retain my mental powers to the last.

EPILOGUE

THOUGHTS ON THE FUTURE OF AMERICAN JUDAISM

There was a time some years ago when at a High Holiday service or a Passover seder in Eagle Pass we had in attendance as many as sixty people. At the present time, we cannot get together a minyan. The older generation has died off, and the children in most cases have moved to larger cities. Even in towns with substantial Jewish communities the same phenomenon is occurring. For one thing there is a lack of opportunity in small towns. How many doctors, lawyers, PhDs, CPAs, and MBAs can even a prosperous small town or city support? Or a Jewish boy meets a Jewish girl at the university, and she refuses to move to his small town. In addition, Jews as a group tend to be interested in cultural activities found only in a large city or suburban area. Jews in America have become an urban cultural group.[1]

American Jews raised in small towns and cities like Eagle Pass develop cultural traits that differ greatly from those traditionally held by the majority of their coreligionists, especially those from a European environment. My mother, for example, was suspicious of gentiles even though she came from an area that had been free of pogroms.[2] When you least expect it, they could turn on you, or so she believed. I used to argue with her at times, pointing out that Christians treated each other as badly as they did Jews, and I gave Magdeburg in the Thirty Years' War or Drogheda at the hands of Cromwell as examples.[3] Entire populations had been massacred—men, women and children—in one case by Catholics and in the other by Protestants. Could Jews have been treated any worse? It's true, Jews have been mistreated over a long period of time and over a greater area, but it is certainly not correct to say that only Jews have been persecuted.

American Jews raised in small towns are more accustomed to living with non-Jews in everyday situations and do not think of themselves as apart from the majority population. They do not have the tension, the constant fear of attack, common among the older generation that came from Europe. In most cases the first Jews to arrive in small towns spoke broken

English. They were considered foreign and many were subjected to ridicule. Unless they were able to adjust quickly, they were not accepted socially. This situation was compounded by the fact that in small towns, religion is very important. Social life is centered around the church to which one belongs. If you do not belong to a church, you are out in the cold, unless the town has a country club to which one can gain acceptance. We had a case years ago when an American vice-consul assigned to Eagle Pass not only refused to join a church, announcing that he and his wife were atheists, but he had the temerity to state that they were nudists. As a consequence, they were ostracized by everyone. Ruth and I alone took pity and befriended them during their stay in Eagle Pass.

By the second generation, the social status of Jews changes. They are often by this time affluent and in most cases are well educated. Instead of being on the fringes of society they are leaders in the town's cultural, political, and social life. At one time, for a non-Jewish local girl to marry a Jew made her someone to pity and gossip about, but this has changed. Jewish boys have become very desirable; a girl who marries one has it made. Jewish husbands are known to be good providers and not prone to mistreat their wives. Not only that, at one time it was taken for granted that children of an intermarriage would become Catholic, Episcopalian, Methodists, or whatever, according to the religion of the mother. That is no longer the case. It depends entirely on whether the Jewish husband or wife truly cares about whether the children are raised as Jews.[4]

There is another factor operating in the present culture, especially in a sophisticated group. Educated non-Jews tend to gravitate toward the educated Jewish element, whether in literary, musical, scientific, or general academic circles, where Jews are present far out of proportion to their numbers in the general population. In these groups, the non-Jew is often apathetic about religion in general and does not object should their spouse wish to raise the children as Jews. Should the children be raised as Jews, the non-Jewish spouse may or may not convert. Where conversion does take place, the convert often becomes more religious than the born Jew.

What has happened in Eagle Pass is, I believe, typical of what has happened elsewhere. First of all, Judaism has changed its nature in that the old tradition of the educated Jewish layman has all but disappeared everywhere except for in some of the bigger cities. Judaism has become more like Christianity in that the masses have to rely on a few clerics for their religious guidance rather than on an educated secular nucleus. Second, more and more Jews are moving to the big cities. They may continue to exist in more substantial smaller cities such as Laredo, but their continued existence in small communities is doubtful. In addition, the inner structure of the Jewish community is changing. For a long time, the trend was to appear non-Jewish, to escape any connection with Judaism or Jews either by converting or blending into the landscape. This is especially true of the better educated. Now the trend seems to have changed. There is a desire on the part of many younger Jews to be identified as Jews, even if they intermarry. In most such cases, the wives or husbands wish to join them, either actively or passively, by raising their children as Jews. This, I believe, is due to the disillusionment or indifference of many Christians with the faith that they were born into.

What does this mean for the future of Judaism in the United States? I am convinced that in the United States we are developing a distinct type of Judaism. You can see this has happened many times before, if one reads Jewish history with an open mind. The majority are not Orthodox in practice, and whether Conservative or Reform, they are following a trend common to both of them.[5] If, God forbid, we "reform" by purging all those who do not meet the requirements of the medieval halakah, then, in my opinion, Judaism is doomed as an American religion.[6] The cultural atmosphere of the United States puts too much pressure on daily life to permit Jews to exist in a vacuum. American Judaism is taking on a distinct character of its own. Conservative Judaism is similar to traditional Orthodoxy but more in line with American needs and conditions. Reform Judaism has moved closer to traditional Judaism and is now very close to the Conservative position. Orthodoxy will be strong in large centers such as New York and Los Angeles; it is attracting many who were estranged from any form of Judaism and now find that the practices and rituals of Orthodoxy give them an inner strength they craved. The great mass of Jews, especially in smaller cities, are Reform or Conservative.

If one looks back at Jewish history, the Babylonian, Alexandrian, Spanish, German, and East European Jews all developed a character of their own. In my opinion, Judaism in America is evolving into a distinct new phase in the long history of the Jewish people. Provided the tolerant atmosphere in the United States continues, in a hundred years most of those who continue to be Jews will be quite distinct from the Orthodox. They will have social acceptability and status similar to a Christian denomination. I am not including in this analysis such groups as the Hasidim, who will remain completely ghettoized.

What all Jews have in common is the Torah, even though it is interpreted diversely. Differences over the interpretation of the Torah are shattering the unity of the Jewish people today. There are those who insist that the *Shulchan Arukh*, adopted five hundred years ago, be enforced to the letter and without amendment, whether consonant with modern society or not.[7] To these people I ask: Do you follow every rule laid down in the Torah without amendment of any kind? Do you, for example, use flint knives for circumcision? If not, shouldn't you be in herem, severe ecclesiastical censure or excommunication?

Furthermore, if the great sage Hillel changed the plain meaning of the Torah through the prosbul, a legal fiction that made it possible to conduct business in a commercial society, why isn't it possible to use his reasoning today to change certain neolithic and Bronze Age laws to fit modern society?[8] Why can't we have an international conference of rabbis and scholars and do what was necessary in the past? Was sixteenth-century Poland more civilized than we are today? The refusal of the extreme Orthodox, not to mention the Hasidim, to do what was done many times in the past—to modernize Jewish law—has created an absurd situation.

Years ago, I found in a hotel room in Tel Aviv some doggerel verse, the substance of which was that an Arab terrorist who knifed a number of innocent bystanders was legally a Jew since his mother was a Jew even though his father was an Arab, but a paraplegic Israeli war hero was not a Jew because of the breach of some idiotic Bronze Age law by his mother. We have reached a point where the modernization of the laws of marriage and divorce and the definition of who is a Jew have become critical.

What is certain to happen if change does not occur? The future, in my opinion, lies with the Conservative and Reform movements. The Hasidim will remain in a world of their own, bypassed by society. The modern Orthodox will adjust or blend in with Conservative and Reform Jews. Those who prefer traditionalism will be Conservative, since they are closer to the Orthodox in their beliefs and practices. Reform Jews, for their part, are becoming more and more traditional; the great difference separating them from Conservatives is over the question of intermarriage. Since intermarriage is becoming more common, even inevitable, this trend can only strengthen the Reform group.[9]

In part the argument against intermarriage comes down to a question of race, the assumption that Jews are a race and must be kept pure. Are the Jews a race? Any reading of history tells us that they are not. If there are any doubters, let them go to Jerusalem and sit down where there are crowds and study the population. They will see Semitic-appearing Jews, European-looking Jews, Africans from Ethiopia, Berbers from North Africa, as well as Slavic-appearing Jews from Poland. The odds are small, but you might even see an Indian or East Asian Jew. The truth is that the Jews are a very mixed people, having in common their history as perpetuated in the Tanakh, the Hebrew language, the Talmud, the Jewish religion, and elements of a common culture, although there are Jews from some areas who did not inherit all such cultural baggage.[10]

The Torah makes it very clear that even in ancient times the Jews were not free of admixture. Did not Moses marry wives who were non-Jews? Does not the Bible say that a mixed multitude of other slaves escaped from Egypt with the Jews? What happened to them? Who is more Jewish than King David? And yet his ancestor is Ruth, a Moabite. What happened to all the Jebusites inhabiting Jerusalem when it was conquered by David? They must have been absorbed into the Jewish people. Did not the prophet of the Jewish people say, "Your mother was a Canaanite and your father a wandering Aramean"?[11] How about the thousands of Idumeans or Edomites who were forcibly converted to Judaism by the Hasmonean king, John Hyrcanus?[12] I doubt very much that they were converted by rituals that are now demanded by the extreme Orthodox.

Referring to the Hasidim, who are vociferously against conversion, it is a strange thing that they bear very little physical similarity to the Jews one sees on ancient monuments. Rather, they have a striking similarity to Poles and Ukrainian Cossacks. It may just be a coincidence that they come from the same area where the Chmielnicki pogroms took place in the seventeenth century.[13] To me it is a strange argument to contend that admixture through rape is fine, but joining the Jewish people by choice is not.

To be fair to the Orthodox, they accept conversion but with a certain reluctance having to do with how the conversion takes place, and they do not agree among themselves on this. It is my personal opinion that the attitude of Jews in Russia arose from the incident in the seventeenth century when several Russian nobles converted to Judaism. The tsar thereupon executed not only those nobles but also the rabbis who converted them. In addition, the tsar threatened dire consequences should such conversions occur in the future. Since then, the rabbis of Eastern Europe have shown no enthusiasm about converting gentiles.[14]

I can think of an incident that occurred some years ago when a friend wished to marry a non-Jew. At that time the policy of Reform Judaism insisted on prior conversion, and the rabbi refused to perform the marriage. The result was that the bride, who had been quite willing to become Jewish, was instead insulted, did not convert, and the children were raised as Christians. From a Jewish standpoint, I cannot see how such a result makes good sense. We risk losing the best and the brightest. Why?

As far as I am concerned, there is a problem facing American Jews even more critical than intermarriage. As far as Jewish learning is concerned, the average Jew is an ignoramus. I take no delight in "corned beef sandwich Jews." How do we educate the young in their Jewish past, that is the problem. To me, the Tanakh, what Christians call the Old Testament, is the core of Judaism. The wonderful stories of the Bible should be the heritage of every Jewish child, preferably in Hebrew, but if that is too utopian, at least in English. And why not in English? It has been read by Jews in Greek, Aramaic, Spanish, Yiddish, and German, to mention only the most important languages. For their own self-respect it is essential that our children be given a Jewish education.

At the same time, I do not believe that Jews should abandon the public schools for parochial schools. In my reading of Jewish history, the survival of the Jewish people, as well as the leading role they have played in Western civilization, has been in large measure due to our insistence on mass education (originally only of males) and the encouragement of continued study throughout adulthood. This was an ideal never fully realized, but depending on the time and location a large enough percentage of Jews was educated and could read and write. In the Middle Ages, when only a few priests were literate, this made Jews a unique cultural group.

I have been asked if we, as Jews, suffered prejudice in Eagle Pass. It is true that Pa was ordered out of the Seco Mines when he was peddling after he first came. He was roughly told that "no Jew peddlers" were allowed. However, what undoubtedly bothered management was not that he was a Jew, but rather that he was infringing on their little monopoly of a company store.

Mother told me that many years ago a woman once came up behind her and patted her head. When Ma asked what she was doing, the woman replied that the padre had said in a sermon that Jews had horns and a tail, and she was only trying to verify if this were true. There is also a story I heard years ago from a member of our Jewish community. He was a Sephardi, a Jew descended from the ancient Spanish Jewish community, whose native language was Spanish. He had moved to a small town in the interior of Mexico and had gotten along very well with the people until one day the padre came to inquire why he did not come to church. When he explained that he was Jewish, he was ordered out of town forthwith. That did not occur on the border, however, and was certainly not typical of this region.

The border has long had an easygoing live-and-let-live atmosphere. Mexicans and Mexican American people have always have been the majority in Eagle Pass. They are now about 95 percent of the population; yet, economic and political power was always in the hands of the Anglos. At the same time there were wealthy Mexican Americans such as Francisco Estrada, and Piedras Negras, with its wealthy aristocracy, was close at hand for all to see. In the old days, the Mexican population was Catholic and almost all the Anglos were Protestant. Such prejudice as existed was Anglo versus Mexican, Protestant versus Catholic, Episcopalian versus Methodist versus Baptist versus Mormon versus Evangelical, and so on. Jews figured very little in the picture—there just weren't enough of us to count. We were treated as members of just another church. In fact, when a sign was put up at the city limits welcoming tourists and inviting them to the various churches, Faye Levine insisted that it had to include the Eagle Pass Jewish community. Had there been, say, a thousand Hasidim in town, there could well have been prejudice. As it was, no one paid any attention to us.

Monsignor Jáuregui was a good friend of my father's. Reuben and I played tennis with some of the younger Catholic priests in Eagle Pass. The Episcopal priest, Mr. Dicus, later a bishop, was a good friend of ours. When Mr. Shulhafer, the Episcopal priest, left for another post, he gave us several books out of his library; when Mr. Parrish, the Methodist minister, moved, he gave me an inscribed Bible. Our relations with the Christian community were always excellent. When an annual ecumenical service was held on Thanksgiving, I was always asked to represent the Jewish community.

The only incident of out-and-out antisemitism I can recall was when a man by the name of Johnson came from out of town and started a weekly periodical listing all the documents recorded, legal cases filed, cattle prices quoted at the various stockyards, and commodity prices at Chicago. One day he printed an editorial blaming the woes of farmers on Jewish speculators in the Chicago commodity market. I had read that such articles were appearing in the Midwest and did not want to see an extension of such filth here. A few of my friends advised me to keep quiet, saying the man was a drunk with no credibility and that no one would pay the slightest attention to him. One of my friends, Johnson's biggest advertiser, did speak to him, and the next issue contained a sort of left-handed retraction. Sometime later, Johnson drank himself to death.

To say there is no prejudice, nor people who dislike or even hate Jews, would be a complete exaggeration—I can truthfully say that as far as the natives of Eagle Pass are concerned it has never been overt or uncomfortable in any way—but from my observation, very few people practice true tolerance. For many Jews, in fact, tolerance refers to them only. The same Jews who complain loudly about antisemitism make derogatory remarks about Mexicans and Blacks. Mexicans complain about discrimination, but as soon as they get the upper hand, they do the same. Blacks complain about racism, which in their definition does not apply to their own conduct or speech. It seems to me that true tolerance applies to all equally. This country became great because people of so many diverse races and religions have learned to coexist. This spirit of tolerance is perhaps our greatest accomplishment as a civilization.

NOTES

FOREWORD

1. Ricardo E. Calderón, "Dr. Hector Ruiz Speaks at Eagle Pass Public Library Foundation Reception," *Eagle Pass Business Journal*, November 20, 2013, accessed August 20, 2022, https://www.epbusinessjournal.com/2013/11/dr-hector-ruiz-speaks-at-eagle-pass-public-library-foundation-reception/.
2. For background on changes to the Mexican and border economies, see Jim Gerber, "Shopping on the Border: The Mexican Peso and US Border Communities," March 2001, accessed March 4, 2023, https://www.academia.edu/3063300/Shopping_on_the_border_the_Mexican_peso_and_US_border_communities.

EDITOR'S INTRODUCTION

1. Ricardo E. Calderón, "City of Eagle Pass Celebrates Groundbreaking Ceremony for Business Incubator Project," *Eagle Pass Business Journal*, April 21, 2023.
2. City of Eagle Pass, "Eagle Pass News: Riskinds Building Announcement," Facebook Live, March 5, 2021, accessed June 17, 2024, https://www.facebook.com/watch/live/?ref=watch_permalink&v=2940917906187906.
3. Ibid.
4. Ibid.
5. I base Morris's completion date on a partial printed manuscript that Peter Riskind provided to me, dated June 27, 1992.
6. Morris's oldest son, John Riskind, offered this recollection of "how gifted our father was." Morris "graduated as president of the honors society at the largest high school in Los Angeles at the age of fifteen, was captain of the chess and tennis teams, passed the California bar at the age of twenty-two (the youngest age of anyone in California up to that time). . . . Our dad was a walking encyclopedia, and it was rare that he wasn't highly informed about any issue that came up in politics, economics, history including cultural history, literature, and archaeology. Our house had huge bookshelves." John Riskind, email message to Bryan Edward Stone, December 2, 2023.
7. "The intimate relationship that developed between Jews and the clothing trade had long-term consequences for both," writes Adam Mendelsohn. "The economic ascent of Jews in America cannot be fully comprehended without understanding the business of stitching and selling garments, and the garment industry cannot be fully understood without following the thread of Jewish involvement in the *shmatte* (rag) business." Adam D. Mendelsohn, *The Rag Race: How Jews Sewed Their Way to Success in America and the British Empire* (New York: New York University Press, 2015), 3.
8. Genealogical documents are from Ancestry.com and will not be cited individually. According to Morris's nephew David Riskind, Rachel roomed with the Riskind family in Chicago, which is how her relationship with Michael began.
9. Peter Riskind, a physician, notes, however, that Mike's quick recovery and subsequent good health suggest that the diagnosis of tuberculosis, usually a lingering and degenerative disease, was a mistake.
10. George J. Sánchez, "'What's Good for Boyle Heights Is Good for the Jews': Creating Multiracialism on the Eastside during the 1950s," *American Quarterly* 56 (September 2004): 635.
11. Lee Shai Weissbach, *Jewish Life in Small-Town America: A History* (New Haven: Yale University Press, 2005), 4–5, 29.
12. Eagle Pass has consistently escaped the notice of Jewish scholars and communal leaders who were *looking* for small Jewish communities. In the early twentieth century, when national Jewish leaders organized efforts to distribute immigrants to small towns, neither the Industrial Removal Office nor the Galveston Movement corresponded with anyone in Eagle Pass or directed a single immigrant there. More recently, the *Encyclopedia of Southern Jewish Communities*, "designed to present a history of every organized Jewish community in the

U.S. South," created entries for fifty-five Texas towns, but Eagle Pass is absent. *Encyclopedia of Southern Jewish Communities*, accessed May 21, 2023, https://www.isjl.org/encyclopedia-of-southern-jewish-communities.html.

13. Ben E. Pingenot, "Eagle Pass, TX," *Handbook of Texas Online*, accessed June 12, 2022, https://www.tshaonline.org/handbook/entries/eagle-pass-tx; "Fort Duncan," *Handbook of Texas Online*, accessed June 22, 2022, https://www.tshaonline.org/handbook/entries/fort-duncan; US Census Bureau, *1910 Census, Volume 3: Population, Reports by States, with Statistics for Counties, Cities, and Other Civil Divisions*, accessed June 21, 2023, https://www.census.gov/library/publications/1913/dec/vol-3-population.html.
14. E. Wolff to Isaac Leeser, December 31, 1850, Isaac Leeser Papers, Jacob Rader Marcus Center of the American Jewish Archives, Cincinnati, Ohio.
15. Jesse Sumpter, *Paso Del Águila: A Chronicle of Frontier Days on the Texas Border*, ed. Ben E. Pingenot (Austin: Encino Press, 1969), 48, 55. The other earliest chronicler of Eagle Pass, Cora Montgomery (pen name of Jane Cazneau), writing in 1852, makes no mention of any Jewish residents, and William J. Munter, who wrote the best history of the Jews of the area, found none earlier than these Sumpter mentions. Cora Montgomery, *Eagle Pass; or Life on the Border*, ed. Alex L. Mauldin (New York: Putnam, 1852); William J. Munter, *History of the Jews of Texas' Middle Corridor* (Laredo, TX: Border Studies Publishing, 1990).
16. "From a Personal Letter," *American Israelite*, July 1, 1881.
17. Henry Cohen, "Settlement of the Jews in Texas," *Publications of the American Jewish Historical Society* 2 (1894): 143–47.
18. "Married," *American Israelite*, February 25, 1887.
19. "San Antonio, Tex.," *American Israelite*, April 20, 1883.
20. "Eagle Pass, Tex.," *American Israelite*, October 31, 1901.
21. Doug Braudaway, "On the Border: A Deck of Cards Led to Del Rio," in Hollace Ava Weiner and Kenneth D. Roseman, eds., *Lone Stars of David: The Jews of Texas* (Waltham, MA: University Press of New England, 2007), 142.
22. The Jewish community poker game seems to have been a commonplace in border communities, as Allison Schottenstein describes a similar game in Brownsville organized by that community's lay leader, Sam Perl. "The only way we could get a minyan to services," according to a Brownsville community member, "was to institute what Perl called a 'Friday night poker tradition.'" Perhaps it's significant that the Eagle Pass game took place on Sunday nights, a supplement to, rather than replacement for, the Friday night service. Allison Elizabeth Schottenstein, "'Perls of Wisdom': 'Rabbi' Sam Perl, New Models of Acculturation, and the 'In-Between' Jew" (master's thesis, University of Texas at Austin, 2011), 93.
23. "Eagle Pass, Tex.," *American Israelite*, October 31, 1901.
24. As Morris tells it, he applied for a teaching position in Bakersfield, and while waiting for an interview with the superintendent, he overheard a pair of teachers discussing a rumor that one of the applicants was Jewish. "And they were talking, and one of them said, 'I wouldn't like that, anyone of that sort to be selected to teach in our schools. He just wouldn't fit in.' And it dawned on me after a while they were talking about me, see? That I was a Jew and I wouldn't fit in with the faculty." Morris Riskind, interview by Peter Riskind, November 8, 1995, video recording in editor's possession, provided by Peter Riskind.
25. Riskind sought to downplay even this apparently straightforward case of antisemitism. "What undoubtedly bothered management was not that he was a Jew," he writes in the epilogue, "but rather that he was infringing on their little monopoly of a company store."
26. Bryan Edward Stone, "West of Center: Jews on the Real and Imagined Frontiers of Texas" (PhD diss., University of Texas at Austin, 2003), 373.
27. Weissbach, *Jewish Life in Small-Town America*, 296, 299–300. Weissbach adds that many small communities were able to survive longer despite declining population by merging congregations or even entire communities, options that were unavailable in Eagle Pass.
28. An excellent memoir that covers similar ground is Stella Suberman, *The Jew Store* (Chapel Hill, NC: Algonquin Books, 2001), set in Concordia, Tennessee. Needless to say, the Upper South offers a distinctly different context for Jewish life and commerce than the Texas border, but Suberman uncovers many of the same concerns as Riskind. See also Lance J. Sussman and Karen Franklin, eds., "Memoirs of Oscar Dreizin of Butler and Macon, Georgia, c. 1948," *Southern Jewish History* 26 (2023): 179–216. Although not a memoir, a revealing study of small-town Texas Jewish retailing in a different regional setting is Jane Bock Guzman, "West of Neiman's: Best Little Department Store in Sweetwater," in Weiner and Roseman, *Lone Stars of David*, 172–81.
29. Hasia R. Diner, *Roads Taken: The Great Jewish Migrations to the New World and the Peddlers Who Forged the Way* (New Haven: Yale University Press, 2015), 61.

30. For brief histories of these retail empires, see Lauraine Miller, "The Zale Story: Diamonds for the Rough," in Weiner and Roseman, *Lone Stars of David*, 148–61, and Hollace Ava Weiner, "Neiman-Marcus: Al Neiman, a Princely Pauper," in Weiner and Roseman, *Lone Stars of David*, 162–71. See also Stanley Marcus, *Minding the Store: A Memoir* (Denton: University of North Texas Press, 1997).
31. Morris Riskind, "Map of Jewish Stores in Downtown Eagle Pass," n.d., copy in editor's possession, provided by Peter Riskind.
32. Alicia M. Dewey documents the growth of the Edelsteins' businesses throughout the region in *Pesos and Dollars: Entrepreneurs in the Texas–Mexico Borderlands, 1880–1940* (College Station: Texas A&M University Press, 2014), 127–28. See also Ben Edelstein and John R. Peavey, *Some Tales of Early Rio Grande Valley History with Memories of My Father, a Valley Pioneer* (n.p: self-published, 2003).
33. See Jerrie Marcus Smith, *A Girl Named Carrie: The Visionary Who Created Neiman Marcus and Set the Standard for Fashion* (Denton: University of North Texas Press, 2021).
34. Morris Riskind interview.
35. Munter, *History of the Jews of Texas' Middle Corridor*, 11.
36. David Riskind, whose father, Reuben, was Morris's brother and partner for decades in the management of the family's enterprises, notes that such civic activism was a common family trait. "From 1945 to Morris's leaving M. Riskind, Inc., the brothers participated broadly in civic, government, community (including Jewish) social and political affairs. They complemented one another to reach out and broadly participate in the community. It was good business, but it also reflected their personal philosophies and interests." David H. Riskind, email message to Bryan Edward Stone, July 24, 2023.
37. Oscar J. Martínez, *Border People: Life and Society in the U.S.–Mexico Borderlands* (Tucson: University of Arizona Press, 1994), 5, 16.
38. Dewey, *Pesos and Dollars*, 1–3.
39. Schottenstein, "'Perls of Wisdom,'" 5, 9.
40. Of Jewish communities on the Texas border, El Paso has received the most scholarly attention, which is fitting as it is the largest and oldest of the Texas border cities and had by far the largest Jewish population. See Floyd S. Fierman, *The Schwartz Family of El Paso: The Story of a Pioneer Jewish Family in the Southwest* (El Paso: Texas Western Press, 1980); Hollace Ava Weiner, *Jewish Stars in Texas: Rabbis and Their Work* (College Station: Texas A&M University Press, 1999), 102–19; Mimi Reisel Gladstein and Sylvia Deener Cohen, "El Paso: The Wild West Welcomes Holocaust Survivors," in Weiner and Roseman, *Lone Stars of David*, 239–54; Erin E. Doran, "The Border Between Remembering and Forgetting: El Paso, Texas, and the Holocaust" (master's thesis, University of Texas at San Antonio, 2008); "El Paso, Texas," *Encyclopedia of Southern Jewish Communities,* accessed June 11, 2023, https://www.isjl.org/texas-el-paso-encyclopedia.html; and the film *People of the Crossing: The Jews of El Paso,* directed by Isaac Artenstein (Cinewest Productions, 2023). On the Jews of Del Rio, see Braudaway, "On the Border," 135–47; Munter, *History of the Jews of Texas' Middle Corridor*. On Eagle Pass, see Munter, *History of the Jews of Texas' Middle Corridor*. On Laredo, see Albert L. Granoff, "To America with Love," unpublished manuscript, n.d., SC-4215, Jacob Rader Marcus Center of the American Jewish Archives, Cincinnati, Ohio; "Laredo, Texas," *Encyclopedia of Southern Jewish Communities,* accessed June 11, 2023, https://www.isjl.org/texas-laredo-encyclopedia.html. On communities of the lower Rio Grande Valley, including Harlingen, McAllen, and Mercedes, see Gabrielle Ryann Lyle, "B'nai Borderlands: The Development of Jewish Communities in the Rio Grande Valley" (master's thesis, Texas A&M University, 2022); "South Texas," *Encyclopedia of Southern Jewish Communities,* accessed June 11, 2023, https://www.isjl.org/texas-south-encyclopedia.html. On Brownsville, see Harriet Denise Joseph, "The Brownsville Jewish Community: From Generation to Generation," unpublished manuscript, 1990, box 3K182, Sam Perl Papers, 1927–2002, Dolph Briscoe Center for American History, University of Texas at Austin, Austin, Texas; Harriet Denise Joseph and Sondra Shands, "Sam Perl: Mr. Friendship and Mr. Temple Beth-El of Brownsville, Texas," *Locus* 5 (Spring 1993): 145–61; Weiner, *Jewish Stars in Texas*, 120–39; Schottenstein, "'Perls of Wisdom'"; and Lyle, "B'nai Borderlands."
41. Villa sightings were a common occurrence among Jewish borderland merchants, as many retailers claimed, probably falsely, to have sold him goods in their stores. In the story Morris relates about his father's own brush with greatness, Mike is honest enough to admit that it was a case of mistaken identity. "It wasn't Pancho Villa," Mike says. "But if they want to believe it was Pancho Villa, why not? It sounds better."
42. Morris Riskind interview.
43. Interactions between Jews and Latinos have received nothing like the treatment scholars have given the relationship between Jews and African Americans, with special emphasis on Jewish involvement in slavery, abolitionism, and civil rights. See, for example, Maurianne Adams and John H. Bracey, eds., *Strangers*

& *Neighbors: Relations between Blacks & Jews in the United States* (Amherst: University of Massachusetts Press, 1999); essays on slavery and abolitionism in Jonathan D. Sarna and Adam D. Mendelsohn, *Jews and the Civil War: A Reader* (New York: New York University Press, 2011); Hasia R. Diner, *In the Almost Promised Land: American Jews and Blacks, 1915–1935* (Baltimore: Johns Hopkins University Press, 1995); Eric J. Sundquist, *Strangers in the Land: Blacks, Jews, Post-Holocaust America* (Cambridge, MA: Harvard University Press, 2009); and P. Allen Krause, Mark K. Bauman, and Stephen Krause, *To Stand Aside or Stand Alone: Southern Reform Rabbis and the Civil Rights Movement* (Tuscaloosa: University of Alabama Press, 2016). By contrast, studies of Latinos and Jews tend to focus either on Jews who *are* Latinos or European Jewish communities in Latin American countries. See, for example, Laura Limonic, *Kugel and Frijoles: Latino Jews in the United States* (Detroit: Wayne State University Press, 2019) and Adina Cimet, *Ashkenazi Jews in Mexico: Ideologies in the Structuring of a Community* (Albany: State University of New York Press, 1997). There are also significant studies of the crypto-Jewish phenomenon, tracing the ancestry of many Latino people to Sephardic Jewish ancestors and their secretive worship practices during the Spanish and Mexican Inquisitions. See Janet Liebman Jacobs, *Hidden Heritage: The Legacy of the Crypto-Jews* (Berkeley: University of California Press, 2002) and Stanley M. Hordes, *To the End of the Earth: A History of the Crypto-Jews of New Mexico* (New York: Columbia University Press, 2005).

There is virtually nothing, however, about the social, cultural, and political interactions of Jewish Americans and Latino or Mexican Americans; even studies of Jews in locations with large Hispanic populations like Texas and California tend to say little about contact between the two groups. Selections from a small number include Steven Windmueller, "Through the Lens of Latino-Jewish Relations," in Ava Fran Kahn and Marc Dollinger, eds., *California Jews* (Hanover, NH: University Press of New England, 2003), 57–64; Bridget A. Kevane, *The Dynamics of Jewish Latino Relationships: Hope and Caution* (Basingstoke, UK: Palgrave Pivot, 2015); and Schottenstein, "'Perls of Wisdom.'" There is a glaring missed opportunity here, as in many ways the Mexican American experience could make a more fruitful comparison than that of Blacks to the Jews' history in America. Like American Jews, Mexican Americans constitute a large group of willing immigrants and refugees; identify deeply with an ancient religious tradition; are part of (or at least intellectually descended from) a global diaspora originating in medieval Spain; grapple with transnational identity; and face continuous uncertainty about their place in America's oversimplified racial schema.

44. This observation is confirmed by Joanne Hershfield in *Imagining La Chica Moderna: Women, Nation, and Visual Culture in Mexico, 1917–1936* (Durham, NC: Duke University Press, 2008), which includes a chapter titled "En México como en París."
45. Original signs from the Riskind's parking lot, recovered and restored by Jeff Taylor Sr., are on display at the Fort Duncan Museum in Eagle Pass. "*Dos horas de Estacionamiento Gratis*," one says. "*Gracias por Comprar en Riskind's.*"
46. Braudaway, "On the Border," 140–41.
47. Schottenstein, "'Perls of Wisdom,'" 22; Joseph and Shands, "Sam Perl: Mr. Friendship," 149.
48. Fierman, *Schwartz Family of El Paso*, 10.
49. For details on the immigration of European Jews in this and other contexts, see Libby Garland, *After They Closed the Gates: Jewish Illegal Immigration to the United States, 1921–1965* (Chicago: The University of Chicago Press, 2018). For Zielonka's activities, see Weiner, *Jewish Stars in Texas*, 102–19. See also Bryan Edward Stone, "Éxodo," *Jewish Herald-Voice*, November 28, 2013, accessed June 18, 2024, https://jhvonline.com/exodo-p16283-271.htm.
50. Riskind describes the Bracero Program in chapter 14. After millions of Mexican workers were recruited to come to the United States during the program's heyday, many remained in the country to live and work after their agreed terms had expired. Immigration enforcement agencies showed little concern for those who had overstayed until federal policy abruptly shifted in the mid-1950s and workers were forcibly rounded up and deported. See John Weber, *From South Texas to the Nation* (Chapel Hill: University of North Carolina Press, 2015), 211–13.
51. Alicia Barrera, "Migrants Cross into US amid Governor Abbott's Visit to Eagle Pass," KSAT.com, June 30, 2022, accessed June 18, 2024, https://www.ksat.com/news/local/2022/06/30/migrants-cross-into-us-amid-governor-abbotts-visit-to-eagle-pass; Office of the Governor of Texas, "Press Release: Governor Abbott Expands Border Security Operations," Office of the Texas Governor, June 29, 2022, accessed June 21, 2023, https://gov.texas.gov/news/post/governor-abbott-expands-border-security-operations.
52. I believe that in every case, Morris's original text was better than the pared-down rewrites. In describing his mother's decision to leave Lithuania, for example, Morris wrote, "There was a second reason why Mother decided to leave her comfortable home to go to America." In the rewritten version that line reads, "A second

factor that persuaded my mother to immigrate to the U.S. is . . ." Perhaps the goal was concision, but the revised version is lifeless, devoid of Morris's voice and sense of narrative style.
53. I have opted to retain previous editors' removal of Morris's occasional use of racial slurs and other outmoded terms like "handicapped." Often he deployed these in the voices of other people, not himself, but they are nonetheless explosive and better removed where possible. In some cases these usages have simply been deleted, in others the word replaced with something less inflammatory. Most such changes are indicated in the notes.

AUTHOR'S INTRODUCTION
1. According to the US Census, there were 5,151 people living in Maverick County in 1910, 3,586 of them (70 percent) within the city of Eagle Pass. Of county residents, 5,055 were identified as white—98 percent of the total—but in 1910 the census counted Latinos as white. Of those whites identified as foreign-born, 2,188, or 42 percent of the total, were born in Mexico; those listed as "native born" but of "foreign or mixed parentage" comprise another 1,719 people, presumably mostly from Mexico. Thus, despite being identified as white, about 76 percent of Maverick County inhabitants were of Mexican birth or ancestry. The largest numbers of non-native whites originated in England, Germany, and Ireland. US Census Bureau, *1910 Census, Volume 3: Population, Reports by States, with Statistics for Counties, Cities, and Other Civil Divisions*, accessed October 30, 2022, https://www.census.gov/library/publications/1913/dec/vol-3-population.html.
2. Riskind was writing between the mid-1970s and early 1990s.

CHAPTER 1
1. Shtetls (from the Yiddish *shtot*, or town) were rural villages with substantial Jewish populations located in the Pale of Settlement, the region of western Russia that included parts of modern-day Poland, Lithuania, Belarus, and Ukraine where, under tsarist rule, Jews were required to live. As Eva Hoffman has written, the shtetl "has become the locus and metaphor of loss. It has often been conceived as the site of greatest Jewish authenticity, defined either as spirituality or as suffering." Eva Hoffman, *Shtetl* (New York: PublicAffairs, 2007), 11. For a classic description of Jewish life and religion in the shtetls, see Mark Zborowski and Elizabeth Herzog, *Life Is With People: The Culture of the Shtetl* (New York: Schocken Books, 1995).
2. Hasidim follow a mystical form of traditional Jewish worship founded in the eighteenth century in Poland by the spiritual leader known as the Baal Shem Tov. The practice emphasizes emotion, individual prayer, and direct devotion to God and the Torah; the word "hasid" means "pious one." Mitnagdim, or "opponents," were their rationalistic rivals. Generally speaking, Hasidism encouraged personal, devotional, and charismatic forms of worship, while Mitnagdim remained committed to an intellectual, disciplined, and scholarly approach to study and ritual. Interpretation of the Talmud, a vast collection of Jewish law, legal commentary, and folklore compiled from oral tradition between 300 BCE and 200 CE, is, as Riskind suggests, an intellectual exercise involving logical disputation, careful examination, and often creative embellishment of the text.
3. Michael Riskind (1877–1969) was born in Orsha, in northeastern Belarus about 13 miles from Dubrovna and 135 miles northeast of Minsk. He immigrated to Chicago about 1893 to rejoin his family, who had traveled ahead of him, married Rachel Edelstein in Chicago in 1907, and moved with her to Eagle Pass in 1910. He founded the M. Riskind department store on Main Street, which he operated until his retirement in the 1950s, along with several other Eagle Pass enterprises. Rachel and Michael had six children, five of whom survived to adulthood, and he died in Eagle Pass in 1969 and is buried in Los Angeles. Morris Riskind, "Riskind, Michael," *Handbook of Texas Online*, accessed July 5, 2022, https://www.tshaonline.org/handbook/entries/riskind-michael.
4. Hanukkah, the eight-day Festival of Lights, commemorates the victory of the Maccabees over the Syrians and the recapture and purification of the Second Temple in Jerusalem beginning in 175 BCE. The holiday usually falls in December, corresponding to Christmas.
5. Judith Sachs Riskind (1850–1933). In Yiddish, a *berye* (or *berrieh*) is a skillful, efficient homemaker. Riskind also uses the description "woman of valor" (*eshet chayil* in Hebrew), a woman who exemplifies traditional Jewish values. The expression is from Proverbs 31:10, "A woman of valor who can find? For her price is far above rubies."
6. Nahum (Nathan) Riskind (1845–1935).
7. The seven surviving children of Nathan and Judith Riskind were Jacob (Jake) Riskind (1869–1968); Aaron Riskind (1874–1949); Michael Riskind (1877–1969); Jennie Riskind Schrager (1884–1925); Albert Isaac Riskind (1885–1982); Rose M. Riskind (1888–1954); and Molly Riskind Schwartz (1889–1986).

8. *Pirkei Avot* (*Ethics of the Fathers*) is a tractate of the Talmud containing memorable sayings of the ancient sages and rabbis. It is the only tractate that is not concerned with the particulars of Jewish law but rather provides folk wisdom of respected scholars.
9. Without doubting the accuracy of Riskind's account of his own family, it is possible to note that this is a somewhat oversimplified stereotype of the financial roles of men and women in the shtetls. For contrast, see the example of Alexander Gurwitz, a contemporary of Nahum Riskind raised nearby in a similar town. Although a devoted Jewish scholar and a product of the finest Lithuanian yeshivahs, Gurwitz struggled constantly with his responsibility to earn a living, eventually abandoning his hope to become a rabbi in order to pursue more remunerative occupations. Alexander Z. Gurwitz, *Memories of Two Generations: A Yiddish Life in Russia and Texas,* ed. Bryan Edward Stone, trans., Amram Prero (Tuscaloosa: University Alabama Press, 2016).
10. The rebbe is the charismatic spiritual leader of a Hasidic community. Regarding "the world to come" (*olam ha-ba*), the Jewish view of the afterlife is complex and inconsistent. Generally speaking, Jews put greater focus on *olam ha-zeh*, the present, living world, and one's obligation to live an ethical and responsible life in the present. The concept of eternal reward and punishment, while present in Jewish thought, is more deeply associated with Christianity. See Simcha Paull Raphael, *Jewish Views of the Afterlife* (London: Rowman & Littlefield Publishers, 2019).
11. The reference is to a Hasidic custom called *tish* ("table") at which the rebbe shares food and drink with his followers accompanied by discourses on Torah, singing, and dancing. The portions of food he shares are thought to have mystical powers and are either eaten by the recipients or held as sacred objects. See Geoffrey W. Dennis, *The Encyclopedia of Jewish Myth, Magic & Mysticism* (Woodbury, MN: Llewellyn Publications, 2007), 262.
12. It isn't immediately clear why this account should be viewed as judgmental, but perhaps Riskind remembers a certain tone in his mother's voice when she told it.
13. Understood as "the day of atonement," Yom Kippur is the most sacred date in the Jewish calendar, observed on the tenth of Tishri, the first month of the Jewish year. It is a time for self-reflective thought, prayer, fasting, refraining from work, and (when possible) day-long attendance at synagogue.
14. The Pale of Settlement was a broad region of tsarist Russia in which Jews were required to live, and their movement and commercial activity outside its boundaries was severely restricted. The region included parts of what is now Poland, Lithuania, Belarus, Ukraine, Romania, Moldova, and western Russia. The move to Shadrinsk, a small industrial town in western Siberia some five hundred miles east of Moscow and more than fifteen hundred miles from Orsha, must have been burdensome to say the least. It may be notable that the distance is roughly the same as Nahum and Judith Riskind later traveled in moving from Chicago to Eagle Pass.
15. Rachel Rose Edelstein Riskind (1880–1979).
16. Kalvaria (today Kalvarija) is in southwestern Lithuania about 115 miles west of Vilnius and 100 miles east of Kaliningrad, Russia (then called Königsberg). There has been a Jewish presence in the town since Jews were first permitted to settle there in 1713. The custom of *kever avot* ("graves of the ancestors") involves visiting the graves of one's parents or close relatives to pray for their eternal rest and for God's help to their living descendants. Masha Greenbaum, *The Jews of Lithuania: A History of a Remarkable Community, 1316–1945* (Jerusalem: Gefen, 1995), 59; "Kever Avot," *Jewish Virtual Library,* accessed June 11, 2022, https://www.jewishvirtuallibrary.org/kever-avot.
17. A mitzvah, or "commandment," is a religious requirement in the Jewish faith to fulfill one's spiritual duty and responsibility to other people. It may be one of the 613 specific obligations described in the Torah or a more general good deed or a kind act toward another person.
18. Payment to liberate Jewish captives (*pidyon shevuyim*) is considered a mitzvah and is highlighted in the Talmud as especially commendable. Jews throughout their history were frequently the targets of false arrest, as well as seized into military service and kidnapped outright in various punitive and extortionist schemes. Natan Efrati, "Ransoming of Captives," *Jewish Virtual Library,* accessed March 14, 2023, https://www.jewishvirtuallibrary.org/ransoming-of-captives.
19. After defeating the English, Austrians, and Russians at the Battle of Austerlitz in 1805, Napoleon moved into Eastern European areas formerly occupied by Russia, including parts of Lithuania, where he extended to the region's Jews the same protections of citizenship that French Jews had received in 1791; some of these rights remained in effect even when Russia regained the area in 1815 after Napoleon's failed attack on Moscow. The right for Jews to own land, however, was not actually a component of the Napoleonic Code, a more generalized body of civil law and procedure, but it was a consequence of the emancipation of the Jews and their acquisition of citizenship as a legacy of the French Revolution. Despite this apparent benevolence, however, Napoleon's policies toward the Jews throughout his empire have been the subject of constant scholarly

debate: to the extent he provided them the benefits of citizenship and political equality, it may have been only in the hope they would assimilate out of existence. Greenbaum, *Jews of Lithuania*, 26–27; Paula Hyman, *The Jews of Modern France* (Berkeley: University of California Press, 1998), 37–52. See also Aubrey Newman, "Napoleon and the Jews," *European Judaism: A Journal for the New Europe* 2 (Winter 1967): 25–32.

20. The Polish nobility rebelled against Russian rule in 1831, and their uprising spread to Lithuania. Caught between the rebels, who bargained for their support, and Russian authorities to whom they had traditionally been loyal, Jews in Poland and Lithuania remained as neutral as possible during the revolt and attempted to support neither side, a position the Russians perceived as loyalty when the uprising was defeated. In the aftermath, rebels' land was confiscated and distributed to loyalists, among whom were probably some number of Jews. Greenbaum, *Jews of Lithuania*, 176; Dov Levin, *The Litvaks: A Short History of the Jews in Lithuania* (Jerusalem: Yad Vashem, 2000), 68.

21. Moses Maimonides, also known as Rambam (an acronym from Rabbi Moses ben Maimon), was an immensely prolific scholar, physician, and the most important philosopher in the Jewish tradition. Born in Spain in 1135, he fled with his family to Egypt, where he served as a court physician to the sultan, wrote numerous books and treatises, and acted as spiritual leader to the Jewish community of Cairo. In his best-known work, *The Guide for the Perplexed*, published in 1190, he attempted to distill the principles of Jewish philosophy into a form accessible to the average reader. It represents, as Riskind suggests, a highly rational approach to the study of Torah. In addition, Rambam's monumental *Mishneh Torah* was the first systematic compilation of Jewish law. "Moses Maimonides (Rambam)," *Jewish Virtual Library*, accessed January 21, 2023, https://www.jewishvirtuallibrary.org/moses-maimonides-rambam.

22. Nicholas II established the Duma as the lower house of the Russian parliament in 1905 in response to the revolution that year, promising it would act as a representative assembly. Almost immediately, however, it was stripped of meaningful power and met only four times between 1906 and its dissolution in the 1917 Bolshevik revolution. "Duma," *Encyclopaedia Britannica*, accessed November 8, 2022, https://www.britannica.com/topic/Duma-Russian-assembly.

23. Königsberg (today the Russian city of Kaliningrad) was the capital of East Prussia and a major port city on the Baltic Sea between modern-day Lithuania and Poland. For most of its history, the majority of its population was German, including a sizable Jewish population dating to the late seventeenth century. In the eighteenth century it became a center of both the European and the Jewish enlightenments and maintained a reputation for intellectual activity, culture, education, and literature. During the era about which Riskind is writing—and until the emergence of Nazism, which led to the near-destruction of the community—the Jews of Königsberg were generally accepted, successful, and integrated with non-Jews. "Koenigsberg," *Jewish Virtual Library*, accessed July 11, 2022, https://www.jewishvirtuallibrary.org/koenigsberg.

24. The yeshivot of Eastern Europe were advanced Jewish academies where select students, always male and usually teenagers, engaged in intensive study of Torah, Talmud, and Jewish law, often in preparation for the rabbinate. The Tanakh is the collection of Hebrew scripture (known in Christianity as the Old Testament) comprising the Five Books of Moses (the Torah); the prophetic books and histories (Nevi'im, or Prophets); and Ketuvim (Writings), poetic and literary works such as the Psalms and the Books of Esther and Job. Tanakh is an acronym of these three parts.

25. The ten surviving children of Chatzkel and Miriam Fried Edelstein, all but the youngest of whom, Isaac, emigrated to the United States, were Abe Edelstein (1879–1933); Rachel Rose Edelstein Riskind (1880–1979); Bertha Edelstein Minsky (1883–1976); Morris Edelstein (1888–1967); Mollie Edelstein Benkaim (1891–1967); Jake Edelstein (1892–1951); Louis Edelstein (1895–1978); Eli Edelstein (1898–1971); David Edelstein (1899–1977); and Isaac Edelstein (?–1940). There is great inconsistency in the ages the Edelstein siblings provided on various documents over the years, a common phenomenon with immigrants of that era, which makes it uncertain exactly what year each was born or in what order. I have done my best to provide the correct information here and in the biographical notes for each of them that follow.

26. A tallis (or tallit in Hebrew) is a fringed shawl worn for prayer. The fringes, called tzitzit, are knotted in representation of the 613 commandments provided in the Torah. It may be plain or embroidered, but its use always signals a sacred moment and the participation in prayer. Michael's everyday garment was probably a *tallit katan*, an undershirt adorned with tzitzit worn by Orthodox Jews as a sign of piety.

27. Because it is forbidden to do any work on the Sabbath, including cooking, Sabbath meals must be composed of items that can be prepared in advance. The *seudah shelishit* (literally "third meal") would typically be served on Saturday evening after the day's final service. The foods Riskind mentions here are typically Ashkenazi, or Eastern and Central European. Latkes are fried potato pancakes, blintzes are thin pancakes similar to crepes filled with fruit or cheese, and kugel is a baked pudding or casserole usually containing noodles with

fruit and nuts.

28. Adela's story bears a conspicuous resemblance to a play by Sholem Aleichem, *The Treasure* (alternatively *The Gold Diggers*), which in turn was based on a common Jewish legend that Napoleon buried a secret trove of stolen Russian gold somewhere in Eastern Europe, possibly in a Jewish cemetery, as he retreated from Moscow. Museum of the Yiddish Theatre, "The Gold Diggers, by Sholem Aleichem," accessed January 14, 2023, https://www.moyt.org/exhibitions/pih/gold-diggers.htm.

29. Hoping to decimate the English economy, Napoleon orchestrated a continental blockade of Britain beginning in 1806 by which British ships could not dock at European ports nor could British goods be sold on the continent. Highly dependent on its trade with England, Russia paid a steep price for this policy. "With its trade with Britain restricted," writes historian Alexander Mikaberidze, "Russia looked to France for trade but the French could provide neither the volume nor the quality of products required in Russia; neither could they replace British spending power when it came to buying raw materials." Under growing economic pressure, the tsar began to relax the enforcement of the blockade, allowing neutral ships to dock at Russian ports, including English vessels traveling under forged papers. English goods unloaded in Russia made their way to Eastern Europe, interfering with the effectiveness of the blockade and providing Napoleon a pretext for his 1812 invasion of Russia. The Neman River (also called the Nieman or Nemunas) begins in Belarus, flows west through Lithuania, and exits into the Baltic Sea north of Kaliningrad. In the 1807 Treaty of Tilsit, Napoleon and Tsar Alexander I accepted the river as the boundary between French and Russian territories in Lithuania, an agreement Napoleon violated when he crossed the river at the outset of his ill-fated invasion. Alexander Mikaberidze, *The Burning of Moscow: Napoleon's Trial by Fire, 1812* (Barnsley, UK: Pen & Sword Military, 2014), 1–2.

30. An 1887 regulation of the Russian Ministry of Education stipulated that only 10 percent of the students in secondary and higher schools within the Pale of Settlement could be Jewish; the proportion was even lower for areas outside the Pale, especially in the capital cities of St. Petersburg and Moscow. The law was (officially) based on the pretext that the Jewish students' rebelliousness and disorderliness posed a threat to the education of gentiles. Among other consequences of the regulation, it became common for Jews to make false conversions to Christianity in order to qualify themselves or their children for state education. Many others fled the country for educational opportunities in Western Europe. S. M. Dubnow, *History of the Jews in Russia and Poland from the Earliest Times Until the Present Day* (Philadelphia: Jewish Publication Society of America, 1918), 2:350–52.

31. Relating tales, legends, and popular stories (*ma'asim*) in Yiddish, *ma'asehbuchs* were composed especially to provide instruction and entertainment for women and girls who were not usually literate in Hebrew. The term originally referred to a multitude of story compilations dating to the Middle Ages from a variety of Central European traditions that contained material not only Jewish in nature, but it later described a single work published in 1602 comprising exclusively Jewish content. Cyrus Adler and Gotthold Weil, "Ma'aseh Books," *Jewish Encyclopedia*, accessed January 21, 2023, https://www.jewishencyclopedia.com/articles/10230-ma-aseh-books.

32. More than eight million immigrants entered the United States through Castle Garden, the processing facility operated by the city of New York from 1855 to 1892. When the federal government took responsibility for receiving immigrants, the facility at Ellis Island was opened, operated from 1892 through 1954, and processed more than twelve million arrivals. I have not been able to confirm with certainty the date of arrival for Nathan and Jake Riskind. Census reports place it between 1890 and 1896, but these are notoriously inaccurate. The references to Benjamin Harrison and Castle Garden, the kinds of narrative color likely to be passed down correctly, narrow the date to somewhere between 1889 and 1892. The family was fully reunited by 1900, when the US Census showed them living together on Maxwell Street in Chicago.

33. Riskind gives voice to the common misconception that US customs officials Americanized immigrants' names upon their arrival, a myth that is demonstrably false. Immigration officials at ports of entry like Ellis Island only checked the names of arriving passengers against ship manifests prepared in Europe before disembarking and recorded the names used there. These officials, furthermore, were often hired for their multilingualism, and languages spoken by Jews, the single largest immigrant group, would have been among the most, not the least familiar. Of course immigrants frequently altered their own names for a variety of reasons after arriving. See Dara Horn, *People Love Dead Jews: Reports from a Haunted Present* (New York: W. W. Norton & Company, 2021), 87–103; Andrew Silow-Carroll, "No One Lost Their Jewish Last Name at Ellis Island. But We Gained a Safe Haven," *Jewish Telegraphic Agency* (blog), September 13, 2021, accessed June 21, 2023, https://www.jta.org/2021/09/13/opinion. For a thorough discussion of American Jewish names and how and why immigrants changed them, see Kirsten Fermaglich, *A Rosenberg by Any Other Name: A History of*

Jewish Name Changing in America (New York: New York University Press, 2018).
34. Morrie Ryskind (1895–1985) was the author of twenty-seven screenplays, including the Marx Brothers' *A Night at the Opera* (1935), *My Man Godfrey* (1936), and *Stage Door* (1937). Politically conservative, Ryskind left Hollywood after testifying in 1947 to the House Un-American Activities Committee about communist infiltration of the film industry. Rabbi Shlomo Riskin (b. 1940), "one of the leading voices of today's Modern Orthodox World," was born in New York, attained ordination at Yeshiva University, and was founding rabbi of the Lincoln Square Synagogue in Manhattan. He moved to Israel in 1983 and became the founding chief rabbi of the city of Efrat. He is a widely published scholar and author. IMDb, "Morrie Ryskind," accessed July 15, 2022, http://www.imdb.com/name/nm0753452/bio; "Shlomo Riskin," *Jerusalem Post*, accessed July 15, 2022, https://www.jpost.com/author/shlomo-riskin.
35. Riskind's observation is that his grandfather chose the name of the Hebrew prophet Nathan—who is described in the books of Samuel, Kings, and Chronicles—rather than keeping his actual name, Nahum, who was also a Hebrew prophet and the author of the Book of Nahum.
36. It's unlikely that the Hebrew Immigrant Aid Society (HIAS) chose the family's destination or paid their way, as Riskind says here, but rather the organization probably sold them discounted rail tickets and perhaps advised on a choice of destination. HIAS was founded in New York in 1881 to assist Jews arriving from Eastern Europe. Originally concerned with providing food, shelter, and jobs, HIAS expanded in 1904 with an Ellis Island bureau that helped immigrants navigate the intake process by providing translation services, guiding them through medical inspections, representing them to agents challenging their admissibility, and locating family members who could supply affidavits of support to facilitate their admittance. In addition, HIAS sold discounted rail tickets to destinations throughout the United States. HIAS, "Our History," accessed November 8, 2022, https://www.hias.org/who/history.
37. Military service under the tsars was a hideously burdensome obligation, sometimes requiring up to twenty-five years of service, and was often a tool used deliberately to destroy Jewish solidarity. "The enrolment of immature lads or practically boys," writes classic historian Simon Dubnow, "their prolonged separation from a Jewish environment, and finally the employment of such methods as were likely to produce an immediate effect upon the recruits in the desired direction—all this was deemed an infallible means of dissolving Russian Jewry within the dominant nation." Dubnow, *History of the Jews in Russia and Poland*, 2:15.
38. A bar mitzvah is the formal induction of a thirteen-year-old Jewish boy into adulthood; in the modern era an identical ritual, bat mitzvah, has become commonplace for girls as well. The ritual marks the point at which a child becomes responsible for fulfilling the requirements of Jewish law. The ceremony usually requires a reading from the Torah (in Hebrew) in front of the congregation and a speech composed by the student or their rabbi. The promise the tailor makes here, therefore, compels religious instruction and training in preparation for the event, as well as imparting his trade.
39. I have not been able to find a passenger list showing the Riskind family's arrival nor to confirm the date they arrived. If Michael was twelve at the time, it was in 1889 or 1890, and several later US Census records show it as 1890.
40. I have not been able to find a passenger list or entry record confirming the date of Michael Riskind's arrival nor his age at the time, and there is uncertainty about his year of birth. Various records state it as somewhere between 1876 and 1880. The information Riskind provides here, which places his father's birth in 1876 or 1877, is likely correct, and Michael's obituary and headstone both claim 1877, which corroborates this reference. It is worth noting, however, that Morris Riskind offered a different year, 1879, in a published biography of his father. Michael Riskind obituary, *Los Angeles Times*, February 14, 1969; Morris Riskind, "Riskind, Michael."
41. "Hinky Dink" is Chicago alderman Michael Kenna, who represented the city's First Ward from 1897 to 1923 and again from 1939 to 1943. His career is detailed in Lloyd Wendt and Herman Kogan, *Lords of the Levee: The Story of Bathhouse John and Hinky Dink* (Evanston, IL: Northwestern University Press, 2005).
42. In February 1896, more than twenty clothing manufacturing firms in Chicago colluded to resist pay increases demanded by the United Garment Workers. Their action drove about seven hundred members of the Chicago Cutters' and Trimmers' Union to strike (although the workers asserted it was a lockout, not a strike). They were later joined by tailors and other garment workers numbering between ten and twenty-five thousand. The stoppage lasted about two months before the cutters and trimmers returned to work with few concessions from their managers and with no guarantee of union recognition. Riskind does not say which firm employed his father, but his observation about the Jewish management of many firms is verified by the list of affected companies, which included Cohn Bros., Stein & Co., J. M. Greenebaum, L. Loewenstein & Sons, and A. L. Singer & Co. "Kick Out the Union; Clothing Manufacturers Enter Into a Hard Fight," *Chicago Chronicle*,

February 18, 1896; "To Break the Union; Clothing Manufacturers Force a Big Strike of Cutters," *Chicago Inter-Ocean*, February 19, 1896; "First Step to Unity; Striking Cutters and Allied Trades Hold a Mass Meeting," *Chicago Chronicle*, February 25, 1896; "Strike of the Tailors," *Chicago Tribune*, March 14, 1896; "Clothing Cutters' and Trimmers' Long Strike Is Off," *Chicago Tribune*, April 22, 1896.

43. Abraham Edelstein (1879–1933) was the oldest of the ten Edelstein children. It's unclear exactly when he immigrated, but in one census record he stated it was in 1900. He was in San Antonio by 1907 and running a furniture store in Eagle Pass by 1908, although he may have remained a resident of San Antonio rather than moving to Eagle Pass to live.

44. This was not an eccentric misconception. "From the time of his presidency to the present day," Gary Zola writes, "American Jews have persistently believed that Lincoln was one of their own. They continuously conceived of Lincoln as a Jewish sojourner and, in certain respects, a Jewish role model." Gary Phillip Zola, ed., *We Called Him Rabbi Abraham: Lincoln and American Jewry, a Documentary History* (Carbondale: Southern Illinois University Press, 2014), 1.

45. In *The Joys of Yiddish*, Leo Rosten defines *yiches* as "more than pedigree or family 'name,' for *yiches* must be deserved, earned as well as inherited. The crucial ingredients of *yiches* are: learning, virtue, philanthropy, service to the community. . . . *Yiches* does not attach itself merely to the successful or the wealthy; wealth or success never warrants or receives the respect accorded knowledge." An attempt to make a marital match, he writes, would involve "a careful listing of the scholars, teachers, rabbis in the family background. The more the learning, the higher the *yiches*." Leo Rosten, *The Joys of Yiddish* (New York: Pocket Books, 1970), 436–37.

46. Riskind says that his mother began thinking about emigrating in 1903, which was also the year of the Kishinev Massacre in present-day Moldova, one of the most violent and notorious pogroms of the era. In attacks fomented by local military and government authorities, forty-nine Jews were killed, more than five hundred injured, seven hundred houses and six hundred Jewish businesses looted, burned, or destroyed, and about two thousand Jewish families left homeless. Theodor Lavi, "Kishinev, Moldova," *Jewish Virtual Library*, accessed November 9, 2022, https://www.jewishvirtuallibrary.org/kishinev-moldova.

47. Riskind correctly reports the name of the ship on which his mother and aunt arrived, but he misremembers or was misinformed about their destination. The *Kaiser Wilhelm der Grosse* docked in New York (not Montreal) on March 1, 1904, and Rachel, age twenty-three, and her sister Beilke, age twenty-one, disembarked there. The ship's manifest stated they intended to go to Chicago to meet A. Edelstein, plainly their brother Abe. It is possible the sisters traveled from New York to Montreal for the visit Riskind describes here before proceeding, but it is hard to make sense of his assertion that they thought it would be easier to travel to Chicago from Montreal than New York.

48. Beilke (Bertha) Edelstein (1883–1976) was born in Kalvaria, the third of ten siblings. She immigrated with her older sister Rachel to New York in 1904 and continued with her to Chicago. After Rachel married Michael Riskind in 1907, Bertha lived alone in Chicago as a boarder and worked in a necktie factory, possibly alongside her younger sister Mollie, who was living with the Riskinds. By 1920, Bertha was in Texas, married to Harry Minsky (1882–1957), and living in Brownsville. They and their three children moved to Corpus Christi by 1930, where Bertha died in 1976 and is buried in the B'nai Israel Cemetery. Bertha was apparently somewhat slippery about her age throughout her life: she claimed to be twenty-one when arriving in 1904 but twenty-three seven years later when she married; similar discrepancies appear in all of her public records. I have opted to use the earliest record available, the passenger list noting her arrival in New York, which suggests her birth year of 1883. If she was born in 1892 as her gravestone records, she would have been only twelve years old when she disembarked.

49. Congregation Knesseth Orthodoxy was known as the Vilner Shul in tribute to its membership of Lithuanian Jews. (Vilna, now called Vilnius, is the capital of Lithuania.) It was located in the North Lawndale neighborhood on Chicago's West Side, an area popular with Jewish immigrants, although it moved north to Albany Park in the 1950s. Its location suggests the part of town where Rachel Edelstein lived. After Rachel married Michael Riskind, the couple moved to Blue Island Avenue, about four miles east of North Lawndale. I'm grateful to Robb Packer and the members of the Synagogues of Chicago Facebook group for help in identifying the congregation.

50. Sarah Block (1874–1948) was born in Russia, immigrated about 1890, and lived on Halsted Street supporting herself as a seamstress. She married Aaron Riskind (1874–1949) on June 17, 1900, and they had five sons, all born in Chicago between 1901 and 1910. For a time, including when the 1910 census was compiled, they shared an address with her parents, Joseph (identified as a Hebrew teacher, possibly not an ordained rabbi) and Taube Block. Aaron's youngest sister, Molly Riskind Schwartz, lived in the building next door with her husband and son.

51. I have corrected their wedding date, which Riskind mistakenly placed in 1905. A Cook County marriage index shows that Michael Riskind and Rose (Rachel) Edelstein were married in Chicago on June 16, 1907. There remains ambiguity about their ages, however. In the marriage record, Michael gave his age as twenty-seven, which is probably correct even if Morris thinks he was a bit older. Rachel, who was nearly twenty-seven, gave her age as twenty-two—three years younger than Morris thought she was and five years younger than she actually was. When she had immigrated three years earlier, she correctly stated her age as twenty-three.
52. A traditional dish of Eastern European Jews consisting of ground whitefish mixed with eggs, matzah meal, and seasonings then poached in broth. It is usually served as an appetizer before holiday meals.
53. Albert Isaac Riskind (1885–1982) figures prominently in the memoir as a partner in the Eagle Pass store operated by his brother Michael and sister Rose. The move to Maroa was in about 1905, but that suggests it was before, not after, Michael and Rachel were married. Albert had moved to Eagle Pass with his wife, Emma, by 1920.
54. Riskind neglects here to mention Albert's wife and children. While in Maroa, he married Emma Leach, who was born there in 1883 to American parents and worked as a clerk in a store, possibly Riskind's. Their children, Gladys and Paul, were born in Maroa; a third child, Rosella, was born in Eagle Pass after they moved there. Emma died in Eagle Pass on June 8, 1958, and is buried at the Congregation Beth-El Memorial Park in San Antonio, where Albert was buried alongside her when he died in 1982.
55. The Panic of 1907, the worst economic contraction in American history other than the Great Depression of the 1930s, began with the failure of a speculative attempt to corner the copper market, which led to the collapse of several investment banks involved in funding the scheme. This was followed by runs on banks throughout the country and a stock market dive. The failure of private banks to regulate their own activities led to the establishment of the Federal Reserve System in 1913. Jon R. Moen and Ellis W. Tallman, "The Panic of 1907," *Federal Reserve History*, accessed November 9, 2022, https://www.federalreservehistory.org/essays/panic-of-1907.
56. Morris's son Peter Riskind, a physician, notes that Michael "must have had a more benign condition [than tuberculosis], as he was not chronically ill later in life."
57. Formed in Odessa, Russia, in 1884, the Chovevei Zion ("Lovers of Zion") brought together disparate groups and clubs operating loosely under that name throughout the Russian Empire. Under Leon Pinsker's leadership, the group oversaw a slow but steady migration of Russian Jews to Palestine, working in the belief that only there could a secure Jewish society exist. As the movement spread into Western Europe in the 1890s, it formed the nucleus of the Zionist movement Theodor Herzl would foster to fruition. See Howard M. Sachar, *A History of Israel: From the Rise of Zionism to Our Time* (New York: Knopf Doubleday, 2013), 16–17.
58. San Antonio was known as the "Sanitarium of the West," a destination frequently prescribed by northern doctors for the dry climate thought to be beneficial for tuberculosis patients. See Chester R. Burns, "Health and Medicine," *Handbook of Texas Online*, accessed March 15, 2023, https://www.tshaonline.org/handbook/entries/health-and-medicine.
59. "Peddling was a common profession for immigrant Jews worldwide during the early twentieth century," noted Peter Riskind in an earlier version of the memoir. "Lithuanian Jews made up the single largest cadre of immigrant Jewish peddlers." Diner, *Roads Taken*, 30.
60. Edward Herman Schmidt Sr. (1876–1968) was born in Eagle Pass to a Prussian immigrant who arrived in Maverick County in the 1870s and ran a store. Schmidt began working as a cashier at the First National Bank in the early 1900s and rose to become its vice president and president. His son, Edward Schmidt Jr. (1913–1997), followed a similar career path and became president of the same bank.
61. Morris Edelstein (1888–1967) was born in Kalvaria, the fourth of ten children, and immigrated in June 1906 through New York. Riskind may be a little off about when exactly the brothers arrived in Eagle Pass. In city directories, Abe is listed as a peddler still living in San Antonio in 1908, residing there with his brother Jake; it's possible that Morris joined them there before they made the move together to Eagle Pass, even though Riskind says later in the memoir that Abe "brought him over from Europe directly to Eagle Pass." In any case, both brothers were in business together in Eagle Pass by 1910.

CHAPTER 2

1. The Galveston, Harrisburg, and San Antonio Railway reached Eagle Pass in 1882, connecting it via the Southern Pacific westward to El Paso and Los Angeles and eastward to New Orleans. From the south, the Mexican International Railroad linked Piedras Negras and Eagle Pass with Durango, Saltillo, and Torreón. Dewey, *Pesos and Dollars*, 51–52.

2. Brothers Rocco, Pasquel, and Leonardo De Bona arrived in San Antonio from Italy in the late nineteenth century and established a fruit and confectionery business. Facing stiff competition in the rapidly expanding San Antonio market, Rocco and Leonardo relocated to Eagle Pass and opened a food market and dry goods store on Main Street as well as a related business in Piedras Negras. The family became and remained prominent commercial and civic leaders in both cities. Dewey, *Pesos and Dollars*, 120.
3. Named Piedras Negras ("black rocks," a reference to nearby coal deposits) soon after its founding in 1849 across the Rio Grande from Eagle Pass, the city was renamed Ciudad Porfirio Díaz in 1888 in honor of the nation's president, who had resumed office in 1884 following a brief hiatus. Díaz held power until he was ousted in the Mexican Revolution in 1911, at which point the city returned to its original name. In 1910, the population of Eagle Pass was 3,536; that of Ciudad Porfirio Díaz was 8,518. "Piedras Negras," *Britannica*, accessed June 13, 2022, https://www.britannica.com/place/Piedras-Negras; Thirteenth Census of the United States, 1910, Maverick County, Texas; INEGI, "Third Census of Population of the United Mexican States, 1910," accessed June 13, 2022, https://en.www.inegi.org.mx/programas/ccpv/1910.
4. Alpine, Texas, lies in the foothills of the Davis Mountains, about 260 miles northwest of Eagle Pass, near the Big Bend region of West Texas. The area's highest peak is 8,378-foot Mount Livermore, only the fifth-highest mountain in the state. Clifford B. Casey, "Alpine, TX (Brewster County)," *Handbook of Texas Online*; "Davis Mountains," *Handbook of Texas Online*, accessed June 13, 2022, https://www.tshaonline.org/handbook/entries/alpine-tx-brewster-county.
5. Originally opened in 1903 in downtown San Antonio, the mission revival Southern Pacific Depot, also known as Sunset Station, was in use as a passenger station until the mid-1990s. It has since been restored and remains in use for entertainment space and other purposes. See Hugh Hemphill, "Restoring Sunset Station," San Antonio Transportation History, accessed March 15, 2023, https://classic.txtransportationmuseum.org/history-rr-southern-pacific-3.php.
6. Álvar Núñez Cabeza de Vaca was, perhaps, more of a refugee than an explorer, but he did leave an account of his eight-year adventure in Texas and Mexico, the first Spanish document of the American Southwest. A survivor of the ill-fated expedition of Pánfilo de Narváez, which attempted to explore Florida and the Gulf Coast in 1527–28, Cabeza de Vaca washed up on the Texas coast near Galveston, ultimately becoming one of only four survivors of the expedition's original three hundred men. In 1532, he and three companions attempted to reach Mexico City by land over a circuitous route that took them across South Texas and northern Mexico to the Pacific, down the coast to central Mexico, and inland to Mexico City, which they reached in 1536 after traveling more than 2,400 miles on foot. Despite Riskind's certainty on this point, the Cabeza de Vaca expedition's exact route through Texas remains in doubt and is the subject of ongoing speculation. Donald E. Chipman, "Cabeza de Vaca, Álvar Núñez," *Handbook of Texas Online*, accessed November 10, 2022, https://www.tshaonline.org/handbook/entries/cabeza-de-vaca-lvar-nunez; Stephen Harrigan, *Big Wonderful Thing: A History of Texas* (Austin: University of Texas Press, 2019), 21–28; Donald E. Chipman, "In Search of Cabeza de Vaca's Route across Texas: An Historiographical Survey," *Southwestern Historical Quarterly* 91 (1987): 127–48.
7. San Juan Bautista Mission was initially established in 1699 in the Mexican interior near the town of Lampazos but was relocated in 1700 to the place Riskind names near the Rio Grande about thirty-five miles south of the site of Piedras Negras. Spanish authorities strengthened it into a garrison called Presidio San Juan Bautista del Rio Grande in 1703, and it served as a base of operations for exploration into Texas and the subsequent establishment of missions there. It later became the location of the town of Guerrero, which in 1836 served as the staging ground for Santa Anna's offensive into Texas to quell the rebellion there. Robert S. Weddle, "San Juan Bautista," *Handbook of Texas Online*, accessed June 13, 2022, https://www.tshaonline.org/handbook/entries/san-juan-bautista.
8. Born in Quebec, Louis Juchereau de St. Denis commanded French forts and conducted explorations along the Mississippi River to the Gulf of Mexico. In 1713, responding to an invitation by a Spanish priest seeking French assistance in pursuing missionary work in East Texas, St. Denis illegally entered Spanish Texas, arriving at San Juan Bautista, where he was arrested, although the cause is unclear: either it was his presence in a forbidden area or his attempt to sell illegal French goods in Spanish territory. He did, as Riskind says, become engaged to the fort commander's granddaughter (or step-granddaughter) and participated in a 1716 expedition to establish Spanish missions in East Texas, marking the frontier between Spanish and French territories in the region. Donald E. Chipman and Patricia R. Lemée, "St. Denis, Louis Juchereau De," *Handbook of Texas Online*, accessed November 10, 2022, https://www.tshaonline.org/handbook/entries/st-denis-louis-juchereau-de; Harrigan, *Big Wonderful Thing*, 63.
9. See Harrigan, *Big Wonderful Thing*, 64.

10. When the United States provoked a war with Mexico in 1846, Lee was dispatched to San Antonio to serve under General John Wool, who was preparing a regiment there. "Wool assigned Lee to an important role," writes historian Carl Coke Rister, "collecting tools for road- and bridge-building and pontoons to throw across the Rio Grande." Lee and his engineers were also ordered to improve a portion of the Old Spanish Road, El Camino Real, a trail the Spanish had forged to link their presidio at Nacogdoches and missions in East Texas through San Antonio to the river below Eagle Pass and beyond to Monclova. The trail was a major thoroughfare under Spanish rule but had fallen into disuse, and Lee's unit was tasked with making the portion from San Antonio to Eagle Pass fit for military transport. In November 1846, Wool led more than two thousands soldiers with their horses and equipment down the route to join Zachary Taylor's force in Mexico. Carl Coke Rister, "Lee, Robert Edward," *Handbook of Texas Online*, accessed November 10, 2022, https://www.tshaonline.org/handbook/entries/lee-robert-edward; "Old San Antonio Road," *Handbook of Texas Online*, accessed June 13, 2022, https://www.tshaonline.org/handbook/entries/old-san-antonio-road; Carl Coke Rister, *Robert E. Lee in Texas* (Norman: University of Oklahoma Press, 1946), chapter 1.
11. The family of Sarah Scott McKellar (1886–1960) owned a ranch in northern Mexico, La Mariposa, adjoining Kickapoo reservation land, and in addition to an interest in regional Texas history, she befriended members of the Kickapoo tribe and became a source of cultural information about them. See Felipe A. Latorre and Dolores L. Latorre, *The Mexican Kickapoo Indians* (New York: Dover Publications, 1976), 93, 241.
12. Placed near the ford across the Rio Grande that became the site of Eagle Pass, Fort Duncan was created after the Mexican War as one of a string of frontier defenses marking the newly established border. It became an important stopping point for travelers making their way to California during the Gold Rush, contributing to the growth of nearby Eagle Pass. The fort was abandoned during the Civil War, occupied by Texan Confederate forces, and used as a point of trade between the Confederacy and Mexico. After US troops reoccupied it in 1868, it was again abandoned in 1883, then reopened with a small force during the Mexican Revolution. It was fully staffed as a training facility during World War I then permanently closed in 1933, after which the city of Eagle Pass acquired the site for a public park and museum. Riskind's account of the settlement of Piedras Negras doesn't align with other explanations, but it comes from Harry Warren's 1906 foreword to Sumpter, *Paso Del Águila*, xxiv; Ben E. Pingenot, *Historical Highlights of Eagle Pass and Maverick County: Maverick County Centennial 1871–1971* (Eagle Pass, TX: Eagle Pass Chamber of Commerce, 1971), 4; "Fort Duncan," *Handbook of Texas Online*.
13. Born in Indiana in 1827, Jesse Sumpter was discharged from the army and settled in Eagle Pass in 1852, where he ran a saloon and kept cattle. During the Civil War he acted as a Confederate customs collector, and upon the creation of Maverick County in 1871, he was elected its first sheriff. When he died in 1910, he was recognized as the city's oldest citizen. Sumpter's memories were published as *Paso Del Águila: A Chronicle of Frontier Days on the Texas Border*. See also Ben E. Pingenot, "Sumpter, Jesse," *Handbook of Texas Online*, accessed May 27, 2022, https://www.tshaonline.org/handbook/entries/sumpter-jesse.
14. Riskind is mistaken on this point. Lee was stationed at a different Texas encampment, Fort Mason in Central Texas, when he heard of the secession of South Carolina in December 1860, and he was still there when Texas seceded and the Confederacy was formed in February 1861. Furthermore, Lee's own involvement in the Confederate cause did not begin until his home state, Virginia, seceded in April 1861. Rister, *Robert E. Lee in Texas*, chapter 10.
15. From the end of the Mexican War in 1848 through the Civil War, Juan Nepomuceno Cortina led a series of raids across the border into South Texas to harass American officials and defend the rights of Mexican workers and landholders. Born into a Tamaulipas ranching dynasty in 1824, his family owned land on both sides of the Rio Grande, and he served in the Mexican Army in South Texas during the US incursion that resulted in the loss of the region. "I never signed the Treaty of Guadalupe Hidalgo," he said by way of explanation for his subsequent actions, referring to the treaty that established the border. In 1859, when the city marshal of Brownsville arrested a vaquero who worked for Cortina, Cortina shot the marshal, rescued the vaquero, and brought a force of men across the river to occupy the Texas border town. While defending his hold on Brownsville against a unit of Texas Rangers, Cortina issued a series of proclamations demanding respect for the rights of Mexican Texans. The Rangers eventually drove him from Brownsville and into hiding in 1860, when Robert E. Lee arrived with a US Army detachment to quell the insurrection and locate Cortina, who remained unfound when the Civil War began. Cortina emerged again after Texas secession, leading a raid into Zapata County, where he was repelled by Confederate troops. His exploits made him a folk hero among borderland Mexicans. Jerry Thompson, "Cortina, Juan Nepomuceno," *Handbook of Texas Online*, accessed November 10, 2022, https://www.tshaonline.org/handbook/entries/cortina-juan-nepomuceno; Harrigan, *Big Wonderful Thing*, 260; Rister, *Robert E. Lee in Texas*, chapter 7. See also Jerry D. Thompson, *Cortina:*

Defending the Mexican Name in Texas (College Station: Texas A&M University Press, 2007).

16. Following France's invasion of Mexico in 1861, Napoleon III installed Maximilian, a Habsburg noble and younger brother of Austrian emperor Franz Joseph, as puppet monarch of the conquered nation. Maximilian served as the first and only emperor of the Second Mexican Empire from 1864 until he was deposed and executed in 1867 by advocates of republican rule. Missouri planter Joseph Shelby raised a brigade at his own expense in 1862 and led Confederate military actions in Arkansas and Missouri. At the time of Lee's surrender Shelby's brigade was in East Texas, and the commander resolved to take them to Mexico to offer their service to Maximilian rather than surrender to Union troops, becoming one of a significant number of unreconstructed Confederates who attempted to flee the country rather than face the consequences of their loss. Loaded with cannons and other equipment, Shelby's force marched through Corsicana, Waco, Austin, and San Antonio and crossed the river at Eagle Pass. Maximilian showed little interest in Shelby's proffer, however, and the brigade disbanded and dispersed, with most returning to the United States by 1867. Art Leatherwood, "Shelby Expedition," *Handbook of Texas Online*, accessed November 10, 2022, https://www.tshaonline.org/handbook/entries/shelby-expedition; Pingenot, *Historical Highlights of Eagle Pass*, 6.

17. The Kickapoo, whose name aptly derives from the Algonquian term *Kiwigapawa*, meaning "he moves about," were a highly mobile and fragmented group native to the Great Lakes region whose members traveled at various times to Wisconsin, Illinois, Indiana, Ohio, Michigan, New York, Pennsylvania, Iowa, Missouri, Kansas, Indian Territory (Oklahoma), Texas, and Coahuila. By the mid-nineteenth century the large, scattered tribe had divided into three primary groups based in Kansas, Indian Territory, and the Texas–Mexico borderland. The largest was the Texas group, invited in during Spanish colonization to help guard against American expansion, but after Mexico's independence in 1810 and the subsequent rise in Anglo-American settlement, many Kickapoo were pressured to move further south. A series of violent assaults against them during the decade of the Texas Republic forced most of the rest into Mexico by 1839 where, with the encouragement of the Mexican government, they engaged in frequent raids into Texas. For these actions Mexico awarded them a grant of land, which they exchanged in 1852 for the tract at Nacimiento they still occupy today. A. M. Gibson, *The Kickapoos: Lords of the Middle Border* (Norman: University of Oklahoma Press, 1963), x; M. Christopher Nunley, "Kickapoo Indians," *Handbook of Texas Online*, accessed November 10, 2022, https://www.tshaonline.org/handbook/entries/kickapoo-indians.

18. Riskind is conflating separate incidents of Kickapoo migration to Mexico. Some arrived in the late 1830s to escape violence by Anglos in the Republic of Texas. Another group, the one referenced here, left Indian Territory in 1864 to avoid entanglement with either side in the US Civil War, each of which was attempting to form alliances in the region against the other. About seven hundred Kickapoo traced a circuitous route across West Texas hoping to evade detection by Confederate forces and to join their relatives in northern Mexico. On January 8, 1865, while camping at Dove Creek, a tributary of the Concho River near present-day San Angelo, three Kickapoo bands were discovered and attacked by a Texan unit of the Confederate cavalry—*not*, as Riskind says, by "frightened white civilians." The Kickapoo lost fifteen warriors but despite being surprised by the sudden attack killed twenty-six Confederates and wounded sixty more, driving the Texans into retreat. It was, according to historian Arrell Gibson, "the most disastrous defeat ever suffered by the Texans in their long history of Indian wars." The viciousness of the attack against them rationalized decades of retaliatory raids by the Mexican Kickapoo into Texas. Gibson, *Kickapoos*, 206–7; Elmer Kelton, "Dove Creek, Battle of," *Handbook of Texas Online*, accessed November 10, 2022, https://www.tshaonline.org/handbook/entries/dove-creek-battle-of.

19. Nacimiento (or El Hacienda Nacimiento) is in Coahuila about thirty miles northwest of the town of Múzquiz and about eighty miles southwest of Piedras Negras. The "deal" to which Riskind refers was struck in 1852 between Seminoles under the leadership of Wild Cat, their Kickapoo allies, and the Mexican government. As Riskind describes, the Indians received land in exchange for their agreement to provide warriors to defend Mexico from attacks by Comanches, Apaches, Mescaleros, and other Indigenous enemies of Mexico. The property, whose possession and use alternated between Seminoles and Kickapoos over the years, is about seven thousand hectares in area, or approximately twenty-seven square miles. Latorre and Latorre, *Mexican Kickapoo Indians*, 45–46; John M. Goggin, "The Mexican Kickapoo Indians," *Southwestern Journal of Anthropology* 7 (1951): 317.

20. According to Allen Lee Hamilton, the Kickapoo in Mexico found it "ridiculously simple" to cross the border and steal horses and cattle, which greatly outnumbered the human population there to protect them. "Mexican government officials," furthermore, "abetted the Indians by steadfastly refusing to allow United States troops to pursue the raiders into Mexico." A. M. Gibson cites a congressional commission report that "estimated that the Kickapoo desolation of south Texas ranches had been so complete that in 1872 there remained only

one-tenth of the livestock population tallied in 1865. Cumulative loss estimates supplied by witnesses revealed that between 1865 and 1872, five hundred thousand head of cattle and fourteen thousand horses had been stolen in Texas by Kickapoo marauders and Mexican outlaws." Allen Lee Hamilton, "Remolino Raid," *Handbook of Texas Online*, accessed November 22, 2022, https://www.tshaonline.org/handbook/entries/remolino-raid; Gibson, *Kickapoos*, 224.

21. Black Seminoles, also known as Muskogees, are descendants of African slaves who escaped from bondage in the British colonies and early American states and found safety among the Seminoles in Florida, with whom they lived and sometimes intermarried. After passage of the Indian Removal Act in 1830, they were forcibly removed along with the Seminoles to Indian Territory where, faced with the constant possibility of being returned to slavery, a faction fled to Mexico in 1849. In part to shield them from American demands for their return, Mexican authorities settled them at Nacimiento in 1852.

    Dissatisfied under Mexican rule, a faction ventured north to Fort Duncan, lured in part by American promises of military employment. From those settled at Fort Duncan, Major Zenas Bliss recruited a few as scouts, and their numbers grew as their service proved valuable. The scouts were transferred to Fort Clark and placed under the command of Lieutenant John Lapham Bullis in 1873, when they participated in the Mackenzie raid on Mexican Kickapoo settlements. "Because [the Kickapoo] village lay forty miles inside Mexico," writes historian Michael L. Tate, "the expedition relied heavily on the Black Seminoles and other scouts to prevent contact with Mexican soldiers and to assure a speedy withdrawal once the mission was accomplished." Riskind originally misidentified Bullis, not Bliss, as the officer who recruited the Seminole scouts in Mexico, an obvious confusion that has been corrected in the text. He revisits the matter of Seminole land claims, in which he played an advisory legal role, in chapter 10. Tracé Etienne-Gray, "Black Seminole Indians," *Handbook of Texas Online*, accessed November 10, 2022, https://www.tshaonline.org/handbook/entries/black-seminole-indians; Michael L. Tate, "Black Seminole Scouts," *Handbook of Texas Online*, accessed November 22, 2022, https://www.tshaonline.org/handbook/entries/black-seminole-scouts; Gibson, *The Kickapoos*, 239. See also Michael L. Tate, "Bullis, John Lapham," *Handbook of Texas Online*, accessed November 10, 2022, https://www.tshaonline.org/handbook/entries/bullis-john-lapham; Jeff Guinn, *Our Land before We Die: The Proud Story of the Seminole Negro* (New York: Tarcher, 2002). For broader studies of Indigenous Americans employed as army scouts, see Thomas W. Dunlay, *Wolves for the Blue Soldiers: Indian Scouts and Auxiliaries with the United States Army, 1860–90* (Lincoln: University of Nebraska Press, 1982) and Robert Marshall Utley, *Frontier Regulars: The United States Army and the Indian, 1866–1891* (Lincoln: University of Nebraska Press, 1984).

22. The immediate order for the May 1873 attack known as the Remolino Raid came from Sheridan—who had been stationed briefly at Fort Duncan in the 1850s, became a hero of the Civil War, led occupying Union troops during Reconstruction, and earned his reputation as a ruthless Indian fighter—but the plan to destroy the Mexican Kickapoo originated with President Ulysses S. Grant, who had grown weary of failed diplomatic attempts to calm their cross-border raids into Texas. Grant ordered the Fourth Cavalry, under the command of Colonel Ranald S. Mackenzie, to Fort Clark in March, where Sheridan visited Mackenzie in April to relay Grant's order. An attack on the Kickapoo inside Mexico would violate Mexican sovereignty, thus it was relayed informally and in person rather than by official written message.

    Mackenzie and his men crossed the river on May 17, 1873, following the Seminole scouts Bliss had recruited. Advance observers noted that the Kickapoo warriors had left their villages near the town of Remolino to hunt, leaving women, children, and older men unprotected. The attack caught them by surprise and alone. Many fled into nearby thickets to hide, but Mackenzie's men hunted them down, captured them, and killed any who resisted; soldiers burned their lodges, destroying more than 180 homes in three settlements. Where a village had been, Mackenzie boasted after the attack, "ruin and desolation now marked the spot—a cyclone could not have made more havoc or a cleaner sweep." The cavalry killed nineteen Indians and captured forty women and children. Fearing further retaliation, the Kickapoo almost completely ceased their raids across the border. Many Kickapoo, furthermore, agreed to return to Indian Territory in exchange for their captured relatives. Joseph G. Dawson III, "Sheridan, Philip Henry," *Handbook of Texas Online*, accessed November 10, 2022, https://www.tshaonline.org/handbook/entries/sheridan-philip-henry; Ernest Wallace, "Mackenzie, Ranald Slidell," *Handbook of Texas Online*, accessed November 17, 2022, https://www.tshaonline.org/handbook/entries/mackenzie-ranald-slidell; Hamilton, "Remolino Raid"; Gibson, *Kickapoos*, 243.

23. Three Black Seminole scouts were awarded the Medal of Honor for rescuing Bullis: Private Pompey Factor, Sergeant John Ward, and Trumpeter Isaac Payne. A fourth scout, Private Adam Paine, also received the award for other service in the Indian wars. All four men are buried in the Seminole Negro Indian Scout Cemetery

near Fort Clark. US National Park Service, "Black Seminole Indian Scouts," accessed November 27, 2022, https://www.nps.gov/articles/000/black-seminole-indian-scouts.htm.

24. In addition to his career as an outlaw, John King Fisher was a Maverick County rancher and the sheriff of Uvalde County. He was killed in a shoot-out in San Antonio in 1884. Webb writes about Fisher in a manner suitable to his usual uncritical and mythic celebration of the Rangers. Walter Prescott Webb, *The Texas Rangers: A Century of Frontier Defense* (1935; repr., Austin: University of Texas Press, 2010), 237; Paul Adams, "Fisher, John King," *Handbook of Texas Online*, accessed November 10, 2022, https://www.tshaonline.org/handbook/entries/fisher-john-king.

25. According to Sumpter, the unlucky merchant was named Stinbock—probably this was Behr Steinbock, born in 1828 in Prussia according to the 1860 Maverick County census—and Riskind greatly undersells the drama of his demise. Says Sumpter: "Stinbock shot himself accidentally while shooting blackbirds in his yard. He shot and wounded one, and then he ran after it trying to kill it with the butt of his gun. He struck so hard with the gun that he broke its stock. This infuriated him, and in a passion he struck the gun against a tree with the muzzle toward him. One of the barrels was discharged, and the shot entered his abdomen, from the effects of which he shortly afterwards died in great agony." Sumpter, *Paso Del Águila*, 57.

26. The resident Sumpter describes was "a very small man by the name of Cain, a Jew, who built a store" on Washington Street. His antagonist was "an American known only by the name of 'Kaintuck,'" and when the men quarreled, Kaintuck insisted that Cain, who was armed with a knife and pistol, put his weapons on a table so they could fight on equal terms. When Cain did so, Kaintuck lunged toward the table, grabbed Cain's pistol, and shot him with it. Sumpter claims to have been present at Cain's funeral, no doubt the first Jewish burial in Eagle Pass. The burial site, according to editor Ben Pingenot, now lies under a supermarket parking lot. Sumpter, *Paso Del Águila*, 20–21, 25n10.

27. Riskind is mistaken on this important detail, as the 1887 Texas state census does not actually indicate a Jewish presence in Maverick County. There were, however, eight "Hebrew" residents in Kinney County, immediately to its north, and eighteen in Val Verde County to its northwest. Conducted by Texas commissioner of agriculture L. L. Foster, the report "contains ethnic data by county unavailable in any other published census of the nineteenth century," according to cultural geographer Terry Jordan, including "the only published enumeration of the Hispanic element in Texas prior to the 1930 census." Jordan's article includes a map indicating "1–9" Jews in Kinney County, which may be the source of Riskind's error. Terry G. Jordan, "The Forgotten Texas State Census of 1887," *Southwestern Historical Quarterly* 85 (April 1982): 401–3, 407; Barbara J. Rozek, ed., *Forgotten Texas Census: First Annual Report of the Agricultural Bureau of the Department of Agriculture, Insurance, Statistics, and History, 1887–88* (College Station: Texas A&M University Press, 2002), 128, 151, 223.

28. San Juan Plaza (or San Juan Park) is a three-and-a-half-acre public park in the center of Eagle Pass.

29. Riskind was writing in the early 1990s, and I have been unable to determine whether any of the buildings now on that corner were the original Riskind family home.

30. Ruben Harold Edelstein (1918–2014) was born in Houston and grew up in Brownsville, where as a young man he worked in the furniture business of his father, Riskind's uncle Morris Edelstein. After serving in the army in World War II, he returned to the business, eventually taking over its management when his father retired. Ruben served as mayor of Brownsville from 1975 to 1979 as well as serving the Brownsville Jewish community as temple president, supervising the cemetery, restructuring the congregation's financial system, and organizing events for Israel Bonds and the United Jewish Appeal. He died in 2014 and is buried near his parents at the Hebrew Cemetery in Brownsville. Ruben H. Edelstein obituary, *Brownsville Herald*, July 23, 2014; Lyle, "B'nai Borderlands," 27–28; Weiner, *Jewish Stars in Texas*, 136.

31. Yetta Wiesenthal Edelstein (1888–1981) immigrated with her parents in 1900 from Austria to Galveston, where she grew up. She married Morris Edelstein in 1916 and moved with him to Brownsville, where they raised six children. She died in Houston in 1981 and is buried next to her husband at the Hebrew Cemetery in Brownsville. Yetta Edelstein obituary, *Brownsville Daily Herald*, August 4, 1981.

32. Edelstein may have been particularly astute in misidentifying the American as German. As Friedrich Katz narrates in breathtaking depth and complexity, world powers competed during World War I for influence among various factions of Mexican revolutionaries, who courted their support. Germany was widely viewed among Mexican insurgents as a potential ally against the detested Americans, so the "bandits" may have felt especially well-disposed toward a passenger they believed was German. See Friedrich Katz, *The Secret War in Mexico: Europe, the United States and the Mexican Revolution* (Chicago: University of Chicago Press, 1985). I'm grateful to Andrew Hernández for this observation.

33. The practice of small-town Jewish retailers acquiring stock in the cities they had left was common, and as Adam

Mendelsohn argues, it not only helped provide a wider array of goods to rural Americans but strengthened Jewish communal and kinship ties over distances. "These connections were useful for trade," he writes, "and trade was useful for the perpetuation of Jewishness." Mendelsohn, *The Rag Race*, 84.

34. Edelstein's Better Furniture eventually grew to thirteen stores, and at least four Edelstein brothers managed locations or worked for the company. Morris Edelstein's success was significant enough to draw the attention of Alicia Dewey, a historian of borderland commerce, who treats him as an exemplar of her observation that "Jews were among the most upwardly mobile entrepreneurs in South Texas." She writes that Morris bought a downtown Brownsville building in 1920 for his furniture business and by 1925 had opened branches in Harlingen and McAllen; by 1930 he owned thirteen stores in towns on both sides of the border. "He found innovative ways to profit in different areas of retail," Dewey writes. "When Studebaker exited horse-drawn vehicle operations in 1920 to focus on automobiles, Edelstein bought some of their remaining buggies, wagons, and harnesses at a fire-sale price and for several years sold them in northern Mexico, where there was still a market." He also showed great ingenuity in advertising and marketing his businesses: "One time he had a woman sleep overnight on a Simmons mattress in the front of the store. On another occasion, he borrowed a large python to place in the main display case, which proved to be quite a draw until the snake disappeared." Allison Schottenstein writes that Edelstein "did not feel the need to recognize class or racial hierarchies" in Brownsville and "became so fluent in Spanish that he was frequently mistaken 'for a Mexican.'" At the end of his life, Edelstein could afford to retire to a ranch in the Texas Hill Country near Kerrville, where he died in 1967. Dewey, *Pesos and Dollars*, 127; Schottenstein, "'Perls of Wisdom,'" 31–32. See also Edelstein and Peavey, *Some Tales of Early Rio Grande Valley History*.

35. The decade-long Mexican Revolution "had a profound impact on formal and informal relations between the United States and Mexico," write Douglas W. Richmond and Sam W. Haynes. "Resulting in the flight of hundreds of thousands of refugees, the rebellion prompted the first major northern migration of Mexican citizens. In so doing, it permanently changed the demographics of the American Southwest, energizing and shaping Latino culture in the United States." Douglas W. Richmond and Sam W. Haynes, preface to *The Mexican Revolution: Conflict and Consolidation, 1910-1940*, ed. Douglas W. Richmond, Sam W. Haynes, and Nicholas Villanueva (College Station: Texas A&M University Press, 2013), vii.

36. The long and complex Mexican Revolution (1910–20) began with the ouster of President Porfirio Díaz, who had governed an authoritarian, business-oriented regime in close alliance with the United States since 1884; Porfirists were his advocates and supporters. Díaz was overthrown and replaced by Francisco Madero in 1911, the same year that partisans of Ricardo Flores Magón—journalist, cofounder of the Mexican Liberal Party (PLM), and radical intellectual leader of the revolution—staged a brief socialist uprising in Baja California. (Despite Riskind's implication here, Flores Magón was exiled in San Antonio, Texas, at the time of the revolt, so it was not him personally but his supporters, the Magonistas, who led the revolt on his behalf.)

With covert encouragement from the Wilson administration, General Victoriano Huerta, Madero's former ally, turned on him and led an armed revolt against federal troops under Madero's authority. Huerta ousted, assassinated, and replaced Madero in a coup d'état in 1913. Although nominally an ally of Huerta, flamboyant militia leader Francisco "Pancho" Villa, who had also fought for Madero at the beginning of the revolution, led a series of insurrectionist attacks throughout northern Mexico, partly in an attempt to compel more radical reform but also in pursuit of self-aggrandizement, which contributed to the destabilization and eventual collapse of the Huerta regime. In 1915 and 1916, Villa's activities threatened not only the safety of northern Mexicans but of Americans living near the border.

37. Riskind does his friend Sam Schwartz (1885–1969) something of a disservice describing him as merely "another Jewish businessman." In fact Schwartz was one of the leading citizens of Eagle Pass, a successful and innovative business owner, for three terms the town's mayor, and cofounder and longtime president of the county irrigation district. Born in Hungary, Schwartz immigrated to El Paso to work for his uncle, Adolph Schwartz, at the Popular Store, one of the city's leading department stores, where he remained for a decade. Hoping to start a similar business somewhere new, he moved to Eagle Pass in 1910. Unable to acquire real estate for a store, he opted instead to present motion pictures, then a new technology, and set up a small theater in a former pool hall, which, surely with some irony, he named the Majestic. According to a biography by his grandson William Munter, "Sam sold the tickets, swept the floors, slept in the theater, and did everything except run the projection equipment."

When thousands of federal troops seeking entertainment were posted in the city during the Mexican Revolution, Schwartz opened a larger venue, the Aztec Theater, in a space on Main Street next to the Riskind store and decorated it in a flamboyant "Mayan" style. In addition to silent films, the Aztec offered a stage for live performances, and it became the first Texas theater to show a talking picture when it screened *The Jazz Singer* on its release in 1927. "The MGM lion came to Eagle Pass," Munter writes, "and Sam had a picture taken with the lion in a cage." In later years, he also opened a Spanish-language movie theater. Schwartz operated the Aztec until the end of his life, after which his family continued its operation until 1982. The building still stands and has been renovated repeatedly for other uses including as an art and performance space. In addition to his theatrical interest, Schwartz served as mayor from 1918 to 1924, invested in real estate and made a large portion of land available to the city for public use, directed a bank, operated a hotel, served on the school board, and helped supervise the management of the International Bridge. He and his wife, Ellen Kranzthor, had three children. William J. Munter, "Sam Schwartz," *Handbook of Texas Online*, accessed July 15, 2022, https://www.tshaonline.org/handbook/entries/schwartz-sam; Munter, *History of the Jews of Texas' Middle Corridor*, 12; Dewey, *Pesos and Dollars*, 127. See also William Munter, "Sam Schwartz and The Aztec," Bullock Museum, July 21, 2014, accessed June 17, 2022, https://www.thestoryoftexas.com/discover/texas-story-project/sam-schwartz-and-the-aztec.

38. Rose Riskind, known throughout the memoir as Aunt Rose, was born in 1887 in Russia, immigrated with her mother in 1890, and lived with her family in Chicago. Moving to Eagle Pass in 1911, she worked at the M. Riskind store with her brothers as a buyer and style consultant until she retired to California. She never married and died in Los Angeles in 1954.
39. The five surviving children of Michael and Rachel Rose Riskind were Bess Adeline Riskind Frank (1909–1998), Morris Samuel Riskind (1911–1996), Ruth Riskind Haberman (1913–1966), Sarah Naomi Riskind Robson (1915–1982), and Reuben Saul Riskind (1919–2010). As Morris mentioned in the previous chapter, their first-born, an infant son, Herschel, died in Chicago in 1908.
40. In a 1998 interview, Morris's wife, Ruth, recalled an incident that reveals the power Aunt Rose wielded over her family and the lingering resentment it caused. "I remember that I made onion soup one night, and Aunt Rose would not let [her brother Michael] eat the onion soup. [She] said, It's not for you, Mike. You won't like it. . . . She doesn't know how to cook and it's lousy and you're going to be sick and you can't have it." Michael obeyed, even though "it was a very good soup. But I still remember Papa smelling it and saying he wanted some, and she said, No, no, no, you can't." More than forty years after her death, Ruth referred to Aunt Rose as "the little hunchback. She was really a horror in many ways, just a true horror." Ruth Riskind, interview by Peter Riskind, 1998, video recording in editor's possession, provided by Peter Riskind.
41. Progressive social worker Jane Addams established the Hull-House social settlement on Chicago's West Side in 1889 to provide an array of services to the city's poor and immigrant communities. The institution's programs included early education, language and citizenship instruction, classes in technical skills like sewing and weaving, and a variety of musical, art, literary, political, and social activities. Addams lived at the institution and managed its programs until her death in 1935.
42. Clara Kimball Young starred in dozens of silent films in the 1910s, first for Vitagraph and later for David O. Selznick. Theda Bara, equally prolific, was one of silent film's most recognizable performers and the first to become a "fabricated star" on the basis of an image entirely concocted by publicity and advertising executives. Both Young and Bara were known for their alluring, "vampish" characters. Errol Flynn achieved swashbuckling immortality with *Captain Blood* (1935) and rapidly became one of the most successful and dashing stars of early American cinema. Jon C. Hopwood, "Clara Kimball Young," IMDb, accessed July 15, 2022, http://www.imdb.com/name/nm0949403/bio; Denny Jackson, "Theda Bara," IMDb, accessed July 15, 2022, http://www.imdb.com/name/nm0000847/bio; Charles Culbertson, "Errol Flynn," IMDb, accessed July 15, 2022, http://www.imdb.com/name/nm0001224/bio.
43. The register is still on display in the Fort Duncan Museum and is still in working order. Jeff Taylor, the former curator, told me he used to let children who visited the museum push the buttons and open the cash drawer. A sign on the display indicates that the register was first used in the 1890s by the Eagle Pass Mercantile Company. Jeff Taylor Sr., telephone conversation with Bryan E. Stone, February 25, 2023; Jeff Taylor Sr., email message to Bryan E. Stone, March 1, 2023.
44. Hart Schaffner & Marx, which specialized in high-quality men's suits, was founded in 1887 and Florsheim Shoes, which sought to provide high-quality footwear at reasonable prices, in 1892. Both firms were established in Chicago by immigrant Jews, giving them perhaps a certain cachet to Michael Riskind, who began his career in the same place and time.
45. As Peter Riskind notes, cursing a woman as a *chaleria* was the Yiddish equivalent of "bitch" or "shrew."
46. Geraldine McCarthy White (1893–1961) and Alfred Lafayette White (1886–1956).
47. Everyone Riskind names here was a longtime M. Riskind employee, several for decades—a testament to a strong personal and professional relationship between management and employees. Riskind's recollection also suggests a number of patterns about the store and its staff. Notably, everyone on this list was Mexican or Mexican American, all either immigrants or the children of immigrants—as, indeed, were the store's owners.

Dolores (Lola) Vela (1895–?) resided in Piedras Negras and crossed the bridge routinely to work at the store; in chapter 16, Riskind says Vela "worked for us for over fifty years and was considered part of the family." Constancia Petronila Miranda (1912–1994) married Albino Diaz, another longtime Riskind's employee. Catarina Santos (1893–1988) and Anacleto Torralba (1894–1961) both had siblings who also worked in dry goods for the Riskinds, Edelsteins, or other Jewish families. At one point five Torralba siblings were all employed in various positions in dry goods businesses, many of which were Jewish-owned. Riskind's recollection of the store's employees also suggests the importance of the Riskind store and other Jewish-owned businesses in providing opportunity and a means of upward mobility to young Mexican American workers in Eagle Pass. The father of Felipe Moncada (1892–1953), for example, was a butcher; the father of Federico Perez (1888–1960) was a day laborer, as was Federico early in his life; Ernesto Garza's (1910–84) father drove the city's water wagon; the fathers of Grien Vann (1888–1977) and Valentin Daniel (1899–1988) were carpenters. The children of these working-class parents became store clerks, salespeople, and bookkeepers, and Grien Vann later moved to Corpus Christi to manage department stores there. Most bought homes in Eagle Pass. M. Riskind, in brief, provided an entry point to the middle class for a significant number of immigrant Mexican families.

48. In a 1995 interview, Morris Riskind indicated that his father frequently recruited Jewish employees from San Antonio to work at the store, and Abraham Leon Seriff (1889–1950) is an example. Seriff was born in Russia and immigrated through New York in 1909. Making his way to Texas, he worked as a salesman in San Antonio, married in Austin in 1918, and was in Eagle Pass working at Riskind's by 1920. His sister, Falla Lapin, was also a member of Eagle Pass's small Jewish community in the 1920s and 1930s. In anecdotes shared later in the memoir, Riskind notes that Seriff left Riskind employment about 1920 and settled with his family in San Antonio. He ran a variety of mercantile businesses of his own and died in San Antonio in 1950. Riskind originally misidentified Seriff by his son's name, Aaron, and I'm grateful to Dr. Suzanne Seriff, Abraham's granddaughter, for confirming his identity so I could correct the error. Morris Riskind interview.

    In describing Albino Diaz (1896–1983) merely as a store employee, Riskind oddly overlooks the fact that he was also a relative—the husband of Riskind's cousin Bessie Schrager. Diaz was born in Múzquiz, Coahuila, in 1907 and entered the United States at Eagle Pass to become a permanent resident in 1929. He and Bessie married the same year, suggesting a prior relationship. They had two children together, one of whom died early, and the marriage apparently failed. Both remarried, Diaz to Constancia Miranda, an Eagle Pass native and another longtime Riskind employee, in 1942. He died in Eagle Pass in 1983. I could not ascertain the identity of Mr. Karp.

49. Emeterio Daniel (1873–1948). Riskind gives Daniel, whose first name he recalls as Demetrio, a more detailed profile in chapter 9.

50. Federico Hernandez Perez (1888–1960) was born in Mexico but moved at an early age to Eagle Pass with his family. His father, Simon, was a day laborer, as was Federico as a teenager. Perez began working for M. Riskind in the 1920s, first as a clerk, later as a salesman. Riskind describes him again in chapter 12 as one of the store's oldest employees. Perez died in Eagle Pass in 1960.

51. According to Peter Riskind, this unnamed employee "was once arrested for running a house of ill repute," suggesting that Mike Riskind's astute business lessons could be usefully applied to a variety of enterprises.

CHAPTER 3

1. *Leche quemada* ("burnt milk") refers to a variety of caramel-like or praline candies made from cooked milk, often with brown sugar and nuts.

2. The Mexican cowboys called vaqueros were part of a ranching tradition in northern Mexico dating back to the Spanish colonial era. They pioneered methods of handling cattle, horseriding techniques, and apparel that were adopted with little change by Anglo ranchers and cowboys when they began to arrive in South Texas after Texas independence in the middle nineteenth century. Respected for their skill, toughness, and expertise, vaqueros initiated the cowboy traditions that permeate American myth, even if in an Anglo context. See Jack Jackson, "Vaquero," *Handbook of Texas Online*, accessed June 8, 2022, https://www.tshaonline.org/handbook/entries/vaquero; Armando C. Alonzo, *Tejano Legacy: Rancheros and Settlers in South Texas, 1734–1900* (Albuquerque: University of New Mexico Press, 1998).

3. Historians Douglas W. Richmond and Sam W. Haynes, editors of a volume of essays about the Mexican Revolution, confirm this analysis of its significance for both Mexico and the United States: "The Mexican Revolution is one of the seminal chapters in the history of Mexico. More than any other single event, the revolution was responsible for creating the modern Mexican nation-state by contributing to a greater degree

of democratization, land reform, anticlericalism, and other far-reaching changes in Mexican society. In addition, the civil war, which began in 1910 and lasted more than a decade, had a profound impact on formal and informal relations between the United States and Mexico." Douglas W. Richmond and Sam W. Haynes, preface to *Mexican Revolution*, vii.

4. Former general Porfirio Díaz served as president of Mexico (with brief interruptions) from 1876 until he was ousted in the Mexican Revolution in 1911. The era, known as the Porfiriato, was characterized by Díaz's authoritarian style, the relative stability of his governance, the influence and power of economic elites, and his cozy relationship with American corporations that invested heavily in Mexico's economic development and became significant owners of Mexican property. Historian Josefina Zoraida Vázquez confirms Riskind's monetary recollection, noting that "the peso and dollar were equivalent until 1895." Josefina Zoraida Vázquez, "War and Peace with the United States," in *The Oxford History of Mexico*, ed. William Beezley and Michael Meyer (New York: Oxford University Press, 2010), 324.

5. Soon after the Mexican Revolution began in 1910, Francisco "Pancho" Villa, the Durango-born son of farm workers, joined the military force of Francisco Madero in his effort to overthrow the long regime of Porfirio Díaz. A brilliant and charismatic leader, Villa contributed greatly to the capture of Ciudad Juárez in spring 1911, which through neighboring El Paso gave the rebels access to American goods and weapons and helped secure Madero's victory. When Madero in turn was overthrown by General Victoriano Huerta in 1913 with covert backing from the United States, Villa, who had become the governor of Chihuahua, joined with Coahuila governor Venustiano Carranza in leading an uprising against Huerta, whom they drove from power in June 1914. In their grappling to succeed Huerta, however, a civil war erupted between the two generals, throughout which Carranza held the advantage. The Woodrow Wilson administration granted de facto recognition to Carranza as Mexico's president in October 1915, which became formal after the ratification of the 1917 Mexican constitution and Carranza's popular election. With Carranza ascendant, Villa lost control of Ciudad Juárez in December 1915, whatever claim he once had to political legitimacy dissolved, and he spent the remainder of his life, until his 1923 assassination, engaged in various forms of banditry and provocation of the United States. Fritz L. Hoffman, "Villa, Francisco [Pancho]," *Handbook of Texas Online*, accessed December 22, 2022, https://www.tshaonline.org/handbook/entries/villa-francisco-pancho; Don M. Coerver and Linda B. Hall, *Texas and the Mexican Revolution: A Study in State and National Border Policy, 1910–1920* (San Antonio: Trinity University Press, 1984), 95–97; John Mason Hart, "The Mexican Revolution, 1910–20," in Beezley and Meyer, *Oxford History of Mexico*, 409–36.

Villa issued paper currency bearing his portrait during his time as governor of Chihuahua. Biographer Friedrich Katz explains that the value of revolutionary currencies depended primarily on the confidence of consumers and merchants that the issuer would succeed in their effort to claim or retain power. "When Villa began issuing such money," for example, "American merchants across the border accepted it at a relatively high value, since they were confident that sooner or later Villa would win, and that his currency would then increase in value and be redeemable at par." As Villa's fortunes fell in late 1914, however, and support from the US government became uncertain, American merchants lost faith in the depreciating paper. Finally, after Villa suffered severe losses against Carranza's army in 1915, "people lost confidence in his currency.... The result was that the Villista peso, which only a few months before had been worth 30 US cents, dropped to 1.5 cents. This led to rapid increases in the prices of all goods, both Mexican and imported. The buying power of Villa's currency reached an all-time low, and many merchants refused to accept it, while workers and soldiers clamored to be paid either in gold or in dollars." The Riskinds were not the only Jewish merchants on the border to express skepticism about Villa's paper money. Adolph Schwartz, owner of the Popular Store in El Paso, who may have had dealings with Villa personally, "was willing to play the game as long as Villa paid his bills," wrote El Paso rabbi and historian Floyd S. Fierman, but he "did not have much faith in Villa's notes or script." Friedrich Katz, *The Life and Times of Pancho Villa* (Stanford: Stanford University Press, 1998), 298, 458, 511; Fierman, *Schwartz Family of El Paso*, 32.

6. Manuel Pérez Treviño, a Coahuila native, was a general in the Mexican federal army, governor of Coahuila, and at one time a contender for president. Riskind describes him in more detail below.

7. Orceneth Samuel Harper (1887–1950), known as Osie, was born in Utopia, Texas, the oldest son of Albert Harper, a cattleman who became the patriarch of a ranching and mercantile dynasty in South Texas and northern Mexico. The family's extensive enterprises also involved Osie's brothers Hite and Paul, whom Riskind mentions elsewhere in the memoir, and several generations of Harper children and grandchildren. In his original manuscript, Riskind spelled Osie's name as "O. C.," no doubt how he heard and imagined it but a mistake I have corrected throughout the text.

8. Octavio Rodolfo Riddle (1910–89); Eduardo W. Riddle (1878–1951).

9. The Chinese Exclusion Act of 1882 barred entry of Chinese laborers into the United States for ten years, a prohibition that later was expanded to include all Chinese and made permanent by subsequent legislation. It is the only piece of American law ever to target an entire ethnic group for exclusion. After its passage, more than sixty thousand Chinese immigrants traveled to Mexico instead and settled in almost every Mexican state. "The exclusion laws of the United States," writes historian Robert Chao Romero, "had the effect of diverting Chinese migration streams to Mexico and resulted in the creation of a new and thriving Chinese diasporic community in North America." The entry of Chinese immigrants was initially encouraged by the government of Porfirio Díaz as part of its effort to modernize the Mexican economy. Many provided agricultural labor, but others became successful landowners, entrepreneurs, and merchants, and by the 1920s, according to Romero, "Chinese merchants developed a monopoly over the grocery and dry goods trade in northern Mexico." Robert Chao Romero, *The Chinese in Mexico, 1882–1940* (Tucson: University of Arizona Press, 2012), 2, 25.

    Ben's father, Wong Foon Chuck, was a conspicuous success, described by Elliott Young as "a well-known merchant, owner of extensive ranch lands, and contractor for mines in San Felipe, Coahuila." Wong immigrated at twelve years old to California before passage of the Chinese Exclusion Act and lived for many years in the American Southwest, where he operated businesses on both sides of the border. He was naturalized as a Mexican citizen. As a wealthy business owner, he was entitled to legal residence in the United States, but American authorities nonetheless arrested him in San Antonio in 1892 for violating the Exclusion Act (which, again, he had not done) and deported him to Mexico. He only grew more prosperous there and continued operating a variety of borderland businesses. According to Young, the "bitter experience of the discriminatory laws in the United States may have prompted Wong to help other Chinese cross the border illegally." He "owned several restaurants along the Mexican International Railroad line, which he used to organize smuggling through El Paso." Wong married a Mexican woman, Cristina Vega Domínguez, in 1895 and had ten children, one of whom, Riskind's friend Ben, was born in 1910 in Piedras Negras. Another brother, Jimmy, is mentioned later in the memoir. Elliott Young, *Alien Nation: Chinese Migration in the Americas from the Coolie Era through World War II* (Chapel Hill: University of North Carolina Press, 2014), 119, 181. See also Elliott Young, "Wong Foon Chuck: Making Home in the Borderlands Between China, the United States and Mexico," in *Forced Out and Fenced In: Immigration Tales from the Field*, ed. Tanya Maria Golash-Boza (New York: Oxford University Press, 2018), 7–20.

10. John A. Bonnet (1838–1917), whose judicial title derives from his two terms in the 1880s as Maverick County judge, the county's chief administrator, was seventy-three years old at the time of the events Riskind recounts. He was born in Prussia in 1838 and immigrated through Galveston with his family in 1845. They made their way to San Antonio, where Bonnet worked as a printer before moving to Georgia and joining the Confederate Army; during the Civil War he was wounded multiple times, including at the battles of Cold Harbor and Antietam. He returned to Texas in 1868 and became tax collector of Bexar County, where his brother was sheriff, and he married and had four children. After the death of his wife, he remarried in 1877 and moved to Eagle Pass, where he opened a general store, later expanded into banking, and was president of the First National Bank of Eagle Pass until 1895. John Henry Brown, *Indian Wars and Pioneers of Texas* (Austin: L. E. Daniell, 1880), 616.

11. Dr. Edith Marguerite Bonnet (1898–1982) was born in Eagle Pass, daughter of Judge Bonnet's son William; she would have been twelve years old at the time of the events she described to Riskind. She graduated from the University of Texas at Austin in 1919 and attended the UT Medical Branch in Galveston, graduating in 1926. She became the first female pediatrics specialist in San Antonio. Dr. Edith Marguerite Bonnet Papers, Portal to Texas History, accessed July 20, 2022, https://texashistory.unt.edu/explore/collections/bonnet/.

12. The Torreón Massacre, the worst ethnic atrocity of the Mexican Revolution, began on May 13, 1911, when forces loyal to revolutionary leader Francisco Madero defeated a small unit of federal troops in Coahuila and occupied the city of Torreón, some 330 miles from Piedras Negras. A week earlier a local Maderista had given a speech condemning the city's six hundred Chinese residents for competing with Mexicans for jobs, hoarding money, and sending it to their families in China. In addition, "he attacked Chinese dominance of the grocery, vegetable, and gardening industries, and called for the expulsion of all Chinese from Mexico." As Maderista troops entered Torreón, a civilian mob rampaged against the Chinese community, "released prisoners from jail, pillaged stores, and attacked inhabitants on the streets." The mob murdered 303 Chinese and 5 Japanese residents. Riskind underplays the extreme risk to the Chuck family personally, whose patriarch, Wong Foon Chuck, was one of the wealthiest men in Coahuila. His properties, businesses, and residences were directly targeted, and "four men were killed in his laundry, nine in his railroad hotel, and thirty-two in his hacienda." Robert Chao Romero describes the massacre of Torreón as "the worst act of violence committed against any Chinese diasporic community of the Americas during the twentieth century," and Elliott Young calls it "the

worst massacre during the entire revolution and the deadliest one-day attack on Chinese in North America ever." Leo M. Dambourges Jacques, "The Chinese Massacre in Torreón (Coahuila) in 1911," *Arizona and the West* 16 (1974): 237, 238, 239–40; Romero, *Chinese in Mexico*, 149; Young, "Wong Foon Chuck," 14.

13. After Victoriano Huerta was deposed as Mexico's president in 1914, conflict erupted over who would replace him. The United States preferred Venustiano Carranza, one of the military leaders behind the overthrow of Huerta, and granted him official recognition in October 1915. Pancho Villa, formerly an ally of Carranza, preferred alternatives who were more radical (and less favorable to the Americans), and engaged in open warfare in northern Mexico against Carranza's supporters. This was the climate in late 1915 when President Woodrow Wilson ordered the delivery of weapons and supplies to *carrancista* fighters through the coastal city of Veracruz and authorized the movement of Mexican troops loyal to Carranza through Texas to Douglas, Arizona. "Carranza brought fresh troops across U.S. territory from as far away as Laredo, Texas, thence through Lordsburg, New Mexico," writes military historian John S. D. Eisenhower. "These troops arrived at the Fifteenth Street station in Douglas and crossed the border immediately into Agua Prieta," a *carrancista* stronghold in Sonora that Villa was threatening. "At a stroke, [the *carrancistas*] jumped from only three thousand men to sixty-five hundred." Villa was soundly defeated in the ensuing fight, securing Carranza's path to the presidency. Hart, "Mexican Revolution," 424; John S. D. Eisenhower, *Intervention! The United States and the Mexican Revolution, 1913–1917* (New York: W. W. Norton, 1995), 191.

14. Álvaro Obregón was a Sonoran general who joined the Carranza cause in 1913 in opposition to President Victoriano Huerta. Seeking to form a constitutional government, Obregón led a force in the Mexican border states alongside Pancho Villa, but after Huerta's fall the generals parted ways when Villa rejected Carranza. In the subsequent civil war, Obregón and Carranza battled revolutionary armies under Villa in the north and Emiliano Zapata in the south. Among Obregón's advantages was his decision to recruit Yaquis native to the border region to join his army on the promise of land when the war was over. Hart, "Mexican Revolution," 426, 443. For the history of the relationship between the Yaqui people and the Mexican government, especially before and during the revolution, see Jeffrey M. Schulze, *"Are We Not Foreigners Here?": Indigenous Nationalism in the Twentieth-Century U.S.–Mexico Borderlands* (Chapel Hill: University of North Carolina Press, 2018), 19–35.

15. Mexican folk songs, called *corridos*, are a crucial aspect of Mexican folk culture and national identity. "Corridos created during the Mexican Revolution," writes Martha I. Chew Sánchez, "were very much a part of the postrevolutionary national project. They were mainly about the qualities of those who fought for social justice and on behalf of the poor, like Emiliano Zapata and Francisco Villa. In a way, these corridos, which were created by *campesinos revolucionarios* [revolutionary rural residents and farmers], were appropriated as part of the national discourse and officialized." Chew writes that many of the songs were later taught in schools, cementing a Mexican national identity in the postrevolutionary era. "La Adelita," notes María Herrera-Sobek, "like 'La Cucaracha,' became one of the most popular musical compositions among revolutionary soldiers. The name Adelita became synonymous with *soldaderas*," female soldiers who joined the revolutionary cause. Herrera-Sobek explains that "La Adelita" was one of a group of songs "reflecting the male-female love relationship in time of war. Most importantly, the women in these corridos are perceived as *soldaderas*." Martha I. Chew Sánchez, *Corridos in Migrant Memory* (Albuquerque: University of New Mexico Press, 2006), 34; María Herrera-Sobek, *The Mexican Corrido: A Feminist Analysis* (Bloomington: Indiana University Press, 1993), 104, 108.

16. Ward Wueste (1907–1992) was not only Riskind's friend and coworker but a relation, married to Riskind's cousin Gladys, the daughter of his uncle Albert. Wueste was born in Eagle Pass and married Gladys Riskind in 1930; they had three children. As Riskind notes elsewhere, Wueste operated a service station in Eagle Pass until he went to work at the Riskind store under Morris's management in the 1950s.

17. Riskind is correct in the outlines, but the Plan de San Diego did not actually originate in the South Texas town that bears its name, nor was it primarily inspired by resentment toward the Texas Rangers, although no doubt their unjustified violence fueled support for the plan among Tejanos. In fact it was written in Monterrey, Nuevo León, and signed there by incarcerated supporters of ousted president Victoriano Huerta in a strategem to return him to power. They called for "war without quarter" against the United States with the express goal of winning the independence of Texas, New Mexico, Arizona, Colorado, and California. The plan called further for the formation of a "Liberating Army of Races and People" comprised of Black, Mexican, and Japanese troops to lead the fight; white males over sixteen years old would all be subject to summary execution. Later revisions of the plan pledged social revolution throughout the American Southwest and the return of Native American land in Oklahoma.

Never a well-organized or effective movement, the plan nonetheless inspired multiple raids across the border into Texas between July and October 1915, which caused the deaths of twenty-one Americans. Worse than the raids, however, was the indiscriminate backlash against Mexican Texans suspected of being involved in the attacks or targeted in vengeance. "As a sign of things to come," writes historian Andrew Hernández, "there was a significant exodus from the region as thousands of *tejanos* fled into Mexico to escape as Texas Rangers and groups of vigilantes retaliated against them, confiscated weapons, and forced them off of their land." On October 2, "the first mass execution of Mexican-Americans was reported," likely by Rangers, evidence of a "climate of fear generated by a purported war without quarter [that] led Anglo-Americans to take their first steps towards reprisals conducted by perpetrators who weren't necessarily concerned about clearly differentiating between bandits and bystanders of the same ethnicity." Andrew Hernández, "'They Will Bring Trouble upon Themselves': The Plan de San Diego and the Question of Hispanic Loyalty in Texas," *Journal of South Texas* 31 (Spring 2018): 82, 86; Don M. Coerver, "Plan of San Diego," *Handbook of Texas Online*, accessed October 19, 2022, https://www.tshaonline.org/handbook/entries/plan-of-san-diego. See also Charles H. Harris III and Louis R. Sadler, *The Plan de San Diego: Tejano Rebellion, Mexican Intrigue* (Lincoln: University of Nebraska Press, 2013); Benjamin Heber Johnson, *Revolution in Texas: How a Forgotten Rebellion and Its Bloody Suppression Turned Mexicans into Americans* (New Haven: Yale University Press, 2003).

18. A strong anticlerical impulse had existed in Mexican government since soon after independence from Spain, culminating in laws in the 1850s prohibiting church involvement in political affairs. Porfirio Díaz, who first assumed power in 1876, allowed these restrictions to lapse and made the church a cornerstone of his authoritarian regime. Thus revolutionists seeking to overthrow the Porfiriato viewed Catholic clergy as integral to the establishment they opposed and sought again to limit their power. Beginning in 1914, large numbers of clergy fled from Mexico to escape revolutionary persecution: American Catholic media, notes David A. Badillo, "reported claims from Mexican nuns that revolutionists had burned statues of saints and confessionals in public squares and shot or otherwise violated numerous church officials." Badillo further observes that ultimately "hundreds of priests, mostly Spaniards, along with dozens of Mexican-born bishops, often disguised as Mexican peasants to evade the authorities, slipped across the border to El Paso or San Antonio, where they often took menial jobs to survive." American Catholics organized and raised funds to support refugee clergy. Most of the refugees returned to Mexico when a new constitution was ratified in 1917 and the violence calmed, but some remained in the United States and contributed to the development of Catholic communities in cities like San Antonio. Fearful of losing clergy to their northern neighbor, ecclesiastical authorities in Mexico urged refugees to seek safety nearby in Texas, where they would be more likely to return when the crisis passed. David A. Badillo, "Between Alienation and Ethnicity: The Evolution of Mexican-American Catholicism in San Antonio, 1910–1940," *Journal of American Ethnic History* 16 (Summer 1997): 67–68.

19. St. Joseph's Convent was probably built in the 1880s, preceding the Mexican Revolution by several decades, but it was located at the site Riskind remembers on Ceylon and Church Streets. The convent operated a school, and a church was also on the site in a separate building. Both were torn down in the early 1970s and Our Lady of Refuge built at the same location. Jeff Taylor Sr., telephone conversation with Bryan E. Stone, February 25, 2023; Jeff Taylor Sr., email message to Bryan E. Stone, March 1, 2023.

20. Beginning in 1918, and likely exacerbated by the diffusion of World War I soldiers back to their home countries, the global influenza pandemic recurred intermittently until at least 1920 and affected hundreds of millions of people, some fifty million of whom died. The casualties included about seven hundred thousand Americans. See John M. Barry, *The Great Influenza: The Epic Story of the Deadliest Plague in History* (New York: Penguin Books, 2005).

21. Smarting from US recognition of Carranza, Villa's depredations against American citizens increased, including attacks on American mine operators in Mexico whose safety Carranza had guaranteed. Riskind is likely referencing an incident in January 1916 when Villista soldiers stopped a train at Santa Isabel, Chihuahua, carrying sixteen American mine workers and engineers who had been granted safe passage by Carranza but not by Villa. Villa's men took the group from the train and executed them. Although Villa was a popular folk hero, Riskind may exaggerate the likelihood of his ever becoming president. Hart, "Mexican Revolution," 431; Don M. Coerver, "'Wire Me Before Shooting': Federalism in (In)Action—The Texas–Mexico Border during the Revolution, 1910–1920," in Richmond and Haynes, *Mexican Revolution*, 47.

22. Arnold Schwartz (1923–1976) was the son of Eagle Pass businessman and civic leader Sam Schwartz, who owned the Aztec Theater next door to Riskind's. Sam's uncle, Adolph Schwartz (1866–1941), was the first in the family to arrive in Texas. He immigrated from Hungary in 1883, traveled widely around the United States, began a retail business in Ciudad Juárez, then moved it to El Paso in 1897. The success of his first business there, a department store called the Fair, attracted a large group of relatives who joined him in expanding the family's activities in El Paso. With a group of partners, Adolph founded the Popular Dry Goods Store in 1902,

which grew into a regional institution. At its peak in the 1950s, the downtown Popular Store was "the largest department store between Denver, Fort Worth and Los Angeles," occupied a six-story building of more than two hundred thousand square feet, and had more than one thousand employees. Fierman, *Schwartz Family of El Paso*; "Popular Dry Goods Co. Organized in 1902; Founders Double as Salesmen," *El Paso Herald-Post*, April 28, 1956.

23. Early in the morning of March 9, 1916, Pancho Villa led a force of 450 men across the Rio Grande to attack the town of Columbus, New Mexico, a trading village with a neighboring army post. The raiders killed seventeen soldiers and civilians and burned and looted several buildings. American troops defended the town, chased the raiders back into Mexico, and exacted a heavy toll of at least seventy-five dead. The raid initiated a harsh American response: the formation of the Punitive Expedition under the command of General John Pershing that pursued Villa and his men inside Mexico for almost a year, and nearly brought the two countries to war.

    There are multiple theories regarding Villa's motives for the raid. It was one of many incidents of increasing violence between Villa and the American government following formal recognition of Carranza, and it was an extension of continuous border raids in the wake of the Plan de San Diego. But the idea Riskind presents, that it was rooted in a personal grievance between Villa and a Columbus storekeeper, is a recurrent theme. John Mason Hart claims that one of Villa's objectives was "revenge on two American arms dealers who had accepted money from Villista representatives but not delivered the goods," although Hart does not identify the dealers. Aligning with Riskind's account, Stacey Ravel Abarbanel identifies her grandfather, Sam Ravel, as the Jewish merchant in question. "Numerous accounts repeat a rumor that Villa had paid for, but never received, weapons from Sam," writes Abarbanel. "Others contend that Sam sold faulty weapons to Villa, or that Sam had ceased selling goods to Villa because the revolutionary leader's fluctuating currency was valueless." Abarbanel recounts that Ravel was in El Paso on the day of the attack but that Villista raiders ransacked his house looking for him and burned the Commercial Hotel, which he owned. Abarbanel also notes, however, that members of the Ravel family deny any connection to Villa, and historians have failed to find evidence that Ravel was a target of the raid. Hernández, "'They Will Bring Trouble upon Themselves,'" 90; Hart, "Mexican Revolution," 431; Stacey Ravel Abarbanel, "Pancho Villa and My Grandfather," *Tablet*, August 26, 2019, accessed June 19, 2024, https://www.tabletmag.com/sections/community/articles/pancho-villa-and-my-grandfather.

24. Clifford Irving's novel *Tom Mix and Pancho Villa* was published in 1982. It is a fictional account of the Western film star joining the Villistas in 1913, serving on Villa's personal staff, and participating in many adventures before leaving Mexico to begin his film career. Edwin B. Burgess, Review of *Tom Mix and Pancho Villa* by Clifford Irving, *Library Journal*, May 15, 1982.

25. William Hollis Fitch (1905–1989) was born in Piedras Negras to American parents, Walter O. (1880–1962) and Elizabeth Hollis Fitch (1884–1932). Educated at the University of the South in Sewanee, Tennessee, Fitch returned to Eagle Pass and ran a drugstore for many years. He died in 1989 and is buried in the Maverick County Cemetery. The grandfather who reportedly owned a share of the International Bridge was William A. Fitch (1853–1934).

26. Molly Riskind (1889–1986) was born in Russia and immigrated to Chicago with her mother and siblings in 1890. In 1907 she married Philip Schwartz (1888–1955), a garment worker born in St. Paul, Minnesota, and they moved into a building next door to Molly's older brother Aaron and his family; a son, Joseph, was born in 1909. In 1920, as Riskind explains, they moved to Eagle Pass to work in her family's businesses, and in 1937 they struck out on their own for Waco, where Philip opened Home Furniture Exchange, which he operated until his death. Nothing in the available record explains what "escapades" Riskind refers to here. Their son Joseph (1909–1983) lived with his parents in Eagle Pass from 1920 to 1937, moved with them to Waco, and lived out his life there. He married Galveston native Edith Tannenbaum (1914–1998), had two daughters, and died in 1983. Like his parents, he is buried in the Agudath Jacob Cemetery in Waco.

27. Not a reference to the fruit liqueurs known by the same name, in Yiddish-speaking households a *schnaps* could be any intoxicating drink, often brandy or whiskey, used for making toasts or celebrating special occasions. The traditional Yiddish toast is "*L'chaim*," "To life," even though the words are actually Hebrew.

28. This appears to be a reference to the Magonista Rebellion of 1911, although it was not centered in Coahuila. The rebellion took place in Baja California and involved the brief seizure by rebels of the cities of Mexicali and Tijuana. Ricardo Flores Magón, an anarchist journalist acting from exile in San Antonio, led the Liberal Party of Mexico (PLM), which Lawrence D. Taylor writes had "transformed itself into a movement with anarchist objectives which sought to effect a thoroughgoing transformation of the Mexican economy and society." The heir to extensive family landholdings in northern Mexico, Francisco Madero led the uprising against Porfirio Díaz that constituted the first phase of the Mexican Revolution and assumed power as president in November

1911. He was never able to consolidate power, however, and was deposed in a coup by General Victoriano Huerta and assassinated in February 1913. Lawrence D. Taylor, "The Magonista Revolt in Baja California," *Journal of San Diego History 45* (Winter 1999).

29. Beginning at the outbreak of hostilities early in the Mexican Revolution, residents of the Mexican border states sought safety on the American side of the Rio Grande. "Thousands of refugees were pouring across the border in response to war conditions in northern Mexico," write Linda Hall and Don Coerver. "It was not unusual for an entire town to cross the border en masse either before or during military clashes in the area." Indeed, in October 1913, they confirm, citing a report by the US Commissioner General of Immigration, "eight thousand inhabitants of Piedras Negras abandoned the town just ahead of a force that was about to attack the city, crossed the line, and entered Eagle Pass, Texas. . . . Despite 'heroic efforts by the Marine Hospital Service and the Army' to prevent them from 'scattering aimlessly over the country,' it proved impossible to keep them together and return them to Mexico." Hall and Coerver, *Revolution on the Border*, 131.

30. Maximilian I, a Habsburg puppet of Napoleon III, reigned as emperor of the Second Mexican Empire from 1864 until his execution in 1867.

31. Napoleon Bonaparte defeated Spain in 1808 and compelled Ferdinand VII to abdicate in favor of the emperor's brother Joseph. There was widespread support for the deposed monarch throughout the Spanish empire, and unrest in Mexico provided an opportunity for long-simmering resentments among *criollos*—those born in Spanish America to Spanish-born parents—to form an independence movement. *Criollos* had been deprived of full participation in government under Spanish rule, which favored *peninsulares*, those born in Spain. Father Miguel Hidalgo de Costilla, a parish priest in Querétaro, organized armed resistance to Spanish dominance, leading a force comprised of *criollos*, Indigenous people, and mixed-race supporters, each of whom had their own reasons to oppose *peninsular* dominance. "The insurgent forces were also made up of many of those lacking a place in the social structure of the viceroyalty," writes Virginia Guedea, "those living on its fringes, and individuals of all sorts who imposed on the armed movement their own peculiar disorder and anarchy." After just six months of armed rebellion, Hidalgo was captured, defrocked, and executed in March 1811. Despite this failure, transfer of power from *peninsulares* to *criollos* was achieved in the independence movement of 1821. Virginia Guedea, "The Old Colonialism Ends, The New Colonialism Begins," in Beezley and Meyer, *Oxford History of Mexico*, 275; Jesús "Frank" de la Teja, "Mexican War of Independence," *Handbook of Texas Online*, accessed December 24, 2022, https://www.tshaonline.org/handbook/entries/mexican-war-of-independence.

32. One of the hallmarks of the Porfiriato, the long reign of Porfirio Díaz, was the president's encouragement of foreign investment in Mexico. "Foreign capital provided the impetus for growth," writes John Mason Hart. "By 1900, foreign investors held some 90 percent of the incorporated value of Mexican industry; Americans alone held 70 percent. Foreigners also held 150 million of Mexico's 485 million acres. Again, the Americans had the largest share among foreigners, with 130 million acres." Thus Riskind is correct about foreign control of Mexican resources becoming a motive for revolution, but he underplays the dominance of American, rather than Spanish, capital. Hart, "Mexican Revolution," 411.

33. *Criollos* were people born in Spanish America to Spanish-born parents, *peninsulares* those born in Spain. Although the two groups were legally equal under Spanish rule, there was a distinct difference in how they were treated in terms of political power and religious authority. *Gachupines*, or "spurred ones," was a derogatory term applied to *peninsulares*, as Richard Grabman explains: "Originally a Náhuatl word referring to the spur on a fighting cock—by analogy, applied to the spurs a horseman wears—it became a rude term for the Spanish overlords: orginally the only people who could ride a horse, and who wore spurs. It is still used to mean an overbearing, foreign, Spanish-speaking twit, especially a Spaniard." Richard Grabman, *Gods, Gachupines and Gringos: A People's History of Mexico* (Albuquerque: Editorial Mazatlán, 2009), 6–7.

34. Despite a promise to cede power in 1909, the long-ruling Porfirio Díaz claimed a seventh term in office, prompting opponents, including revolutionary leader Francisco Madero, to form the National Anti-Reelection Party. Madero won in 1911 on a platform of "effective suffrage and no reelection." The slogan remained potent even after Madero's assassination and the failed and overthrown regime of Victoriano Huerta, and the principle of limited, single-term governance was enshrined in the Constitution of 1917, "arguably the most progressive charter in the world" at that time. Accordingly Venustiano Carranza, the first president elected under the new constitution, served just one term (1917–1920), as did his successor, Álvaro Obregón (1920–24). Plutarco Calles, minister of the interior under Obregón, won election and served until 1928. Over the next six years, as Calles stubbornly retained power despite officially leaving office, "the country saw three presidents wrestle politically with the strongman Calles." These were Emilio Portes Gil (1928–1930), Pascual Ortiz Rubio (1930–1932), and Abelardo Rodríguez (1932–1934). Residents of Mexico City were said to joke of the president's residence at Chapultepec Castle that "the president lives here, but the man who

gives the orders lives across the street," *calle* being the Spanish word for "street." As the presidential election of 1934 approached to replace the outgoing Rodríguez, Calles narrowed his choice for a nominee to two loyal generals, Manuel Pérez Treviño and Lázaro Cárdenas. "Of the two," writes Jürgen Buchenau, "Pérez Treviño more closely followed Calles's political views, and he had been mentioned as a possible candidate for interim president after the assassination of Obregón. A veteran *obregonista* [and] former president of the PNR ... Pérez Treviño appeared to enjoy the inside track for the nomination." Buchenau offers a different explanation than Riskind for why the choice settled on Cárdenas instead: Rodríguez, the outgoing president, "loathed Pérez Treviño, a former rival for the affections of the woman who was now his wife, and hence supported an alternative," a preference to which Calles acceded. Thomas Benjamin, "Rebuilding the Nation," in Beezley and Meyer, *Oxford History of Mexico*, 441, 447–48; Jürgen Buchenau, "From the *Caudillo* to Tata Lázaro: The *Maximato* in Perspective, 1928–1934," in Richmond and Haynes, *Mexican Revolution*, 153.

35. Jacob Kranzthor (1857–1935) and his wife, Mary (1863–1943), were born and married in Hungary and emigrated in 1886 with two daughters. Their grandson, William J. Munter, writes that they settled first in the West Texas mining town of Shafter, where Jacob sold goods provided by his brother Sam, a wholesale dry goods dealer in San Antonio. They relocated briefly to a Mexican mining town, El Oro, returned briefly to Europe, then moved to Purcell in Indian Territory and afterward to Eagle Pass. Jacob opened a dry goods store on Main Street in 1905, the Fair, which he operated until his retirement in 1928, passing its management to his son. Upon retirement, the Kranzthors moved to Los Angeles, where both died. Their daughter Ellen married Sam Schwartz, another pioneering Eagle Pass Jewish merchant. Munter, *History of the Jews of Texas' Middle Corridor*, 8–9; "Jacob Kranzthor Taken by Death," *El Paso Times*, October 15, 1935; "Guarantee Shoe Company Opens New Store Tomorrow," *El Paso Herald-Post*, September 9, 1957.

36. Born in Russia, Herman Brenner (1886–1970) was in Eagle Pass by the time of World War I. He was married but there is no record of his wife's name. She apparently died or the couple divorced, as Herman married again in San Antonio in 1925 to Ida Shapiro (1904–1983), who had immigrated there with her parents in 1908. The couple engaged in a number of ready-to-wear establishments and other ventures in Austin, Fort Worth, and San Antonio. After immigrating from Russia to Rock Island, Illinois, in 1902, Edward Goldburg (1885–1966) married Iowa native Lena Paul (1881–1974), and they had come to Texas by 1912, when their first child was born in Corpus Christi. They were in Eagle Pass operating the store Riskind describes by 1918 and stayed about a decade; by 1934 they were in San Antonio operating a new department store (Riskind says later that they moved to Corpus Christi, but I found no record of that). Both are buried in the Agudas Achim Cemetery in San Antonio. Sam (1882–1971) and Jessie Stark Grossman (1887–1969) were married in Houston in 1909; he immigrated from Austria in 1898, and she was born in Syracuse, New York. They arrived in Eagle Pass around the time of the First World War and ran their store there for about a decade before moving to Corpus Christi, where Sam operated the Economy Booterie, a discount shoe and boot store, until 1946. They relocated again to Houston, where they remained.

Originally from Hungary, the brothers Sam (1890–1958) and Louis Hausman (1888–1978), along with their older brother Adolph (1886–1930), operated the Hausman Brothers Packing Company. William J. Munter writes of the Hausman family: "Louis, Sam, and Adolph Hausman came to Eagle Pass from Vancouver, British Columbia, where they were in the cattle business. Louis Hausman first came to visit Eagle Pass on a cattle buying trip in the early 1900's. In Eagle Pass he did business with a prominent family, the Harpers, who persuaded him to come settle on the border, which he and his two brothers did. They went into the cattle business. Louis married Gabrella, a Hungarian known as Ella, in 1918, to whom he was introduced by my grandfather, Sam Schwartz. Eventually Adolph, Sam and Louis all left Eagle Pass. Louis lived in Laredo from 1922 until the death of his wife in 1940. He then decided to move back to Eagle Pass and went into the meat packing business and other ventures including real estate development and farming." After leaving Eagle Pass, Sam Hausman settled in Corpus Christi, Adolph in Mercedes. I have been unable to identify "Red" Harris. Munter, *History of the Jews of Texas' Middle Corridor*, 15–16.

37. *In drerd gai*, literally "go into the earth." I was unable to identify Mr. Epstein.

38. Max (1888–1954) and Falla (1898–1988) Lapin were both born in Russia; she immigrated in 1921, he in 1922. They married in 1922 and arrived in Eagle Pass by 1930. Riskind may be mistaken about Falla's relationship to Abraham Seriff—her maiden name was not Seriff—but there certainly may have been a family connection that brought the couple to Eagle Pass, where, as Riskind describes below, Lapin went into business with Solomon Libson. The couple's departure for Austin was in about 1944, and they operated a laundry business there until Max's death in 1954. Falla remained in Austin and worked in real estate and property management but later moved to Bowie, Maryland, where her daughter lived and where she died in 1988. Solomon Libson (1891–1957), born in Vitebsk, Russia, and Eloisa Maldonado (1902–1989), born in Monclova, Coahuila,

were married in Piedras Negras in 1921. As described below, they lived in Eagle Pass, where they raised four children, and Solomon ran a fruit business with Max Lapin on both sides of the border. The Libsons apparently remained a mixed-faith family: when Solomon died in 1957, he was buried in Agudas Achim Cemetery in San Antonio under a headstone bearing a Star of David and a Hebrew inscription; Eloisa is buried in Our Lady of Refuge Cemetery in Eagle Pass beneath an image of the Virgin Mary. Falla G. Lapin obituary, *Austin American-Statesman*, July 10, 1988.

39. The Mikulisnkys were close friends of the Riskinds, and Morris has much more to say about them elsewhere in the memoir. There's a Mikulinski Road in Eagle Pass named for them, even if spelled differently. Owsey Mikulinsky (1892–1968) was born in Russia and married Tanya (or Traina, 1897–1980) in Minsk in 1923. Their son, Sam, was born in Minsk in 1925. As Riskind describes in chapter 8, Owsey fled to Mexico that year and established himself as a peddler in the area around Rosita, about sixty miles southwest of Eagle Pass. After Tanya and Sam joined him there, they remained in Mexico until 1938, when they made the move to Eagle Pass. Owsey worked in various occupations, including farming, until his death in 1968. He was buried in Pittsburgh, Pennsylvania, where Sam was then living; Tanya lived until 1980, moved to Pittsburgh to live with Sam, and was buried alongside her husband in Rodef Shalom Cemetery. Sam Mukulinsky (later Sam Michaels) attended Texas A&M University, lived in New York where he married in 1939, then relocated to Pittsburgh.

Ira (or Isidore, 1892–1974) and Helen Goldstein Morgenstern (1903–1971) were married in Brooklyn in 1937; he was born in Poland, she in New York. They lived briefly in San Antonio, then in Rosita, Coahuila, and crossed into the United States at Eagle Pass in 1939. Ira was the owner of a Philco electronics and radio shop.

40. In a 1995 interview, Morris explained that the company, based in Piedras Negras, was called the California Fruit Company because the produce they sold was grown in California then shipped through northern Mexico to Piedras Negras and across the river back into the United States. Morris Riskind interview.

41. The laws Riskind refers to, preventing non-Mexican citizens from owning land in Mexico, were probably related to a revolutionary backlash against US and other foreign-owned investment in the country. The Constitution of 1917, enacted as a consequence of the Mexican Revolution, "drastically restricted the rights of foreigners in Mexico," according to historian Friedrich Katz, "and under certain circumstances made their holdings subject to confiscation." Katz, *Secret War in Mexico*, 569.

42. This was the Guarantee Shoe Store. Aron Emanuel (Manny) Schwartz (1899–1977), born in Hungary, arrived in New York in 1920 and joined his family and the constellation of Schwartz businesses in Texas, opening the Guarantee in Eagle Pass. After several years Manny closed the store, moved to El Paso, married Ethel Robbins in 1974, and worked in the insurance business. He's buried in the B'nai Zion Cemetery in El Paso. Nandor Neuman (1903–1991) was born in Czechoslovakia and arrived in the United States in 1921. He worked as a salesman in El Paso, ran the Texas Furniture Company in Del Rio with partner Mack Goldberg, then joined Manny Schwartz in operating the Guarantee Shoe Store in Eagle Pass. When Neuman petitioned for citizenship in 1927, his uncle Sam Schwartz stood as his witness. He married Eagle Pass native Bessie Williams (1908–1985) in 1940 at the home of Rabbi David Jacobson in San Antonio, and the couple is buried next to Morris and Ruth Riskind in Eagle Pass's small Jewish cemetery, although Bessie's headstone bears the image of a cross.

43. Theodore Greenberg (1912–2008) was born in Buffalo and grew up in nearby Jamestown, New York. His father was a tailor; both of his parents immigrated from Russia in the middle 1910s. Ted was in San Antonio by 1935, where he met and married Gertrude Briskman (1912–1969), whose family, originally from Russia by way of New York, had been in the city since 1914. By 1940 the couple was in Eagle Pass, where Ted established Western Auto on Main Street near the Riskind store. The couple raised two children there, Larry and Billy. Gertrude died in 1969 and was buried in the Agudas Achim Cemetery in San Antonio with her parents, who were members of that congregation. Ted died in North Carolina in 2008.

44. Benjamin (1913–1986) and Faye Entner Levine (1921–2013) were both originally from the Northeast. Ben was born in Jersey City and became a poultry farmer in New York State before serving in World War II. Faye was born and raised in Peekskill, New York. After marrying in 1945, the couple moved to Eagle Pass in 1947 where, as Riskind describes, Ben engaged in farming and ranching while Faye ran the Pan American Fabrics shop in town. They remained in Eagle Pass for more than fifty years and raised their three sons there. After Ben's death in 1986, Faye relocated to Houston. They are both buried in the Beth Yeshurun Cemetery in Houston.

Improbably, there were *two* Jewish men named Bennie Spiegal (or Spiegel) living in Eagle Pass at the same time. This Bennie Spiegal (1905–1984) was born in Poland and was active in South Texas dry goods businesses by World War II, probably traveling frequently, and never married. It's unclear when Riskind wrote this passage, but Spiegal died in Eagle Pass in 1984, earlier than Riskind indicates here. The other Bennie Spiegel is mentioned in chapter 10. I've been unable to identify the Bargs, Pimentelli, or Herzberg. Barg is

one of two Holocaust survivors Riskind says lived in Eagle Pass; the other, Spiller, is mentioned in chapter 13.
45. The High Holidays (or High Holy Days) are the sacred days of Rosh Hashanah, Yom Kippur, and the period between them. Rosh Hashanah, the Jewish New Year, is the first day of the Hebrew month of Tishri, corresponding to September or October. Yom Kippur, the Day of Atonement, is the most sacred event in the Jewish calendar, a twenty-four-hour period of fasting and prayer that occurs ten days after Rosh Hashanah. Many Jews who don't regularly attend services throughout the year are inclined to attend on these days, accounting for the overflow Riskind describes. The Knights of Columbus Hall at the corner of Adams and Ford is still in use. The Marquez Grocery building still stands across the street but is not in use.
46. Galician Jews (*Galitzianers*) were from a region of southeastern Poland and northwestern Ukraine. In their long-standing rivalry, Lithuanian Jews (*Litvaks*) considered *Galitzianers* to be overly emotional and anti-intellectual, a view related to the prevalence of Hasidism in the region. In contrast, Galicians viewed *Litvaks* as cold, reactionary, and pedantic.
47. Originally sold in 1885 as a treatment for catarrh, Peruna was a patent medicine later offered as an all-purpose panacea. In 1906, journalist Samuel Hopkins Adams exposed the product, which had become massively popular, as a quack medicine containing 28 percent alcohol. Abraham Seriff is described in chapter 2. Lena Sebakijje, "Research Guides: Catarrh Remedy and Peruna Scandal: Topics in Chronicling America: Introduction," accessed October 19, 2022, https://guides.loc.gov/chronicling-america-peruna-scandal-catarrh-remedy/introduction.

CHAPTER 4

1. William Stanley Chichester (1908–1982) was born in Eagle Pass, married Harlingen native Willa Mae Perkins in 1937, and lived most of his life in San Antonio, where he was a grocer. His father, John William Chichester (1875–1937) was born in Washington, DC, and moved with his parents to San Antonio. In 1910, the US Census recorded him at Amakarak Island, Alaska, working for the North American Commercial Company. By 1920, he was married and raising his children in Eagle Pass, where he worked as an electrician.
2. This is Charles Wesley Hartup (1840–1937), the father of Willie's mother, and he did indeed fight in the Civil War from 1861 to 1864, but Riskind puts him in the wrong army. Hartup was born in Wayne County, Indiana, and served in the Nineteenth Indiana Infantry. He moved to Texas after the war, was in Eagle Pass with his wife and daughter by 1900, and is buried in the Maverick County Cemetery.
3. Webb's coverage of King Fisher is described in chapter 2.
4. Florencio Meza (or Mesa) (1881–1973) was born in Zacatecas, Mexico, and died in Eagle Pass.
5. Best known for the adventure serial *The Perils of Pauline* (1914), Pearl White enjoyed brief international fame but was unable to translate it into a lasting film career. Jim Beaver, "Pearl White," IMDb, accessed July 20, 2022, http://www.imdb.com/name/nm0925310/bio.
6. The Hasid, or the Pious One, is the Baal Shem Tov, the founder of Hasidism. A story often told of him, though in various versions, regards his becoming stranded in Constantinople with his daughter in the course of an attempt to reach Jerusalem. Arriving in the city the evening before Passover, his daughter was worried they would have nothing for their Pesach meal. "God will provide for us," he responded. In one version of the legend, the next morning, still without matzah or wine, his daughter met a wealthy man who invited them to his home, fed them, and became deeply impressed by his guest's obvious holiness. Needless to say, Mrs. Riskind makes this reference with a deep sense of irony. Yitzhak Buxbaum, *The Light and Fire of the Baal Shem Tov* (New York: Continuum, 2006), 132–34.
7. *Birth of a Nation* (1915), a paean to the Ku Klux Klan, and *Intolerance* (1916), a sweeping historical epic covering events from the fall of Babylon to the present, were the two most successful and influential silent films by pioneering American director D. W. Griffith. All of Griffith's films, but *Intolerance* in particular, were renowned for their large casts, massive sets, and grandiose scene design. Elmo Lincoln was a popular stage and screen actor who appeared in more than a hundred films, including four directed by Griffith. Michael Kaminsky, "D. W. Griffith Biography," IMDb, accessed June 19, 2023, https://www.imdb.com/name/nm0000428/bio/?ref_=nm_ov_bio_sm; IMDb, "Elmo Lincoln (1889–1952)," accessed June 19, 2023, https://www.imdb.com/name/nm0511104/bio/?ref_=nm_ov_bio_sm.
8. Charles J. Pilgrim (1909–1983) later worked for Dallas Power & Light; Fred F. Pilgrim (1911–1987) worked at a car dealership in Brownsville.
9. Minnie Hielscher Pilgrim (1887–1952) was born and died in Eagle Pass. Her father, Charles Hielscher (1861–1958) lived many years in Eagle Pass and died in Fredericksburg, Texas. Charles F. Pilgrim (1890–1947) was born in Montreal and died in Eagle Pass.

10. Dr. Van Earl McFarland appears in chapter 5. US Air Force Major General Homer I. "Pete" Lewis (1919–2015) was born in Asheville, North Carolina, moved to Texas in 1932, and entered the US Naval Academy in 1938. He served in Europe during World War II, then moved to Eagle Pass in 1950 to pursue farming, ranching, and retail enterprises. He remained active in the Air Force Reserves until he retired in 1975 and continued living in Eagle Pass until his death in 2015. Obituary, "Homer I. 'Pete' Lewis," *San Antonio Express-News*, October 27, 2015.
11. Peter John Luderus (1872–1934) was born in Fredericksburg, Texas, to parents who were German immigrants. He worked as a baker in San Antonio until the 1910s, when he moved with his wife and children to Eagle Pass, where he operated a bakery and what the US Census calls a "poultry house." He is buried in the Maverick County Cemetery.
12. Dr. Evan Shelby Easton (1875–1951) was born in Austin, served in the Texas infantry in Cuba during the Spanish-American War, and was in medical practice in Eagle Pass by 1910, where he remained until the late 1920s. As Riskind notes below, Easton's life after Eagle Pass was unhappy. He lost a leg in a railroad accident, and his marriage failed (or his wife died; records differ) by 1929. He spent four years in a residential veterans' hospital in South Dakota, and then lived alone in Southern California until his death in 1951. He is buried in the Veterans Administration Cemetery in Los Angeles.
13. Abe Edelstein died of tuberculosis on December 29, 1933, but he was a resident of a hospital in San Antonio, not Denver.
14. Ellen Williams (1869–?), identified in the census as a school teacher, and her husband, Joseph (1866–?), a railroad worker, were longtime residents of Eagle Pass, arriving there from San Antonio in the late 1890s. They had four children. For background on the separation of enslaved families and their efforts to reunite after emancipation, see Heather Andrea Williams, *Help Me to Find My People: The African American Search for Family Lost in Slavery* (Chapel Hill: University of North Carolina Press, 2012).
15. Although public education, as opposed to parochial or private school, was the preferred path for Mexican American children in Texas, in 1900 only 18 percent of Tejano children were enrolled in public schools. When they attended, furthermore, they were segregated by race. "At first, segregation was confined to the elementary grades, because of the high withdrawal rates of Mexican children," writes historian Guadalupe San Miguel. "When these children sought secondary schooling, officials established segregated facilities in these grades." The quality of the Latino schools, furthermore, was decidedly inferior: "The buildings generally were older and dilapidated, recreation space was minimal and substandard, and school equipment was inadequate," San Miguel writes. "Expenditures per pupil in the Hispanic schools were extremely low. The teaching staff lacked training, credentials, and experience." A series of midcentury Supreme Court decisions, including *Del Rio ISD v. Salvatierra* (1930), which demonstrated the inferior quality of Hispanic schools, and *Delgado v. Bastrop ISD* (1948), which prohibited the segregation of Mexican American children, catalyzed a move toward greater equity and access to education for Tejanos. Guadalupe San Miguel, "Mexican Americans and Education," *Handbook of Texas Online*, accessed January 2, 2023, https://www.tshaonline.org/handbook/entries/mexican-americans-and-education.
16. Students from Piedras Negras could attend school in Eagle Pass, but they were required to pay tuition for the privilege. This was a practice that continued into the twenty-first century. See Karla Adelina Garza and M. R. Graham, "Eagle Pass High School," *American Educational History Journal* 47 (2020): 188.
17. The daughter of South Texas farmers, Dena (or Rhoda Hardena) Kelso (1867–1955) married Charles Graves in Maverick County in 1890 and they had two children. Charles died in 1898 at just thirty-five years old, and Mrs. Graves never remarried. (Riskind appears mistaken about her superintendent husband.) She remained in Eagle Pass for the rest of a long teaching career, retired there, and is buried in the Maverick County Cemetery. An elementary school in Eagle Pass is named after her.
18. Shabbat is the Jewish day of rest, the Sabbath, beginning at sunset on Friday evening and continuing until sunset on Saturday.
19. The first modern children's encyclopedia, *The Book of Knowledge* was produced by Englishman Arthur Mee, published in Britain in 1910 as *The Children's Encyclopaedia*, then published under its American name in the United States in 1912. According to *Encylopaedia Britannica*, its "contents comprised vividly written and profusely illustrated articles." It remained in print in multiple editions for decades. Riskind refers to it again in chapter 10. Robert L. Collison, "Encyclopaedia: The Kinds of Encyclopaedias," *Encylopaedia Britannica*, accessed October 29, 2022, https://www.britannica.com/topic/encyclopaedia/The-kinds-of-encyclopaedias.
20. An older institution, the Eagle Pass Public School, was built about 1909 on Madison Street across from San Juan Plaza; its cornerstone is now at the Fort Duncan Museum. It was replaced about 1917 with the imposing three-story Stephen F. Austin School that Riskind attended, which housed grades one through twelve. As

Riskind recalls, that building was torn down in 1975 and replaced with a newer, modern Stephen F. Austin Elementary School at the same location, which operated until 2011. That building is still in use by the school district. Jeff Taylor Sr., telephone conversation with Bryan E. Stone, February 25, 2023.

21. In an earlier draft of the memoir, Riskind recommended, "to those interested," T. R. Fehrenbach's renowned *Lone Star*, a monumental Texas history first published in 1968. Fehrenbach does indeed acknowledge the Tejano presence among the Texas revolutionaries and at the Alamo, but his anglocentric view of Texas history has long been surpassed by modern studies that give proper attention not only to a Tejano presence but, critically, to settler hostility toward Indigenous Texans and to the pivotal role of slavery in motivating the Texian rebellion. For example, an excellent modern interpretation of the Battle of the Alamo, which delves deeply into the motivations of independence-minded Tejanos (and how they were ultimately betrayed by their white allies), as well as the contested legacy of the battle and the historic site, is Bryan Burrough, Chris Tomlinson, and Jason Stanford, *Forget the Alamo: The Rise and Fall of an American Myth* (New York: Penguin Press, 2021). See also Stephen Harrigan's *Big Wonderful Thing: A History of Texas*, an outstanding and engrossing narrative that grapples effectively with the state's rich ethnic diversity and the stubborn anglocentric myth that none such existed. In addition, Gregg Cantrell and Elizabeth Hayes Turner, eds., *Lone Star Pasts: Memory and History in Texas* (College Station: Texas A&M University Press, 2007) provides an excellent overview of the efforts of professional Texas historians to tell a more complete and accurate story of the state's past.

22. The Supreme Court ruled in *Engel v. Vitale* (1962) that school-sponsored prayer in public schools violates the establishment clause of the First Amendment.

23. Born in 1910 or 1911 in Piedras Negras, James Wong Chuck was one of ten children of Wong Foon Chuck and Cristina Vega Domínguez, who are described in chapter 3. Jimmy's football skill apparently earned him a spot at the University of the South in Sewanee, Tennessee, where he was a student and athlete in 1923 and 1924.

24. Cultural historian Joel Huerta, who has studied high school football in South Texas, notes similar racialized abuse directed at Mexican American players. He writes, for example, of Everardo Lerma, who played for King High School in Kingsville in the early 1930s. "Lerma endured repeated abuse," Huerta writes, primarily from his white teammates who were jealous he claimed athletics scholarships to which they felt entitled. "He was thrown into the pool, his teammates knowing he could not swim. He took cheap shots on the field. And he had to tolerate venomous remarks like 'kill that Mexican!' not from opponents or hecklers, but from certain members of his own team." Joel Huerta, "Friday Night Rights: South Texas High-School Football and the Struggle for Equality," *International Journal of the History of Sport* 26 (June 2009): 989.

25. The Nueces Strip—the region in South and West Texas between the Nueces and Rio Grande—was disputed territory after Texas independence in 1836: Mexico claimed the boundary was at the Nueces, Texas at the Rio Grande, which resulted in a significantly larger Texas Republic. After annexation to the United States, which adopted Texas's view, the dispute supplied a pretext for American provocation of war with Mexico in 1846. American victory and the Treaty of Guadalupe Hidalgo in 1848 established the Rio Grande as the international boundary. Riskind's theory that Mexico could have negotiated a permanent border at the Nueces seems unlikely given the expansionist ambitions of both Texas and the United States.

26. This is Dr. Lea Hume (1875–1939), the brother of Eagle Pass attorney David E. Hume Sr., whom Riskind describes later in the memoir. Dr. Hume was born in Southeast Texas near Houston, studied medicine in Galveston, married, and moved to Eagle Pass to establish a medical practice by 1900. A newspaper report of his death indicates he "was killed when the horse he was riding was struck by a truck." "Nuns Say Prayers at Funeral for Laredo Physician," *El Paso Herald-Post*, August 8, 1939.

27. Devils River runs for ninety-four miles from Sutton County toward the southwest, emptying into the Amistad Reservoir northwest of Del Rio. "The area's generally dark, calcareous, stony clays and clay loams," notes the *Handbook of Texas Online*, "support oak, juniper, grasses, mesquite, and water-tolerant hardwoods and conifers." The river was dammed in 1969 at its confluence with the Rio Grande to create Amistad Reservoir, which provides flood control, irrigation, hydroelectric power, and recreation to the region. The international border now runs through the middle of the lake. "Devils River," *Handbook of Texas Online*, accessed June 21, 2022, https://www.tshaonline.org/handbook/entries/devils-river; "Amistad Reservoir," *Handbook of Texas Online*, accessed June 20, 2022, https://www.tshaonline.org/handbook/entries/amistad-reservoir.

28. Heavy rainfall throughout Texas in April 1922 caused overflows of most of the state's rivers and streams and flooding across the state, although the greatest damage was in the vicinity of Fort Worth. Riskind describes the flood's impact on Eagle Pass in chapter 5.

29. Born in Kalvaria, David Edelstein (1899–1977) was the ninth of ten Edelstein children and the youngest of the siblings to immigrate to the United States. (As Riskind writes later, the youngest brother, Isaac, stayed behind with his father in Lithuania and was murdered by the Nazis.) David traveled to Mexico about 1923

and entered Texas across the International Bridge in Eagle Pass in October 1924. Riskind originally erred in writing that David's store was in Weslaco when in fact it was his brother Eli who operated that branch; David's store was nearby in the town of Mission. David never married, lived the rest of his life in Mission, and died in neighboring McAllen. He is buried with much of his family in the Hebrew Cemetery in Brownsville.

30. The Emergency Quota Act of 1921 limited the number of immigrants from any country to 3 percent of the 1910 population from that country already living in the United States. The 1924 Johnson-Reed Act augmented the restrictions by lowering the quota to 2 percent of the population based on the 1890 census. These restrictions were openly preferential toward Western and Northern Europeans, who received larger quotas, and severely curtailed immigration from Southern and Eastern Europe, where most Jews originated. The extensive but unsuccessful effort by Jewish and Italian Americans to block passage of these acts is described in Maddalena Marinari, *Unwanted: Italian and Jewish Mobilization against Restrictive Immigration Laws, 1882–1965* (Chapel Hill: University of North Carolina Press, 2020).

31. Jacob (Jake) Edelstein (1892–1951) was born in Kalvaria, the sixth of ten Edelstein children. He immigrated in 1908, lived briefly with his brother Abe in San Antonio, then joined Abe, brother Morris, and sister Rachel Riskind in Eagle Pass. Around 1913, when Morris Edelstein left to begin his own furniture business in Brownsville, Jake joined him and worked alongside him in Edelstein's Better Furniture store. He married Sophye Harris in Austin in 1923 and moved to McAllen, where he opened the J. Edelstein furniture store. He and Sophye had one daughter, Betty Jean, born in San Antonio in 1925. He died in 1951. His brother Morris Edelstein is described in chapter 1.

32. Most likely this house was at 2810 Buena Vista Street in San Antonio, the address where Jennie was living when she died in 1925 at the age of forty-one. Jacob (Jack) Schrager (1883–1959) was born in Galicia (sometimes identified as Poland or Austria in official records) and immigrated to the United States about 1895. He met Jennie Riskind in Chicago and married her on January 9, 1910. By 1920, the couple had moved to Mission, Texas, in the lower Rio Grande Valley, where he peddled and later operated a dry goods store. They had two children, Bessie, born in 1911 in Chicago, and Norman, born in 1913 in Laredo. After Jennie's death, Jack returned to the Rio Grande Valley, living in Edinburg until his death in 1959.

33. San Antonio's Orthodox congregation, formed in 1908, is Rodfei Sholom (Seekers of Peace). Its origin and early twentieth-century history is partially described in Gurwitz, *Memories of Two Generations*. See also "San Antonio, Texas," *Encyclopedia of Southern Jewish Communities*, accessed June 20, 2022, https://www.isjl.org/texas-san-antonio-encyclopedia.html.

34. It appears that Morris's grandparents returned to Chicago late in life; they are both buried there. Judith Riskind died on February 28, 1933, Nathan Riskind on July 2, 1935.

35. These are Bessie (1911–2005) and Norman Schrager (1913–2009). Bessie Schrager was born in Chicago, moved to the Rio Grande Valley with her family by 1920, and settled in Eagle Pass where she married Albino Diaz, a window dresser at the M. Riskind store, in 1929. After having two children, one of whom died, the marriage apparently failed some time during World War II, as both partners soon remarried. Bessie married a World War II veteran, George Shifrin, in 1945, and they lived in San Antonio. She died in 2005 and is buried next to Shifrin at the Fort Sam Houston military cemetery in San Antonio. Norman Schrager was born in Laredo and grew up in the Rio Grande Valley. He went to work for his father at his Edinburg store and later operated a western wear store there. He died in Edinburg in 2009.

36. All three hotels are in downtown San Antonio and remain in use today; all are listed on the National Register of Historic Places. The Gunter, on Houston Street, was built in 1909 and greatly expanded and remodeled in 1926. The Menger, one of the oldest hotels in Texas, opened in 1859 on Alamo Square as a brewery and boardinghouse and expanded continuously through the nineteenth and twentieth centuries; its famous guests include General Philip Sheridan, President Ulysses S. Grant, and the author William Sydney Porter (O. Henry). The Travelers Hotel faces Broadway Avenue, which was the city's major commercial thoroughfare when the hotel was built in 1914. Texas Historical Commission, "Gunter Hotel," accessed June 24, 2022, http://www.thc.texas.gov/preserve/projects-and-programs/historic-texas-highways/place-of-interest/hotel-205-e-houston-st-san; Eleanor Stuck, "Menger Hotel," *Handbook of Texas Online*, accessed June 24, 2022, https://www.tshaonline.org/handbook/entries/menger-hotel; Texas Historical Commission, "Travelers Hotel," accessed June 24, 2022, http://www.thc.texas.gov/preserve/projects-and-programs/historic-texas-highways/place-of-interest/hotel-220-broadway-ave-san.

37. Formed in 1892 to preserve Texas historic sites, the Daughters of the Republic of Texas gained custodianship of the Alamo in 1905. The group's long internal and external struggle to refurbish and maintain the site is documented in Burrough, Tomlinson, and Stanford, *Forget the Alamo*.

38. Jewish merchant Julius Joske arrived in San Antonio in 1867 from Germany, opened a small dry goods store in

1869, sold it, and began a new business, J. Joske, in 1873 that offered penny pricing and the latest fashions from New York. Sons Alexander and Siegfried arrived and joined the business, renamed Joske Brothers; Alexander bought out his brother in 1903 and operated the business himself, expanding it into the largest department store in the region before selling it in 1929. The large metal sign and framework had existed atop the Conroy Building, adjacent to Alamo Square, since 1913, and Joske's adapted it to their use when they purchased the building. The caption accompanying a photograph of the sign in the UTSA digital collection describes it as the "largest neon sign in State of Texas, erected by Texas Outdoor Adv Co, San Antonio." Alternating lights animated the image of a cowboy roping a steer. The sign was removed in 1939 when the building was demolished to permit the store's expansion. "San Antonio, Texas," *Encyclopedia of Southern Jewish Communities*; UTSA Libraries Special Collections, "Joske's Sign, San Antonio, Texas," accessed January 2, 2023, https://digital.utsa.edu/digital/collection/p9020coll008/id/4639; San Antonio Conservation Society Foundation, "Alamo Plaza History," accessed January 2, 2023, https://www.saconservation.org/VirtualExhibits/AlamoPlaza/82873E32-AF52-486B-B566-185253770420.htm.

39. Albert Friedrich of San Antonio was a noted collector of animal horns and antlers, which he displayed at a bar he opened on Dolorosa Street before relocating to the corner of West Houston and Soledad in 1896. This may be the location Riskind visited in the early 1920s, although Friedrich moved again in 1922 during Prohibition to 400 West Houston, where he operated the business as a curio shop, museum, and restaurant. In addition to hides and other hunting trophies from around the world, Friedrich displayed a massive collection of animal horns, including a chandelier constructed of more than four thousand of them. Donald Everett, "Buckhorn Saloon," *Handbook of Texas Online*, accessed June 24, 2022, https://www.tshaonline.org/handbook/entries/buckhorn-saloon.

40. Located at the headwaters of the San Antonio River, Brackenridge Park consists of about 350 acres north of downtown San Antonio. It was named for George W. Brackenridge, who had acquired the land that provided the city's water supply. When the springs diminished, Brackenridge donated two hundred acres to the city for a public park. It was later expanded and improved with botanical gardens, a zoo, and other recreational features. Brackenridge Park Conservancy, "History of the Park," accessed June 24, 2022, https://www.brackenridgepark.org/visit-the-park/history-of-the-park.

41. "Katie over the Cowshed" was a World War I–era popular song about a soldier missing his girl at home, composed and recorded by Billy Murray.

CHAPTER 5

1. On February 15, 1919, amid the violence of the Russian Civil War, Ukrainian troops under Ataman Ivan Semosenko slaughtered more than two thousand Jews in three hours in Proskurov, Ukraine. The soldiers were part of a Ukrainian nationalist movement fighting both Bolsheviks and tsarist White forces in pursuit of Ukrainian independence; anti-Jewish pogroms were a routine aspect of their activities. "As long as the [nationalists] had a foothold in the country," writes Peter Kenez, "they continued to carry out pogroms. In the course of [several] months they killed tens of thousands of people." The massacre at Proskurov was "the single bloodiest pogrom" of this era. I'm grateful to Peter Riskind for making this identification. Peter Kenez, "Pogroms and White Ideology in the Russian Civil War," in *Pogroms: Anti-Jewish Violence in Modern Russian History*, ed. John D. Klier and Shlomo Lambroza (Cambridge, UK: Cambridge University Press, 1992), 295.

2. The Emergency Quota Act of 1921 did not specifically target Jews for restriction, but as the largest distinct immigrant group of the previous decades it affected them disproportionately. Illegal European immigration was common across the Rio Grande from Mexico, whose entry requirements were far more generous than those of the United States, and Jews were conspicuous among those attempting the crossing. The most common point of passage was El Paso, where hundreds of Jewish refugees were detained. Some were subsequently returned to Mexico, others deported back to their countries of origin, and, as Hollace Ava Weiner describes, thousands opted to remain in Mexico and became the core of significant Ashkenazic communities in Mexico City and other places. Weiner, *Jewish Stars in Texas*, 102–19. See also Garland, *After They Closed the Gates*, 43–88.

3. It is unclear exactly when Isaac Ramberg (1904–1985) moved to Mexico, but according to his US naturalization record, he and his wife, Rebeca, were married in Mexico City in 1931, had two children in Monterrey, and entered the United States together through Laredo in 1939. Isaac died in 1985 in Los Angeles, and his death certificate notes that his mother's last name was Fried, linking him to Rachel Edelstein Riskind, whose mother was also named Fried. In this case, Isaac and Rachel were first cousins, and Morris is technically incorrect to refer to Isaac as his uncle; they were second cousins.

4. This is William A. Fitch (1853–1934), an Eagle Pass businessman and the grandfather of Riskind's

contemporary Hollis Fitch.
5. Francisco Pasquale Estrada (1881–1949) was born in San Luis Potosí and died in Piedras Negras. As Riskind indicates, he owned a lumber distributorship in Eagle Pass.
6. Charros are participants in *charrería*, displays of competitive horsemanship and the origin of American rodeo. Riders compete in elaborate costume including embroidered sombreros and decorated chaps that are themselves a reflection of the sport's long cultural legacy. The tradition is celebrated in the annual Charro Days festival in Brownsville, which Jewish business owner Sam Perl played a key role in establishing in 1937. María-Cristina García, "Charrería," *Handbook of Texas Online*, accessed January 2, 2023, https://www.tshaonline.org/handbook/entries/charreria; Joseph and Shands, "Sam Perl," 150–51.
7. After a number of failed attempts in the nineteenth century to build a canal system to transport water from the Rio Grande to adjacent farmland, the Maverick County Water Control and Improvement District was established in 1926. Supported by a public issue of more than four million dollars in bonds, the first canal went into operation in 1932, drawing from an intake forty miles from Eagle Pass and distributing it from the Quemado Valley north of town to El Indio to the south. By the 1940s, expansion of the network made it possible to water more than forty thousand acres of land in the county, and by the early 1970s the main canal was more than 108 miles long, the longest in the state. Ben E. Pingenot, "Maverick County Irrigation Canal," *Handbook of Texas Online*, accessed September 27, 2022, https://www.tshaonline.org/handbook/entries/maverick-county-irrigation-canal.
8. While the outlines of this gossipy story about the Estradas seem accurate, Riskind (or whomever he heard it from) has applied some embroidery. Estrada's wife, Encarnación Garrido Estrada (1887–?), was indeed born in Spain, but she was only a few years younger than her husband Francisco, and they were married more than thirty years when he died. After Estrada died in 1949, his widow, now in her sixties, traveled to Mexico City and returned with Ignacio Frías Yague, about fifteen years her junior, who was also of Spanish birth, had lived in San Antonio and Los Angeles, and had indeed been a Catholic priest. They were married by 1954, when they embarked on a series of European trips together. I could not confirm the details about the family's business interests, nor could I find when or where Encarnación or Ignacio died.
9. Francis G. Aldridge (1898–1985) was a bookkeeper for the Eagle Pass Lumber Company and for the Riskind store; Riskind writes about him in detail in chapter 12. The Viguera Banking Company in Eagle Pass was owned by a resident of Piedras Negras, F. N. García, who also held an 85 percent interest in the Citizens Bridge Company that built and operated a toll bridge connecting Del Rio, Texas, with Villa Acuña, Mexico. García's estate was declared bankrupt in 1950, and after an extended legal tangle with his coinvestors, he was required to relinquish his remaining property. See *Citizens Bridge Co. et al. v. Guerra*, 258 S.W.2d 64 (Supreme Court of Texas, 1953), in which Aldridge is named as receiver.
10. Whether he realizes it or not, Riskind is quoting Jesus: "A prophet is not without honour, save in his own country, and in his own house." Matthew (KJV) 13:57.
11. Dr. Van Earl McFarland (1873–1942) was born and raised in southeast Texas, attended medical school in St. Louis, and arrived in Eagle Pass in 1899. In addition to acting as a physician in the town for decades, he was a founder of the Maverick County Irrigation District and served as president of that organization for twelve years. Despite Riskind's assertion that McFarland "was broke and moved from town" after the failed wildcatting scheme he describes here, McFarland appears to have lived out his life comfortably in Eagle Pass, died there in 1942, and is buried in the Maverick County Cemetery. "Dr. M'Farland, 69, Dies at Eagle Pass," *Victoria Advocate*, June 29, 1942.
12. The Spindletop oil field near Beaumont, Texas, was discovered on January 10, 1901, initiating a statewide boom in oil exploration and production, not to mention the emergence of the modern petroleum industry.
13. Harry Spitz (né Uspitz, 1894–1972) was born in Lithuania and immigrated to the United States in 1914. It's unclear exactly how he was related to Rachel Edelstein Riskind, but they both had mothers named Fried; if Miriam and Judith Fried were sisters, then Harry and Rachel were first cousins, as Riskind implies here. By 1917, Spitz was in Eagle Pass working at M. Riskind until he left to join the army, serving overseas during World War I. Upon returning, he settled in El Paso and married Hannah Atkin (1899–1943) in 1921. Hannah was born in New York to immigrant parents from Russia and moved with her family to El Paso about 1917. The couple had a daughter, Leona. Hannah died in 1943 and is buried at the Temple Mount Sinai Cemetery. Harry then married Mildred Lefkowitz of El Paso in 1945. No doubt influenced by his association with the Edelsteins, Spitz operated an El Paso furniture store, Central Furniture, which he purchased and ran until he retired in 1968.
14. Sometimes described as the Lower East Side of Los Angeles, Boyle Heights, southeast of downtown, was home to some twenty-five or thirty thousand Jews, about 25 percent of the city's Jewish population, in

the decades preceding World War II. It was also, however, a highly heterogeneous area, where about fifteen thousand Mexicans (40 percent of the city's total) and about five thousand Japanese also lived, along with smaller populations of Italians, Armenians, and other groups. "In its prime, between the two world wars," claims an article in the *Los Angeles Times*, it was "a vibrant community of Jews, Latinos and Japanese. During that period, dozens of kosher restaurants, bakeries and cafes with Yiddish and Hebrew signs lined Brooklyn Avenue. . . . Mariachi and klezmer tunes drifted from apartment windows. Socialists and Zionists argued on street corners in Yiddish and Spanish." Most of the area's residents, including Jews, were immigrants, giving the neighborhood a distinctly working-class and multiethnic atmosphere. Many of the Jews of Boyle Heights continued to speak Yiddish, worshipped traditionally, and engaged in radical and unionist politics. Orthodox congregations were abundant, and kosher restaurants like the famous Canter's Deli, which opened in 1931, thrived there. The Jewish population of the Eastside diminished rapidly, however, after the war, as newcomers to the city, mostly from New York and the East Coast, were drawn to newer and more middle-class enclaves like the Beverly-Fairfax neighborhood on the Westside and parts of the San Fernando Valley. Freeway construction in Boyle Heights further displaced the population, driving those Jews who could afford them to more affluent parts of town. As they moved out, they were replaced mostly by incoming Mexican and Mexican American residents. The Riskinds joined this trend, settling first on South Boyle Avenue in Boyle Heights, where Morris and his siblings attended school, but moving by 1930 to North Mansfield Avenue in Fairfax. Reed Johnson, "The Afterlife of an East L.A. Shul," *Los Angeles Times*, December 31, 2000; Deborah Dash Moore, *To the Golden Cities: Pursuing the American Jewish Dream in Miami and LA.* (New York: Free Press, 1994), 55–57; Sánchez, "'What's Good for Boyle Heights Is Good for the Jews,'" 635.

15. Sophye Marie Harris (1899–1972) was born in San Antonio and married Jake Edelstein in Austin in 1923. They raised two children, David and Betty Jean, in McAllen, and Sophye taught at the Sunday school. Sophye died in 1972 and is buried in the Temple Emanuel Cemetery in McAllen with her husband. Lyle, "B'nai Borderlands," 27.

16. Reuben Riskind, Morris's younger brother, confirmed and elaborated on Rachel's reason for the move: "In the 1920's Rachel made a decision that her children should have a Jewish education. She was adamant that her children be schooled in the Torah. Mike agreed. Rachel had cousins in Los Angeles and was influenced by them to move to the city." Reuben Riskind, "Texas Border Merchant," *Texas Jewish Historical Society Bulletin*, August 2002, 18.

17. Bourbon producer Waterfill & Frazier moved its operations from Bourbon County, Kentucky, to Juárez, Mexico, during Prohibition and continued supplying the American market. Fusel alcohols, or fusel oils, are a natural byproduct of fermentation but considered a contaminant if present in a significant amount; very high concentrations can cause illness or even death. Fred Minnick, "Cross Border Bourbon," *Whisky Magazine*, July 20, 2012, accessed October 20, 2022, https://whiskymag.com/articles/cross-border-bourbon/.

18. After immigrating with his father to Chicago in 1888, Jake Riskind (1869–1968) settled on the South Side and married Ida Wechsler in 1896. The US Census confirms his trade as a watchmaker in 1900; later, he was a jeweler and diamond broker. He was a few months shy of a hundred years old when he died in Chicago in 1968. Ida Wechsler (1873–1958) was born in Russia, immigrated about 1890, and had six children with Jake between 1897 and 1909. She died in 1958 and is buried in Oak Woods Cemetery in Chicago alongside her husband.

19. Mollie Edelstein Benkaim (1889–1967), born in Kalvaria, was the fifth of ten Edelstein children. She married Harry Benkaim (1886–1970), a clothing merchant, in Chicago in 1913, and the couple moved to Scranton, where Harry opened Salben's, a ladies' wear store he ran until he retired in 1960. They had three sons. The Benkaims' home in Scranton became a receiving point for several Edelstein siblings as they made their way to America, similar to the way Eagle Pass served as a landing point for various Riskind relations.

20. Louis Edelstein (1895–1978) was born in Kalvaria, the seventh of ten Edelstein children. He immigrated through New York in 1913 to Scranton, where his sister Mollie Benkaim lived with her family, and worked in the garment trade. He served in the US Army during World War I and was posted overseas for seven months before returning to Scranton. In 1928, he married Florence Lipsky, and they had two daughters, Phyllis and Adelle. He died in Las Vegas in 1978. His daughter Adelle Edelstein Alexander (1930–95) was born in Scranton, married Joseph Alexander and had two children, Helen and Norman. She died in Los Angeles in 1995.

21. Eli (or Hillel) Edelstein (1898–1971) was born in Kalvaria, the seventh of ten Edelstein children. He immigrated through New York in 1914 and briefly lived with his sister, Mollie Benkaim, and her family in Scranton before heading out for Eagle Pass. He moved to Brownsville in 1925, presumably to work with his brother Morris at Edelstein's Better Furniture, then to Mercedes in 1928 to open his own store, the Edelstein Furniture

Company, in neighboring Weslaco. Eli served stateside in World War II, as Riskind describes, never married, and died in Harlingen in 1971. He is buried at the Hebrew Cemetery in Brownsville.

22. Charles d'Artagnan, later Le Comte d'Artagnan, is a swashbuckling, handsome young soldier featured in Alexandre Dumas's trilogy beginning with *The Three Musketeers* (1844). "He is always the soldier," according to one literary authority, "quick-witted, quick-tempered, and extraordinarily brave." The Jacobite hero of Robert Louis Stevenson's novel *Kidnapped* (1886), Alan Breck Stewart is a dashing swordsman, "considered one of Stevenson's most interesting and best-drawn characters." William Rose Benet, *Benet's Reader's Encyclopedia* (New York: Harper & Row, 1987), 50, 529.

23. Ida Ramberg (1901–1994), the sister of Isaac Ramberg mentioned previously, was Rachel Riskind's first cousin: presumably their mothers were sisters. Ida was born in Lithuania, married Herbert Siegel, a dentist, and worked for more than fifty years as a nurse in his New Jersey practice. They had two daughters. Ida died in Richmond, Virginia.

24. A small range in the Trans-Pecos region of West Texas, the Davis Mountains are near Fort Davis, for which they were named. They lie about twenty miles off both major routes to El Paso. The second-highest range in the state, they are somewhat ironically nicknamed the Texas Alps. "Davis Mountains," *Handbook of Texas Online*, accessed June 13, 2022, https://www.tshaonline.org/handbook/entries/davis-mountains.

25. Tefillin, or phylacteries, are leather boxes containing passages of scripture that are bound with leather straps to the forehead and left hand for morning services most days of the year except Sabbaths and some holidays. The source of the tradition is Exodus 13:9: "And it shall be for a sign unto thee upon thy hand, and for a memorial between thine eyes, that the law of the Lord may be in thy mouth; for with a strong hand hath the Lord brought thee out of Egypt."

26. King Ranch is an immense agricultural estate comprising some 825,000 acres (or thirteen hundred square miles) in South Texas between Corpus Christi and Brownsville; it includes land in six counties. It began in 1852 when Richard King, later in partnership with his son-in-law Robert Kleberg, began ranching in the region, gradually buying up old Mexican land grants to accumulate the family's vast holdings. Originally involved primarily in ranching cattle and other livestock, the King family later converted some of the land to oil production, timber, and farming. As Riskind suggests here, the property also became a tourist destination, known for wildlife conservation programs and protection of natural habitat for deer, quail, ducks, wild turkeys, antelope, and a variety of other native species. John Ashton, Edgar P. Sneed, and Bob Kinnan, "King Ranch," *Handbook of Texas Online*, accessed June 24, 2022, https://www.tshaonline.org/handbook/entries/king-ranch. See also Don Graham, *Kings of Texas: The 150-Year Saga of an American Ranching Empire* (Hoboken, NJ: Wiley, 2004).

27. Meaning "joy" or "happiness" in Yiddish, a simcha is a festive event or celebration—a wedding, bar or bat mitzvah, or the birth of a child.

CHAPTER 6

1. Ida Bel Eby (1888–1974), to whom Riskind dedicated this memoir, was born in Los Angeles and raised by a single mother, Adelia; over the years they lived with various relatives and sometimes alone together until Adelia died in 1947. Ida started teaching around 1920 and remained at Roosevelt High School, where Riskind studied with her, for decades. She never married and, as Riskind suggests, did not fail to live her best life, frequently traveling to Europe and Asia, including transatlantic voyages on the RMS *Olympic* in 1923 and the RMS *Queen Mary* in 1949. She died in Santa Clara (or perhaps Cupertino), California, in 1974.

2. Riskind entered Theodore Roosevelt High School (RHS), located on Mathews Street in Boyle Heights, upon arriving in Los Angeles in 1923 at age twelve, and on the accelerated schedule he describes here, attended for four years and graduated at age sixteen in 1927. He appears as a senior in the 1927 RHS yearbook, *The Round-Up*. As he reports, he was named an Ephebian, and his other activities were listed as president of the Aldebaran Society (the honor society), the yearbook staff, president of the Latin Club, President's Forum, and Boys' Self-Government. Roosevelt High School was comprised, like its surrounding neighborhood, of an ethnically mixed student body: a significant number of Riskind's classmates were Jewish, many were Mexican, a few were Asian or Black. In 1931, four years after he graduated, a number of Jewish students at Roosevelt were suspended for speaking, writing, or organizing on behalf of communism and other "radical" views as the Great Depression worsened; the principal who disciplined them, Thomas Elson, was the same who had been in that position when Riskind attended. This political activism among the students offered a preview, as one historian notes, of the school's later participation in the Chicano student walkouts of 1968. To be sure, Riskind was not a participant in any of this, but it demonstrates at the school and in the surrounding

community an atmosphere of social activism and liberalism that could well have affected his own views. *Round-Up* (Roosevelt High School yearbook), Los Angeles, CA, 1927, accessed June 17, 2024, https://www.ancestrylibrary.com/imageviewer/collections/1265/images/43135_b171734_00000?ssrc=&backlabel=Return; Abraham Hoffman, "Jewish Student Militancy in the Great Depression: The Roosevelt High School Blowouts of 1931," *Branding Iron* 121 (March 1976): 6–10.

3. Riskind's paraphrase is extensive enough to make the reference uncertain, but it's possible he is thinking of *Pirkei Avot* 4:12, "Let the honor of your student be as dear to you as your own, and the honor of your colleague as the reverence for your teacher, and the reverence for your teacher as the reverence of heaven."
4. Abraham Mirkin (1872–1937) arrived in the United States at Baltimore in 1904 from Russia, where he was born in Bobruisk. His wife, Ida, and their son joined him in Baltimore in 1905, and three more children were born there before they moved to Washington, DC, where he served briefly as a rabbi (although apparently not ordained). The family was in Los Angeles by 1926, when Mirkin obtained citizenship. Mirkin died in 1937 and is buried in the Agudath Achim Cemetery in Los Angeles.
5. Saul N. Rittenberg (1912–2005) was born in Chicago and raised in Boyle Heights, where he attended Roosevelt High School with Riskind and later graduated from UCLA and Northwestern University Law School. He took a break from his Los Angeles law career to serve in the army during World War II then returned to legal work, representing motion picture studios including MGM. He died in Los Angeles in 2005. "Saul N. Rittenberg," *Los Angeles Times*, September 1, 2005.
6. Riskind is underplaying the importance of the Breed Street Shul, which was at one time the largest Orthodox congregation west of the Mississippi River. Located in Boyle Heights, Congregation Talmud Torah occupied a synagogue built in 1915 in a Byzantine revival style that reflected the Eastern European origin of most of its members. It thrived until the postwar years, when the Jewish population of Boyle Heights drifted rapidly out to newly developing parts of the city and its membership dwindled to nearly nothing. Congregants stopped using the main sanctuary in 1987 when it suffered irreparable earthquake damage, and the building was soon after deeded to the city's Jewish historical society for renovation and preservation. Those efforts continue today. Ryan Torok, "Why California Just Gave the 100 Year-Old Breed Street Shul $15 Million," *The Forward*, August 11, 2021; Reed Johnson, "The Afterlife of an East L.A. Shul," *Los Angeles Times*, December 31, 2000; Sánchez, "'What's Good for Boyle Heights Is Good for the Jews,'" 655–56. See also Jonathan L. Friedmann, *Jewish Los Angeles, Images of America* (Charleston, SC: Arcadia Publishing, 2020).
7. The hazan is a cantor, the clergy member who chants or sings the prayers during synagogue worship.
8. The Hebrew word for Germany, *Ashkenaz*, supplies this term for the Jews of Central Europe and their descendants who migrated to Eastern and Western Europe. The expression is primarily used to distinguish Central European Jewry and its distinctive customs and language from those of Sephardim, the Jews of Spain and Portugal, and Mizrachim, those of the Mideast and North Africa. Riskind notes here the variations in Hebrew pronunciation that derive from the many places Ashkenazim have lived.
9. Simchat Torah, literally "rejoicing in the Torah," is a holiday celebrating the gift of the Torah ("Law") to the Jewish people. It marks the conclusion of the annual cycle of Torah reading. As part of its celebration, the Torah scrolls are removed from the ark and carried by congregants around the synagogue.
10. "You've probably never heard of Yossele (Josef) Rosenblatt unless you're a serious fan of Jewish cantorial music," wrote NPR correspondent Ina Jaffe. "But if you have, you know he's the equivalent of Elvis Presley, Frank Sinatra, Luciano Pavarotti." Rosenblatt was born in Ukraine in 1882 and was a major cantorial figure in the United States by 1920. Talented enough to find success in secular entertainment, Rosenblatt remained committed to liturgical music exclusively. (He turned down an opportunity to play the major role of a cantor in *The Jazz Singer*, the first talking movie, alongside Al Jolson, and opted instead to appear as himself in the background in one brief scene.) Rosenblatt recorded his performances and traveled worldwide singing at concerts and in synagogues until dying of a heart attack in Palestine in 1933. He is buried in Jerusalem. Ina Jaffe, "Yossele Rosenblatt: The Cantor With The Heavenly Voice," NPR, September 6, 2010, accessed June 20, 2024, https://www.npr.org/templates/story/story.php?storyId=129635330; Jeffrey Shandler, *Jews, God, and Videotape: Religion and Media in America* (New York: New York University Press, 2009), 29–31.
11. Talmud Torahs were public primary schools for Jewish boys, similar in curriculum to the private elementary schools called heders but available to those who could not afford tuition for teachers. Providing instruction in Hebrew, the Bible, and the Talmud, their purpose was to prepare young men for yeshiva study. The particular school to which Riskind refers was the Modern Talmud Torah and Social Center, founded in 1924 in Boyle Heights. Norma Levenson, "A Study of the Jewish Community Centers of Los Angeles, California" (master's thesis, University of Southern California, 2015), 37–38. See also Jewish Histories in Multiethnic Boyle Heights, "The Modern Talmud Torah and Social Center," accessed July 23, 2022, https://scalar.usc.

edu/hc/jewish-histories-boyle-heights/the-modern-talmud-torah-and-social-center.

12. Moses Tolchinsky (1895–1969) was born in Ukraine and took the unusual route of immigrating to the United States through Seattle via Kobe, Japan. He arrived in 1917, worked in Seattle as a Hebrew teacher, and married in 1919. He and his wife, Sarah (or Sadie), moved to Los Angeles in 1923, where he was hired by the Modern Talmud Torah in Boyle Heights soon after its founding as its first Hebrew teacher. (This is probably the school Riskind describes visiting, although Tolchinsky was not its principal.) In 1929, Tolchinsky resigned his position there to open a school of his own, the Menorah Center, of which he was principal, in a more upscale part of the neighborhood where Jews were beginning to migrate. Under Tolchinsky's direction, the Menorah Center became "the largest Jewish educational institution in Los Angeles, and perhaps the entire West Coast, at the time." Tolchinsky died in 1969. Jewish Histories in Multiethnic Boyle Heights, "The Menorah Center: 3218 Wabash Ave.," accessed July 23, 2022, https://scalar.usc.edu/hc/jewish-histories-boyle-heights/the-menorah-center-3218-wabash-ave; Jewish Histories in Multiethnic Boyle Heights, "The Modern Talmud Torah and Social Center."

13. Usually performed at the conclusion of Shabbat, *Adon Olam* praises God as the creator and ruler of the world. As Riskind indicates, the lyrics are medieval, but there are a variety of melodies, some of recent composition.

14. Literally "head of the year," Rosh Hashanah is the Jewish new year, falling on the first day of the Hebrew month of Tishri. A joyful celebration of the conclusion of one year and the beginning of the next, Rosh Hashanah initiates the Days of Awe, a ten-day period of self-reflection and self-abnegation culminating in the day of atonement, Yom Kippur. Hillel International sponsors facilities for Jewish prayer, study, dining, and social activities near college and university campuses worldwide.

15. Roman orator, statesman, and consul Marcus Tullius Cicero achieved fame with a series of orations in 63 BCE exposing and denouncing the antigovernment conspiracy led by the patrician Catiline, which as a result was overcome and its leaders executed.

16. Located at 131 South Boyle Avenue, the Jewish Home for the Aged opened in 1915 as the Hebrew Sheltering and Home for the Aged. It grew through purchases of nearby property and the addition of an on-site synagogue, Tiferes Israel, which relocated there permanently from its shul across the street in 1923; this would be where Riskind's bar mitzvah took place. The institution's proximity to Hollywood made it a favorite charity for people in the film industry, Jewish and non-Jewish, throughout the 1940s and 1950s. As the Jewish population left Boyle Heights in the 1950s, though, it merged with other Jewish institutions to provide care in the San Fernando Valley and other areas where Jews had moved, and in 1975 the Boyle Street facility was purchased by a Japanese American community organization, Keiro, to provide eldercare in their community. Jewish Histories in Multiethnic Boyle Heights, "Hebrew Sheltering and Home for the Aged," accessed June 25, 2022, https://scalar.usc.edu/hc/jewish-histories-boyle-heights/hebrew-sheltering-and-home-for-the-aged-origins.

17. We may view Riskind's reflexive use of the Christian term "Old Testament" (which only has meaning if there is a New Testament) as a byproduct of his long participation in a Christian-dominated society. Jews usually refer to the Hebrew scripture (as Riskind does elsewhere) simply as the Bible or the Tanakh, an acronym derived from the Hebrew names for the Torah, Prophets, and Writings that comprise it.

18. The passage is from Judges 5:10. The JPS translation of the same verse is thus: "You riders on tawny she-asses, you who sit on saddle rugs, and you wayfarers, declare it!"

19. The Book of Isaiah was likely compiled from the work of several authors over centuries. First Isaiah refers to the first thirty-nine chapters, thought to be the work of the prophet himself.

20. The Disputation of Barcelona took place in 1263 at the palace of James I of Aragon. Nachmanides (Moshe ben Nachman, or the Ramban), the leading Spanish talmudist of his age, was required to debate single-handedly four Dominican friars, in particular Pablo Christiani, a convert from Judaism, on the question whether the truth of Christianity could be proven from biblical and talmudic sources. After offering a variety of explanations for the Jews' rejection of Jesus, Nachmanides was awarded the victory but fled Spain immediately to avoid retaliation, settled in Jerusalem, and founded a synagogue. "Disputation of Barcelona," *Jewish Virtual Library*, accessed January 2, 2023, https://www.jewishvirtuallibrary.org/disputation-of-barcelona.

21. Gandhi's views on Jews and the Holocaust are the subject of ongoing debate. See, for example, Dusty Sklar, "Mahatma Gandhi on Zionism and the Holocaust," *Blog-Schmog* (blog), March 19, 2016, accessed June 21, 2023, https://jewishcurrents.org/mahatma-gandhi-on-zionism-and-the-holocaust.

22. Recorded in written form in the second century CE, the Mishnah, or Oral Law, consists of law and rabbinical commentary compiled into the central text of the Talmud. Additional rabbinical commentary on the Mishnah forms the remainder of the Talmud, called the Gemara. Various tractates, or volumes, deal with ritual observance of holidays, rules governing the Sabbath, dietary restrictions, criminal law, and other matters pertinent to daily Jewish life.

23. Hillel the Elder (or Hillel HaGadol, Hillel the Great) lived in Babylon during the first century BCE. Perhaps the most famous Jewish scholar and sage of any era, he led a school of interpretive thought that provided much of the source material for the Talmud. Hillel is also responsible for the original form of the saying that became known as the Golden Rule. The quote Riskind cites comes from *Pirkei Avot* 1:14.
24. The Pharisees (Perugim in Hebrew) were a religious party active in Palestine during the Second Temple period (515 BCE–70 CE). Their position was characterized by the view that oral tradition was as binding a source of law as the Torah itself; they maintained that Moses received both an oral and written law at Sinai. Their interpretations of biblical text became a key source for the code of law compiled in the Mishnah, the core of the Talmud. Rather than relying exclusively on the written text—as their rivals the Sadducees did—the Pharisees emphasized that the law could change and adapt through interpretation and discussion. See Jacob Neusner and Bruce D. Chilton, eds., *In Quest of the Historical Pharisees* (Waco: Baylor University Press, 2020).
25. Riskind may be conflating two legends regarding scholarly Jewish women. Rabbi Meir, a Talmudic sage, did have sons, but according to the Midrash for Proverbs 31:10, they died. Nothing is said of any daughters, but Meir's wife, Beruriah (or Beruryah), whose father and husband were both sages of note, is renowned as one of the few women named in the Talmud and the only one identified as a Torah student. The other legend, probably the one Riskind means to refer to, involves the medieval Talmudist Rashi (Rabbi Shlomo Yitzhaki), who had no sons but three daughters. His daughters, Yocheved, Miriam, and Rachel, are reported to have prayed like men, studied Torah, and worn tefillin. They each married Talmudic scholars and mothered a dynasty of Talmudists. See Shoshana Pantel Zolty, *And All Your Children Shall Be Learned: Women and the Study of Torah in Jewish Law and History* (Northvale, NJ: Jason Aronson, Inc., 1993); Elie Wiesel, *A Life of Rashi* (New York: Schocken, 2009); Tal Ilan, "Beruryah," *Jewish Women's Archive,* accessed June 7, 2022, https://jwa.org/encyclopedia/article/beruryah; and Dvora Weisberg, "Desirable But Dangerous: Rabbis' Daughters in the Babylonian Talmud," *Hebrew Union College Annual* 75 (2004), 121–61. For background on Riskind's observation about Jewish women in the rabbinic era, see Tal Ilan, "Post-Biblical and Rabbinic Women," *Jewish Women's Archive,* accessed June 7, 2022, https://jwa.org/encyclopedia/article/post-biblical-and-rabbinic-women.
26. This is Hollenbeck Park at Saint Louis and Fourth in Boyle Heights, a few blocks from Riskind's high school.
27. Louis Rittenberg (1889–1936) was born in Russia and immigrated about 1920. His brother William, who had immigrated several years before, died in 1919, leaving a widow, Lena, and the children named here. When the family moved to Los Angeles, Louis joined them and took work as an electrician. He never married, died in 1936, and is buried in the Agudath Achim Cemetery in Los Angeles.
28. The five acres of Pershing Square Park, located in downtown Los Angeles, have been in continuous use since Spanish rule, when the land was ceded to the new city of Los Angeles in 1781. Continuously improved through the nineteenth century, it was named after General John Pershing in 1918 following World War I and a refurbishment of the park. According to the Los Angeles Conservancy, "From the 1920s through the 1960s," including, that is, the years Riskind writes about, "Pershing Square anchored the 5th Street corridor known as 'The Run' because of its close proximity to gay friendly establishments and cruising areas." Bars, the city library, and other nearby locations provided sites for intimate recreation, and "Pershing Square's relatively open and tolerant social atmosphere attracted large numbers of gay and bisexual men, though women tended not to gather there. In addition to cruising," the conservancy notes, "the park provided activists with a place to discuss social issues." This latter observation explains Riskind's comparison to London's Hyde Park, known for its Speaker's Corner, a long-standing forum for public discussion and argument. The rest of this context, however, may also be relevant in regard to Riskind's description of Louie Rittenberg as "a middle-aged bachelor" who was frequently arrested at the park for reasons Riskind leaves unclear. Los Angeles Conservancy, "Pershing Square," accessed June 25, 2022, https://www.laconservancy.org/locations/pershing-square.
29. In his study of the Jewish community of Boyle Heights in the 1950s, historian George J. Sánchez notes that the neighborhood "had a long tradition of working-class politics and was home to various labor unions before World War II." After the war it "was increasingly associated with political radicalism . . . as political ideologies in greater Southern California moved decidedly to the right." The sense that Boyle Heights was "sympathetic to liberal and leftist causes" may have led left-leaning residents to remain while their more politically moderate neighbors left; it may also have drawn more leftists into the community from less hospitable parts of Southern California. Although Jews were hardly the only liberals in Boyle Heights, they were conspicuous among them. Sánchez, "'What's Good for Boyle Heights Is Good for the Jews,'" 646.
30. According to historian Frank Donner, "More than any other single individual," Captain William F. "Red" Hynes "was influential in shaping the agenda of the modern red squad and in exploiting the career opportunities of its chief." Less objectively, the director of the Los Angeles district of the National Labor Relations

Board, Towne Nylander, testified to Congress in 1937 that Hynes "has not only done more to interfere with the legitimate self-organization of workers than any other man in Southern California, but he is distinctly psychopathic on the question of communism." Born in Chicago in 1896, Hynes was hired by the Los Angeles Police Department in 1922 and began infiltrating labor and other left-leaning organizations in an apparent attempt to provoke them from within into illegal activity. He became director of the department's Intelligence Bureau in 1927 and for more than a decade supervised a brutal and often violent suppression of the civil liberties of workers and political activists. He retired in 1943 and died in 1952. Frank Donner, *Protectors of Privilege: Red Squads and Police Repression in Urban America* (Berkeley: University of California Press, 1992), 59; US House of Representatives, *Hearings Before the Special Committee to Investigate National Labor Relations Board* (Washington, DC: US Government Printing Office, 1940), 3:5635; "W. F. Hynes, Noted Foe of Reds, Dies," *Los Angeles Times*, May 18, 1952.

31. The wedding between Riskind's sister Bess and Samuel Frank took place at the Beverly Hills Hotel on January 7, 1931.

32. Dr. Ernest C. Moore was a founder of UCLA as well as its first provost. Born in Youngstown, Ohio, in 1871 and educated at Columbia University and the University of Chicago, he taught at Harvard and Berkeley before becoming superintendent of the Los Angeles public school system in 1906. He helped found UCLA in 1919 by facilitating a merger of the State Normal School in Los Angeles, where he was then teaching, with the University of California, and he worked as an administrator and professor of education and philosophy at the new institution, supervising its relocation to its present site in Westwood, until retirement in 1941. He died in 1955. The Homburg hat, made of felt with a circular brim and a strong crease through the center of the crown, is German in origin but perhaps most associated with Winston Churchill. "Dr. Ernest C. Moore, Founder of UCLA, Dies," *Los Angeles Times*, January 24, 1955.

33. The English philosopher, mathematician, and radical social reformer Bertrand Russell condemned the *Republic*—in which Plato describes his vision of an ideal (undemocratic) society whose citizens are assigned roles by class and are obliged to fulfill only their designated functions—as a "totalitarian tract." Plato desired a state, Russell writes, in which the "government is to be in the hands of a small oligarchy, who are to practice trickery and lying . . . to persuade the population that there are biological differences between the upper and lower classes." Bertrand Russell, "Philosophy and Politics," in *Unpopular Essays* (London: Routledge, 1995), 17.

34. The famous passage is Isaiah 2:4: "Thus He will judge among the nations and arbitrate for the many peoples, and they shall beat their swords into plowshares and their spears into pruning hooks; nation shall not take up sword against nation; they shall never again know war."

35. The utopian novel *Looking Backward*, published by Massachusetts writer Edward Bellamy in 1888, tells of a Bostonian who falls asleep in 1887 and awakens in 2000 in an America that has solved all its social problems through a combination of technology and socialist governance. Widely popular in its day, the book inspired a number of short-lived political organizations attempting to implement its vision of the future. Margaret Drabble, ed., *The Oxford Companion to English Literature* (New York: Oxford University Press, 1985), 83.

36. In *The Intelligent Woman's Guide to Socialism and Capitalism* (1928), Irish playwright George Bernard Shaw addressed his sister-in-law, who had asked for his views on socialism. He replied with a long and detailed summary of multiple aspects of the subject, including the observation that the true equality promised by socialism would bring about women's economic independence from men. There were, however, readers at the time of its publication who shared Miss Eby's interpretation of Shaw's tone as condescending to the "intelligent" women he imagined himself to be instructing. See Thelma McCormack, Review of *The Intelligent Woman's Guide to Socialism and Capitalism, American Journal of Sociology* 91 (July 1985): 209–11.

37. Henry George, a Philadelphia-born political philosopher, California journalist, and one-time candidate for New York City mayor, became one of the most influential writers on politics and economics of the Gilded Age, laying the intellectual foundation for a number of subsequent Progressive Era reform movements. The widely read *Progress and Poverty* (1879) advocated "radical land reform (via land-value taxation that came to be called 'the single tax') as a means of eliminating the crushing mass poverty, restricted opportunity, and increased inequality that accompanied industrial progress." Edward T. O'Donnell, *Henry George and the Crisis of Inequality: Progress and Poverty in the Gilded Age* (New York: Columbia University Press, 2015).

38. Scotsman Adam Smith in the eighteenth century and Englishman John Stuart Mill in the nineteenth laid the foundations of classical economic and political liberalism. Smith's *The Wealth of Nations* (1776) advocated an economy determined solely by individual self-interest, free of all government restraint or regulation. In the essay "On Liberty" (1859), Mill argued that individuals should be free to act without interference unless their actions interfered with others. The monumental *Das Kapital*, its first volume published in 1867, is

a systematic critique of capitalism and contains Marx's argument for the abolition of private property. In contrast to the revolutionary communism of Marx and Engels, members of the Fabian Society, founded in London in 1884, urged a gradualist approach to socialist reform through the channels of normal constitutional government. Through the writings and political careers of twentieth-century advocates including G. D. H. Cole and Harold Laski, the view became a primary influence on the prewar Labour Party in Britain.

39. Riskind here names the leading lights of classical history. The eighteenth-century English historian Edward Gibbon—the only name on this list who was not an ancient Greek or Roman—published his magisterial *History of the Decline and Fall of the Roman Empire* between 1776 and 1788, covering thirteen centuries of Roman history. Herodotus, the Greek scholar widely viewed as the first true Western historian, documented the wars between Persia and Greece; Thucydides, also Greek, chronicled the Peloponnesian War in a narrative notable for its engaging style and critical objectivity. Livy, a resident of Roman Padua, was the author of an expansive history of Rome from its mythic origins to the early first century CE. Polybius, a Greek statesman of the Hellenistic period, was captured by Rome, where he thereafter lived and produced a history of the rise of the Roman Republic and the Punic Wars through about 150 BCE.

40. Born in 1632 in Amsterdam to a Sephardic family that had returned to Judaism after forced conversion, Baruch Spinoza became a forerunner of the Enlightenment and a philosophical critic of all established religion. Accused of atheism and shunned from Jewish society, Spinoza's views were nonetheless rooted in Jewish tradition, notably the Torah and the Jewish conception of monotheism. "Baruch Spinoza," *Jewish Virtual Library*, accessed June 19, 2023, https://www.jewishvirtuallibrary.org/baruch-spinoza.

41. Far and away the leading figure in medieval Jewish thought, Moses Maimonides (or Rabbi Moses ben Maimon, or Rambam) was born in Córdoba, Spain, about 1135, but the rise of a hostile Muslim regime forced his family to flee to North Africa, where Maimonides received training as a physician in the city of Fez. In addition to a career as a doctor, Maimonides was a remarkably prolific scholar, producing crucial works on halakah (Jewish law), including the *Mishneh Torah*, a massive synthesis of all Jewish law. *The Guide for the Perplexed*, written in Arabic in 1190, applies Aristotelian analysis to the interpretation of halakah, ostensibly to help Jews confused by the modern world navigate the conflict between faith and reason. His melding of a rational, Aristotelian method with Jewish scripture and belief made it a landmark in Jewish religious philosophy. "Moses Maimonides (Rambam)," *Jewish Virtual Library*, accessed January 21, 2023, https://www.jewishvirtuallibrary.org/moses-maimonides-rambam.

42. Primarily an economist as well as sociologist, Vilfredo Pareto included his ideas about "residues" in *The Mind and Society*, published in 1916. These are inherited attitudes—perhaps cultural, perhaps biological—that affect people's motivations and actions. Pareto was attempting to explain why people behaved in irrational ways that mathematical conceptions of economics and social action could not accurately predict. It's intriguing to consider why this view appeals so much to Riskind, a Jew living among Christians, who must have been continually aware of the impact of the "residue" of his Jewish background on all of his actions. See Zbigniew Bokszański, "On the Concept of Residues in the Theory of Vilfredo Pareto," *Polish Sociological Bulletin* 54 (1981): 39–50.

43. Bobby Riggs was born in 1918 in the Lincoln Heights neighborhood of Los Angeles and as a teenager dominated competition at the L.A. Tennis Club. He played on the 1938 US team that took the Davis Cup against Australia and the next year, at twenty-one years old, won at Wimbledon. He also won the US Open twice, in 1939 and 1941. He is undoubtedly best known, however, for losing in straight sets to Billie Jean King in 1973 in a much-hyped and widely viewed "Battle of the Sexes" at Houston's Astrodome. He finished his career as a tennis promoter, established a museum in California, and died in 1995 at his home in Leucadia, California. Bob Oates, "Star Turned Hustler Bobby Riggs Is Dead," *Los Angeles Times*, October 26, 1995.

44. Congress established the nation's land-grant colleges in 1862 with the Morrill Act, which contained a stipulation that such schools must provide their students military training. By 1900 more than forty schools required it. With Europe at war in 1916, Congress passed the National Defense Act, which formally established the ROTC to prepare military officers in the event of US entry into the war. Under that act, a two-year officer training program was theoretically mandatory but never fully enforced. ROTC requirements were expanded, however, in the National Defense Act of 1920, and by 1928, when Riskind was a participant, mandated ROTC units were operating at 225 colleges and universities. When the stock market crash in 1929 diverted attention from matters of national defense, universities began to push back against the compulsory nature of military training, arguing that it conflicted with academia's mission to inculcate critical thinking and freedom of thought. Simultaneously student peace movements organized anti-ROTC protest that continued until the program was suspended in 1940 in favor of a military draft and shorter officer training programs. Reinstated after the war, some schools again made ROTC training a compulsory part of the curriculum, which inevitably

became a target of 1960s-era antiwar campus protest. When again made voluntary, ROTC programs suffered significant setbacks in enrollment. Woolf Gross, "The Army Reserve Officers' Training Corps: A Hundred Years Old and Still Going Strong," *On Point* 23 (Fall 2017): 10, 11; David L. Leal, "Students in Uniform: ROTC, the Citizen-Soldier, and the Civil-Military Gap," *PS: Political Science and Politics* 40 (July 2007): 479–83; Richard M. Abrams, "The U.S. Military and Higher Education: A Brief History," *Annals of the American Academy of Political and Social Science* 502 (March 1989): 15–28.

45. In February 1933, students at Oxford University, in a sign of lingering disenchantment following the violence of the Great War, supported a resolution stating they would "in no circumstances fight for King and Country." Despite a strong backlash against such an apparently extreme and unpatriotic statement, the Oxford Oath was adopted by an emerging American campus peace movement, rephrased "to refuse support for any war that the United States government might conduct," and spread widely among American universities. In 1935, delegates from more than two hundred campuses formed the American Student Union (ASU) to promote and organize campus antiwar activism, and the group adopted the Oxford Oath as its guiding plank. The ASU also organized opposition to the presence of ROTC programs and compulsory military service at American universities. "Underlying the opposition to compulsion," writes historian Eileen Eagan, "was the assumption that ROTC was inherently undemocratic and authoritarian and contradictory to the aims of liberal education." Eileen Eagan, *Class, Culture, and the Classroom: The Student Peace Movement of the 1930s* (Philadelphia: Temple University Press, 1981), 59, 134, 110–11.

46. The incident Riskind describes—known depending on the source as the Ford Hunger March or the Ford Massacre—occurred in March 1932. The Ford Motor Company, one of the nation's largest employers, laid off about two-thirds of its work force in the wake of the 1929 economic crash, and in response some three thousand current and former employees gathered in Detroit for a march to Dearborn, Michigan, the site of Ford's River Rouge plant. The protesters' demands included income for laid-off workers, collective bargaining, and increased wages. As the group arrived in Dearborn, city police blocked their path and launched tear gas at the protesters, who responded by throwing rocks at the police. Officers retreated and the march proceeded to the plant, where Dearborn police and Ford's private security detail again blocked their way. The city fire department sprayed the crowd with high-pressure water to get them to disperse, but protesters continued throwing stones. Finally, police fired into the group of marchers, killing four, all members of the Young Communist League. The demonstration had no immediate impact on Ford's employment policies, but it was one of several events that paved the way for passage of the 1935 Wagner Act assuring workers' right to collective bargaining. The *Daily Worker*, published in Chicago from 1921 through 1924 then in New York through 1958, was a newspaper sponsored by the Communist Party USA. Global Nonviolent Action Database, Swarthmore College, "Unemployed Detroit Auto Workers Conduct Hunger March to Protest Ford Motor Company's Policies, United States, 1932," accessed October 26, 2022, https://nvdatabase.swarthmore.edu/content/unemployed-detroit-auto-workers-conduct-hunger-march-protest-ford-motor-companys-policies-un.

47. Now located on the USC campus, the historic Hoose Library of Philosophy, built in 1930, the year he started law school, was new when Riskind visited. Its main reading room features a high vaulted ceiling and is elaborately decorated with stained glass windows, wooden carvings, and mosaics depicting important philosophers in the Western tradition. USC Libraries, "About the Hoose Library of Philosophy," accessed March 31, 2023, https://libraries.usc.edu/locations/hoose-philosophy-library/hoose-philosophy-library-history.

48. Founded in 1946 in England, Mensa is a "round-table society" whose qualification for membership is "scoring within the upper 2% of the general population on an approved intelligence test." Mensa International, "About Us," accessed October 25, 2022, https://www.mensa.org/mensa/about-us.

49. Orville P. Cockerill was born in Missouri in 1871, raised in Ohio, and attended the Ohio State University law school. He practiced law in Columbus, began teaching in 1910, and was subsequently hired by the University of Washington. He married and had a child in Seattle, then accepted an appointment as Dean of Law at the University of Idaho, followed by a deanship at the University of North Dakota in 1923. By 1930, he was at USC, where he remained for the rest of his career. He died in Los Angeles in 1961. Charles L. Crum, "The History of the University of North Dakota School of Law," *North Dakota Law Review* 35 (1959): 15.

50. The author of several authoritative texts on business and property law, William E. Burby was born in Michigan in 1893 and attended the University of Michigan. Following military service during World War I, he returned to Ann Arbor, married, graduated from law school in 1922, and took a job teaching law at Notre Dame. He later taught for three years at the University of North Dakota School of Law alongside his future USC colleague Orville Cockerill, then joined the faculty at USC in 1926, where he remained for the rest of his career and died in Los Angeles in 1982. "Students, Appointed by the Faculty," *Michigan Law Review* 20 (June 1922): 887; Crum, "History of the University of North Dakota School of Law," 15.

51. In a 1995 interview, Riskind elaborated on the hardships of a Depression-era legal career: "I was already finished [with] law school, and after a while I was having a terrible time because during the Depression, lawyers were all starving to death. There was just no way to make a living. Nobody had any money. If you got a client he couldn't pay you. And unless you had some sort of a job like working for the government or teaching or something of that nature, you had a difficult time." Morris Riskind interview.
52. The reference is probably to the bankruptcy of the Owl Drug Company, which operated a chain of retail drugstores in California, Washington, Oregon, Nevada, and Utah. The company was declared bankrupt in 1932 in Reno. Despite the memorable details Riskind presents below about attorney Abe Gold, including the extraordinary circumstances of his demise, I have been unable to identify him or find any reference to his involvement in the Owl Drug case. It's possible that Riskind altered his colleague's name. *In re Owl Drug Co.*, 21 F. Supp. 907 (D. Nev. 1937).
53. Signed into law by Franklin Roosevelt on July 5, 1935, the National Labor Relations Act, also known as the Wagner Act, guaranteed American employees "the right to self-organization, to form, join, or assist labor organizations, to bargain collectively through representatives of their own choosing, and to engage in concerted activities for the purpose of collective bargaining or other mutual aid and protection." The act led to a dramatic increase in the membership, influence, and effectiveness of organized labor. National Archives, "National Labor Relations Act (1935)," accessed June 21, 2023, https://www.archives.gov/milestone-documents/national-labor-relations-act.
54. Born in Saskatchewan in 1912, David L. Mohr settled in Los Angeles with his American parents, graduated from USC in 1935, then finished at the USC law school two years later. After two decades in private practice, Governor Edmund G. Brown appointed Mohr a judge of the Los Angeles Municipal Court in 1964. He held that position until his premature death in 1972, as Riskind describes. Bob Martin, "Gov. Appoints Mohr to Court," 1964, Los Angeles Public Library Photo Collection, accessed June 21, 2023, https://calisphere.org/item/1674ef1370641d2eb8c84d3e1e2cadc7; "Judge David L. Mohr, 59, Dies," *Los Angeles Times*, January 8, 1972.
55. The song in which the singer "fell in love with a rich attorney's elderly, ugly daughter" is "When I, Good Friends, Was Called to the Bar" (or "The Judge's Song") from Gilbert and Sullivan's 1875 comic opera *Trial by Jury*.
56. Dr. Samuel Max Melamed, writer, scholar, and for twelve years the editor of the *Jewish Courier* in Chicago, was educated at Leipzig, Germany, and wrote and published widely in Europe before coming to the United States in 1915. A dedicated Zionist, he was the author, among other works, of *On the Eve of Redemption* (1918) and *Spinoza and Buddha: Visions of a Dead God* (1933). He died in New York in 1938. "Dr. S. M. Melamed, Writer and Editor, Dead at 52," *Jewish Telegraphic Agency*, June 21, 1938; "Dr. S. M. Melamed, 54, Dies; Noted Jewish Scholar and Editor," *Chicago Tribune*, June 20, 1938.
57. John Sholtz, Riskind's future father-in-law, was born in Kansas City in 1892; his father was a butcher. He married Ann Lehman in Kansas City, and after the birth of their first daughter, Riskind's wife Ruth, the couple moved to Chicago where John began teaching in a public high school. They moved on to Los Angeles, where a second daughter, Jeanne, was born in 1924. Sholtz continued teaching in Los Angeles–area public schools throughout the rest of his career, particularly Venice High School, although he was a social studies teacher at Roosevelt at the same time Riskind was a student there. Sholtz died in 1969, Ann in 1987.

CHAPTER 7

1. Isaac Edelstein appears to have been the youngest of ten Edelstein children, although little information is readily available about him as he was the only one of the siblings not to immigrate to the United States. Morris makes clear in the memoir that Isaac was killed by the Nazis in 1940 along with his father, Chatzkel, Morris's grandfather.
2. According to a Riskind family genealogical record, Miriam Fried Edelstein died in 1931.
3. Under the terms of the German-Soviet Nonaggression Pact (the Molotov-Ribbentrop Pact) of August 1939, Poland and the Baltic states were partitioned between Germany and the USSR, although the affected nations retained nominal independence and were not initially notified of the agreement. Upon the German invasion of Poland on September 1, Lithuania proclaimed its neutrality. The Soviets occupied their designated portions of Poland on September 15, including the Lithuanian capital of Vilnius, which Poland had annexed in 1922. In October, the Soviets demanded Lithuanian agreement to the stationing of Red Army forces in the country, offering in exchange the return of Vilnius to Lithuanian control, a proposal the barely independent Lithuanian government accepted. Despite such pretenses of diplomacy, the Soviet Union fully annexed Lithuania in

August 1940 and began a brutal process of "Sovietization" that continued until the surprise Nazi invasion of the USSR in 1941. Lithuania, lying along the German front, bore the brunt of the Nazi assault in its opening days, beginning on June 21, 1941. A brief Lithuanian uprising emerged, signifying a futile attempt to regain independence, but the country was overrun by German forces within a week, accompanied by wide-scale pogroms against the nation's Jews. The Soviets reoccupied the country in July 1944, but by then the Holocaust had claimed some 90 percent of the Lithuanian Jewish population. Of a prewar Jewish population of about 250,000, only 6,000 to 7,000 survived. Greenbaum, *Jews of Lithuania*, 302, 336, 338, 345.

4. Jack Benkaim (1917–1998) was born to Rachel Riskind's sister Mollie and her husband, Harry Benkaim, in Scranton and attended the University of Scranton and the University of Wisconsin. He married Helen Tapper in Wilkes-Barre in 1941 and they had two daughters. He died in Sarasota, Florida.

5. The Yiddish originals of these letters are in the Riskind family's possession. It is unknown who translated them into English, and I have been unable to identify most of the people named or to correct a number of apparent errors in names and dates.

6. Syanno (Senno) and Pinsk are in modern-day Belarus; Suvalki is in northern Poland. Jewish refugees from Nazi-occupied Poland began arriving in Lithuania immediately after the German invasion on September 1, 1939. "In all," writes historian Masha Greenbaum, "some 25,000 Polish and a small number of German Jews found temporary refuge in Lithuania." Although some managed to emigrate again ahead of the 1941 Nazi incursion into Lithuania, "the remainder shared the fate of the Lithuanian Jews, first under the Russians and then at the hands of the Germans." Greenbaum, *Jews of Lithuania*, 288–89.

7. As Yom Kippur occurs in the fall (it was on September 22, 1939, and October 11, 1940), there appears to be an error in the date of this letter.

8. A traditional Yom Kippur blessing, literally "a good final sealing" or "good inscription." The blessing refers to the belief that on Rosh Hashanah our names (or our fates) are written in the Book of Life and are sealed for the coming year on Yom Kippur.

9. Isaac's older sister Mollie lived in Scranton, Pennsylvania, with her husband, Harry Benkaim, but as they only had sons, this reference is unclear. It must refer to someone in another branch of the family.

10. As seen in this letter, it was a common practice in overseas mail for several people to append messages to a single correspondence.

11. Vilkovshisk (now Vilkaviškis), Lithuania is about fifty miles southwest of Kaunas (Kovno) and twenty-five miles north of Kalvaria (Kalvarija).

12. Celebrated fifty days after Passover, on the sixth of Sivan (in May or June), Shavuot (or *Shavuos* in Yiddish) commemorates the anniversary of God's gift of the Torah to the Israelites at Sinai.

13. The Germans occupied Kalvaria on June 22, 1941, took local Jewish residents and the Polish refugees they had sheltered to the nearby barracks at Marijampole, and murdered them on August 30. A memorial marks the site at Marijampole: "Here the blood of about 8000 Jews was spilled—men, women, and children; and about 1000 people of other nationalities that the Nazi murderers and their local collaborators killed in a gruesome fashion." "Kalvarija," *Jewish Virtual Library*, accessed January 3, 2023, https://www.jewishvirtuallibrary.org/kalvarija; "Kalvarija," JewishGen, accessed January 3, 2023, https://kehilalinks.jewishgen.org/Kalvarija/Kalvarija.html#holocaust.

14. Founded in 1775, the US Army Judge Advocate General's Corps is the army's legal unit, providing legal services to the army and its officers. The office experienced significant staff growth during and after World War II, which "increased the complexity of the legal problems facing the United States Army." From a prewar level of 115 in 1940, the corps grew to nearly 1,000 by 1960. Lewis T. Sweet and Harvey Paticoff, "The Education of an Army Lawyer: The Judge Advocate General's School," *American Bar Association Journal* 45 (May 1959): 463.

15. J. Edgar Hoover led the Bureau of Investigation beginning in 1924, founded the FBI in 1935, and headed it until his death in 1972.

16. The Selective Training and Service Act, enacted on September 16, 1940, required American men between twenty-one and thirty-six years old to register with local draft boards. After US entry into World War II, the registration age was expanded to between eighteen and sixty-five, although only men between eighteen and forty-five were eligible for active duty. See James A. Huston, "Selective Service in World War II," *Current History* 54 (June 1968): 345–84.

17. In 1941 Maverick County was in Texas's Fifteenth Congressional District, which was represented by Congressman Milton West. He held the seat from 1933 until his death in 1948.

18. Dr. Raul M. Montemayor (1911–1990) had a private medical practice in Eagle Pass.

19. Fort Sam Houston is a US Army installation in the northeast part of San Antonio. There has been a continuous

military presence in the city since the days of the Texas Republic, including during the Civil War, when its military facilities were under Confederate control. Expanded greatly in the late nineteenth century, the facility became the second-largest army base in the country and in 1890 was named in honor of Texas president and governor Sam Houston. Theodore Roosevelt's Rough Riders mobilized at Fort Sam during the Spanish-American War, and more than two hundred thousand troops passed through on their way to fight in World War I. During World War II, it provided headquarters for the Third, Fourth, Sixth, Ninth, Tenth, and Fifteenth Armies, which trained and deployed from San Antonio; General Dwight Eisenhower was stationed there at the war's beginning. After the war the fort became a center for medical training and has continued to serve a variety of medical, troop training, equipment, and deployment purposes in the decades since. John Manguso, "Fort Sam Houston," *Handbook of Texas Online*, accessed June 25, 2022, https://www.tshaonline.org/handbook/entries/fort-sam-houston.

20. Eagle Pass Army Air Field was activated in 1942 as a single engine flying school but was converted to a general flight school in 1944. Training stopped in April 1945 with the conclusion of the war. It was used for a while as a radar station, which has since closed and now serves as public housing. Art Leatherwood, "Eagle Pass Army Air Field," *Handbook of Texas Online*, accessed June 25, 2022, https://www.tshaonline.org/handbook/entries/eagle-pass-army-air-field.

21. This is Laughlin Army Air Field, seven miles east of Del Rio and about fifty-three miles north of Eagle Pass, which was commissioned in 1942 for bomber training and closed at war's end in 1945. It was reopened in 1952 as Laughlin Air Force Base as a training center for F-84 fighter pilots and later for pilots of reconnaissance aircraft, including the U-2. It remains a flight-training center today. Art Leatherwood, "Laughlin Air Force Base," *Handbook of Texas Online*, accessed June 25, 2022, https://www.tshaonline.org/handbook/entries/laughlin-air-force-base.

22. The shooting occurred at the Eagle Pass Army Air Field on November 2, 1942. Sixty-six-year-old former guard Calvin C. Taylor was killed. Chief guard Charles M. Lindenborn, forty-five years old and a veteran of World War I, survived until 1962 and is buried in the Maverick County Cemetery. "Former Guard at Air Base Killed," *Corpus Christi Caller*, November 3, 1942.

23. Riskind's misgivings about Wallace Mendelson (1911–2004) obscure a life of tremendous accomplishment. Born in Dubuque, Iowa, in 1911, Mendelson attended the University of Wisconsin, took a law degree at Harvard, then returned to Madison to complete a PhD in 1940. After his wartime service, during which he rose to the rank of lieutenant colonel, he embarked on a career practicing and teaching law, including serving as an assistant to Supreme Court justice Felix Frankfurter and publishing extensively. He joined the law faculty at the University of Texas in 1957 and remained there through retirement in 1991. He died in Austin in 2004. Margery Janet Rosen Mendelson (1921–2017) was born in St. Joseph, Missouri, attended the University of Missouri, and earned a degree in journalism. She met Wallace Mendelson in Missouri and married him in 1942 in Eagle Pass during his deployment there. They eventually had three children. She died in Austin in 2017. Wallace Mendelson, "ERA, the Supreme Court, and Allegations of Gender Bias," *Missouri Law Review* 44 (Winter 1979): 1; Dignity Memorial, "Wallace Mendelson Obituary," November 19, 2004, accessed July 25, 2022, https://www.dignitymemorial.com/obituaries/austin-tx/wallace-mendelson-8211125; Dignity Memorial, "Margery Mendelson Obituary," May 31, 2017, accessed July 25, 2022, https://www.dignitymemorial.com/obituaries/austin-tx/margery-mendelson-8209838.

24. The Yolanda Hotel was owned by Sam Schwartz and named for his daughter, as was the Yolanda Theater he operated nearby. Jeff Taylor Sr., telephone conversation with Bryan E. Stone, February 25, 2023.

25. Holman Irwin ("Ozzie") Baum (1905–1986) operated a printing company in San Antonio.

26. Edgar A. ("Eddie") Klein (1912–2000) was born in Pennsylvania, attended Rice University in Houston, worked for the San Antonio Independent School District, and owned the George Mendlovitz Store in Seguin, Texas. He also served as a legislative assistant to a longtime member of the Texas Senate. "Eddie A. Klein Obituary," *Austin American-Statesman*, April 20, 2000.

27. Jaffe's mural was also described in the *Eagle Eye*, the newsletter of the Eagle Pass Army Air Field. Made possible by "a combination of rare artistry and superb willingness on the part of Mrs. Sue Jaffe," the mural "depict[s] a typical cross-section of life and activities in the interior of Mexico" and "will add much to the beauty of the U.S.O. Patio." I have been unable to find additional information about Jaffe or her lieutenant husband. Albert Shank, "At the U.S.O.," *Eagle Eye*, August 14, 1943.

28. Colonel John H. Bundy (1902–1983), a California native, earned a civil engineering degree from Santa Clara University in 1927. He enlisted in the army the next year and trained as a pilot at Kelly Field in San Antonio. Bundy served at posts in California and in the Philippines, and from 1936 to 1942 supervised pilot training at Kelly Field. He took command of the Eagle Pass Army Air Field in 1942 and remained throughout the war. He

retired from the military in 1954, settled in San Antonio, and died in 1983. He is buried at Fort Sam Houston in San Antonio. Army Air Forces Flying Training Command, *Eagle Pass Army Air Field Class Book*, 1943, accessed June 17, 2024, https://aafcollection.info/items/documents/view.php?file=000483-01-00.pdf, 29.
29. Descended from Jewish retailers on both sides of his family, Samuel Alexander Meyer (1917–2005) was born in Rochester, New York, his father a longtime sales representative for Stein-Bloch clothing manufacturers. Two of his mother's uncles, Ike and Louis Alexander, established the I. Alexander men's store in Laredo in 1886, and Sam made frequent visits as a child, deciding he would eventually live in Laredo. He attended the University of Rochester and the University of Texas, earning a master's degree in Spanish and Latin American civilization. He joined the navy in 1942, serving in the South Pacific until 1946. After returning to Austin to complete his thesis, he joined the faculty at Laredo Junior College, married Olga Rosenbaum in 1952, and had three children. In 1956 he became manager of the Alexander store, where he remained until it closed in 1988. He was a leading member of the Laredo business community, supported Jewish charitable and advocacy causes, helped promote trade between Texas cities and Mexico, and traveled widely throughout the world, including many international trips with his friend Morris Riskind. Meyer died in 2005. "Samuel Alexander Meyer," *Laredo Times*, September 16, 2005.
30. Riskind clearly intends for "border *pocho*" to mean a regional dialect blending Spanish and English (like Spanglish), in contrast to the "pure" Castilian of Spain, but he is misconstruing the term. Literally meaning "faded" or "off-color," *pocho* is derogatory, describing a person (not a language) of Mexican descent who is overly Americanized, especially one who does not speak Spanish. It is certainly a word Riskind would have heard in use, but he may have misinterpreted its pejorative meaning. Chad Richardson and Michael J. Pisani, *Batos, Bolillos, Pochos, and Pelados: Class and Culture on the South Texas Border* (Austin: University of Texas Press, 2017), x.
31. This is Private Morris N. Goldberg (1915–2004), then about twenty-eight, four years younger than Riskind, and from Buffalo. According to a 1943 item in his hometown newspaper, Goldberg was promoted to sergeant, led High Holiday services at the airfield chapel, and had been "a youth leader in the Labor Zionist Movement" in Buffalo. Army Air Forces Flying Training Command, *Eagle Pass Army Air Field Class Book*, 76; "Sergeant Conducts Services," *Buffalo Evening News*, September 17, 1943.
32. I had no luck identifying or learning more about Ruza.
33. Fort Ringgold was established in 1848 at the close of the Mexican War in Rio Grande City, forty miles upstream of McAllen and about 220 miles downstream of Eagle Pass. Built to defend the newly defined international boundary and to secure the region from Mexican border incursions, it was an important garrison during the Mexican Revolution in 1910. During World War II it became the headquarters of the 124th Cavalry, the last horse cavalry regiment in the US Army, assigned to patrol the border. The fort was closed in 1944 when the unit was converted to ordinary infantry and transferred to Fort Riley, Kansas. Garna Christian, "Fort Ringgold," *Handbook of Texas Online*, accessed June 26, 2022, https://www.tshaonline.org/handbook/entries/fort-ringgold; Texas Military Department, "1st Squadron, 124th Cavalry Regiment," accessed June 26, 2022, https://tmd.texas.gov/1st-squadron-124th-cavalry-regiment.
34. The reference here is unclear. There was a Lieutenant Ammon A. Augur who served at Ringgold, but that was in the 1870s and 1880s, and he died long before the era Riskind writes about.
35. *El Diario de Juárez* is the daily newspaper in Ciudad Juárez, Chihuahua, across the river from El Paso.
36. An ukase was an autocratic edict by the tsar under the Russian imperial system. Riskind's usage is plainly ironic.

CHAPTER 8

1. Riskind's brother Reuben described El Retiro as "a 1,100 acre ranch not too far from the city." He said that their father purchased it because ranching "was the principal economic activity of the area, [centering] mostly on sheep and to a lesser extent on cattle," and he "concluded that he would have a side business." Riskind, "Texas Border Merchant," 17.
2. Owsey Mikulinsky and his wife, Tanya, were introduced in chapter 3.
3. Bessie Davies Kennedy was married to Robert Kennedy of Maverick County, a state-paid trapper of coyotes and other wildlife. "Mrs. Kennedy, however," according to a 1937 report, "is the more amazing of the two." In March 1937, "she hauled into town a huge mountain lion on the running board of her dust-covered car," then brought in a second a few weeks later. The first catch "weighed 160 pounds and was 7 feet 8 inches long." "Young Mother Is Southwest's Clever Trapper," *Waxahachie Daily Light*, April 6, 1937.
4. The nation's county extension service experienced rapid growth in the decades prior to Riskind's endeavor, making support available to him as a novice farmer that did not exist previously. "The nation's extension programs continued to expand markedly between the 1920s and the 1950s," writes agriculture historian Derek S.

Oden. "The demands of the Great Depression, environmental stress, and wartime emergency produced a need for larger staff, expanded publication services, and new communication tools, including radio. Thus, by the onset of the Second World War, extension programs had been transformed from their beginnings into a vigorous rural education network." Walter Monroe Sellers (1885–1957), a graduate of the University of Texas at Austin, was born in Alabama to a father who was a Methodist minister. After working as an agricultural extension agent in Alabama and Mississippi, he arrived in Eagle Pass about 1940, where he remained for life. He died in 1957 and is buried in the Maverick County Cemetery. Derek S. Oden, *Harvest of Hazards: Family Farming, Accidents, and Expertise in the Corn Belt, 1940–1975* (Iowa City: University of Iowa Press, 2017), 83. I'm grateful to my colleague Derek Oden for pointing this context out to me and for his observation that Riskind's agricultural experience highlights "the era's transitional nature."

5. Maverick County judge Robert (or Roberto) Edward Bibb (1904–1969) figures prominently throughout the memoir, and Riskind has more to say about his life and career in chapter 13.

6. Born in Chihuahua, Mexico, Atanacio Cruz García (1885–1978) immigrated to El Paso in 1902 and was a railroad worker there. He married in 1910, began working in agriculture, applied for US citizenship in 1914, and crossed the border frequently through various towns, including Eagle Pass, throughout the 1920s and 1930s, presumably seeking work. The US Census shows him living in Uvalde in 1920, and his 1942 World War II draft registration shows him employed by Morris Riskind in Eagle Pass as a farm foreman. He died in Los Angeles.

7. Riskind is employing terminology he heard in use, but it's informal. *Víbora* is a more general term for a snake (or viper); *víboras de cascabel* more specifically refers to rattlesnakes. *Alicantres* are, specifically, a Mexican species also known as the Sonoran whipsnake, seen often in the American Southwest. Unlike the American coral snake (*coralillo* or *serpiente de coral* in Spanish), it is not venomous.

8. Hite Thorne Harper (1894–1965) and Paul Lawrence (Larry) Harper (1897–1964) were the brothers of Osie Harper, mentioned frequently in the memoir. They and their family were fixtures in the Eagle Pass business community across generations, and they also operated ranchland in northern Mexico. A syndicated 1965 news item credits Eagle Hardware with "outfitting an army" when, in 1915, the Mexican president sent troops to Eagle Pass for equipment. "In one week," the story reports, "the border store sold the Mexicans almost 5,000 horses and mules and hundreds of saddles." "Post Exchange?," *Austin American*, March 28, 1965.

9. Riskind described in a 1995 interview how he acquired this engine: "A regular pump engine was very, very expensive, and I was trying to conserve my resources because Papa was paying for all of this and I was trying to hold costs down as much as possible. So I went to San Antonio, to a junk automobile place. Horsepower was not what it is today, the biggest car that Buick made was a straight eight, I think they call it the Century. It had an engine something like 120 horsepower, which it was a huge, long thing. It was an inline, eight-cylinder engine. . . . So I had him deliver this engine, I think I paid a couple of hundred dollars for it in a junkyard. I had it delivered and I had it checked over to see that it was in good mechanical condition, and I had it attached . . . to run the pump." Morris Riskind interview.

10. Born in Coahuila to American parents (his father was a mine superintendent), Edward Wilson Ritchie Sr. (1896–1973) settled in Maverick County with his family in 1903 and was working his own farm by 1924. With his brother John, he established Tiro Tres Farms, which grew and shipped spinach from Eagle Pass and Crystal City, eventually acquiring the nickname "The Spinach Kings." Ritchie remained in the profession for life, and so important was it to him that his family placed a memorial plaque on his grave in the Maverick County Cemetery: "Spinach was his gain. Spinach was his fame. Spinach made his name." Ritchie's descendants are still active in spinach production in South Texas today. FindaGrave, "Edward Wilson Ritchie, Sr.," accessed June 19, 2024, https://www.findagrave.com/memorial/51249686/edward-wilson-ritchie; Tiro Tres Farms, "History," accessed August 12, 2022, https://www.tirotresfarms.com/about1; "Meet a Farmer | Texas Spinach," 2018, accessed June 21, 2023, https://www.youtube.com/watch?v=7Ha-LVvN_HI.

11. Manuel Sánchez Moncada (1896–1975) was born in Eagle Pass; his father, Teodoro, was a butcher. (It is unclear if Felipe Moncada, a Riskind store employee mentioned elsewhere in the memoir, whose father Felipe Sr. was also a butcher, was related to Manuel, but the appearance of a family trade suggests they were.) Manuel was engaged in the grocery business by 1918, when he registered for the draft, and was married by 1920; his wife, María García, was born in Mexico in 1901. They had five sons, some of whom followed their father into the grocery, fruit, and vegetable businesses. Manuel died in Eagle Pass in 1975.

12. As Riskind indicates (and as Alvarez was apparently given to emphasizing), Joe Gonzalez Alvarez (1888–1962) was born in Doiras, in Asturias, Spain. It is uncertain when he arrived in the United States or in Eagle Pass, but multiple records identify him as a produce buyer, broker, and shipper. Alvarez died in Eagle Pass and is buried in the Maverick County Cemetery. The fruit and vegetable brokerage A. J. Tebbe & Sons was formed

by Albidie J. Tebbe of New Orleans and his two sons, Cyril and Frederick. Originally based simultaneously in Michigan, where the family had lived since about 1906, and Texas—working in Michigan in the summers and Texas in the winters—the company closed its northern operation in 1929 to focus exclusively on Texas. A. J. lived in Carrizo Springs at the time of his death in 1942, and his sons continued the business out of San Antonio, Cotulla, and Carrizo Springs. "Obituary: Frederick J. Tebbe," *Press-Herald* (St. Joseph, MI), November 30, 1956.

13. *Morado* is Spanish for "purple."
14. Often called sticker burrs in English, or simply stickers, these grow from a grass called sand burr and are a familiar nuisance to most Texans—rural, urban, and suburban. See Mimi Swartz, "Texas Primer: The Sticker Bur," *Texas Monthly*, January 1985.
15. "Shoes" was included in the short story collection *Cabbages and Kings*, published in 1904 by Texas author William Sydney Porter, better known by his pseudonym O. Henry. In the story, Porter calls the dreaded items "cockleburrs" and writes that they were "as hard as filberts, and bristling with spines as tough and sharp as needles." Connie Patterson, "Porter, William Sydney," *Handbook of Texas Online*, accessed April 7, 2023, https://www.tshaonline.org/handbook/entries/porter-william-sydney.
16. Riskind mentions Osie Harper and other members of the Harper family many times throughout the memoir in a wide variety of roles and circumstances, indicating the family's reach and importance. Richmond Chase Harper (1923–1993), Osie's middle son, was born in Eagle Pass, attended Texas A&M University, served in the army during World War II, and worked in the family's various operations throughout his life. He died in Laredo and is buried in the Eagle Pass Catholic Cemetery.
17. Antonio Coasa Mello (1907–1993) was born in Bermuda and was living with his family in Eagle Pass by 1910. He must have returned to Bermuda, as his naturalization petition indicates a later arrival of 1916 through New York, but in any case he settled again in Eagle Pass, married, and raised a son there. He died in San Antonio in 1993.
18. Also known as the collared peccary, the javelina is distantly related to the South American tapir, although on account of its pig-like appearance it was long assumed to be a relative of wild hogs or boars. Native to Texas and most common in the state's southern and border regions, it is an omnivorous animal that favors prickly pear cactus, also native to the area. They are often aggressive toward dogs but rarely toward humans unless startled or cornered, and they do have large canine-like teeth that can inflict serious damage. Art Leatherwood, "Javelina," *Handbook of Texas Online*, accessed October 26, 2022, https://www.tshaonline.org/handbook/entries/javelina.
19. The wartime agricultural labor shortage was a severe national problem, as Derek Oden confirms: "The nation's leaders quickly discovered potentially serious obstacles to achieving victory in the production battle. These challenges included the problem of labor scarcity, as farmworkers migrated to cities and men enlisted into military service. A study by the Bureau of Agricultural Economics highlighted the dilemma, reporting that approximately two million men had been diverted from agricultural work to other employment or military service." The shortage motivated federal responses such as the Women's Land Army and the Bracero Program, which Riskind describes later in the memoir. Oden, *Harvest of Hazards*, 89.
20. John C. Carraway (1898–1963) was a freight and passenger agent for the Southern Pacific Railroad.
21. A lug is a shallow wooden container, in a variety of sizes according to product, used for packing and transporting produce.

CHAPTER 9

1. A native Texan and resident of Eagle Pass and Uvalde, Hal L. Mangum owned the San Geronimo ranch near Múzquiz, which he acquired and began expanding in the early 1920s, in addition to extensive holdings in Texas. The San Geronimo was described in a 1941 profile as "one of the major ranch properties in Northern Mexico," and a visitor in 1944 claimed it was 581,000 acres. The *latifundio* (estate) of the Sánchez Navarro family, established in 1765 near Monclova and confiscated by the Mexican government in 1866, was the largest private estate in North America, more than 16.5 million acres. In addition to amassing magnificent wealth in ranching and other enterprises, the Sánchez Navarro family was prominent, if perhaps somewhat misguided, in Mexican politics, siding with Spain during Mexico's independence revolution and later with the French in their failed 1862 invasion of Mexico. It was in retaliation for this activity that Benito Juárez, who led Mexican resistance to the invasion, ordered the state confiscation of the family *latifundio*.

Luis Terrazas, governor of Chihuahua intermittently over decades beginning in the 1850s, was an ally of President Benito Juárez and later of Juárez's rival, Porfirio Díaz. During his long political career, he amassed an almost unimaginable amount of personal wealth and property. "Take a Mexican Central train at El Paso, Texas," claimed a 1923 *New York Times* profile of Terrazas, "travel south . . . for ten hours, and if your train is following schedule time you will be traveling for the entire period through the ranch of one man," Luis Terrazas, the nation's "wealthiest citizen." As a consequence of the Mexican Revolution, in which Terrazas supported the overthrown Díaz regime, revolutionary leader Pancho Villa confiscated Terrazas's property in Chihuahua—approximately five to seven million acres and more than a million head of cattle—to redistribute as small private farms for working-class Mexicans. Terrazas and his family fled to the United States, where he lived in exile in El Paso and Los Angeles. In 1920, at ninety-one years old, he returned with his sons to Chihuahua to attempt to reconstitute his holdings but died before it could be accomplished. Riskind's reference to "Old man Meir" is unclear. Frank Reeves, "Chuck Wagon Gossip," *Fort Worth Star-Telegram*, December 12, 1941; Fred S. Mathias, *The Amazing Bob Davis: His Last Vagabond Journey* (New York: Longmans, Green, 1944), 16; "H. Mangum, Runnels Native, Dies; Funeral Set Saturday," *San Angelo Weekly Standard*, August 11, 1950; Charles H. Harris, *A Mexican Family Empire, the Latifundio of the Sánchez Navarros, 1765–1867* (Austin: University of Texas Press, 1975); "Gen. Terrazas Dies; Once Cattle King," *New York Times*, June 16, 1923; "Luis Terrazas; Former Governor of Mexico," *Busy Man's Magazine*, March 1907, 9–11.

2. The three sons of Osie and Mary Black Harper were Osie Harper Jr., Richmond Chase Harper, and Hite Lawrence (Tito) Harper.
3. This appears to be the same proposal Mike Riskind dismissed as *"kunkel-munkel* business" in chapter 3.
4. Francisco Madero led the revolt in 1910 to overthrow Porfirio Díaz and subsequently became president of Mexico. His family was one of the nation's wealthiest. His grandfather, Evaristo Madero, built a fortune through a variety of enterprises including agricultural production of rubber, cotton, and wine, mining, banking, and textile manufacture. In addition, the family possessed multiple haciendas and massive quantities of land in Coahuila and elsewhere in northern Mexico. See Stanley R. Ross, *Francisco I. Madero: Apostle of Mexican Democracy* (New York: Columbia University Press, 1955).
5. Felipe and Dorothy Latorre, in their study of the Kickapoo tribe of northern Mexico, identify Las Rusias as one of two Anglo-owned ranches (the other was La Mariposa, whose owners, the McKellars, were acquaintances of the Riskinds in Eagle Pass) that were established on land the Kickapoo believed was taken from them unjustly. In the 1930s, write the Latorres, the Kickapoo "revived an old suspicion, which had rankled among them for years, that they had been despoiled of some of their land. Not only did the neighboring ranchers refuse them hunting privileges; they refused them privileges on land taken away from them and given to the adjoining ranches of La Mariposa and Las Rusias." Latorre and Latorre, *Mexican Kickapoo Indians*, 139.
6. This is Albert Buckner Harper (1860–1953), whose parents moved to Texas from Tennessee and established a family ranching dynasty in Texas and northern Mexico that continues today. At the time of this meeting, Harper was about eighty years old.
7. La Consolidada was an American-owned scrap metal company that began producing steel from scrap in Mexico City in 1914. Its plant was relocated to Piedras Negras in 1937, where it used scrap iron and steel procured in the United States to produce steel ingots, which were transported to Mexico City for final processing. At one point the La Consolidada plant in Piedras Negras was responsible for producing 15 percent of Mexico's crude steel. The facility closed in 1991. Robert Andrew Kennelly, "The Location of the Mexican Steel Industry," *Revista Geográfica* 14 (September 1954): 54, 59; Salvador C. Corrales, "Notas Sobre La Historia Económica de La Consolidada, S.A. (1936–1991)," *Estudios Fronterizos* 37–38 (January 1996), accessed June 26, 2022, http://ref.uabc.mx/ojs/index.php/ref/article/view/323.
8. *Zonas de tolerancia* ("tolerance zones"), known colloquially as Boy's Towns, are red-light districts in several Mexican border towns.
9. Unfortunately Riskind never provides Agapito's other name, so it has proven impossible to identify him in more detail.
10. *Feeds and Feeding: A Hand-Book for the Student and Stockman* by Frank Barron Morrison was first published in 1898 and reprinted in revised editions until 1950. A 2012 review by a working farmer described it as "the bible of feeding animals," in which "horses, mules, dairy cattle, beef cattle, goats, sheep, and swine are covered in extensive detail." It is, the reviewer writes, "a book no person involved in husbandry can do without" and remains timely and useful long after its original publication. George Wright, "Book Review: Feeds and Feeding by Frank B. Morrison," *The Ruminant* (blog), January 4, 2012, accessed June 21, 2023, http://www.theruminant.ca/blog/2012/01/04/book-review-feeds-and-feeding-by-frank-b-morrison.
11. John Thornton Mason, Sr. (1890–1973).
12. Opened in Wisconsin in the 1850s and later reestablished in Denver, the Herman H. Heiser Saddlery Company became the largest manufacturer of saddles in the West. Colorado Virtual Library, "Hermann H. Heiser:

Saddlery Manufacturer," accessed June 21, 2023, https://www.coloradovirtuallibrary.org/digital-colorado/colorado-histories/boom-years/hermann-h-heiser-saddlery-manufacturer/.

13. Widely considered the foremost chronicler of Texas myth and legend, particularly stories of cowboy life and the frontier, folklorist and author James Frank Dobie published more than twenty books. Born and raised in South Texas, he was educated at Southwestern University in Georgetown, Texas, and at Columbia University, and then began a long career as a literature professor at the University of Texas at Austin. He took a break from teaching to serve overseas during World War I, then returned to teaching, only to quit again to manage his family's ranch, where he gained the experience and heard many of the stories that would become his subject matter. He returned to the university in 1921, published his first book in 1929, and maintained one of the state's most prolific literary careers until his death in 1964. He is one of a small number of writers buried in the Texas State Cemetery in Austin. Francis Edward Abernathy, "Dobie, James Frank," *Handbook of Texas Online*, accessed August 11, 2022, https://www.tshaonline.org/handbook/entries/dobie-james-frank.
14. Peter Riskind notes, "Morris Riskind never taught his children how to ride horses. He said they were 'stupid and dangerous animals.'"
15. I could locate no certain information on either Dovalina brother.
16. The daily newspaper comic *Mutt and Jeff* ran from 1907 until 1982, long past the death of its creator, Bud Fisher. The mismatch between tall, lanky Mutt and short, stocky Jeff was often a source of the strip's humor. Library of Congress, "Mutt and Jeff—An Unlikely Pair," Comic Art: 120 Years of Panels and Pages, accessed October 26, 2022, https://www.loc.gov/exhibitions/comic-art/about-this-exhibition/early-years-1890s-to-1920s/mutt-and-jeff-an-unlikely-pair/.
17. Leo Carrillo was a motion picture and television actor from the 1930s through 1950s. Born in California, he specialized in portraying Mexican characters in various Westerns. He was best known as Pancho, the Cisco Kid's trusty (and thinly mustachioed) sidekick, whom he played in several films and a long-running 1950s television series. IMDb, "Leo Carrillo: Biography," accessed January 29, 2023, https://www.imdb.com/name/nm0140504/bio.
18. Daniel is described in chapter 2.
19. William Christopher Bond (1893–1965) was born and lived his entire life in Eagle Pass; both of his parents were native Texans. As Riskind writes, Bond served in the US Army motor transportation corps during World War I (as indicated on his military headstone) and returned to Eagle Pass after the war to work as an auto repairman and truck driver; he later worked as a hunting guide. Bond is buried in the Maverick County Cemetery.
20. As related in Genesis 41, Pharaoh dreamed of seven grazing cows, "handsome and sturdy," who were approached by "seven other cows [that] came up from the Nile close behind them, ugly and gaunt" and devoured them. Pharaoh asked his Hebrew prisoner, Joseph, to interpret this dream, and Joseph told him it portended that seven years of plenty were on the way to be followed by seven years of famine.

CHAPTER 10

1. Maria Isabel Riddle (1907–2008) was the older sister of Morris Riskind's friend Octavio Riddle, mentioned earlier, and taught Spanish for many years in the Eagle Pass High School where Ruth Riskind was also a teacher.
2. Riskind appears mistaken about the order of events. According to Peter Riskind, Ruth became friendly with Eduardo Riddle *after* marrying and moving with Morris to Eagle Pass, and when she learned that his daughter Maria was planning a trip to Mexico, Ruth arranged to join her for a trip she had long desired because so many artists were going there at the time. The two women didn't know each other before the trip and didn't room together while traveling, but Maria had taught Spanish at the University of Texas and was fluent in the language while Ruth was not. Ruth spent about six weeks in Mexico City in addition to the time they spent together in Oaxaca. Peter Riskind, email message to Bryan Edward Stone, January 22, 2023.
3. A professor of philosophy at the University of California at Berkeley, Isabel Creed Hungerland was born in Berkeley, studied at Oxford, and earned a PhD at Berkeley in 1936. She taught at UCLA from 1936 to 1940, when Ruth Sholtz was a student there. Hungerland returned to join the faculty at Berkeley after the war and remained there until her retirement in 1967. Her research, which focused on aesthetics, the philosophy of language, and the history of philosophy, resulted in numerous publications including two books. She served, as Riskind notes, as the president of the American Society for Aesthetics, but not until 1965, later than he recalls; she held similar positions in various other professional organizations during the era of her association with Ruth. Berkeley awarded her the title of professor emerita prior to her death in 1987. Donald Davidson Benson Mates, "Isabel Creed Hungerland, Philosophy: Berkeley," in *University of California: In Memoriam, 1992*, ed. David Krogh, accessed June 17, 2024, http://texts.cdlib.org/view?docId=hb7c6007sj;NAAN=13030&doc.

view=frames&chunk.id=div00025&toc.depth=1&toc.id=&brand=calisphere.

4. Otto Klemperer, one of the foremost modern German conductors and composers, was born in Breslau in 1885, trained in Frankfurt and Berlin, and conducted orchestras in Prague, Hamburg, Berlin, and London among other places. From 1933 to 1939, after fleeing the Nazis, he conducted the Los Angeles Philharmonic Orchestra, presumably where his daughter met Ruth Sholtz. Lotte Klemperer was born in Cologne in 1923, came to the United States with her refugee family in 1934, and spent the rest of her father's life managing his complicated career and public image in America and postwar Europe. After his death she became a lifelong and full-time guardian of his reputation and legacy. Her brother, Werner Klemperer, was an actor famous for playing a Nazi colonel in the television series "Hogan's Heroes." "Otto Klemperer," *Britannica*, accessed August 13, 2022, https://www.britannica.com/biography/Otto-Klemperer; Martin Anderson, "Lotte Klemperer (1923–2003)," *The Independent* (UK), July 10, 2003.

5. Following the attack on Pearl Harbor, President Franklin Roosevelt signed Executive Order 9066 on February 19, 1942, authorizing the designation of geographical zones from which people of Japanese descent could be excluded. As a consequence, some 120,000 Japanese Americans—about two-thirds of them US citizens, about half of them children—were required to leave their homes in California, Oregon, Washington, and Arizona and spend the duration of the war in custody under the supervision of the War Relocation Authority (WRA). Ten "relocation centers" were constructed across the western states to house them, along with seventeen "assembly centers," mostly in California, where "evacuees" were received and held temporarily before assignment to a camp. There were also a number of army bases and Justice Department facilities throughout the country used for this purpose, including one in Crystal City, Texas, less than fifty miles from Eagle Pass.

Riskind's observation that the relocation centers were in fact concentration camps—and that America's treatment of its Japanese citizens was comparable to Nazi atrocities toward Jews—is an accurate if provocative thing to say. Historian Roger Daniels has shown that some Americans, including FDR, freely used the term "concentration camp" to describe the American facilities, as did the inmates themselves on occasion. But the policy of the WRA, which administered the camps, was to "put the best possible face on what it did" by adopting less inflammatory language. "The captive Japanese had been 'evacuated,' a word associated with rescue," Daniels writes. "The people who were in 'relocation centers' were 'residents,' not inmates." Daniels argues that "internment" is a term describing a specific legal status enacted in wartime that relates to legitimate prisoners of war; it is a status embedded in due process and international law. To Daniels, most Japanese American prisoners did not meet these criteria and were definitively *not* internees; he prefers to say they were "incarcerated" rather than "interned." Daniels admits, however, that after the Holocaust, a program of deliberate genocide that was worse by orders of magnitude than anything the Americans did, it is confusing to describe the American facilities as concentration camps, even if that is what they were. "The general practice, especially after the liberation of the Nazi death camps," he writes, "was to avoid the blunt term." Daniels notes with frustration how the continuing use of euphemistic language allows Americans to believe their actions were not so terrible. Roger Daniels, "Words Do Matter: A Note on Inappropriate Terminology and the Incarceration of the Japanese Americans," in *Nikkei in the Pacific Northwest: Japanese Americans and Japanese Canadians in the Twentieth Century*, ed. Louis Fiset and Gail M. Nomura (Seattle: University of Washington Press, 2005), 1, 7, 8, 11. See also Jeffery F. Burton, Mary M. Farrell, Florence B. Lord, and Richard W. Lord, *Confinement and Ethnicity: An Overview of World War II Japanese American Relocation Sites* (Seattle: University of Washington Press, 2011), 1, 3, 18, 25.

6. The Gila River Relocation Center was one of ten internment camps scattered mostly around the western states. Located on 16,500 acres of land leased from the Gila River Indian Reservation about fifty miles south of Phoenix, its two residential camps reached a maximum population of 13,348 in November 1942, making it the fourth largest city in Arizona at that time. At Gila River, twenty-four buildings were dedicated as school facilities, although it is uncertain how much space or time was devoted to art instruction specifically.

Art and art education were important components of camp life not only at Gila River but at all of the camps. As multiple books and exhibitions have demonstrated, the prisoners often used art as a coping mechanism, and many highly talented artists were among the incarcerated. "Most of the artists in the camps did not simply wish to illustrate the internment experience for the historical record," writes art historian Kristine C. Kuramitsu. "Art, as an expression of free creativity, provided a venue for a kind of spiritual empowerment as well." To a degree, teachers working in the camps tried to replicate the curriculum of peacetime schools, part of an effort "on the part of captor and captive alike," Kuramitsu writes, "to maintain a sense of normalcy behind the barbed wire." Incarcerated parents worried that their children would fall behind their peers if camp instruction was of lower quality than what was offered outside, and they took great interest in the teachers' qualifications and experience. In fact many of the teachers, like Ruth Sholtz, were recent college graduates with little experience, and turnover was high. Art programs in particular were underfunded, teachers underpaid, and materials in short supply. "There were NO desks or seats," remembered an art instructor at the Rohwer War Relocation Center in Arkansas, "except for two little benches about five feet long. . . . A few had tablets or notebooks or pencils. That was it!"

Compounding the teachers' frustration, their curriculum had to align with the objectives of the WRA, which emphasized vocational skills like printing and woodworking and promoted patriotic themes. Indeed, children's art programs were expected to serve the propaganda purposes of the government. "Art assignments were designed not only to give students vocational skills," writes art historian Gina Mumma Wenger, "but to be publicly displayed outside the camps in order to illustrate the values being taught to the young Japanese Americans." While adult internees could find art a meaningful source of self-expression and spiritual escape, for children and their teachers, bound by strict curricular requirements, it was often frustrating. As Wenger observes, "There was far too much irony between the teaching of democratic ideals and the denial of the children's American-born citizenship." Burton, Farrell, Lord, and Lord, *Confinement and Ethnicity*, 59, 61, 65; Arthur A. Hansen, "Cultural Politics in the Gila River Relocation Center 1942–1943," *Arizona and the West* 27 (1985): 327–62; Gila River Relocation Center, "A Year at Gila Anniversary Booklet," July 20, 1943, accessed June 17, 2024, https://www.jstor.org/stable/community.31046820; Kristine C. Kuramitsu, "Internment and Identity in Japanese American Art," *American Quarterly* 47 (December 1995): 622, 629; Gina Mumma Wenger, "History Matters: Children's Art Education Inside the Japanese American Internment Camp," *Studies in Art Education* 54 (2012): 28, 31, 35. Multiple studies exist of art produced by the prisoners. See, for example, Delphine Hirasuna, *The Art of Gaman: Arts and Crafts from the Japanese American Internment Camps 1942–1946* (Berkeley, CA: Ten Speed, 2013).

7. In a 1998 conversation recorded by her son Peter, Ruth Riskind remembered being interviewed by the administrator responsible for staffing the camps. "So he interviewed me, wanted to know why I wanted to go and I told him why. And he said, Did I think it was right that the Japanese were being shipped off like that? And I said I thought it was a terrible thing. And he said that's what he wanted. He didn't want anybody there who was looking at the Japanese as a captive audience to politicize or 'religisize' or change their viewpoint in anything. He simply wanted to, you know, be understanding." She also told of camp administrators sleeping outside so inmates could use their quarters until the inmates' barracks were complete. Ruth Riskind interview.

8. Born in Buffalo in 1903 to a father who was a pioneering motion picture exhibitor, Frederick Ullman Jr. graduated from Yale in 1925 and immediately embarked on a career as a film producer. Head of the Pathé News Agency, which produced newsreels, from 1942 to 1947, he then became a producer at RKO Pictures when it purchased Pathé. While at Pathé he partnered with Gilbert Seldes to produce *This Is America* (1933), a seventy-minute compilation of newsreel footage that provided a "kaleidoscopic cross-section of American life" and inspired a series of 112 short documentary films on the same principle, initially produced by Ullman and exhibited from 1942 to 1951. Many of the series' episodes centered on small towns during World War II, contributing to Hollywood's program to build and maintain civilian support for the war effort. "Frederick Ullman, 75, Theater Owner, Dies," *New York Times*, November 12, 1939; "Movie Producer Dies," *York (PA) Dispatch*, December 27, 1948; Richard Meran Barsam, "'This Is America': Documentaries for Theaters, 1942–1951," *Cinema Journal* 12 (1973): 23.

9. "I was supposedly being trained as someone who would take over as the assistant to the main cheese," Ruth later said of her job at RKO Pathé. "And I started off, I was supposed to write scripts having to do with 'This Is America,' you know, inspiring scripts. I wrote one script and they told me immediately that was not my forté." Ruth Riskind interview.

10. "So I was the first female executive, or [assistant to] any executive, they'd ever had," Ruth remembered in 1998. "And the men were furious because they saw their jobs flying out of a window, and they saw visions of women coming in there and taking over their work. So they didn't like this idea. So they were just horrible to me, just absolutely unbearable. . . . They were, they were sort of too oily, you know, in their ways of behaving toward me. . . . Everybody in the studio thought that I was Ullman's mistress. They couldn't figure out why the hell he'd hired me if I wasn't a mistress." Ruth Riskind interview.

11. This is Luis and Elena Follaman Ávalos. Luis was born in 1872 in Michoacán, making him about seventy-one during these visits. Elena was born in the state of Mexico in 1901, making her about forty-two. The 1930 national census identifies Luis as a *joyero*, or jeweler.

12. Cora Chambers Ostrom (1871–1956) was born in Arkansas and married Clark Ostrom, a civil engineer, in 1896. After they settled in Eagle Pass, he began working as an immigration inspector. They had four children, one of whom, reporter and local historian Dorothy Ostrom Worrell, was a friend of the Riskinds also mentioned in the memoir. Cora was active in the Rio Grande Valley Art League, which met regularly

in various South Texas cities. See, for example, "Art League Has First Conclave in Harlingen," *Brownsville Herald*, October 26, 1934.

13. Founded in San Antonio in 1916, the Pan American Round Table sought "to provide mutual knowledge and understanding and friendship among the peoples of the Western Hemisphere, and to foster all movements affecting the women and children of the Americas." Local chapters, or Tables, proliferated throughout Texas and Mexico to sponsor projects related to education. Helen B. Frantz, "Pan American Round Table," *Handbook of Texas Online*, accessed September 19, 2023, https://www.tshaonline.org/handbook/entries/pan-american-round-table.

14. In addition to working as a teacher, principal, and superintendent in Eagle Pass, Clarence James Garland Sr. (1903–1996) was a teacher and administrator in several other South Texas school districts, including Floresville and Carrizo Springs, and he later served as president of Texas Southmost College in Brownsville. Garland left Eagle Pass for the Southmost job in 1953 and did not return to Eagle Pass, so it would appear that Riskind is misremembering the time frame of these events by a pretty significant margin. "College President Since 1953: After 13 Years, Garland Still Looks Ahead," *Brownsville Herald*, November 20, 1966; "Obituary: Clarence J. Garland, Jr.," *Victoria Advocate*, January 25, 1996.

15. In Ruth's telling, she "looked at the book, and the book was horrendous, all about these terrible Mexicans and the wonderful Texans and how always thousands of Mexicans would come and five brave Texans would destroy them. And it was just very one-sided, to say the very least. So when I told this to Morrie, he said, 'Don't pay attention to that, I'll tell you what happened.'" Ruth Riskind interview.

16. Riskind elaborated in a previous draft on his dispute with published versions of Texas history. In particular, he criticized Mexican narratives for failing to acknowledge that Spain and Mexico "invited" empresarios Moses and Stephen Austin to colonize the province to help defend against Apache and Comanche attacks, suggesting Mexicans' complicity in their eventual loss of Texas. White historians, he continued, neglected the involvement of Tejano (Mexican Texan) supporters of independence, whose actions were motivated by Santa Anna's dissolution of the federal constitution and his imposition of what they viewed as centralist tyranny. "Mexicans such as De Zavala and Seguin," Riskind wrote, "joined in the Texas Revolution because of this. The flag above the Alamo had only *1824* on it, signifying that the defenders of the Alamo were not fighting for independence but for the return of the Mexican Constitution of 1824. Mexicans died in the Alamo alongside Anglos, not to separate from Mexico but for the return of the old, more liberal federal constitution."

17. The four children of Morris and Rachel Riskind are John Haskell Riskind (b. 1948); Peter Nathaniel Riskind (b. 1950), Susan Elizabeth Riskind (b. 1951), and Lorin Jeremy Riskind (b. 1954). Louis Bernal, a native of San Antonio and graduate of the University of Houston, worked for the Eagle Pass schools for twenty-two years, teaching Spanish starting in 1949 and proceeding to a series of administrative roles: Riskind describes in chapter 15 the thorny political circumstances that led to Bernal's appointment as coordinator of federal programs for the district. About 1971 he returned to San Antonio to a similar administrative position at the Southside ISD in southern Bexar County and was elevated to superintendent there in 1975. "Bernal Gets Southside Position," *San Antonio Express*, July 10, 1975.

18. The Book of Genesis describes how Joseph, one of the sons of Jacob, brought his brothers to Egypt and, as a close adviser to the Pharaoh, oversaw the flourishing of the Jewish people there. Many generations later, however, by the era of Exodus, the new Pharaoh "knew not Joseph" (Ex. 1:8) and was disinclined to treat the desendants of Joseph and his brothers, the Israelites, favorably. They were thus subjugated in slavery, where they remained until their liberation and escape under Moses.

19. The Riskinds' return to Eagle Pass—leaving practicing attorney Morris behind in Los Angeles—may actually have been somewhat earlier than this. In the anecdote below, Riskind says his parents lived in an apartment adjoining the one they leased to Pappy O'Daniel, and it's verifiable that O'Daniel arrived in Eagle Pass in November 1935 and stayed into early 1936. Gene Fowler and Bill Crawford, *Border Radio: Quacks, Yodelers, Pitchmen, Psychics, and Other Amazing Broadcasters of the American Airwaves* (Austin: Texas Monthly Press, 1987), 85–86.

20. All of these participants are introduced in chapter 3.

21. A minyan, a quorum of at least ten adult Jewish men, is required for prayer, although Reform, Reconstructionist, and many Conservative congregations also count women. Gathering a minyan can present an impossible obstacle to small Jewish communities like the one in Eagle Pass, and it is a requirement often dispensed with when it cannot be fulfilled.

Solomon Charles Freed (1891–1950) was born in Russia, immigrated to New York in 1905, and joined relatives in their mercantile business in Laredo by 1913. He was sufficiently successful by 1919 to apply for a US passport to carry on cross-border trade in Mexico. In 1921, he married Rosalie Kalvorisky (1898–1969), born in Texas and living in San Antonio, and they moved to Crystal City to operate a dry goods store and later the cannery, Freed Packing Company. They had three children. Both are buried in the Agudas Achim Cemetery in San Antonio.

22. Born in Cincinnati and ordained at Hebrew Union College, Rabbi David Jacobson (1909–2001) completed a PhD at Cambridge University and served at congregations in London and Indianapolis before accepting the associate rabbi position at Temple Beth-El in San Antonio, the city's oldest and largest congregation, where he remained until he retired in 1976. In addition to serving on a wide variety of civic boards and commissions, Jacobson played a pivotal role in helping to peaceably desegregate San Antonio during the civil rights era. Porter Loring Mortuary, "David Jacobson Obituary," November 4, 2001, accessed June 21, 2023, https://www.porterloring.com/obituaries/obituary-listings?obId=18277967. See also "San Antonio, Texas," *Encyclopedia of Southern Jewish Communities*; Bryan Edward Stone, *The Chosen Folks: Jews on the Frontiers of Texas* (Austin: University of Texas Press, 2010), 212–13; and Weiner, *Jewish Stars in Texas*, 178.

23. During Jewish services, the rabbi (or prayer leader) will select members of the congregation to call up to the altar to recite blessings in Hebrew and to read or chant from the Torah. Receiving this invitation for an *aliyah* is considered a great honor, and in larger congregations there could be fierce competition—often including financial contributions—to determine who would get the call. Clearly small groups like Eagle Pass faced no such difficulty.

24. Riskind's brother Reuben (1919–2010) was born and grew up in Eagle Pass until 1938, when he was recruited as a tennis player by the University of Texas and moved to Austin. There he met Esther Swirce (1921–2011), a Brownsville native, and the couple were married in Mercedes in 1941; they had three children. The same year Reuben enlisted in the Army Air Force and served in China, Burma, and India. Reuben and Esther returned to Eagle Pass in 1945, and Reuben became co-owner with Morris of M. Riskind, Inc., and the company's vice president. Like Morris, Reuben was active in a wide variety of social, political, and charitable organizations throughout his life. "Reuben Riskind Obituary," *San Antonio Express-News*, March 25, 2010; Munter, *History of the Jews of Texas' Middle Corridor*, 14–15; David H. Riskind, email message to Bryan Edward Stone, July 24, 2023.

25. Lloyd Theodore Munter (1924–1989), born in Brooklyn, served in the army during World War II and settled in Eagle Pass after the war. In 1946 he married Yolanda Schwartz (1921–1997), the daughter of Eagle Pass stalwart Sam Schwartz, and for a time Lloyd worked for Sam in his theater business. According to Munter's son William, Lloyd was instrumental in acquiring the Torah scroll for use by the Jewish community of Eagle Pass that Riskind mentions earlier. Both Lloyd and Yolanda are buried in the cemetery of Congregation Beth-El in San Antonio. Bennie (1913–1986) and Faye Levine (1921–2013) arrived in Eagle Pass in 1947; they are described in chapter 3. Harry Kaback (1909–1980) was born in New York to Russian immigrant parents and trained as a doctor in New York and Zurich. He practiced medicine in New York until World War II, when he enlisted in the army medical corps. Edna Bartsch (1919–2009), born and raised in Shamokin, Pennsylvania, trained as a nurse and joined the nursing corps during the war. Harry and Edna were both stationed in Thomasville, Georgia, where they met and married in 1943. After the war Harry opened a private practice near Binghamton, New York, where a son was born in 1946, and then (for reasons unknown) they moved to Eagle Pass, where their daughter was born in 1949. They remained in Eagle Pass until Harry's death in 1980; Edna resettled in Fort Worth and died in 2009. Arnold Schwartz (1921–1976), the son of Sam and Ellen Kranzthor Schwartz and Yolanda's twin brother, was born and raised in Eagle Pass, served overseas during the war, and went to work for his father's movie theater company after the war. He married El Paso native Edythe Guez (1925–1983) in 1946 and they settled in Eagle Pass, where they raised two sons. Rosalie Strum (1912–2005), a native of San Antonio, married Bennie Spiegel (1910–52), born in Portland, Oregon, in 1931. In Eagle Pass, where they moved by 1940, Ben became the manager of the Texas Gas Utilities Company and they had two sons. Like many Jewish families in small towns, the Spiegels maintained synagogue membership at a larger city's congregation nearby, in this case Orthodox congregation Rodfei Shalom in San Antonio. When Ben died in 1952, Rosalie returned to San Antonio and subsequently remarried. Munter, *History of the Jews of Texas' Middle Corridor*, 14.

In many ways the Stool family (originally Ctyl or Stul) were to Del Rio what the Riskinds and Edelsteins were to Eagle Pass—a large immigrant family that arrived sibling-by-sibling and became leading merchants and the core of the town's small but dedicated Jewish community. Max Stool (1882–1972), the uncle of the Max Stool named here, arrived in the border town in 1904. According to family legend, the Chicago resident and immigrant from Ukraine was traveling by train to California, but he disembarked in Del Rio to continue a poker game he had begun on the train and ended up staying permanently. Max began as a peddler, then opened the Guarantee Store in 1905; his family operated the Guarantee for nearly a century. Max's brother

Nathan (1898–1976) arrived in 1911 and opened another clothing store, which he sold to a third brother, David (1884–1971), who arrived in 1921 with his wife Esther. David renamed the business La Estrella (or the Star Store), which his family operated for about eighty years. David's son Max (1922–2012), mentioned here, was born in Del Rio two years after his parents arrived, served in the army in World War II, and worked alongside his father at the Star, taking over the business after David's death. He married Oklahoma native Libbie Polsky (1927–2006) in 1947. His nephew Michael, mentioned here with his wife Ann, represent the next generation: Michael was the son of William Stool, whose father Max was the family's original Del Rio patriarch. For a comprehensive study of the Stool family and their impact on Del Rio, see Braudaway, "On the Border: A Deck of Cards Led to Del Rio," 135–47.

26. Meaning "conclusion," the haftarah is a selection from the biblical Prophets that corresponds to the Torah portion for the week and is recited at a Shabbat service after the Torah is read. Bar and bat mitzvah recipients are given the honor of reciting that week's Torah portion and haftarah.

27. Sherri Riskind (b. 1955) married Riskind's youngest son, Lorin.

28. This was in November 1935, when O'Daniel broadcast for several months on station XEPN in Piedras Negras and lived in Eagle Pass with his wife, Merle, and their children, Pat, Mike, and Molly, who was then thirteen. Certainly one of the most unusual and colorful figures in Texas political history (which is saying something), Wilbert Lee "Pappy" O'Daniel was a native midwesterner who moved to Fort Worth in 1925 and became sales manager for the mill that produced Light Crust Flour. To advertise the product, O'Daniel managed a "hillbilly" band, the Light Crust Doughboys, which featured legendary Texas musician Bob Wills. O'Daniel also broadcast on air as the band's announcer, adding a heavy touch of cornpone along with religious and political commentary. Despite the program's enormous popularity, the company fired O'Daniel, who formed his own band, the Hillbilly Boys, and his own flour company for it to advertise; his sons became band members. The group's statewide broadcasts were hugely popular, and O'Daniel played up its rural, "hillbilly" appeal: he bestowed on himself the nickname "Pappy" and adopted a flour-based slogan, "Pass the Biscuits, Pappy," that became a familiar catchphrase. With the successful band and radio program as his platform, O'Daniel ran for governor in 1938, stressing "the Ten Commandments, the virtues of his own Hillbilly Flour, and the need for old-age pensions, tax cuts, and industrialization." He won election and was reelected in 1940 (Texas then had two-year gubernatorial terms), but his administration lacked much in the way of accomplishments. Nonetheless, he edged out a young congressman, Lyndon B. Johnson, for the Democratic nomination for US senator in 1941 in a race generally acknowledged to have been corrupt. O'Daniel served in the Senate until 1949 as an outspoken opponent of FDR, the New Deal, and communism. He failed to reclaim the governor's office in 1956 and 1958, when he ran on the claim that the *Brown* desegregation decision was a communist plot. O'Daniel died in Dallas in 1969. George N. Green, "O'Daniel, Wilbert Lee [Pappy]," *Handbook of Texas Online*, accessed January 3, 2023, https://www.tshaonline.org/handbook/entries/odaniel-wilbert-lee-pappy; Charles R. Townsend and John B. Bratcher II, "Hillbilly Boys," *Handbook of Texas Online*, accessed January 4, 2023, https://www.tshaonline.org/handbook/entries/hillbilly-boys; Albert J. Knabe, "O'Daniel, Merle Estella Butcher," *Handbook of Texas Online*, accessed January 4, 2023, https://www.tshaonline.org/handbook/entries/odaniel-merle-estella-butcher. See also John Mark Dempsey, *The Light Crust Doughboys Are on the Air: Celebrating Seventy Years of Texas Music* (Denton: University of North Texas Press, 2002).

29. Riskind is probably referring to the Communications Act of 1934, which created the Federal Communications Commission (FCC) to regulate the nation's airwaves, although it was focused more on systematizing radio frequencies, licensing, and call signs than content. In 1937, however, the National Association of Broadcasters, an industry group, distributed a set of broadcast standards providing guidelines for appropriate programming that would promote "spiritual harmony and understanding of mankind" and discouraged "advertising of fortune-telling, occultism, spiritualism, astrology, phrenology," and other quackeries. As broadcasters complied with such guidelines, American radio became canned and lifeless, leading to the eventual establishment of "border blaster" stations, usually operated by Americans, at sites in Mexico that could broadcast more freely and with enough power to be heard throughout the United States. Fowler and Crawford, *Border Radio*, 6.

30. The first of the border stations, XER, opened in Villa Acuña across the river from Del Rio, in 1931 by John R. Brinkley, a doctor of suspect credentials who had established a highly profitable medical clinic and radio station in Kansas. His claim to fame was a unique procedure he had developed to cure male impotence that involved extracting sections from the testicles of billy goats and implanting them into the scrotums of human subjects. The procedure made Brinkley wealthy enough to set himself up as a pioneer of American radio from his base in Kansas City, from where he dispensed information about the benefits of "goat glands" and other questionable medical advice. When the state threatened to shut his station down, he relocated to Acuña, from where he continued his venture until 1941, when the station was nationalized by President

Manuel Ávila Camacho. By then Brinkley's success had inspired a number of imitators along the length of the border, including station XEPN in Piedras Negras, established in 1932 under the management of Coahuilan businessman Claudio M. Bres. The business communities of Eagle Pass and Piedras Negras were strongly in support of the station, and Michael Riskind is reported to have said that "the station will put our towns on the map, modernize them, keep them abreast of the times. We must keep up." XEPN was, in fact, twice as powerful as Morris remembers, broadcasting at 100,000 watts. Fowler and Crawford, *Border Radio*, 78, 80. For more on Brinkley, see Pope Brock, *Charlatan: America's Most Dangerous Huckster, the Man Who Pursued Him, and the Age of Flimflam* (New York: Crown Publishers, 2008).

31. The garrison that became Fort Duncan was established on March 27, 1849, at the site that grew into Eagle Pass, providing the town's origin story. Ben E. Pingenot, *Historical Highlights of Eagle Pass and Maverick County*, 4.

32. *Li'l Abner* was a popular comic strip created by Al Capp that ran from 1900 to 1979 and featured a family in the rural Appalachian community of Dogpatch. Historian A. M. Gibson provides an earlier example of commercial exploitation that made *Kickapoo* "a common household word throughout America." In the late nineteenth century, "Healy and Bigelow of New Haven, Connecticut, organized the Kickapoo Medicine Company and peddled Kickapoo Indian Cough Cure, Kickapoo Indian Salve, and Kickapoo Indian Sagwa (a panacea guaranteed to cure symptoms of dyspepsia including neuralgia, headache, constipation, kidney disease, various stomach and liver ailments, and female disorders) through the peripatetic medicine show." It could be that this well-known real-life quackery inspired Al Capp's invention. It's unfortunate that Riskind doesn't seem aware of the implicit disrespect and co-optive nature of his proposal, but he is hardly alone in such insensitivity: there is currently available a commercial product called "Kickapoo Joy Juice" whose producer, the Monarch Beverage Company, advertises with the slogan "Weirdly Refreshing, Refreshingly Weird." (The company's website contains a link labeled "Click here to locate a Kickapoo near you!") Gibson, *Kickapoos*, ix; "Kickapoo Joy Juice," accessed June 20, 2023, https://drinkkickapoo.com/.

33. The Kickapoo Removal of Restrictions Act of 1906 was not as benign as Riskind implies. About two hundred Kickapoo families who owned allotments on the Kickapoo Reservation in Oklahoma had opted to join their kinspeople in Nacimiento, leaving their Oklahoma lands vacant. Anglo speculators and ranchers were anxious to acquire these properties but were prevented by laws protecting tribal ownership of lands. The 1906 act removed such barriers and allowed the Kickapoos' Oklahoma land to be sold out from under them without their knowledge or consent. After a lengthy legal fight, they were granted regular payments in nominal compensation. A. M. Gibson provides a detailed account of the years-long legal battle to obtain restitution for "Oklahoma Kickapoo land frauds." The long process was, Gibson says, "a legal circus which cluttered federal and state dockets from Oklahoma to Texas and Mexico and included counter suits; civil and criminal proceedings; charges of libel, bribery, fraud, and forgery; and heated extradition hearings." See Gibson, *Kickapoos*, 331–46, 347, 357.

34. Ethnographers Felipe and Dolores Latorre, writing in 1976, note that the Kickapoo "make two types of moccasins. The most popular is the one made from a single piece of skin, slightly puckered at the front and heel, cut in such a way that the skin turns like a cuff in the back and on either side of the instep, forming a flap. The other variety is made of two pieces, with uppers of buckskin and a sole of bovine leather. These are used strictly for hard wear or when going into the *monte* or sierra, where thorns and rough stones are a hazard. The one-piece moccasin is decorated on the instep with beading in angular geometric designs; the two-piece one is unadorned but has a thong intercalated in the upper part which can be tightened around the ankle for better security." Latorre and Latorre, *Mexican Kickapoo Indians*, 99.

35. The Latorres confirm many of Riskind's observations about changes in Kickapoo attire. "Today the majority of the older men wear nondescript work clothes. Trousers may be either Levis or wool slacks; shirts may be anything from T-shirts to heavy flannel plaids.... For footwear they use high work boots, oxfords, or cowboy boots." Men's hair styles, the Latorres write, "are an interesting study in variety." Older men "wear a long bob to the earlobes and, in the back, a thin queue, sometimes two feet long, tied at the end with a narrow ribbon." Women's dress consisted "of a flounced skirt and a loose overblouse of printed or solid cotton.... This dress was probably copied from that of the American pioneer women of the nineteenth century." Women "display as much variety in footgear as the older men do in clothing. They may be seen in moccasins of their own making, moccasins made by Indians from the United States, oxfords, loafers, tennis shoes, slippers, or boots." Latorre and Latorre, *Mexican Kickapoo Indians*, 99–102.

36. The Kickapoo shifted to migrant labor in the United States as a result of a severe drought in northern Mexico in the 1940s. By 1960, 98 percent of the Mexican Kickapoo lived part of the year in the United States, mostly at a seasonal campsite under the International Bridge between Eagle Pass and Piedras Negras. "In late April,"

write ethnographers Felipe and Dolores Latorre, "entire families traveled to Eagle Pass, where they set up flimsy camps under the International Bridge or rented substandard houses in the ghetto area of the city." They traveled widely during harvest season, working for "producers of beet sugar in Montana, cherry and apple growers in Utah, cucumber growers in Wisconsin, tomato growers in Indiana, and cotton growers in the Southwest," after which they returned to their reservation in Mexico for the winter. Jan Reid provides a discouraging depiction of the Kickapoos' living conditions at their campsite in "the long flood plain under the bridge at Eagle Pass." They built for themselves, Reid writes, "wickiups, but not with the cattail reeds and finely detailed craft of their ceremonial houses at Nacimiento. As if to acknowledge their transience and diminished state, they cobbled the domed structures together with plywood and tarp. They had no water, bathrooms, or privacy. Pedestrians on the bridge hurled down insults and trash." In 1985, historian T. R. Fehrenbach offered an intriguing analysis of the situation: "In a way, the Kickapoo are like the Jews wandering in the wilderness," he told the *Los Angeles Times*. "These people have been outsiders for more than a century. They've been treated like pariahs by everyone." Latorre and Latorre, *Mexican Kickapoo Indians*, 54, 111; Jan Reid, "The Forgotten People," *Texas Monthly*, February 1997; Fehrenbach quoted in J. Michael Kennedy, "Kickapoos Live Under Texas Bridge: Tribe Clings Stubbornly to a Way of Life Long Past," *Los Angeles Times*, April 8, 1985.

37. Christobal M. Benavides (1910–77) was an insurance and real estate agent in Eagle Pass. During their years of residency at Nacimiento the Kickapoo were technically Mexican citizens, but various documents over the years provided them freedom to cross the border and traverse the United States at will. Major William Whistler, commander of Fort Dearborn in Illinois, issued "safe-conduct" to the Kickapoo on September 28, 1832, and "with this document, repeatedly copied," wrote Felipe and Dolores Latorre in 1976, " the Indians enjoy free and unmolested access to both the United States and Mexico." To prevent forgery of these ancient documents, however, the US Immigration and Naturalization Service began issuing cards showing each individual's name in Algonquian and Spanish with a photograph and the statement "Member of the Kickapoo Indian tribe, pending clarification of status by Congress." In 1983, the Texas Band of Kickapoo Act extended American citizenship to the Kickapoo, paving the way for their Eagle Pass reservation and permanent American residency, but Congress continued to provide for their right to "pass and repass the borders of the United States." Latorre and Latorre, *Mexican Kickapoo Indians*, 62; "Texas Band of Kickapoo Act," Pub. L. No. 97–429, § Stat, 96 2269 (1983).

38. See chapter 2.

39. Born in 1921 in the South Texas town of Mission, Lloyd Bentsen grew up on one of the largest ranches in the Rio Grande Valley, his father a major player in oil and ranching. After completing law school, Bentsen flew bombers in World War II, after which he was elected Hidalgo County judge then, in 1948, congressman for the Fifteenth Texas Congressional District, which included Maverick County. After serving four terms, he took a hiatus from politics, moved his family to Houston, and focused on his law career. In 1970 he reembarked on political life, upsetting Democratic incumbent US senator Ralph Yarborough in the Democratic primary then defeating Republican nominee George H. W. Bush in the general election. Bentsen remained in the Senate for twenty-two years; ran and lost in 1988 as Michael Dukakis's running mate; and served as President Bill Clinton's Secretary of the Treasury from 1993 to 1994. He died in Houston in 2006. Maury Maverick would have been invited to the centennial event because his grandfather, Samuel, was the county's namesake. Maury, born in 1895, was a San Antonio native, World War I veteran, congressman for San Antonio from 1935 to 1938, and mayor of that city from 1939 to 1941. During World War II he served as member of the War Production Board and chairman of the Smaller War Plants Corporation. By the time of his visit to Eagle Pass, Maverick had retired from politics and died five years later in San Antonio. George Slaughter, "Bentsen, Lloyd Millard, Jr.," *Handbook of Texas Online*, accessed September 27, 2022, https://www.tshaonline.org/handbook/entries/bentsen-lloyd-millard-jr; Richard B. Henderson, "Maverick, Fontaine Maury," *Handbook of Texas Online*, accessed September 27, 2022, https://www.tshaonline.org/handbook/entries/maverick-fontaine-maury.

40. Born and raised in Eagle Pass, Dorthy Ostrom Worrell (1904–1995) was the daughter of Cora Ostrom, mentioned earlier as Ruth Riskind's friend and mentor. She married John Worrell about 1924 and they had three children. As Riskind notes, Dorothy wrote for the *Eagle Pass News Leader* then, after moving to San Marcos, began work as city secretary and occasional interim city manager. She died in 1995 and is buried in Eagle Pass.

41. There were, in fact, three Seminole Wars with the aim of forcing the Seminoles to leave Florida and cede their land to the United States. The reference here is to the Second Seminole War (1835–1842), a consequence of the Indian Removal Act of 1830, which compelled the Seminoles' forced removal to Indian Territory.

Most refused to leave and waged a bitter defensive war against the US Army. Wild Cat (Coacoochee) was born in Florida about 1810, a direct descendant of previous Seminole leaders, and became a leading figure in the tribe's resistance to removal, second only to Osceola. After several years of fighting, he was captured in 1841, forced to settle on a reservation in Arkansas, then brought to Texas in 1845 to attempt to make peace between the United States and the Comanches. Instead, he began traveling around the state promoting an intertribal confederation and unified Indigenous rebellion. He partnered closely in this sojourn with Juan Caballo (John Horse), a Black Seminole and, at least in his youth, an enslaved person. After the Indian Removal Act, Caballo relocated to Indian Territory along with a large number of other Black Seminoles, but they were dissatisfied with conditions there and joined Wild Cat's group to flee Oklahoma for Texas and eventually Mexico. The band made the crossing at Eagle Pass on July 12, 1850, and were, as Riskind suggests, well-received by Mexican and Coahuilan authorities. Brackettville, Texas, about forty-five miles north of Eagle Pass, is the site of Fort Clark, where the Seminole scouts employed by the army in the 1870s were stationed, and it remains home to a sizable community of their descendants. The 1852 memoir by Cora Montgomery (the pen name of Jane Cazneau) recounts her life as an early inhabitant of Eagle Pass and provides the earliest narrative history of the area. Donald A. Swanson, "Coacoochee [Wild Cat]," *Handbook of Texas Online*, accessed January 7, 2023, https://www.tshaonline.org/handbook/entries/coacoochee-wild-cat; E. Douglas Sivad, "Caballo, Juan," *Handbook of Texas Online*, accessed January 7, 2023, https://www.tshaonline.org/handbook/entries/caballo-juan; Guinn, *Our Land before We Die*, 1–8, 162–69; Montgomery, *Eagle Pass*. A fascinating analysis of Cazneau's book and the racial and expansionist theory behind it is provided in William T. Kerrigan, "Race, Expansion, and Slavery in Eagle Pass, Texas, 1852," *Southwestern Historical Quarterly* 101 (January 1998): 275–301.
42. The Fugitive Slave Act, passed by Congress in 1850 as part of the package of compromise bills that brought California into the union, committed the federal government to the policy that enslaved people did not become free by escaping to a free state, territory, or foreign nation. It required, furthermore, that fugitives be returned to their owners, and it penalized Americans who helped enslaved people escape.
43. Details about the Black Seminole scouts are in chapter 2.
44. It is unclear what 1910 act of Congress Riskind has in mind, but he may be thinking of the 1903 Supreme Court decision in *Lone Wolf v. Hitchcock* or some legislative consequence of it. Here the court ruled that Congress retains the power to abrogate treaties with Native American tribes without their agreement and with no judicial recourse. "Plenary authority over the tribal relations of the Indians has been exercised by Congress from the beginning," wrote Chief Justice Edward White, "and the power has always been deemed a political one, not subject to be controlled by the judicial department of the government." Even where Indian ownership of property has been established, White continued, "Congress possessed a paramount power over the property of the Indians, by reason of its exercise of guardianship over their interests, and that such authority might be implied, even though opposed to the strict letter of a treaty with the Indians." *Lone Wolf v. Hitchcock*, 23 S. Ct. 216 (1903).
45. The 1983 congressional act that granted American citizenship to the Kickapoo and recognized them as a subgroup of the Oklahoma Kickapoo tribe also permitted the purchase of 125 acres of land along the Rio Grande about eight miles south of Eagle Pass to establish the reservation of the Kickapoo Traditional Tribe of Texas (KTTT). I can find no confirmation of Riskind's supposition about Hollywood, but a syndicated UPI story from the time indicates that funds were raised privately to purchase the necessary land. "Initially, the land was used by Kickapoo daylaborers to rest on their way to U.S. fields," writes Elisabeth A. Mager Hois, "but, when in the mid-1990s they were largely replaced by machines, they had to seek another source of income. So, in August 1996, they set up the Kickapoo Lucky Eagle Casino on the [KTTT] reservation." Leon Daniel, "Wandering Indians May Receive Reservation Site," *Tyler Courier-Times*, January 8, 1984; Elisabeth A. Mager Hois, "The Kickapoo of Coahuila/Texas: Cultural Implications of Being a Cross-Border Nation," *Voices of Mexico* 90 (Spring–Summer 2011): 37.

CHAPTER 11

1. In *Gideon v. Wainwright* (1963), the Supreme Court ruled that criminal defendants in state courts are entitled to legal counsel, which the court must provide if they can't afford it. *Miranda v. Arizona*, in 1966, required law enforcement officials to advise suspects under arrest of their rights to remain silent and to legal counsel.
2. Riskind employed a pejorative in this sentence that was once commonly used, often without ill will or intent but is inflammatory today; to avoid misunderstanding I have followed the example of previous editors and replaced it with "illegal immigrants." Roger H. Thurmond (1904–1970) was born in Del Rio. His father, George M. Thurmond, was the district attorney of Val Verde County and a member of the Texas House of

Representatives, a seat that Roger would hold briefly in 1929 followed later by both of his sons. He served as a Val Verde county judge and district attorney before being appointed to the Sixty-Third District Court by Governor Coke Stevenson, with whom he had served in the legislature. He remained on the bench until his death in 1970. "Thurmond Service Is Set Thursday," *San Angelo Standard-Times*, March 25, 1970.

3. The trial took place in Beardstown, Illinois, on May 8, 1858. Lincoln represented Duff Armstrong, accused of murder. The crime occurred outdoors at night, but a witness testified that he saw Armstrong commit the murder by the light of the full moon. Lincoln "floored the principal prosecuting witness," according to his law partner William Herndon, "by showing from an almanac that the moon had set." Quoted in Duncan Ferguson, "True Story of the Almanac Used by Abraham Lincoln in the Famous Trial of Duff Armstrong," *Journal of the Illinois State Historical Society* 15 (October 1922): 689.

4. Established in 1849, the Texas State Penitentiary in Huntsville, north of Houston, was the state's first enclosed penitentiary and is legendary for its harshness. Donald R. Walker, "Texas State Penitentiary At Huntsville," *Handbook of Texas Online*, accessed June 28, 2022, https://www.tshaonline.org/handbook/entries/texas-stat e-penitentiary-at-huntsville.

5. Confusion such as Riskind describes here is common as there are great differences between an American notary public and a Mexican *notario público*, despite the similar names. Texas attorneys Jonathan A. Pikoff and Charles J. Crimmins note that the two titles "convey vastly different responsibilities upon their respective officeholders." Whereas in Texas, "virtually anyone can qualify and become a Notary Public," certification in Mexico as a *notario público* is rare and difficult to obtain. *Notarios públicos* act as arbitrators and mediators, issue judicial opinions, intervene in judicial proceedings, ensure the consistency and legality of legal documents, and certify public deeds. "In many respects," they write, "the Mexican Notario Publico serves not only as a lawyer but also as a judge in his role as protector of the law." By contrast, a notary public "only certifies the identity of [a document's] signer." Jonathan A. Pikoff and Charles J. Crimmins, "Lost in Translation: Texas Notary Public v. Mexico Notario Publico," accessed June 11, 2022, https://www.sos.state.tx.us/statdoc/notariopublicoarticle.shtml. See also Fred V. Perry, "Understanding the Mexican Attorney: Legal Education and the Practice of Law in Mexico," *International Lawyer* 10 (1976): 167–79.

6. The son of a prominent lawyer and president of the Texas Bar Association, David Elmer Hume Sr. (1886–1965) was born in Galveston, attended the University of Texas Law School, and served as county attorney and assistant district attorney in Houston before moving to Eagle Pass around 1916. He served there as county attorney in the early 1920s and again in the early 1950s and maintained a private legal practice until the end of his life. "Obituary: David Elmer Hume," *Austin American-Statesman*, November 18, 1965.

7. Elected to Del Rio's Sixty-Third Judicial District Court in 1932, Judge Brian Montague (1892–1972) presided over that bench until 1946. Born in Bandera, Texas, he served in World War I, studied at the University of Texas, and practiced law in San Angelo, Del Rio, and Alpine, where he served as district attorney. He died in Fort Worth. "[Brian] Montague Services Are Held," *San Angelo Standard-Times*, October 10, 1972.

8. Alfonso Leon Bres Burckhardt was the son of Claudio M. Bres, the Mexican radio entrepreneur Riskind mentioned in chapter 10.

9. David Hume Jr. (1915–1972) was born in Eagle Pass, where his father was county attorney. The younger Hume attended the University of Texas and the Southern Methodist University law school, then he enlisted in the navy and served in the submarine corps during World War II. He married Farlee Eaton in Waterford, Connecticut, near where he was stationed at New London; they had two sons. They settled in Maryland after the war, and Hume worked as a Justice Department attorney before entering private practice in Washington, DC. In 1962, he ran for the Democratic nomination for Maryland governor, opposing incumbent governor J. Millard Tawes (not, as Riskind remembers, Spiro Agnew, who was elected in 1966). Hume placed third in a field of seven, considered a run for the Senate, opted against it, and soon after divorced and returned to Eagle Pass. He worked there in private practice until his death in 1972. "David Hume Dies in Texas at 57, Ran for Governor of Md. in '62," *Baltimore Evening Sun*, October 7, 1972.

10. Born in Nova Scotia in 1883, Cyrus Eaton established himself in Cleveland and amassed a fortune, lost it in the 1929 crash, and rebuilt it, coming to own controlling interests in Goodyear Tire, Republic Steel, Detroit Steel, and other industrial firms. He became active in Cold War diplomacy and advised several presidents, holding that a beneficial working relationship could be established with the Soviet Union. When he died in 1979, President Jimmy Carter credited him with beginning the process that led to détente. "Cyrus S. Eaton Sr., Multimillionaire, 95," *Baltimore Evening Sun*, May 11, 1979.

11. Riskind's comments here about "legitimate" molestation are problematic to be sure; indeed, a previous editor opted to delete this passage. I have restored it from Riskind's original manuscript: it is not an editor's role to protect the author from himself.

12. The Battle of Flodden was an English victory over the Scots that took place in September 1513 in Northumberland. It was at the time the largest battle the two countries had fought against each other and is considered the last medieval battle fought in Britain. Simon Adams, "Battle of Flodden," *Britannica*, accessed January 7, 2023, https://www.britannica.com/event/Battle-of-Flodden.
13. Leopoldo Samaniego de la Sota (1899–1976) was born in Guanajuato, Mexico, became a radio broadcaster in Mexico City in 1930, and was sent to Eagle Pass as Mexican consul in 1946. He and wife, María (1910–70), had three children. María died in 1970, Leopoldo in 1976, both in Piedras Negras.
14. This was XEW, a five-thousand-watt station in Mexico City that launched in 1930. It "eventually became the most powerful and most popular station in the country," known as *La Voz de la América Latina desde México* (The Voice of Latin America from Mexico). Samaniego was the station's inaugural broadcaster. Fowler and Crawford, *Border Radio*, 150; Fernando Avedoy Guerrero, "XEW: 'La Voz de la América Latina desde México,'" W Radio, January 10, 2006, accessed June 21, 2023, https://web.archive.org/web/20060110144117/http://www.wradio.com.mx/historia.asp.
15. From the Spanish *picaro*, or "rogue," picaresque is a literary genre, typically in the form of novels, recounting the exploits of roguish adventurers in their travels from place to place. Often the protagonist thrives through criminal activity and by outwitting his rivals and social betters. Although elements of picaresque are present in some classical literature, the form reached its peak in seventeenth-century Spain, notably in the work of Guzmán de Alfarache and Miguel de Cervantes. Benet, *Benet's Reader's Encyclopedia*, 761.
16. William Kane (1906–1979) was born in New York and joined the US foreign service in the early 1930s. While posted in Prague, he married Czech national Dagmar Odehnal in 1936. They were posted in Washington during World War II, followed by assignments in London and Prague. William became the US consul in Piedras Negras in 1948 and remained until 1951, when they were sent to Caracas, Venezuela. Details of their lives are available in an oral history Dagmar gave in 1987, although she says little about their time in Piedras Negras and Eagle Pass. See Dagmar Odehnal Kane, interview by Mary Louise Weiss, March 9, 1987, Library of Congress, accessed June 21, 2023, https://www.loc.gov/item/mfdipbib001570/.
17. Richard N. Lane (1903–1966) was a realtor, accountant, and county auditor in Eagle Pass.
18. The policy dubbed Operation Intercept was "the nation's largest peacetime search and seizure operation by civil authorities," implemented in September 1969. The Nixon Administration had concluded that Mexico was the main source of marijuana, heroin, and other narcotics entering the United States and that the actions of Mexican authorities in response were "inadequate." Intercept was superficially a blunt interdiction campaign, but it had a deeper purpose of inflicting economic hardship on Mexico in order to pressure them into a more cooperative antidrug stance. Deploying "intensified land, sea, and air surveillance along the entire 1,945-mile U.S.-Mexico border," writes historian Richard B. Craig, enforcement agents inspected more than 4.5 million individuals and their belongings. "Vehicles, their component parts, personal baggage, purses, books, lunch boxes, jackets, and in some cases even blouses and hairdos were searched. . . . No person or object was spared, including diplomatic and consular officials, their children, possessions, and even their diplomatic cargo." The inevitable result was long lines at crossing points and enormous cost to businesses that relied on cross-border patronage, much to the consternation of the business community in both countries. "In the words of an American consular official," Craig writes, "'the architects of Operation Intercept failed to recall a small but very significant fact—there are two sides to this damn border!'" Within months, following public outcry in both countries, the inspections were severely curtailed and Nixon apologized to the Mexican president for "the friction" the strategy had caused between them. Despite its harshness, however, Intercept did have its intended effect, leading to bilateral talks about increasing drug enforcement within Mexico. "While Intercept proved a short-term diplomatic blunder," Craig concludes, "it indirectly and somewhat ironically became a long-term catalyst to an accelerated Mexican antidrug campaign and a springboard to more effective international cooperation." Richard B. Craig, "Operation Intercept: The International Politics of Pressure," *Review of Politics* 42 (October 1980): 556–80. See also Lawrence A. Gooberman, *Operation Intercept: The Multiple Consequences of Public Policy* (New York: Pergamon Press, 2013).
19. Born in Chicago and a longtime resident of Indianapolis, the Reverend Charles P. Shulhafer (1912–1985) accepted a position as rector of Eagle Pass's Church of the Redeemer in 1969. He remained there until 1977 when he left for a church in Edenton, North Carolina. "Rev. Shulhafer Resigns as Redeemer Ch. Rector," *Eagle Pass News Guide*, December 16, 1976.
20. According to Peter Riskind, the family "lived in an apartment in Mexico City for six weeks during the summer of 1966."

CHAPTER 12

1. Francis George Aldridge (1898–1985) was born in Eagle Pass. His father, Ernest, was a bookkeeper for a number of local businesses, and Francis followed him into that profession. He never married, served in the army during World War II, and was active in the American Legion for the remainder of his life. He died in Eagle Pass in 1985 and is buried in the Maverick County Cemetery.
2. Garza was introduced in chapter 2.
3. Joanne Hershfield addresses the appeal Riskind notes here of Parisian fashion to Mexican women, particularly in the 1920s and 1930s, when European modernity seemed to speak to the emerging feminism of postrevolutionary Mexico. Describing an advertisement illustration from 1929, Hershfield notes that "la chica moderna" pictured there "is 'up-to-date' in her appearance, her dress, and her attitudes. . . . She is the personification of feminine elegance and Parisian chic. This resemblance can be linked to the transnational distribution of the ideologies and commodities of style and fashion." Fashion magazines from New York and Paris were consumed throughout Mexico, Hershfield says, and "modeled how to be modern." Hershfield, *Imagining La Chica Moderna*, 19, 66.
4. The Missouri, Kansas & Texas Railroad (MKT), also known as the Katy, connected Denison, Texas, to points north beginning in 1872 but rapidly expanded to provide passenger service to Dallas, Fort Worth, Waco, San Antonio, Houston, Galveston, and Wichita Falls. The San Antonio MKT Depot on Durango and South Flores streets, a magnificent Spanish-style structure with steeples and a vaulted ceiling, was built in 1917. It remained in operation until 1964 when the Katy ceased passenger service and was demolished in 1969. Donovan L. Hofsommer, "Missouri-Kansas-Texas Railroad," *Handbook of Texas Online*, accessed October 28, 2022, https://www.tshaonline.org/handbook/entries/missouri-kansas-texas-railroad; Hugh Hemphill, "Missouri Kansas Texas," San Antonio Transportation History, accessed October 28, 2022, https://classic.txtransportationmuseum.org/history-rr-missouri-kansas-texas.php.
5. When it opened in 1910, the Adolphus Hotel was the tallest building in Dallas. Designed in a rich beaux arts style and located in the heart of downtown at the corner of Commerce and Akard, it remains one of the city's most luxurious hotels. Despite expansion and remodeling, the original portion of the Adolphus building "has been called one of the city's most beautiful commercial structures." The Baker Hotel, opened in 1925 across the street from the Adolphus, was the city's other premier hotel until it closed in 1979. Prominent members of Dallas society and American presidents were guests there. Liz Carmack, *Historic Hotels of Texas: A Traveler's Guide* (College Station: Texas A&M University Press, 2007), 153; City of Dallas Office of Historic Preservation, "Baker Hotel," April 9, 2019, accessed June 21, 2023, https://cityofdallaspreservation.wordpress.com/tag/baker-hotel.
6. The Dallas Civic Opera was established in 1957. Jewish business leaders including Arthur Kramer and Herbert and Stanley Marcus were critical to its founding. See Stone, *Chosen Folks*, 200.
7. The Dallas Apparel Mart opened in 1964 as part of the magisterial Dallas Market Center, a six-building complex devoted to marketing goods and connecting wholesale suppliers with retail buyers. It closed in 2003, but at its peak in the 1980s it was the largest wholesale fashion market under one roof in the world, comprising 1.8 million square feet with nearly two thousand separate showrooms featuring more than ten thousand individual apparel lines. "It is a place," according to a *Texas Monthly* writer in 1981, "where every year, in ten furious major market weekends, 100,000 buyers . . . order an estimated $2 billion worth of merchandise. It is a place where the fashion consciousness of New York and Paris can be transmitted to the heart of America." As Riskind describes, this flashy, world-class system entirely replaced the personalized relationship between small buyers like Riskind's and the traveling salesmen who visited their stores in person. "Clearly the Apparel Mart and its innovation of bringing together thousands of clothing lines under one roof marked the beginning of the end for the traveling salesmen," according to a 1984 *D Magazine* feature on the Dallas Apparel Mart. "In [the old] days, we were constantly on the road," said one distributor. "It was really a traveling man's occupation. Today, you have the luxury of the customer coming to you." These observations certainly conform with what Riskind has to say about his changing business. Michael Ennis, "Rags to Riches," *Texas Monthly*, January 1981; Clarissa Tartar, "Anatomy of the Apparel Mart," *D Magazine*, April 1, 1984.
8. This was Hurricane Alice, the first major storm of the 1954 Atlantic hurricane season, which made landfall just south of Brownsville on June 25 and proceeded directly up the line of the Rio Grande, crossing over Laredo then into West Texas. Although damage from wind was slight—the storm's highest winds were measured near Brownsville at eighty miles per hour, a Category 1 hurricane by today's standards—heavy rainfall caused severe flooding on the Rio Grande and the Pecos River. Walter R. Davis, "Hurricanes of 1954," *Monthly Weather Review*, December 1954, 370.
9. In fact, catastrophic flooding is common in the Rio Grande Valley and in the memoir: even while speaking

of their rarity, Riskind describes the effects of three major floods he experienced personally in 1922, 1932, and 1954. In early September 1932, heavy rains across South Texas caused extensive flooding along the Rio Grande, Devils Creek, and Nueces River. Eagle Pass and Piedras Negras were inundated, and several buildings in downtown Eagle Pass collapsed. A new bridge linking the cities was spared, but a similar crossing in Del Rio was badly damaged. The flood he describes here, which occurred in late June 1954, was noted at the time as "the Rio Grande's greatest flood in history." "Eagle Pass and Piedras Negras Flooded Friday," *Corsicana Daily Sun*, September 2, 1932; "Giant Crest Expected at Laredo Tomorrow," *Corpus Christi Times*, June 29, 1954.

10. The agents Riskind encountered were considering adjustments to the international border based on the flooded condition of the river, which designates the boundary. The International Boundary and Water Commission was formed in 1889 by joint agreement between the United States and Mexico to enforce boundary and water agreements between the two nations and settle disputes between them. The course and width of the Rio Grande change frequently, making it difficult to locate the border in times of flood or drought. "As the settlements grew along the boundary rivers and the adjoining lands began to be developed for agriculture in the late Nineteenth Century," states the commission's current website, "questions arose as to the location of the boundary when the rivers changed their course and transferred tracts of land from one side of the river to the other. The two Governments by the Convention of November 12, 1884 adopted certain rules designated to deal with such questions." International Boundary and Water Commission, "Mission, Organization and Procedures for Solution of Boundary and Water Problems," accessed January 5, 2023, https://www.ibwc.gov/about_us/about_us.html. See also Douglas R. Littlefield, *Conflict on the Rio Grande: Water and the Law, 1879–1939* (Norman: University of Oklahoma Press, 2014).
11. Longtime Riskind employee Federico Perez (1888–1960) was sixty-six years old at the time of the flood.
12. The 1954 flood was devastating, but Riskind exaggerates its deadliness. The head of the Weather Bureau office in Miami estimated casualties from Hurricane Alice at fifty-five—seventeen in the United States and thirty-eight in Mexico. Davis, "Hurricanes of 1954," 370.
13. As noted in chapter 2, Vela lived in Piedras Negras and crossed the border daily to work at Riskind's.
14. Harold Hausman (1922–1992), whose immigrant Jewish family is described in chapter 3, was born in Laredo, where his parents lived for a period between stints in Eagle Pass. He attended Texas A&M University and returned to Eagle Pass to run an appliance store. He died and is buried in San Antonio.
15. Alejo B. Vann (1882–1954) owned the Sabinas Inn, a beer hall next to the Hotel Eagle in a historic building that once housed the city's first customshouse and post office. In addition to the Merchant's Cafe, a drinking establishment on Main Street a few blocks from Riskind's, Mike Chorgas (1892–1976), an immigrant from Greece, owned and operated a number of other establishments in town.
16. This is Oscar Flores Tapia, who served as governor of Coahuila from 1975 until his resignation in 1981 amid corruption charges. Riskind is incorrect on a couple of details: Flores Tapia founded a society of journalists and writers but was not the president of a teachers union, and he was never actually arrested on corruption charges, only investigated and forced out of the PRI, his political party. Nevertheless, the extent of Flores Tapia's alleged corruption was extreme, amounting to some thirty million dollars amassed over his five years in office, much of it stemming from an agency he created to obtain low-cost, government-subsidized housing loans for the poor, which he used instead to purchase luxury homes he sold to wealthy buyers. When these activities were exposed by a Saltillo newspaper, President José López Portillo—himself no stranger to massive corruption—called for an investigation. Facing impeachment, Flores Tapia resigned instead. He later wrote a book detailing his perceived mistreatment by the president. Juan M. Vásquez, "Hard Times for Corrupt Mexican Politicians," *Spokane Review*, September 6, 1981; Mark Seibel, "Coahuila Governor's Plight Signals Change," *Corpus Christi Times*, August 27, 1981; Oscar Flores Tapia, *José López Portillo y Yo: Historia de Una Infamia Política* (México, DF: Editorial Grijalbo, 1983).
17. I have been unable to determine which president this was.
18. Riskind is mistaken about the legal hierarchy in Mexico, where it is *more* difficult to become a *notario público* (notary public) than to obtain a *licenciado en derecho* (licentiate in law). Indeed, a *licenciado*, which requires years of schooling and examinations and is therefore roughly equivalent to the requirements for attorneys in the United States, is a prerequisite for becoming a *notario*. According to legal scholar Fred V. Perry, "In the Federal District (Mexico City) and over one-half of the Mexican states, this degree [*licenciado en derecho*] must be acquired either to practice law or to be a notary." Perry, "Understanding the Mexican Attorney," 173.
19. Albert D. Eidson (1886–1953) was born in South Carolina and had settled in Texas by 1914, when he married Alice Viola Winters in Corpus Christi. His brother, E. B. Eidson, remained in Corpus Christi and operated a department store there, as Albert did upon reaching Eagle Pass by 1918. Eidson was serving as mayor of Eagle Pass when, as Riskind describes below, his store was destroyed by fire in December 1952. Riskind appears

to be mistaken about Eidson reentering business after the fire, as he died just three months later. "Eagle Pass Fire Razes Three Stores," *San Angelo Standard-Times*, December 15, 1952.

20. Monsignor José Jáuregui-Yañez was born in Michoacán in 1901, studied in Spain and Italy, and was ordained in 1930. Returning to Mexico, he served churches in Guadalajara and various towns in the Saltillo diocese before being assigned to the Piedras Negras parish in 1941. A Saltillo newspaper profile described him as "a strong, dynamic, cheerful, charismatic, loving, joking, generous, tireless man, with a cleft brow, with a stentorian and well-modulated voice, and almost invincible." Otto Schrober, "Monseñor José Jáuregui—Parts I and II," *Zócalo*, n.d., accessed June 20, 2024, https://www.zocalo.com.mx/monsenor-jose-jauregui-i-parte, https://www.zocalo.com.mx/monsenor-jose-jauregui-ii-parte. Translation by Google.

21. Alice Viola Winters Eidson (1892–1968) was born in Ohio and married Albert D. Eidson in Corpus Christi in 1914. She lived with him in Eagle Pass until his death in 1953, after which she moved to San Antonio, where she lived another fifteen years. Her obituary notes that she was "active in opera circles." "Mrs. Alice Eidson," *San Antonio Express*, August 18, 1968.

22. Carolina Cerna (1906–2000).

23. Bertha Flores Riojas (1900–95) was born in Veracruz, Mexico, and was married to another Eagle Pass retailer. She died in Eagle Pass and is buried at Our Lady of Refuge Cemetery.

24. Devaluation occurs when a national government adjusts the value of its currency relative to that of another nation's currency or against an index or standard; it is a tactic nations employ in times of economic or fiscal crisis in an attempt to revive their domestic economy by making imported goods less desirable for their citizens to buy. In the 1970s, the discovery of vast Mexican oil reserves at just the moment global oil prices were soaring momentarily supercharged the Mexican economy, but declining prices in the early 1980s quickly cooled it off and led to a massive federal deficit, 30 percent unemployment, and 100 percent inflation. In February 1982 the Mexican government devalued the peso by about 40 percent, down to 2.1 US cents per peso; a second devaluation in August took it down to 1.43 cents per peso. As a result, the purchasing power of pesos in the United States declined sharply: in January 1982, five thousand pesos would buy $185 worth of American goods, in December, just $33 worth. It was no longer affordable or advantageous for Mexican customers to cross the border to shop in American stores.

   The effect of the devaluation on businesses in US border towns, where Mexican nationals comprised a significant share of the clientele, was devastating. In the 1970s, during the boom in Mexico, border businesses reaped the benefits, and Eagle Pass was a standout beneficiary. Philip N. Diehl cites data showing that retail sales in Maverick County increased by 17.1 percent in 1979, another 18.5 percent in 1980, and a breathtaking 52.6 percent more in 1981, greater growth than any other Texas border town. But with the crash in the peso's value and the consequent disappearance of Mexican customers, Maverick County businesses lost 79 percent of their retail sales between 1981 and 1982, greater again than any other Texas border community.

   The problem Riskind describes regarding customers' credit accounts reveals a different consequence of devaluation. Customers were hard-pressed to repay debts to American merchants once the pesos they earned at home were worth only a fraction of the dollars they had borrowed in Texas. The Riskind store's policy to require repayment in dollars would not have eased the problem for their Mexican customers, but of course it would have been enormously costly to the store to accept payment in devalued pesos. Christina Majaski, "Devaluation: Definition, How It Works, and Examples," Investopedia, August 29, 2021, accessed June 21, 2023, https://www.investopedia.com/terms/d/devaluation.asp; Philip N. Diehl, "The Effects of the Peso Devaluation on Texas Border Cities," *Texas Business Review* 57 (June 1983): 120, 121, 122. See also Jim Gerber, "Shopping on the Border: The Mexican Peso and US Border Communities," March 2001, accessed June 21, 2023, https://www.academia.edu/3063300/Shopping_on_the_border_the_Mexican_peso_and_US_border_communities.

CHAPTER 13

1. There is some confusion in Riskind's recollection of Salinas and this World War II squadron. In May 1942, a German submarine sank a Mexican oil tanker near Miami, drawing Mexico into the war. Lacking a significant military force of its own, Mexican president Manuel Ávila Camacho offered to supply a unit of fighter pilots to the American war effort, Escuadrón 201, nicknamed the Aztec Eagles. The men trained in Texas and deployed to the Philippines in March 1945; they flew fifty-nine combat missions, and five of their pilots were killed. There was not, however, a Juan Salinas among them. It's possible that Riskind is mistaking the name of Alberto Salinas Carranza, a pioneer of Mexican aviation, organizer of Mexico's Department of Aviation, and frequent military air attaché. A memorial listing the names of the members of the 201st is in Chapultepec, Mexico City. Dana Calvo, "The Saga of the Aztec Eagles," *Los Angeles Times*, July 25, 2004.

2. The Hotel Regis was built in 1914 as a luxury hotel in a flamboyant neoclassical style on the Avenida Juárez

next to Alameda Park, the oldest public park in the Americas. Across the park, the Palacio de Bellas Artes was built in 1934 as a cultural center, which includes the city's main art collection. The Regis collapsed during the devastating earthquake that struck the city in 1985, and a memorial park, the Plaza de la Solidaridad, now stands on its former location.
3. The legendary Prendes opened in 1892 in downtown Mexico City and remains a leading fine dining establishment today. Famous diners include Diego Rivera and Frida Kahlo, Pancho Villa, Walt Disney, and Octavio Paz. Prendes, "Nuestra Historia," accessed June 28, 2022, https://prendes.mx.
4. Born in Mexico City, Cantinflas (real name Mario Moreno) was one of Mexico's most popular movie actors, starring in more than fifty films between 1937 and 1978. American audiences knew him best as Passepartout, Phileas Fogg's valet, in *Around the World in Eighty Days* (1956). His stage name derived from a Spanish expression for talking much and saying little, which captured his rapid-fire, nonsensical comedic banter. IMDb, "Cantinflas: Biography," accessed January 5, 2023, http://www.imdb.com/name/nm0134594/bio.
5. A broad avenue running diagonally through Mexico City's center, the Paseo de la Reforma is where many of the city's tallest buildings, most luxurious hotels and restaurants, and major monuments and other tourist attractions are located.
6. Río Bravo (or Rough River) is the name commonly used in Mexico for the Rio Grande.
7. Written and directed by American Jewish filmmaker Jules Dassin, *Never on Sunday* (1960) tells of an American intellectual (played by Dassin) who falls in love with a Greek prostitute on a trip to Athens and attempts to reform her. The film was produced in Greece, where Dassin was living after being subjected to the McCarthy-era Hollywood blacklist. Its soundtrack featured the bouzouki, a Greek stringed instrument with a round body and fretted neck resembling a lute.
8. The Plaka is a historic neighborhood in Athens, built above the ruins of the ancient city's agora and residential district, on the northeast slope of the Acropolis. It is the most frequently visited part of Athens and is where many of the city's most important museums are located.
9. A port city on the outskirts of Athens, Piraeus lies on the Saronic Gulf about five miles from the Acropolis and is the busiest port in Greece.
10. Meknes is in northern Morocco, fifty miles east of Rabat. It was an imperial capital in the seventeenth century, which led to the construction of a number of notable mosques and monumental gates.
11. Mark Robson (1913–1978), the director of thirty-three Hollywood films including *Peyton Place*, *Valley of the Dolls*, and *Earthquake*, was born in Montreal and married Sarah Riskind in Los Angeles in 1937; they had three daughters. Robson traveled widely to filming locations around the world and died while filming in London. I. S. Mowis, "Mark Robson: Mini Bio," IMDb, accessed July 6, 2022, https://www.imdb.com/name/nm0733476/bio/?ref_=nm_ov_bio_sm; Eleanor Blau, "Mark Robson, Film Director, Dies; Did 'Champion' and 'Earthquake,'" *New York Times*, June 22, 1978.
12. In 1945, the Jewish Agency established ZIM—the name is a Hebrew word from the Book of Numbers referring to a fleet of ships—to carry European refugees and supplies to Israel. It became a regular passenger carrier offering service to Israel and remains a major provider of cargo shipping in the region. ZIM Integrated Shipping Services, "Once upon a time—The story of ZIM," accessed October 27, 2022, https://www.zim.com/about-zim/history.
13. The King David Hotel was opened in 1931 in central Jerusalem near the Old City and became the city's premier luxury hotel. In 1946, in the last years of the British Mandate prior to Israeli independence, it housed a portion of the British military and administrative headquarters, making it a symbol of lingering British power in the emerging state. On July 22, 1946, in an apparent attempt to pressure the British to withdraw more quickly and recognize Israeli autonomy, Zionist paramilitary groups bombed a wing of the hotel, killing twenty-eight Britons, forty-one Arabs, seventeen Jews, and five others. Although roundly condemned, the attack may have encouraged greater UN involvement in the dispute and furthered Israel's claim to independence. Paul Johnson, *A History of the Jews* (New York: Perennial Library, 1988), 523–24.
14. The Six-Day War began on June 5, 1967 (two days before Riskind's scheduled arrival in Jerusalem), and lasted through June 10. The conflict broke out, writes Anita Shapira, "without premeditation on either side and without anyone having predicted that it would occur when it did." Egypt, Israel's hostile western neighbor, had signed a defense agreement the previous year with Syria, a Soviet client state to Israel's northeast. On May 16, 1967, responding to false Soviet warnings of an Israeli troop buildup on its Syrian border, Egyptian president Gamal Nasser ordered armored troops to reinforce the Sinai Peninsula between Egypt and Israel; he further demanded the withdrawal of UN peacekeeping forces from the peninsula and closed to Israel the Straits of Tiran, which offer an essential outlet from the Gulf of Aqaba and the Red Sea. These provocative actions initiated a dramatic three-week period of intensifying threat as media

throughout the Arab world "hailed Nasser's triumph and predicted the imminent end of the Zionist entity," Shapira writes. "In the streets of the Arab capitals, there were stormy rallies of support for Nasser, with slogans calling for him to throw the Jews into the sea." On May 30, Jordan's King Hussein, previously the mildest Arab leader in his posture toward Israel, bowed to pan-Arab pressure and agreed to a mutual defense agreement with Nasser that left Israel effectively surrounded and isolated. Sensing an existential threat, and receiving only tepid encouragement from the United States and Europe, Israel took swift unilateral action. On June 5 the Israeli Defense Forces (IDF) launched an offensive that destroyed Egyptian, Syrian, and Jordanian air power in a matter of hours, forced Egypt to retreat from Sinai, captured the peninsula and the Egyptian-occupied Gaza Strip, and seized the Golan Heights in the north from Syria.

At the outbreak of fighting, Israel urged Hussein to remain neutral, but Jordan initiated shelling of Jerusalem from across its border that compelled Israel to siege and occupy the West Bank and the entirety of Jerusalem, the eastern portion of which, including the Old City, had been under Jordanian control. Israel's decisive six-day victory, says Shapira, "changed the face of the Middle East," as "Israel was transformed from an underdog under threat of destruction to a regional power whose positions had to be taken into account." Israel held out hope of bargaining back the land it had taken in exchange for peace, but its Arab opponents viewed their losses as humiliations to be avenged only through further conflict, setting the stage for the 1973 Yom Kippur War. Israel's occupation of the West Bank, furthermore, initiated its long-standing conflict with the territory's Palestinian population and fueled the rise of the nationalist Palestinian Liberation Organizaton (PLO), which "now embraced the idea of a protracted armed struggle in the form of guerrilla warfare." Anita Shapira, *Israel: A History* (Waltham, MA: Brandeis University Press, 2012), 295, 297, 302, 305.

15. As a consequence of the 1948 Arab-Israeli War, neighboring Jordan seized control of the West Bank, which abuts it, including the eastern portion of the city of Jerusalem where the Old City and the Temple Mount are located; Israel claimed the city's western side. As Riskind explains, Jordan held East Jerusalem and prohibited Jews from entering sacred sites there until 1967, when Israel took it back in the Six-Day War. The President Hotel, in the upscale Talbiyeh neighborhood, a short distance from the Old City, was built in 1954 and was a popular destination for diplomats and official guests of the government. When its appeal dimmed it was purchased for redevelopment in 1988, but the plans never materialized and the building remained vacant and abandoned. Raz Smolsky, "Vacant Hotel in Jerusalem to Get New Lease on Life," *Haaretz*, August 6, 2014; Greer Fay Cashman, "Grapevine: Ahad Ha'am Harmony," *Jerusalem Post*, June 10, 2022.

16. Founded in 1939, the United Jewish Appeal was formed in a combination of philanthropies dedicated to supporting Jewish refugees and others in need in Europe, Israel, and the United States. The group was again part of a merger in 1997 that created the United Jewish Communities.

17. The Federation of American Zionists, formed in 1898 to support the establishment of a Jewish state in Palestine, merged in 1918 with other American Zionist groups to form the Zionist Organization of America (ZOA). It became an important fundraising and advocacy group for the eventual establishment of Israel, and after World War II, ZOA members and officers were instrumental in bringing about US recognition of the nascent Jewish state. In later years, with the Jewish state a fait accompli, ZOA shifted its focus to fundraising and public relations in support of Israel, advocating Hebrew culture in the United States, and initiating various Israel-based cultural programs. The group's seventieth convention was held in Israel in July 1967, with about a thousand Americans acting as delegates from various local chapters and councils. "Zionist Organization of America," *Jewish Virtual Library*, accessed October 27, 2022, https://www.jewishvirtuallibrary.org/zionist-organization-of-america.; "Columbia Co. Couple Tours All of Israel," *Danville* (PA) *News*, August 7, 1967.

18. The Balearic island of Majorca in the Mediterranean off the east coast of Spain was home to a thriving Jewish population in the Middle Ages. The establishment of the Inquisition on the island in 1488, however, began a long period of suppression, persecution, executions, and forced conversion. Under such pressure, many Jewish Majorcans became crypto-Jews, officially converting to Catholicism while retaining Jewish customs and identity in secret: they were called *chuetas,* from the Catalan word for "pig," a reference to their consumption (under duress) of pork. Despite their conversion, chuetas faced ongoing discrimination by the Majorcan and Spanish majorities and were required to marry within their group, a fact that helped them maintain a distinct identity and Jewish lineage. On this basis, and in recognition of centuries of discrimination, Israeli religious authorities officially recognized the descendants of the chuetas as Jewish in 2011, even though they are mostly Christians today, and they were offered an opportunity to rejoin the Jewish community. Gotthard Deutsch and Meyer Kayserling, "Chuetas," *Jewish Encyclopedia*, accessed January 5, 2023, https://www.jewishencyclopedia.com/articles/4376-chuetas; Jeremy Sharon, "Chuetas of Majorca Recognized as Jewish," *Jerusalem Post*, July 12, 2011. See also Baruch Braunstein, *The Chuetas of Majorca: Conversos and the Inquisition of*

Majorca (New York: Ktav Publishing House, 1972).

19. A cleansing bath filled with fresh natural water, a mikveh is used for a number of Jewish ritual purposes. Traditional Jewish married women visit the mikveh monthly following their menstrual periods; Jewish women also bathe at the mikveh prior to marriage and following childbirth. Riskind's reference is to the practice of immersing converts to Judaism as a sign of their entry into the Jewish faith. It is not, needless to say, literally a baptism.
20. Nablus is in the West Bank thirty miles north of Jerusalem, within the region occupied by Israel in 1967 in consequence of the Six-Day War.
21. The Cave of the Patriarchs (Me'arat Ha-Machpelah) is in Hebron, thirty miles south of Jerusalem in the West Bank. All three Abrahamic faiths recognize the site as the burial place of Abraham and his family; Abraham's purchase of the site to bury his wife, Sarah, is described in Genesis 23. A Byzantine-era basilica stands over the caves, built originally as a Christian church but which has changed hands and been repurposed many times since its construction. The British Mandate, which governed the region from the end of World War I through Israeli independence in 1948, imposed severe restrictions on Jewish access to holy sites in an attempt to maintain peace with the Arab population. Under Jordanian occupation, after 1948, as Riskind says, the basilica was rededicated as a mosque and remained inaccessible to Jews. A short time after the Israeli occupation began as a consequence of the Six-Day War (and after the Riskinds' visit), half the building was converted into a synagogue. Arriving so soon after Israel took control of the region, the Riskinds were among the first Jews to visit the site in decades. "Tomb of the Patriarchs and Matriarchs (Ma'arat HaMachpelah)," *Jewish Virtual Library*, accessed June 20, 2023, https://www.jewishvirtuallibrary.org/tomb-of-the-patriarchs-ma-arat-hamachpelah.
22. Following the 1948 Arab-Israeli War, Jordan captured, occupied, and later annexed the West Bank, including the eastern half of Jerusalem, which includes the Old City. Jerusalem was forcibly divided, as historian Simon Goldhill writes, and "the city became to all intents and purposes two cities." Under Jordanian rule, furthermore, East Jerusalem was scrubbed of signs of its previous Jewish life, and "the Mount of Olives cemetery," which originated in the sixteenth century and is the oldest Jewish burial place in the city, "was desecrated and the gravestones used for building work." The extent of the depredation was revealed when Israel reclaimed the area after the Six-Day War, and a Jewish Telegraph Agency report from that time confirms the specific offenses Riskind describes. "One of the most shocking reported episodes of the nineteen-year occupation by Jordan of Mount of Olives Cemetery near Jerusalem was confirmed today," it explains, "when Israeli officials found that tombstones from the historic burial ground had been used in the construction of an Arab Legion camp near Jericho. . . . Nearly the entire camp was built with tombstones carted from the cemetery and used for the main parade ground, roads, buildings and even the lavatory structure." Simon Goldhill, *Jerusalem: City of Longing* (Cambridge, MA: Harvard University Press, 2010), 320; "Jordanian Desecration of Mount of Olives Cemetery Described," Jewish Telegraphic Agency, July 5, 1967.
23. Jericho is a city in the West Bank about ten miles east of Jerusalem. According to the biblical account, the ancient city was defended by impenetrable stone walls. When the Israelites arrived in the Promised Land under their leader Joshua, God commanded them to blow their trumpets, at which point the walls miraculously fell, opening the city to Israelite conquest. Archaeological research has discovered evidence of a walled city at the site, but nothing on the scale described in the Bible. The biblical narrative appears in Joshua 6.
24. Hisham's Palace (or Khirbet al-Mafjar) is in the vicinity of Jericho and is among the most important early Islamic sites in Palestine. Built in the eighth century by Umayyad Caliph Hisham bin Abd el-Malik, who used it as a winter retreat, it included a palace, residence, thermal bath, mosque, audience hall, monumental fountain, and protective walls and gates. It was destroyed by earthquake in 749 CE. Excavation of the site began under the British Mandate in 1935. UNESCO World Heritage Centre, "Hisham's Palace/ Khirbet al-Mafjar," accessed June 28, 2022, https://whc.unesco.org/en/tentativelists/6546.
25. Qumran is an ancient settlement and archaeological site in the West Bank near the northwestern shore of the Dead Sea. In 1947, under the British Mandate, a set of ancient manuscripts was discovered there, mostly in Hebrew, mostly on papyrus, comprising eight hundred to nine hundred documents broken into thousands of small fragments. When reconstituted, these fragments revealed, among other works, the earliest extant versions of many entire books of the Bible.
26. Ein Gedi is a natural oasis and nature preserve near the Dead Sea. Although the preserve was not created until 1971, it has long been a popular destination for hikers and other visitors. The kibbutz (collective farm) near the site was founded in 1953, barely on the Israeli side of the border with the Jordanian-occupied West Bank.
27. The Romans under King Herod built a fortress (*masada* in Hebrew) and palatial residence for the king atop a 1,500-foot-high plateau at the western edge of the Judaean desert. As the Jewish historian Josephus describes, a group of Jewish rebels seized the fortress at the beginning of the Great Revolt against Roman rule in 66 CE.

Nearly a thousand rebels held the site for three years against Roman attack, finally committing suicide rather than submit to capture. The site was identified in 1842 but not fully excavated until the mid-1960s. Masada has become a physical symbol of Israeli determination, courage, and defiance, and it is one of the most-visited tourist sites in Israel.

28. Eilat is a port and resort town at the northern tip of the Red Sea. It shares a coastline with the Jordanian city of Aqaba.

29. Arad is an Israeli city on the edge of the Negev and Judaean deserts, sixteen miles west of the Dead Sea. In antiquity there had been a Canaanite city nearby that was used as a military outpost during the reign of Solomon, but Arad was founded in 1962, the first city planned and built under Israeli rule. Excavation of the site began in 1962 and uncovered, among other things, the only Israelite temple complex known outside Jerusalem.

30. Held in Khartoum, Sudan, in September 1967, three months after the Israeli victory in the Six-Day War, the Khartoum Conference offered an opportunity for enduring peace between Israel and the Arab states it had defeated. The eight Arab nations in attendance, however, "declared three 'Nos,'" writes Anita Shapira, "no recognition of Israel, no negotiations, and no peace." Nasser and his allies doubled down on their commitment to recapturing by force the lands they had lost. "Although Israel had proved itself capable of defeating the Arabs," Shapira concludes, "it could not force peace upon them. The basic balance of power between the small state and its numerous powerful neighbors was not altered by the Six-Day War." The failure at the conference to secure permanent peace set the stage for the 1973 Yom Kippur War. Shapira, *Israel*, 304.

CHAPTER 14

1. This is probably Willie Dan Russell (1895–1972), who was married to George H. Russell (1895–1961), a USDA crop inspector. She was active in a variety of civic and church programs while in Eagle Pass.

2. Born in Italy and raised in Brooklyn, José Greco was a renowned performer of Spanish dance, flamenco in particular. He formed his troupe, Ballet y Bailes de España de José Greco, in 1947 and toured widely throughout the world. He died in 2001. Jennifer Dunning, "José Greco, 82, Fiery Master Of Spanish Dance, Is Dead," *New York Times*, January 4, 2001.

3. The son of an Alabama farmer, Jake Marshall Mabe Sr. (1886–1985) became a grocer in several small Texas towns before settling in Eagle Pass in the 1930s. He held an administrative job with the chamber of commerce; his wife, Floy (1894–1974), was a school teacher. Rodolfo Leo Marquez (1904–1976) was a lifetime Eagle Pass resident, the operator of the grocery business founded by his father; as noted earlier in the memoir, some of the first Jewish religious services in Eagle Pass were held in an upstairs room above the Marquez store on Adams Street. Born in Fort Worth, Henry Max Medley (1909–1971) worked in the oil business in Harlingen before opening an automobile dealership in Eagle Pass after the war. Robert Bruce Thomson (1894–1982) was born in Eagle Pass to Scottish immigrant parents and lived his entire life there except for service during World War I; he was an oil and gasoline distributor.

4. This is Edward Herman Schmidt Sr. (1876–1968), whose son, Edward Herman Schmidt Jr. (1913–97), is mentioned below. Both were career bank officers at First National Bank.

5. The National Housing Conference (formerly Public Housing Conference) met for an annual convention, usually in Washington, DC. Riskind does not say, and it is impossible to determine, which year's meeting he attended, but his comment below about visiting his congressman on this or a similar trip while the Voting Rights Act (VRA) was being considered suggests that it was in or around 1965. The 1965 convention was held in March, the month the VRA was introduced in the House, but no significant votes on it were taken that month. "National Housing Parley," *Baltimore Sun*, March 7, 1965; James Bryan Spell Jr., "The Voting Rights Act of 1965: A Summary of Its Legislative History" (master's thesis, University of Richmond, 1966).

6. For much of Riskind's tenure, the Eagle Pass Public Housing Board operated under the provisions of the Housing Act of 1949, signed into law by Harry Truman on July 15, 1949. On the principle that "the general welfare and security of the Nation and the health and living standards of its people require housing production and related community development," the act provided federal funds to local housing boards to build 810,000 low-rent residential units over six years, clear slums and blighted areas, and rehabilitate farm housing in rural areas, a component that assured the support of southern Democrats. Although it was widely opposed by congressional Republicans and predictably decried as "socialistic," many prominent Republicans, such as Senator Robert Taft of Ohio, recognized its value and supported it, especially as it left decision-making power in the hands of local rather than federal authorities. Housing Act of 1949, 63 Stat 413 (1949); Charles Hurd, "President Signs Housing Bill; Orders Work Begun At Once," *New York Times*, July 16, 1949; Marjorie

McKenzie, "Pursuit of Democracy: Taft's Housing Stand Something of a Paradox of Usual Philosophy," *Pittsburgh Courier*, May 23, 1953.

7. The Voting Rights Act, which eliminated a variety of methods states employed, especially in the South, to prevent Blacks from voting, passed the House of Representatives on July 9 and was signed by LBJ on August 6, 1965. At that time the representative for the Fifteenth Congressional District of Texas, which included Maverick County, was Kika de la Garza (1927–1997), a Democrat elected to the seat in 1964. Despite Riskind's observation, however, and whatever the merits of his conclusion about personal integrity, de la Garza actually voted in favor of the VRA. Perhaps Riskind observed consideration of a different matter or something procedural preliminary to the final VRA vote. See roll call at GovTrack, "To Pass H.R. 6400, the 1965 Voting Rights Act.—House Vote #87—Jul 9, 1965," accessed February 1, 2023, https://www.govtrack.us/congress/votes/89-1965/h87; Spell, "The Voting Rights Act of 1965," 17.

8. Robert Edward Bibb (1904–1969), longtime county judge of Maverick County, was once described in a newspaper account as "the political leader of his area, comparable to Boss George Parr of Duval [County], without the controversy." Born in Monclova, Coahuila, Bibb's father was the Anglo-American manager of an iron mine (it is unclear whether he was also a rail conductor or if Riskind is mistaken), his mother a Mexican national. Although regarded as Anglo, Bibb was fluent in Spanish and was known locally as Roberto throughout his life. "He spoke Spanish and that is why he was able to exercise so much control over people's lives here," remembered David Riojas, an Eagle Pass attorney, activist, and former city council member. "He was able to interact not only with the money element, on the Anglo and business side, but he was also able to interact with the working class of Mexicanos." Bibb served as tax assessor for the Eagle Pass school district, deputy county sheriff, and deputy county tax assessor-collector before his election as Maverick County judge in 1938. He held that post until he was defeated in 1962 but was reelected in 1966; he died in 1969 before the completion of his final term. José Ángel Gutiérrez, Oral History Interview with David Riojas, July 9, 1996, accessed June 21, 2023, https://library.uta.edu/tejanovoices/xml/CMAS_017.xml; Raymond Brooks, "Shivers Hits CIO along Citrus Belt," *Austin American-Statesman*, July 19, 1954; John Bennett, "Bibb Eyes Return to Political Wars," *San Antonio Express*, February 25, 1965; "County Judge at Eagle Pass Dies at 64," *Fort Worth Star-Telegram*, March 26, 1969.

9. County judges in Texas are not primarily judicial officers, although as Riskind says their many duties could occasionally include adjudicating legal disputes. The main function of the county judge is to supervise the county commissioners court, manage the county budget, and oversee elections. Such responsibilities, especially in remote and rural counties, gave county judges inordinate power and opportunity to forge durable political machines. Writing about the county judge of Zapata County, downriver from Eagle Pass, J. Gilberto Quezada summarizes a situation similar to that of Maverick: "In his role as county judge, [Manuel] Bravo assumed total responsibility for the political, social, and economic affairs of the county. Without the bureaucracy of a city council, a city manager, or a mayor, the only governmental entity in Zapata County centered around the county judge and the commissioners' court. Therefore, his decision-making authority, which rested on his public office in the form of county government, constituted considerable power and control over local affairs." J. Gilberto Quezada, *Border Boss: Manuel B. Bravo and Zapata County* (College Station: Texas A&M University Press, 1999), 9.

10. One of the most enduring programs of Franklin Roosevelt's New Deal, the Works Progress Administration (later renamed the Work Projects Administration) was created in 1935 to provide federal funds to local communities to pay for a variety of building, infrastructure, recreational, educational, and arts projects. Before its termination in 1943, the WPA employed about 8.5 million Americans, including about six hundred thousand in Texas. WPA projects in Eagle Pass included a public library in 1937, a high school in 1938, and the conversion of Fort Duncan into a public park in 1939. Mallory B. Randle, "Work Projects Administration," *Handbook of Texas Online*, accessed January 11, 2023, https://www.tshaonline.org/handbook/entries/work-projects-administration; Eagle Pass Public Library, "History," accessed January 11, 2023, https://eaglepasspubliclibrary.org/history-1; Garza and Graham, "Eagle Pass High School," 177–79; "Old Texas Fort To Become Park," *Brownsville Herald*, July 6, 1939.

11. Bibb was typical among South Texas political bosses in his careful attention to the large Mexican American electorate, both in terms of turning out their vote and in winning and keeping their support. Indeed, as Evan Anders wrote in his classic study of South Texas political machines, bosses like Bibb "provided basic social and economic services to an economic elite of ranchers and merchants and to a lower-class mass of Mexican American laborers, farmers and ranch hands. Political success rested upon control of the Hispanic votes and access to patronage." J. Gilberto Quezada adds the observation, citing John Peavey, that in addition to getting out the Tejano vote, it "was common practice to count votes cast by Mexican citizens." Mexican Americans

12. in Texas generally had family in Mexico, "and this connection made it feasible to solicit their votes." The frequency of legal disputes involving Mexican nationals also provided ample opportunity for border bosses to extend favors to their American relatives to be repaid at the ballot box. Evan Anders, *Boss Rule in South Texas: The Progressive Era* (Austin: University of Texas Press, 1979), viii; Quezada, *Border Boss*, 8.

12. There is no doubt that the up-and-coming Lyndon Johnson, whom Stephen Harrigan superbly describes as "that ever-revving human ambition machine," cultivated relationships with every local source of influence in Texas. It seems notable, though, that Roberto Bibb's name does not appear in any major biography of Johnson, including Robert Caro's massive and exquisitely detailed multivolume work. The men certainly knew each other—there are photographs of them together—but Bibb was not one of LBJ's closer friends or contacts. Harrigan, *Big Wonderful Thing*, 601.

13. Every LBJ biography closely documents the legendary feat of "Landslide Lyndon" (a title that biographer Robert Dallek claims LBJ bestowed upon himself) in barely winning his 1948 election to the US Senate. As Riskind reports, Johnson lost his first Senate bid in a 1941 special election to Governor Lee "Pappy" O'Daniel, who edged Johnson out by just over a thousand votes statewide. Most of O'Daniel's margin mysteriously appeared at the last moment in East Texas ballot boxes. Determined not to be out-corrupted, Johnson arranged in his 1948 run for enough votes similarly to materialize for him in the Democratic primary—the only race that mattered in an effectively one-party state. He had help in this scheme from many quarters, but the pivotal returns came from Duval County in South Texas, where George Parr, the son of the county's original boss, Archie Parr, held sway. "Returns from Duval on election day," Dallek writes, "showed Johnson ahead, 4,197 to 40. The following day—during which Johnson turned an overall 2,119-vote deficit into a 693-vote lead—Duval added 425 ballots to his total." In the process of "correcting" the vote over the following days, officials in Alice, in Duval County, added nearly another 25 percent to LBJ's column. "It was," Dallek observes dryly, "an astonishing vote total." Robert Dallek, *Lyndon B. Johnson: Portrait of a President* (New York: Oxford University Press, 2005), 47, 67, 68. For detail on the Parr dynasty, see Anders, *Boss Rule in South Texas*; Dudley M. Lynch, *The Duke of Duval: The Life & Times of George B. Parr: A Biography* (Waco: Texian Press, 1976); Anthony R. Carrozza, *The Dukes of Duval County: The Parr Family and Texas Politics* (Norman: University of Oklahoma Press, 2017).

14. The agricultural labor shortage began during the war (as Riskind observes in chapter 8), as did the Bracero Program, which was implemented by an agreement with Mexico (not by Congress) in August 1942. Although originally a wartime measure, the program to permit short-term immigration of Mexican farm workers into the United States continued until 1964. In total, about four million braceros migrated to the United States; some estimates suggest as many as three hundred thousand entered the country each year through the 1950s. A significant number remained in the United States after their terms had expired, leading to a notorious operation in the mid-1950s to deport massive numbers of Mexican immigrants: many of those who were repatriated in the indiscriminate sweep had never been braceros. It is notable, furthermore, that Texas's participation in the program was delayed due to the reluctance of Mexican authorities to permit braceros to work in Texas "because of the number of cases of extreme, intolerable racial discrimination" there. Otey M. Scruggs, "Texas and the Bracero Program, 1942–1947," *Pacific Historical Review* 32 (August 1963): 254; Fred L. Koestler, "Bracero Program," *Handbook of Texas Online*, accessed January 8, 2023, https://www.tshaonline.org/handbook/entries/bracero-program; Deborah Cohen, *Braceros: Migrant Citizens and Transnational Subjects in the Postwar United States and Mexico* (Chapel Hill: University of North Carolina Press, 2011).

15. There were several such "reception centers" or "recruiting points" along the Texas border, including stations at Brownsville, McAllen, Eagle Pass, and Laredo, as well as a headquarters in El Paso. Through these stations, farmers throughout the country could contract for workers to be selected at the border and sent to them to work. It is understandable that Riskind would focus his attention on the economic benefit to Eagle Pass of housing such a facility, but it should be noted that the reception centers were also sites of severe discomfort and dehumanization for the migrants. In addition to intensive medical and mental evaluations, including invasive inspections for lice and venereal disease, migrants were stripped and sprayed with DDT, a powerful (and later discovered to be carcinogenic) insecticide. "Bracero Recruiting In Valley Centers Mapped," *McAllen Monitor*, August 7, 1949; Cohen, *Braceros*, 98–100.

16. This is probably Fred Freeman Smith (1901–1965), a San Antonio native and South Texas oil distributor.

17. Bibb had a contract with the US Department of Labor to provide food for braceros staying temporarily at the Eagle Pass reception center while they waited for work assignments. Anonymous letters to the Mexican consul in Eagle Pass revealed that Bibb was supplying the workers with canned meat marked "dog food—unfit for human consumption." The scandal became national news in October 1951, and despite lurid headlines about a Texas official feeding dog food to people, Riskind is correct that the product was actually canned

for human consumption and was safe to eat. Much of the meat was Marshall Plan surplus, "not dog food," reported the *Chicago Tribune*, "but an edible beef and gravy preparation frequently purchased by Eagle Pass residents for their own use." Bibb "had imported some 2,000 cases of the meat," according to the *Tribune*, and by altering the labels to mark it as animal food, he evaded a customs charge of about two thousand dollars. When the fraud was discovered, customs agents confiscated 728 remaining cases and the labor department canceled Bibb's contract. I could not confirm LBJ's intervention. "Judge's Little Meat Deal Goes to Dogs," *Chicago Tribune*, October 8, 1951; "Judge Poses," *Corsicana Daily Sun*, October 10, 1951.

18. The 1950 US Census recorded a population of 7,247 in Eagle Pass and 12,246 in Maverick County. Seventeenth Census of the United States, 1950, Maverick County, Texas.

19. I was unable to identify Spiller. It's possible that Riskind gave him a pseudonym to protect his anonymity. Lane's was one of the city's largest department stores. This is one of two mentions in the memoir of a Holocaust survivor who resided in Eagle Pass; the other was named Barg and is mentioned in chapter 3.

20. Daniel Ryan McDuff (1915–2002) was born in Brownsville; his father worked for the US Customs Service in several border communities. The family was in Eagle Pass by 1930, and McDuff attended college at Schreiner Institute in Kerrville and Tyler Commercial College in Tyler, Texas. He worked for Shell Oil in Kilgore and Standard Oil in Venezuela before marrying in 1942 and enlisting in the Army Air Corps, with which he flew missions in Italy. He and his wife, Gladys, resettled after the war back in Eagle Pass and raised two sons. McDuff was in the insurance business, as Riskind indicates, but devoted considerable time to civic activities. When he ran successfully against Roberto Bibb for Maverick County judge in 1962, newspaper coverage made much of the "names right out of Shakespeare" of Bibb's leading competitors: McBeath and McDuff. Dorothy Richter, "Weekly News Events of Tyler Commercial College," *Tyler Courier-Times*, March 19, 1939; "Shakespearean Names Leading 'Los Nuevos' in Maverick County Races," *San Antonio Express and News*, April 29, 1962.

21. Born in Los Angeles, Jeremiah "Jerry" Ingels Rhodes (1915–1988) came to Texas with his family in the 1920s. His father was a teacher and later superintendent of the San Antonio public schools. After graduating from Harvard Law School in 1941, Jerry served two years in the navy then returned to Texas, married Susie Gates of Eagle Pass, and began a legal practice there. He was active throughout his life on all manner of boards, commissions, and elective local offices.

22. Riskind's implicit defense of boss rule is notable given the de facto criticism such methods usually attract, and it may have something to do with Roberto Bibb's particular way of practicing it. In his study of South Texas bossism, William Curtis Bryson defined a spectrum of the region's counties ranging from "boss-free" (Hidalgo, Cameron) to "boss-ridden" (Duval, Starr, Zapata), and he identified Maverick County as "moderately boss-run." Perhaps Bibb's personal charm and relative lack of overt corruption made his autocratic methods more palatable to his electorate. William C. Bryson, "The Social Basis of South Texas Bossism," quoted in Quezada, *Border Boss*, 31, 234n71.

23. Riskind's memory of the Texas Democratic Convention is a little murky. He recalls traveling to Austin, where Texas Democrats gathered in 1960, but this cannot be the convention he attended, as neither Governor John Connally nor Eagle Pass mayor Art Flores, both of whom figure prominently in his account, had been elected then. The 1968 convention, which met in Dallas starting on June 10, is more likely, as Connally's supporters were indeed out in force as Riskind describes, to secure his selection for the nomination left open by the assassination of Robert Kennedy only the previous week. The main convention was held at the Dallas Municipal Auditorium, not in a hotel ballroom, but there were preliminary meetings at the city's Adolphus Hotel, no doubt what Riskind remembers. His observation below that his "recollection is probably incorrect in detail" is accurate, but this account nevertheless provides a revealing insight into the workings of state politics at that time. Rodger Duncan, "Democrats Eye Delegate Rows," *Fort Worth Star-Telegram*, June 10, 1968.

24. Arturo Flores (1928–2006) was born in Eagle Pass, graduated from Eagle Pass High School in 1945, and attended Texas A&M and Sul Ross State Universities. He served with the marines in Korea and was released from active duty in 1960, returning to Eagle Pass to work at La Consolidada steel mill in Piedras Negras and to pursue other metal businesses. Appointed to the Eagle Pass school board in 1959, Flores became board president in 1963 and was elected mayor in 1966. He served as Eagle Pass mayor until 1972. Throughout his life he held a wide variety of appointed positions on various civic boards, commissions, and councils. He died in Eagle Pass in 2006. Mission Park Funeral Chapels, "Obituary for Arturo Flores," June 14, 2006, accessed June 20, 2023, https://www.missionparks.com/obituaries/Arturo-Flores-37440.

25. Community action programs (CAPs) were created under the Economic Opportunity Act of 1964, a cornerstone of LBJ's War on Poverty that also established the Job Corps, Neighborhood Youth Corps, various programs to relieve impoverished farmers and support small businesses, and Volunteers in Service to America (VISTA), billed as a "domestic Peace Corps." Under the CAP provision, local community agencies could

determine needs in a variety of areas and apply directly for federal grants, bypassing elected local and state officials. The law required that each local CAP be "developed, conducted, and administered with the maximum feasible participation of residents of the areas and members of the groups served," the intent being to bring into the process as many of the poor as possible, those who would be most affected by the programs being developed. Predictably, the mayors and governors whom these agencies sidestepped opposed them and complained bitterly that their poorer constituents were embracing the opportunity to organize against them. "We ought not to be in the business of organizing the poor politically," one adviser argued to Johnson, while another warned that local CAPs were "using public funds to *instruct* people how to protest." Such concerns—not to mention the diversion of Vietnam and its cost to LBJ's concentration and influence—led to a gradual decline in the administration's support for the CAPs. Joshua Zeitz, *Building the Great Society: Inside Lyndon Johnson's White House* (New York: Penguin, 2019), chapter 4; Susan Abrams Beck, "The Limits of Presidential Activism: Lyndon Johnson and the Implementation of the Community Action Program," *Presidential Studies Quarterly* 17 (Summer 1987): 544.

26. Sociologist and criminologist Lloyd E. Ohlin, who led the Center for Education and Research in Corrections at the University of Chicago in the 1950s, worked within a school of thought that placed the blame for crime and "juvenile delinquency" on environmental factors like poverty and lack of economic opportunity rather than on the moral qualities of individuals. The "opportunity theory" Ohlin developed with Richard Cloward "held that an individual unable to achieve socially acceptable goals because of insufficient opportunities will strive to achieve those goals through alternative means, often illegal." This view later became the basis of the Johnson administration's attempt in efforts like community action to involve the poor more fully in organizing to improve their lives and communities. Margalit Fox, "Lloyd E. Ohlin, Expert on Crime and Punishment, Is Dead at 90," *New York Times*, January 3, 2009; Beck, "The Limits of Presidential Activism," 542; Richard A. Cloward and Lloyd E. Ohlin, *Delinquency and Opportunity: A Theory of Delinquent Gangs* (New York: Free Press, 1960).

27. Enriqueta Díaz (b. 1942) was elected county judge in 1990 but was removed from office and "convicted of a misdemeanor for concealing court records from the county attorney." As recently as 2018, she was endorsing (and criticizing) candidates in local elections and hosting a regular radio program. "I may be 75, but I'm still kicking butt," she said. John McCormack, "Old Scores, New Charges Enliven Maverick County Judge Race," *San Antonio Express-News*, February 25, 2018.

28. The value of this sketch of George de Mohrenschildt is in Riskind's personal reflections and impressions, though it contains a mixture of truth and inaccuracy—to the extent it may be possible to discern the truth about this mysterious and evasive man. It does appear that over the course of his life, de Mohrenschildt associated with both Jacqueline Bouvier Kennedy and Lee Harvey Oswald. George de Mohrenschildt (1911–1977) was born in Belarus of aristocratic ancestry and fled with his anti-Bolshevik parents to Poland in the early 1920s. He earned an economics PhD in Belgium, then immigrated to New York in 1938. There he befriended Jack Bouvier and met his teenage daughter, Jacqueline. Following a brief marriage, de Mohrenschildt enrolled at the University of Texas and earned a master's degree in petroleum engineering in 1945. After a second failed marriage and in the course of a third, George arrived in Dallas in 1952 to work as a petroleum geologist, where he socialized with many of the city's oil elite. In 1959, following his third divorce, he married Jeanne LeGon (1914–1993), a dancer of Russian parentage born in China where her father directed a railroad. The couple, both fluent in Russian, participated in the Russian immigrant community in Dallas, and through those contacts met Lee Harvey Oswald and his Russian-born wife Marina in 1962. The de Mohrenschildts moved to Haiti in June 1963, five months before the Kennedy assassination, and no known evidence implicates de Mohrenschildt in Oswald's later activities. He was, however, friendly with Oswald during the two years prior to the assassination and therefore became a key witness before the Warren Commission investigating the assassination. In 1977, while visiting a friend in Florida, he learned he was about to be called again to testify to another congressional committee. It was also revealed in Dallas news reports that he had been hospitalized for depression, a revelation he feared would cost him business and professional credibility. The strain of both developments drove him to kill himself in a bedroom of the house where he was staying. In the decades since his death, he has figured in a variety of allegations and conspiracy theories related to the assassination. George McMillan, "The Man Who Knew Oswald," *Washington Post*, April 3, 1977; Nancy Wertz Weiford, *The Faux Baron: George de Mohrenschildt: An Aristocrat's Journey from the Russian Revolution to the Assassination of John F. Kennedy* (n.p.: CreateSpace Independent Publishing Platform, 2014).

29. De Mohrenschildt biographer Nancy Wertz Weiford describes George's relationship with the young Tito Harper: "Hite Lawrence Harper [was] the 19 year old son of a wealthy multi-generational family of Eagle Pass, Texas. The Harper family's holdings included cattle ranching, banking and real estate. Called Tito by

his friends, Harper was drawn to the older de Mohrenschildt who represented adventure and rebellion." In a further note about Tito's troubled life, Weiford writes that he "had a terrible temper, was an alcoholic and prone to physical fights with little provcation. He became alienated from the Harper family, and renounced his American citizenship in 1965. He moved to Mexico City where he died in 1970, while under psychiatric care." Weiford, *The Faux Baron*, 117, 730n195.
30. This is Bishop College, founded in Marshall, Texas, to serve Black Baptist students in East Texas and then relocated to Dallas in 1961. De Mohrenschildt taught French and Russian (not engineering) there for nearly ten years. After the college closed, its campus was acquired by the Dallas-based HBCU Paul Quinn College. Jack Herman and Peggy Hardman, "Bishop College," *Handbook of Texas Online*, accessed October 14, 2022, https://www.tshaonline.org/handbook/entries/bishop-college; Weiford, *The Faux Baron*, 15.
31. This is Alexandra de Mohrenschildt (b. 1944), the daughter of George's first wife. George had two other children by his third wife, both of whom died young of cystic fibrosis.
32. A graduate of West Point and veteran of World War II and the Korean War, General Edwin Walker was an avid anticommunist and segregationist who resigned from the army in 1961 after being censured for distributing right-wing literature to soldiers under his command. He settled in Dallas, from where he directed a public relations crusade against all manner of liberalism and ran unsuccessfully for Texas governor in 1962. He was also arrested for inciting rioting at the University of Mississippi in opposition to the integration of the school. In April 1963, Dallas police responded to a shooting at his home, an apparent assassination attempt, which slightly injured him. The incident looms large in Kennedy assassination lore as it is widely suspected that Lee Harvey Oswald was the shooter. As George de Mohrenschildt biographer Nancy Wertz Weiford describes, George was instantly persuaded his friend Oswald was responsible. "First, he knew that Oswald disliked General Walker intensely, and second, that Oswald owned a rifle." Speaking to Oswald about the crime soon after, George "did not have to work hard to get the truth out of Oswald about the Walker shooting. . . . [He] found a young man who was proud of his involvement." Weiford, *The Faux Baron*, 353–54.
33. Jeanne LeGon de Mohrenschildt (1914–1993) and her husband divorced in 1973, but they continued to live together as a married couple. After George's death, she provided congressional investigators with testimony and documentary evidence about his relationship with Lee Harvey Oswald. She died in Los Angeles in 1993.

CHAPTER 15

1. The son of Greek immigrants who originally ran a candy store in Eagle Pass, Pete Mathiwos (1914–1987)—his Maverick County birth certificate identifies him as Pedro—grew up in Eagle Pass, attended college at St. Mary's in San Antonio, and became a restaurateur and bar owner.
2. In 1949, the Texas Legislature adopted the Gilmer-Aikin Laws, a series of bills reforming public education in the state. Among other changes, the laws consolidated public education into fewer local independent school districts, supplemented local school taxes with equalizing funding from the state, increased teacher salaries, created an appointed state education commissioner, and, as Riskind explains, tied school funding to attendance. Oscar Mauzy, "Gilmer-Aikin Laws," *TSHA Handbook of Texas Online*, accessed April 20, 2023, https://www.tshaonline.org/handbook/entries/gilmer-aikin-laws.
3. Riskind mistakenly appears to be referring to school construction in the 1930s. In the early twentieth century, Eagle Pass and Piedras Negras high school students all attended together a series of buildings in Eagle Pass, including the "new" high school Riskind mentions here, built in 1930 at 649 Webster. In 1938, using WPA funds, a newer building was constructed, as he says, at 1619 Del Rio Boulevard; the Webster site became a junior high. That building served as the community's only high school until a replacement was built in 1973, at which point it also became a junior high. Riskind describes below his involvement in the design and construction of the 1973 building at 2020 Second Street, which is still in use today as Eagle Pass High School. A second high school, C. C. Winn, was added in 2003, located east of town on Foster Maldonado Boulevard. Garza and Graham, "Eagle Pass High School," 174, 176, 189.
4. No proof is needed of Texans' obsession with football, but Joel Huerta, a scholar of the sport's cultural impact particularly among Tejanos, provides a poetic analysis of where that obsession came from: "The backwater Texan was many things, but overcivilized he was not. With the Mexican Revolution to the south, protracted Texas-Mexican resistance in the borderlands and the chaos of the oil boom, much of early-twentieth-century Texas retained the restless and nervous energy of the frontier. Mobs still lynched, trains still got ambushed and derailed. Bandits, posses, rebels, smugglers, wildcatters and lawmen still shot it out in saloons, on courthouse steps and sun-drenched middles-of-nowhere. The pistons of frontier democracy still fired and misfired. What the Texan needed was some taming. He needed a controlled outlet for aggression and energy. Something like

(reformed) football could teach the Texan boy how to cooperate, how to win and lose honourably; it could give the rustic boy structure, polish and a public role without making him soft and sweet. Where the Yankee bourgeoisie had employed strenuous competition to toughen, [Texas advocates] saw in it a tonic to sublimate 'the fighting instinct.'" Huerta, "Friday Night Rights," 986.

5. The year after Faubus's failed standoff against President Eisenhower, the US Army, and nine Black high school students to block the integration of Central High, the governor ordered the closure of all the city's schools for the entire 1958–1959 academic year, unilaterally prohibiting both integration and education. The Little Rock school board accordingly canceled all related school activities, including football. "To the city's legions of sports fans," writes Elizabeth Jacoway in her narrative history of the Little Rock crisis, "this was a sacrilege." White citizens began to argue that the schools should be reopened, even if on an integrated basis, only so that football could resume immediately. Perceiving his position eroding, Faubus accused the board of engineering a backlash against him, and they reinstated the games—but not the classes. "Ironically," Jacoway observes, "although the high schools remained closed all year, a team from the darkened Little Rock Central High went on to place second in the state championship." Elizabeth Jacoway, *Turn Away Thy Son: Little Rock, the Crisis That Shocked the Nation* (Fayetteville: University of Arkansas Press, 2008), 269–70.

6. A different, unsourced version of this anecdote appears in another version of Riskind's manuscript: "When my son Pete asked at the high school for college application information on MIT or Cal Tech, the answer was, 'I am sure those are good schools. If you'll tell me what states they're in, I will help you as much as I can.'" Founded as a land-grant college in 1876 with a focus on agricultural and mechanical instruction, Texas A&M University in College Station is the largest public university in the state.

7. Garland was introduced in chapter 10.

8. Mary Elizabeth "Susie" Gates Rhodes (1913–1978) was born in rural South Texas but lived most of her life in Eagle Pass, where her father was a physician. She attended Tulane University and married Jerry Rhodes, who was introduced in the previous chapter, in the late 1930s.

9. Dr. Ellis Franklin Gates (1886–1979) was raised on a ranch in rural Atascosa County, Texas, studied medicine in Tennessee, and practiced in Mexico and several small Texas towns before joining the army medical corps in World War I. He was stationed near Eagle Pass and remained there permanently after the war. He founded the city's first hospital in 1922, worked there until 1968, and established a second practice in Piedras Negras. In a newspaper profile near the end of his life, Gates recalled rowing through floodwaters to deliver a baby, once receiving payment in the form of a cow, and making "about a million house calls" in a career spanning seventy years. "Texas Country Doctor Recalls House Calls," *Victoria Advocate*, June 1, 1977.

10. Julius I. "Curly" James (1908–1993) was born in San Antonio and graduated from St. Edward's University in Austin in 1929. A member of an athletic family—his brother, Byrne "Bernie" James, played professional baseball for the New York Giants—James stayed on at St. Edward's, coaching the school's basketball team until 1934, when he decided to coach high-school football instead. He worked for high schools in Laredo and Raymondville, becoming the principal of Raymondville High School in 1947. In 1953, when Jimmy Garland left to lead Texas Southmost College in Brownsville (he may or may not have been "summarily fired"), James arrived in Eagle Pass to head the school district. As Riskind describes, James was fired and replaced as superintendent in 1964, shortly before an election that brought in new trustees who immediately rehired him. Two years later, shortly after Riskind's election to the board in April 1966, James was again removed, this time permanently. He died in San Antonio in 1993. "Olivia Taylor to Wed Austin Man April 13," *Abilene Daily Reporter*, April 2, 1933; "Coach to Leave School Here at Close of Term," *Austin American*, January 31, 1934; "New School Heads," *Valley Morning Star*, May 30, 1947; "Pro-James Slate Wins in Maverick," *San Antonio Express and News*, April 5, 1964; "Eagle Pass Incumbent Voted Out," *San Antonio Express and News*, April 3, 1966.

11. Joseph (Jack) Walton Spence (1912–1995) was born in Uvalde but moved to Eagle Pass as a child with his family; his father was a salesman in an automobile dealership. He graduated from Rice University in Houston in 1938, married Clara Mae Carson, an Eagle Pass native, and they settled in Eagle Pass and ran the Style Shop, a ready-to-wear clothing store, on Main Street. Spence and Riskind were elected to the Eagle Pass school board in April 1966. "Class of 1938," *Sallyport* (Rice University student newspaper), May 1958.

12. This is undoubtedly a reference to the Elementary and Secondary Education Act of 1965 (ESEA), one of LBJ's Great Society initiatives and described in one study as "the most important piece of educational legislation in U.S. history." Best known for its Title I, which provided nearly a billion dollars in federal funds "for the education of children from low income families," the law also subsidized school libraries; textbooks and other educational materials; supplementary educational programs in music, science, physical education, and remedial skills; educational research and teacher training and recruitment; and the establishment of state departments of

education. David A. Gamson, Kathryn A. McDermott, and Douglas S. Reed, "The Elementary and Secondary Education Act at Fifty: Aspirations, Effects, and Limitations," *RSF: The Russell Sage Foundation Journal of the Social Sciences* 1 (December 2015): 1; Lee W. Anderson, *Congress and the Classroom: From the Cold War to "No Child Left Behind"* (University Park: Pennsylvania State University Press, 2007), 63; Zeitz, *Building the Great Society*, chapter 7. See also Lyndon B. Johnson, "Remarks in Johnson City, Tex., Upon Signing the Elementary and Secondary Education Bill," April 11, 1965, accessed June 21, 2023, https://www.presidency.ucsb.edu/documents/remarks-johnson-city-tex-upon-signing-the-elementary-and-secondary-education-bill.

13. The voucher system would permit taxpayers with school-aged children to contribute to tuition at private or parochial schools by diverting a portion of their educational taxes away from the public schools they choose not to attend. The notion remains a hotly contested proposal today in Texas and throughout the country. Riskind's concern is that such a system would benefit wealthier families, who could afford the remainder of private tuition not covered by the tax diversion, or those whose children are more successful, while starving the public schools of necessary funds and leaving behind those students who could not afford to take advantage of the program or would not be admissible to selective schools.

14. Born in Chihuahua, Mexico, Ofelia Sepulveda (1927–2006) was two years old when she moved to Eagle Pass with her family; her father was an attorney. She graduated as valedictorian from Eagle Pass High School and went to work for the school district as the superintendent's secretary. She married Joseph L. Martine in 1954, a Kerrville native and veteran of World War II and the Korean War who was teaching in the Eagle Pass schools. His subsequent work as a linguist with the Department of Defense may be what took them to Turkey as well as to Morocco. They had three children and settled in Santa Fe, New Mexico, where Joseph died in 1991, Ofelia in 2006. "Kerrville Young Man Engaged," *Kerrville Mountain Sun*, September 30, 1954; "Martine, Joseph L.," *Albuquerque Journal*, July 30, 1991; "Martine, Ofelia Drucila," *Albuquerque Journal*, March 28, 2006.

15. Kenneth Eugene Moore (1929–2001) was born in the North Texas town of Bailey. His family later settled in New Mexico where he met and married Byrna Hicks in 1954. They moved to Eagle Pass in 1961, where Moore became the head basketball coach and assistant football and track coach at Eagle Pass High School. He became principal and eventually district superintendent in 1966. He served in that role about two years, then moved to Marble Falls, Texas, where he died in 2001. "Curriculum Director Employed by Local School District," *Eagle Pass News Guide*, September 1, 1966; "New Sch. Superintendent Takes Over Duties July 1," *Eagle Pass News Guide*, June 29, 1967; "Byrna Dean Hicks," *Eastern New Mexico News*, August 25, 2005.

16. The vote on the bond issue, for $3.8 million, was held on January 31, 1967. Riskind had been elected to the board the previous April. "School Bond Vote in Maverick Today," *San Angelo Standard-Times*, January 31, 1967.

17. At the urging of President Lyndon B. Johnson as part of his Great Society project, Congress passed the Child Nutrition Act in 1966. According to Johnson, the act expanded earlier school nutrition programs by providing money for "schools that simply cannot afford to finance the basic equipment for food service." For "thousands of children [who] arrive at school hungry because they have no breakfast," the act "provides for breakfasts at school." Historian Joshua Zeitz explains that the program grew significantly over time, experiencing "steady growth under successive Democratic and Republican initiatives." Between 1970 and 2010, "the number of disadvantaged youth benefiting from free or subsidized breakfasts grew from 450,000 to 11.7 million, while those receiving free or reduced-price lunches grew from 22 million to 32 million." Lyndon B. Johnson, "Remarks at the Signing of the Child Nutrition Act of 1966," October 11, 1966, accessed June 21, 2023, https://www.presidency.ucsb.edu/node/238283; Zeitz, *Building the Great Society*, chapter 9.

18. The reference is to the construction of the new Eagle Pass High School (EPHS), opened in 1973 at 2020 Second Street and still in use. The "existing high school" Riskind mentions was built in 1938 at 1610 Del Rio Boulevard. It became a junior high when the new EPHS opened, and the "existing junior high," at 649 Webster, which itself was a former high school built in 1930, became an elementary. See Garza and Graham, "Eagle Pass High School," 173–92.

19. This bond issue, in the amount of $3.1 million, was put to Maverick County voters on March 28, 1969. This one passed, providing funding for the construction of a new high school. "Eagle Pass Bond Election Is Today," *San Angelo Standard-Times*, March 28, 1969.

20. With more than six hundred thousand acres to his name, Dolph Briscoe was at one time the largest individual landholder in Texas. Born in Uvalde in 1923, he was a conservative Democrat, protégé of Vice President John Nance Garner, and served in the Texas House of Representatives from 1948 to 1957. He sought and lost the 1968 Democratic nomination for governor but was successful at securing the nomination and the governorship in 1972. He was reelected in 1974 but did not receive the 1978 Democratic nomination, returning to his career in banking and ranching in Uvalde, where he died in 2010.

Riskind misremembers the name of the lawsuit in which he was involved—*Briscoe Ranches, Inc. v. Eagle Pass Independent School District*—which did not name him personally in the title. As Riskind correctly explains, Briscoe and a group of other ranchers sued Eagle Pass Independent School District over the mechanism by which property was assessed for the payment of school district taxes. The district was upheld in the Sixty-Third District Court in September 1968 and affirmed on appeal to the Court of Criminal Appeals of Texas on April 2, 1969. The ranchers were ordered to pay taxes at the agreed rate but most still resisted, leading to a settlement in June 1970 in which they made partial payment. During the campaign for the Democratic nomination for governor in 1972, supporters of one of Briscoe's opponents, Lieutenant Governor Ben Barnes, tried to make an issue of the case, implying that Briscoe and his coplaintiffs had withheld payment in order to push the district to the brink of insolvency so it would accept a less generous settlement. George Slaughter, "Briscoe, Dolph, Jr.," *Handbook of Texas Online*, accessed October 14, 2022, https://www.tshaonline.org/handbook/entries/briscoe-dolph-jr; *Briscoe Ranches, Inc. v. Eagle Pass Independent School District*, 439 S.W.2d 118, Court of Criminal Appeals of Texas, San Antonio, April 2, 1969; "Ranchmen Fight Maverick Taxes," *Del Rio News-Herald*, January 29, 1970; "Eagle Pass Trustees Accept Tax Settlement," *Corpus Christi Times*, June 27, 1970; "What They Say About Ben Barnes," *Victoria Advocate*, May 2, 1972.

21. Moore resigned at the board's request in May 1967 and was replaced the next month by Kenneth Flory, a nineteen-year veteran school administrator who was principal of San Antonio's Robert E. Lee High School. "New Sch. Superintendent Takes Over Duties July 1," *Eagle Pass News Guide*, June 29, 1967.
22. This may refer to educational programs offered under the Veterans' Readjustment Benefits Act, or the Cold War GI Bill, which Congress approved unanimously in 1966. Authored by Texas senator Ralph Yarborough and signed into law by Lyndon Johnson, the bill extended the benefits of the World War II–era GI Bill to veterans of the conflicts in Korea and Vietnam.

CHAPTER 16

1. Shneur Zalman (1745–1813) of Lyady, in present-day Belarus, founded Chabad, a version of Hasidism in which "the mystical relationship of man and his Creator is intellectualized to the maximum and the Hasidic principles of love and compassion toward human beings are based not on emotional sentimentality but on rational principles of ethics and philosophy." In 1813, his son and successor, Dov Baer (1773–1827), moved from Lyady to Lubavich and established a center of Chabad Hasidism. His descendants, in a hereditary line of the family name Schneersohn, led the movement as it expanded globally, including communities in Palestine and the United States. Quotation from Zborowski and Herzog, *Life Is With People*, 186.
2. Riskind previously listed Vela among the store's longtime employees and described his brother Reuben's concern for her when Piedras Negras experienced devastating flooding in 1954.
3. Leo Rosten was the author of several books explaining and extolling the Yiddish language, notably *The Joys of Yiddish*, first published in 1968. He was also the author of a series of fictional works featuring the character Hyman Kaplan, whose mangled Yiddish-inflected English was a source of humor but also of constant exasperation for others. "Leo Rosten; wrote 'Joys of Yiddish,'" *Chicago Tribune*, February 21, 1997.
4. Diaz was introduced in chapter 2.
5. Literally "interpretation," the Midrash consists of rabbinical explication, discussion, argument, clarification, and definition of Torah text. The term refers to all such interpretation, including what continues to be produced today, so midrash represents a constantly evolving and growing body of thought. Riskind refers to a narrative in Tanchuma, Noach 13, which elaborates on Genesis 9:20, the story of Noah's drunkenness. In the midrash, Satan visits Noah, shows him how to plant grapes and make wine, and deceives him into overdrinking, leading to a lasting curse on his household.
6. Agustín Lara was one of Mexico's most popular songwriters and musical performers. "Te Vendes" was recorded in 1953.
7. Blackouts in New York were frequent, but this probably refers to the wide-scale power outage of June 12, 1961, as that date most closely fits the ages Riskind provides for his sons. There was another, smaller outage on August 16, 1959, but it doesn't seem to have affected the part of the city where the Riskinds were staying, nor does he seem to be referring to the Great Northeast Blackout of 1965, a much more severe outage that affected the entirety of New York State as well as several other states and provinces. Originally located on Delancey Street on the Lower East Side, Gluckstern's Kosher Retaurant relocated to Broadway and 48th in Midtown; the Manhattan Hotel is nearby at Seventh Avenue and Fifty-Second Street. Homer Bigart, "Power Cut Off for 500,000 in Manhattan," *New York Times*, August 18, 1959; Peter Kihss, "Power Fails, Tying Up Midtown 4 1/2 Hours," *New York Times*, June 14, 1961.

8. Written by Jean Schwartz and William Jerome in 1903 and recorded by, among others, Billy Murray, "Bedelia" was a widely popular song that originated in minstrelsy. Library of Congress, "Bedelia," accessed October 29, 2022, https://www.loc.gov/item/ihas.100007925/.
9. A greenhorn (*grine* or *griner* in Yiddish) was a newcomer to America. Written for the New York Yiddish theatrical stage in 1921 by composer Abe Schwartz, "*Di Grine Kuzine*" ("The Greenhorn Cousin") is "one of the best known in the category of 'disillusionment' songs of the immigrant era." It tells of the singer's beautiful young cousin who arrived from the old country "happy and merry," but after finding work only in sweatshops "turned into a wreck." Riskind doesn't quote the song's final stanza, which reads in English: "Nowadays, when I meet my cousin / and I ask her, 'How are you, greenhorn?' / She answers me with a crooked expression: / 'Columbus's land can go to hell!'" Neil W. Levin, "*Di Grine Kuzine*/The Greenhorn Cousin," Milken Archive of Jewish Music, accessed October 29, 2022, http://www.milkenarchive.org/music/volumes/view/great-songs-of-the-american-yiddish-stage/work/di-grine-kuzine.
10. An ancient figure in Jewish myth, and appearing prominently in mystical Kabbalistic writings, a golem is "a man-made being, usually an anthropoid, animated through the power of the Hebrew alphabet." According to Geoffrey Dennis, "the golem became a staple of Jewish folk legends in Europe, the most famous golem being the one created by Rabbi Loew of Prague"—that is, Rabbi Judah Loew ben Bezalel, a sixteenth-century mystic and leader of the Prague Jewish community—"to protect the community against anti-Semitic violence. Like many other golem tales, over time the Prague golem grew in power and in unpredictable behavior, and the creator was forced to destroy his creation, thus curbing his own hubris and teaching him humility." Dennis, *Encyclopedia of Jewish Myth, Magic and Mysticism*, 111, 139.
11. Kabbalists, followers of the Jewish mystical tradition called Kabbalah, hold that God gave Moses a set of mystical teachings alongside the Torah at Sinai. The movement's central text, the *Sefer ha-Bahir*, was compiled in France in the twelfth century and its other central text, the *Zohar*, in the thirteenth. Adherents examine the numeric value of Hebrew letters inscribed in the Torah, uncover allegorical meanings of texts, and develop distinctive concepts of creation, good and evil forces on earth, and death and reincarnation.
12. It's unclear from the context what book this might have been, perhaps a collection of European fairy stories, but "East of the Sun and West of the Moon" is, in fact, a Norwegian folktale, not French. It tells of a beautiful maiden who falls in love with a white bear later revealed to be a human prince.
13. *The Book of Knowledge* is described in chapter 4.
14. The Haggadah is the book containing the order of events and prayers conducted during a Passover seder, the annual family meal at which the Jews' freedom from slavery in Egypt is recounted and celebrated. The Haggadah relates the story of their escape along with prayers, scripts, and songs unique to the occasion, and it guides participants in ritualized consumption of foods chosen for their symbolic value as reminders of ancient events and emotions.
15. Peter Riskind writes, "Rachel Riskind's signature dish, served as an appetizer at all family gatherings, was her pirogen (similar to Russian *piroge*). These were small, baked, savory pastries filled with finely chopped beef tongue mixed with bell peppers, onions, and spices. These were an eagerly awaited treat, almost instantly devoured as they came out of the oven. Over time she adapted the recipe, including the use of prepared biscuit dough, and added jalapeños to the filling. Toward the end of her life the pirogen were made by her caretaker, Licha Torres. Unfortunately the recipe for Grandma's pirogen has been lost."
16. The famous story Riskind refers to, relating a challenge issued to the great teacher Hillel and his major rival, Shammai, is found in the Talmudic tractate Shabbat 31a: "On another occasion it happened that a certain heathen [Riskind says Greek] came before Shammai and said to him, 'Make me a proselyte, on condition that you teach me the whole Torah while I stand on one foot.' Thereupon [Shammai] repulsed him with the builder's cubit [a wooden measuring tool] which was in his hand. When [the heathen] went before Hillel, [Hillel] said to him, 'What is hateful to you, do not to your neighbor: that is the whole Torah, while the rest is commentary thereof; go and learn it.'"
17. Sholem Yankev Abramovich, popularly known by the name of his fictional persona, Mendele Mocher Sforim ("Mendele the Book Peddler"), and Solomon Rabinovich, who published under the pseudonym Sholem Aleichem, were among the founders of modern Eastern European Yiddish literature. Best known for "Fishke der Krumer" ("Fishke the Lame"), Mendele deployed a wry, folksy humor and, in the voice of the unlettered character Mendele, depicted the lives of Jewish vagrants and beggars as they shifted among the shtetls of Russia. Sholem Aleichem merged factual accounts of mundane shtetl life with Jewish myth and legend, building a vibrantly Jewish world populated by a cast of recurring archetypal characters. Among these, most famously, was Tevye, the talkative dairyman struggling to provide for his large family. The Tevye stories, as Riskind notes, became the basis of the 1964 Broadway and 1971 Hollywood musical productions *Fiddler on the Roof*. Dan

Miron, "Sh. Y. Abramovitsh and His 'Mendele,'" in Dan Miron, *The Image of the Shtetl and Other Studies of Modern Jewish Literary Imagination* (Syracuse, NY: Syracuse University Press, 2000), 81–127; "Sholem Aleichem," *YIVO Encyclopedia of Jews in Eastern Europe*, accessed January 14, 2023, https://yivoencyclopedia.org/article.aspx/sholem_aleichem.
18. *H.M.S. Pinafore* is an 1878 comic opera by Gilbert and Sullivan.
19. Michael Riskind died in Eagle Pass on February 12, 1969, and was buried at Mount Sinai Memorial Park in Los Angeles.
20. According to artist Teresa Villegas, for whom *lotería* cards have been a recurring subject, the game was introduced to Mexico from Spain in the late eighteenth century. A deck contains fifty-four cards, each displaying a colorful image and a word in Spanish corresponding to the image. Each player has a game board, a *tabla*, resembling an American bingo board, and cards are drawn from the deck matching images on the players' boards. The game would be familiar to American bingo players, Villegas writes, but "players will quickly realize how much more visually and intellectually engaging and fun it is to play *Lotería* than the American Bingo game." Whereas in the American game the announcer simply declares the letter-number combination drawn, a *lotería* announcer "gives an improvised short poem or familiar phrase alluding to the image on the card (e.g., 'the coat for the poor' for the image of the sun, or 'the one who dies by the mouth' for the image of the fish)." As Riskind describes, *lotería* cards often serve an educational purpose. "Because the *Lotería* cards include the name of the pictured character," Villegas writes, "they are used to teach reading, writing, history, and social values. Many bilingual teachers use the game as a teaching tool in the United States." Teresa Villegas, "History of La Lotería," accessed June 10, 2022, https://teresavillegas.com/history-of-la-loteria.
21. Rachel Riskind died in Eagle Pass on September 22, 1979. She was buried next to her husband at Mount Sinai Memorial Park in Los Angeles.

EPILOGUE

1. This has been true since the early twentieth century and has only become more so since Riskind wrote the memoir. A study of the American Jewish population in 1990, at the time Riskind was writing, found that about three-quarters of Americans who identified as Jewish lived in metropolitan areas including suburbs (as opposed to rural areas or small towns). A 2013 Pew Research Center study found a significantly higher portion: 49 percent of American Jews were living in urban areas and another 47 percent in the suburbs, a total of 96 percent. To provide a Texas context, my own research found that in 2000, 97 percent of Texas Jews lived in urban areas, up from about 47 percent in 1900. Sidney Goldstein, "Profile of American Jewry: Insights from the 1990 National Jewish Population Survey," *American Jewish Year Book* 92 (1992): 100; Pew Research Center, *A Portrait of Jewish Americans* (Washington, DC: Pew Research Center, 2013); Stone, "West of Center," 369.
2. Peter Riskind rightly notes, "Unfortunately this suspicion was validated by murderous wartime antisemitic behaviors of some Lithuanians and others during the Nazi occupation."
3. Magdeburg, a city in east-central Germany, embraced the Protestant Reformation in 1524. In 1630, amid the Europe-wide series of religious and monarchal conflicts known as the Thirty Years' War, the city was attacked by a Catholic force led by Count von Tilly of the Netherlands. After a fierce defense, Magdeburg fell and Tilly's men, contrary to his orders, proceeded to massacre the citizenry, killing more than twenty thousand residents. Drogheda, north of Dublin, was sieged by Cromwell's army in the course of an Irish uprising against British Protestant and parliamentary rule in 1649. After taking the city in September, according to *Britannica*, "Cromwell's troops killed priests and monks on sight and set light to a Catholic church sheltering some soldiers. Civilians as well as soldiers were massacred, and [its governor Arthur] Ashton was bludgeoned to death with his own wooden leg." Jacob F. Field, "Battle of Magdeburg," *Encyclopaedia Britannica*, accessed January 15, 2023, https://www.britannica.com/event/Battle-of-Magdeburg; Amy Tikkanen, "Magdeburg," *Encyclopaedia Britannica*, accessed January 15, 2023, https://www.britannica.com/place/Magdeburg-Germany; Simon Adams, "Siege of Drogheda," *Encyclopaedia Britannica*, accessed January 15, 2023, https://www.britannica.com/event/Siege-of-Drogheda.
4. A 1990 US Jewish population study conducted by the Council of Jewish Federations found that of children raised in "mixed households" (one Jewish and one non-Jewish parent), 28 percent were being raised Jewish, 31 percent with no religion, and 41 percent in a non-Jewish faith. Barry A. Kosmin, Sidney Goldstein, et al., *Highlights of the CJF National Jewish Population Study* (New York: Council of Jewish Federations, 1991), 16.
5. There are four major movements (or branches, or denominations) of Jewish practice common in the United States and Canada: Orthodox, Conservative, Reform, and Reconstructionist. Orthodoxy represents the most

traditional branch, putting the greatest emphasis on strict adherence to Jewish laws and ritual practice such as keeping a kosher diet and home (kashrut), Sabbath observance, head covering, division of worship by gender, and reliance on Hebrew exclusively in worship services. Reform emerged in the early nineteenth century in Central Europe and the United States as an attempt to accommodate with modern, secular society. Long the most popular branch in American Judaism, it curtails the ritual requirements of the faith—eliminating dietary restrictions, for example, introducing more vernacular language into services, and providing greater gender equality—and it allows latitude for individual and congregational interpretation of scripture. The Conservative movement, founded in the United States in the nineteenth century, sought a middle ground between Orthodoxy and Reform. It reimposed kashrut and Sabbath observance along with an array of other traditional practices, but it retained some of Reform's adaptations, including joining women alongside men in worship. Reconstructionism, founded in the early twentieth century in the United States, is the newest and smallest branch and views Judaism as a cultural and ethical tradition more than a set of specific restrictions or obligations. Its adherents emphasize individual responsibility and ethical behavior rather than strict observance of scriptural commandments. In 1990, when Riskind was writing, Reform Jews constituted 38 percent of the American Jewish population, Conservative 35 percent, Orthodox 6 percent, and Reconstructionist 1 percent; those of no stated denomination, those who identified as secular, and miscellaneous categories accounted for the remainder. Goldstein, "Profile of American Jewry," 129.
6. Halakah is Jewish law, the commandments, requirements, rituals, and restrictions outlined in the Torah, Talmud, and interpretive texts. Like many adherents of the Reform movement in Judaism, Riskind argues here for the necessity of adjusting these ritual behaviors to modern life and contexts rather than demanding strict observance of ancient customs that made sense only in different circumstances. Orthodox Jews, on the other hand, and many Conservative Jews, place value in adherence to traditional halakhic rules as a sign of Jewish continuity regardless of their efficacy in the contemporary setting.
7. The *Shulchan Arukh*, meaning "prepared table," is a compilation of Jewish law produced by Joseph Karo in the sixteenth century. Based on the Talmud and later commentaries, it is considered the most authoritative version of halakah.
8. Rooted in Leviticus, Jewish law required all debts to be forgiven every seventh year, the sabbatical year (or shemittah). In order to encourage the wealthy to continue loaning funds, however—a practice clearly beneficial to the development of business and commerce as well as support for the poor—Hillel the Elder introduced a legal formula in the first century BCE, *prosbul*, that created an exception and allowed creditors to continue collecting on debts. See Yair Ettinger, "Religious Jews Sign Prozbul, Promise to Pay Off Debts," *Haaretz*, October 3, 2008.
9. Riskind's observation that intermarriage between Jews and non-Jews was "becoming more common" is demonstrably true. In 1970, approximately 8 percent of Americans born Jewish were married to non-Jews, but by 1990, when Riskind was writing, that figure had risen to 31 percent. "The magnitude of the change that has occurred in the extent of mixed marriages," wrote demographer Sidney Goldstein in 1992, "is indicated by the fact that among those marrying before 1965, five times as many Jewish marriages were homogamous as mixed." More recent statistical studies show that trend continuing. A Pew Research Center survey conducted in 2020 found that Jewish intermarriage has increased dramatically since the 1980s. Of American Jews married before 1980, only 18 percent had a non-Jewish spouse; that figure rose to 61 percent of those married in the 2010s. The same report also indicated, encouragingly, that the children of mixed marriages were increasingly likely to be raised as Jews.

It's harder to quantify Riskind's view that this trend would strengthen the Reform movement, especially to confirm intermarriage as a cause of denominational growth or reduction. Pew does provide data on "denominational switching" that shows a movement of American Jews out of the more traditional branches, especially the Conservative, toward Reform. "Within Judaism," according to the authors of a 2021 Pew report, "denominational switching has led to the largest net losses for the Conservative movement, which, in the 1950s and 1960s, was the largest branch of American Jewry.... By contrast, Reform Judaism—now the largest American Jewish denomination—has experienced a net gain.... Nearly half (46%) of today's Reform Jews have come from outside the Reform movement. A quarter of today's Reform Jews were raised as either Conservative or Orthodox." Goldstein, "Profile of American Jewry," 126–27; Pew Research Center, *Jewish Americans in 2020* (Washington, DC: Pew Research Center, 2021), 39, 43; Jacob Ausubel, Gregory A. Smith, and Alan Cooperman, "Denominational Switching among U.S. Jews: Reform Judaism Has Gained, Conservative Judaism Has Lost," June 22, 2021, Pew Research Center, accessed June 21, 2023, https://www.pewresearch.org/fact-tank/2021/06/22/denominational-switching-among-u-s-jews-reform-judaism-has-gained-conservative-judaism-has-lost/. See also Louis Keene, "Intermarriage Increasingly Leads to Jewish

Children, Pew Study Shows," *Forward*, May 12, 2021.

10. In raising the question whether Jews constitute a race, Riskind enters upon fraught terrain. His conclusion they are not a distinct race due to the obvious fact that there are Jews among all of the various groups identified as races is a common one. Indeed, Frederick Douglass observed in 1854 that "The Jews, who are to be found in all countries, never intermarrying, are white in Europe, brown in Asia, and black in Africa." Melanie Kaye/Kantrowitz rightly observes, however, that "to say, simply, *Jews are not a race*, while accurate, overlooks the confusion, the waffling and uncertainty about Jewish racial identity, and the anxiety created by this uncertainty." Whether a race or not, Jews have been treated and discriminated against as if they were a race, making it impossible to fully divorce Jewish identity from racial categories. Eric L. Goldstein has shown, furthermore, that Ashkenazic American Jews were largely accepted into the white mainstream even though many would have preferred to have remained a distinct racial group, as they were assumed to be in the nineteenth century when it was common for Jews to describe themselves as a race. "Even as Jews pursued whiteness," Goldstein writes, "they wrestled with its consequences and tried to preserve other cherished means of self-definition that resided uneasily within its confines. . . . [T]he ultimate loss of 'race' as a term for self-description rendered inarticulate some of their deepest feelings of group solidarity and difference."

    In a more localized Texas example, Allison Schottenstein has analyzed the racial context behind the 1943 schism at Congregation Beth Israel in Houston, the state's oldest and, at that time, largest Reform congregation. The congregation's leadership developed a set of "Basic Principles" that included the statement, "Our race is Caucasian." Schottenstein explains that the congregation's leadership viewed this simply as an observation of reality given the demographics of the Houston Jewish community at that time, but she also reveals the leaders' worries about being excluded from political power in Houston, especially in the state's whites-only Democratic primary elections, if they were viewed as anything other than white. "A stress on their Caucasian identity," Schottenstein writes, "was an attempt to secure their position with their white Gentile peers." Frederick Douglass, *The Claims of the Negro, Ethnologically Considered. An Address, Before the Literary Societies of Western Reserve College, at Commencement, July 12, 1854* (Rochester, NY: Lee, Mann, and Co., 1854); Melanie Kaye/Kantrowitz, *The Colors of Jews: Racial Politics and Radical Diasporism* (Bloomington, IN: Indiana University Press, 2007), 27–28; Eric L. Goldstein, *The Price of Whiteness: Jews, Race, and American Identity* (Princeton, NJ: Princeton University Press, 2008), introduction; Allison E. Schottenstein, *Changing Perspectives: Black-Jewish Relations in Houston during the Civil Rights Era* (Denton: University of North Texas Press, 2021), 40, 42, 65. See also Karen Brodkin, *How Jews Became White Folks and What That Says about Race in America* (New Brunswick, NJ: Rutgers University Press, 1998).

11. Riskind is correct that the Bible provides numerous examples of cultural mixing and intermarriage. His quotation here is mistaken, however, as he seems to conflate two passages. Ezekiel, the prophet he means to cite, writes at 16:3, "Thus saith the Lord God unto Jerusalem: Thine origin and thy nativity is of the land of the Canaanite; the Amorite was thy father, and thy mother was a Hittite." The rest of Riskind's quote comes from Deuteronomy 26:5: "And thou shalt speak and say before the Lord thy God: 'A wandering Aramean was my father, and he went down into Egypt, and sojourned there, few in number; and he became there a nation, great, mighty, and populous.'"

12. The Hasmonean (or Maccabean) dynasty ruled Judea during the second and first centuries BCE, prior to Rome's acquisition of the region. Hyrcanus I, a son of Simon Maccabee, ruled from about 135 BCE during a prosperous era when the Pharisee scholars and Sadducee priests became prominent elites. As king, Hyrcanus led a series of offensives to expand Judean boundaries, including capturing neighboring Samaria and Idumaea (Edom). To underscore his conquest, he compelled the conversion of the Edomites to Judaism. It was the first case of Jews forcibly imposing their religion on the entirety of another group. "In John Hyrcanus' view," historian Menahem Stern explains, "this operation was designed to strengthen the Jewish nation, [which] fell on fertile soil in Idumea; their upper classes occupied key social and governmental positions in the Hasmonean Kingdom. From then on the Judaization of the whole of Palestine became a permanent element of Hasmonean policy." "John Hyrcanus I," *Encyclopaedia Britannica*, accessed January 15, 2023, https://www.britannica.com/biography/John-Hyrcanus-I; Menahem Stern, "The Period of the Second Temple," in *A History of the Jewish People*, ed. H. H. Ben-Sasson (Cambridge, MA: Harvard University Press, 1976), 218–19.

13. Peter Riskind notes that "Bogdan Chmielnicki [or Khmelnitsky] led a Cossack rebellion against Polish rule in Ukraine in 1648 and was responsible for pogroms that destroyed over three hundred Jewish communities and caused the deaths of over one hundred thousand Jews." Jews often acted as financial agents for the Polish aristocracy and so were identified in the minds of the rebelling Cossacks as synonymous with the order they opposed. Chmielnicki, who led the uprising to establish an independent Ukraine, probably was not personally responsible for the anti-Jewish violence that erupted in the eastern half of Ukraine, but nevertheless

"in the annals of the Jewish people," according to the *Jewish Virtual Library*, "Chmielnicki is branded as 'Chmiel the Wicked,' one of the most sinister oppressors of the Jews of all generations." John D. Klier, "The Pogrom Paradigm in Russian History," in Klier and Lambroza, *Pogroms*, 14; "Bogdan Chmielnicki," *Jewish Virtual Library*, accessed January 15, 2023, https://www.jewishvirtuallibrary.org/chmielnicki-khmelnitski-bogdan-x00b0.

14. This is probably a slightly mistaken reference to a pair of executions in St. Petersburg in 1738 during the reign of Empress Anna Ivanovna. Borukh Leibov, a Jewish merchant in Smolensk, who had previously been arrested for building a synagogue in a small Russian village and proselytizing Christians there, made the acquaintance of Alexander Voznitsyn, a retired naval officer. The men traveled together to Dubrovna where, according to court records, Voznitsyn was "converted to Judaism and circumcised by the Jew Baruch Leibov." Voznitsyn's wife denounced him to Russian authorities after noticing not only his circumcision but his strange new prayer and dietary habits. The two men were arrested, tortured, and burned at the stake in a public spectacle in central St. Petersburg. Voznitsyn's estate was transferred to his wife in gratitude for her informing on him. Herman Rosenthal, "Baruch Leibov," *Jewish Encyclopedia*, accessed January 15, 2023, https://www.jewishencyclopedia.com/articles/2580-baruch-leibov; Mikhail Beizer, *The Jews of St. Petersburg: Excursions Through a Noble Past* (Philadelphia: Jewish Publication Society, 1989), 50–51.

BIBLIOGRAPHY

Abarbanel, Stacey Ravel. "Pancho Villa and My Grandfather." *Tablet*, August 26, 2019. Accessed June 19, 2024. https://www.tabletmag.com/sections/community/articles/pancho-villa-and-my-grandfather.

Abernathy, Francis Edward. "Dobie, James Frank." *Handbook of Texas Online*. Accessed August 11, 2022. https://www.tshaonline.org/handbook/entries/dobie-james-frank.

Abrams, Richard M. "The U.S. Military and Higher Education: A Brief History." *Annals of the American Academy of Political and Social Science* 502, no. 1 (March 1989): 15–28.

Adams, Maurianne, and John H. Bracey, eds. *Strangers and Neighbors: Relations between Blacks and Jews in the United States*. Amherst: University of Massachusetts Press, 1999.

Adams, Paul. "Fisher, John King." In *Handbook of Texas Online*. Accessed November 10, 2022. https://www.tshaonline.org/handbook/entries/fisher-john-king.

Adams, Simon. "Battle of Flodden." *Encyclopaedia Britannica*. Accessed January 7, 2023. https://www.britannica.com/event/Battle-of-Flodden.

———. "Siege of Drogheda." *Encyclopaedia Britannica*. Accessed January 15, 2023. https://www.britannica.com/event/Siege-of-Drogheda.

Adler, Cyrus, and Gotthold Weil. "Ma'aseh Books." *Jewish Encyclopedia*. Accessed January 21, 2023. https://www.jewishencyclopedia.com/articles/10230-ma-aseh-books.

Alonzo, Armando C. *Tejano Legacy: Rancheros and Settlers in South Texas, 1734–1900*. Albuquerque: University of New Mexico Press, 1998.

"Amistad Reservoir." *Handbook of Texas Online*. Accessed June 20, 2022. https://www.tshaonline.org/handbook/entries/amistad-reservoir.

Anders, Evan. *Boss Rule in South Texas: The Progressive Era*. Austin: University of Texas Press, 1979.

Anderson, Lee W. *Congress and the Classroom: From the Cold War to "No Child Left Behind."* University Park: Pennsylvania State University Press, 2007.

Army Air Forces Flying Training Command. *Eagle Pass Army Air Field Class Book*, 1943. Accessed June 17, 2024. https://aafcollection.info/items/documents/view.php?file=000483-01-00.pdf.

Artenstein, Isaac, dir. *People of the Crossing: The Jews of El Paso*. Oceanside, CA: Cinewest Productions, 2023.

Ashton, John, Edgar P. Sneed, and Bob Kinnan. "King Ranch." *Handbook of Texas Online*. Accessed June 24, 2022. https://www.tshaonline.org/handbook/entries/king-ranch.

Ausubel, Jacob, Gregory A. Smith, and Alan Cooperman. "Denominational Switching among U.S. Jews: Reform Judaism Has Gained, Conservative Judaism Has Lost," June 22, 2021. Pew Research Center. Accessed June 21, 2023. https://www.pewresearch.org/fact-tank/2021/06/22/denominational-switching-among-u-s-jews-reform-judaism-has-gained-conservative-judaism-has-lost/.

Badillo, David A. "Between Alienation and Ethnicity: The Evolution of Mexican-American Catholicism in San Antonio, 1910–1940." *Journal of American Ethnic History* 16, no. 4 (Summer 1997): 62–83.

Barrera, Alicia. "Migrants Cross into US amid Governor Abbott's Visit to Eagle Pass." KSAT.com, June 30, 2022. https://www.ksat.com/news/local/2022/06/30/migrants-cross-into-us-amid-governor-abbotts-visit-to-eagle-pass/.

Barry, John M. *The Great Influenza: The Epic Story of the Deadliest Plague in History*. New York: Penguin Books, 2005.

Barsam, Richard Meran. "'This Is America': Documentaries for Theaters, 1942–1951." *Cinema Journal* 12, no. 2 (1973): 22–38.

"Baruch Spinoza." *Jewish Virtual Library*. Accessed June 19, 2023. https://www.jewishvirtuallibrary.org/baruch-spinoza.

Beaver, Jim. "Pearl White." IMDb. Accessed July 20, 2022. http://www.imdb.com/name/nm0925310/bio.

Beck, Susan Abrams. "The Limits of Presidential Activism: Lyndon Johnson and the Implementation of the

Community Action Program." *Presidential Studies Quarterly* 17 (Summer 1987): 541–57.
Beezley, William H., and Michael C. Meyer, eds. *The Oxford History of Mexico*. New York: Oxford University Press, 2010.
Beizer, Mikhail. *The Jews of St. Petersburg: Excursions Through a Noble Past*. Philadelphia: Jewish Publication Society, 1989.
Benet, William Rose. *Benet's Reader's Encyclopedia*. 3rd ed. New York: Harper & Row, 1987.
Benjamin, Thomas. "Rebuilding the Nation." In *The Oxford History of Mexico*, edited by William Beezley and Michael Meyer, 438–70. New York: Oxford University Press, 2010.
Ben-Sasson, H. H., ed. *A History of the Jewish People*. Cambridge, MA: Harvard University Press, 1976.
"Bogdan Chmielnicki." *Jewish Virtual Library*. Accessed January 15, 2023. https://www.jewishvirtuallibrary.org/chmielnicki-khmelnitski-bogdan-x00b0.
Bokszański, Zbigniew. "On the Concept of Residues in the Theory of Vilfredo Pareto." *Polish Sociological Bulletin* 54 (1981): 39–50.
Brackenridge Park Conservancy. "History of the Park." Accessed June 24, 2022. https://www.brackenridgepark.org/visit-the-park/history-of-the-park.
Braudaway, Doug. "On the Border: A Deck of Cards Led to Del Rio." In *Lone Stars of David: The Jews of Texas*, edited by Hollace Ava Weiner and Kenneth D. Roseman, 135–47. Waltham, MA: University Press of New England, 2007.
Braunstein, Baruch. *The Chuetas of Majorca: Conversos and the Inquisition of Majorca*. New York: Ktav Publishing House, 1972.
Briscoe Ranches, Inc. v. Eagle Pass Independent School District, 439 S.W.2d 117. Court of Civil Appeals of Texas, San Antonio, 1969.
Brock, Pope. *Charlatan: America's Most Dangerous Huckster, the Man Who Pursued Him, and the Age of Flimflam*. New York: Crown Publishers, 2008.
Brodkin, Karen. *How Jews Became White Folks and What That Says about Race in America*. New Brunswick, NJ: Rutgers University Press, 1998.
Brown, John Henry. *Indian Wars and Pioneers of Texas*. Austin: L. E. Daniell, 1880.
Bryson, William C. "The Social Basis of South Texas Bossism." Master's thesis, Harvard University, 1969.
Buchenau, Jürgen. "From the Caudillo to Tata Lázaro: The Maximato in Perspective, 1928–1934." In *The Mexican Revolution: Conflict and Consolidation, 1910–1940*, edited by Douglas W. Richmond, Sam W. Haynes, and Nicholas Villanueva, 135–60. College Station: Texas A&M University Press, 2013.
Burgess, Edwin B. Review of *Tom Mix and Pancho Villa* by Clifford Irving. *Library Journal*, May 15, 1982.
Burns, Chester R. "Health and Medicine." *Handbook of Texas Online*. Accessed March 15, 2023. https://www.tshaonline.org/handbook/entries/health-and-medicine.
Burrough, Bryan, Chris Tomlinson, and Jason Stanford. *Forget the Alamo: The Rise and Fall of an American Myth*. New York: Penguin Press, 2021.
Burton, Jeffery F., Mary M. Farrell, Florence B. Lord, and Richard W. Lord. *Confinement and Ethnicity: An Overview of World War II Japanese American Relocation Sites*. Seattle: University of Washington Press, 2011.
Buxbaum, Yitzhak. *The Light and Fire of the Baal Shem Tov*. New York: Continuum, 2006.
Cantrell, Gregg, and Elizabeth Hayes Turner, eds. *Lone Star Pasts: Memory and History in Texas*. College Station: Texas A&M University Press, 2007.
Carmack, Liz. *Historic Hotels of Texas: A Traveler's Guide*. College Station: Texas A&M University Press, 2007.
Carrozza, Anthony R. *Dukes of Duval County: The Parr Family and Texas Politics*. Norman: University of Oklahoma Press, 2017.
Casey, Clifford B. "Alpine, TX (Brewster County)." *Handbook of Texas Online*. Accessed June 13, 2022. https://www.tshaonline.org/handbook/entries/alpine-tx-brewster-county.
Chipman, Donald E. "Cabeza de Vaca, Álvar Núñez." *Handbook of Texas Online*. Accessed November 10, 2022. https://www.tshaonline.org/handbook/entries/cabeza-de-vaca-lvar-nunez.
———. "In Search of Cabeza de Vaca's Route across Texas: An Historiographical Survey." *Southwestern Historical Quarterly* 91 (1987): 127–48.
Chipman, Donald E., and Patricia R. Lemée. "St. Denis, Louis Juchereau De." *Handbook of Texas Online*. Accessed November 10, 2022. https://www.tshaonline.org/handbook/entries/st-denis-louis-juchereau-de.
Christian, Garna. "Fort Ringgold." *Handbook of Texas Online*. Accessed June 26, 2022. https://www.tshaonline.org/handbook/entries/fort-ringgold.
Cimet, Adina. *Ashkenazi Jews in Mexico: Ideologies in the Structuring of a Community*. Albany: State University of New York Press, 1997.

Citizens Bridge Co. et al. v. Guerra, 258 S.W.2d 64. Supreme Court of Texas, 1953.
City of Dallas Office of Historic Preservation. "Baker Hotel," April 9, 2019. Accessed June 21, 2023. https://cityofdallaspreservation.wordpress.com/tag/baker-hotel/.
City of Eagle Pass. "Eagle Pass News: Riskinds Building Announcement." Facebook Live, March 5, 2021. Accessed June 17, 2024. https://www.facebook.com/watch/live/?ref=watch_permalink&v=2940917906187906.
Cloward, Richard A., and Lloyd E. Ohlin. *Delinquency and Opportunity: A Theory of Delinquent Gangs*. New York: Free Press, 1960.
Coerver, Don M. "Plan of San Diego." *Handbook of Texas Online*. Accessed October 19, 2022. https://www.tshaonline.org/handbook/entries/plan-of-san-diego.
———. "'Wire Me Before Shooting': Federalism in (In)Action—The Texas–Mexico Border during the Revolution, 1910–1920." In *The Mexican Revolution: Conflict and Consolidation, 1910–1940*, edited by Douglas W. Richmond, Sam W. Haynes, and Nicholas Villanueva, 35–57. College Station: Texas A&M University Press, 2013.
Coerver, Don M., and Linda B. Hall. *Texas and the Mexican Revolution: A Study in State and National Border Policy, 1910–1920*. San Antonio: Trinity University Press, 1984.
Cohen, Deborah. *Braceros: Migrant Citizens and Transnational Subjects in the Postwar United States and Mexico*. Chapel Hill: University of North Carolina Press, 2011.
Cohen, Henry. "Settlement of the Jews in Texas." *Publications of the American Jewish Historical Society* 2 (1894): 139–56.
Collison, Robert L. "Encyclopaedia: The Kinds of Encyclopaedias." *Encyclopaedia Britannica*. Accessed October 29, 2022. https://www.britannica.com/topic/encyclopaedia/The-kinds-of-encyclopaedias.
Colorado Virtual Library. "Hermann H. Heiser: Saddlery Manufacturer." Accessed June 21, 2023. https://www.coloradovirtuallibrary.org/digital-colorado/colorado-histories/boom-years/hermann-h-heiser-saddlery-manufacturer/.
Corrales, Salvador C. "Notas Sobre La Historia Económica de La Consolidada, S. A. (1936–1991)." *Estudios Fronterizos* 37–38 (January 1, 1996): 157–76. Accessed June 26, 2022. http://ref.uabc.mx/ojs/index.php/ref/article/view/323.
Craig, Richard B. "Operation Intercept: The International Politics of Pressure." *Review of Politics* 42, no. 4 (October 1980): 556–80.
Crum, Charles L. "The History of the University of North Dakota School of Law." *North Dakota Law Review* 35, no. 1 (1959): 5–35.
Culbertson, Charles. "Errol Flynn." IMDb. Accessed July 15, 2022. http://www.imdb.com/name/nm0001224/bio.
Dallek, Robert. *Lyndon B. Johnson: Portrait of a President*. New York: Oxford University Press, 2005.
Daniels, Roger. "Words Do Matter: A Note on Inappropriate Terminology and the Incarceration of the Japanese Americans." In *Nikkei in the Pacific Northwest: Japanese Americans and Japanese Canadians in the Twentieth Century*, edited by Louis Fiset and Gail M. Nomura, 183–207. Seattle: University of Washington Press, 2005.
"Davis Mountains." *Handbook of Texas Online*. Accessed June 13, 2022. https://www.tshaonline.org/handbook/entries/davis-mountains.
Davis, Walter R. "Hurricanes of 1954." *Monthly Weather Review*, December 1954.
Dawson III, Joseph G. "Sheridan, Philip Henry." *Handbook of Texas Online*. Accessed November 10, 2022. https://www.tshaonline.org/handbook/entries/sheridan-philip-henry.
De la Teja, Jesús "Frank." "Mexican War of Independence." *Handbook of Texas Online*. Accessed December 24, 2022. https://www.tshaonline.org/handbook/entries/mexican-war-of-independence.
Dempsey, John Mark. *The Light Crust Doughboys Are on the Air: Celebrating Seventy Years of Texas Music*. Denton: University of North Texas Press, 2002.
Dennis, Geoffrey W. *The Encyclopedia of Jewish Myth, Magic and Mysticism*. Woodbury, MN: Llewellyn Publications, 2007.
Deutsch, Gotthard, and Meyer Kayserling. "Chuetas." *Jewish Encyclopedia*. Accessed January 5, 2023. https://www.jewishencyclopedia.com/articles/4376-chuetas.
"Devils River." *Handbook of Texas Online*. Accessed June 21, 2022. https://www.tshaonline.org/handbook/entries/devils-river.
Dewey, Alicia M. *Pesos and Dollars: Entrepreneurs in the Texas–Mexico Borderlands, 1880–1940*. College Station: Texas A&M University Press, 2014.
Diehl, Philip N. "The Effects of the Peso Devaluation on Texas Border Cities." *Texas Business Review* 57 (May–June 1983): 120–25.
Dignity Memorial. "Margery Mendelson Obituary." May 21, 2017. Accessed July 25, 2022. https://www.dignitymemorial.com/obituaries/austin-tx/margery-mendelson-8209588.

———. "Wallace Mendelson Obituary." November 19, 2004. Accessed July 25, 2022. https://www.dignitymemorial.com/obituaries/austin-tx/wallace-mendelson-8211125.

Diner, Hasia R. *In the Almost Promised Land: American Jews and Blacks, 1915–1935*. Baltimore: Johns Hopkins University Press, 1995.

———. *Roads Taken: The Great Jewish Migrations to the New World and the Peddlers Who Forged the Way*. New Haven: Yale University Press, 2015.

"Disputation of Barcelona." *Jewish Virtual Library*. Accessed January 2, 2023. https://www.jewishvirtuallibrary.org/disputation-of-barcelona.

Donner, Frank. *Protectors of Privilege: Red Squads and Police Repression in Urban America*. Berkeley: University of California Press, 1992.

Doran, Erin E. "The Border Between Remembering and Forgetting: El Paso, Texas, and the Holocaust." Master's thesis, University of Texas at San Antonio, 2008.

Douglass, Frederick. *The Claims of the Negro, Ethnologically Considered. An Address, Before the Literary Societies of Western Reserve College, at Commencement, July 12, 1854*. Rochester, NY: Lee, Mann, and Co., 1854.

"Dr. Edith Marguerite Bonnet Papers." Portal to Texas History. Accessed July 20, 2022. https://texashistory.unt.edu/explore/collections/bonnet/.

Drabble, Margaret, ed. *The Oxford Companion to English Literature*. New York: Oxford University Press, 1985.

Dubnow, S. M. *History of the Jews in Russia and Poland from the Earliest Times Until the Present Day*. 3 vols. Philadelphia: Jewish Publication Society of America, 1918.

"Duma." *Encyclopaedia Britannica*. Accessed November 8, 2022. https://www.britannica.com/topic/Duma-Russian-assembly.

Dunlay, Thomas W. *Wolves for the Blue Soldiers: Indian Scouts and Auxiliaries with the United States Army, 1860–90*. Lincoln: University of Nebraska Press, 1982.

Eagan, Eileen. *Class, Culture, and the Classroom: The Student Peace Movement of the 1930s*. Philadelphia: Temple University Press, 1981.

Eagle Pass Public Library. "History." Accessed January 11, 2023. https://eaglepasspubliclibrary.org/history-1.

Edelstein, Ben, and John R. Peavey. *Some Tales of Early Rio Grande Valley History with Memories of My Father, a Valley Pioneer*. Self-published, 2003.

Efrati, Natan. "Ransoming of Captives." *Jewish Virtual Library*. Accessed March 14, 2023. https://www.jewishvirtuallibrary.org/ransoming-of-captives.

Eisenberg, Joyce, and Ellen Scolnic. *Dictionary of Jewish Words*. Philadelphia: Jewish Publication Society, 2006.

Eisenhower, John S. D. *Intervention! The United States and the Mexican Revolution, 1913–1917*. New York: Norton, 1995.

"El Paso, Texas." *Encyclopedia of Southern Jewish Communities*. Accessed June 11, 2023. https://www.isjl.org/texas-el-paso-encyclopedia.html.

"Encyclopedia of Southern Jewish Communities." *Encyclopedia of Southern Jewish Communities*. Accessed May 21, 2023. https://www.isjl.org/encyclopedia-of-southern-jewish-communities.html.

Ennis, Michael. "Rags to Riches." *Texas Monthly*, January 1981.

Etienne-Gray, Tracé. "Black Seminole Indians." *Handbook of Texas Online*. Accessed November 10, 2022. https://www.tshaonline.org/handbook/entries/black-seminole-indians.

Everett, Donald. "Buckhorn Saloon." *Handbook of Texas Online*. Accessed June 24, 2022. https://www.tshaonline.org/handbook/entries/buckhorn-saloon.

Ferguson, Duncan. "True Story of the Almanac Used by Abraham Lincoln in the Famous Trial of Duff Armstrong." *Journal of the Illinois State Historical Society* 15, no. 3–4 (October 1922): 688–91.

Fermaglich, Kirsten. *A Rosenberg by Any Other Name: A History of Jewish Name Changing in America*. New York: New York University Press, 2018.

Field, Jacob F. "Battle of Magdeburg." *Encyclopaedia Britannica*. Accessed January 15, 2023. https://www.britannica.com/event/Battle-of-Magdeburg.

Fierman, Floyd S. *The Schwartz Family of El Paso: The Story of a Pioneer Jewish Family in the Southwest*. El Paso: Texas Western Press, 1980.

FindaGrave. "Edward Wilson Ritchie, Sr." Accessed June 19, 2024. https://www.findagrave.com/memorial/51249686/edward-wilson-ritchie.

Fiset, Louis, and Gail M. Nomura, eds. *Nikkei in the Pacific Northwest: Japanese Americans and Japanese Canadians in the Twentieth Century*. Seattle: University of Washington Press, 2005.

Flores Tapia, Oscar. *José López Portillo y Yo: Historia de una Infamia Política*. México, DF: Editorial Grijalbo, 1983.

"Fort Duncan." *Handbook of Texas*. Accessed June 22, 2022. https://www.tshaonline.org/handbook/entries/

fort-duncan.
Fowler, Gene, and Bill Crawford. *Border Radio: Quacks, Yodelers, Pitchmen, Psychics, and Other Amazing Broadcasters of the American Airwaves*. Austin: Texas Monthly Press, 1987.
Frantz, Helen B. "Pan American Round Table." *Handbook of Texas Online*. Accessed September 19, 2023. https://www.tshaonline.org/handbook/entries/pan-american-round-table.
Friedmann, Jonathan L. *Jewish Los Angeles*. Charleston, SC: Arcadia Publishing, 2020.
Gamson, David A., Kathryn A. McDermott, and Douglas S. Reed. "The Elementary and Secondary Education Act at Fifty: Aspirations, Effects, and Limitations." *RSF: The Russell Sage Foundation Journal of the Social Sciences* 1, no. 3 (December 2015): 1–29.
García, María-Cristina. "Charrería." *Handbook of Texas Online*. Accessed January 2, 2023. https://www.tshaonline.org/handbook/entries/charreria.
Garland, Libby. *After They Closed the Gates: Jewish Illegal Immigration to the United States, 1921–1965*. Chicago: The University of Chicago Press, 2018.
Garza, Karla Adelina, and M. R. Graham. "Eagle Pass High School." *American Educational History Journal* 47, no. 2 (January 2020): 173–92.
Gerber, Jim. "Shopping on the Border: The Mexican Peso and US Border Communities," March 2001. Accessed June 21, 2023. https://www.academia.edu/3063300/Shopping_on_the_border_the_Mexican_peso_and_US_border_communities.
Gibson, A. M. *The Kickapoos: Lords of the Middle Border*. Norman: University of Oklahoma Press, 1963.
Gila River Relocation Center. "A Year at Gila Anniversary Booklet." July 20, 1943. Accessed June 17, 2024. https://www.jstor.org/stable/community.31046820.
Gladstein, Mimi Reisel, and Sylvia Deener Cohen. "El Paso: The Wild West Welcomes Holocaust Survivors." In *Lone Stars of David: The Jews of Texas*, edited by Hollace Ava Weiner and Kenneth D. Roseman, 239–54. Waltham, MA: University Press of New England, 2007.
Global Nonviolent Action Database, Swarthmore College. "Unemployed Detroit Auto Workers Conduct Hunger March to Protest Ford Motor Company's Policies, United States, 1932." Accessed October 26, 2022. https://nvdatabase.swarthmore.edu/content/unemployed-detroit-auto-workers-conduct-hunger-march-protest-ford-motor-companys-policies-un.
Goggin, John M. "The Mexican Kickapoo Indians." *Southwestern Journal of Anthropology* 7 (1951): 314–27.
Golash-Boza, Tanya Maria. *Forced Out and Fenced In: Immigration Tales from the Field*. New York: Oxford University Press, 2018.
Goldhill, Simon. *Jerusalem: City of Longing*. Cambridge, MA: Harvard University Press, 2010.
Goldstein, Eric L. *The Price of Whiteness: Jews, Race, and American Identity*. Princeton, NJ: Princeton University Press, 2008.
Goldstein, Sidney. "Profile of American Jewry: Insights from the 1990 National Jewish Population Survey." *American Jewish Year Book* 92 (1992): 77–173.
Gooberman, Lawrence A. *Operation Intercept: The Multiple Consequences of Public Policy*. New York: Pergamon Press, 2013.
GovTrack. "To Pass H.R. 6400, the 1965 Voting Rights Act.—House Vote #87—Jul 9, 1965." Accessed February 1, 2023. https://www.govtrack.us/congress/votes/89-1965/h87.
Grabman, Richard. *Gods, Gachupines and Gringos: A People's History of Mexico*. Albuquerque: Editorial Mazatlán, 2009.
Graham, Don. *Kings of Texas: The 150-Year Saga of an American Ranching Empire*. Hoboken, NJ: Wiley, 2004.
Granoff, Albert L. "To America with Love." Unpublished manuscript, n.d. SC-4215. Jacob Rader Marcus Center of the American Jewish Archives, Cincinnati, Ohio.
Green, George N. "O'Daniel, Wilbert Lee [Pappy]." *Handbook of Texas Online*. Accessed January 3, 2023. https://www.tshaonline.org/handbook/entries/odaniel-wilbert-lee-pappy.
Greenbaum, Masha. *The Jews of Lithuania: A History of a Remarkable Community, 1316–1945*. Jerusalem: Gefen, 1995.
Gross, Woolf. "The Army Reserve Officers' Training Corps: A Hundred Years Old and Still Going Strong." *On Point* 23, no. 2 (Fall 2017): 6–13.
Guedea, Virginia. "The Old Colonialism Ends, The New Colonialism Begins." In *The Oxford History of Mexico*, edited by William Beezley and Michael Meyer, 265–84. New York: Oxford University Press, 2010.
Guerrero, Fernando Avedoy. "XEW: 'The Voice of Latin America from Mexico.'" W Radio, January 10, 2006. Accessed June 21, 2023. https://web.archive.org/web/20060110144117/http://www.wradio.com.mx/historia.asp.

Guinn, Jeff. *Our Land before We Die: The Proud Story of the Seminole Negro*. New York: J. P. Tarcher/Putnam, 2002.

Gurwitz, Alexander Z. *Memories of Two Generations: A Yiddish Life in Russia and Texas*, edited by Bryan Edward Stone, translated by Amram Prero. Tuscaloosa: University of Alabama Press, 2016.

Gutiérrez, José Ángel. Oral History Interview with David Riojas, July 9, 1996. Accessed June 21, 2023. https://library.uta.edu/tejanovoices/xml/CMAS_017.xml.

Guzman, Jane Bock. "West of Neiman's: Best Little Department Store in Sweetwater." In *Lone Stars of David: The Jews of Texas*, edited by Hollace Ava Weiner and Kenneth D. Roseman, 172–81.

Hall, Linda B., and Don M. Coerver. *Revolution on the Border: The United States and Mexico, 1910–1920*. Albuquerque: University of New Mexico Press, 1988.

Hamilton, Allen Lee. "Remolino Raid." *Handbook of Texas Online*. Accessed November 22, 2022. https://www.tshaonline.org/handbook/entries/remolino-raid.

Hansen, Arthur A. "Cultural Politics in the Gila River Relocation Center 1942–1943." *Arizona and the West* 27, no. 4 (Winter 1985): 327–62.

Harduf, David Mendel. *Harduf's Transliterated English-Yiddish, Yiddish-English Dictionary*. Brookline, MA: Israel Book Shop, 2003.

Harrigan, Stephen. *Big Wonderful Thing: A History of Texas*. Austin: University of Texas Press, 2019.

Harris, Charles H. *A Mexican Family Empire: The Latifundio of the Sánchez Navarros, 1765–1867*. Austin: University of Texas Press, 1975.

Harris, Charles H. III, and Louis R. Sadler. *The Plan de San Diego: Tejano Rebellion, Mexican Intrigue*. Lincoln: University of Nebraska Press, 2013.

Hart, John Mason. "The Mexican Revolution, 1910–20." In *The Oxford History of Mexico*, edited by William Beezley and Michael Meyer, 409–36. New York: Oxford University Press, 2010.

Hemphill, Hugh. "Missouri Kansas Texas." San Antonio Transportation History. Accessed October 28, 2022. https://classic.txtransportationmuseum.org/history-rr-missouri-kansas-texas.php.

———. "Restoring Sunset Station." San Antonio Transportation History. Accessed March 15, 2023. https://classic.txtransportationmuseum.org/history-rr-southern-pacific-3.php.

Henderson, Richard B. "Maverick, Fontaine Maury." *Handbook of Texas Online*. Accessed September 27, 2022. https://www.tshaonline.org/handbook/entries/maverick-fontaine-maury.

Herman, Jack, and Peggy Hardman. "Bishop College." *Handbook of Texas Online*. Accessed October 14, 2022. https://www.tshaonline.org/handbook/entries/bishop-college.

Hernández, Andrew. "'They Will Bring Trouble upon Themselves': The Plan de San Diego and the Question of Hispanic Loyalty in Texas." *Journal of South Texas* 31, no. 2 (Spring 2018): 78–105.

Herrera-Sobek, María. *The Mexican Corrido: A Feminist Analysis*. Bloomington: Indiana University Press, 1993.

Hershfield, Joanne. *Imagining La Chica Moderna: Women, Nation, and Visual Culture in Mexico, 1917–1936*. Durham, NC: Duke University Press, 2008.

HIAS. "Our History." Accessed November 8, 2022. https://www.hias.org/who/history.

Hirasuna, Delphine. *The Art of Gaman: Arts and Crafts from the Japanese American Internment Camps 1942–1946*. Berkeley, CA: Ten Speed, 2013.

Hoffman, Abraham. "Jewish Student Militancy in the Great Depression: The Roosevelt High School Blowouts of 1931." *Branding Iron* 121 (March 1976): 6–10.

Hoffman, Eva. *Shtetl*. New York: PublicAffairs, 2007.

Hoffman, Fritz L. "Villa, Francisco [Pancho]." *Handbook of Texas Online*. Accessed December 22, 2022. https://www.tshaonline.org/handbook/entries/villa-francisco-pancho.

Hofsommer, Donovan L. "Missouri-Kansas-Texas Railroad." *Handbook of Texas Online*. Accessed October 28, 2022. https://www.tshaonline.org/handbook/entries/missouri-kansas-texas-railroad.

Hopwood, Jon C. "Clara Kimball Young." IMDb. Accessed July 15, 2022. http://www.imdb.com/name/nm0949403/bio.

Hordes, Stanley M. *To the End of the Earth: A History of the Crypto-Jews of New Mexico*. New York: Columbia University Press, 2005.

Horn, Dara. *People Love Dead Jews: Reports from a Haunted Present*. New York: W. W. Norton & Company, 2021.

Housing Act of 1949, 63 Stat 413 (1949).

Huerta, Joel. "Friday Night Rights: South Texas High-School Football and the Struggle for Equality." *The International Journal of the History of Sport* 26 (June 2009): 981–1000.

Huston, James A. "Selective Service in World War II." *Current History* 54, no. 322 (June 1968): 345–84.

Hyman, Paula. *The Jews of Modern France*. Berkeley: University of California Press, 1998.

Ilan, Tal. "Beruryah." *Jewish Women's Archive*. Accessed June 7, 2022. https://jwa.org/encyclopedia/article/beruryah.

———. "Post-Biblical and Rabbinic Women." *Jewish Women's Archive*. Accessed June 7, 2022. https://jwa.org/encyclopedia/article/post-biblical-and-rabbinic-women.

IMDb. "Cantinflas: Biography." Accessed January 5, 2023. http://www.imdb.com/name/nm0134594/bio.

———. "Elmo Lincoln: Biography." Accessed June 19, 2023. https://www.imdb.com/name/nm0511104/bio/?ref_=nm_ov_bio_sm.

———. "Leo Carrillo: Biography." Accessed January 29, 2023. https://www.imdb.com/name/nm0140504/bio.

———. "Morrie Ryskind: Biography." Accessed July 15, 2022. http://www.imdb.com/name/nm0753452/bio.

In re Owl Drug Co., 21 F. Supp. 907. United States District Court, D. Nevada, 1937.

INEGI. "Third Census of Population of the United Mexican States, 1910." Accessed June 13, 2022. https://en.www.inegi.org.mx/programas/ccpv/1910.

International Boundary and Water Commission. "Mission, Organization and Procedures for Solution of Boundary and Water Problems." Accessed January 5, 2023. https://www.ibwc.gov/about_us/about_us.html.

Jackson, Denny. "Theda Bara." IMDb. Accessed July 15, 2022. http://www.imdb.com/name/nm0000847/bio.

Jackson, Jack. "Vaquero." *Handbook of Texas Online*. Accessed June 8, 2022. https://www.tshaonline.org/handbook/entries/vaquero.

Jacobs, Janet Liebman. *Hidden Heritage: The Legacy of the Crypto-Jews*. Berkeley: University of California Press, 2002.

Jacoway, Elizabeth. *Turn Away Thy Son: Little Rock, the Crisis That Shocked the Nation*. Fayetteville: University of Arkansas Press, 2008.

Jacques, Leo M. Dambourges. "The Chinese Massacre in Torreón (Coahuila) in 1911." *Arizona and the West* 16, no. 3 (1974): 233–46.

Jaffe, Ina. "Yossele Rosenblatt: The Cantor with the Heavenly Voice." *NPR*, September 6, 2010. Accessed June 20, 2024. https://www.npr.org/templates/story/story.php?storyId=129635330.

Jewish Histories in Multiethnic Boyle Heights. "Hebrew Sheltering and Home for the Aged." Accessed June 25, 2022. https://scalar.usc.edu/hc/jewish-histories-boyle-heights/hebrew-sheltering-and-home-for-the-aged-origins.

Jewish Histories in Multiethnic Boyle Heights. "The Menorah Center: 3218 Wabash Ave." Accessed July 23, 2022. https://scalar.usc.edu/hc/jewish-histories-boyle-heights/the-menorah-center-3218-wabash-ave.

Jewish Histories in Multiethnic Boyle Heights. "The Modern Talmud Torah and Social Center." Accessed July 23, 2022. https://scalar.usc.edu/hc/jewish-histories-boyle-heights/the-modern-talmud-torah-and-social-center.

"John Hyrcanus I." *Encyclopaedia Britannica*. Accessed January 15, 2023. https://www.britannica.com/biography/John-Hyrcanus-I.

Johnson, Benjamin Heber. *Revolution in Texas: How a Forgotten Rebellion and Its Bloody Suppression Turned Mexicans into Americans*. New Haven: Yale University Press, 2003.

Johnson, Lyndon B. "Remarks at the Signing of the Child Nutrition Act of 1966." The American Presidency Project, October 11, 1966. Accessed June 21, 2023. https://www.presidency.ucsb.edu/node/238283.

———. "Remarks in Johnson City, Tex., Upon Signing the Elementary and Secondary Education Bill," April 11, 1965. Accessed June 21, 2023. https://www.presidency.ucsb.edu/documents/remarks-johnson-city-tex-upon-signing-the-elementary-and-secondary-education-bill.

Johnson, Paul. *A History of the Jews*. New York: Perennial Library, 1988.

Jordan, Terry G. "The Forgotten Texas State Census of 1887." *Southwestern Historical Quarterly* 85, no. 4 (April 1982): 401–8.

Joseph, Harriet Denise. "The Brownsville Jewish Community: From Generation to Generation." Unpublished manuscript, 1990. Box 3K182. Sam Perl Papers, 1927–2002, Dolph Briscoe Center for American History, University of Texas at Austin, Austin, Texas.

Joseph, Harriet Denise, and Sondra Shands. "Sam Perl: Mr. Friendship and Mr. Temple Beth-El of Brownsville, Texas." *Locus* 5 (Spring 1993): 145–61.

Kahn, Ava Fran, and Marc Dollinger, eds. *California Jews*. Hanover, NH: University Press of New England, 2003.

"Kalvarija." JewishGen. Accessed January 3, 2023. https://kehilalinks.jewishgen.org/Kalvarija/Kalvarija.html#holocaust.

"Kalvarija." *Jewish Virtual Library*. Accessed January 3, 2023. https://www.jewishvirtuallibrary.org/kalvarija.

Kaminsky, Michael. "D. W. Griffith: Biography." IMDb. Accessed June 19, 2023. https://www.imdb.com/name/nm0000428/bio/?ref_=nm_ov_bio_sm.

Kane, Dagmar Odehnal. Interview by Mary Louise Weiss, March 9, 1987. Library of Congress. Accessed June 21, 2023. https://www.loc.gov/item/mfdipbib001570/.

Katz, Friedrich. *The Life and Times of Pancho Villa*. Stanford: Stanford University Press, 1998.

———. *The Secret War in Mexico: Europe, the United States and the Mexican Revolution*. Chicago: University of Chicago Press, 1985.

Kaye/Kantrowitz, Melanie. *The Colors of Jews: Racial Politics and Radical Diasporism*. Bloomington, IN: Indiana University Press, 2007.

Kelton, Elmer. "Dove Creek, Battle Of." *Handbook of Texas Online*. Accessed November 10, 2022. https://www.tshaonline.org/handbook/entries/dove-creek-battle-of.

Kenez, Peter. "Pogroms and White Ideology in the Russian Civil War." In *Pogroms: Anti-Jewish Violence in Modern Russian History*, edited by John D. Klier and Shlomo Lambroza, 293–313. Cambridge, UK: Cambridge University Press, 1992.

Kennelly, Robert Andrew. "The Location of the Mexican Steel Industry." *Revista Geográfica* 14 (September 1954): 51–80.

Kerrigan, William T. "Race, Expansion, and Slavery in Eagle Pass, Texas, 1852." *Southwestern Historical Quarterly* 101, no. 3 (January 1998): 275–301.

Kevane, Bridget A. *The Dynamics of Jewish Latino Relationships: Hope and Caution*. Basingstoke, UK: Palgrave Pivot, 2015.

"Kever Avot." *Jewish Virtual Library*. Accessed June 11, 2022. https://www.jewishvirtuallibrary.org/kever-avot.

Kickapoo Joy Juice. "Kickapoo Joy Juice—The Original Citrus Soft Drink." Accessed June 20, 2023. https://drinkkickapoo.com/.

Klier, John D. "The Pogrom Paradigm in Russian History." In *Pogroms: Anti-Jewish Violence in Modern Russian History*, edited by John D. Klier and Shlomo Lambroza, 13–38. Cambridge, UK: Cambridge University Press, 1992.

Klier, John D., and Shlomo Lambroza, eds. *Pogroms: Anti-Jewish Violence in Modern Russian History*. Cambridge, UK: Cambridge University Press, 1992.

Knabe, Albert J. "O'Daniel, Merle Estella Butcher." *Handbook of Texas Online*. Accessed January 4, 2023. https://www.tshaonline.org/handbook/entries/odaniel-merle-estella-butcher.

"Koenigsberg." *Jewish Virtual Library*. Accessed July 11, 2022. https://www.jewishvirtuallibrary.org/koenigsberg.

Koestler, Fred L. "Bracero Program." *Handbook of Texas Online*. Accessed January 8, 2023. https://www.tshaonline.org/handbook/entries/bracero-program.

Kosmin, Barry A., Sidney Goldstein, et al. *Highlights of the CJF National Jewish Population Study*. New York: Council of Jewish Federations, 1991.

Krause, P. Allen, Mark K. Bauman, and Stephen Krause. *To Stand Aside or Stand Alone: Southern Reform Rabbis and the Civil Rights Movement*. Tuscaloosa: University of Alabama Press, 2016.

Kuramitsu, Kristine C. "Internment and Identity in Japanese American Art." *American Quarterly* 47, no. 4 (December 1995): 619–58.

"Laredo, Texas." *Encyclopedia of Southern Jewish Communities*. Accessed June 11, 2023. https://www.isjl.org/texas-laredo-encyclopedia.html.

Latorre, Felipe A., and Dolores L. Latorre. *The Mexican Kickapoo Indians*. New York: Dover Publications, 1976.

Lavi, Theodor. "Kishinev, Moldova." *Jewish Virtual Library*. Accessed November 9, 2022. https://www.jewish-virtuallibrary.org/kishinev-moldova.

Leal, David L. "Students in Uniform: ROTC, the Citizen-Soldier, and the Civil-Military Gap." *PS: Political Science and Politics* 40, no. 3 (July 2007): 479–83.

Leatherwood, Art. "Eagle Pass Army Air Field." *Handbook of Texas Online*. Accessed June 25, 2022. https://www.tshaonline.org/handbook/entries/eagle-pass-army-air-field.

———. "Javelina." *Handbook of Texas Online*. Accessed October 26, 2022. https://www.tshaonline.org/handbook/entries/javelina.

———. "Laughlin Air Force Base." *Handbook of Texas Online*. Accessed June 25, 2022. https://www.tshaonline.org/handbook/entries/laughlin-air-force-base.

———. "Shelby Expedition." *Handbook of Texas Online*. Accessed November 10, 2022. https://www.tshaonline.org/handbook/entries/shelby-expedition.

Levenson, Norma. "A Study of the Jewish Community Centers of Los Angeles, California." Master's thesis, University of Southern California, 2015.

Levin, Dov. *The Litvaks: A Short History of the Jews in Lithuania*. Jerusalem: Yad Vashem, 2000.

Levin, Neil W. "Di Grine Kuzine/The Greenhorn Cousin." Milken Archive of Jewish Music. Accessed October 29, 2022. http://www.milkenarchive.org/music/volumes/view/great-songs-of-the-american-yiddish-stage/work/di-grine-kuzine/.

Library of Congress. "Bedelia." Accessed October 29, 2022. https://www.loc.gov/item/ihas.100007925/.

———. "Mutt and Jeff—An Unlikely Pair." Comic Art: 120 Years of Panels and Pages. Accessed October 26, 2022. https://www.loc.gov/exhibitions/comic-art/about-this-exhibition/early-years-1890s-to-1920s/mutt-an

d-jeff-an-unlikely-pair/.
Limonic, Laura. *Kugel and Frijoles: Latino Jews in the United States*. Detroit: Wayne State University Press, 2019.
Littlefield, Douglas R. *Conflict on the Rio Grande: Water and the Law, 1879–1939*. Norman: University of Oklahoma Press, 2014.
Lone Wolf v. Hitchcock, 23 S. Ct. 216. Supreme Court of the United States, 1903.
Los Angeles Conservancy. "Pershing Square." Accessed June 25, 2022. https://www.laconservancy.org/locations/pershing-square.
"Luis Terrazas; Former Governor of Mexico." *Busy Man's Magazine,* March 1907.
Lyle, Gabrielle Ryann. "B'nai Borderlands: The Development of Jewish Communities in the Rio Grande Valley." Master's thesis, Texas A&M University, 2022.
Lynch, Dudley M. *The Duke of Duval: The Life & Times of George B. Parr, A Biography*. Waco: Texian Press, 1976.
Mager Hois, Elisabeth A. "The Kickapoo of Coahuila/Texas: Cultural Implications of Being a Cross-Border Nation." *Voices of Mexico* 90 (Spring–Summer 2011): 36–40.
Majaski, Christina. "Devaluation: Definition, How It Works, and Examples." *Investopedia*, August 29, 2021. Accessed June 21, 2023. https://www.investopedia.com/terms/d/devaluation.asp.
Manguso, John. "Fort Sam Houston." *Handbook of Texas Online*. Accessed June 25, 2022. https://www.tshaonline.org/handbook/entries/fort-sam-houston.
Marcus, Stanley. *Minding the Store: A Memoir*. Denton: University of North Texas Press, 1997.
Marinari, Maddalena. *Unwanted: Italian and Jewish Mobilization against Restrictive Immigration Laws, 1882–1965*. Chapel Hill: University of North Carolina Press, 2020.
Martin, Bob. *Gov. Appoints Mohr to Court*. 1964. Los Angeles Public Library Photo Collection. Accessed June 21, 2023. https://calisphere.org/item/1674ef1370641d2eb8c84d3e1e2cadc7/.
Martínez, Oscar J. *Border People: Life and Society in the U.S.–Mexico Borderlands*. Tucson: University of Arizona Press, 1994.
Mates, Donald Davidson Benson. "Isabel Creed Hungerland, Philosophy: Berkeley." In *University of California: In Memoriam, 1992*, edited by David Krogh. Accessed June 17, 2024. http://texts.cdlib.org/view?docId=hb7c6007sj;NAAN=13030&doc.view=frames&chunk.id=div00025&toc.depth=1&toc.id=&brand=calisphere.
Mathias, Fred S. *The Amazing Bob Davis: His Last Vagabond Journey*. New York: Longmans, Green, 1944.
Mauzy, Oscar. "Gilmer-Aikin Laws." *Handbook of Texas Online*. Accessed April 20, 2023. https://www.tshaonline.org/handbook/entries/gilmer-aikin-laws.
McCormack, Thelma. Review of *The Intelligent Woman's Guide to Socialism and Capitalism*, by George Bernard Shaw. *American Journal of Sociology* 91, no. 1 (July 1985): 209–11.
"Meet a Farmer | Texas Spinach," 2018. Accessed June 21, 2023. https://www.youtube.com/watch?v=7Ha-LVvN_HI.
Mendelsohn, Adam D. *The Rag Race: How Jews Sewed Their Way to Success in America and the British Empire*. New York: New York University Press, 2015.
Mendelson, Wallace. "ERA, the Supreme Court, and Allegations of Gender Bias." *Missouri Law Review* 44, no. 1 (Winter 1979): 1–11.
Mensa International. "About Us." Accessed October 25, 2022. https://www.mensa.org/mensa/about-us.
Mikaberidze, Alexander. *The Burning of Moscow: Napoleon's Trial by Fire, 1812*. Barnsley, UK: Pen & Sword Military, 2014.
Miller, Lauraine. "The Zale Story: Diamonds for the Rough." In *Lone Stars of David: The Jews of Texas*, edited by Hollace Ava Weiner and Kenneth D. Roseman, 148–61. Waltham, MA: University Press of New England, 2007.
Minnick, Fred. "Cross Border Bourbon." *Whisky Magazine*, July 20, 2012. Accessed October 20, 2022. https://whiskymag.com/articles/cross-border-bourbon/.
Miron, Dan. "Sh. Y. Abramovitsh and His 'Mendele.'" In Dan Miron, *The Image of the Shtetl and Other Studies of Modern Jewish Literary Imagination*, 81–127. Syracuse, NY: Syracuse University Press, 2000.
Mission Park Funeral Chapels. "Obituary for Arturo Flores," June 14, 2006. Accessed June 20, 2023. https://www.missionparks.com/obituaries/Arturo-Flores-37440/.
Moen, Jon R., and Ellis W. Tallman. "The Panic of 1907." *Federal Reserve History*. Accessed November 9, 2022. https://www.federalreservehistory.org/essays/panic-of-1907.
Montgomery, Cora. *Eagle Pass; or Life on the Border*, edited by Alex L. Mauldin. New York: Putnam, 1852.
Moore, Deborah Dash. *To the Golden Cities: Pursuing the American Jewish Dream in Miami and L.A.* New York: Free Press, 1994.
"Moses Maimonides (Rambam)." *Jewish Virtual Library*. Accessed January 21, 2023. https://www.jewishvirtuallibrary.org/moses-maimonides-rambam.
Mowis, I. S. "Mark Robson: Mini Bio." IMDb. Accessed July 6, 2022. https://www.imdb.com/name/nm0733476/

bio/?ref_=nm_ov_bio_sm.

Munter, William J. "Sam Schwartz and the Aztec." Bullock Texas State History Museum. Accessed June 17, 2022. https://www.thestoryoftexas.com/discover/texas-story-project/sam-schwartz-and-the-aztec.

———. *History of the Jews of Texas' Middle Corridor*. Laredo, TX: Border Studies Publishing, 1990.

———. "Schwartz, Sam." *Handbook of Texas Online*. Accessed July 15, 2022. https://www.tshaonline.org/handbook/entries/schwartz-sam.

Museum of the Yiddish Theatre. "The Gold Diggers, by Sholem Aleichem." Accessed January 14, 2023. https://www.moyt.org/exhibitions/pih/gold-diggers.htm.

National Archives. "National Labor Relations Act (1935)." Accessed June 21, 2023. https://www.archives.gov/milestone-documents/national-labor-relations-act.

Neusner, Jacob, and Bruce D. Chilton, eds. *In Quest of the Historical Pharisees*. Waco: Baylor University Press, 2020.

Newman, Aubrey. "Napoleon and The Jews." *European Judaism: A Journal for the New Europe* 2, no. 2 (Winter 1967): 25–32.

Nunley, M. Christopher. "Kickapoo Indians." *Handbook of Texas Online*. Accessed November 10, 2022. https://www.tshaonline.org/handbook/entries/kickapoo-indians.

Oden, Derek S. *Harvest of Hazards: Family Farming, Accidents, and Expertise in the Corn Belt, 1940–1975*. Iowa City: University of Iowa Press, 2017.

O'Donnell, Edward T. *Henry George and the Crisis of Inequality: Progress and Poverty in the Gilded Age*. New York: Columbia University Press, 2015.

Office of the Governor of Texas. "Press Release: Governor Abbott Expands Border Security Operations," June 29, 2022. Accessed June 21, 2023. https://gov.texas.gov/news/post/governor-abbott-expands-border-security-operations.

"Old San Antonio Road." *Handbook of Texas Online*. Accessed June 13, 2022. https://www.tshaonline.org/handbook/entries/old-san-antonio-road.

"Otto Klemperer." *Encyclopaedia Britannica*. Accessed August 13, 2022. https://www.britannica.com/biography/Otto-Klemperer.

Patterson, Connie. "Porter, William Sydney." *Handbook of Texas Online*. Accessed April 7, 2023. https://www.tshaonline.org/handbook/entries/porter-william-sydney.

Perry, Fred V. "Understanding the Mexican Attorney: Legal Education and the Practice of Law in Mexico." *International Lawyer* 10, no. 1 (Winter 1976): 167–79.

Pew Research Center. *A Portrait of Jewish Americans*. Washington, DC: Pew Research Center, 2013.

———. *Jewish Americans in 2020*. Washington, DC: Pew Research Center, 2021.

"Piedras Negras." *Encyclopaedia Britannica*. Accessed June 13, 2022. https://www.britannica.com/place/Piedras-Negras.

Pikoff, Jonathan A., and Charles J. Crimmins. "Lost in Translation: Texas Notary Public v. Mexico *Notario Publico*." Accessed June 11, 2022. https://www.sos.state.tx.us/statdoc/notariopublicoarticle.shtml.

Pingenot, Ben E. "Eagle Pass, TX." *Handbook of Texas Online*. Accessed June 12, 2022. https://www.tshaonline.org/handbook/entries/eagle-pass-tx.

———. *Historical Highlights of Eagle Pass and Maverick County: Maverick County Centennial 1871–1971*. Eagle Pass, TX: Eagle Pass Chamber of Commerce, 1971.

———. "Maverick County Irrigation Canal." *Handbook of Texas Online*. Accessed September 27, 2022. https://www.tshaonline.org/handbook/entries/maverick-county-irrigation-canal.

———. "Sumpter, Jesse." *Handbook of Texas Online*. Accessed May 27, 2022. https://www.tshaonline.org/handbook/entries/sumpter-jesse.

Porter Loring Mortuary. "David Jacobson Obituary," November 4, 2001. Accessed June 21, 2023. https://www.porterloring.com/obituaries/obituary-listings?obId=18277967.

Prendes. "Nuestra Historia." Accessed June 28, 2022. https://prendes.mx/.

Quezada, J. Gilberto. *Border Boss: Manuel B. Bravo and Zapata County*. College Station: Texas A&M University Press, 1999.

Randle, Mallory B. "Work Projects Administration." *Handbook of Texas Online*. Accessed January 11, 2023. https://www.tshaonline.org/handbook/entries/work-projects-administration.

Raphael, Simcha Paull. *Jewish Views of the Afterlife*. London: Rowman & Littlefield Publishers, 2019.

Reid, Jan. "The Forgotten People." *Texas Monthly*, February 1997.

Richardson, Chad, and Michael J. Pisani. *Batos, Bolillos, Pochos, and Pelados: Class and Culture on the South Texas Border*. Austin: University of Texas Press, 2017.

Richmond, Douglas W., and Sam W. Haynes. Preface to *The Mexican Revolution: Conflict and Consolidation*,

1910–1940, edited by Douglas W. Richmond, Sam W. Haynes, and Nicholas Villanueva, vii–x. College Station: Texas A&M University Press, 2013.

Richmond, Douglas W., Sam W. Haynes, and Nicholas Villanueva, eds. *The Mexican Revolution: Conflict and Consolidation, 1910–1940*. College Station: Texas A&M University Press, 2013.

Riskind, Morris. Interview by Peter Riskind, November 8, 1995. Video recording in editor's possession, provided by Peter Riskind.

———. "Map of Jewish Stores in Downtown Eagle Pass." n.d. Copy in editor's possession, provided by Peter Riskind.

———. "Riskind, Michael." *Handbook of Texas Online*. Accessed July 5, 2022. https://www.tshaonline.org/handbook/entries/riskind-michael.

Riskind, Reuben. "Texas Border Merchant." *Texas Jewish Historical Society Bulletin*, August 2002, 17–19.

Riskind, Ruth. Interview by Peter Riskind, 1998. Video recording in editor's possession, provided by Peter Riskind.

Rister, Carl Coke. "Lee, Robert Edward." *Handbook of Texas Online*. Accessed November 10, 2022. https://www.tshaonline.org/handbook/entries/lee-robert-edward.

———. *Robert E. Lee in Texas*. Norman: University of Oklahoma Press, 1946.

Romero, Robert Chao. *The Chinese in Mexico, 1882–1940*. Tucson: University of Arizona Press, 2012.

Rosenthal, Herman. "Baruch Leibov." *Jewish Encyclopedia*. Accessed January 15, 2023. https://www.jewishencyclopedia.com/articles/2580-baruch-leibov.

Ross, Stanley R. *Francisco I. Madero: Apostle of Mexican Democracy*. New York: Columbia University Press, 1955.

Rosten, Leo. *The Joys of Yiddish*. New York: Pocket Books, 1970.

Round-Up (Roosevelt High School yearbook). Los Angeles, CA, 1927. Accessed June 17, 2024. https://www.ancestrylibrary.com/imageviewer/collections/1265/images/43135_b171734_00000?ssrc=&backlabel=Return.

Rozek, Barbara J., ed. *Forgotten Texas Census: First Annual Report of the Agricultural Bureau of the Department of Agriculture, Insurance, Statistics, and History, 1887–88*. College Station: Texas A&M University Press, 2002.

Russell, Bertrand. "Philosophy and Politics." In *Unpopular Essays*, 11–31. London: Routledge, 1995.

Sachar, Howard M. *A History of Israel: From the Rise of Zionism to Our Time*. New York: Knopf Doubleday, 2013.

San Antonio Conservation Society Foundation. "Alamo Plaza History." Accessed January 2, 2023. https://www.saconservation.org/VirtualExhibits/AlamoPlaza/82873E32-AF52-486B-B566-185253770420.htm.

"San Antonio, Texas." *Encyclopedia of Southern Jewish Communities*. Accessed June 20, 2022. https://www.isjl.org/texas-san-antonio-encyclopedia.html.

San Miguel, Guadalupe. "Mexican Americans and Education." *Handbook of Texas Online*. Accessed January 2, 2023. https://www.tshaonline.org/handbook/entries/mexican-americans-and-education.

Sánchez, George J. "'What's Good for Boyle Heights Is Good for the Jews': Creating Multiracialism on the Eastside during the 1950s." *American Quarterly* 56, no. 3 (September 2004): 633–61.

Sánchez, Martha I. Chew. *Corridos in Migrant Memory*. Albuquerque: University of New Mexico Press, 2006.

Sarna, Jonathan D., and Adam M. Mendelsohn. *Jews and the Civil War: A Reader*. New York: New York University Press, 2011.

Schottenstein, Allison E. *Changing Perspectives: Black-Jewish Relations in Houston during the Civil Rights Era*. Denton: University of North Texas Press, 2021.

———. "'Perls of Wisdom': 'Rabbi' Sam Perl, New Models of Acculturation, and the 'In-Between' Jew." Master's thesis, University of Texas at Austin, 2011.

Schulze, Jeffrey M. *"Are We Not Foreigners Here?": Indigenous Nationalism in the Twentieth-Century U.S.–Mexico Borderlands*. Chapel Hill: University of North Carolina Press, 2018.

Scruggs, Otey M. "Texas and the Bracero Program, 1942–1947." *Pacific Historical Review* 32, no. 3 (August 1963): 251–64.

Sebakijje, Lena. "Research Guides: Catarrh Remedy and Peruna Scandal: Topics in Chronicling America: Introduction." Accessed October 19, 2022. https://guides.loc.gov/chronicling-america-peruna-scandal-catarrh-remedy/introduction.

Shandler, Jeffrey. *Jews, God, and Videotape: Religion and Media in America*. New York: New York University Press, 2009.

Shank, Albert. "At the U.S.O." *Eagle Eye*, August 14, 1943.

Shapira, Anita. *Israel: A History*. Waltham, MA: Brandeis University Press, 2012.

"Sholem Aleichem." *YIVO Encyclopedia of Jews in Eastern Europe*. Accessed January 14, 2023. https://yivoencyclopedia.org/article.aspx/sholem_aleichem.

Silow-Carroll, Andrew. "No One Lost Their Jewish Last Name at Ellis Island. But We Gained a Safe Haven." *Jewish Telegraphic Agency* (blog), September 13, 2021. Accessed June 21, 2023. https://www.jta.org/2021/09/13/opinion/no-one-lost-their-jewish-last-name-at-ellis-island-but-we-gained-a-safe-haven.

Sivad, E. Douglas. "Caballo, Juan." *Handbook of Texas Online*. Accessed January 7, 2023. https://www.tshaonline.org/handbook/entries/caballo-juan.

Sklar, Dusty. "Mahatma Gandhi on Zionism and the Holocaust." *Blog-Schmog* (blog), March 19, 2016. Accessed June 21, 2023. https://jewishcurrents.org/mahatma-gandhi-on-zionism-and-the-holocaust.

Slaughter, George. "Bentsen, Lloyd Millard, Jr." *Handbook of Texas Online*. Accessed September 27, 2022. https://www.tshaonline.org/handbook/entries/bentsen-lloyd-millard-jr.

———. "Briscoe, Dolph, Jr." *Handbook of Texas Online*. Accessed October 14, 2022. https://www.tshaonline.org/handbook/entries/briscoe-dolph-jr.

Smith, Jerrie Marcus. *A Girl Named Carrie: The Visionary Who Created Neiman Marcus and Set the Standard for Fashion*. Denton: University of North Texas Press, 2021.

"South Texas." *Encyclopedia of Southern Jewish Communities*. Accessed June 11, 2023. https://www.isjl.org/texas-south-encyclopedia.html.

Spell, James Bryan, Jr. "The Voting Rights Act of 1965: A Summary of Its Legislative History." Master's thesis, University of Richmond, 1966.

Stern, Menahem. "The Period of the Second Temple." In *A History of the Jewish People*, edited by H. H. Ben-Sasson, 185–303. Cambridge, MA: Harvard University Press, 1976.

Stone, Bryan Edward. *The Chosen Folks: Jews on the Frontiers of Texas*. Austin: University of Texas Press, 2010.

———. "West of Center: Jews on the Real and Imagined Frontiers of Texas." PhD diss., University of Texas at Austin, 2003.

Stuck, Eleanor. "Menger Hotel." *Handbook of Texas Online*. Accessed June 24, 2022. https://www.tshaonline.org/handbook/entries/menger-hotel.

"Students, Appointed by the Faculty." *Michigan Law Review* 20 (June 1922): 887.

Suberman, Stella. *The Jew Store*. Chapel Hill, NC: Algonquin Books, 2001.

Sumpter, Jesse. *Paso Del Águila: A Chronicle of Frontier Days on the Texas Border*, edited by Ben E. Pingenot. Austin: Encino Press, 1969.

Sundquist, Eric J. *Strangers in the Land: Blacks, Jews, Post-Holocaust America*. Cambridge, MA: Harvard University Press, 2009.

Sussman, Lance J., and Karen Franklin, eds. "Memoirs of Oscar Dreizin of Butler and Macon, Georgia, c. 1948." *Southern Jewish History* 26 (2023): 175–216.

Swanson, Donald A. "Coacoochee [Wild Cat]." *Handbook of Texas Online*. Accessed January 7, 2023. https://www.tshaonline.org/handbook/entries/coacoochee-wild-cat.

Swartz, Mimi. "Texas Primer: The Sticker Bur." *Texas Monthly*, January 1985.

Sweet, Lewis T., and Harvey Paticoff. "The Education of an Army Lawyer: The Judge Advocate General's School." *American Bar Association Journal* 45 (May 1959): 463–508.

Tartar, Clarissa. "Anatomy of the Apparel Mart." *D Magazine*, April 1, 1984.

Tate, Michael L. "Black Seminole Scouts." *Handbook of Texas Online*. Accessed November 22, 2022. https://www.tshaonline.org/handbook/entries/black-seminole-scouts.

———. "Bullis, John Lapham." *Handbook of Texas Online*. Accessed November 10, 2022. https://www.tshaonline.org/handbook/entries/bullis-john-lapham.

Taylor, Lawrence D. "The Magonista Revolt in Baja California." *Journal of San Diego History* 45, no. 1 (Winter 1999). Accessed June 18, 2024. https://sandiegohistory.org/journal/1999/january/magonista/.

Texas Band of Kickapoo Act, Pub. L. No. 97–429, § Stat, 96 2269 (1983).

Texas Historical Commission. "Gunter Hotel." Accessed June 24, 2022. http://www.thc.texas.gov/preserve/projects-and-programs/historic-texas-highways/place-of-interest/hotel-205-e-houston-st-san.

———. "Travelers Hotel." Accessed June 24, 2022. http://www.thc.texas.gov/preserve/projects-and-programs/historic-texas-highways/place-of-interest/hotel-220-broadway-ave-san.

Texas Military Department. "1st Squadron, 124th Cavalry Regiment." Accessed June 26, 2022. https://tmd.texas.gov/1st-squadron-124th-cavalry-regiment.

Thompson, Jerry. "Cortina, Juan Nepomuceno." *Handbook of Texas Online*. Accessed November 10, 2022. https://www.tshaonline.org/handbook/entries/cortina-juan-nepomuceno.

———. *Cortina: Defending the Mexican Name in Texas*. College Station: Texas A&M University Press, 2007.

Tikkanen, Amy. "Magdeburg." *Encyclopaedia Britannica*. Accessed January 15, 2023. https://www.britannica.com/place/Magdeburg-Germany.

Tiro Tres Farms. "History." Accessed August 12, 2022. https://www.tirotresfarms.com/about1.

"Tomb of the Patriarchs and Matriarchs (Ma'arat HaMachpelah)." *Jewish Virtual Library*. Accessed June 20, 2023. https://www.jewishvirtuallibrary.org/tomb-of-the-patriarchs-ma-arat-hamachpelah.

Townsend, Charles R., and John B. Bratcher II. "Hillbilly Boys." *Handbook of Texas Online*. Accessed January 4, 2023. https://www.tshaonline.org/handbook/entries/hillbilly-boys.
UNESCO World Heritage Centre. "Hisham's Palace/Khirbet al-Mafjar." Accessed June 28, 2022. https://whc.unesco.org/en/tentativelists/6546/.
US Census Bureau. "1910 Census: Volume 3. Population, Reports by States, with Statistics for Counties, Cities, and Other Civil Divisions: Nebraska-Wyoming, Alaska, Hawaii, and Porto Rico." Accessed June 21, 2023. https://www.census.gov/library/publications/1913/dec/vol-3-population.html.
US House of Representatives. *Hearings Before the Special Committee to Investigate National Labor Relations Board*. Washington, DC: US Government Printing Office, 1940.
US National Park Service. "Black Seminole Indian Scouts." Accessed November 27, 2022. https://www.nps.gov/articles/000/black-seminole-indian-scouts.htm.
USC Libraries. "About the Hoose Library of Philosophy." Accessed March 31, 2023. https://libraries.usc.edu/locations/hoose-philosophy-library/hoose-philosophy-library-history.
Utley, Robert Marshall. *Frontier Regulars: The United States Army and the Indian, 1866–1891*. Lincoln: University of Nebraska Press, 1984.
UTSA Libraries Special Collections, Digital Collections. "Joske's Sign, San Antonio, Texas." Accessed January 2, 2023. https://digital.utsa.edu/digital/collection/p9020coll008/id/4639.
Vázquez, Josefina Zoraida. "War and Peace with the United States." In *The Oxford History of Mexico*, edited by William Beezley and Michael Meyer, 319–48. New York: Oxford University Press, 2010.
Villegas, Teresa. "History of La Lotería." Accessed June 10, 2022. https://teresavillegas.com/history-of-la-loteria/.
Walker, Donald R. "Texas State Penitentiary at Huntsville." *Handbook of Texas Online*. Accessed June 28, 2022. https://www.tshaonline.org/handbook/entries/texas-state-penitentiary-at-huntsville.
Wallace, Ernest. "Mackenzie, Ranald Slidell." *Handbook of Texas Online*. Accessed November 17, 2022. https://www.tshaonline.org/handbook/entries/mackenzie-ranald-slidell.
Webb, Walter Prescott. *The Texas Rangers: A Century of Frontier Defense*. Austin: University of Texas Press, 2010.
Weber, John. *From South Texas to the Nation: The Exploitation of Mexican Labor in the Twentieth Century*. Chapel Hill: University of North Carolina Press, 2015.
Weddle, Robert S. "San Juan Bautista." *Handbook of Texas Online*. Accessed June 13, 2022. https://www.tshaonline.org/handbook/entries/san-juan-bautista.
Weiford, Nancy Wertz. *The Faux Baron: George de Mohrenschildt: An Aristocrat's Journey from the Russian Revolution to the Assassination of John F. Kennedy*. np: CreateSpace Independent Publishing Platform, 2014.
Weiner, Hollace Ava. *Jewish Stars in Texas: Rabbis and Their Work*. College Station: Texas A&M University Press, 1999.
———. "Neiman-Marcus: Al Neiman, a Princely Pauper." In *Lone Stars of David: The Jews of Texas*, edited by Hollace Ava Weiner and Kenneth D. Roseman, 162–71. Waltham, MA: University Press of New England, 2007.
Weiner, Hollace Ava, and Kenneth D. Roseman, eds. *Lone Stars of David: The Jews of Texas*. Waltham, MA: University Press of New England, 2007.
Weisberg, Dvora. "Desirable But Dangerous: Rabbis' Daughters in the Babylonian Talmud." *Hebrew Union College Annual* 75 (2004): 121–61.
Weissbach, Lee Shai. *Jewish Life in Small-Town America: A History*. New Haven: Yale University Press, 2005.
Wendt, Lloyd, and Herman Kogan. *Lords of the Levee: The Story of Bathhouse John and Hinky Dink*. Evanston, IL: Northwestern University Press, 2005.
Wenger, Gina Mumma. "History Matters: Children's Art Education Inside the Japanese American Internment Camp." *Studies in Art Education* 54, no. 1 (2012): 21–36.
Wiesel, Elie. *A Life of Rashi*. New York: Schocken, 2009.
Williams, Heather Andrea. *Help Me to Find My People: The African American Search for Family Lost in Slavery*. Chapel Hill: University of North Carolina Press, 2012.
Windmueller, Steven. "Through the Lens of Latino-Jewish Relations." In *California Jews*, edited by Ava Fran Kahn and Marc Dollinger, 57–64. Waltham, MA: Brandeis University Press, 2003.
Wright, George. "Book Review: *Feeds and Feeding* by Frank B. Morrison." *The Ruminant* (blog), January 4, 2012. Accessed June 21, 2023. http://www.theruminant.ca/blog/2012/01/04/book-review-feeds-and-feeding-by-frank-b-morrison.
Young, Elliott. *Alien Nation: Chinese Migration in the Americas from the Coolie Era through World War II*. Chapel Hill: University of North Carolina Press, 2014.
———. "Wong Foon Chuck: Making Home in the Borderlands Between China, the United States and Mexico." In *Forced Out and Fenced In: Immigration Tales from the Field*, edited by Tanya Maria Golash-Boza, 7–20.

New York: Oxford University Press, 2018.

Zborowski, Mark, and Elizabeth Herzog. *Life Is with People: The Culture of the Shtetl*. New York: Schocken Books, 1995.

Zeitz, Joshua. *Building the Great Society: Inside Lyndon Johnson's White House*. New York: Penguin, 2019.

ZIM Integrated Shipping Services. "Once upon a Time—The Story of ZIM." Accessed October 27, 2022. https://www.zim.com/about-zim/history.

"Zionist Organization of America." *Jewish Virtual Library*. Accessed October 27, 2022. https://www.jewishvirtuallibrary.org/zionist-organization-of-america.

Zola, Gary Phillip, ed. *We Called Him Rabbi Abraham: Lincoln and American Jewry, a Documentary History*. Carbondale: Southern Illinois University Press, 2014.

Zolty, Shoshana Pantel. *And All Your Children Shall Be Learned: Women and the Study of Torah in Jewish Law and History*. Northvale, NJ: Jason Aronson, Inc., 1993.

INDEX

Abbreviations: **EP**: Eagle Pass; **J**: Jewish; **MR**: Michael Riskind; **MSR**: Morris S. Riskind; **PN**: Piedras Negras; **R's**: Riskind's (store); **RSR**: Ruth S. Riskind; **RER**: Rachel Edelstein Riskind

Note: Page numbers in italics refer to images.

Abbott, Greg, xxxix
Abramovich, Sholem Yankev (Mendele Mocher Sforim), 237, 323n17
Abrams family, 151
Ackerman, Bill, 92
Acropolis (Athens), 195
Adan Olam (liturgical song), 86
Addams, Jane, 266n41
Adolphus Hotel (Dallas), 178
African Americans, in EP, 59
Agapito (MSR's vaquero), 115, 137, *137*–38, 141
Agnew, Spiro, 166
agricultural workers: during WWII, 126–27; from Mexico, xxxix, 126; recruitment of, 118–19, 126. *See also* Bracero Program; migrant workers
agriculture: county extension service, 117–18, 293n4; during WWII, 117–30; equipment, 129, 138–39; harvest, 121, 126–27, 127–28, 129; irrigation, 117, 118; MSR in, 117–30; pricing, 122–23; thrip, 121, 123; workers (*see* agricultural workers)
  crops: castor beans, 128–29; cotton, 62, 117, 124; hegari, 129, 138–39, 189; oats, 142; onions, 120–23; peanuts, 129; spinach, 125–27; tomatoes, 127–28. *See also* agricultural workers; ranching
Agua Prieta, Sonora, Mexico, 41
Alamo, 62, 67, 278n21, 300n16
Alaska, xviii
Aldridge, Francis, 63, 73, 173, 175
Aleichem, Sholem (Solomon Rabinovich), 237, 256n28, 323n17
Alexander, Adelle Edelstein, 77, 229
Alexander, Ike, 293n29
Alexander, Joseph, 282n20

Alexander, Louis, 293n29
Alexander the Great, 236
Alexander the Great, Life of, 61
Alfonso the Wise, 87
Alger, Horatio, 61
Alice in Wonderland (Carroll), 61
Allende, Coahuila, Mexico (San Miguel de Allende), xvi, 43, 63
Alpine, Texas, 22
Altman, Jack, 179
Alvarez, Joe, 149; as produce broker, 122–23, 124, 127, 128
American Legion, 175
American Smelting and Refining, 31
American Society for Aesthetics, 145
American Student Union, 289n45
Anabasis (Xenophon), 83
Anglos: political dominance of, 207–8, 218, 247
animals: alligator, 67; burro, 51; Colonel Cootie (cat), 51; ducks, 58, 141–42; horses, 37, 114, 115, 137–38, 139–40, 297n14; Morris Edelstein's cat, 27; mules, 120; pigeons, 13; roosters, 51; Tippie (dog), 136–37; tortoise, 51. *See also* wildlife
antisemitism, 203, 243; in army, 114; in California, 250n24; in EP, xxxii, 25, 220, 247–48; in legal profession, 96; in Lithuania, 103; in Mexico, 247; social, 215, 243–44. *See also* pogroms
Apology (Plato), 90
Arabian Nights, The, 236
Arab-Israeli War (1948), 313n22
Aristotle, 91
Armstrong, Duff, 306n3
Army Corps of Engineers, 185
art: in EP, 111, 147, 148; in internment camps, 298n6; RSR as artist, 145, 147, 148

art education: in internment camps, 298n6
arts. *See* art; music
assimilation. *See* Jews: assimilation
Athens, Greece, 195–96
Augur, General (Fort Ringgold commander), 114
Aunt Rose. *See* Riskind, Rose
Austin, Texas, xxxiii, 212–13
automobiles: Buick, 179; Chrysler, 171; Dodge, 74, 119; Essex Phaeton, 65; Ford, 119; Ford Model T, 54, 79–80; Hudson, 65, 68; International Harvester, 134; Kaiser-Frazier, 179; Pontiac, 119; Studebaker, 63
Ávalos family, 147
Ávila Camacho, Manuel, 302n30, 310n1
Aztec Eagles, 310n1
Aztec Theater, 28, 265n37; customers, 30, 52; location, xxxi, xxxiv, 30, 39
Azulejo Ranch, 133–35

Baal Shem Tov (the Hasid), 53, 253n2. *See also* Jews: Hasidim
Baer, Dov, 322n1
Baker Hotel (Dallas), 178
bar/bat mitzvah: in EP, 86, 150–51; MSR's, 84, 86–87
Bara, Theda, 30
Barnes, Ben, 321n20
Barrera, Héctor, 45, 72–73
Barrientos, René, 36
Bartók, Béla, 204
Baum, L. Frank, 236
Baum, Ozzie, 111
Baum family, xxx
Benavides, Chris, 154
Benkaim, Jack, 103
Benkaim, Mollie (Malke) Edelstein, 77, 103
Bentsen, Lloyd, 156
Bernal, Louis, 148, 191, 224
Beverly Hills Hotel, 89
Bibb, Edna, *208*, 212
Bibb, Robert (Roberto), *208*; community action program, 213–14; criminal court, 211; declining power, 211–12, 212–13, 213–14; EP city limits, 210–11; friendship with MR, xxxiv, 118, 232; friendship with MSR, 210–211; in 1954 flood, 185; Latino voters, 208–9; rise to power, 208–9; sketch of, 207–12; WPA, 208
 and LBJ: 1948 senate race, 209–10; Bracero Program, 210; favors from, 211
 as Maverick County boss, 118, 183, 185, 209–10, 212; and LBJ, 209–10; city elections, 217; Latino enfranchisement, 208–9; tax assessments, 226; teachers, 223
Bible. *See* Tanakh
Big Bend, flooding in, 182
bilingualism: in public education, 60, 224–25
Bill of Rights, 166–67
Birth of a Nation (Griffith), 54
Bishop College (Dallas), 319n30
Black Seminoles, xlv, 24, 159; cavalry scouts, 24, 159–60; legal situation, 159–61; reservation, 154; racial identity, 160. *See also* Seminoles
Blacks, in EP, 59
Bliss, Zenas, 24, 159
Block, Joseph, 16
Block, Sarah. *See* Riskind, Sarah Block
Bonaparte, Napoleon, 7, 11
Bond, Bill, 141–42
Bonnet, Dudie, 39
Bonnet, Edith, 41
Bonnet, John, 41
Bonnet, Rafael, 54
Bonnet family, 27
Book of Knowledge, The, 61, 236
border, US-Mexico: diversity and tolerance of, xiii, xxxii, 247; during Civil War, 23; International Boundary Commission, 182, 309n10; International Bridge, *32*; Jewish refugees, xxxviii, 71–72; Kickapoo, 154; location, 63, 182, 278n25, 309n10; Operation Intercept, 307n18; red-light districts, 136, 152, 296n8; violent history of, 23–25
 commerce: cross-border shopping, 31, 40; Jewish merchants, xxxv–xxxvi; peso devaluation, xviii, xxiii, 191, 310n24
 enforcement: Greg Abbott/Operation Lone Star, xxxix; in EP, 163–64; intensification, xxxix; Operation Intercept, xxxix, 307n18. *See also* Border Patrol
 immigration: illegal, 194; Jewish, xxxviii, 71–72
 legal issues: bigamy, 165; drug enforcement, 169–70, 307n18; Mexican police, 171
border blasters. *See* radio

Border Patrol, xiv, xxxix, 126. *See also* border enforcement
boss system, 212–13, 315n11
Botega de Leon, El (Brownsville), xxxviii
Bouvier, Jack, 318n28
Boyle Heights (Los Angeles): as Jewish neighborhood, xxvi, 76, 291n14
    Jewish institutions: Breed Street Shul, 84; Canter's Deli, 291n14; Jewish Home for the Aged, 86; Menorah Center, 284n12; Modern Talmud Torah, 284n11, 284n12
Bracero Program: dog food scandal, 210; in EP, xxxix, 210; and labor unions, 210. *See also* agricultural workers
Brackenridge Park (San Antonio), 67
Brackettville, Texas: Black Seminoles, 24, 159–60
Breed Street Shul (Los Angeles), 84
Brenner family, 47
Brentwood (Los Angeles), 229
Bres, Alexia, 151
Bres, Alfonso, 166
Bres, Carlos, 151
Bres, Claudio, 152, 302n30
Bres, Stephanie, 151
Brinkley, John R., 152
Briscoe, Dolph, 227
Briscoe Ranches, Inc. v. Eagle Pass Independent School District, 321n20
Brownsville, Texas, 23, 27; J businesses in, xxxiii, xxxviii, 28; Jews in, 250n22
Buckhorn Saloon (San Antonio), 67
Bullis, John, 24
Bundy, John H., 112–13, 114–15
Burby, William, 95
Butler, Cliff, 220

Caballo, Juan (John Horse, Gopher John), 159, 304n41
Cabeza de Vaca, Álvar Núñez, 22
Cain (J EP resident), xxx, 264n25
Caine Mutiny, The, 178
California: antisemitism in, xxxii, 250n24; Riskinds move to, 79–80
California Camp (EP), 22
California Fruit Company, xxxviii, 48, 123
California Gold Rush, 22–23, 74
Calles, Plutarco, 46
Camino Real, 22
Canada, 15
Canter's Deli (Los Angeles), 291n14

Cantinflas (Mario Moreno), 194, 311n4
Cantú, Dr. (R's customer), 66
Capitanachi, Aurora, *36*
Capp, Al, 153
Cárdenas, Lázaro, 46
CARES Act (2020), xxiii
Carranza, Venustiano: limited to single term, 273n34; Mexican Revolution, 268n5, 270n14; recognized by US, 43, 270n13
Carraway, J. C., 127, 295n20
Carrillo, Leo, 140
Carrizo Springs, Texas, 24, 65
Carter, Jimmy, 306n10
Castle Garden (New York), 12
Catholic Church, 40, 165, 271n18
cattle. *See* ranching
Cave of Machpelah (Israel), 199, 313n21
Cazneau, Jane, 159, 304n41
Census, US, for Maverick County, 210–11
Central High School (Little Rock), 218
Central Power and Light, 39
Cerna, Carolina, 148, 191, 204
Cerna's Money Exchange, 26
Cervantes, Miguel de, xiii
Chabad, 322n1
chalanes (rowboats on Rio Grande), 72, 185
Chicago, Illinois: Edelsteins in, xxv, 15, 18; garment strike (1896), 14–15; garment trade, xxv, 14–15; in commercial network, xxiv, xxxvi; kosher food, 17–18; MR buying in, xxvi, xxxi, 27–28; politics, 14
    Riskinds in, xxiii, 77; arrival, 12–13, 14–15; businesses, 14–15, 17; departure, 25, 66–67; marriage, 16–17
Chichester, John W., 52
Chichester, William (Willie), 51–52
Child Nutrition Act (1966), 321n17
Chinese Exclusion Act (1882), 268n9
Chmielnicki, Bogdan, 326n13
Chorgas, Mike, 187, 232
Chovevei Zion (Lovers of Zion), 18
Christiani, Pablo, 185n20
Chuck, Ben, 41
Chuck, James (Jimmy), 62–63
Chuck, Wong Foon, 268n9, 269n12
Chuck family, xxxvii, 41, 62–63
Chuetas (Majorcan Jews), 198
Cicero, 86
Cirilo, Jesusita, 36
Ciudad Juárez, Chihuahua, Mexico: captured by Villa, 43, 268n5; Jews in, xxxviii
Ciudad Porfirio Díaz. *See* Piedras Negras

Civil War, US, on border, 23
Cloward, Richard, 318n26
Coacoochee. See Wild Cat
Cockerill, Orville P., 95
Cohen, Henry, xxx
Cold War GI Bill, 322n22
Colonel Cootie (cat), 51
colonias (unincorporated rural communities), 211
Columbus, New Mexico, 43
Comanches, 23; vs. Kickapoo, 24; vs. Seminole, 159
commerce. *See* retail
Communications Act (1934), 302n29
community action programs, 213–14
Connally, John, 213
Conservative Judaism. *See* Jews: identity, denominations
Corpus Christi, Texas, xxxiii, 48
Cortina, Juan, 23
Cossacks, 71
county extension service, 117–18, 293n4
county judges: in Texas, 207–8, 315n9
cowboys. *See* vaqueros
credit. *See* retail
Cromwell, Oliver, 237, 243
Cruz (Moderno Café waiter), 233
Crystal City, Texas, 150, 298n5
currency: Confederate, 52; devaluation, 310n24; during Mexican Revolution, 40

Dallas, Texas, xxxiii, 108, 215; buying trips to, xxxv, 177–80; in commercial network, xxiv
Dallas Apparel Mart, xxxv, 180
Dallas Shoe Show, 177
Daniel, Demetrio, 36, 141; background, 140–41
Daniel, Valentín, *36*, 36
Darwin, Charles, 91
Das Kapital (Marx), 90, 91
Dassin, Jules, 311n7
Daughters of the Republic of Texas, 67
Davis Mountains, 79
De Bona, Rocco, 21
De Bona family, 76
De Bona's, 21, 28, 173; closure, 30–31, 39, 173
de la Garza, Kika, 315n7
de Mohrenschildt, Alexandra, 319n31
de Mohrenschildt, George: sketch of, 214–16
de Mohrenschildt, Jeanne, 214–15
Dead Sea (Israel), 199
Dead Sea Scrolls, 199

Decline and Fall of the Roman Empire (Gibbon), 89, 91
Del Rio, Texas, 38, 62–63, 66, 111; Jews in, xxxviii, 301n25
Del Rio Bridge, 73
Del Rio ISD v. Salvatierra (1930), 277n15
Delgado v. Bastrop ISD (1948), 277n15
Deming, New Mexico, 75
desegregation: Little Rock, 218
devaluation: of peso, xviii, xxiii, 191, 310n24
Devils River, 66, 74–75, 80
Devine, Texas, 65
Dewey, Alicia, xxxvi
Diamond, Ken, 179
Diaz, Albino, *36*, 36, 232
Díaz, Constancia, *36*, 36
Díaz, Porfirio: as Mexican president, 40, 45, 273n34; Mexican Revolution, 265n36, 268n5, 272n28
Díaz, Queta, 213
Díaz (band leader), 233
Dicus, Mr. (priest), 247
Dilley, Texas, 65
Diner, Hasia, xxxiii
Disney, Walt, 311n3
Disputation of Barcelona, 185n20
Dobie, Frank, 138
Douglas, Arizona, 41
Dovalina, Natividad, 138
Dovalina, Salvador, 138
Dove Creek, Battle of, 24
Dozier, Miss (MSR's teacher), 83
Drogheda, Ireland, 243
drug enforcement. *See* border, US-Mexico: legal issues
Dubrovna, Belarus, 327n14; Riskinds in, 3, 6, 13
ducks, Muscovy, 141–42
Duma, 10
Dumas, Alexandre, 283n22
Durango, Mexico, 23

Eagle Coffee Shop, 127
Eagle Drugstore, 191, 219
Eagle Hardware, 120, 191
Eagle Hotel, 131, 132, 169, 184, 186, 220, 222
Eagle Pass, or Life on the Border (Montgomery), 159
Eagle Pass, Texas: antisemitism in, 220, 247–48; Army Day (1949), 153–54; Bracero Program, xxxix, 210; Centennial Celebration (1949), xxvi, 152–59; chamber

of commerce, xxxiv; character of, xiii; community center, 214; downtown business district, xxiii, *xxviii–xxix*, 39–40, *174*; during Civil War, 23; during WWII, 111–15; Edelsteins in, xxv, 19; ethnic diversity of, xlv, xxvi, xxxvii; flood of 1922, 72; flood of 1954 (*see* flood of 1954); history, *xxvii*, xxvii–xxviii, *xlv*, 21–25; interfaith relations, 247; Jews in (*see* Jews: in Eagle Pass); legal system, 163–65, 166; library board, 228; Mexican refugees in, 28, 42–43, 45; Paso del Águila, xxvii; poor in, 34; racism in, xxvi; remoteness, 21–22; Riskind Building, xxiii–xxxiv; Riskind family in, xx, xxvi, 19; tourism, 152; working conditions, 35

    art and music: art education, 148; Civic Music, 204; Jaffe, Sue, 111; Latino students, 148; Ostrom, Coco, 148; reception of, 111, 147

    businesses. *See* individual names: Aztec Theater; California Fruit Company; Central Power and Light; Cerna's Money Exchange; De Bona's; Eagle Coffee Shop; Eagle Drugstore; Eagle Hardware; Eagle Hotel; Eagle Pass Lumber Company; Edelstein's Better Furniture; El Palacio de Hierro (the Iron Palace); First National Bank; Fort Duncan Club; Holly Inn; Imperial Novelty Company; International Grocery; Kress; La Barata; Lane's; Lorin's; Los Chilenos; M. Riskind (*see* Riskind's); Marquez Wholesale Grocery; Merchant's Cafe; Mesquite Club, 39–40; Mike's Cafe; Murray Hardware; National Grocery; New Furniture Company; Pan American Fabric; Pilgrim Jewelry; Riskind Furniture Company; Riskind's; Sabinas Inn; San Miguel Saloon; Schuessler's Men's Store; Seco Mines; Star Theater; Style Shop; Taylor's Saloon; Three Sisters; Velásquez Body Shop; Western Auto Parts; Yolanda Hotel; Yolanda Theater

    International Bridge, 25, *32*, 136, 170–71, 265n37; cattle drives across, 42; immigration across, 163–64; 1922 flood, 72; 1954 flood, 183, 185; Kickapoo camp under, 72, 153, 160–61, 303n36; ownership of, 72–73; refugees across, 41, 43, 45, 71; workers across, xiv, 126

    politics: Anglo dominance, 207–8; boss rule, 207–8; city council, 217; community action program, 213–14; congressional representative, 110, 206; Latino voters, 208–9; influence of ranchers, 226–27; MSR's career in, 217–28. *See also* Bibb, Robert

public housing board: activities of, 204–7; MSR's service on, 204–7, 228. *See also* public housing

public schools: administration and staff, 220, 223; athletics, 62–63; districting, 218–19; Elementary and Secondary Education Act (1965), 320n12; enrollment, 217–18, 222, 225; ethnic composition of, 60; facilities, 218, 222–23, 225–26; financing: bond elections, 222–23, 225–26; financing: enrollment, 217–18; financing: lawsuit, 226–27; financing: tax assessments, 226–27; immigrants, 218; Latino students, 60; MSR as student, 60–63, 83; school board (*see* school board); Spanish prohibited, 60; superintendents (*see* school superintendents); teachers, disrespect toward, 223; teachers, grievances, 223; teachers, recruitment of, 218; test scores, 220

school board: elections, 225–26; Hume as attorney, 166; MSR's service on, xxxiv, 60, 166, 218–28; responsibilities, 221; vocational training program, 227

school superintendents: Bernal, Louis, 148; Flory, Kenneth, 322n21; Garland, James, 148, 218–19; James, Curly, 219, 220, 221–22, 224; Moore, Kenneth, 222, 224, 225, 227

Eagle Pass Army Air Field, 111, 112–13

Eagle Pass Creek, 27

Eagle Pass High School, xvi, 62, 321n18

Eagle Pass Independent School District. *See* Eagle Pass, Texas: public schools

Eagle Pass Lumber Company, 166, 173

Eagle Pass News Guide, 111; and school politics, 223, 225, 227–28

Easton, Evan S., 50, 59, 236

Eaton, Cyrus, 166
Eby, Ida Bel, 90, 91, 83–84
Economic Opportunity Act (1964), 317n25
Edelstein, Abe, xxv, 10, 15, 18–19, 28, 59; EP, xxv, 18, 19, 25, 26, 27, 47
Edelstein, Bertha (Beilke), 16, 77
Edelstein, Chatzkel, *8*, 9–10, 11–12, 16, 18, 103; death, 108; letters, 104–8
Edelstein, David, 66, *78*, 80, 82, 103
Edelstein, Deborah, 11
Edelstein, Eli, 12, *78*, 79–80, 81, 137, 138; sketch of, 77–82
Edelstein, Hirsch, 10
Edelstein, Isaac, 103; death, 108; letters, 104–8
Edelstein, Jacob (Jake), 10, 66, 74–76
Edelstein, Louis, 77
Edelstein, Miriam Fried, 7–8, *9*, 10–11
Edelstein, Morris, xxxvi, 12, 27, 28, 103; in business, 27, 28, 66, 72; EP, 19, 123
Edelstein, Rachel. *See* Riskind, Rachel Edelstein
Edelstein, Ruben, 27, 59, 264n30
Edelstein, Yetta, 27, 103
Edelstein, Yossel, 7
Edelstein family: and Holocaust, 103–8; Lithuania, 3, 6–12, 103–8; Rio Grande Valley, xxxiii; letters, 104–8; origin of name, 6
Edelstein's Better Furniture (Brownsville), 28
Edelstein's Better Furniture (EP), 123
education: MSR's views on, 89–90, 218; school prayer, 62
education, in Eagle Pass. *See* Eagle Pass, Texas: public schools
education, Jewish. *See* Jews: education
education, public. *See* Public education
Eidson, A. D., 188–89
Eidson, Alice, 189, 191, 204
Eidson, E. B., 309n19
Ein Gedi kibbutz (Israel), 199
Eisenhower, Dwight D., 291n19
El Fenix (Los Angeles), 72
El Fenix (Monterrey), 72
El Palacio de Hierro (the Iron Palace), 123
El Paso, Texas, xxxiii, xxxviii, 22, 43, 75, 79
El Retiro, 115, 140–42, 173; cattle, 133, 137–39, 189; description, 118, 136–37; farming, 120–30; preparation for use, 117–20, 138–39, 143; vegetation and wildlife, 136–37
Elementary and Secondary Education Act (1965), 320n12

Ellington, Duke, 204
Ellis Island (New York), 12, 256n33
Emergency Quota Act (1921), 71, 279n30, 280n2
Encyclopaedia Britannica, xv, 167
English as a Second Language, 60, 224–25
Episcopal Church, 36
Epstein (soldier), 47–48
Escuadrón 201 (Aztec Eagles), 310n1
Estrada, Encarnación Garrido, 73, 281n8
Estrada, Francisco, 72–73, 247
Ethics of the Fathers, The (Talmud), 5
Exposition Park (Los Angeles), 94
extension service. *See* county extension service

Fabian socialism, 91
farming. *See* agriculture
Faubus, Orval, 218
FBI, 110, 206–7, 208
Federal Communications Commission (FCC), 302n29
Federation of American Zionists, 312n17
Feeds and Feeding (Morrison), 137, 138, 139
Ferguson, Travis, 141, 142
Fiddler on the Roof, 237
First National Bank (EP), 205, 208
Fisher, King, 24, 52, 117
fishing. *See* hunting and fishing
Fitch, Floyd, 55
Fitch, Hollis, 43–44, 47, 153
Fitch, William A., 72
Fitzpatrick, Cowboy, 132
Flodden, Battle of, 167
flood of 1922, 66, 72
flood of 1954, 182–86, *183*, *184*
Flores, Art, 59, 212–13
Flores Magón, Ricardo, 28, 272n28; Magonista Rebellion (1911), 45, 265n36, 272n28
Flores Tapia, Oscar, 309n16
Florsheim shoes, 31, *32*, 188, 266n44
Flory, Kenneth, 322n21
Flynn, Errol, 30
food: Azulejo ranch, 135; Moderno Café, 232–33; deli, 180, 232; duck, 58; kosher, 17–18, 49, 236; MR and, 180, 197, 232–33; pirogen, xiv, 323n15
football: high school, 62–63, 218, 222
Ford Motor Co.: Hunger March (Ford Massacre, 1932), 94, 289n46
Fort Clark (Brackettville), 114; and Black Seminoles, 24, 159
Fort Dearborn (Chicago), 154

Fort Duncan (EP), 39, 42, 43, 47, 59; Black Seminoles, 24, 159; closure, 40, 55; founding, xxvii, 23, 154
Fort Duncan Club, 40, 148, 209
Fort Duncan Museum, 31, 277n20
Fort Ringgold (Rio Grande City), 114
Fort Sam Houston (San Antonio), 110
Fox, Morris, 27
Fox family, 27
Frank Brothers (San Antonio), xxx
Frank, Bess Riskind, 25, *85*, 89, 229; childhood, 26, 29, 40, 52, 59, 68
Freed family, 150
Freud, Sigmund, 7
Frías Yague, Ignacio, 281n8
Fried, Adela, 11
Fried, Moshe, 11
Fried, Reuben, 7–8, 16
Fuentes, Marcos, 224
Fugitive Slave Act (1850), 159, 305n42

Galindo (R's salesman), 230
Galveston Movement, 249n12
Garcia, Atanacio, 118, 120, 139, 141, 147, 189
García, Chema, 229–30, 239
García, F. N., 281n8
Garland, James (Jimmy), 148, 218–19
garment trade, 77–78; in Chicago, xxv, 14–15; Jews in, 14–15, 249n7; MR in, xiii, 13, 77–78
Garza, Ernesto, 35, 36, *176*, 178; as salesman, 176–79; buying trips, 177–79
Gates, Ellis, *53*, 218
Gates, W. C., 55
Gayle, Carolyn, 241
Genesis, Book of, 87
George, Henry, 91
German, 82
GI Bill, 322n22
Gibbon, Edward, 91
Gideon v. Wainwright (1963), 163, 164
Gila River Relocation Center, 145–47
Gilbert and Sullivan, 98, 204
Gilmer-Aikin Laws (1949), 319n2
Gluckstern's Restaurant (New York), 233–34
Gold Diggers, The (Aleichem), 256n28
Gold, Abe, 96–97
Goldberg, Morris, 114, 293n31
Goldburg family, 47, 48
Golem, 234, 323n10
González, Eugenio, 179
Gopher John. *See* Caballo, Juan

Grand Canyon, 80
Grant, Ulysses S., 263n22, 279n36
Graves, Dena, 60
Great Depression: law practice during, 96, 97
Greece, 195–96
Greek, 83
Green Davidson Ranch, 66
Greenberg, Gertrude, 48, 149
Greenberg, Ted, 48, 149; as MSR's farm partner, 121, 122–23
Greenberg family, 151
Griffith, D. W., 54
Grimms' Fairy Tales, 236
Grossman family, 47
Guanajuato, Mexico, xvi
Guerrero, Coahuila, Mexico, 54, 134, 136, 232
Guerrero, Texas, 22, 38, 65
Guide for the Perplexed, The (Maimonides), 91, 255n21, 288n41
Gulliver's Travels (Swift), 236
guns, 42; MSR's use of, 93, 115, 137, 138
Gunter Hotel (San Antonio), 67
Gurwitz, Alexander, 254n9
Gutiérrez family, 27

Haberman, Ruth Riskind, *85*; childhood, 29, 40, 52, 59, 68
Haggadah, 236
Haifa, Israel, 197
Hanukkah, 3
Har El Synagogue (Jerusalem), 86
Harper, Albert Buckner, 135, 296n6
Harper, Concha, 215
Harper, Hite, 120
Harper, Hite Lawrence (Tito), 134, 214–15, 222
Harper, Larry, 120
Harper, Osie, 125, 214; as agent, 41, 120, 134; dealings with MR, 41, 134; dealings with MSR, 133–35, 142, 222; sketch of, 133–34
Harper, Osie, Jr. (Junior), 55, 134
Harper, Richmond, 125, 134, 135, 222
Harris, "Red," 47
Harris, Sophye, 76
Harrison, Benjamin, 12
Hart Schaffner & Marx, 31, 33, 188
Hartup, Charles Wesley, 276n2
Harvard Hillel, 86
Hasid, The (Baal Shem Tov), 53, 253n2
Hasidim. *See* Jews: Hasidim
Hausman, Harold, 186
Hausman, Louis, 47, 149

INDEX   349

Hausman, Sam, 47
Hebrew, 60, 246; MSR's study of, 49, 84–87; RER's study of, 12, 49; Tanakh, 87
Hebron, Israel, 199
Herod, King, 313n27
Herodotus, 91
Herzberg, Mauricio, 49
Herzl, Theodor, 259n57
HIAS, 12, 14
Hickey Freeman, xiv, 187
Hidalgo de Costilla, Miguel (Padre Hidalgo), 45
Hielscher, Charles, 54
High Holidays. *See* Jews: holidays
Hillel the Elder, 88, 237, 245
"Hinky Dink" (Kenna, Michael), 14, 257n41
Hisham bin Abd el-Malik, 313n24
Hisham's Palace (Israel), 199, 313n24
History of the Peloponnesian War (Thucydides), 91
History of the Russian Revolution (Trotsky), 89
holidays, Jewish. *See* Jews: holidays
Hollenbeck Park (Los Angeles), 286n26
Hollis, William, 208
Holly Inn, 186
Hollywood Bowl (Los Angeles), 145, 237
Holocaust, 108–9; Edelsteins, 103–8; EP survivors, 211, 317n19; Lithuania, 103–8, 290n3; Poland, 104, 108–9; vs. internment camps, 145, 298n5
Homer, xiii, 90
Hondo, Texas, 68
Hoose Library of Philosophy, 289n47
Hoover, J. Edgar, 110, 208
Horse, John. *See* Caballo, Juan
horses, 137–38, 139–40
Hotel Regis (Mexico City), 193
housing. *See* housing, public
Housing Act (1949), 314n6
housing, public, 204–6. *See also* Eagle Pass, Texas: public housing board
Houston, Texas, xxxiii, 22
Huerta, Victoriano, 28, 265n36, 268n5, 270n13, 270n14
Hull-House (Chicago), 30, 266n41
Hume, David (philosopher), 167
Hume, David, Jr: school board attorney, 166, 227; sketch of, 166–68; trial skills, 166–68
Hume, David, Sr: sketch of, 165–66; trial skills, 169
Hume, Lea, 65, 278n26
Hume, Margaret, 167

Hungerland, Isabella Creed, 145
Hunt, Joe, 92
hunting and fishing, 54–55, 58, 137, 141–42
Huntsville, Texas: penitentiary in, 164, 165
Hussein, King of Jordan, 197–98
Hutton & Company, 89
Hyde Park (London), 89
Hynes, William F. ("Red"), 89

Iliad (Homer), 83
immigration, xxxviii; Emergency Quota Act (1921), 71, 279n30, 280n2; Immigration Act (1924), 279n30; US-Mexico border, 71, 194, 211
Immigration Act (1924), 279n30
Imperial Novelty Company, 48
Imperial Valley, California, 75
Indian Removal Act (1830), 263n21
Indian Territory, 47, 159, 262n18, 263n21, 304n41
Indio Ranch, 117, 133
influenza epidemic (1918), 43
Innsbruck, Austria, 6
Intelligent Woman's Guide to Socialism, An (Shaw), 91
Intercontinental Hotel (Jerusalem), 199
intermarriage. *See* Jews, intermarriage
Internal Revenue Service (IRS), 173–74
International Boundary and Water Commission, 182, 309n10
International Bridge. *See* Eagle Pass, Texas: International Bridge
International Grocery, 39, 49, 54
International Harvester, 175
internment camps, 145, 298n6; RSR at, xv, 145–47
Intolerance (Griffith), 54
Ireland, 15
Irondale (Chicago), 18
Isaiah (prophet), 86, 87, 91
Israel, xxiv, xxvi, 114, 197–201, 233; Six-Day War, 197–98, 200–201

Jacobson, David, 150
Jaffe, Sue, 111
Jake the American (Yankel der Amerikaner), 15
James I of Aragon, 87, 185n20
James, Bernie, 320n10
James, Curly: as EP superintendent, 219, 220, 221–22, 224
Jáuregui-Yañez, José, 189, 231, 247
Jazz Singer, The (film), 284n10

Jefferson, Thomas, 167, 203
Jericho, 199–201
Jerusalem, Israel, 86, 197–99, 246; Arab conflict, 199, 201; Six-Day War, 197–98
Jesús (Riskinds' driver), 66, 68–69, 74–76
Jewish Agency, 199, 311n12
"Jewish Community Center" (EP), xiv, 49, 150, *150*
Jewish Home for the Aged (Los Angeles), 76, 86
Jewish Publication Society, 87
Jewish Welfare Board, 49, 111, 113
Jews: and Latinos, xxxvii–xxxviii; antisemitism (*see* antisemitism); as merchants, xxxiii, 25; as urbanites, 56, 243, 244, 324n1; humor, 237; immigration, 12, 15–16, 71; in agriculture, 10, 127, 139; in garment trade, 14–15; in small towns, 243–44; in the military (Russia), 13; in the military (US), 111–15; kabbalah, 234; messiah, 87; politics, 203; racism of, 248; San Antonio, xxvii, xxx–xxxi, 279n33
    education, 5, 10, 11–12, 88, 246–47; formal, 10, 84, 86; importance of, 5, 88, 246–47; in EP, xxxi, 49, 151; MSR's, 84–88; 11–12
    Hasidim: 85, 245, 246, 253n2; and Riskind family, xxv, 3, 5, 231, 234; Baal Shem Tov, 53, 253n2
    holidays: High Holidays, 49, 113, 150, 151, 243; Passover (Pesach), 106, 107, 108, 151, 243; Rosh Hashanah, 86; Shavuos, 107; Simchat Torah, 85; Yom Kippur, 5, 104
    identity: adaptability, 245; assimilation, 243–44, 244–45; conversion, 246; denominations, 244–45, 324n5; identifiable traits, 112, 200; "in between," xiii, xxxvi; intermarriage, 244, 245, 246, 325n9; kashrut, 17–18, 49, 236; observance, 235, 236–37, 244–45; race of, 246, 326n10
    in Eagle Pass: adaptability of, xxxix–xl; antisemitism, 220, 247–48; billboard, xxiv, 247; changes, 244; community, 47–49, 149–51; disappearance, xxxix–xl, 51, 151, 243; early, xxvi, 25; Hebrew school, xxxi, 49, 151; identity of, xiii, xiv, xxvi–xxvii, xxxvii, 244; "in between," xiii, xxxvi; "Jewish Community Center," xiv, xxiv, 49, 150, *150*; merchants, *xxviii–xxix*, 25, 47–49; poker game, 149; public acceptance, 247–48; refugees, xxxviii, 71–72; religious observance, 49, 149–51, 150, *150*; servicemen, 111–15. *See also* individual names: Abrams; Baum; Brenner; Bres; Cain; Edelstein; Freed; Goldburg; Greenberg; Grossman; Harris; Hausman; Herzberg; Kaback; Kranzthor; Lapin; Levine; Libson; Mello; Mendelson; Mikulinsky; Morgenstern; Munter; Neuman; Oppenheimer; Phillips; Pimentelli; Riskind; Schwartz; Spiegal; Spiegel; Spiller; Steinbock; Sulzbacher; Toziewitz; White; Wolff
Job Corps, 317n25
Johnnie (horse), 137–38
Johnson, Charlie, 36, 44
Johnson, Lyndon B., 209–10; and Bibb, 209–10, 211; community action programs, 213, 317n25; education policy, 320n12, 321n17, 322n22
Johnson (EP journalist), 247–48
Johnson-Reed Act (1924), 279n30
Jolson, Al, 284n10
Jones, Ralph, 179
Jordan: occupation of East Jerusalem, 199
José Greco Dance Group, 204
Joske's (San Antonio), 67
Juárez, Benito, 295n1
Judaism. *See* Jews
Judge Advocate General (JAG), 109
Justin Boot Company, 112

Kaback, David, 151
Kaback, Edna, 150
Kaback, Harry, 150
Kahlo, Frida, 311n3
Kaiser Wilhelm der Grosse (ship), 16
Kalvaria, Lithuania (Kalvarija), *7*, 68, 89; Edelsteins in, 6, 10, 16, 103–8
Kane, William, 168
Karp, Mr. (R's employee), 36
Kelso, Martin, 119
Kenna, Michael ("Hinky Dink"), 14, 257n41
Kennedy, Bessie Davies, 293n3
Kennedy, Jacqueline, 214
Kennedy assassination, 214, 216
Khartoum Conference (1967), 200–201
Kickapoo: and border, 154; as migrant

workers, 156, 303n36; as R's customers, 35, 153; bigotry toward, 153, 156; camp in EP, 72, 153, *160*, 160–61, 303n36; reservation in Mexico, 23–24, 35, 154, 262n17; reservation in Texas, 160–61, 305n45
    Eagle Pass Centennial Celebration (1949), xxvi, 152–59; cultural program, 156–59; "Minnehoa," 155–59
    history and culture: dress and behavior, 153; history in Texas, 23–24, 159; moccasins, 153, 303n34; payments from US, 35, 153; vs. Seminoles, 159
Kickapoo Removal of Restrictions Act (1906), 303n33
Kickapoo Traditional Tribe of Texas (KTTT), 305n45
Kidnapped (Stevenson), 283n22
King, Billie Jean, 288n43
King Cotton (book), 62
King David Hotel (Jerusalem), 197
King James Bible, 87
King Lear (Shakespeare), 231
King Ranch, 81
Kishinev Massacre (1903), 258n46
Klein, Edgar, 111
Klemperer, Lottie, 145
Klemperer, Otto, 145
Klemperer, Werner, 298n4
Knights of Columbus Hall, 49, 113
Königsberg (Kaliningrad, Russia), 10, 13
Kraft, Mr. (agricultural inspector), 140
Kramer, Arthur, 308n6
Kranzthor, Ellen, 47
Kranzthor, Jacob, xxxi
Kranzthor, Mary, xxxi
Kranzthor family, 39, 47
Krasnow, Peter, xvi
Kress, 48, 56, 156, 195
Ku Klux Klan, 148

"La Adelita" (song), 41–42
La Barata, 48, 189
La Consolidada (PN), 136, 193
La Estrella (Del Rio), xxxviii
La Pryor, Texas, 63, 120
La Villita, Coahuila, Mexico, 66
Lane, Dick, 169
Lane's, 211
Lapin, Falla, xxxi, 48, 149
Lapin, Max, xxxviii, 48
Lapin family, 149
Lara, Agustín, 233
Laredo, Texas, 23, 134
Laredo National Bank, 205
Las Rusias (ranch), 134
Last Chance Saloon (San Antonio), 65
Latin, 83
Latinos: and Jews, xxxvii–xxxviii, 251n43; as artists, 148; education, 60, 277n15; in Texas history, 62, 300n16; political influence, 208–9, 212, 219, 247, 315n1; prejudice against, xiv, 60, 68–69; San Antonio, 67; violence against, xxxvii, 42
law. *See* legal system
Lee, Robert E.: in Texas, 22, 23, 65, 154
Leeser, Isaac, xxix
legal system: California bar, 84, 96; civil liberties, 166–67; drug trade, 167–68; in EP, 163–65, 166; in Mexico, 163, 164, 169–71, 309n18; Indigenous rights, 159–61, 304n37, 305n44, 305n45; MSR's career, 96–98; Texas bar, 163, 166
Leibov, Baruch, 327n14
Lerma, Everardo, 278n24
Lermontov, Mikhail, 11
Les Misérables (Hugo), 237
Levine, Bennie, 48, 150
Levine, Faye, 48, 150, 247
Levine family, 151
Levi's, xiv, 153
Levitansky, Sonya, 76
Lewis, Homer I. (Pete), 55
Libson, Eloisa, 48, 149
Libson, Solomon, xxxviii, 48, 49, 123, 149
Li'l Abner, 153
Lincoln, Abraham, 15, 164, 203
Lincoln, Elmo, 54
Lindenborn, Charles, 111
Lipan Apache, 23, 24, 159
Lithuania: Edelsteins, xxv, 6–12, 103–8; Holocaust, 108; pogroms, 290n3; WWII era, 103–8, 290n3
Lithuanian, 80
Little Rock, Arkansas, 218
Livy, 91, 203
Locke, John, 167
Loew of Prague, Rabbi, 234
Loma Linda (ranch), 136; description, 117, 124, 125; farming on, 125–27
Lone Wolf v. Hitchcock (1903), 305n44
Lonesome Dove (McMurtry), 131
Looking Backward (Bellamy), 91
López Portillo, José, 309n16
Lorin's, xviii

Los Angeles County Museum, 94
Los Angeles Philharmonic, 98–100, 204
Los Angeles, California, xxvi, 72, 74–76, 79–80; Jewish neighborhoods, 76; MSR in, 83–101, 145; Riskinds move to, 79–80
Los Chilenos, 167
lotería cards, 240
Lovers of Zion (Chovevei Zion), 18
Luderus, Peter John, 58

M. Riskind (store). *See* Riskind's
M. Riskind, Inc. *See* Riskind's
Mabe, Jake, 205
machine politics. *See* boss system
Mackenzie, Ranald, 24
Mackenzie's Raid, 159
Mackey, E. O., 190
Macy's, 33–34
Madero, Evaristo, 296n4
Madero, Francisco: Mexican president, 45, 273n34; Mexican Revolution, 265n36, 268n5, 272n28, 273n34
Madero family: as R's customers, 187; wealth of, 134, 296n4
Mafia, 167
Magdeburg, Germany, 243
Magonista Rebellion (1911). *See* Flores Magón, Ricardo
Maimonides, Moses, 9, 91, 255n21, 288n41
Mallorca, Jews in, 198, 312n18
Mandel, Max, 111
Mangum, Hal, 132
Manhattan Hotel (New York), 233
maps, MSR's interest in, *xxviii–xxix*, 62, 74, 93
Marcus, Herbert, 308n6
Marcus, Stanley, 308n6
Maroa, Illinois, 17–18, 30
Marquez, Rudy, 205
Marquez Wholesale Grocery, 49
Marshall Plan, 210
Martine, Joseph L., 321n14
Martínez, Oscar J., xxxvi
Marx Brothers, 232
Marx, Karl, 90, 91
Masada (Israel), 199–200
Mason, John, 137
Mason, "Pockets" (agricultural inspector), 140
Matamoros, Tamaulipas, Mexico, 23
Mathiwos, Pete "The Greek," 217
Maverick, Maury, 156
Maverick County Cemetery, xxi
Maverick County Courthouse, 220

Maverick County irrigation canal, 182
Maverick Irrigation District, 73
Maximilian I, 23
Mazatlán, Sinaloa, Mexico, 23
McAllen, Texas: Edelsteins in, 76, 81; Riskind's in, xviii
McDuff, Dan, 212
McFarland, Van Earl, 55, 73–74
McKellar, Sarah, 22
McMurtry, Larry, 131
Medal of Honor, 24
Medley, Max, 205
Meir, Rabbi, 88, 286n25
Melamed, S. M., 98
Mello, Tony, 125
Mello family, 55
Mendelson, Margaret, 111
Mendelson, Walter, 111
Menger Hotel (San Antonio), 67
Menorah Center (Los Angeles), 284n12
Merchant's Cafe, 44, 187, 230, 232
Mesquite Club, 39–40
Mexican Americans. *See* Latinos
Mexican Revolution (1910), xiii, xlv; and Harpers, 120, 134; effect on EP and region, xxxvi–xxxvii, 28, 40–47; finance and economy, 21, 40, 46–47, 49; MSR memories of, 40–47; refugees, xxxvii, 42–43, 45
Mexicans. *See* Latinos
Mexico, xvi, xxiv, 54–55, 134, 135–36; antisemitism, 247; class system, 45; fashion, 28, 176–77; independence (1810), 22, 40, 45; legal system, 163, 164, 169–71, 309n18; Mexican War (1846), 22, 278n25; police, 171, 187; politicians as R's customers, 170, 187–88; presidential campaigns, 45–47; radio stations, 151–52, 166, 168, 302n30; red-light districts, 63, 136, 152, 296n8; regional conflict, 46; travel in, xvi, xxiv, xxxv, 23, 54–55, 63, 66, 84, 134, 135–36, 145, 154, 170, 175, 193–94, 194–95, 307n20; women in, 28, 176–77. *See also* Latinos
Mexico City, Mexico, xvi, xxxviii, 38, 170, 193, 307n20
Meyer, Sam, *113*; friendship with MSR, xviii, 113–14, 145, 154–55, 205; sketch of, 113–14
Meza, Florencio, 52
Michaels, Sam (Sam Mikulinsky), 48, 125
Midrash, 232, 286n25
migrant workers, 119, 203, 218, 219, 303n36

See also agricultural workers
Mike's Cafe, 26, 155, 156
Mikulinsky, Owsey, 48, 149, *150*; as farmer, 117, 124–27, 128; as R family friend, 189; immigration, 124–25; peddling, 125; PN, 125; sketch of, 124–25
Mikulinsky, Tanya, 48, 149, *150*; business, 189; immigration, 125
Mikulinsky (Michaels), Sam, 48, 125
military service (Russia), 257n37
Mill, John Stuart, 91, 287n38
Miller, Leon, 225–26
Mind and Society (Pareto), 288n42
"Minnehoa" (Kickapoo tribal member), 155–59
Minsky, Bertha (Beilke) Edelstein, 16, 77
Miranda v. Arizona (1966), 163
Mirkin, Abraham, 84–88
Mishnah, 88
Mishneh Torah (Maimonides), 255n21, 288n41
Mission Concrete Pipe Company, 118, 119
Mission, Texas, 66
Modern Talmud Torah (Los Angeles), 284n11, 284n12
Moderno Café (PN), 149, 179, 209; described, 232–33; frequented by MR, xxxiv, 232–33
Mohr, Dave, 97–98, 101
Molière, xiii
Molotov-Ribbentrop Pact (1939), 290n3
Monaco, 7
Moncada, Felipe, 36
Moncada, Manuel, 122
Monclova, Coahuila, Mexico, 23, 170, 207
Monet, Claude, 94
Montague, Brian, 166
Montemayor, Raul, 110
Monterrey, N. L., 72
Montgomery, Cora (Jane Cazneau), 159, 304n41
Montgomery, Monty, 154
Montreal, Quebec, Canada, 16
Moore, Ernest Carroll, 90
Moore, Kenneth, 222, 224, 225, 227
Morgenstern family, 48
Morocco, 196–97
Morrison, Frank Barron, 137, 138, 139
Mount of Olives (Jerusalem), 199
movies, 52–54
Mozart, Wolfgang, 204
Munter, Lloyd, 150, *150*
Munter, Yolanda Schwartz, 150

Murray Hardware, 40
music: Civic Music of EP, 204; Eidson, Dottie, 189, 191; MSR's appreciation, xxi, 85–86, 204
Múzquiz, Coahuila, Mexico, 134, 168

Nablus, Israel, 199
Nachmanides, 87
Nacimiento, Coahuila, Mexico, 154; Kickapoo, 35, 153, 154; Seminole, 24, 159
Napoleonic Code, 7
"Napoleon's Treasure" (story), 11
Nasser, Gamal Abdel: and Six-Day War, 198, 311n14, 314n30
Natchez, Mississippi, 112
Nation, The, 47
National Grocery, 153
National Housing Conference, 205–6, 314n5
National Labor Relations Act (Wagner Act), 97
Needles, Arizona, 80
Neighborhood Youth Corps, 317n25
Neiman, Carrie Marcus, xxxiv
Neiman Marcus, xxxiii
Neman River (Lithuania), 11
Neuman, Nandor, 48, 149
Never on Sunday (film), 195
New Furniture Company, 19
New Orleans, Louisiana, 22
New York, NY, 33–34, 233–34; blackout, 233–34; Edelsteins in, 18; in American J history, xxvi; in commercial network, xxiv, xxxvi; Riskinds in, 12, 147
Nixon, Richard M.: and drug enforcement, 169, 170, 307n18
Nonaggression Pact (1939), 290n3
Nueces River, 63, 69, 79
Nueva Rosita, Coahuila, Mexico, 35
Nuevo Laredo, Tamaulipas, Mexico, 46

O. Henry (William Sydney Porter), 124, 279n36
Oaxaca, Mexico, 84, 145, *195*
Obregón, Álvaro: Mexican Revolution, 41, 46
O'Daniel, Molly, 152
O'Daniel, Wilbert Lee (Pappy): and LBJ, 209–10; as R neighbor, 151–52
Odehnal, Dagmar, 307n16
Odyssey, The (Homer), 90
Ohlin, Lloyd E., 318n26
oil drilling, 73–74
Oklahoma, 24, 155

Old City (Jerusalem), 197–98
Olivares, Enriqueta, 36
Olympia, SS, 197, 198
"On Liberty" (Mill), 287n38
Operation Intercept, xxxix, 307n18
Operation Lone Star, xxxix
Oppenheimer, Max, xxx
Oppenheimer, Rachel Ganz, xxx
Organ Pipe Cactus National Monument, 75
Orsha, Belarus, xxiii, 3, 13
Orthodox Judaism. *See* Jews: identity, denominations
Ostrom, Cora (Coco), 148, 304n40
Oswald, Lee Harvey, 214, 215, 216
Oswald, Marina, 214, 215
Our Lady of Refuge (EP), 43, 271n19
Overland Furniture Company (El Paso), 75, 79
Owl Drug Company, 290n52
Oxford peace movement, 93
Ozona, Texas, 75

Padre Island, Texas, 55, 81
Palacio de Bellas Artes (Mexico City), 310n2
Pale of Settlement (Russia), 6
Palestine (Israel), 18, 103, 108
Pan American Fabric, 48
Pan American Highway, xvi
Pan American Round Table, 148
Panic of 1907, xxv, 18
Pareto, Vilfredo, 92, 288n42
Parr, Archie, 316n13
Parr, George, 210, 316n13
Parra, Santos, 167–68
Parrish, Mr. (Methodist minister), 247
Parthenon (Athens), 196
Paseo de la Reforma (Mexico City), 194
Passover (Pesach). *See* Jews: holidays
Pátzcuaro, Michoacán, Mexico, xvi
Paz, Octavio, 311n3
Pearl, Gabriel, xxxviii
Pearsall, Texas, 129
Pecos River, 182
peddling, 67, 259n59; vicinity of EP, xiii, xxiii, xxxii, 19, 25, 125
Pérez Treviño, Manuel: as R's customer, 41, 168; sketch of, 46
Perez, Federico, *36*; as R's employee, 36, 37–38, 153, 182, 183, 185; during 1954 flood, 182, 183, 184, 185
Perl, Sam, xxxvi, xxxviii, 250n22
Pershing Square (Los Angeles), 89
Pershing, John, 272n23

Pesach (Passover). *See* Jews: holidays
peso: devaluation, xviii, xxiii, 191, 310n24
Petrified Forest, 80
Pharisees, 88
Phillips, Ada, xxx
Phillips, Jacob, xxx
Phillips, Yetta (Toziewitz), xxx
Piedras Negras, Coahuila, Mexico, xxxiv, 25, 44, 175, 194; Americans jailed in, 170–71; as destination, 21, 38, 40, 78, 147, 152; Chuck family, 62–63; during Civil War, 23; during Mexican Revolution, 45–47; during Prohibition, 54, 72; establishment, xxvii; flood of 1954, 184–85; Jews in, xxx, 48, 66; politics, 45–47, 247; R's employees from, xiv, xxxvii, 183, 185
   businesses: California Fruit Company, xxxviii, 48, 123; La Consolidada, 136, 193; Moderno Café, xxxiv, 149, 179, 209, 232–33; San Carlos Hotel, 175; XEPN (radio station), 152
Pilgrim, Charles (Charlie), 54–56, *56*
Pilgrim, Charles F., 54–55, 72
Pilgrim, Fred, 54–56, 175
Pilgrim, Minnie Hielscher, 54
Pilgrim, Ruby, 56
Pilgrim family, 54–56
Pilgrim Jewelry, 54
Pimentelli, David, 49
Pinsk, Poland, 104
Pinsker, Leon, 259n57
Piraeus, Greece, 196, 197
Pirkei Avot (Ethics of the Fathers), 5, 84, 88
pirogen, xiv–xv, 323n15
Plaka (Athens), 195
Plan de San Diego (1915), xxxvii, 42
Plato, 90–91
pogroms: as motive to emigrate, 15–16, 258n46; legacy of, 243; Lithuania, 290n3; Poland, 86; Ukraine, 71, 246, 326n13. *See also* antisemitism
poker, 149, 180, 250n22
Poland, 290n3; Holocaust in, 104, 105, 108–9; refugees from, 104
politics: in EP (*see* Eagle Pass, Texas: politics); MSR views on, 203, 228; Texas Democratic Convention, 212–13
politics, machine. *See* boss rule
Polybius, 91
Popular Dry Goods Store (El Paso), xxxviii, 271n22; and Villa, 43, 268n5
Porter, Cole, 204

Porter, William Sydney (O. Henry), 124, 279n36
Prendes restaurant (Mexico City), 194
President Hotel (Jerusalem), 198
Presidio del Rio Grande, 22
Progress and Poverty (George), 91
prohibition, 49, 54; drinking in PN, 54, 72, 232; violations of, 66, 117
Proskurov, Ukraine, 280n1
public education: and Jews, 247; MSR's views on, 220–21; rights of students, 221. *See also* Eagle Pass, Texas: public schools
    financing: as "socialism," 223; enrollment, 217–18; test scores, 218; voucher system, 221
        programs: English as a second language, 60, 224–25; federal funding, 220–21, 224; free breakfast, 224; special education, 224
public schools. *See* public education; Eagle Pass, Texas: public schools
Pushkin, Alexander, 11

Quemado, Texas, 130, 237
Qumran, Israel, 199

Rabinovich, Solomon (Sholem Aleichem), 237, 256n28, 323n17
race: of Jews, 246, 326n10; segregation, 69, 218
racism, 248; vs. Asians, 62–63; vs. Indigenous, xxvi, 153, 154, 156; vs. Latinos, xiv, 68–69, 278n24
radio: border stations, 151–52, 166, 302n29, 302n30; in Mexico, 168
railroad, 178, 194; Southern Pacific, 22, 25, 41, 42, 166, 182
Ramberg, Ida, 79, 80
Ramberg, Isaac, 72, 229
ranchers. *See* ranching
ranching: Azulejo, 133–35; cattle buyers, 139; changes in, 131–32; land use, 131; MSR in, 133–36, 137–39; ranchers, 131–32, 226–27; tax assessment, 226–27. *See also* agriculture
    cattle: breeds, 131, 135; drives, 42, 131; feeding, 138–39, 142–43; pricing, 139, 142; purchasing, 135
Ravel, Sam, 272n23
Red Cross, xxxiv, 185, 189, 203–4
red-light districts. *See* Mexico: red-light districts
Reform Judaism. *See* Jews: identity, denominations

refugees: in Lithuania, 104; Jewish, xxxviii, 71–72; from Mexican Revolution, xxxvii, 28, 42–43, 45
relocation centers. *See* internment camps
Remolino Raid (1873), 263n22
Republic (Plato), 90
retail, xxxiii; changes in, xxxv, 191; credit, 18, 30, 120, 191, 310n24; salesmen, 14, 179, 180–82, 194
Rhodes, Jerry, 212, 219, 220
Rhodes, Susie, 218–19
Rice University (Houston), 219
Riddle, Eduardo, 41
Riddle, Maria, 145
Riddle, Octavio, 41
Riggs, Bobby, 92
Rio Escondido, 54, 66
Rio Grande, 24, 39, 137; as border, 22, 63, 182, 278n25, 309n10; *chalanes* (barges), 72, 185; crossings, 43, 71, 194; flooding, 72, 182, 185, 308n9
Rio Grande Valley, 42; Edelsteins in, xxxiii, 28, 66
Riojas, Bertha, 191
Riskin, Shlomo, 12
Riskind, Aaron (Otto), 5, 13, 16, 77
Riskind, Albert, 5, 13, 186; and family, 14, 17–18, 38; and Pérez Treviño, 46, 168; at R's, 33, 34–35, 38, 41, 77, 112–13, 173; EP, xxxiv, 30, 71, 73, 133, 149
Riskind, Bess. *See* Frank, Bess Riskind
Riskind, Dan, xviii, 151
Riskind, David, 151
Riskind, Esther Swirce, 150
Riskind, Herschel, 18
Riskind, Ida Wechsler, 77
Riskind, Jacob (Jake), 5, 12, 77
Riskind, Jennie. *See* Schrager, Jennie Riskind
Riskind, John, xxi, 55, *78*, 148, 151, 215, 233, *238*
Riskind, Judith, xxiii, *4*; as cook, 4–5, 14, 17, 67; Chicago, xxv, 13; San Antonio, 66–67; sketch of, 3–5
Riskind, Lorin, xviii, 11, 151, 55, *238*; birth, 183, 184, 185, 186; Dallas, xviii, xxi, 108
Riskind, Michael, 5, 51, *64*, 72, *157*, *176*, *238*, 302n30; as parent, 231; Chicago, 14–15; courtship and marriage, 15, 16–17, *17*; food preferences, 180, 197, 232–33; immigration, 14; later years, xv, 186, 229–30, 238–39; Los Angeles, 149, 229; Russia, xxv, 13; Six-Day War, 197–98; travels (*see*

Riskind family: travels)
  as Jewish, 203; refugees, xxxviii, 71–72; religious practice, 229; trips to Israel, 197–98, 199, 233; use of Yiddish, 34, 113, 180, 187, 233–34; Yiddish theater, 231
  business: cautiousness, 30, 41, 112–13, 134, 203; innovation, xxxiii–xxxiv, xxxv, 14–15, 28; merchandising strategies, 30, 33–34, 197
  career: Chicago, 14–15; EP, xxv, 3, 25; Panic of 1907, 18; peddling, xiii, xxiii, xxxiii, 25, 28, 56, 117, 123; separated from family, xvi, 76; tailoring, 13, 14–15
  in EP: arrival, xxv, 3, 25; as institution, 38; Bibb, 209; civic leader, xxxiv; Harpers, 134; Pérez Treviño, 46; refugees, 45, 71–72; Villa, 44–45
  personality: drinking, 232; food preferences, 232–33; generosity, 231; guns, 42; health, 18, 74; horse, 37, 51; humorlessness, 78, 231–32; malapropisms, 16–17, 187, 231; movies, 52; pigeons, 13; poker, 44, 66, 149, 180; politics, 203, 219–20; sketch of, 230–34, 35, 230; use of English, xxxvii, 231; use of Spanish, xiii; use of Yiddish, 34, 113, 180, 187, 233–34; with Latinos, xiii, 42
  Riskind's: as manager, 29, 33–34, *36*, 176, 229–30; building, xli; buying trips, 179–80, 197; with customers, xxxiv, 35, 41, 112–13; with employees, 34–38, 229–30; with salesmen, 33, 180
Riskind, Miriam, 151
Riskind, Molly. *See* Schwartz, Molly Riskind
Riskind, Morris Samuel, *xix, xx, 57, 78, 85, 113, 133*; birth, xxv, *26*, 27; character, xiii, xv, xxv–xxvi; childhood, 51–63, 56–58, 71; courtship and marriage, 98–101, 145, *146*, 147; drinking, 49–50; during WWII, 109–111; health, 59, 110; intelligence, 249n6; later years, xviii–xxi; Los Angeles, 83–101; memoir, xxi, xxiv, xli–xliii; voice, 60, 86, 151
  as Jewish: bar mitzvah, 86–87; EP community leader, xxi, xxxi, 5, *150*, 150–51; Hebrew teacher, 86, 151
  career: ambition to create, 94–95, 98; cattle rancher, 133–36, 137–39; farmer, 117–30; law practice, 96–98, 101, 160–61, 163–65; Riskind's: xiv, xxxiv, 173, 176–77, 177–80, 186–87
  education: EP public schools, 60–63, 83; intellectual development, 90, 94–95; Roosevelt High School (Los Angeles), 83–84, 89; ROTC, 93–94; UCLA, 89–93; USC law school, 94–96; views on, 62, 89–90, 220–21
  in EP: civic activity, xxxiv, 203–7, 210–11, 212–13, 213–14, 228; flood of 1954, 182–86; home, 26–27, 183, 186; map of Jewish businesses, *xxviii–xxix*, xxxiii; public housing board, 204–7, 228; with Kickapoo, 154–59; with Seminoles, 159–61
  interests and opinions: animals, 51, 136–37, 137–38, 140–42, 297n14; guns, 56–58, 93, 115, 138; history, xiii, 148, 167; hunting and fishing, 54–55, 58, 137; movies, 52–54; music, xxi, 85–86, 98–100, 204; reading, xv, 61, 94, 236; tennis, 92–93, 148, 215, 218; use of Spanish, 119, 194
  politics, 217–28; Bibb, 210–11; city council run, 217; community action program, 213–14; moderating influence, 227; school board, xxxiv, 60, 166, 218–28; school board, as president, 223–28; Texas Democratic Convention, 212–13; views on, 203; visits congressman, 206
  travels: Alaska, xviii, *113*; Austin, 212–13; Durango, 23; Guerrero, 54, 134, 136; Israel, xxiv, 199–201; Jericho, 199–201; Jerusalem, 86, 199; Mazatlán, 23; Mexico City, 193–94; Mexico, xxiv, 54–55, 134, 135–36; Monclova, 23; New York, 33–34; Oaxaca, *195*; Padre Island, 55; Qumran, 199; Saltillo, 194; San Antonio, 177–78; Tel Aviv, 245; Teotihuacán, xvi; Torreón, 23; Washington, DC, 205–6. *See also* Riskind family: travels
  travels, with RSR: Athens, 195–96; Dallas, 108, 215; Greece, 195–96; Hebron, 199; Israel, 198–99; Jerusalem, 198–99; Morocco, 196–97; Nablus, 199; Nacimiento, 154; Oaxaca, 84; Piraeus, 196; Taxco,

194–95; Veracruz, 175. *See also*
	Riskind family: travels
Riskind, Nathan, xxiii, *4*; Chicago, 14; immigration, xxv, 12–13; Maroa, 17–18; San Antonio, 66–67; sketch of, 4–5
Riskind, Peter, xxxvi, 151, 233, *238*, 241; as student, 86, 218; MSR memoir, xxi–xxii, xxxii, xli–xlii
Riskind, Rachel (MSR's granddaughter), xviii
Riskind, Rachel Edelstein, *85*, *238*; and O'Daniel, 152; Chicago, 15–16, 25; cooking, xiv–xv, 17, 58, 323n15; courtship and marriage, 15, 16–17, *17*; education, 11–12, 49; immigration, xxv, 15–16; later years, xviii, 238–41, *240*; Los Angeles, 74–76, 149; Six-Day War, 197–98; travels (*see* Riskind family: travels)
	as Jewish: frustrating missionaries, 239; community leader, xxxi, 149; kashrut, 49, 236; religious practice, 229; trips to Israel, 197–98, 199, 233; use of Yiddish, 59, 234, 235
	family, 14; Edelstein, Abe, 27, 59; Edelstein, Eli, 80; Edelstein, Morris, 27; history, 6–12; in Lithuania, 103–8; MR's drinking, 232; MR's health, 74; Schwartz, Phil, 44
	in EP, 149, 229–30; arrival, xxv, 3, 26; gardening, 51, 239; help in fields, 124; help with business, xiii, 28; raising ducks, 141; refugees, 45, 71
	personality: and Blacks, 59; and doctors, 59; care for others, 236; guns, 56; health, 29, 76; humor, 237; indifference to arts, 12, 237–38; learnedness, 9, 236, 239; love of nature, 235; movies, 52; needle work, 12, 16, 241; nondemonstrative, 59, 236; reading, 236; sketch of, 234–38; suspicion of non-Jews, 243; theater, 237–38; use of Spanish, 239–40
	stories: aphorisms, 237; criminals, 237; family history, 5, 68; from Midrash, 232; from Talmud, 237; from Tanakh, 86–87; "Greenhorn Cousin, The," 234, 323n9; golem, 234; Napoleon's Treasure, 11; "Pretty Penny," 235–36
Riskind, Reuben, 29, *85*; at El Retiro, 118, 128; civic activity, xxxiv, 213–14, 219, 251n36; family trips, 68, 74–76; Hebrew school, xxxi, 151; in EP, 150–51; military service, 134; relationship with MSR, xvi; tennis, xvi, 92, 247
	Riskind's: flood of 1954, 182–84, 185; manager, 176, 185, 230; partner, 34, 229; vice president, xiii, xvi, xxiv, 186–87
Riskind, Rose (Aunt Rose), 5, *36*, 142, 149; and family, xxxiv, 29, 34, 38, 53, 60, 76, 78, 232, 233; at R's, xxxiv, 33, *36*, 41, 173, 176, 177; sketch of, 29–30
Riskind, Ruth (MSR's sister). *See* Haberman, Ruth Riskind
Riskind, Ruth Sholtz, *100*, *150*; and MSR, xv, 177; appearance, 147; courtship and marriage, 98–101, 145, *146*, 147; later years, xxi; Lorin's birth, 183, 184, 185, 186; Oaxaca, 145; Passover, 108; questioned by FBI, 206–7; school board, 219; youth, 145–47
	career: artist, 145, 148; Gila River, 145–47; RKO Pictures, 147; teacher, xv–xvi, 148, 223
	in EP: acceptance in, 147–48; adjustment, 147; arrival, xxvi, 145; Civic Music of EP, 204; de Mohrenschildt, 215; decision to stay, 145, 173; Kickapoo cultural program, 158–59; school board, 220, 228; social life, 147, 244
	personality: bargaining skills, 194–95, 196–97; sketch of, xv–xvi, 147–49; use of Spanish, xv–xvi, 147
	travels, with MSR: Athens, 195–96; Dallas, 108, 215; Greece, 195–96; Hebron, 199; Israel, 198–99; Jerusalem, 198–99; Morocco, 196–97; Nablus, 199; Nacimiento, 154; Oaxaca, 84; Piraeus, 196; Taxco, 194–95; Veracruz, 175
Riskind, Sarah (MSR's sister). *See* Robson, Sarah Riskind
Riskind, Sarah Block, 16, 77
Riskind, Sherri, xxi, 151
Riskind, Susan, 16, 233
Riskind building, xxiii, 17, 28, *29*; apartment, 28, 51, *150*; renovations, *xvii*, xxiii, xl–xli, *xl–xli*, 30; site of J services, xiv, xxiv, xxxi, 49, *150*, 150
Riskind family: immigration, 6, 12–13; EP, xxv–xxvi, 19, 26–27, 51; Russia, 3–6; move to California, 76, 79–80; origin of name, 3; social life, 39, 149

as Jews: community, 49; hosting J servicemen, 47–48, 111–15; kashrut, 49, 236. *See also* individual names
travels: auto trips, 63–69, 74–76, 79–80. *See also* individual names: Allende, xvi, 63; Carrizo Springs, 65; Deming, 75; Devils River, 66, 74, 75, 80; Devine, 65; Dilley, 65, 69; El Paso, 69, 75, 79; Grand Canyon, 80; Guanajuato, xvi; Hondo, 68; Israel, xxvi, 197–98, 199, 233; La Pryor, 63; Los Angeles, 74–76, 79–80; Mexico City, xvi, 170, 307n20; Needles, 80; New York, 233–34; Organ Pipe Cactus National Monument, 75; Ozona, 75; Pátzcuaro, xvi; Petrified Forest, 80; Sabinal, 68; Saltillo, xvi; San Antonio, 63–65, 66–69; San Bernardino, 80; San Diego, 76; San Luis Potosí, xvi; Sheffield, 75; Spofford, 69; Springerville, 80; Taxco, xvi, xxxv; Tohono O'odham reservation, 75; Tucson, 75; Uvalde, 65, 69; Van Horn, 75; Yosemite National Park, 235; Yuma, 75

Riskind Furniture Company, 123

Riskind's (the store), xxxiv, xxxv, xxxvi; building (*see* Riskind Building); cash register ("the organ"), 31, *32*, 33, 173; decline and closure, xvi–xviii; described, xiv, 33–34, 176; flood of 1954, 182–86, *183*; history, xxiii, xxv, 27–28, 31, location, *31*, 39, *174*, *190*; peso devaluation, xviii, 191

  business practices, xxxiii–xxxiv, 173; acquisition of merchandise, 177–80, 186, 197; advertising, *32*, *37*, *190*; credit, 30, 173, 191, 310n24; salesmen, 179; shoe department, 176–77, 194; special orders, 187–88

  customers: airmen, 112–13; complaints, 188; from Mexico, xiv, 31; preferences, 176–77; variety of, xxxvii–xxxviii

  employees: from Piedras Negras, xiv, 183; MSR recollections of, 34–38; nature of, xxxvii; wages, 35. *See also* individual names: Barrientos, René; Cirilo, Jesusita; Daniel, Demetrio; Daniel, Valentín; Diaz, Albino; Díaz, Constancia; García, Chema; Garza, Ernesto; Johnson, Charlie; Karp, Mr.; Meza, Florencio; Moncada, Felipe; Olivares, Enriqueta; Perez, Federico; Riojas, Bertha; Santos, Cata; Seriff, Abraham; Torralba, Anacleto; Vann, Grien; Vela, Lola; White, Geraldine; Wueste, Ward

  product lines, 31, 33; Florsheim, 31, *32*, 188, 266n44; Hart Schaffner & Marx, 31, 33, 188, 266n44; Hickey Freeman, xiv, 187; Levi's, xiv; Stetson, xiv, 189, 232

Ritchie, Bill, 137
Ritchie, Ed, 121
Ritchie Brothers, 127
Rittenberg, Bea, 88–89
Rittenberg, Lena, 88
Rittenberg, Louis (Louie), 88–89, 90, 91
Rittenberg, Saul, 83, 84, 87, 88, 98
Rittenberg, Syd, 88
Rivera, Diego, 311n3
RKO Pictures, 147
Roberts, Thurman, 73
Robson, Mark, 197, 229, 231
Robson, Sarah Riskind, 29, *85*, 231; with family, 68, 197, 229, 239, 241
Robles (farm worker), 122
Rochester, New York, 113
Rodfei Sholom (San Antonio), 279n33
Rodríguez, Cecilio, 220
Rodríguez, Chilo, 21, 25
Rodríguez, Pablo, 59
Rodríguez, Raul "Peanuts," 212
Roosevelt, Franklin D., 298n5, 315n10
Roosevelt High School (Los Angeles), 98, 283n2; MSR at, 83–84, 89
Rosh Hashanah. *See* Jews: holidays
Rotary Club, 73
ROTC, 93–94
Rover Boys (book series), 61
Ruby, Jack, 214
Ruiz, Hector, xiv
Russell, Bertrand, 91
Russell, Willie Dan, 203, 314n1
Russia, military service in, 257n37
Russian, 71, 215
Russian Cossack Choir, 71
Russian Revolution, 6, 16, 89, 124, 214
Ruza, Ladislas, 114–15
Ryskind, Morrie, 12

Sabinal, Texas, 68
Sabinas Inn, 209, 232
Sabinas, Coahuila, Mexico, 43

Sadducees, 286n24
Salinas, Juan, 193
Salinas Carranza, Alberto, 310n1
Saltillo, Coahuila, Mexico, xvi, 21, 22, 65, 194; R's advertisement, xxxviii, 31
Salvation Army, 185
Samaniego, Leopoldo de, 25; sketch of, 168–69
Samaniego, Señora, 168
San Antonio, Texas, 23, 28, 45, 59, 63–65, 66–69, 177–78, 185; Edelstein, Abe, 18–19; Jews, xxvii, xxx–xxxi, xxxiii, 48, 150, 279n33; Latinos, 66–68; travel conditions, 21–22, 65, 152
San Antonio de Béxar, 22
San Antonio River, 67
San Antonio Symphony, 204
San Bernardino, California, 80
San Carlos Hotel, 175
San Diego, California, 76, 166, 200
San Juan Bautista (Guerrero), 22
San Juan Plaza (EP), 25, 61, 156, 158–59
San Luis Potosí, S.L.P., xvi, 73
San Miguel Saloon, 30, 39, 49–50, 53–54
Sánchez Navarro family, 132
Sanderson, Texas, 182
Santa Monica (Los Angeles), 229
Santos, Cata, 36
Sawyer, Tom (litigant), 163–64
Schmerber, Mrs. (property owner), 40
Schmidt, Edward, Jr., 205
Schmidt, Edward, Sr., 19, 189, 205, 221
Schoenberg, Arnold, 145
school board. *See* Eagle Pass, Texas: school board
schools. *See* Eagle Pass, Texas: public education; public schools
Schottenstein, Allison, xxxvi
Schrager, Bessie, 68
Schrager, Jack, 66–67
Schrager, Jennie Riskind, 5; illness, 66–67, 74, 236
Schrager, Norman, 68
Schrager family, 66–67, 236
Schuessler's Men's Store, 39, 54
Schwartz, Adolph, xxxviii; Villa, 43, 268n5
Schwartz, Arnold, 43, 150
Schwartz, Edythe, 150
Schwartz, Ellen Kranzthor, xxxi, 47
Schwartz, Joe, 44, 48, 52
Schwartz, Manny, 48
Schwartz, Molly Riskind, 5, 44, 48
Schwartz, Phil, 44, 48

Schwartz, Sam, xxxiv, xxxviii, 40, 47, *53*; as property owner, 28, 30, 39, 52; businesses, 53, 111, 128; poker, 44, 149; use of Yiddish, 128
Schwartz, Yolanda. *See* Munter, Yolanda Schwartz
Schwartz family, 151
Scranton, Pennsylvania, 77
Seco Mines, xxxii, 25
Seldes, Gilbert, 299n8
Sellers, Walter, 117–18, 128–29, 137
Seminole Wars, 159, 304n41
Seminoles: reservation in Mexico, 24, 159; tribal conflicts, 159; Wild Cat (Coacoochee), 159, 262m10, 304n41. *See also* Black Seminoles
Semosenko, Ataman Ivan, 280n1
Senno, Poland, 104
Sephardim, 6, 198, 247
Sepulveda, Ofelia, 220, 221–22
Seriff, Abraham, 36, 48, 50, 63, 65
Sforim, Mendele Mocher (Sholem Yankev Abramovich), 237, 323n17
Shadrinsk, Russia, 6
Shafter, Texas, 47
Shalashudes, Michael, 10
Shammai, 323n16
Shavuos. *See* Jews: holidays
Shaw, George Bernard, 91, 168
Sheffield, Texas, 75
Shelby, Joseph, 23; brigade, 23
Sheridan, Philip, 24, 154, 279n36
Shoah. *See* Holocaust
"Shoes" (O. Henry), 124
Sholtz, Ann Lehman, 290n57
Sholtz, Jeanne, 145, 290n57
Sholtz, John, 87, 98, 151
Shotz, Orv, 93
Shulchan Arukh, 245
Shulhafer, Charles P., 170–71, 247
Sifuentes, Luis, xxiii
Simchat Torah. *See* Jews: holidays
Simnas, Lithuania, 8
Six-Day War, 197–98, 200–201
Smith, Adam, 91, 287n38
Smith, Fred, 210
Sneed, L. F., 28
Socrates, 90
South Africa, 15
Spanish: and Anglos, 147; in public education, 60, 224–25; use by EP Jews, xiii, xvi, xv–xvi, 34, 71, 81, 113, 119 121, 147, 154, 218,

219, 239–40; use by MSR, 119, 194; use by RSR, 198
Spanish Civil War, 94
Spector (produce buyer), 149
Spence, Jack, 58, 226; on school board, 219, 222, 223
Spiegal, Bennie, 49
Spiegel, Bennie, 150
Spiegel, Rosalie Strum, 150
Spiller (J EP resident), 211
Spindletop, 73
Spinoza, Baruch, 91
Spitz, Harry and Hannah. *See* Uspitz
Spofford, Texas, 69
Springerville, Arizona, 80
St. Denis, Louis Juchereau de, 22
St. Edward's University, 214
Stalin, Josef, 91
Stanford University, 218
Star Theater, 53–54
Steffens, Lincoln, 212
Steinbock, Behr, xxx, 264n25
Stephen F. Austin School, *61*, 61–62
Stetson, xiv, 189, 232
Stevenson, Coke, 210
Stevenson, Robert Louis, 283n22
Stool, Ann, 150
Stool, Libbie, 150
Stool, Max, 150
Stool, Michael, 150
Stool family, xxxi, xxxviii, 151
Stravinsky, Igor, 204
Style Shop, 219
Sulzbacher, Nathan, xxx
Sumpter, Jesse, xxx, 23, 25
Sunset Limited, 69
Suvalki, Poland, 104
Swirce, Esther, 150
Switzerland, 200

tailoring. *See* garment trade
Talmud, 10, 236–37, 246; *Pirkei Avot*, 5, 84, 88
Tanakh, 10, 285n17; and Jewish identity, 246–47; MSR and, 86–88, 151; RER and, 12, 49, 236, 241
Tarlow, Peter, xxi
Tawes, J. Millard, 306n9
Taxco, Guerrero, Mexico, xvi, xxxv, 194–95
Taylor, Calvin C., 292n22
Taylor, Zachary, 22
Taylor's Saloon, 39, 49–50
Teotihuacán, Mexico, xvi

"Te Vendes" ("You Sell"), 233
Tebbe, A. J., 294n12
Tebbe (produce buyer), 122, 124
Tejanos. *See* Latinos
Tel Aviv, Israel, 245
Temple Beth-El (San Antonio), 150
tennis: MSR, 92–93, 148, 215, 218, 247; Reuben Riskind, xvi, 92–93
Terrazas family, 132
Tevye the Milkman (character), 237
Texas A&M University, xxi, 62, 118, 218
Texas Democratic Convention, 212–13
Texas Employment Office, 153
Texas Fine Arts Commission, xviii
Texas history, 300n16; MSR's interpretation, 62, 148
Texas Rangers, 25, 220; violence against Latinos, xxxvii, 42
Texas Rangers, The (movie), 237
Texas Rangers, The (Webb), 52
Texas War for Independence, 63; historiography, 62, 278n21, 300n16
Thirty Years' War, 243
This is America (documentary series), 147
Thompson, Kenneth, 179
Thompson's Tank (EP), 58
Thomson, Bruce, 205
Three Musketeers, The (Dumas), 283n22
Three Sisters, 56
Thucydides, 91
Thurmond, Roger, 163–65
Tippie (MSR's dog), 136–37
Toch, Ernst, 145
Tohono O'odham reservation, 75
Tolchinsky, Moses, 86
Toledo, Spain, 6
Tom Mix and Pancho Villa (Irving), 43
Tom Sawyer (Twain), 61, 236
Tom Swift (book series), 61
Torah, 245, 246; MSR's study, 60, 86
Torah scroll (*sefer Torah*): acquired by EP Jews, xxvii, 150
Torralba, Anacleto, 36, 123
Torralba, Humberto, 220
Torreón Massacre, 269n12; Chuck family, xxxvii, 41
Torreón, Coahuila, Mexico, 21, 23
Torres, Licha, xiv–xv, 239–40, 241, 323n15
Toziewitz, Adolph, xxx
Toziewitz, Yetta Phillips, xxx
travel. *See* Riskind family; MSR; RSR
Travelers Hotel (San Antonio), 67

Treasure, The (Aleichem), 256n28
Treaty of Guadalupe Hidalgo, and border, xxvii, 278n25
Tres B (Juárez), xxxviii
tuberculosis, xxv, 29, 236; Edelstein, Abe, 18, 59; Riskind, Michael, 18; Schrager, Jennie, 66, 74
Tucson, Arizona, 75
Twain, Mark, 237
Tweed, William, 212

UCLA: MSR at, 89–93; RSR at, xvi, 145–46
Ukraine, 71; pogroms, 16, 326n13
Ullman, Frederick, 147
United Garment Workers, 257n42
United Jewish Appeal, 198
United Nations, 199
University of Southern California (USC): MSR at, xxiv, 94–96
University of Texas, 62, 166, 214
Ural Mountains, 6
US Department of Justice, 166, 227
USO, 111–12
Uspitz (Spitz), Hannah, 75, 79
Uspitz (Spitz), Harry, 75, 79–80, 103
Uvalde, Texas, 24, 65, 69, 138, 227

Van Horn, Texas, 75
Vann, Alejo, 187
Vann, Grien, 36
vaqueros: at Azulejo, 135; at El Retiro, 137; tradition, 131, 132, 137, 138. *See also* Agapito
Vela, Lola, 36, 36, 185, 231
Velásquez Body Shop, 40
Venice, California, 77
Venitzky, Mr. (Jewish Agency), 198, 199
Veracruz, Mexico, 175
veterans, 227
Veterans' Readjustment Benefits Act (Cold War GI Bill), 322n22
Vielke, Abele, 5
Viguera Banking Co., 73, 281n8
Villa Acuña, Coahuila, Mexico, 152
Villa, Francisco (Pancho), 46, 311n3; as customer, 43; Mexican Revolution, 28, 40, 41, 47, 265n36, 270n14; rumors about, xxxvii, 43–45
Vilner Shul (Chicago), 16
Virgin Islands, 15
Vivaldi, Antonio, 204
Volunteers in Service to America (VISTA), 317n25

von Tilly, Count, 324n3
Voting Rights Act (1965), 206
Voznitsyn, Alexander, 327n14

Wadsworth, T. C., 28
Wagner, Richard, 204
Walker, Edwin, 216
Walmart, 191
War Relocation Authority, 298n5
Warsaw, Poland: Holocaust in, 108
Washington, DC, 205–6
Washington, George, 203
Waterfill & Frazier (whiskey), 77
Wealth of Nations, The (Smith), 287n38
Webb, Walter Prescott, 24, 52, 237
Weissbach, Lee Shai, xxvi, xxxii
Weslaco, Texas, 81
West, Milton, 291n17
West Bank, 313n22
Western Auto Parts, 48, 121
Westsmith, Frank, 93
Weyrich (blacksmith), 40, 51, 56
White, Alfred, 35–36
White, Edward, 305n44
White, Geraldine, 35–36
White, Harold, 153, 156
White, Pearl, 52–53
White, Samuel, xxx
Wichita Falls, Texas, xxxiii
Wild Cat (Coacoochee), 159, 262n19, 304n41
wildlife: armadillos, 136; beavers, 136; coyotes, 66, 136, 142; deer, 66; foxes, 136, 142; hawks, 134; jackrabbits, 66, 136; javelina, 66, 125; mountain lions, 117, 137; opossums, 136, 142; quail, 134, 137; rabbits, 134, 136, 142; raccoons, 136, 142; snakes, 120; starlings, 138; turkeys, 66, 137; turtles, 136. *See also* animals
Williams, Ellen, 59
Wilson, Woodrow, 43, 268n5, 270n13
Wizard of Oz, The (Baum), 61, 236
Wolff, E., xxix–xxx
women: education of, 11, 88; in work force, 147; Mexican, taste and style, 28, 176–77, 308n3
Woodruff, Victoria, xxi
Wool, John, 22, 65
Works Progress Administration (WPA), 208
World War I, 55, 61, 113, 141
World War II, 109–15, 145–47; agriculture, 117–30, 189–214; enlistment, 81, 109–11; EP Jews, 111–15, 150; in EP, 111–15;

Mexico in, 193, 310n1; retailing, xxxv, 181–82
Worrell, Dorothy, 158–59, 159–60
Wueste, Ward, 42, 62, 191; gas station, 139; R's management, 40, 187, 188, 230, 232

Xenophon, 83
XEPN (radio station in PN), 302n30
XER (radio station in Villa Acuña), 302n30
XEW (radio station in Mexico City), 307n14

Yankel der Amerikaner (Jake the American), 15
Yaqui people, 41
Yarborough, Ralph, 322n22
Yiddish: expressions, 13, 33, 34, 44, 87–88; *ma'asehbuchs*, 12, 256n31; MSR and, 80, 84; theater, 231; use by Edelsteins, 80, 104, 233–34, 235; use by EP Jews, xlii, 13, 126, 128, 187; use by MR, 34, 113, 180, 187, 233–34; use by RER, 59, 234, 235; use in store, xxxvii, 33, 34, 48, 178
Yolanda Hotel, 111
Yolanda Theater, 53, *184*
Yom Kippur. *See* Jews: holidays
Yom Kippur War, 311n14
Yosemite National Park, 235
Young, Clara Kimball, 30
Yuma, Arizona, 75

Zale's Jewelry, xxxiii
Zalman, Shneur, 322n1
Zapato, Emiliano, 270n14
Zielonka, Martin, xxxviii
ZIM line, 197
Zionism, 98
Zionist Organization of America, 198–99
Zionist youth groups, 98, 100

ABOUT THE AUTHOR

Morris S. Riskind was born in 1911 in Eagle Pass, Texas, a Rio Grande border town about 140 miles southwest of San Antonio. His parents, Russian Jewish immigrants, arrived there the previous year from Chicago and opened a large retail clothing store on Main Street. Morris grew up in the family apartment above the store. For three generations, the Riskinds were at the heart of the town's small but active Jewish community and of its lively and multilingual downtown commercial district. Riskind died in 1996, but his memoir preserves his recollections of how Jewish identity, family business, and the border environment intersected in a small binational community.

ABOUT THE EDITOR

Bryan Edward Stone is a professor of history at Del Mar College, where he teaches courses in US history. He was named a 2024 Piper Professor by the Minnie Stevens Piper Foundation, which recognizes ten Texas college and university faculty annually. He also received the 2019 Aileen Creighton Award for Teaching Excellence and the 2021 Teacher of the Year award from Del Mar College. Stone is the author of *The Chosen Folks: Jews on the Frontiers of Texas* (2010), which won the Southern Jewish Historical Society Book Prize in 2011, and the editor of Alexander Gurwitz's historical memoir *Memories of Two Generations: A Yiddish Life in Russia and Texas* (2016). He lives in Corpus Christi, Texas.

Milton Keynes UK
Ingram Content Group UK Ltd.
UKHW031954281024
450365UK00009B/535